Hankow: Commerce and Society in a Chinese City, 1796-1889

WILLIAM T. ROWE

HANKOW

Commerce and Society in a Chinese City, 1796–1889

STANFORD UNIVERSITY PRESS 1984
STANFORD, CALIFORNIA

Published with the assistance of the
National Endowment for the Humanities

Stanford University Press
Stanford, California

Printed in the United States of America
ISBN 0-8047-1204-2
LC 82-61784

FOR BILL, BETTY, AND JILL

Preface

THIS IS THE first part of a projected two-part study of nineteenth-century Hankow, which began with my dissertation research at Columbia University. Although I have tried to make this volume in itself a coherent and satisfying whole, some themes introduced here must inevitably await fuller treatment in the sequel, and certain issues important to understanding Hankow society have been deliberately played down. Chief among them is social conflict, which will be a central concern of the subsequent volume. Hankow was a notoriously violent place; nevertheless, it was also remarkable for the degree to which the temptations to divisiveness and conflict were overcome, and to which the city genuinely worked as a social unit. It is this aspect of local history that I have chosen to emphasize here.

In the course of this study, many teachers, friends, and colleagues have generously offered me their assistance and support. Foremost among them were my three successive dissertation advisors at Columbia: C. Martin Wilbur, James Polachek, and Andrew Nathan. Each contributed a different set of concerns to my understanding of my subject, and I have profited greatly from them all. To Andy especially I can never adequately convey my thanks. During my various research sojourns I was aided by John Dolfin of the Universities Service Center, Hong Kong; Chang P'eng-yüan and Su Yün-feng of the Institute of Modern History, Academia Sinica, Taiwan; Ichiko Chūzō of the Tōyō Bunko, Tokyo; Shiba Yoshinobu of Osaka University; Mark Elvin of the University of Oxford; Hsiao Chih-chih, Kao Shang-yin, and P'eng Yü-hsin of Wuhan University; P'an Hsin-tsao of the Hupeh Cultural and Historical Office; Hsu Ch'ing-an and Chai Hsüeh-ch'ao of the Wuhan Municipal Archives; Chu Te-yuan and Liu Kuei-lin of the Ming-Ch'ing Archives, Peking; and P'eng Tse-i of the Institute of Economics, Chinese Academy of Social Sciences. I especially thank Professor Hsiao, Professor Shiba, and Mr. Su for their bibliographic guidance.

For assistance at various stages of the project I am indebted to Beatrice Bartlett, Steven Butler, Joshua Fogel, Susan Naquin, David Strand, and Tang Tsou. Myron Cohen, Jerry Dennerline, Robert Gardella, Winston Hsieh, James Lee, Tetsuo Najita, William Parish, Thomas Rawski, Carl Riskin, and Lyman Van Slyke each read portions of the manuscript and offered useful advice. Heartfelt thanks for their repeated (and often badly needed) encouragement go to Susan Mann Jones, G. William Skinner, and J. G. Bell, as well as to Edward Perzel and my colleagues in the History Department of the University of North Carolina at Charlotte. Sandra Bergo and Mary Bottomly typed the manuscript with the highest standards of professionalism. Jefferson Simpson and Tran Van Ra prepared the maps.

In these days when academic research is threatened with economic and political adversity, it is a special pleasure to be able to thank the funding agencies that contributed so generously to this project: the Foreign Area Fellowships Program of the American Council of Learned Societies and the Social Science Research Council, the National Endowment for the Humanities' Modern China Project at the University of Chicago, and the Committee on Scholarly Communication with the People's Republic of China.

Finally, my deepest gratitude goes to Jill A. Friedman, who as classmate, colleague, and spouse shared the assorted joys and griefs of this endeavor. To her, and to my parents, this volume is dedicated.

W. T. R.

Contents

Maps and Figures

Hankow

Greatest of markets, crossroads of land and river trade,
A speck of earth that dominates all Ch'u:
To the south it holds the reins of Szechwan,
From east to west, links Honan and Wuchang.

Wealthy merchants unite here to control the trade,
Bringing their local speech from all parts of the Empire;
From every famous, far-flung border town
One by one they answer to its call.

A brace of donkeys swish their tails together,
Horses' hooves thump as they gallop by.
The crowd buzzes, people jammed shoulder to shoulder
Shuffle along, necks drawn in like snails.

The squawking of a flock of chickens,
The lazy strength of a dog stretching out in the sun:
Fish and prawns skitter along the river's edge,
And the scent of herbs drifts off into the hills.

There government salt wrapped in yellow rush mats;
Here bitter tea in green bamboo baskets.
The sluice-gates holding firm on all sides
Amid a panorama of buildings, large and small.

The clamor of the market starts early in the morning;
The smoke is blinding by the break of day.
A hundred thousand households of one determination—
How else can one run a business?

The confluence of two great rivers
Where three mountains meet to form a tripod:
Here traffic is drawn, like spokes to the hub of a wheel—
And yet, a startlingly lonely town.

Yellow sand strikes my face;
From it my fan is no protection.
But still I like to walk beside the clear rivers
And watch the reflections of those washing clothes at the shore.

CHA SHEN-HSING, 1650–1727

Introduction: Cities in the History of Europe and China

In the second half of the nineteenth century, Hankow, the major commercial city of central China, was among the largest urban places in the world. It was the hub of an intensely active marketing system spanning thousands of miles and involving scores of commodities, as well as a port of international trade. It hosted a cosmopolitan, ethnically diverse population of great industry and skill. And yet, a full century after its European counterparts had begun to enter the industrial age, Hankow was essentially without steam-powered manufacture. Whereas Western states had undergone sweeping political changes, whether gradual or revolutionary, Hankow was still administered by an ancient imperial regime incapable of responding effectively to severe international pressure.

Despite the size, economic centrality, and social complexity of Hankow and other Chinese cities of the time, an influential school of Western historiography came to identify the inadequate development of urban institutions as the principal cause of China's "backwardness." According to this view, urban places in China had failed to perform the catalytic function necessary to bring about the sorts of social, economic, and political change that had transformed the West since medieval times and provided the basis of its superior material civilization in the nineteenth and early twentieth centuries.

A basic assumption underlying this argument is that the type of central place we commonly recognize as a "city" had its genuine origins only in the *commune*, a relatively autonomous form of urban settlement that first appeared in northern Italy during the eleventh century and spread soon after to France, Germany, and the Low Countries. The classic treatment of the commune's development is Henri Pirenne's *Medieval Cities* (1925); although many elements of Pirenne's argument have since provoked considerable debate, his view of the commune's broad historical significance remains widely accepted.[1] More important, perhaps, the renowned German sociologist Max Weber wove Pirenne's basic argument into a web of theoretical validation and cross-cultural analysis in his roughly contemporaneous essay *The City* (*Die Stadt*).[2] The views expounded by Weber in this work have retained their appeal for students of urban history down to the present day.

For both Pirenne and Weber, to qualify as a city a central place needed to do much more than function as an administrative capital. Pirenne, for example, noted of the "burgs" or "boroughs" of ninth- and tenth-century Europe that:

> The burg did not show the slightest urban character. Its population comprised, aside from the knights and the clerics who made up its essential part, only men employed in their service and whose number was certainly of very little importance. It was a fortress population; it was not a city population. Neither commerce nor industry was possible or even conceivable in such an environment. It produced nothing of itself, lived by revenues from the surrounding country, and had no other economic role than that of a simple consumer. It is therefore a safe conclusion that the period which opened with the Carolingian era knew cities neither in the social sense, nor in the economic sense, nor in the legal sense of that word.[3]

Similarly, Weber required that any candidate for true city status qualify as an "urban community." To do so, a settlement must "display a relative predominance of trade-commercial relations, with the settlement as a whole displaying the following features: 1. a fortification; 2. a market; 3. a court of its own and at least partially autonomous law; 4. a related form of association; and 5. at least partial autonomy and autocephaly, thus also an administration by authorities in the election of whom the burghers participated."[4]

In discussing the reasons the newly risen European middle class sought this "urban autonomy," Pirenne remarked that:

> What they wanted, first of all, was personal liberty, which would assure to the merchant or artisan the possibility of going and coming, of living where he wished. . . . Next came the creation of a special tribunal by means of which the burgher would at one stroke escape the multiplicity of jurisdictions to which he was amenable and the inconvenience which the formalistic procedures of ancient law imposed upon his social and economic activity. Then came the instituting in the city of a "peace"—that is to say, of a penal code—which would guarantee security. And then came the abolition of those prestations most incompatible with the carrying on of trade and industry, and with the possession and acquisition of land. What they wanted, in fine, was a more or less extensive degree of . . . local self-government.[5]

Weber elaborated upon the "special urban law," secured for the urban populace by means of "city revolutions":

> The burgess was particularly anxious to exclude irrational means of proof, particularly the duel—as illustrated in numerous grants of privilege of the eleventh

century. . . . Among other legal gains by the burghers was the prohibition of summons of burghers to non-urban courts. They also pressed for the codification of a special rational law for urbanites to be applied by the court of the consuls.

Among the products of such revolutionary urban movements was the development of a permanent political association the members of which were legal colleagues enjoying special legal status as urbanites. . . . Materially, [this] involved the breaking up of the fief-system and patrimonial estates, but not yet in favor of an institutionalized territorial corporation. Burgher law, thus, is a halfway house between the old feudal law and the law of territorial units.[6]

To sum up, then, the urban commune movement in medieval Europe has been held to have left numerous legacies, not all of which were seized upon by the immediately succeeding ages, but all of which have become part of the general cultural myth we cherish as describing modern Western society. Legally, it created the ideal of the freedom and equality of individuals before the law ("city air makes men free"), and of the free alienation of property. Thus it hastened the demise of the feudal system.[7] Politically, it left a heritage of democracy and widespread enfranchisement, as well as the concept of a corporate political body with a clearly demarcated public sector in terms of both budgetary accounting and professional civil service.[8] Intellectually, it fostered the primacy of rationality, both in legal procedure and in an economic focus on calculability of returns on investment—in Weber's words, the medieval urbanite was well "on the way to becoming an economic man (*homo oeconomicus*)."[9] Finally, in the area of economic organization, the urban communities of the Middle Ages laid the groundwork for early capitalism. As one sinologist and comparative historian puts it: "We have come to believe that the industrial civilization in which we now live was essentially created by a 'middle class' who lived in the cities of Europe. We believe that it is the city with its condensation of population, its greater division of labor, its mixed population that made it possible to create the first industries and the first great accumulations of capital which were necessary for an industrial society. This view [is] based on detailed historical research."[10]

These factors, then, constitute the historical significance of the development of urban autonomy in the medieval West. But what of Chinese cities? How did they differ from their Western counterparts? Could they in fact be considered "cities" at all, or did they more closely resemble the urban *non*-cities of the early European Middle Ages? And how did such differences affect the diverse courses of Chinese and Western social evolution?

Until remarkably recently the prevailing conception of late imperial Chinese cities has been that elaborated by Max Weber, both in *The City* and in his *The Religion of China* (*Konfuzianismus und Taoismus*, 1915). Weber knew no Chinese and never visited China, but he had read widely in the Western-language literature then available. This left him constrained by something of a treaty-port view of Chinese society; he relied heavily, for instance, on such knowledgeable but jaundiced observers as H. B. Morse and E. H. Parker. That the resulting work has commanded so much attention for so long is a tribute to insights that only a man of Weber's great genius could elicit from his sketchy data. Nevertheless, Chinese cities emerge from Weber's writings less as historical realities than as an ideal type to be counterposed to his view of European urban development. Whereas European society had made the successful passage from "traditional" to "rational" (or, in the words of some of Weber's heirs, "modern") principles of behavior and organization, Chinese society had not.

The major reason identified by Weber for China's failure in this regard was the nature of the Chinese city itself. In China, true "cities" never came into being, since the "urban community" that was their necessary prerequisite never existed. Weber attributed this to two causes, one deriving from the nature of the political system and the other stemming from the structure of society.

Politically, he argued that the hand of the central administration was consistently too heavy for urban autonomy ever to have developed. Urbanism in China did not originate as a natural product of the process of economic exchange, as it largely did in Europe, but rather in the conscious design of imperial rulers. "The Chinese city was predominantly a product of rational administration, as its very form indicated."[11] A political function as the seat of a local field administration and the site of a military garrison remained paramount throughout Chinese urban history; the city was always the "princely city," whose primary function was that of "princely residence."[12] This political dominance extended into the economic sphere as well: "The prosperity of the Chinese city did not primarily depend upon the citizens' enterprising spirit in economic and political ventures, but rather upon the imperial administration, especially the administration of the rivers."[13] Weber did not altogether discount the existence of trade, but he held the city's role as a market to be decidedly secondary to that as garrison.[14]

As a direct result of the primacy of its administrative function, political autonomy could never develop in the city. Although he did not dwell on the point, Weber seems to have been aware that Chinese cities failed to constitute discrete and exclusive territorial units for bureaucratic administration. He emphasized that the imperial government deliberately discouraged urban solidarity by selecting subunits such as urban wards to be the major administrative units below the county level.[15] Moreover, the Chinese government, unlike that of the Holy Roman Empire in Europe, was able to maintain its monopoly of military force in the cities. Weber pointedly remarked that this ability did not extend to the Chinese countryside: "Actually, not the city but the village was the armed association capable of defending the interests of those in its orbit."[16] More important still was the fact that the administration effectively quashed the development of institutions of local autonomy in urban centers, although it specifically fostered them in rural areas. Charters of municipal incorporation were never granted. Weber summarized his views to the effect that "a 'city' was the seat of the mandarin and was not self-governing; a 'village' was a self-governing settlement without a mandarin."[17]

Beyond the coercive power of the administration, however, there were even more compelling socioreligious factors in China to inhibit the development of any urban community that might effectively press for political rights. Chief among these was the unusual degree of attachment of all Chinese to an idyllically conceived natural village, both in formal terms (by means of legal requirements for home-district registration) and in informal terms (by sentimental native-place and kinship ties). In Weber's view, "The Chinese urban dweller legally belonged to his family and native village, in which the temple of his ancestors stood and to which he conscientiously maintained affiliation."[18] As a result, the urban population was made up overwhelmingly of sojourners who formed no identification with their place of temporary abode. "The 'city' was . . . never the 'hometown' but typically a place away from home for the majority of its inhabitants."[19] This precluded the development of any Chinese urban class.

The customary modes and channels of collective action also inhibited urban development. Weber was among the first to call attention to an excessive reliance upon particularistic ties in Chinese business practice. This reliance was both reflected in and reinforced by the total absence of legislation enforcing principles of "contractual autonomy" in major commercial centers.[20] Particularism in business was carried over into all areas of collective endeavor: "In Asiatic and Oriental settlements of an urban economic character, only extended families and professional associations were vehicles of communal actions."[21] Despite his use in this context of the word "association," it seems clear that Weber saw all such groups as essentially preassociative in nature. He argued: "True 'communities' were absent, especially in the cities, because there were no economic and managerial forms of association or enterprise which were purely purposive. Almost none of these originated from purely

Chinese roots. All communal action there remained engulfed and conditioned by purely personal, above all, by kinship relations."[22] The net result was that, even had a proper urban class come into existence in China, individual cities could never have given rise to legitimate urban communities: "There was ordinarily no joint association representing a community of city burghers *per se*; even the concept of such a possibility is completely lacking. Citizenship as a specific status quality of the urbanite is missing."[23]

Thus for Weber the communal principle in Chinese cities was embodied not in the urban population as a whole but in smaller, particularistic kinship groups ("sibs") and guilds. The problem with such groups was not that they were ineffective—they could be very successful in achieving private, nonpolitical aims—but that they worked against "the fusion of urban dwellers into a homogeneous status group."[24] Specifically, Chinese guilds (as well as sibs) were simultaneously submunicipal and extramunicipal in their orientations; they served only a restricted segment of the urban population, and not all of their constituents lived within the city. The fact that the headquarters of such groups were frequently located in cities was for Weber no more than coincidence—a matter of convenience rather than an indication of the group's orientation.[25] At the same time, Weber was unequivocal that in practice, in the absence of either a "polis" or "commune" organization uniting all of a city's inhabitants for political purposes, the Chinese city was in effect controlled almost entirely by such kinship groups and guilds.[26]

Weber's notions of the nature of Chinese society, developed primarily to provide a contrast to his concept of European social development, immensely influenced specialists in the fields of Chinese history and social science from the 1920's through the 1960's. His identification of the intensely particularistic character of Chinese economic behavior, for example, passed into the realm of conventional wisdom through the medium of classic studies by Marion Levy and Albert Feuerwerker.[27] Meanwhile, his related arguments on the failure of Chinese urban development were elaborated in detail by Etienne Balazs, Wolfram Eberhard, and Rhoads Murphey, among others.[28] Although these scholars focused on different concerns, collectively their writings present a consistent set of assumptions about the Chinese city, which can be traced either directly or indirectly to Weber.

Eberhard, for example, blames the city for China's failure to industrialize:

> During several centuries, it seemed that an industrial era was pending in China—in the Sung period, when the necessary conditions for capitalism and

> industry were developed, and some necessary steps already taken towards industrialization. What prevented the Chinese from going further? Judging from the relation between industry and city in Europe, it may be postulated the difference was in the very structure of the Chinese city.[29]

Chinese cities, according to Balazs, "were never able to play the same role of social catalyst" as their European counterparts.[30] In large measure this resulted from the oppressive bureaucratic domination of urban life. Chinese cities were first and foremost the seat of the administration and the home of the garrison; their commercial functions remained wholly dependent upon administrative patrons. The city was created by and existed for the officials, who retained a "despotic" control over all facets of its existence.[31] Moreover, the Chinese city retained an unhealthy degree of dependence upon the countryside and upon rural elites.[32] This dependence perpetuated rural attitudes within even the largest urban centers, which in turn arrested the development of an urban class.[33] In the political sphere, dependence on the countryside was reflected in the failure of the cities to be granted, or even to press for, the urban autonomy that was such a potent historical force in medieval Europe.[34] Indeed, Chinese cities were not discrete units of bureaucratic administration, but were governed only as part of predominantly rural county units.[35]

Apart from its cultural self-satisfaction, the Weberian model incorporates several conceptual problems that more recent detailed research on Chinese cities has brought to the fore. First among these is its forced dichotomization between "city" and "village," which takes no notice of important marketing (or even subordinate administrative) centers below the county-seat level, or of the potential variance between social conditions at the levels of county, province, or imperial capital. Second, the Weberian model is insensitive to differentiation of urban function and possible specialization among types of Chinese cities. For example, it seems impossible to reconcile the existence of a major manufacturing town like Ching-te-chen with Weberian hypotheses. Third, Weberian thinking assumes that, beginning in at least the Sung, for urban China time stood still. Even the historically sensitive Wolfram Eberhard spoke of "the pre-industrial period" of Chinese urban history as an undifferentiated unit, and the geographer Glenn Trewartha could baldly state (in 1952) that "Chinese cities did not change fundamentally in function and form from the period when Polo and Odoric reported on their numbers and magnificence down to about the middle of the nineteenth century, when Western influences began to enforce some modifications."[36] Like other followers of Weber, Trewartha took for granted a stagnant, backward China, jogged out of its lethargy only by the progressive, expanding West.

A recognition of these conceptual problems in Weberian thinking, along with the discovery of numerous details in which Weber's specific assumptions regarding Chinese cities were clearly in error, has led historians and social scientists in recent years to search for a more satisfying alternative approach. This search has tended to emphasize (1) the continuing historical development of cities in the postmedieval period, (2) the wider geographic and human context of Chinese cities, and (3) the primacy of the economic rather than political role of the city in Chinese society.

Our more sophisticated understanding of the late imperial city can perhaps be said to have begun with a turning away from the image of the rigid, T'ang-style city that clearly was foremost in the minds of Weber and subsequent writers in his tradition.[37] Recent scholarship, such as that of Shiba Yoshinobu, has given us a fuller appreciation of the fundamental changes in urban character that occurred during the Sung. The major commercial revolution of this period led to a new type of city for which trade rather than administration was the chief determinant of population size and level of prosperity. Internally, such cities were characterized by the rise of extramural trading quarters, a decrease in official control of market operations, and a corresponding rise in the role of guilds and other voluntary associations.[38] But if the Sung commercial revolution affected urban roles, an even more significant change seems to have taken place during the late Ming, when domestic commerce began to progress beyond an interurban exchange of luxury goods to a major interregional circulation of staple grains and commercial crops such as cotton, which for the first time brought rural dwellers into the national market on a large scale as both producers and consumers.[39] Far from being simply a center of administration and military control, or even a commercial island in a noncommercial agrarian hinterland, the Chinese city now came to relate directly to its surroundings as a center of commodity extraction and distribution.

The study of Chinese cities within this context of commodity circulation, and the more general appreciation of their economic role, took a quantum leap forward with the initial application of "central-place" theory to China, in G. William Skinner's celebrated studies of rural marketing.[40] One major contribution of this line of thinking has been to free us from the false dualism of city and countryside so long dominant in the field. Where once we saw only the extremes of capital city and agrarian village, we are now coming to perceive a graded hierarchy of more or less urban localities spaced along the contours of the extraction and distribution chain (Frederick Mote has called it the "rural-urban continuum" in Chinese society).[41] The development of this continuum has, moreover, been given a historical dimension by Mark Elvin and by Skinner himself, who see the process of Chinese urbanization since the Sung as basically a filling in of the intermediate levels in the central-place hierarchy, accompanying an overall commercialization of the society.[42] Other social scientists, like Gilbert Rozman and Rhoads Murphey (in his more recent work), have tended to stress the place of individual Chinese cities in national or even international "urban networks."[43] The common denominators in these approaches are of course the emphases on context and commerce lacking in Weber.

Two specific contributions of this new line of thinking are particularly useful for understanding first-magnitude central places, such as the subject of the present study, Hankow. First, Skinner's conceptualization of a hierarchy of commercial central places that overlay but did not correspond to the hierarchy of administrative central places[44] allows us to array systematically varying types of cities, even those of the same general size. Thus, an urban center whose position in the administrative hierarchy was disproportionately higher than its position in the marketing hierarchy would be likely to have a very different social structure from one in which the relative hierarchical rankings were reversed (it might, in fact, closely resemble the sort of urban society Weber believed to exist in all Chinese cities). We will shortly examine in detail how Hankow's place in these hierarchies affected its social history.

Second, we have become increasingly aware, particularly through the work of Elvin, of nonadministrative structures of social and even political power within large urban centers.[45] The subject of Elvin's own case study, Shanghai, not surprisingly occupied a position in the marketing hierarchy far higher than that it held in the administrative hierarchy; as Elvin's work suggests, its variance from the Weberian ideal type in this regard was probably almost as significant a determinant of its remarkable social history as was its relatively heavy subjection to outside, Western influences.

We have thus come a long way from reliance upon Weber's undifferentiated model of the late imperial Chinese city. Yet, as Shiba Yoshinobu has recently pointed out, his influence today remains strong—even when unacknowledged.[46] In part this is due to the fact that many of Weber's specific predictions for Chinese urban behavior have seemed verified by subsequent research; partly it is because we simply do not yet know enough about the subject to liberate us from inherited patterns of thought.

The present study of Hankow society will highlight a variety of specific areas in which Weber's assumptions are contradicted in at least this case. In the area of commercial behavior, for example, contractual guarantees *were* actively provided by the administration, particularly for creditors. Chinese merchant firms operated along principles of rational capital accounting, close calculation of returns on investment, and a concern for quality control based on a faith in a rational, orderly market that would reward a superior and unvarying quality of merchandise. Businesses were often conducted along universalistic principles, so that particularistic ties (such as those of kinship or native place) did not dictate the selection of partners, investors, contractors, employees, and buyers. The state, moreover, far from suppressing trade, took an active interest in its well-being and even stimulation.

As for local society, Weber's assumption that most city dwellers were rapacious sojourners appears unfounded. The sojourner mentality did exist, but its content needs to be redefined. Organizationally, the influence of the "sib" in Hankow was negligible. Guilds, on the other hand, were all-important, but they took their urban location as far more than a matter of convenience. Indeed, when such groups did maintain ties outside Hankow, these ties were far less often to a rural native place than they were to other major urban centers (e.g., Shanghai) within the developing national market economy. The guilds were internally constituted along increasingly nonparticularistic lines, and tended to become proto-capitalist corporations.

Despite its many officials, Hankow was able to escape the heavy-handed bureaucratic domination posited by Weber. Guilds and other voluntary associations (such as benevolent halls) became progressively more powerful, but they did not necessarily do so at the expense of the rest of the urban population. Rather, such groups increasingly sought to identify their interests with those of a broader urban community and to devise methods of broad, extrabureaucratic coordination to achieve communal goals. At the same time, new lines of schism started to form: between established and upstart commercial interests, between long-standing residents and threatening interlopers, and, eventually, among the different economic classes just coming to self-awareness.

Although I will periodically highlight specific points of divergence from the Weberian model, my more basic concern will be to offer a fully developed picture of a particular city against which to measure the myth. As the anthropologist Donald DeGlopper has recently noted, after himself conceding the necessity of taking Weberian views as a point of departure, "Only when we know something about the internal order of a number of cities and about the kinds of variations in their structures may we proceed beyond the delusively simple picture of 'the Chinese city' that trapped Weber."[47]

This study of Hankow, then, is an attempt to identify the major social forces in a first-magnitude urban center of late imperial China, and to present as complete a picture as possible of the manner in which those forces interacted to affect the city's vital functions. It is precisely this comprehensiveness, or three-dimensionality, that has been lacking in recent studies of specific urban institutions. The few full-length studies we do have of individual cities (Murphey's on Shanghai, Buck's on Tsinan, Lieberthal's on Tientsin)[48] are helpful, but each remains restricted to a rather limited range of concerns. More encompassing studies, such as DeGlopper's on Lukang, Elvin's on Shanghai, and the collaborative "Ningpo project" have until now appeared only in fragmentary form.[49] As a result, nothing on Chinese cities has approached the complex institutional and social analyses provided by Geertz for Indonesian towns, by Lapidus for medieval Muslim cities, and by numerous authors for individual cities of preindustrial Europe.[50] The present work is an attempt to fill this gap.

Because of its unusually commanding commercial position and other peculiarities of its history, such as its late founding, Hankow can hardly be viewed as a typical case for the study of social change in China. Rather, its interest lies in its role as a vanguard locality. Precisely this feature led me to select Hankow in the first place. Wishing to examine what Rhoads Murphey has aptly termed "the city as a center of change," I was drawn away from cities in which the hand of the central administration seemed overly strong, such as Peking or Wuchang. At the same time, I wanted to focus on a locality that was as yet only slightly a party to "China's response to the West," and so rejected outright any coastal city, including such inviting commercial centers as Shanghai, Canton, or Tientsin. As the following chapters will argue, my choice of Hankow proved well-founded on both counts, although in neither case was the issue as clear-cut as one might expect.

This study basically covers the period from 1796 through 1889. Of course, my beginning and ending dates reflect certain assumptions about the periodization of local history, which require some defense. I chose to begin around 1796 because in that year the Ch'ien-lung Emperor retired, and it closes the era conventionally designated "high Ch'ing." More important, it saw the outbreak of the White Lotus Rebellion, which speeded the financial decline of all levels of Chinese administration. Susan Jones and Philip Kuhn note that "the accumulated [central imperial] surplus of the late Ch'ien-lung period, perhaps

78 million taels, was wiped out by the cost of suppressing the rebellion, estimated at 120 million."[51] The Hupeh provincial administration was even more impoverished, since in its hill country much of the White Lotus fighting had taken place. When Pao Shih-ch'en was invited by the provincial governor early in the nineteenth century to assist in drawing up antirebel strategies, he reported quite frankly that Hupeh was broke.[52] Counterinsurgent fighting and its expenses did not cease in Hupeh with the formal suppression of the White Lotus in 1804, moreover, but continued throughout the Chia-ch'ing (1796–1820) and Tao-kuang (1821–50) reigns. Somewhat paradoxically, these very reigns are usually cited in local sources as the Golden Age of commercial prosperity in Hankow, which had been spared the brunt of the rebel attacks. The combination of administrative exhaustion and local economic vitality makes 1796 a convenient baseline for analyzing initiatives from within local society.

Our study ends with the installation of Chang Chih-tung as Hukwang Viceroy in December 1889. As Su Yun-feng and others have shown, the broad-ranging reforms of Chang's administration transformed virtually every area of local and regional society. Most significantly, we may take Chang's arrival as the starting point of the industrial era in local history. In 1889, the only steam-powered machinery in the Wuhan cities was located in Hankow's British Concession, and it was limited to three or four small plants owned and managed by foreigners. Chang's Hupeh Arsenal and Hanyang Iron and Steel Works of 1890, as well as his several Wuchang cotton mills of the next few years, marked the beginnings of an extremely rapid development of local mechanized industry. A 1909 Japanese survey of the Chinese economy, for example, discussed dozens of modern industries at Hankow and recorded the year of origin of each; without exception these plants had been founded since 1890.[53] In the process of industrial expansion, the number of local Chinese employed in modern industrial plants greatly multiplied. In Hankow alone, the total jumped from about one thousand in 1889 to ten times that number five years later, and more than thirty thousand by the early years of the Republic.[54]

Most of these new factories were owned and run by foreigners. The principal watershed here, of course, was the 1895 signing of the Treaty of Shimonoseki, which for the first time formally legitimated the establishment of foreign factories in the interior. The same decades also saw the introduction of the railroad (effectively completed in 1906) and the rapid expansion of steamship lines—technological breakthroughs that resuscitated the then-stagnant foreign trade of the port. According to

Joseph Esherick, direct overseas shipments to and from Hankow quadrupled between 1890 and 1911.[55] As a result of the new opportunities for industry and trade, there were many more foreigners in the city, stimulating both conflict and imitation. The British Concession had stood alone at Hankow for some thirty-five years before the Russians, French, Germans, and Japanese all decided to set up concessions of their own within two years after Shimonoseki. Accordingly, the city's foreign population grew from about one hundred in 1889 to almost three thousand less than a quarter century later.[56]

The Chinese population also grew dramatically in these years, and with it the physical boundaries of the city itself.[57] Although Hankow had been growing steadily ever since its recovery from the Taipings, it seems to have received an extraordinary population influx around the turn of the twentieth century, in response to the new employment opportunities it began to offer. More important, the new population differed from that of earlier periods both in composition and in character. It was a newly urbanized, industrial work force. Although it is possible to detect the slow rise of a consciousness of horizontal stratification (and an accompanying weakening of vertical ties) for a few decades before 1890, the rapid introduction of factory labor conditions after that time clearly brought with it major alterations in economic and social relationships between individuals and between groups within Hankow.

All these changes occurred after the period treated in this study. However, I will argue that the social and economic structures characteristic of Ch'ing Hankow, and the gradual change that those structures underwent in the course of the nineteenth century, led directly into the industrial revolution of the 1890's and the political revolution of 1911. (The Wuhan cities were among the very first localities in China to experience these radical events.) Of course, intervening and exogenous factors also came into play. The technology of industrialization was wholly imported, and it was initially sponsored by an imposed bureaucratic administration (that of Chang Chih-tung) and by non-Chinese entrepreneurs. The direct instruments of the 1911 Wuchang Uprising were the "New Armies," an institution founded by central government directive, at a time subsequent to our period of study. Despite the importance of these outside factors, however, it should become clear in the course of this study that conditions indigenous to the city made it a likely—perhaps necessary—candidate for national leadership in China's industrial and political revolutions. This account of the life of nineteenth-century Hankow represents the long prologue to those events.

More generally, the study is designed to portray a locality that reflected the highest stage of the indigenous development of Chinese urbanism before wholesale imitation of Western models arguably deflected this process into a new era of pan-cultural urban history. I hope that by doing so it will contribute not only to a better understanding of social change in modern China, but also to a more accurate view of the role of cities in human history.

PART ONE

THE EMPORIUM

CHAPTER ONE

Hankow in the Nineteenth Century

Hankow! Marketplace that links Yangtze and Han,
Defiled by troops, but once more gaily on display:
Red rafters loom amid surrounding hills;
Bright-painted hulls and a thousand masts adorn the harbor.
With northern goods and southern treasures hidden away in their vaults,
Great merchants of Szechwan and Kiangsu make up its household.

P'an Lei, "Han-k'ou"

When western diplomats and traders first beheld Hankow in the 1860's, they saw a city differing little from that described by the early Ch'ing poet P'an Lei. At both times, the locality was struggling to recover from the ravages of military pillage and occupation, in the mid-seventeenth century by the conquering Manchus and in the mid-nineteenth by both Taiping rebels and dynastic defenders. These were not to be the last of such devastations, nor was the brutal decimation of the 1911 Revolution. In years of relative peace the town still found itself threatened by the armies of White Lotus sectarians, European invaders, and Nien rebels. It also withstood frequent and severe attacks by flood and fire. Yet through it all Hankow's commanding geographical position and the overwhelming mercantile impetus of late imperial society combined to produce and sustain a remarkable commercial metropolis, a city that represented the highest expression of indigenous urbanism achieved before China's first assimilation of European cultural norms.

The triple cities of Wuchang, Hanyang, and Hankow lay at the gateway to the vast plains of Hukwang, which comprised most of southeast and south central Hupeh province and adjacent northern Hunan. More important, they formed the hub of a gigantic drainage system extending far beyond these plains into the mountains and basins more than a thousand miles to the north, west, and south. The cities straddled the Yangtze at a point, some 680 miles from its mouth, that marked the transition between the easily navigable lower river and its treacherous upper reaches in western Hupeh and Szechwan. They stood at the confluence of the great river and its largest tributary, the Han, flowing in from the uplands of northwest China. A short way up the Yangtze lay the mouth of the Hsiang River, the central artery of Hunan province, which linked central China with the south and southeast.[1] The three Wuhan cities thus constituted a center of communications for almost three-fourths of the territory of China proper, relaying goods, persons, and information from these regions to the empire's administrative headquarters in the northeast and its key commercial area in the Yangtze delta.[2]

This joining of flat plains and powerful waterways was the chief topographical feature of Wuhan. The modest "surrounding hills" of which P'an Lei wrote were largely confined to the Hanyang third of the triad, west of the Yangtze and south of the Han. (Although the Yangtze's general direction is west to east and the Han's north to south, at their point of confluence the Yangtze has veered sharply northward and the Han flows into it from the west.) Wuchang, on the east bank of the Yangtze, and Hankow, west of the Yangtze and north of the Han, were built on flat, low-lying ground subject to annual flooding and known popularly as "the marshy kingdom" (*tse-kuo*). In the words of one local resident, Hankow "has no hills or mounds to shield it when in distress. In fall and winter the waters dry up so that one can see farther across the plains than even a horse galloping like the wind could reach in a day."[3] In spring and summer, however, Hankow was far from dry. The town was perched on a liver-shaped stretch of sand, bounded on all sides by water. The Han lay to the south and the Yangtze to the east, whereas on its landward side the town was belted by the Yü-tai "river" (Yü-tai ho), a heavily diked canal and tributary of the lower Han. Slightly beyond the canal and linked to it by smaller channels lay the large backwater pool known as Back Lake (Hou-hu), a formidable reservoir capable of overflowing its banks and inundating the town from behind. Even in the driest of seasons the town was dotted with dozens of collecting pools (*shui-tang*) for stagnant river water and streaked by tiny rivulets that demanded a host of internal bridges. An 1818 artist's rendering of the confluence, in which Hankow appears as a mere strip of sand (Figure 1), depicts the precariousness of the town's site in a manner topographically exaggerated but no doubt experientially accurate.

The climate of the Wuhan cities was (and remains) no less a mixed blessing than their riverine site. Although they are situated at about the same latitude as New Orleans (30°38′ N), they are exposed to far greater extremes of temperature—indeed, sudden shifts of thirty to forty degrees Fahrenheit are not unusual. In the spring and summer the weather is genuinely tropical, and when periods of burning sun followed the spring floods, epidemics frequently came in their wake. Frosts, freezing rains, and snows of up to a foot exacerbated the shortages of food usual in winter months. On occasion the Han River itself freezes over. Throughout the year the cities are subject to high winds and sudden gales, which in the nineteenth century took a regular toll of river craft.[4]

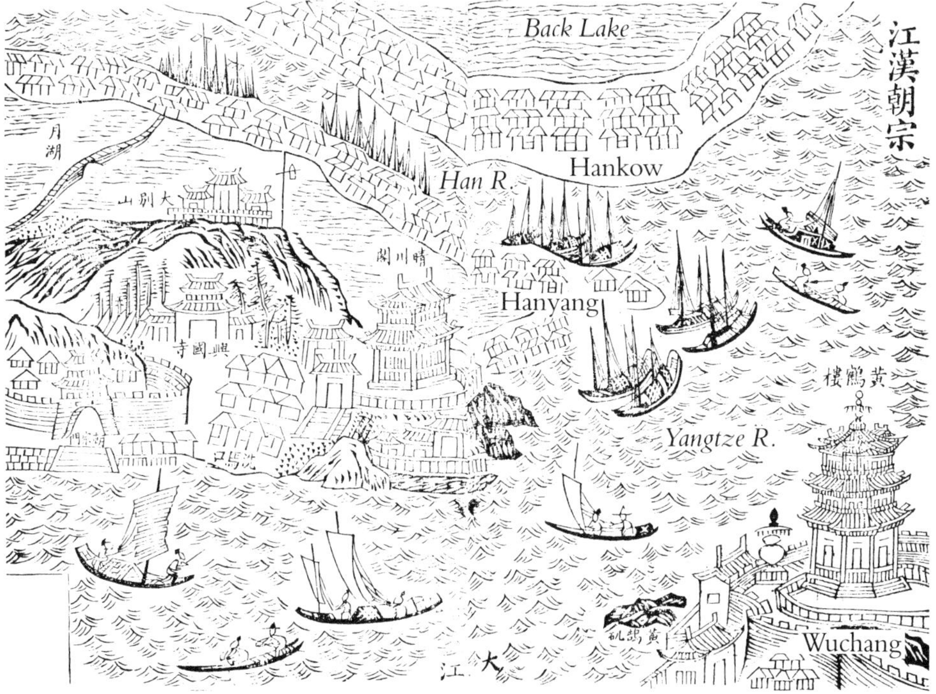

Fig. 1 The Yangtze-Han confluence, 1818. (Source: *1818 HC*.)

The Three Cities

To official eyes by far the most significant of the Wuhan cities was Wuchang, an ancient town that under the Ch'ing served as the seat of the Hupeh governor and the governor-general of Hukwang (Hupeh and Hunan). Early Western knowledge of the city, as summarized in 1738 by Du Halde, adjudged it "the Center of the whole Empire, and the place from which it is easiest to keep a Communication with the rest of the provinces."[5] The walled city was consistently hailed by pioneering Western visitors as among the most magnificent in all China.[6] But as late as the end of the nineteenth century the city walls were seen to "enclose more vacant than occupied surface."[7] This was typical of the general pattern of urban land use in China and reflected Wuchang's fulfillment of a typical urban role: it was a city that specialized in the administration of its surrounding territory. An authoritative Western writer described it in 1883 as first and foremost "the residence of provincial officers, the Manchu garrison, and a literary population of influence."[8] Indeed, it was a city totally dominated by officialdom. According to the report of a longtime resident, 48 government yamens were located at Wuchang. The largest of these, that of the Hukwang governor-general, was said to govern some fifty-five million Chinese subjects, and several offices employed staffs of well over a hundred persons.[9] As the center of administration, Wuchang was also the site of the triennial provincial examinations. The one time it became densely crowded, in fact, was during the exams, when as many as ten thousand aspirants for civil service degrees might converge upon its great testing halls.

For centuries before the founding of Hankow, Wuchang had been the major commercial city of central China as well as its administrative capital, and it remained an important trading center long afterwards. In 1835, for instance, the Lazarist father M. Baldus described his first impressions of the city in these terms: "This city, nearly as populous as Paris, is notable for its commerce and for the number of its ships, which are more numerous than those of all the ports of France put together. Apart from the incalculable number of commercial junks, whose masts form a vast forest, one sees here at all times, symmetrically arranged, between fifteen hundred and two thousand ships carrying salt alone. . . . It presents a rather impressive appearance."[10] Baldus's description of Wuchang's harbor suggests that even at this late date the city continued to function as a major marketplace in its own right. In contrast, an Englishman attached to the treaty-port opening party not thirty years later recorded that "Wu-chang-foo . . . is a large provincial city . . . but it has no special connection with commerce."[11] This was probably an exaggeration. Nevertheless, the Taiping occupation of the 1850's may have provided the housecleaning required to rationalize more fully the division of labor among the three cities. With few qualifications we can characterize post-Taiping Wuchang as an administrative center that held only a modest position in the commercial life of the region and the empire.

Hanyang, the second of the three cities in official rank, was a small prefectural and county capital, surrounded by a well-built wall. Although its administrative functions remained intact, throughout the period of this study it was in decline. During much of the Ming (and probably before) it had assumed a major role in the trade of the Yangtze-Han confluence, but its commercial functions, even more than those of Wuchang, had been usurped by the rise of Hankow. Early Ch'ing reports that drifted to Europe held it to be "not inferior to the most populous cities in France,"[12] yet the first mid-nineteenth-century European visitors found it disappointing. Then, of course, it had been decimated by years of rebel and imperial campaigns, but apparently even before the rebellion the county seat had become no more than "an aristocratic, quiet place, chiefly inhabited by officials and their retainers."[13] A less sympathetic reporter in 1861 described it bluntly as "a place of no importance."[14] Indeed, because of its modest administrative and commercial roles, Hanyang languished in its post-Taiping rubble far longer than did either of its more illustrious neighbors, and not until Chang Chih-tung chose it as the site of his steel mills and arsenal in the 1890's did it begin again to exhibit signs of genuine urban vigor.

These then were the two cities that with Hankow made up the great triple metropolis of central China. (See Map 1.) Throughout the Ch'ing the three were customarily known by the acronym "Wu-Han," the name later given to the single municipality they today comprise. However, during the period of this study they seem to have been three independent localities, and I have found it surprisingly easy to study Hankow in nearly complete isolation from the other two. Wuchang was distinct in terms of local administration (it belonged to a different prefecture and county), and it was physically separated from the other towns by the formidable Yangtze River, swift-flowing and some eleven hundred yards across. Ferries connected the two shores, but did not bring about a significant interpenetration of elites, labor force, or urban culture. As late as 1914, a local source could note of Hankow and Wuchang that "communication between the two cities is extremely inconvenient."[15] Relations between Hankow and Hanyang were somewhat closer, but still, perhaps due to the insignificance of Hanyang or to the dramatic contrast between its provincialism and Hankow's cosmopolitanism, the two seem to have been remarkably distinct. The Han River, though narrow, was notoriously hazardous to ford. Even at the turn of the twentieth century, local officials complained that an urgent message usually could not be passed from the county seat to Hankow and back in a single day.[16] Thus apparently the industrialization after 1890 laid the groundwork for the social integration of the three cities. Not until the beginnings of Communist administration in the area (1950) did Wuhan as a united municipality come into being, and not until the completion of the famous Yangtze River Bridge (1957) did large-scale intracity mobility become a reality.

If Hankow in the nineteenth century was less well integrated with its neighboring cities than one might expect, it was also less continuous with the surrounding countryside than its lack of a circumscribing wall

Map 1 The Wuhan cities, ca. 1865–90.

1. Office of the Hukwang governor-general.
2. Office of the Hupeh governor.
3. Office of the Hupeh salt taotai.
4. Office of the Hanyang prefect.
5. Office of the Hanyang magistrate.
6. Office of the Hankow taotai and Maritime Customs superintendent.
7. Office of the Hankow subprefect.
8. Office of the Jen-I submagistrate.
9. Office of the Li-Chih submagistrate.
10. Office of the Liang-Huai salt superintendent.
11. Chü-jen Gate.
12. Yu-i Gate.
13. Hsün-li Gate.
14. Ta-chih Gate.
15. Lung-wang Temple.
16. Shen Family Temple.
17. Hui-chou Guildhall.
18. Shansi-Shensi Guildhall.
19. Chekiang-Ningpo Guildhall.
20. Kwangtung Guildhall.
21. Medicine God Temple and guildhall.
22. British Consulate.
23. U.S. Consulate.
24. Russian Consulate.
25. Yü-tai Canal.
26. T'u-tang Inlet.
27. Parrot Island.

(for much of the period) would have suggested. Wall or no wall, the town's boundaries were rigidly set, fixed by the rivers on two sides and by the diked canal on the other. Although the outer districts fronting the rivers were more densely populated than the landward side, the concentration of population did not gently decrease as one moved inland; rather, it plummeted dramatically. Outside the canal were a few vegetable gardens cultivated chiefly by enterprising townsmen, then a large ring of sparsely populated marshland known as Ti-wai ("outside the dike"), whose contrast to the densely built-up port could not have been more striking. Only quite a way beyond this, in the more luxuriant area known as Huang-hua ("the dandelions"), did one begin to encounter peasant villages.[17] Isolation from the immediate hinterland, in which geography was abetted by the town's function and its subethnic composition, was one of the basic characteristics of Hankow in our period.

Hankow's raison d'être was trade, and trade of a particular sort: it was the central entrepôt at which the bulk of China's domestic circulation of goods was overseen and in large measure controlled. A Chinese merchant guidebook of the early Ch'ing described it as "the single greatest port for the collection and sale of commodities in all of the empire,"[18] and American observers readily associated its position in the national commodities market (and its continental location) with Chicago.[19] The British party sent to open the treaty port in 1861 reported that: "The appearance of the town was not merely that of a wealthy place of residence, but we saw ample proofs that it actually was, as it has generally been supposed to be, the great commercial centre of the Chinese Empire. . . . Merchandize of the most various kinds, and from all quarters of China, were to be found."[20] In subsequent years, resident missionaries described it as "the largest mart in China, and one of the largest in the world,"[21] and summarized its role in these terms: "Commercially considered, Hankow is one of the most important cities of the East. To it, the native merchants, not only from all parts of Hupeh Province, but from all the surrounding Provinces for hundreds of miles, go up. It is the rendezvous of the foreign merchant and the native buyer in central China—a wonderful emporium for trade—a Chinese cosmopolitan city."[22]

Impressions of the Cityscape

Looking around Hankow one was continually reminded of the primacy of commerce. Far from being the orderly square grid of a planned administrative city, the town's physical layout was marked by a pragmatic asymmetry and irregularity. A Western visitor remarked that "possibly there may have been a plan on which Hankow's streets were built, but it must have been outgrown for some centuries, and at present there is little suggestion of design."[23] The city was constructed along three major thoroughfares that echoed the curve of the Yangtze-Han shoreline, paralleled by a few truncated secondary arteries and crossed by dozens of lanes and alleys leading to and from the riverbanks. In contrast to the rustic spaciousness of its neighboring administrative centers (the Abbé Huc found "lakes and wildfowl" scattered within the walls of Hanyang, and Lord Elgin was startled in Wuchang to discover that when walking "in the very center of the walled town we put up two brace of pheasants!"),[24] because of intense pursuit of the best commercial sites Hankow was far more densely built-up. With the exception of a belt of gardening land along the inside of the canal, virtually all real estate in the town was heavily developed. If, as Kung-chuan Hsiao has suggested, density of construction is the best real measure of the "urbanness" of a late imperial city, Hankow was among the most urban localities in China.[25]

Both native and foreign sources consistently remarked that crowding in Hankow—in its residence patterns, its thoroughfares, and in the concentration of its buildings—attained a level almost unique among Chinese cities. The Ch'ien-lung (1736–95) *Consolidated Gazetteer of the Ch'ing Empire* (*Ta Ch'ing i-t'ung-chih*) described it as "crammed with inhabitants," and because of its crowding, in 1747 the Hupeh governor intervened directly to eliminate fire hazards—an unusual step that he apparently did not feel was necessary for the provincial capital.[26] The local gazetteer of 1818 recorded that: "Those living on the shore are like bees in a hive or ants in an anthill. Those living on boats are as closely packed as the scales of a fish. Within one small entryway inside a crooked alley, ten or more households may be unceremoniously thrown together."[27] According to one foreign visitor, along the city's thoroughfares "to stop was to be lost: [the] only chance of escaping the pressure was to keep moving at a smart pace."[28] Another noted that:

> The Main Street of Hankow . . . would be thirty feet wide, but for numerous stalls and stands along its sides. The remaining space is thronged like the footway of one of the bridges of London; but besides the foot passengers are sedan-chairs, an occasional wheelbarrow, and a rider on horseback. It need not surprise us that there are so few women about. It would be difficult for the gentler sex to make way in such a crowd.[29]

And the Abbé Huc, visiting the town a decade before its opening to the West, found it "incredibly bustling. . . . In all parts of the city you meet with a concourse of passengers, often pressed so compactly together that you have the greatest difficulty to make your way through them."[30] Quite possibly Hankow was the most densely populated piece of land in all of nineteenth-century China. Relying on Chinese and early missionary accounts, the pioneering scholar S. Wells Williams wrote in 1850 that "London and Yedo alone can compare to it, for no other place in China presents an equal number of human beings on the same area."[31]

For all of its closeness and asymmetry, the city seems to have presented a reasonably attractive appearance nonetheless. At mid-century, for instance, a local literatus could write wistful verses celebrating its plum and apricot blossoms.[32] Laurence Oliphant, visiting the town in 1858, commented that: "The streets themselves were superior to any I had seen in any other city of the empire. They were well-paved, and roofed over with mats as they are in Persian or Egyptian cities, but still broad enough to be bright and cheerful. The shops were well-stocked, and upon a much grander and handsomer scale than those at Canton or any of the open ports."[33] Another reporter wrote of the shops, saying:

> Some of them are really fine. You will hardly see higher shop fronts in England, for here the upstairs apartments are merely lofts. They have no very broad frontage, but many of them go back a long way. They are suggestive of arcades rather than shops. Plateglass is unknown; a few shops have glazed shutters, but the great number are quite open to the street, and we can see as much of the goods and customers within as a passing glance can give us.[34]

Several decades later, "A New Arrival" wrote to the *North-China Herald* that "Hankow strikes me as fairly clean, considering how crowded its streets are" and speculated that those who deplored Chinese urban squalor must "know very little of London."[35]

Despite densely packed buildings, the cityscape remained quite flat, for only around the turn of the nineteenth century did many structures of more than a single story begin to appear. Even thereafter, the occasional multistory guildhall could dominate a section of town, looming over low-lying roofs for many blocks around. It was symptomatic of Hankow's commercial orientation that throughout the Ch'ing its chief multistory structures were just such guildhalls, warehouses, and mercantile emporia, whereas government offices remained squat, humble affairs hidden away on back streets. The handsome, broad main avenues belonged to trade, particularly to the city's great wholesale warehouses. This visual hierarchy was reflected in the selection of building materials: the red-lacquered rafters celebrated by P'an Lei, the tile roofs and dazzling tile facades, belonged almost exclusively to the palaces of commerce. For most structures, such as offices and residences, simple materials like brick, earth, bamboo, and wood sufficed.[36]

Among the most picturesque of the wooden buildings were the stilted houses that lined the riverbank, merging directly into the congested harbor. These delighted the missionary Henrietta Green, who wrote of them in her journal: "May 1st, 1885. I wish I could give any idea of the *queer* houses the people live in by the waterside; more than anything they are like Punch and Judy shows, the lower part having only wooden props; many are very much on the slant, and often come down altogether; few, if any, are straight."[37] The harbor was, if possible, more densely populated than the city it had spawned. (An idea of this density can be gathered from the 1871 report that when one of Mrs. Green's "Punch and Judy" houses collapsed upon the inhabited boats tied up beneath it, more than a hundred lives were lost.)[38] Conventionally described as "a forest of masts," Hankow harbor was an unsheltered stretch of riverbank extending about twenty *li* (nearly seven miles) along the Han and Yangtze. In peak summer months, all the way across to Hanyang and Wuchang the river seemed a solid mass of boats, a mass that at times came to surround the city totally, when high water in the canal behind allowed boats to moor there as well. At any given time as many as ten thousand boats could be found tied up at Hankow, and an estimated seventy to eighty thousand called at the port each year.[39]

The sights, sounds, smells, and general intensity of the city made an intoxicating blend. Residents and visitors congregated at the town's innumerable wineshops, opium dens, bathhouses, restaurants, and teahouses—the latter ranging from serene gathering spots for poetry clubs along the shore of the lake to sleazy, rowdy haunts out on the piers. Between these extremes lay the sprawling marketplace teahouses, the noisy, smoke-filled mah-jongg parlors "into which people of all classes seemed crowded" until all hours of the night.[40] According to an 1822 Chinese reporter, "for a distance of thirty *li* [ten miles] east to west, markets and bazaars are strung together like the teeth of a comb. . . . Rare commodities are set out in the open for display, and the shops exhibit treasures of inestimable value."[41] Near the river confluence lay the city's famous all-night market, where colored lanterns dazzled the eye and the smell of spices and exotic foodstuffs filled the air. In the markets one heard a cacophony of local speeches, as merchants from various parts of the empire competed with each other to buy or sell. Around the fringes itinerant peddlers announced their wares by characteristic drums, rattles, bells, and gongs.[42] Beneath it all rumbled, incessant and inescapable, the drone of the city's labor force. As Mrs. Green reported, "The coolies who carry all the tea, etc., etc., keep up a continual sort of song; in the distance it sounds rather pretty, but near to, that is, if the load is at all heavy, it is too loud to be pleasant; as a rule the heavier the load the louder they call out."[43]

Constant noise, bright lights, fabulous merchandise, painted boats, street entertainers, glittering guildhalls, rickety huts, exotic aromas, livestock of all descriptions, and, above all, throngs of mankind of the most diverse sorts: the city was indeed, as one European summed it up, "a wonderful variety show."[44]

Hankow's Early History

Much of Hankow's uniqueness derived from the circumstances of its origin. The city was never truly "founded" in any official sense, nor was it brought into being by a process of slow organic development like other major marketing centers. Rather, it appeared, virtually full-grown, as the result of a sudden act of nature in the late Ming.

The revival of interregional trade in the T'ang and Sung drew a large urban population to the commercially indispensable Yangtze-Han confluence. In an attempt to maintain an orderly circulation of grain, the Sung rulers divided their empire into three regional commercial systems, each dominated by a "central regional market." One such market was established at the city of O-chou (present-day Wuchang), which became the headquarters of the Hukwang General Commissariat.[45] At the same time, nonofficial commercial functions began to aggregate at a number of suburban markets surrounding the city. One of these was located on Parrot Island (Ying-wu chou) in Wuchang harbor, where by Sung times large-scale merchants from six or more provinces were said to congregate.[46] Apparently even larger was Wuchang's commercial suburb South Market (Nan-shih), claimed to host merchants from nine provinces and described in the Sung History as the site of tens of thousands of commercial houses.[47]

During the mid-fourteenth century the Han River for some reason became less turbulent, making its mouth at the Yangtze a safer and more attractive commercial harbor than it had been in the past. For this reason, after Wuchang's South Market was razed during the fighting at the founding of the Ming, many merchants chose to reestablish themselves at a different location on the Hanyang side.[48] At this time, the Han flowed into the Yangtze at a point south of Hanyang city, about five miles from its present mouth, and a commercial suburb grew up in the area between the county seat and the river's northern bank. Like its predecessor on the Wuchang side, this suburb became known as South Market. The new South Market quickly became a flourishing center of interregional trade, and many of the major commercial houses of later Hankow were already established there by the mid-Ming. In the low-lying marshland north of Hanyang city—the site of modern Hankow—there was only a tiny fishing village during these years.[49]

Although scattered references turn up in early sources to cities known as Han-k'ou-ch'eng or Hsia-k'ou (presumed to be the ancient name for the same area), by all accounts these were not lineal ancestors of Ming-Ch'ing Hankow.[50] That city came into being around 1465, in the Ming Ch'eng-hua reign, when the Han River suddenly shifted its lower course and came to enter the Yangtze at a point just north of Hanyang city.[51] Almost immediately, commercial activity was relocated to the Han's new northern bank, opposite the county seat. As a seventeenth-century local literatus reconstructed the early years of the new town:

> People had first come during the T'ien-shun reign [1457–64], when Chang T'ien-chüeh and others began to break ground and set up shops. By the fourth year of Chia-ching [1525] there were already 630 houses along the upper bank belonging to Chang T'ien-chüeh and another 651 along the lower bank belonging to Hsü Wen-kao and others. Hankow became increasingly prosperous. Because it possessed a number of small interior waterways, merchants were able to moor their boats easily. As a result, the city has developed into a place famous throughout the empire.[52]

The new commercial center became so busy and populous that in 1497 it was formally designated a *chen* (nonadministrative town), with its own governing deputy officials, fiscal obligations, and internal ward structure. By the sixteenth century, Hankow's "tens of thousands of households" made it larger than the provincial capital, and indeed the largest city in Hupeh.[53]

The town's continuing growth was greatly stimulated in 1535 by the construction, at the initiative of Hankow Subprefect Yüan Ch'ang, of a dike that stretched for nearly twenty miles along the city's inner border. Some time later a canal, known as the Yü-tai ho, was dredged along the dike's far side in order to channel off some of the seepage of the Han River from the deltalike terrain of Hankow and its backwater environs. The canal provided not only a degree of flood control, but also passage and anchorage for small merchant vessels and, via the so-called T'u-tang Inlet, access to the small internal rivulets of the city itself.[54] Not surprisingly, these capital improvements in Hankow's commercial facilities coincided with what many historians have identified as the period of greatest overall intensification of China's interregional trade, the Ming Wan-li reign (1573–1619).

Then, following a pattern that would recur some two centuries later, the town was repeatedly demolished by rebellion and imperial reconquest. The rebel leader Chang Hsien-chung pillaged it in transit several times during the Ming's final decade, occupying it for a longer time in early 1643. At the beginning of that year, Chang broke out of a trap set by Ming forces and launched a predawn surprise attack on Hankow. The townspeople, with no time either to flee or to hide their valuables, were thrown into a panic. Nevertheless, we are told, they stoically resisted the rebels and refused them supplies or other cooperation; in retaliation, the angry Chang put the *chen* to the torch. Imperial troops arrived to drive him out, too late to save the city. The rebels returned for the final time four months later and made Hankow into their provisional capital; this time, however, it was the conquering Manchus who dislodged them. Once again, the town was pillaged and devastated by the victors.[55]

In spite of this punishing setback, the town recovered rapidly, and most local historians have seen the early Ch'ing as roughly the "takeoff point" for Hankow's national prominence as a center of trade. Hsiung Po-lung, a local literatus of the Shun-chih period (1644–61), claimed that it was "situated at the very crossroads of traffic from all directions," and the Ch'ien-lung *Consolidated Gazetteer of the Ch'ing Empire* found it to be "an essential thoroughfare . . . the hub of merchants and trades, and the most prosperous place in the region."[56] The town escaped serious damage in the White Lotus campaigns when, ironically, a flash flood protected it from rebel marches. Thus it could greet the nineteenth century in full stride. Under the long tenure of county magistrate Ch'iu Hsing-shu (in office from 1807 to 1810 and from 1812 to 1820), by all reports an extremely vigorous administrator and builder, this prosperity was turned to full account. According to Ch'iu's biography in the county gazetteer, "this was a time of great stability and peace within the empire, and human resources could all be turned to productive purposes. Hankow in particular was booming. Thus Hsing-shu spared no effort to repair everything that he saw required it."[57] With Ch'iu's administration the stage was fully set for Hankow's preeminent position in nineteenth-century commerce.

Administration

For all its size, national importance, and truly urban density of construction and population, in Chinese eyes (at least official eyes) Hankow was never in our period classed as a "city" (*ch'eng*). The determinant of city status in imperial China was a simple one: to qualify, a locality needed to be the capital of an administrative area of at least county level. Owing to Hankow's relatively late and sudden appearance on the imperial map, central authorities did not get around to accommodating administrative rank to the realities of urban development for more than four hundred years. Thus, until the very close of the nineteenth century the expedient solution undertaken at the end of the fifteenth remained in force: Hankow was not a *ch'eng* but a *chen*. This placed it in the company of innumerable market towns of quite modest size, but also of a handful of other major noncities—the so-called "four great *chen*," including Ching-te in Kiangsu and Fo-shan in Kwangtung—whose administrations were similar anomalies.[58] Until the end of the Ch'ing, then, Wuchang served as viceregal, provincial, prefectural, and county capital; Hanyang served as seat of its own prefecture and county; Hankow remained legally no more than a suburb of Hanyang city, which it dwarfed.

This administrative status was deeply appreciated by the inhabitants of nineteenth-century Hankow and had a profound effect on their lives. Psychologically and culturally it was brought home by the absence of a city god (*ch'eng-huang*), that focus of community life common to even the humblest of county seats. Architecturally the town lacked not only a city-god temple, but also such accoutrements of urban status as a bell tower and a drum tower, which by rallying citizens to action served (in theory at least) as further tokens of urban identity. Moreover, for most of its history Hankow lacked a city wall, a fact that had not only deep ritual significance but a drastic effect on the military vulnerability of the town and regional officials' willingness to expend their energies in its defense. When in the mid-1860's the people of Hankow undertook to build their own wall, they did so not with the purpose of making their town into a "city," but rather with the pragmatic goal of taking their physical security into their own hands.

But if the Ch'ing administration failed to admit Hankow into its hierarchy of administrative central places, it hardly ignored the town or the problems of governing it. As Skinner has reminded us, the late imperial rulers could demonstrate their awareness of the importance of any given locality by various means. One was the system of "post designations" for evaluating the difficulty of a governing official's billet. There were four such designations, which Skinner interprets as follows: "*Fan* ('troublesome, abundant') was conventionally taken to signify a great deal of official business at the yamen in question. *Ch'ung* ('thoroughfare, frequented') was held to indicate a center of communications. . . . *Nan* ('difficult, vexatious') purportedly referred to a post that had to cope with an unruly, crime-prone populace. *P'i* ('fatiguing, wearisome') referred to the difficulty of collecting taxes."[59] At the turn of the nineteenth century (that is, well before the opening of central China to foreigners), the county and prefectural posts governing the great regional capital at Wuchang were assigned only the first three of these designations, whereas both the prefect and county magistrate stationed at Hanyang city were granted all four.[60] Whether or not the difficulty of tax collection (*p'i*) was felt to plague officials at Wuchang less than their counterparts across the river, the greater responsibility recognized for the Hanyang posts can only have resulted from the fact that they, rather than the Wuchang officials, were charged with governing Hankow.

The throne could acknowledge the importance of a local administrative area by more concrete methods, notably by increasing the number of officials on the scene. This was the solution adopted for Hankow, and consequently, although it was not a formal administrative unit, the town was governed by a plethora of overlapping, centrally appointed bureaucratic functionaries.

The Hanyang Prefect. This official, whose yamen was located in Hanyang city, held jurisdiction over four counties and one independent department (*chou*). Thus, although he was the senior local official in the regular hierarchy with territorial powers over Hankow, the scope of his duties led him to take less of a direct interest in the *chen*'s affairs than his proximity to it might indicate. Sources for the nineteenth century reveal only a few instances in which prefects actually intervened in the city's affairs; nearly all involved local projects or crises of some magnitude.[61] Even then, the prefect normally seems to have been involved only in conjunction with (and apparently at the invitation of) the county magistrate.

Subprefects. According to the 1780 *Schedule of Official Designations* (*Li-tai chih-kuan piao*), ten subprefects (*t'ung-chih*) and assistant subprefects (*t'ung-p'an*) were assigned to the various prefectures of Hupeh province. Both categories of officials held fairly high rank: a *t'ung-chih* carried the upper fifth and a *t'ung-p'an* the upper sixth rank, which made both superior to a county magistrate's seventh rank. Both were charged generally with "assisting the prefect," with special competences assigned as needed in areas such as grain transport, local defense, prosecution of criminals, and maintenance of waterways and irrigation works. They might where necessary be attached to specific territorial subunits within their assigned prefecture.[62] This was the case with the subprefect and assistant subprefect allocated to Hanyang prefecture.

The subprefect, whose duties were more encompassing, was a centrally appointed official whose jurisdiction was coterminous with the boundaries of the *chen* of Hankow (thus belying the widely held notion that territorially discrete urban officials did not exist in late imperial China). The position of subprefect for Hankow had been established very early in the Ch'ing, when the town's commercial role seemed clearly to demand a full-time local official, and it remained in existence until the end of the nineteenth century. In 1863 an assistant subprefect was also assigned to the port. Both officials seem to have concentrated on problems of law enforcement and public security within the increasingly complex urban milieu.[63]

The Hanyang Magistrate. Like the prefect, this official was situated across the river from Hankow in the county seat, but he seems to have had a far greater interest in the day-to-day affairs of the port. Local sources reveal his regular attention to the entire spectrum of urban concerns in Hankow, including fire prevention, education, property rights, and local philanthropy. In particular, a succession of active magistrates in the late 1870's devoted a great deal of energy to the growing problems of crime, commercial expansion, and a growing marginal population in the city, not only in their handling of civil and criminal yamen cases but by increasingly aggressive legislative intervention into such areas as public security and commercial liability.[64]

Submagistrates. As the Hanyang prefect had representatives assigned to the *chen*, so the magistrate had three direct subordinates stationed there. One was a deputy submagistrate (*hsien-ch'eng, chün-ch'eng*), whose specific duty was to oversee water-control projects designed to prevent flooding and maintain harbor facilities. This position was something of a sinecure, as one Hanyang magistrate found to his chagrin when, dropping by unannounced one day at his deputy's office, he discovered the entire staff involved in running a lively gambling operation.[65] The other two county-level officials at Hankow, the Li-Chih and the Jen-I submagistrates, filled more demanding positions.

The very existence of the post of submagistrate (*hsün-chien*) disproves the widely held belief that the regular Ch'ing bureaucracy seldom penetrated below the county level. According to the Ch'ien-lung *Schedule of Official Designations*, a *hsün-chien* was an official of the lowest (lower ninth) rank whose duties were to prevent crime and to apprehend criminals and "disloyal elements." Sixty-eight submagistrates were allocated to the various counties of Hupeh province;[66] of these, the Hanyang magistrate was allotted five. As was customary throughout the empire, these men were assigned territorial jurisdictions at important market towns outside the county seat—jurisdictions coterminous with the boundaries of the towns. Thus, in assigning submagistrates the Chinese state treated urban settlements as discrete political units (in contradiction to the Weberian view). Hanyang county had four such urban centers outside the county seat: the four *chen* of Hankow, Ts'ai-tien, Ch'uan-k'ou, and Hsin-t'an. Two of its five submagistrates were assigned to Hankow, the rest one each to the other three towns.[67] Although these men were low in rank and reported to the county magistrate, they were regular bureaucratic officials, centrally appointed by the Board of Civil Office (Li-pu), and, in Hankow at least, their assignments complied with the normal Ch'ing "law of avoidance."[68]

One of the two submagistrates at Hankow was the organizational descendant of an official who before the shift of the Han River's lower course had been stationed at Hanyang city's great commercial suburb, Nan-shih. Shortly after the shift, in the late Ming, he had been reassigned to the newly created market on the opposite bank.[69] In the Ch'ien-lung period a second submagistrate was added, and by the nineteenth century the two officials were assigned to discrete jurisdictions that divided the town between them. The entire county of Hanyang was divided into eight districts, or wards (*fang*); one comprised the county seat, and four lay wholly within the *chen* of Hankow.[70] Reading east to west, these four were Chü-jen ward, Yu-i ward, Hsün-li ward, and Ta-chih ward—all names derived from classical Confucian mottoes. Of the four, the two western wards made up an area known popularly as the "upper circuit" or "uptown" (*shang-lu*), and the two eastern an area known as the "lower circuit" or "downtown" (*hsia-lu*).[71] These circuits made up the jurisdictions of the two submagistrates, and their official titles (Jen-I hsün-chien, Li-Chih hsün-chien) incorporated acronyms for the two-ward units each administered. It was typical of the inelegant and rather unwieldy system gradually evolved to govern Hankow that although the jurisdictions of these two men divided that of the Hankow subprefect, the latter was wholly outside of their chain of reporting or command. The submagistrates served the county and the subprefect the prefecture, and despite the fact that all three were concerned with matters of public security in Hankow, I have found no evidence that they ever effectively cooperated in any local project.

The two submagistrates of Hankow had substantial powers and responsibilities. Their yamen staffs were large (some said too large) and included armed guards as well as more than a hundred civil functionaries.[72] Their duties included supervising local *pao-chia* matters, controlling influxes of refugees from the countryside, arresting and interrogating criminal suspects, investigating land title disputes, hearing litigation, and other affairs requiring an intimate familiarity with the population and territory they governed.[73] In the second half of the century, the establishment of the British concession adjacent to Ta-chih ward seems to have measurably increased the workload of the Li-Chih submagistrate, and this elevated him to a position of considerable influence; his growing, independent power is perhaps best revealed by the customary foreign translation of his title as "the magistrate of Li-Chi township."[74]

The Hankow Taotai. The foreign presence brought about another change that more profoundly affected the structure of administrative authority at Hankow by introducing a new figure who became the most senior official not only in the *chen* but in the county and indeed the prefecture of Hanyang. This was the Han-Huang-Te taotai, later to be known informally as the taotai of Hankow. At least since the beginning of the Ch'ing, this official had existed as one of the four circuit intendents assigned to Hupeh province; as the acronym prefixed to his title implied, he was responsible for overseeing the administration of the three prefectures of Hanyang, Huang-chou, and Te-an. His seat was not at Hanyang but at the prefectural and departmental city of Huang-chou. As an official with a prescribed territorial jurisdiction, he was responsible for supervising all matters of general administration within the three prefectures; thus, for example, we find him in 1838 corresponding with Hukwang Governor-general Lin Tse-hsü on the subject of irregularities in the local civil service examinations in the department of Ch'i-chou.[75]

In the spring of 1861, however, Governor-general Kuan-wen, reporting to the throne the first visit of foreign ships and merchants to the newly declared treaty port of Hankow, requested the transfer of the Han-Huang-Te taotai from Huang-chou to Hankow for the specific purpose of "supervising matters of trade with the foreigner." Imperial permission was granted, and on 8 June 1861 Taotai Cheng Lan established his yamen at the port.[76] Although the "Han-Huang-Te" prefix was retained in his title, after 1861 the taotai largely gave up in practice his responsibilities as a territorial administrator (*fen-hsün tao*) in exchange for the functionally specific duties associated with a diplomatic and customs taotai (*kuan tao*).[77] Although he became popularly known as the "Hankow taotai," he was never in the nineteenth century assigned the role of chief administrator of that town. If, as Skinner has asserted, a trend did develop in the nineteenth century for taotais to be more regularly assigned to each "regional metropolis," in Hankow at least this development was purely incidental. It was not the *chen*'s enormous and long-standing economic importance that precipitated the transfer of the taotai, but rather the opening of the port to foreign trade and foreign residence.[78]

Aside from supervising customs revenues, the Hankow taotai's major duties were (1) establishing commercial policy and negotiating disputes involving foreign trade, and (2) serving as diplomatic liaison with the foreign consular officers located at the port. These duties made him a very busy man. A survey of U.S. consular correspondence, for example, indicates that the Americans dealt far more frequently with the taotai than with any other local official, not merely for matters of trade but in all aspects of their contact with the Chinese. Any local Chinese accused of crimes against a foreigner was routinely turned over to the taotai for hearing and sentencing; in the early 1870's one U.S. consul reported that this had led to the taotai's having to sit through over ten cases per day dealing with the theft of foreign cargo alone.[79] On the Chinese side, the taotai was charged with preparing extensive reports of all incidents or legal cases involving either foreigners or Chinese in foreign employ, which were submitted via the Hukwang governor-general to the Tsungli yamen.

Because of the centrality of his post, the taotai gradually came to assume a number of collateral appointments, such as Hupeh salt taotai, grain tribute taotai (*ts'ao-yün tao*), co-director with the provincial treasurer of the Hupeh Bureau of Military Supply (*chün-hsu chü*), and standing member of the Hupeh Provincial Board for Salt, Tea, Brokerage, and Likin Matters (Hu-pei t'ung-sheng yen-ch'a-ya-li tsung-chü).[80] All of these collateral posts, of course, reflected the provincial (and to some extent the central) government's growing acknowledgment of its fiscal reliance on the commercial vitality of Hankow *chen*.

Other Officials. The various civil officials whose duties we have been detailing far from exhaust the formal administrative presence in Hankow. There was, for example, a similar array of military officials assigned to land and river duty at the port.[81] In addition, a type of functionally specific management unit known as the *chü* (bureau) began to appear in many areas of urban governance in the postrebellion decades; it seems to have been a carry-over into the civil sphere of the military staff offices familiar to Hu Lin-i, Kuan-wen, and other Restoration officials from their anti-Taiping campaigns. Hankow first hosted Hu's Likin Bureau (Li-chin chü), then an Official Ferry Bureau (Kuan-tu chü), a Pao-chia Bureau (Pao-chia chü), and in 1885 its first Telegraph Bureau (Tien-pao chü), to say nothing of its Chao-shang chü, better known as the China Merchants' Steam Navigation Company. All such "bureaus" were governmental or quasi-governmental organs, and most represented local branches that plugged into a higher functional network overseeing a particular sort of activity in various localities. In other cases, quasi-governmental *chü* were established on a temporary, task-specific basis; such were the Hankow Wall Construction Bureau (Pao-kung chü) of the mid-1860's and the Shansi Famine Relief Bureau (Chin-chüan chü) of the late 1870's. Similar organizations not designated *chü* were the city's Harbor Anchorage Office (Ho-po so) and the several domestic customs collection stations (*kuan*, *k'a*) scattered along the town's approaches.[82]

A great deal of urban administration at the level below the centrally appointed bureaucrats was in the hands of gentry managers (*shen-tung*) and gentry deputies (*wei-yüan*). By the close of our period, for example, each of the submagistrates had at least one gentry deputy assisting him in matters of public security (*hsün-szu wei-yüan*), the subprefect had one specializing in the affairs of the foreign concession (*yang-chieh wei-yüan*), and a variety of specialized deputies were handling administrative tasks in the service of the Hankow taotai. (One such deputy, named Ch'en Ch'eng-tse, was an expectant magistrate at the time of his service in Hankow; such a situation may have been common.)[83] Less respectable but far more numerous were those bêtes noires of late imperial reformers and social critics, the sub-bureaucratic yamen functionaries. Under a variety of designations (*ya-i*, *men-tou*, *kung-ch'ai*, *pu-k'uai*, *tsao-li*, *shu-pan*), these men numbered in the hundreds and perhaps the thousands in the government offices of Hankow. In the city as in the countryside, they were popularly believed (and often proven) to be involved in any number of profitable systematic abuses of authority, such as padding government payrolls, colluding with gamblers and local gangsters, falsifying local registration and other public documents, selling brokerage licenses and commercial tax exemptions, and so on.[84] Many such opportunities for corruption were specific to the urban milieu, and we will return to them in the chapters that follow. Most if not all were included under the blanket charge of *chung-pao* (gorging at the middle), the act of siphoning off financial resources at a level between the populace and the state treasuries.[85] Indeed, the continual outcry against such clerical abuses in the latter half of the century, which in rural areas has been linked by Philip Kuhn and others to a tradition of support for a "feudal" (*feng-chien*) local autonomy, may perhaps be seen in its urban context to represent one tentative beginning of a movement for urban autonomy similar to that in medieval Europe.[86]

To recapitulate, Hankow's sudden creation, as it were ex nihilo, presented late imperial rulers with an administrative dilemma they were never fully able to resolve. Had the town undergone a more natural and prolonged course of development, it is likely it would at some point have been designated a county capital, that is, a city in the orthodox sense. But at the time of its appearance it no doubt seemed already too late for such a move, and thus the administration contented itself with a series of improvisations, which became more and more complex as Hankow continued to grow in size and importance. First a submagistrate, then a subprefect, then a second submagistrate, then a taotai, and finally an assistant subprefect, as well as an array of military officials and sub-bureaucratic functional specialists, successively entered the local scene, in a chain of command that was unusually diffuse even by Ch'ing standards. The first bold step toward the rationalization of this administrative morass did not come until 1898, when Hukwang Governor-general Chang Chih-tung succeeded in having the portion of Hanyang county north of the Han River declared a separate administrative unit, Hsia-k'ou t'ing, with Hankow as its capital.[87] A *t'ing* was generally designed as a transitional administrative unit in the formation of a new county, and in the case of Hsia-k'ou full county status indeed followed very quickly, being conferred in August 1900.

With its assumption of formal administrative rank, Hankow became for the first time in its history a legitimate "city" (*ch'eng*) in the eyes of the bureaucracy. To do so it had been required to assume administrative authority over its surrounding countryside—the office of the subprefect, which formerly governed the city alone, was hastily converted into that of a county magistrate governing all of Hsia-k'ou county. The administration of a hinterland, however, was a task for which Hankow had never been well suited, perhaps least so at this time of maximum treaty-port utilization (the Treaty of Shimonoseki had only a few years earlier precipitated a spate of foreign factory foundings in the town). The city's ties—personal, professional, and even of food supply—were less to its immediate environs than to a greater interregional network. (Of course, it is probably also true that the failure to develop close hinterland ties *resulted* in part from the town's lack of any commanding administrative relationship with the countryside.) Culturally and economically as well as geographically, Hankow was to all intents and purposes an island. In recognition of this situation, and more generally to allow for the better administration of urban affairs, the conquering Nationalist armies in 1927 withdrew Hankow from Hsia-k'ou county and established it instead as an independent administrative unit, a "special municipality" (*t'e-pieh shih*).[88]

Thus the attempt to incorporate the administration of the city with that of a surrounding rural hinterland proved abortive. Part of the reason for this failure may be rooted in the tradition of discrete urban administration that seems to have existed in Hankow. Several formal officials who throughout our period were stationed at Hankow could claim jurisdictions either wholly contained within Hankow proper (the two submagistrates) or precisely coterminous with the boundaries of the *chen* (the subprefect). When a more senior official (the Hankow taotai) was transferred to the town after 1861, his duties were in practice limited to the management of Hankow affairs. Thus Hankow avoided what Weber identified as one of the principal stumbling blocks to the emergence of a "modern" urban society in China: the fact that the jurisdictions of urban-based administrations were not the city alone, but the city as of a piece with the surrounding county or some other larger territorial unit. This tradition of discrete urban administration seems to have bequeathed to the city a sense of itself as a separate political entity, and thus to have fostered the development of an incipient "urban autonomy."

A major factor that prevented this autonomy from being realized, say early in the nineteenth century, was the care taken by the bureaucratic administration to keep Hankow under its control. The city had an unusual number of officials, and the post-designation system insured the greater-than-average competence of those officials.* So long as the Ch'ing bureaucracy chose to monopolize political authority within Hankow, it was probably capable of doing so. But, as later chapters will show, in its attempt to manage an ever-more-complex urban society while remaining itself relatively small in terms of budget and personnel, the administration progressively conceded to that society ever greater powers of economic, social, and ultimately political self-governance.

Population

As might be expected, it is impossible to arrive at reliable population figures for nineteenth-century Hankow. Not the least reason for this is the fact that the population was subject to great seasonal fluctuations between periods of high and low market activity.[89] Moreover, the mobility of the inhabitants rendered contemporary Chinese (as well as Western) census-taking machinery totally inadequate to the task of compiling their number. Thus official figures in periodic *pao-chia* enrollments yield a population size so understated that they have served more to mislead modern scholars than to enlighten them.

*Hankow Customs Commissioner R. B. Moorhead speculated that the proximity of the provincial capital, Wuchang, may have served as a further deterrent to local autonomy (IGC, *Decennial Reports, 1892*, p. 167). (Abbreviations in this and other footnotes and notes to tables can be found on p. 349.)

Three such *pao-chia* enrollment totals survive for Hankow (that is, the combined enrollments of the Jen-I and the Li-Chih submagistracies). The 1721 census reported a population of 99,381; that of 1813 a total of 129,182; and that of 1888 a figure of 180,980.[90] Possibly these figures can supply a rough index of the rate of population *growth* in the city, if we are willing to concede a degree of consistency in their underreporting. On their testimony we find an aggregate growth of about 30 percent over the course of the century ending in 1813, and a growth of 40 percent in the 75 years following. The 1813 census, moreover, provides us with a total Hanyang county enrollment of 428,526.[91] Thus, if we allow for the probability that the Hankow figures were underreported by a considerably greater margin than were those from elsewhere in the county (see below), and grant further that the town's population continued to grow at a rate exceeding that of the surrounding countryside, we may surmise that over the course of the nineteenth century the population of the *chen* of Hankow alone was approaching or exceeded half of that of the entire county. These are interesting speculations; however, they seem to represent the limits of the utility of *pao-chia* enrollment figures for formulating population estimates.

Certainly they can give us little idea of the absolute totals of the town's population. The authorities undertaking the 1813 census noted frankly that they had been unable to count the boat dwellers, and that they had been almost as unsuccessful with most of the Hankow merchants.[92] They also noted that as many as half of those included in their totals were registered local natives, a percentage that, as we shall see, did not reflect the true situation. However, the magnitude of underreporting in the *pao-chia* figures is driven home only when we compare them to even very conservative estimates of the city's population by local Chinese observers. For example, the late Ming resident Kuo Wen-i already credited the town with "several tens of thousands of households." Hupeh Governor Yen Ssu-sheng in 1745 estimated its population as two hundred thousand persons. And a resident in 1806 reported "several hundred thousand households."[93] Even supposing that household size in a city with a large transient work force was somewhat smaller than the average of five persons normally assumed for late imperial China,[94] this last estimate suggests a Hankow population already near the million mark at the start of the nineteenth century. Small wonder, then, that Chao Yü could boast in his preface to the 1818 county gazetteer that Hankow was the "largest of the 'four great *chen*' of the empire."[95]

By most contemporary accounts, at this very time the city was beginning to undergo the greatest period of population growth it had yet

TABLE 1

Foreign Estimates of Hankow Population

Year	Estimated population (*millions*)	Source
1737	1.0–1.4[a]	Loppin, Jesuit missionary
1850[b]	1.0+	Oliphant, British official (citing Chinese accounts)
1850[b]	1.5	John, Protestant missionary (citing Chinese accounts)
1858	0.6	Oliphant, British official
1861	1.0	Parkes, British official
1864	0.8–1.0	John, Protestant missionary
1867	0.6	Mayers, guidebook author
1869	0.7	Oxenham, long-term resident
1885[b]	2.0	Simon (citing "European resident")
1890[b]	0.8	John, Protestant missionary

SOURCES: John to London office, 13 July 1861, and John to London office, 1 January 1864, LMS; John, *A Voice from China*, p. 90; Loppin to Radominski, 7 December 1737, *Lettres édifiantes*, 12: 355–56; Mayers, p. 446; Oliphant, pp. 560, 579; Oxenham, *Yangtze-Kiang*, p. 1; Parkes to Bruce, 10 May 1861, *BPP 1862*, 63, no. 2976, p. 31; Simon, *La Cité chinoise*, p. 7.

[a]The latter figure includes the harbor-dwelling population, estimated by Loppin at 400,000.

[b]Approximate year.

TABLE 2

Foreign Estimates of Wuhan Population

Year	Estimated population (*millions*)	Source
1737	2.6–3.0[a]	Loppin, Jesuit missionary
1850[b]	2.0	Oliphant, British official (citing Chinese accounts)
1858	1.0	Oliphant, British official
1867	1.0	Mayers, guidebook author
1881	1.0+	Hill, missionary

SOURCES: Hill, *Hoopeh*, p. 1; Loppin to Radominski, 7 December 1737, *Lettres édifiantes*, 12: 355–56; Mayers, p. 446; Oliphant, p. 560.

NOTE: Abbé Huc's unbelievable figure of 8,000,000 in 1850 is not included. (Huc, 2: 111.)

[a]The latter figure includes the harbor-dwelling population, estimated by Loppin at 400,000.

[b] Approximate year.

seen. The best way to get an idea of its true size and growth over the nineteenth century is by tabulating the often inconsistent estimates of its population offered by Western reporters. Table 1 lists several of these by year and source; Table 2 does the same for estimates for the combined Wuhan cities. A composite of these estimates might accord to Hankow a population of close to a million at the beginning of the nineteenth century, growing to almost a million and a half by about 1850, dropping over the next decade by more than half, and perhaps regaining the million mark by around 1890. In comparison, one Western urbanologist has estimated that only two cities in the world had populations of over a million in 1850 (London, which had over two million, and Paris), and that but eleven had populations of over one million in 1900 (including Tokyo and Calcutta, but no Chinese cities).[96] Clearly even fairly conservative estimates of Hankow's population would have placed it at both times in this exclusive company.

The sudden drop in population during the 1850's was due, of course, to the devastation of the Taipings, who on their last occupation of the town razed it completely. The ramifications of this event in many areas of local history will be a recurring theme of this study. As regards population and commercial prosperity, we may simply cite the remarks of Governor Hu Lin-i shortly before he retook the city for the imperial cause the final time: "Hankow in the past was known as the most flourishing place in the entire region; today it is reduced to mere rubble, like a piece of shattered pottery. It will indeed be difficult to reconstruct it quickly."[97]

Yet Western observers of the early treaty-port years, even as they noted the Taiping devastation, commented also on the city's amazing recuperative ability. The following reports are typical:

Lord Elgin (1858): [Hankow] seems to have been almost entirely destroyed by the Rebels; but it is recovering rapidly, and exhibits a great deal of commercial activity.[98]

An unnamed journalist accompanying the Elgin mission (1858): [Hankow has] a persevering and industrious population, who cannot afford to let the mercantile emporium of this section of the empire follow the example of its large walled cities [in slowness to rebuild].[99]

The Times *(1861):* It is an enormous place, though not half the size it once was, as seen by the ruins. Life and activity prevailed, and, if not interfered with by the revolutions, is likely to increase.[100]

Protestant missionary Robert Wilson (1862): During my month's stay here last year it was easily perceptible that the place was filling up. It has apparently continued to do so and is indeed still doing so, for the less important streets which were then very thinly peopled now have every house occupied. There are also numerous houses rising in all directions.[101]

British Consul Arthur Gingell (1863): Hankow still continues steadily to increase in magnitude and busy life. Large numbers of Chinese of different grades are flocking to the place, either returning to their homes, from which they had been scared by the rebels, or in search of employment which they readily find. Buildings of every size and description are being erected on all sides; and it is believed by all, both foreign and native residents, that Hankow will shortly regain its once far-spread celebrity and importance.[102]

As similar reports from the succeeding years make clear, however, the process of recovery from the drastic depopulation of the Taiping interregnum was more gradual than these initial reports anticipated. In large measure this was due to the fact that the military security of the port remained in doubt. For a full decade after Hu Lin-i's final recovery of Hankow in 1856, even non-native observers were aware that the city's continued population growth was principally a matter of returning to prerebellion levels, and foreigners reporting on the town's growing population through the very close of our period saw this as a gradual recuperative process rather than as an unprecedented boom resulting from the foreign trade.[103]

Official census figures for Hupeh province as a whole (Table 3) allow an additional check on our population estimates for Hankow. In general, the provincial population grew rapidly over the eighteenth century, grew more slowly in the early nineteenth, plummeted during the Taiping disorders, and only by the mid-twentieth century had begun again to approach pre-Taiping levels. Given the likelihood that official Chinese figures were considerably underestimated and the certainty that Hankow was Hupeh's largest city, our estimates of a Hankow population of around a million in 1800, a million and a half at mid-century, and again a million by about 1890 seem increasingly plausible. The fact that the city recovered its population in the post-Taiping period at a rate faster than that of the province as a whole, moreover, conforms with other evidence (see Chapter 7) that in the late nineteenth century Hankow reflected a process of substantial regional urbanization, drawing persons from other areas within Hupeh.

The rapid growth of Hankow from its fifteenth-century founding to the late nineteenth century is thus a counter-example to Mark Elvin's argument that "what would seem to have happened between about 1300 and 1900 is that the trend towards the growth of great cities stopped or reversed itself."[104] The experience of Hankow, however atypical, demonstrates the continuing capacity of the Chinese economy to spawn new first-magnitude cities, where geographic and commercial factors dictated. More dramatically, the experience of Hankow contradicts both the assertions and the underlying assumptions of Rhoads Murphey's 1954 statement on the Western impact: "In bureaucratic China, trade alone could not rival administration as an urban foundation. Outstanding locations for trade, such as Hankow . . . were frequently not put to full use until European traders built major cities there."[105] In late imperial China, Hankow proves, "trade alone" could indeed support cities as large as the very biggest then existing in the West. No doubt the Western presence did, by the military security it af-

TABLE 3
Official Census Reports of Hupeh Population

Year	Population
1786	18,556,000
1819	28,807,000
1851	33,810,000
1908	24,777,000
1953	27,789,693

SOURCE: Su, *Hsien-tai-hua*, pp. 33, 69.

forded, contribute to the speed of Hankow's post-Taiping repopulation (although the construction of the town wall on purely Chinese initiative in the mid-1860's did quite as much in this regard); yet the key fact is that much of the city's population growth between 1856 and 1889 was repopulation. Even with the new opportunities for foreign trade, it is unlikely that after almost three decades of treaty-port status the population had regained its size during the *chen*'s heyday, on the eve of the Taiping invasion. Thus "European traders" could not possibly have been the first to build a major city on the site of Ch'ing Hankow. Let us, then, conclude this chapter with an attempt to put the Western presence into a more accurate perspective.

"Hankow Hotel": The Effect of the Western Presence

On 11 March 1861, British Vice Admiral James Hope and Chief Diplomatic Officer Sir Harry Parkes arrived in Hankow to open the port for foreign residence and trade in pursuance of the provisions of the Treaty of Tientsin and the Peking Convention. To what extent did the results of this action alter the social fabric and the world view of the indigenous population of the city? I will attempt to answer this extremely complex question in two parts. In the following chapter I will treat the problem of foreign trade and its effect on the commodity flows, occupational structure, and general level of economic prosperity of the city. Here I want to look at the possible effects, whether in the form of imitation or disruption, of the intrusion of the foreigners themselves into an established urban society.

We must first of all recognize that the dichotomy between a pristine, purely "Chinese" city before the opening of the treaty port and a wholly new world of foreign influence afterwards is a false one. Since at least the first part of the eighteenth century, the city had played host to a European community small in number yet deeply committed to propagating its influence: Roman Catholic missionaries. According to one local Chinese source, as early as the late Ming a Roman Catholic mission (T'ien-chu chiao) was set up in Hankow, where it dispensed medical and other public welfare services to the local population. Although the foreign priest who headed this mission was said to be on speaking terms with many local literati, around 1700 the Hanyang magistrate ordered him expelled and the building that housed the mission destroyed. In fact, however, a small group of local faithful continued to practice Christianity, at least until 1724, when the Yung-cheng Emperor began to enforce more strictly a prohibition of heterodox religious practices.[106]

By the early eighteenth century, however, we have firm evidence in the writings of missionaries themselves that other foreigners had come. The Jesuit order first appeared in central China around the end of the seventeenth century, and by 1730 one Jesuit father, Etienne Le Couteux, could report that he had lived for seventeen years in Hankow.[107] Throughout the middle decades of the eighteenth century, the correspondence of a number of Jesuit priests continued to flow out of the city, where they claimed a substantial Chinese Christian community had been established. Their relations with the local authorities vacillated, but at times could be cordial. One Hanyang magistrate was said to have actively patronized the foreign mission and to have sought its aid in the delivery of public welfare services such as emergency grain disbursements.[108] Much of the Jesuits' success in this period was achieved among the city's boat dwellers, although they had also been able to open a branch mission in the administrative capital, Wuchang.[109] One source estimates that by the mid-eighteenth century there were as many as two or three thousand practicing Chinese Christian families in the Hukwang provinces, but in 1768–69 a campaign of renewed government persecution seems again to have been successful in both drastically reducing this number and decreasing foreign proselytization in Hankow.[110] The dissolution of the Jesuit order in 1773 probably put an end to this phase of foreign residence in the city.

Evidence that Christianity had not been totally rooted out at Hankow and indeed may have undergone an early-nineteenth-century revival there is supplied in the records of the Lazarist order. Upon receiving a letter signed by eight Chinese in the name of the "chrétiens de Hou-pe" in 1831, the Lazarist superior at Macao dispatched Father Baldus, who arrived in 1835. Three years later Baldus was followed by one Joseph Rizolati, who was designated "Vicaire apostolique du Hu-Quam." Rizolati established his vicariate at Wuchang, but assigned several European clerics to serve as his deputies in Hankow. Although Rizolati was expelled by the provincial authorities in 1847 (he continued to hold the

TABLE 4
Population of the British Concession, 1861–71

Year	Population	Source
1861	40	Mayers, guidebook author
1862	127	Gingell, British consul
1863	150±	Mayers, guidebook author
1864	300	Breck, U.S. consul
1866	125	Mayers, guidebook author
1871	110	Reid, concession physician

SOURCES: Breck to U.S. Embassy, Peking, 2 September 1864, *DUSCH*; Gingell, "Report on the Trade at Hankow," 30 June 1862, *BPP 1863*, 73, no. 3104, p. 135; Mayers, p. 444; Reid, in *Customs Gazette*, 11, p. 45.

seals of his office in exile at Hong Kong), the Wuhan Christian mission continued to function under a number of Chinese priests.[111] Apparently a few Europeans also managed to remain, for Thomas Blakiston, who visited Hankow in 1861, came away convinced that a "disguised priest or two of the Romish Church" could be found secreted among the native population.[112]

Roman Catholic missionaries were not the only Europeans who made their presence felt in Hankow in pre–treaty-port days. An overland tea trade with Siberia had been conducted from Wuhan since the twelfth century, and although Shansi Chinese usually acted as intermediaries (or compradores) for foreign merchants in this trade, some Russians probably visited or even resided in the area in the course of these centuries.[113] As early as 1842, the town seems to have experienced a taste of British military might when a naval vessel under the command of a Captain Collinson visited there while some of his countrymen were drawing up the Treaty of Nanking.[114] In general, then, 1861 was not an absolute watershed.

The opening of the port did of course bring about a significant increase in the number of foreigners at Hankow. Nevertheless, throughout the period the foreign population remained smaller than one might imagine. (See Table 4.) It peaked early, in about 1864, and did not regain that level until the 1890's. Indeed, writers from the mid-1860's on reported a falling Western population, and British Consul Clement Allen, returning to the town in 1888 after an absence of twenty years, lamented that "the British Community has gone down to less than one-half of what it used to be then."[115] Much of this decline can be attributed to disappointments in the trade, as will be explained in Chapter 2. Whereas Alexander Bowers could boast confidently in 1863 of the forty or so foreign firms at the port, "including all the leading names at Hong Kong and Shanghai," only three years later the British consul reported that the "large [foreign] commercial failures of 1864–65 had their effect in . . . inducing several firms and individuals to cease their connection with [this port]."[116]

Probably more important than any specific trade reversals, however, was an increasing tendency to treat Hankow as a commercial outpost rather than a home away from home, like Shanghai and many of the other treaty ports. This distinction is clearly evident in the tone of the reporting in the foreign-language press at Shanghai. The 127 foreign Hankow residents of 1862 included only eight women and six children—almost all in missionary families—and the concession consistently resembled less a community than a business office, to be visited only by those who had little choice but to do so. In 1879, for instance, British Consul Chalconer Alabaster reported that "for three months of the year [the tea-trading season] the settlement is crowded and busy, while during the other nine it is deserted by three fourths of its residents."[117] And in the early 1880's Maritime Customs Commissioner Francis White described the Western presence at Hankow in these terms: "There has been no change in the foreign community. The tea season brings with it a contingent of some 70 or 80 business people from Shanghai, but they remain only for a few weeks, and the number of foreigners then gradually dwindles down to the few whose occupations necessitate permanent residence."[118]

If Western influence in Hankow before 1890 was limited by the smallness of the foreign community, it was further diminished by the residence pattern of this group. In the first few years after 1861 there was a considerable intermingling of foreign and Chinese worksites and residences. The British consul, for example, reported in 1862 that foreign traders were buying up many tracts of riverfront land outside of the designated concession area, not only in Hankow but along the opposite shore in Hanyang; another source reports the opening of a French consulate and the establishment of several European residences in the walled county seat itself.[119] These early years were something of an experiment in Sino-foreign contact at the port, sometimes with unsatisfactory results. For instance, American Consul Williams reported in 1862: "Observing that all the evidence tends to prove that a building called the Hankow Hotel situated upon the Yangtze is the depot for many lawless foreigners . . . I have instructed the [Western?] proprietor of the same with a reprimand for this affair [the shooting of a Chinese by an American national] and warned him either to conduct his house upon an orderly scale or suffer the pain of being broken up."[120]

But for a variety of reasons, including Sino-Western friction of the sort referred to by Williams, the experiment in intermingled living seems to have ended rather quickly. Disappointments in the trade also contributed to this outcome, as a foreign resident wryly noted in 1865:

> In the palmiest days of old Hankow the native town extended over but a small portion of the upper part of the present British concession, whilst land for more than a mile beyond its lower limits is now foreign-owned. This spirit of speculation was doubtless engendered by the marvellous way in which paddy fields were transmuted into crowded streets in Shanghae, and was fostered by the large profits yielded by the trade of the port during the first two years, which induced many to look forward to an extra-ordinary increase in the foreign population. . . . [However] the depressing effect of net losses of the last two years has prevented the realization of expectations.[121]

According to a number of reports, as early as 1862 and 1863 foreigners had begun to abandon wholesale the properties they had built or rented in the Chinese city and to retreat to the more amenable confines of the British Concession. As the concession area was rapidly improved in these years, it quickly became both home and workplace of virtually the entire foreign population of Hankow,[122] which it was to remain until the late 1890's. In 1871 a concession doctor noted that it was "solely occupied by foreigners and their Cantonese servants, who are thus cut off from close contact with the other inhabitants" of the city.[123] In 1886 a visitor noted that the concession was "almost completely cut off" from the rest of Hankow, and in an 1892 summary of the treaty port's history the local Maritime Customs commissioner observed that "nearly all the European residents" had confined themselves to the concession limits.[124]

There seem to have been two exceptions to this general rule. First, of course, were the missionaries. Catholic priests, as we have seen, had probably already been active in the town at the time of the opening of the port, but they took advantage of their new legitimacy to establish a missionary hospital in Hankow immediately, and to expand into Wuchang and other surrounding areas in the succeeding years.[125] Protestant missionaries appeared for the first time in 1861 with the arrival of the London Missionary Society's Griffith John, and a Wesleyan Mission was established under Joseph Cox the following year. The two groups worked in relative cooperation, and their modest successes encouraged both to augment slightly their foreign staffs in Hankow and to expand their operations slowly into contiguous areas.[126]

The second class of foreign residents that opted to live and work within the Chinese city were the Japanese, who are reported to have first appeared in Hankow around the beginning of 1874.[127] In these early years the few Japanese seem to have been private traders, but this changed with the arrival of one Arao Kiyoshi in 1885. Arao posed as a merchant, the proprietor of a branch of the Tokyo and Shanghai shop known as the Le-shan t'ang (Japanese: Rakuzendō), which imported books, foreign medicines, and Japanese manufactures. He soon built up a sales staff of seven Japanese and five Chinese assistants. The true mission of Arao and his idealistic young disciples, however, was not commerce but spreading the gospel of Pan-Asianism and transmitting intelligence on trade conditions in the interior to their associates in Shanghai and Japan. Like Western traders and missionaries before him, Arao hoped to use Hankow as a base from which to open all of central China to the propagation of his ideology. However, even his hagiographer admits that he met with little but frustration in the period covered by this study.[128] In general, then, we may conclude that foreigners living outside the concession, though fervid proselytizers, remained inconsequential in number and modest in influence.

What about Chinese inside the concession? These, too, were few in number and severely restricted in their range of influence. In fact, Chinese dwelling within the concession served, if anything, less as a bridge between cultures than as further insulation for the Chinese city. All were domestic servants, and most had accompanied their employers from Shanghai and had few ties to their countrymen in Hankow. (A guidebook for prospective foreign visitors warned that bringing along one's own domestics was imperative, "as the [Hankow] natives do not readily adapt themselves to attendance upon Europeans.")[129] Since personal servants were the only Chinese permitted to reside within the British Concession, its establishment in 1861–62 necessitated the evacuation of some 2,500 Chinese families. This was not by local standards a large population, however, nor did these residents have any long-standing attachment to their homesites. Once they were recompensed for the inconvenience of moving, by all accounts the evacuation was accomplished without either conflict or lingering animosity.[130] In fact, the site chosen for the concession was not favored by permanent Chinese settlers for very good reasons—it was subject to flooding, and its sandy foundation was poorly suited to large-scale construction, as the foreigners themselves soon came to realize. Once evicted, the local Chinese were expected not to return, either to reside or to do business in the concession area. As Taotai Cheng reminded the British consul in 1870, "This port differs from Shanghai inasmuch as here Chinese neither occupy hongs or shops within the settlement nor land goods upon the jetties."[131] This situation seems to have prevailed until after the destruction of the Chinese city in the revolutionary battles of 1911, when some favored Chinese began to establish businesses in the concession grounds.[132] Moreover, in notorious treaty-port fashion, most Chinese were prohibited from even entering the concession precincts. The missionary Henrietta Green, writing of Chinese exclusion from the bund, lamented the cruel necessity of so doing: "It seems rather hard to keep the Chinese off, but if it were not so, ladies could not walk out alone at all."[133]

Although local natives could not set up private businesses within the concession, a number of Chinese did find employment there. Many of these were compradores, almost all of whom hailed from other areas of the empire. Like domestic servants, such men often served less to convey foreign influence than to isolate the Westerners more fully. As the Maritime Customs commissioner remarked in 1865: "It may not be out of place to remind Foreigners that here they have not yet attained the position of their countrymen in the South, but that they are still in old China, where they are comparatively little known or appreciated, except by a class in whose interest it is to keep them isolated from the mass of the population."[134] Of more positive importance in the process of cultural interpenetration were the menial and industrial laborers who were recruited from the Chinese city for employment in concession businesses. The number of such individuals, however, was small. Even in 1888, British Consul Clement Allen could report that only a total of two thousand local Chinese were employed by foreigners in any capacity, including coolies, dockhands, warehouse employees, and industrial workers.[135] The last group found work within the mechanized Russian brick-tea compression plants (set up locally in 1875 and 1878), the British hide-pressing factory (1876), and the one or two other very modest industrial experiments undertaken within the concession in these years. These factory workers would seem to have been best situated to effect a transfer of technology and to form the germ of a new, Western-style working class, but their numbers remained small and their influence within Chinese Hankow almost nonexistent before 1890. At the height of their activity, for example, the brick-tea compression plants, which were by far the most ambitious foreign industrial enterprises in the city before 1895, employed only a hundred-odd local laborers.[136] As noted in the Introduction, the size of the incipient urban proletariat was to expand dramatically in the decade or two after 1890.

To be sure, there were signs of foreign contact and influence in the early treaty-port decades. The public sermons of Griffith John and other missionaries continually attracted large crowds of curious, if not credulous, listeners, and in later years John could write that "missionaries passing through Hankow often tell us that they are astonished to meet with so many people in the interior who have heard the Gospel at Hankow."[137] The rise in antiforeign incidents in the 1870's and 1880's testifies to an increasing Chinese awareness of the foreign encroachment and its effects, although it is clear that at Hankow the principals were more frequently transient visitors than local residents.[138] A few foreign-imitative institutions, like the telegraph office (1884), made their appearance in the city, but most were sponsored by nationally prominent Chinese who had gained their inspiration and technological expertise elsewhere. Personal contacts between Chinese and foreigners increased slightly over the course of our period (necessitating, for example, the 1888 founding of a Hankow Home for Eurasian Children!),[139] and several Western observers noted the rise in population density and general level of activity in the portion of Ta-chih ward directly adjoining the concession, as well as occasional instances of Sino-Western cooperation to make civic improvements in this neighborhood.[140]

Moreover, it would be naive to deny that the seeds of truly momentous changes in local consciousness and social structure were being sown during the early treaty-port decades. Perhaps the pattern of these changes can best be seen in the following personal histories. T'u Tzu-sung, a Hupeh native, and Lo K'ai-hsüan, a Hunanese, were both Christian converts who had studied English from missionary teachers during the 1840's. During the Taiping Rebellion, they served in the private secretariat of Tseng Kuo-ch'üan, who drew upon their language skills to coordinate his lower Yangtze campaigns with officials of the Shanghai International Settlement. After the rebellion had been put down, Tseng recommended both men for official posts, but for some reason the court refused to grant these appointments. Instead, Tseng got them jobs as translators in the Hankow office of the Maritime Customs, and while at Hankow T'u and Lo opened a school of English for local Chinese boys. Most of their students graduated into compradorial posts with local foreign firms, and many became extremely rich. The most celebrated was Liu Hsin-sheng (Liu Jen-hsiang), who became a contract labor broker and eventually compradore for the French Banque de l'Indochine et Suez. Liu's elder brother, a compradore for the bank's Saigon office, convinced him that Hankow was destined to expand and that local real estate would be an excellent investment. On this advice, and largely capitalized by his French employers, Liu bought up large tracts of marshland northeast of the town. When the Peking-Hankow railroad was built in the first decade of the twentieth century, he developed these sites for warehouses, stockyards, and railroad-worker housing. (In an orgy of self-congratulation, he saw to it that *all* the streets in his "new town" were named after himself.) After the 1911 Revolution, unable to assess adequately the size and value of the Liu family properties, county authorities pragmatically opted to appoint Liu's grandson Yao-ch'ing director of the newly created Hankow Land Survey and Assay Office (Ch'ing-chang chü).[141]

The stories of T'u, Lo, and Liu show that isolated local Chinese were indeed responding to the West; nevertheless, such men were rare, and although the impact on local society of a man like Liu Hsin-sheng was great, it did not begin to be felt until after the rapid commercial-industrial growth of the 1890's. Before then, these seeds of change had not yet sprouted. This is clearly reflected in the remarks of the local customs commissioner in 1892 who, asked to evaluate the cumulative effect of the opening of Hankow to foreign residence thirty years before, concluded that "the Native population, no doubt, has increased, but . . . the composition, character, and occupation of the people have not been the subject of any considerable change."[142]

Thus the Western presence did not dramatically alter the course of social history in Hankow during the first three decades of the treaty-port period. Foreigners had been known in the town well before 1861, and though their numbers later increased, they remained remarkably few and severely isolated (mostly by choice) from the local population. This isolation was made even more dramatic by the peripheral and insulated position into which they were forced in the conduct of the trade (as we will see in the following chapter). Before 1890, then, direct foreign influence was held within very narrow limits, and the evidence for this early period supports Rhoads Murphey's recent conclusion that in the treaty ports "there was no blending of China and the West, but only a sharpening of the confrontation."[143]

A passage of rare understanding written by one Hankow concession resident brings home how striking this confrontation was, and can serve as a fitting conclusion for our setting of the local stage:

> The half mile of "bund" or embankment is impressive to ourselves, and more so to the Chinese. From behind this fine row of willows, across the broad road, loom massive buildings, suggestive of power and wealth. They are too massive to appear home-like to us. They claim our attention, rather than appeal to the English heart. They are the offspring of a massive ruler and compasses. Our impressions of them, multiplied by ten, give us the Chinaman's first impression of us. . . . We in his eyes are mechanical, exact, and powerful.[144]

Given the contrast between this picture and the warm irregularity of the Chinese city, with the very human scale of its pleasing closeness and largely single-story houses, it is hardly surprising that it would be several decades before the architectural models of these barbarians and the social models behind them would invite concerted imitation.

CHAPTER TWO

The Trade of Hankow

NINETEENTH-CENTURY Hankow was a product of the "circulation economy" that had been evolving in China for several centuries. According to Fujii Hiroshi, author of the first major theoretical treatment of the rise of this economy,[1] it was in the Sung dynasty that long-distance, interregional trade was first conducted within China in commodities other than luxury goods and the few items of popular consumption (such as salt) in whose distribution the state played a direct role.* By the mid-Ming, largely because of such massive, government-franchised projects as the colonization of the northwest frontier and the roughly concurrent development of the cotton-cloth industry in the lower Yangtze valley, this trade was so highly evolved that peasant households in remote villages throughout the country both produced commodities for the national market and relied upon the interregional trade for many of their daily necessities. Areas of the country began to specialize in certain items and to seek a national market for their produce through professional interregional traders, such as those from Hui-chou, Anhwei, studied by Fujii. By the mid-nineteenth century, China could impress Abbé Huc as "the most commercial nation in the world."[2]

One consequence of this commerce was the creation of a new type of mercantile metropolis. As Huc noted: "There are in all the great towns important commercial establishments into which, as into reservoirs, the merchandise of all provinces discharges itself. To these great store-houses people flock from all parts of the empire."[3] The Yangtze-Han confluence had hosted one such metropolis since Sung times, but it was the great intensification of domestic commerce in the sixteenth and sev-

*In Fujii's work, "circulation economy" (*ryūtsū keizai*) appears to convey roughly the same meaning as "commodity economy" (*shang-p'in ching-chi*), as used by Mao Tse-tung and subsequent writers in the People's Republic. See Mao, "The Chinese Revolution and the Chinese Communist Party," *Selected Works* (Peking, 1965), 2: 305–29.

enteenth centuries that gave the area its modern national importance. The Ch'ing *pax sinica*, following the widespread and prolonged chaos at the close of the Ming, contributed even more to Hankow's development as one of the greatest commercial entrepôts in the land. An early Ch'ing commercial handbook referred to the city as "the single largest port for the collection of merchandise in the empire."[4] It has retained its position in the first rank of Chinese trading centers to the present day.

In examining the shape of the Hankow trade in the nineteenth century, I have used the central-place analysis of late imperial China pioneered by G. William Skinner. Skinner divides all Chinese settlements above the rural village into an eight-level hierarchy, based on the scale and intensity of their marketing operations, and sees each as the node of a hinterland (or "marketing system") of corresponding size.[5] The fact that these marketing systems were "nested" meant that, as a rule, a central place at a higher level in the marketing hierarchy automatically also fulfilled the roles of centers at lower levels. Skinner further argues that in China marketing systems at the same level were discrete—that is, exchange activities in a given locale tended to attach to one and only one central place at each level. It is my belief, however, that as one ascended the central-place hierarchy this discreteness tended to break down, so that a village producing, say, both tea and hemp might market its produce through two different regional cities, each of which controlled the regional market in one of the two commodities. For this reason, it is probably more accurate to speak of higher-level central places as accruing commodity-specific functions associated with a given level rather than as categorically belonging to that level. Of course, certain central places accrued more functions than did others, and this permits the convenient shorthand of speaking of a city as, for example, a "regional metropolis."

Sitting at the apex of China's domestic trade, Hankow could be expected to fulfill some functions associated with all eight levels of the central-place hierarchy. However, for simplicity's sake, we will consider its trade in terms of only four levels: central metropolis, regional metropolis, greater city, and local city (levels one, two, four, and five in Skinner's hierarchy, respectively). The first two levels were relevant because of Hankow's dominant position within what Skinner calls the "Middle Yangtze macroregion"—essentially Hupeh and Hunan, with portions of Kiangsi, Honan, and Shensi appended.[6] Hankow's role as a *central metropolis* would entail providing linkage services for goods produced in one regional system outside the Middle Yangtze and destined for consumers in a second external system. As a *regional metropolis*, it would import extraregional goods into the Middle Yangtze system, export Middle Yangtze products to other systems, and control the redistribution of goods both produced and consumed within the regional system. Its role as a *greater city* and *local city* would replicate these regional functions within smaller areas. As we shall see, Hankow in fact performed all of these functions, but concentrated on some far more than on others.

In addition, Hankow of course served as a direct producer (or at least processor) of commercial commodities and as a consumer of imported goods. Contrary to the assumptions of analysts who divide urban places into "producer cities" and "consumer cities," however, it is clear that Hankow directly added or withdrew only a very small percentage of the total volume of traffic that passed through its markets. Its residents produced handicrafts and consumed foodstuffs in great quantities, but most devoted their labors primarily to the import, storage, sale, and export of transiting goods.

The Shape of the Hankow Trade: The National Market

What transformed Hankow from a large regional market specializing in luxury goods into a crucial link in an integrated national commercial network was its role as rice exporter to the Lower Yangtze region. As Kiangnan became increasingly urbanized and devoted to commercial crops in the late Ming, it became reliant for its grain supply on other areas of the country, which in turn began to cultivate rice as a cash export crop. These areas included Hunan, Szechwan, and to a lesser extent parts of Hupeh.[7] Virtually all of this rice passed through Hankow en route to the Lower Yangtze, and most of it changed vessel and ownership while at the port, supplying the city both with huge profits as a middleman and with employment for a substantial number of porters and dockworkers. All reports indicate that this trade had peaked by the first half of the eighteenth century. In a single four-month period in 1730, for example, Hukwang Governor-general Mai-chu noted over four hundred large rice boats passing through the city, and three years later the annual volume of rice handled by the great Hankow dealers was estimated at ten million piculs.[8] The city, moreover, played a central role in the grain tribute system of the late imperial period. The Hukwang provinces furnished so much of this tribute that the Yung-cheng Emperor dubbed them "the rice storehouse of the Ch'ing court."[9] The Wuhan cities were the chief collection point on the route north.

The huge and continually growing population of Hankow itself was also fed from the rice collected in its markets. Hupeh province was never in recent centuries self-sufficient in grain, and only two of its prefectures consistently produced a surplus. Hanyang prefecture was one of them, yet most of its produce was committed to other markets, especially the tribute. A 1728 memorial of Mai-chu says that Wuhan was then supported by rice primarily from Szechwan and secondarily from Hunan. In normal years the sheer volume of rice passing through Hankow dealerships was sufficient to keep grain prices in the city low.[10] Thus for its grain supply the city was almost completely independent of its natural hinterland and was supported by the national market in which it played a pivotal role. In fact, Hankow supplied grain for much of the rest of Hupeh province; most significantly, it was a major purchase point for rations to feed the large military contingents stationed in the grain-deficient and rebel-plagued provincial highlands.[11]

Japanese historians chronicling the Hankow rice trade have noted a sharp decline in exports to the Lower Yangtze at the end of the eighteenth century, for reasons they cannot totally explain. Although the trade picked up again in the second and third decades of the nineteenth century, we are told that it never quite regained its previous proportions.[12] However, local sources throughout this later period attest to large numbers of rice boats coming up from the grain baskets of Hunan and to a prosperous rice market in the city.[13] Moreover, after Hankow was recaptured from the Taipings in the late 1850's, the rice trade underwent a revival, brought about by the need to divert grain from the repacified Middle Yangtze to feed troops and civilians in the war-devastated Lower Yangtze.[14] As late as 1907 the Japanese consul ranked rice second among the commodities traded at the port (with an estimated annual value of 18 million taels) and reported that between one and three hundred Hunanese rice boats were unloaded at the city's piers every day.[15]

Although the grain trade was the foundation of Hankow's commercial power and remained one of its major components throughout our period, the city's location gave it a central role in the distribution of other commodities as well, among them salt and tea. Throughout most of the late imperial period, Hankow was the primary distribution center for the Huai-nan salt district and by government mandate the location for the sale of salt destined for most of the Middle Yangtze region. Although grain was traded at the port in greater volume, it was the lordly salt merchants of Hankow who were primarily responsible for its national reputation as the most commercially oriented of Chinese cities.[16] A large percentage (although probably not the majority) of the rice shipped downriver to Kiangnan traveled aboard the fleets of these merchants as they returned from carrying their cargoes of salt up from Yangchow to Hankow. Although the share of the total local trade claimed by salt declined rapidly in the second half of the nineteenth century, in 1907 it still amounted to an estimated four to five million taels per year, placing it seventh among commodities in overall commercial value.[17] The collection and distribution of tea from Hunan and other regional production areas became a principal function of Hankow immediately upon its founding. Throughout the Ming and Ch'ing, it supplied a large and growing market both within China and in Mongolia and Asiatic Russia to the north. After 1861 tea became the staple item of Hankow's overseas trade, and it was as a center of the tea trade that the city was seen by the West.

Although Hankow served as a center of the domestic trade in an estimated 360 distinct commodities,[18] local Ch'ing sources speak of the city's "eight great trades," usually identified as grain, salt, tea, oils, medicinal herbs, hides and furs, cotton, and Cantonese and Fukienese miscellaneous goods (*tsa-huo*).* During the Ch'ing, both domestic and foreign demand for oil (especially tung oil and tallow oil) grew steadily, so that by the early twentieth century it was reported to have the largest annual sales volume of any item traded at the port, including grain and tea.[19] In the trade in native medicines, Hankow remained the largest collection point in the empire, its large wholesale druggists controlling the shipment of various local specialities to apothecaries throughout China. Both cotton and silk were traditionally traded in bulk at Hankow in many forms: raw, dyed and undyed, and as thread, piece goods, and finished manufactures. Every day several hundred junks congregated alongside the cotton marketplace to discharge and receive their cargoes.

The trade in cotton had particular significance for the Middle Yangtze macroregion, and especially for the Han River valley, where cotton had been an important cash crop and item of trade since the Yuan. It was grown along the river from southern Shensi to the Yangtze-Han confluence, but was most closely associated with the economy of the "T'ien-Mien" area (the county of T'ien-men and the independent department of Mien-yang) on the Han's south bank just upriver from Hanyang. The trade in cotton was one of the few in which Hupeh merchants were dominant—especially the group known as the "Huang-pang," which hailed largely from Ma-ch'eng county and operated out of the Yangtze port Huang-chou (Huang-kang). A considerable portion of this crop was spun, woven, and dyed in Hankow itself, where cotton handicraft workshops lined such thoroughfares as Cotton Street (Mien-hua chieh)

*The term *pa-ta-hang* (eight great trades) was used sometimes to refer to the guild structures governing these trades, and sometimes simply to designate the trades themselves. (See Chapter 10, below, for an analysis of the guild organization bearing this name.) Occasionally other trades, such as timber, replace the ones given in this listing.

and Calico Street (Hua-pu chieh). Moreover, since at least the late eighteenth century Hankow had played a major role in marketing hand-woven cotton cloth from various other production centers in Hanyang, Huang-chou, and Ching-chou prefectures. Some of this product was redistributed within the Middle Yangtze macroregion, but much of the better-quality cloth entered the interregional trade.[20]

Beyond the "eight great trades," the city did a major national business in such agricultural produce as beans, hemp, sugar, and vegetable wax (for which the city developed a "monopoly" in the foreign trade).[21] Parrot Island, in Hankow harbor, was the largest wholesale bamboo and timber market in the empire. The amount of coal traded at the town astounded Lord Elgin in 1859; it was traditionally carried downriver by returning salt boats, and eventually became a major item in the port's foreign trade.[22] Local manufactures from all parts of the empire also found their way to Hankow for sale.

These, in brief, were the major commodities traded at the port. Their mere listing makes clear that the city served as the central market for a wide range of geographic areas. In fact, even in the absence of reliable figures by which to assess the domestic trade, we may confidently conclude from the available evidence that interregional linkage was by far the single most important commercial function fulfilled by nineteenth-century Hankow, followed by extraction from and distribution to the Middle Yangtze macroregion. The port was both a transfer point between overland and water routes, and a cargo-breaking point where goods were loaded from deeper-draught to shallower-draught vessels (or the reverse) in order to adapt to the differing depths and currents of the lower Yangtze, the upper Yangtze, the Han, and the Hsiang. In most cases, merchandise passing through Hankow was repackaged and sold from one shipper to another while at the port.

Table 5 breaks down by Skinner's macroregions the flow of interregional trade through Hankow in the second half of the nineteenth century. The regions are listed roughly in descending order of their volume of trade with Hankow, and the various commodities associated with each region are also given, likewise in descending order of volume. (This tabulation represents only an estimate, and the relative volumes of trade in individual items may have shifted over the course of the period.)

As the table suggests, Hankow's central location made it a crossroads for many of the most-frequented trade routes in late imperial China. Many if not most of the goods traded there simply arrived along one of these routes and departed via another. The routes radiated spokelike

TABLE 5

Hankow's Regional Trading Partners, ca. 1855–1900

Region	To Hankow	From Hankow
Middle Yangtze	rice, millet, tea, oil, coal, timber, metals, medicinal herbs, lacquer, hemp, tobacco, raw and processed cotton, sesame	salt, raw cotton, sugar, rice, textiles, manufactured goods, foodstuffs
Lower Yangtze	salt, cotton thread, tea, textiles, ceramics, lacquer, ink, marine products, foodstuffs	rice, other grains, beans, oil, coal, hides, hemp, dyed cotton, medicinal herbs, timber, textiles
Upper Yangtze	rice, medicinal herbs, oil, salt, sugar, wax, silk, hemp, foodstuffs	textiles, cotton thread, other manufactures
Northwest China	hides, wool, animal products, lacquer, beans, oil, wine, raw cotton	cotton thread, textiles, tea, foodstuffs
North China	millet, beans, hides, hemp, oil, medicinal herbs, wheat, opium, coal, textiles, native manufactures	cotton thread, textiles, rice, foodstuffs
Ling-nan	foreign and native manufactures, sugar, foodstuffs, opium	medicinal herbs, grain, beans, oil, hemp
Southeast Coast	tea, marine products, foodstuffs	grain, beans, oil, coal, hemp, medicinal herbs
Yun-Kwei	lacquer, oil, wax, timber, opium	cotton thread, textiles

SOURCES: Adapted from P'eng Yü-hsin, "Yang-hang," p. 23; with modifications derived from Yeh, *Chu-chih tz'u*; Mizuno, *Kankō*; British consular reports; Maritime Customs reports; Su, *Hsien-tai-hua*; and other sources.

from the city; the five most important, reading clockwise from the south, were as follows.[23]

1. *The Hsiang River valley through Hunan, and thence overland to Kwangtung.* This was traditionally one of the major trade routes in China, as energetic Cantonese merchants from the late Ming on came to market spices and foodstuffs from the tropical south, local manufactures such as iron cooking utensils, and, eventually, imported Western goods (including opium) throughout central China. In return they carried a share of Hunan's rice export. Cities along the Canton-Hankow route such as Hsiang-t'an and Changsha were among the most active

marketplaces in the country. Hunan itself sent rice, tea, timber, and coal to Hankow along the northern sections of this route, and the city was thus host to thousands of Hunanese boatmen. As Canton's role in the foreign trade declined, first in favor of the lower Yangtze ports and then when Hankow was opened to the West, the southern portion of this route was used less frequently. At the same time, however, the growing foreign demand for Hunanese tea led to an increase in the traffic along its northern sections.

2. *The upper Yangtze.* Large numbers of Szechwanese boatmen also collected at Hankow. They brought agricultural produce such as rice, sugar, and (perhaps most profitably) the native medicines for which Szechwan was noted. Szechwanese buyers at Hankow purchased foreign textiles that had arrived via Canton (and later Shanghai), but by the time Hankow itself was opened, more and more of them were choosing to bypass the city and purchase goods directly at Shanghai.[24] Major stops along the Hankow-Chungking route were I-ch'ang, Wu-hu, and Sha-shih. Western merchants long sought to tap into the upper Yangtze trade by opening these "stages," and they succeeded in 1877.[25]

3. *The Han River and overland north to Shensi, Shansi, Mongolia, and Siberia.* Land and water routes separately and in combination brought the produce of the fertile Han River valley and the furs, hides, and animal products of northwest China into the markets of Hankow. Chapter 4 will discuss the great traffic in tea that had followed this route north since at least the Sung, and which was at least partially responsible for the rise to national prominence of the great Shansi merchant groups. The Han River from Hankow to Han-chung (Shensi) and beyond was one of the great arterial waterways of the empire; in the latter half of the nineteenth century great embankments were built along it specifically to facilitate the Hankow trade.[26] The city's most direct relationship with its hinterland involved the fertile counties located immediately upstream along the Han.

4. *Overland to Honan and Hopeh.* This was the largest of the strictly overland trade routes feeding into Hankow, and the city received a steady stream of horse and mule trains and human porters bearing the manufactures of the imperial capital (shoes, for example) and the agricultural produce of the dry northern plains. Honan was frequently stricken by famine, and there are periodic reports of a female-slave trade, bringing into Hankow the daughters of destitute peasants of that province.[27]

5. *The lower Yangtze to Kiangnan and Shanghai.* This was probably from the city's founding the most heavily trafficked of Hankow's trade routes, largely because of the rice-for-salt exchange with Kiangnan. A

wide variety of other merchandise supplemented this primary commercial relationship with such downriver cities as Kiukiang, Wuhsi, Yangchow, and Nanking, and with Ningpo and other delta seaports. After the rise of Shanghai, that city became Hankow's single largest trading partner, in both foreign and domestic goods.

Up to this point I have implied that the interregional trade focused on Hankow made up a "national marketing system" or "national market." It is now necessary to defend this suggestion more explicitly, especially since Skinner (whose work provides so much of the theoretical framework for this study) denies the existence of such a market before 1895. He and other scholars, such as Frances Moulder, who have addressed the issue in recent years base their denials largely on the assumption that interregional trade in late imperial China, although it existed, remained insignificant in comparison with the population and aggregate product of the society. They defend this assumption by reference to the costs of transport in the preindustrial era. Skinner argues: "Transactions between centrally located cities of one region and those of another were minimized by the high cost of unmechanized transport and the great distances involved. . . . [High transport costs] effectively eliminated low-priced bulky goods from interregional trade."[28]

Recent research in the People's Republic supports an opposing view, however. The consensus of Chinese scholars, based on their perception of a relatively high volume of interregional trade, is that an integrated national market emerged in China by at least the mid-eighteenth century.[29] P'eng Tse-i, for example, has estimated that by mid-century interregional commodity circulation had reached an annual value of 86 million taels.[30] (This figure excludes the interregional smuggling trade, which we know to have been very large.) Although P'eng believes that this trade probably contracted somewhat in the late eighteenth century and early in the nineteenth, he and other Chinese scholars agree that the level of trade resumed its upward trend in the post-Taiping era.

A study of Hankow leads inescapably to agreement with the Chinese point of view. Although I do not believe that meaningful statistics on the late imperial domestic trade are at present available, overwhelming nonquantitative evidence points to the existence of a national market at least throughout the period of this study. The leading items in the trade that supported Hankow's huge commercial workforce were those of interregional transshipment. These items, moreover, were not luxury goods bearing high per-unit prices, but low-priced, bulk commodities such as rice, other grains, vegetable oil, beans, and raw cotton, as well as the only slightly more precious tea, salt, and timber. This clearly suggests that a significant percentage of a given region's output, even of staple commodities, was marketed extraregionally.* Further evidence of this may be seen in the commodities Hankow collected from its own macroregional hinterland (Hunanese rice and timber, Hupeh beans and cotton, etc.), most of which were destined for extraregional shipment rather than intraregional redistribution.

More telling still is the pervasive phenomenon of "internal colonization," whereby merchant groups from one part of China staked out territories in other parts (often fairly distant ones), in which they developed the production of commodities primarily or solely for extraregional marketing. P'eng Tse-i cites as examples the eighteenth-century exploitation of Szechwan forests by Kiangsi merchants, of Shensi forests by Szechwanese and Hunanese, and of Yunnan copper and lead mines by merchants from Szechwan, Hunan, and Kwangtung. In later chapters of this study, we will see several nineteenth-century examples, such as the exploitation by Kiangsi merchants of Hunan medicinal herbs and Kweichow timber, and by Shansi merchants of Hupeh tea and tobacco.[31]

This relatively high level of interregional exchange became a truly integrated national market (at least in many of the key commodities of Chinese material life) through the central direction given it by a number of mercantile groups based on local origin, notably those from Huichou, Shansi, Ningpo, and Kwangtung. Such groups were widely dispersed geographically, well organized internally, and (as we will repeatedly observe in this study) able to cooperate effectively with one another for mutual advantage. The empire-wide dispersion of such groups was facilitated by rapidly developing networks of commercial intelligence, and even more by the emergence from the late eighteenth century through the early nineteenth of a sophisticated and flexible system of native banking. Evidence from Hankow thus demonstrates the remarkable responsiveness of Chinese commercial capital to empire-wide market conditions, in an ability to shift investments fluidly from one commodity to another, and indeed from one macroregion to another, as prospects warranted.[32]

*This extraregionally marketed produce was not, however, drawn uniformly from all parts of the macroregion. Rather, the production of commodities for nonlocal markets was concentrated heavily in those parts favored by relatively direct links into the intricate and extensive empire-wide water-transport system. (For a clear example of how access to water routes differentially affected a region's development, see the discussion of eighteenth-century Hunan agriculture in Rawski, chap. 5.) The favored areas within macroregions centered on those Skinner identifies as "regional cores." Beyond these, of course, the inhibiting costs of overland transportation (stressed by Skinner, Moulder, and others) became a key factor in preventing significant participation in the national market. Nevertheless, it seems clear to me that both population and productivity were so heavily concentrated in the favored parts of regions (again, see Rawski) that interregional trade between these parts alone was easily sufficient to support the emergence of a national market.

In summary, the uniquely efficient water-transport system and marketing mechanisms of preindustrial China allowed it to overcome the barriers of distance and low technology, and to develop a national market by the mid-Ch'ing, even though in Europe and elsewhere such a development may have been conditional upon the advent of steam-powered transportation. If there was a single node of mediation and integration within this Chinese national market, it was the "central metropolis" of Hankow.

The Shape of the Hankow Trade: Local Systems

Although, as Skinner argues, a central place at a given level in the marketing hierarchy is likely simultaneously to fulfill roles at each lower level, it does not necessarily do so. Or, to put it more accurately, certain functions appropriate to lower-level marketing systems will tend to aggregate at the node of a higher-level system if that node is located within the spatial range of the lower-level system, but other commodity-specific functions appropriate to the lower-level system may be dispersed among more convenient sites. Skinner himself suggests one possible exception to the principle of concentric nesting: "Higher levels of the economic hierarchy saw a departure from this general [nesting] pattern in that it was not the city per se that served as the center of low-level marketing systems but rather the various marketplaces located at the city's major gates. Thus a large city might have four central marketing systems arrayed sectorally around it."[33] Hankow was an exaggerated case of the departure from the norm that Skinner suggests here, with lower-level functions diffused to satellite markets. That is, its roles within interregional and regional marketing systems were far more active than its role in the local marketing systems of Hanyang county and its vicinity.

Here we should remind ourselves of an obvious principle: on the small scale, a river is not an asset to marketing flows but a barrier. Thus the Yangtze, the great transport artery of China's interregional trade, was a virtually insuperable obstacle to trade of less than regional scale. Although Hankow served as entrance point into the national market for certain commodities (e.g., tea) produced on the river's southern shore, for more localized trade the same areas relied almost exclusively on Wuchang and other south-bank marketing centers. In contrast, all greater-city and local-city marketing systems in which Hankow directly participated lay wholly on the river's north bank. The same principle applied with respect to the Han. That narrower (though treacherously swift-flowing) river proved somewhat less insuperable, but given the technology of traditional water transport it too served to circumscribe rather than to integrate low-level marketing systems.

The result was that at both the greater-city and local-city levels Hankow tended to straddle marketing systems rather than to serve as their node. To say that the city fulfilled no marketing functions at these levels would be an exaggeration, but several geographic factors did combine to discourage its use on a merely local scale. To the difficulty of Han and Yangtze River transport for small punts were added the special problems of navigating and mooring in Hankow's harbors, designed for and crowded with larger, long-distance river craft. Moreover, the demand created by large-bulk shippers drove the costs of mooring, storage, and market facilities well beyond the means of local-system traders. In general, then, Hankow's commercial relationship with its immediate hinterland tended to be limited to the goods that its own urban population consumed or those it entered directly into the national market, rather than goods for intralocal exchange.

What shape did these systems take? Along the Yangtze's northern bank, Hanyang county was flanked by marketing systems centered on two greater cities: Huang-chou and Hsien-t'ao. (See Map 2.) Huang-chou, some 130 *li* down the Yangtze, was the administrative seat of Huang-kang county and of Huang-chou prefecture. It was also the headquarters of the "Huang-pang," an enterprising group of merchants who held a commanding position in the trade of the entire Han River valley. Enough Huang-pang merchants congregated in Hankow to create a subethnic neighborhood, and by at least 1738 they had constructed a guildhall there. Huang-chou was also the node of its own greater-city marketing system, which concentrated on commercial production of beans, vegetable oil, and rice. A portion of this produce also entered the national market at Hankow. Over the course of the mid- and late Ch'ing, as more and more Huang-pang merchants shifted their operations to Hankow, a portion of Huang-chou's greater-city market activity seems to have been redirected there as well. For this reason, at some point the intermediate Huang-p'i county was administratively detached from Huang-chou and assigned instead to Hanyang prefecture.[34]

Hsien-t'ao was a nonadministrative city in the independent department of Mien-yang. It was situated on the southwest bank of the Han about 150 *li* (50 miles) upriver from Hanyang city, at the mouth of some dozen tributary streams and canals that drained the rich cotton- and rice-growing T'ien-Mien area. Like Huang-chou, Hsien-t'ao was the headquarters of several powerful merchant families, whose activities spread throughout the Han River valley and the area of the Yangtze-

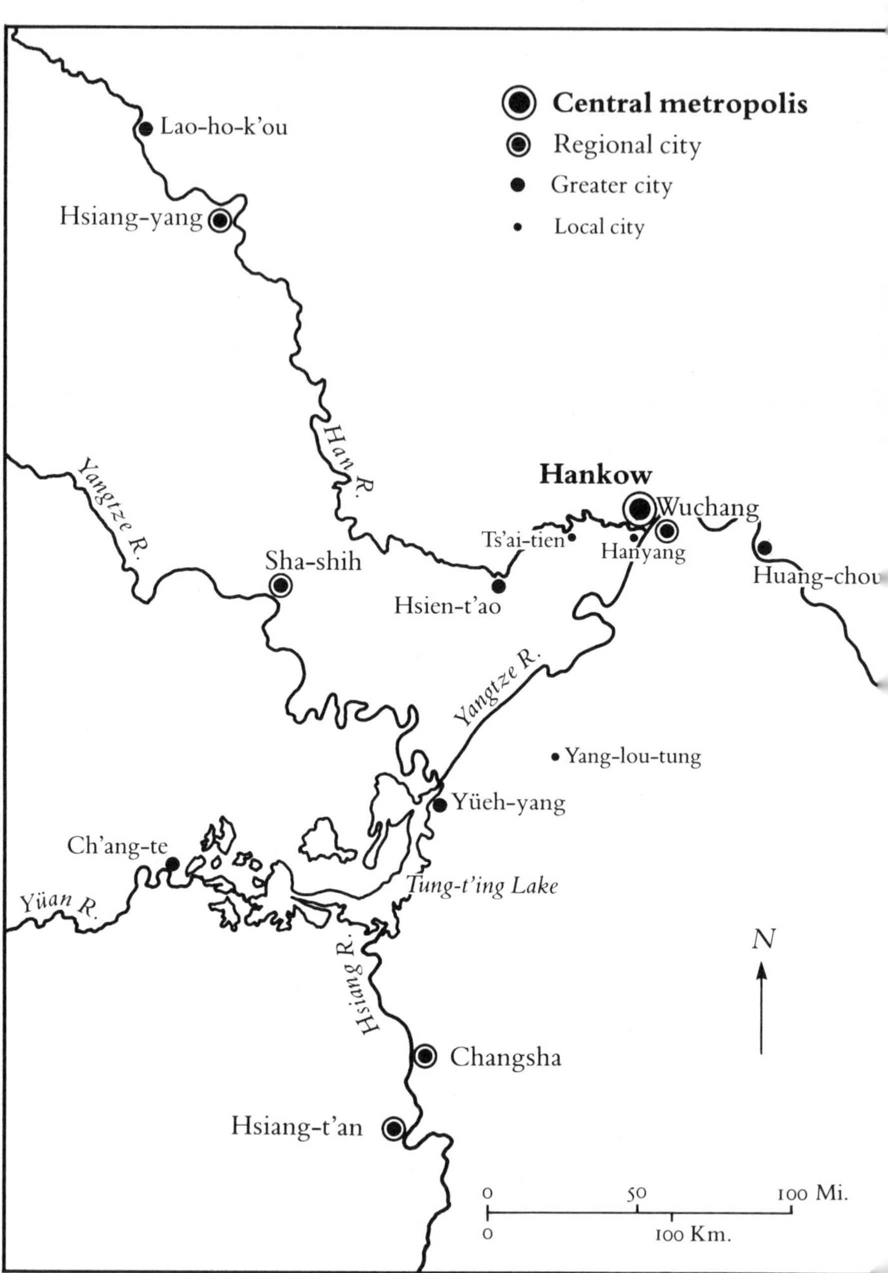

Map 2 A portion of the Middle Yangtze Macroregion, showing Hankow's major trading partners.

Han confluence. The city's commercial centrality was acknowledged in a twentieth-century administrative rationalization that moved the departmental seat there from sleepy, declining Mien-yang city.[35]

At the local-city level, Hanyang county was split into two discrete marketing systems, divided by the Han River. (See Map 3.) Hankow maintained links with both. Of the two, the area on the Hanyang-city side south of the river, known popularly as "Han-nan," was the larger and by far the more agriculturally developed. Although it comprised less than three-quarters of the county's territory, Han-nan contained seventeen of its nineteen tax-assessment districts (*li*). By 1894, moreover, it hosted all but four of the county's 23 recognized market towns (*shih-chi*).[36] Although somewhat hilly, Han-nan was well integrated as a marketing system by a network of tributary streams and public roads. In addition to its crops of rice and cotton, since the K'ang-hsi reign the area had developed a modest national market for its cotton cloth. A market town known as So-ho, some 85 *li* (somewhat more than 26 miles) west of Hanyang city, was the most important center to which peasants of the area brought the products of this cottage industry. As reports from the early eighteenth century to the later nineteenth reveal, small Hankow-based merchants made daily sorties to So-ho to purchase this cloth for resale in the city, where it was dyed, processed, rolled into bolts, and resold to large interregional traders.[37]

Apart from So-ho and Hanyang city (whose role even in local commerce was surprisingly modest),* Han-nan contained three marketing centers of sufficient importance to host submagistrates' yamens. Hsin-t'an, a Yangtze port some 110 *li* (around 40 miles) upriver from the county seat, was the chief market for the county's extreme southern portion. Ch'uan-k'ou, a strategic outpost on the Yangtze at the outlet of a small rivulet, was a subdepot for tribute-grain collection; with the blanket commutation of tribute payments in the mid-nineteenth century, it fell into decline and ultimately lost its submagistrate to nearby P'u-t'an.[38] The third market, Ts'ai-tien, located some 60 *li* (20 miles) up the Han River from Hanyang, was the major economic center of the entire Han-nan area. Moreover, it combined this role as node of a local marketing system with important functions in regional and even interregional trade. A local writer in the 1850's described Ts'ai-tien as an "appended state" of Hankow.[39] Like Hsien-t'ao further upstream, the

*Hanyang can be classed as a "local city." It did fulfill some functions appropriate to central places a level or two higher up the economic hierarchy, however, because of (1) its administrative status as a prefectural seat, requiring it to cater to resident bureaucrats and literati, (2) its proximity to Hankow, from which there was a spillover of interregional trade, and (3) its historical role as a regional market before the rise of Hankow.

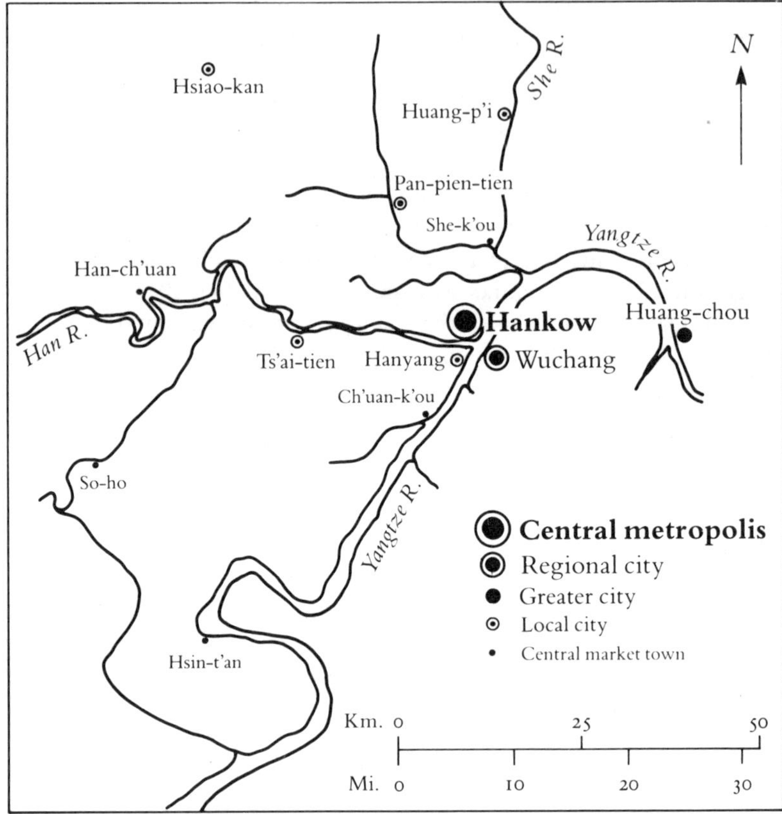

Map 3 Hankow's greater-city hinterland, showing major commercial centers.

town served as the drainage point for numerous small waterways that ran like veins through the fertile T'ien-Mien area. It was also the southern terminus for many Han River merchants who preferred, for either economy or convenience, not to enter Hankow itself. The town's name suggests an origin connected with the Ts'ai clan, whose powerful local influence peaked in the late Ming. In 1670 its commercial importance made it the site for the clan temple of the prominent Liu clan, and the Yaos, who were perhaps the most commercially oriented of the leading local kinship groups, were also headquartered there. Yao Yü-kuei, a major local mercantile force in the first half of the nineteenth century, reportedly divided his working hours between Hankow and Ts'ai-tien; several decades later his kinsman Yao Ch'ao-tsung ran a chain of dry goods emporia in Ts'ai-tien and Sha-shih.[40] By 1818, the town already hosted several thousand merchant houses, and its development was further spurred when it remained virtually untouched by the Taipings, although all nearby commercial centers were repeatedly despoiled. Toward the end of the century it was known as "a major crossroads of land and river traffic," and was the site of a lucrative likin station.[41] Since 1950, it has succeeded Hanyang city as the administrative seat of Hanyang county.

The quadrant of Hanyang county west of the Yangtze and north of the Han, the portion in which Hankow itself was situated, belonged to a marketing system discrete from that of Han-nan. This area was marshy (its principal topographic feature being the large backwater pool known as Back Lake), and as late as the early nineteenth century largely uncultivated. Although it became more populated in the 1820's and 1830's, its agriculture remained limited to subsistence farming, with some production of melons and other vegetables for Hankow retail markets. Fishing constituted an important sideline, with the catch likewise marketed largely in Hankow.[42] Northern Hanyang's economic isolation from the rest of the county facilitated its independent establishment as "Hsia-k'ou t'ing" and subsequently Hsia-k'ou county at the turn of the twentieth century, but it never truly made up an economic system unto itself. Rather, it linked into a local marketing system incorporating much of the neighboring counties to the north, Huang-p'i and Hsiao-kan. Besides sharing a common Yangtze shoreline with Huang-p'i, Hankow was linked to both counties by a network of small but navigable rivulets, most of which spilled into the Yü-tai Canal in the vicinity of the city's T'u-tang Inlet and Liu-tu Bridge. The T'u-tang neighborhood was also the terminus of a major public road connecting Hankow with Huang-p'i. By the 1820's a number of daily, open-air markets had sprung up at regular intervals along the length of the canal—that is, along Hankow's landward boundary. As local trade intensified over the latter half of the century, small-scale dealerships and brokerage operations were devised by neighborhood people to manage with greater sophistication the flow of foodstuffs to the city.[43]

Hankow, then, occasionally drew items for consumption directly from this local hinterland. It also provided entry into the national market for handicraft products (tobacco pouches, copper jewelry) produced in Huang-p'i workshops and peasant households, as well as opening urban employment opportunities for the hinterland population. Although Hankow was thus a great asset to the local system, comprising Huang-p'i, Hsiao-kan, and northeast Hanyang, it would be a mistake to see the city as its central node. Intralocal marketing functions seem rather to have been diffused between several smaller central places. Perhaps the most important was Pan-pien-tien, a nonadministrative local city in Huang-p'i county that served as the hub of the local vegetable-oil trade, drawing peasants and petty traders to its oil presses from several surrounding counties. Hankow was completely bypassed by this traffic.[44]

To sum up, although Hankow was not entirely isolated from its hinterland, its role in the economy of south-central Hupeh was remarkably restricted. Its orientation was almost exclusively to the interregional trade, both in supplying linkage between external regions and in mediating between the Middle Yangtze region and the national market. Even in feeding its population, although the city did draw fresh fish and vegetables from its suburban backwater, it gathered the bulk of its food supply—including virtually all of its grain—from farther afield via the interregional trade. In other words, Hankow exhibited an unusually low degree of embeddedness in its surrounding territory, and this fact had critical implications for its social history.

In his recent work *The Outsiders*, Rhoads Murphey takes a similar argument even further. He states:

> The relations between the treaty ports and their supposed hinterlands, in contrast to the Indian experience, was severely limited. They were confined for the most part to the extraction via Chinese agents of a few predominantly agricultural goods for export and the distribution, again through Chinese agents, of relatively small amounts of imported or treaty port manufactured goods. There was some increase in commercialization of some sectors of the economy through the indirect agency of the treaty ports, and a substantial increase in the foreign trade, but none of these changes bulked large in the context of the Chinese economy as a whole.[45]

We may quarrel with the degree of disjunction Murphey claims to have existed between the city and the rural economy, but our findings for Hankow generally confirm his view of the independence of town and hinterland. However, there would appear to be no reason to attribute this situation to a city's becoming a treaty port. The remarkable volume and extent of Hankow's interregional trade predated the Opium War by several centuries and remained the city's most vital concern even after the port had been opened. It was Hankow's rise to national prominence, rather than the Western impact, that increasingly divorced the city from its role in local systems of exchange. That divorce was a natural consequence of the development in Ming and Ch'ing China of an integrated national commercial economy.

The Conduct of Trade

Cities of late imperial China generally belied the claims of urbanologists that "preindustrial cities" necessarily exhibit a relatively low division of labor and occupational specialization. In China, as Skinner has argued, the division of labor intensified as one proceeded up the scale of economic central places. Thus a city like Hankow, occupying the highest rung in the marketing hierarchy, hosted a workforce that was extremely diversified both across the range of occupations and within the commercial sector itself.[46]

Within the Hankow trade, there was an intricate division of labor, specialized both by product and by function. Financial speculators and transport contractors might, it is true, shift their investments and haulage contracts from one commodity to another in response to market conditions,[47] but merchants more directly involved in the marketing of goods tended to concentrate on a single commodity. Newspaper reports of local fires in the 1870's and 1880's enumerate a dizzying array of retail shops, specializing in items like hats, headbands, wine, tobacco, fireworks, cooking oil, and rope and cable. Government-licensed brokers were restricted by law to operating in a single commodity. Wholesale dealers might, like the phenomenally successful Wang Shih-liang and his wife, begin with a single product (a local variety of tea leaf), branch out into related lines (other foodstuffs), and then open subsidiary firms to deal in nonrelated products (cotton cloth).[48] But the increasing trend for merchant guilds to organize by product rather than local origin reflects the fact that individual wholesalers themselves were moving toward more, rather than less, specialization in their commodities.

Even more dramatically, the Hankow trade's intricate division of labor was seen in the system by which merchants assumed narrowly defined roles within a particular commodity's chain of collection and distribution. This system—which one Chinese writer has dubbed the "naturally generated business structure" (*tzu-jan hang-yeh*), as opposed to "modern-style enterprise" (*ch'i-yeh*)[49]—was characterized by a network of contractors and subcontractors who operated as middlemen between producer and consumer. It had evolved to meet the needs of the domestic trade, but was eventually adopted in the foreign trade as well. Examining the overseas export of tung oil from Hankow, for example, P'eng Yü-hsin has isolated seven distinct levels of traders through whose hands the oil passed between producer and foreign buyer.[50] Merchants at each stage of the chain of collection and distribution had sharply delineated spheres of competence and responsibility.

Many links in this chain were headquartered in the major commercial cities, but this does not imply that most were highly capitalized. Rather, most were "petty native traders who work on a commission basis," as they were described by British Consul Medhurst in 1867.[51] Nearly all the considerable Chinese and Japanese scholarly literature on the subject has condemned the system for its "feudal" character, insofar as it was built upon bonds of financial dependency between traders at lower and higher levels.[52] In a recent revisionist article, however, Ramon Myers has suggested that it was precisely this system that permitted the impressive level of commercialization in late imperial China, since it "encouraged parties with little savings to become productive and engage in contracting and sub-contracting."[53] Both points of view may be justified; but commercial networks utilizing a low level of overall capitalization could prove a serious shortcoming when confronted with international competition, as happened in the Hankow tea trade.

The merchant community of Hankow may be divided for analytic purposes into five general types, which I will discuss in roughly descending order of centrality within the trade.[54]

1. *Factors or brokers.* Depending on the commodity in which they specialized, brokers fell into two overall categories: those known as *ya-hang*, who held government licenses, and those known as *ching-chi*, who did not. Both were independent businessmen whose basic function was to manage the market in a particular item of trade and to serve as middlemen between buyers and sellers. The broker either owned or was partner in a warehouse (*chan*, *chan-hang*), where the goods of his clients were stored and transactions closed, usually with an attached hostel (*shu-hang*), where merchants and their staffs might lodge while doing business at the port. These warehouse-hostels were the true heart of Hankow; according to an 1867 commercial guidebook they were virtually the only structures to be seen along the city's main thoroughfares.[55] Brokers derived their handsome incomes from rental fees for these premises, from commissions charged for overseeing sales and guaranteeing the principals' good faith, and occasionally from interest charged on advances made to underwrite the transaction. Moreover, brokers often dealt on their own account in the commodities they brokered.

2. *Other commission agents.* In addition to the brokers, a wide variety of commission agents operated in Hankow. These men also served primarily to bring buyer and seller together in return for a percentage of the transaction price, but unlike the brokers they were not substantially capitalized, independent businessmen. Rather, they were contract employees of the buying or selling party who offered assistance in soliciting business. (A special type of commission agent was hired by the brokers themselves to perform the more routine aspects of their job.) The names by which commission agents were known varied according to their specific function, but as a class they were referred to as *ching-shou* or *ching-shou-jen*. One type of *ching-shou* was the well-known comprador (*mai-pan*), an institution that reached full maturity in the Sino-for-

eign trade of treaty-port days, but which had a long history before 1861 in such an ethnically diverse marketplace as Hankow. Nieh Tao-p'ing, a native of Hsiang-t'an, for example, was a compradore involved in a wholly domestic trade. Nieh was employed by a large Hsiang-t'an coal dealership that relied upon him to market its product to Hankow merchants from various provinces.[56] Like the broker, the commission agent at times augmented his profits by speculating on his own account.

3. *Wholesale dealers.* These businesses were known variously as *chuang*, *hao*, or *tien*. They specialized in a single item or line of items, which they often marketed under their firm's own name, or "chop" (*hao*). They normally bought and sold goods on their own account, and in some cases engaged in partial processing of their merchandise. Consequently a *chuang* was usually a rather large operation; a late Ch'ing source estimated that in Hankow its normal capitalization ranged between ten and sixty thousand taels. The larger dealers employed their own buyers on a full-time basis; the smaller bought from independent traveling merchants. It was not uncommon for a Hankow *chuang* to be affiliated with similar firms in other commercial centers. For example, the famous Fang lineage of Chen-hai (Ningpo) established a wholesale dealership in foreign calicos at Hankow around 1840 as part of a conglomerate enterprise that included sugar, tea, silk, and cotton *chuang* in Shanghai, Hangchow, and other cities. Hanyang county's Yao clan likewise ran cotton and silk dealerships in Hankow, Ts'ai-tien, and Sha-shih. Yet a third example was a dealer in Cantonese and Szechwanese specialty foodstuffs, whose Hankow branch was linked with others at Chungking, Chengtu, Canton, Shanghai, and Yangchow.[57]

4. *Itinerant merchants.* These were usually known as *k'o-shang* (guest merchants) or *fan* (peddlers). Whereas in smaller markets such individuals may also have engaged in retail sales, in Hankow they were almost exclusively wholesale jobbers, who carried merchandise to or from other major urban centers or rural markets. Few *k'o-shang* were Hankow natives, but large numbers of them dwelt in the city at all times, and in several neighborhoods they made up the majority of the population. Individual *k'o-shang* varied greatly in their scale of operations, but collectively they formed the lifeblood of the Hankow marketplace and were responsible for providing almost all of the merchandise traded there. They either bought and sold on their own account or operated on a commission basis. The larger might own their own means of transport, but most relied on contracted boats or porterage. Typical of the larger *k'o-shang* of the city was the Ningpoese Shih Fu-jun, who in partnership with his uncle, his brother, and a Hangchow native named Ch'en Chung-chi ran a lorcha trade between I-ch'ang and several down-

river ports such as Chinkiang. Shih and his partners bought timber with their own capital for shipment downriver and brought back cargoes of tung oil. Because of the higher per-unit cost of the oil, they resorted to syndicate financing for their upriver trip.[58]

5. *Retail shopkeepers*. These were known as *p'u* or occasionally *tien* (a term shared with certain wholesale dealers). To support its huge population Hankow required a great number of local merchants. Their shops were of all sorts and sizes, from the packs of street peddlers, to open-air booths, to long-standing establishments with capitalizations of up to several thousand taels. In general, the retail trade was sharply distinguished from the major interregional commerce of the city. Interface between the two was usually effected by the individual shopkeeper, who made the rounds of warehouses that stored goods for transshipment and there purchased job lots for retail.[59] As has been noted, however, Hankow was only a very modest consumer of the goods in which it traded.

Let us now turn to a brief consideration of the structure of Hankow commercial firms. As Japanese researchers have pointed out, most late imperial merchant houses were constructed along ascriptive (or what the Japanese term "feudal") lines, with employees normally recruited through ties of kinship or local origin. In the Hankow trade, one finds repeated evidence of these practices. They were useful for reinforcing the loyalty of employees, particularly in such geographically diversified firms as some of the Hankow *chuang* just noted. Fujii Hiroshi describes a hypothetical firm of this type, such as might have been set up in Hankow by his Hui-chou merchants, as a family outfit run by the head of the household assisted by his immediate blood relations, with lesser jobs held by unrelated persons who were usually from the same home village and were often hereditary servants of the proprietor.[60] Hired employees who were not kin often had sharply restricted duties; for example, a British official noted during a Taiping scare at Hankow that "the heads of Hongs have nearly all deserted their places of business, and but few men are left who can buy, they being principally clerks left in charge of the Hongs."[61]

To a considerable extent, however, the model of the family-owned, family-run commercial firm was being displaced in late imperial Hankow. By the mid-eighteenth century, for instance, we find the Hui-chou native Wang Shih-liang turning over his multifarious Hankow enterprises to a professional manager of Shantung origin, so that he can retire to his native place.[62] By the mid- and late nineteenth century, perhaps the majority of business firms that for one reason or another came under investigation by the Hankow taotai were made up of partners from diverse regions of the country.[63] These firms, moreover, were often organized along lines of joint-stock ownership that look extremely modern.

Clearly, the commercial world of nineteenth-century Hankow fully met the major test of "economic rationality" proposed by Max Weber: the widespread and sophisticated use of capital accounting.[64] By the nineteenth century, the joint-stock business firm already had a long history in Chinese commerce. According to the chronology suggested by Imahori Seiji, the "classic type" of partnership dated from the mid-Ming and featured a system of accounting that divided profits in accordance with the percentage of capitalization put up by each investing partner (these were sharply differentiated from salaried employees). By the first quarter of the nineteenth century—that is, before the Opium War—a further differentiation had become widely recognized between managing partners (*huo*), who had responsibility for business operations, and purely investing partners (*tung*), who did not.[65] In a study of early Ch'ing coal-mining operations recently reissued in the People's Republic, Teng T'o showed in detail how capital-account books were employed to calculate the distribution of profits to stockholders according to percentage of capital investment, managerial responsibilities, and a wide range of other factors. The system, moreover, had a built-in capability for expansive refinancing when new capital was needed.[66]

In Hankow itself, sophisticated forms of partnership and capital accumulation existed on surprisingly modest levels. A local source from 1850, for example, describes Hankow firms of all sorts and sizes as "each having its capitalists (*ts'ai-tung*) and each its poorer employees."[67] Participation in the trade by nonworking investors had become so routine by the 1860's that the local Maritime Customs commissioner could write that "Chinese speculators" at the port, having suffered from the preceding year's poor tea crop, were shifting their capital quite fluidly to the salt trade in an effort to recoup their losses.[68]

The sophistication of business organization, as well as the principle of legal recourse to enforce personal liability, was perhaps nowhere more clearly revealed than in the report of an 1887 symposium conducted by the Royal Asiatic Society's China Branch on the legal culpability of Chinese trading firms in bankruptcy proceedings.[69] Most of the symposium's participants were veterans of long experience at Hankow (Alabaster, Gardner, Parker) and no doubt based their comments on observations made there. The symposium concurred that there were no fixed, statutory rules in China for assessing the amount of liability of each individual partner, but that the official judging the case decided what he himself felt to be an equitable settlement. Usually the partners were held liable according to the percentage of the original capital that they had advanced. One partner, however, was always designated the "managing partner," and in some cases funds advanced by other partners might be considered to have been merely loans to him, in which case the other partners' liabilities were limited to these original amounts. In any case, the managing partner was likely to be held liable for more than his share of the capital if negligence on his part was determined to have been a cause of the firm's failure.

Business practices in Hankow varied widely according to the item of trade, and even such basic factors as weights and measures differed with each commodity. Yet certain common denominators can be identified in most of the trades carried on in the city. Chief among these was the use of mediators (*ts'ung-chung*), who functioned at all levels of the economic spectrum, from the wholesale brokers and commission agents described above to the neighborhood go-between who arranged private small business or personal loans. Mediators usually served a dual function: as guarantors for the parties involved in the transaction and as impartial arbiters of the details of sale. Much has been made (by Marion Levy[70] and others) of the former function as evidence of a residual particularism in nineteenth- and twentieth-century Chinese business practices; here I would like to stress the mediator's more "rational" function of maintaining an orderly market.

One of the mediator's strategies for doing so is illustrated in the 1880 attempt by some British concession residents to purchase paving stones, needed for local repairs, from a stone-carrying boat in Hankow harbor. The boat's master was anxious to sell, but said that the mediation of the local stone dealers' guild would be required. When they sought out the guild's manager, the perplexed foreigners were informed that in order to assure continuity in the market and stability of prices, stone-carrying boats were assigned sequential numbers upon arrival at Hankow and were allowed to strike bargains only when all prior boats had completed their sales.[71] This had the effect of eliminating excessive competition among sellers and thus supporting prices, but it did not imply that the price had been *fixed* by the mediator. Testimony to this fact is provided by no less a witness than Yü-t'ai, Hukwang governor-general at the time of the Opium War. Yü-t'ai had been ordered by the imperial government to procure iron at Hankow to be cast into cannon for use against the British in Kwangtung. When he approached some local iron brokers as mediators for the transaction, the governor-general was aghast at the price the metal commanded on the market, and initiated an investigation. Yet the investigation proved to Yü-t'ai's satisfaction that the price was neither fixed nor artificially inflated, but was kept up merely by the mechanisms of supply and demand, as successfully mediated by Hankow's iron brokers.[72]

In other ways as well the maintenance of an orderly market was a common denominator throughout the Hankow trade. The city's great marketplaces, each dominating the trade in a single item, retained several features of the government-regulated markets of T'ang times. The controlling authority was now private, the collective trade guild, but control was still ever present. The great markets were all seasonal affairs, since passage of the river in winter months was hazardous for the countless *min-ch'uan* (independently owned junks) bearing merchandise for sale. The guild governing each trade would meet to determine the auspicious day for the opening of its trading season; the day differed from year to year, but frequently all or most markets of the town would settle upon the same opening day for a particular season. Once the market was opened, brokers supervising that trade struggled to keep bids and offers in good order and within a stable price range. In most trades, incoming sellers were not strictly prohibited from disposing of their merchandise at sites other than the recognized market for a commodity, but since these markets were usually at the location most convenient for incoming junks bearing that type of goods, and moreover offered both the assurance of loading and unloading facilities and a reasonable expectation of buyers, most incoming merchants were willing to submit to the market and its managers.[73]

Despite persistent efforts at regulation and self-regulation within the Hankow trade, in the nineteenth century the city remained a remarkably free-wheeling marketplace. Trades were closely supervised, but control could never be complete. Charlatans, fast-buck operators, and would-be market manipulators all flourished in the city. Yet the abuses and inefficiencies present in the Hankow trade were seldom those for which the Chinese city (or the "preindustrial city") has usually been stigmatized in Western literature. Primitive haggling in lieu of rational market control mechanisms, excessive particularism in the treatment of trading partners, inadequate stock and storage facilities, as well as the lack of "contractual autonomy" that characterized these cities for Max Weber[74]—none applied to the great wholesale trade of late imperial China as manifest in the markets of Hankow. All manner of written commercial agreements, from shipping orders (*ch'uan-p'iao*) to bills of lading (*pao-tan*, *ch'ing-tan*) to promissory notes (*p'ing-p'iao*, *chieh-chü*) to contracts of sale (*ting-tan*, *ch'eng-tan*) were routinely circulated and, as Chapter 5 will argue, enforceable in Hankow.[75] Indeed, without them the bulk trade of the port would hardly have been conceivable. The consistent efforts by merchants and guilds at quality control evidence a faith in, rather than an ignorance of, the rational market. In consideration of these facts Weber's definition of a rational economy as "a functional organization oriented to money-prices which originate in the interest-struggles of men in the market"[76] seems to describe almost perfectly the situation in nineteenth-century Hankow.

The Trade Transformed?

At the beginning of the present century, longtime China Hand Archibald Little wrote of the Wuhan cities:

> To those residents in China who can still remember the utter ruin and desolation of the triple cities after their evacuation by the Taipings in 1855 . . . their revival is astonishing; a revival due, unquestionably, not alone to the great recuperative power of the Chinese themselves, but in the main to the opening of the port to the foreign settlement. This measure, so bitterly opposed by the official Chinese and so welcomed by the people, has been the salvation of Hupeh, by the introduction of foreign capital, and energy stimulated by international rivalry.[77]

These self-satisfied musings are echoed in all but the most recent Western scholarship on Hankow and similar cities. But was the Hankow trade really transformed during the half-century or so following the Opium War? It should be evident from the foregoing discussion, as it was to the Western merchants who pushed energetically for the opening of the as-yet-unseen "celebrated commercial emporium of Hank'how,"[78] that before 1850 the city was already one of the largest and most sophisticated trading centers of China, and of the world. Trade with the West brought a few notable changes, such as the steamship and the international tea trade. However, we must be careful to distinguish between changes that can be ascribed directly to Western contact and the results of an ongoing process of indigenous development that, although accelerated by the catalyst of foreign trade, considerably predated that trade. Until the introduction of steam-powered industry after 1889, the continuities seem more important than the changes.

In order to determine the effect of foreign trade on Hankow before 1890, we must first differentiate the city of that period from the city of several decades later, when it was far more the focus of Western attention. Writers on both sides of the Pacific have tended to extend conditions from this later, better-known period back into the early years of the Western trade at Hankow. There has therefore been a tendency to attribute the changes these conditions represented to the opening of the port, rather than to subsequent developments. However, even P'eng Yü-hsin, who argues strenuously for the pernicious effects of foreign domination of the Hankow trade, concedes that in the first three decades after the opening of the port the Western trade "remained in but the first stage," characterized by relatively little foreign influence.[79]

In the Introduction, I noted the dramatic changes in Hankow society that followed Chang Chih-tung's self-strengthening industrialization projects of the early 1890's and the development of foreign-capitalized industry after the Treaty of Shimonoseki. The decades from 1890 to 1910 were a turning point for local commerce as well. During these years the beginnings of the most predatory forms of imperialism, combined with the strains produced by the Sino-Japanese war and by early industrialization efforts, appear to have genuinely shifted to its Western participants the controlling position in the Hankow trade that they had long sought. For a number of reasons, not least the construction of the first railroad links to Hankow, the city's foreign trade greatly increased during this period. One contemporary source reported that Hankow's foreign trade tripled in annual value (from 69 to 202 million taels) between 1897 and 1916; other accounts claim even greater increases in these years.[80] As the trade intensified, foreigners appeared on the scene in ever greater numbers. The British concession was joined by the Russian in 1895, by the German later the same year, and by the French in 1898. Also in 1898, the Japanese opened their first concession in the city, and within seven years they needed to nearly double it in size. This, then, was the period in which the centuries-old trade of Hankow was subjected most radically to the forces of foreign-induced change.

If the Hankow trade in the decades before 1890 was a different creature from that in the years thereafter, it also differed qualitatively from the trade of the first half of the nineteenth century. However, the first dramatic set of changes in the trade seems to have been brought about, not by the coming of the West either in 1842 or in 1861, but by the Taiping Rebellion. In the early 1850's rebel armies began to interrupt the flow of merchandise to and from the city, and by 1853 they had effectively sealed off Hankow's single most important trade route, the Yangtze downriver to Kiangnan.[81] During this period the Taipings, in the words of a local resident, "used Hankow like a treasury," visiting the city once a year to plunder and to build up their food and cash reserves.[82] Their depredations altered the national commodity traffic, forcing many merchants to bypass the city. The final blow came in 1854, when Taiping armies razed the Wuhan cities to the ground, and the huge Hankow trade was suddenly and completely brought to a halt. Upon recapturing the city the next year, Hu Lin-i commented that "Hankow was known in the past as the most prosperous place in the region, but today it is reduced to rubble like a piece of shattered tile."[83]

Recovery efforts began almost at once, and their speed astonished

Western observers.[84] However, the Taiping Rebellion did have long-range and even permanent effects on the commerce of the port. Some trades such as salt, although they later again reached tremendous proportions, by all evidence never quite regained their prerebellion levels. The overall composition of the Hankow trade was altered somewhat, and, more importantly, the mercantile elite of the town experienced significant turnover. Merchant groups such as those from Hui-chou, whose influence had already begun to decline in the 1830's and 1840's, found it extremely difficult to start again from scratch. This change in commercial leadership was probably most evident in the pivotal salt trade, but no less an authority than Hu Lin-i testifies that across the full spectrum of trades at Hankow the firms most prominent in the aftermath of the military crisis were seldom those that had been most prominent before it.[85]

Considerable evidence indicates that, although Hankow began its recovery immediately upon being retaken by government forces in 1855, it was many years before the city began even to approximate the national economic position it had occupied before the war. As long as the Taipings continued to hold Nanking, which they did until 1864, Hankow's utility as a point of entry into the Yangtze for native goods destined downriver was severely curtailed. Throughout the late 1850's and early 1860's the rebels continued to block other important avenues to and from the city as well. Moreover, both Taiping and Nien rebel armies regularly threatened the city itself in these years, periodically disrupting the conduct of business. Because of the city's demonstrated vulnerability to attack, many of its leading merchants took more than a decade to decide in favor of reestablishing there.[86] One index to the gradualness of Hankow's recovery is provided by the value of commercial property in the city: a Maritime Customs report from 1892 gives credence to the assertions of local Chinese that only then did urban land values reach the same point as before the rebellion.[87] Despite the prodigious opportunities for foreign trade at the port, it seems that only some thirty years after the opening did the city appear to major Chinese merchants as attractive a locus of business as it had in the period of peaceful domestic commerce.

This information underscores the fact that foreign writers like Archibald Little had simply never observed pre–treaty-port Hankow in anything approaching its normal state. There can be no doubt that the Western presence at Hankow both militarily and diplomatically discouraged further rebel attacks upon the city and thereby contributed to the growth of its trade after 1861, but it may be concluded with equal certainty that the steady rise in the town's total commercial activity in the

1860's, 1870's, and even 1880's was more the result of a belated commercial recovery from the Taiping devastation than of any marvelous effect of the foreign trade.

In assessing the actual effects of this trade, we must consider first of all its impact before the opening of the treaty port. The products of industrial Europe probably began to reach Hankow around the beginning of the nineteenth century through Kwangtung merchants plying the Hsiang River route to central China. An 1822 Chinese visitor to Hankow noted "Western goods, new and novel" among the items for sale in the city's markets.[88] The opening of the northern ports after the Opium War gave impetus to this trade, for transport of foreign goods into the interior could now be accomplished by the more convenient Yangtze route. Wholesale dealerships specializing in these imports began to appear in Hankow about this time; for example, the Ningpo entrepreneur Fang Chen-chi began to trade in British calico there in the 1840's.[89] Members of the British opening party in 1861 saw many foreign articles displayed in local shops, among them Japanese seaweed and several varieties of British and American textiles.[90]

What was the net effect of foreign trade on Hankow before 1861? Visiting the city in the 1850's, the Abbé Huc concluded that "trade with foreigners might cease suddenly and completely without causing any sensation in the interior provinces."[91] This, like other of Huc's contentions, was something of an overstatement. Foreign cotton goods, at least, had by then become a minor staple in the Hankow economy, and an early British customs official there attributed a failure to sell many new imports in the 1860's to the "overstocked market" in foreign cloth that existed at the port before its opening.[92] Moreover, the local dyeing industry, which provided an important source of income for residents of both the city and its surroundings, had begun sometime before 1861 to use British cotton cloth.[93] Thus by mid-century Hankow already had made significant contact with the European trade, in more than selected luxury items.

If the city had gradually accommodated to the expansion of China's overall foreign trade before the opening of the port in 1861, what significance can be assigned to the inauguration of direct foreign trade at Hankow? The experience of this port, at least, seems to confirm Rhoads Murphey's conclusion that "the real growth of . . . trade was modest, and . . . the treaty port impact on the Chinese economy was very much less than the trade figures and many people who have used them would suggest."[94] The reason for this is simple: foreign officials had no way of measuring, and indeed no adequate conception of, the domestic trade of the cities in which their customs stations were established. As the offi-

TABLE 6
Monetary Value of Trade Goods Monitored by the Maritime Customs Service at Hankow, 1880
(in Haikwan taels)

Goods	Value
Foreign trade	
Foreign goods imported from abroad	27,841
Foreign goods imported from Chinese ports	13,303,494
Native products exported abroad	5,099,638
TOTAL	18,430,973
Domestic trade	
Native products imported from Chinese ports	13,513,967
Native products exported to Chinese ports	15,549,933
TOTAL	29,063,900

SOURCE: Adapted from IGC, *Reports on Trade*, 1880, p. 47.

cial Customs Regulations for Hankow (and the repeated testimony of local commissioners) make clear, the cargo subject to Maritime Customs monitoring and assessment was limited to that carried by three classes of vessels: (1) oceangoing steamers and sailing vessels, (2) river steamers, and (3) lorchas or junks owned or chartered by foreigners.[95] This meant in effect that the annual "Reports on Trade" issued by the Hankow Customshouse neither included nor were ever intended to include what was by far the greatest portion of the city's trade—the local, regional, and interregional traffic carried aboard native-owned and native-operated sailing vessels. Thus the customs figures from Hankow, which have inspired later analysts to posit a geometric growth rate for the overall trade of Hankow following its opening, give no indication of real trade volumes at the port.

In reality, from 1861 to 1890 Hankow's domestic trade remained much larger in volume than its foreign trade. Even the Maritime Customs figures—despite their built-in bias toward foreign trade—bear this out. Table 6 gives the customs figures for 1880 (a good year for the tea trade, and hence for the foreign trade in general). It shows a preponderance of domestic over foreign trade of 29,063,900 taels to 18,430,973 taels, or a domestic share of the total trade of 61.3 percent. If we consider foreign-produced goods shipped to Hankow from other Chinese ports as "domestic" rather than "foreign" trade, the domestic share becomes an even more dramatic 89.3 percent. In either case, the addition to the domestic total of the substantial amount carried in Chinese-owned, Chinese-operated vessels (an amount, as we have seen, wholly unrepresented in the Maritime Customs figures) would make the domestic share of Hankow's total trade for 1880 an overwhelming majority.

In the early years of Hankow's foreign trade, the accounts of foreign officials and journalists, despite occasional bright moments, consistently reflect the dissatisfaction of initially hopeful promoters.[96] In its first three years the foreign trade was almost exclusively in tea; this trade grew so rapidly that the town soon surpassed Canton to stand second only to Shanghai in total value of export trade. At the same time, however, all other aspects of the trade (such as carriage of freights on foreign vessels to and from the city) failed to answer earlier anticipations. Starting in 1864, the foreign trade began to show signs of stagnation, in part because of the continuing activity of rebel bands in the surrounding countryside. The British consul wrote in 1865 that "the past two years will hardly be regarded as bright ones in the commercial annals of the port,"[97] and these sentiments were echoed by foreign observers for several years thereafter. In 1866 British Consul Walter Medhurst referred to "the stagnation of the trade both local and general," and the following year a British guidebook warned potential investors of a "commercial depression" at the port.[98] By the early 1870's, Western reports show a qualified optimism, but later in the decade serious reversals again occurred, bringing about the failure of hundreds of Chinese export merchants in the 1877 and 1878 seasons alone.[99] Chinese sources continue to report an extremely depressed export market through the early 1880's, and by 1886 British Consul Gardner, seeking to dispel foreign fears of a continued depression in the Hankow trade, was nevertheless obliged to acknowledge that foreign imports remained at a disappointingly low level and had, in fact, been steadily declining in recent years.[100] A *North-China Herald* correspondent summed up the situation in an 1885 dispatch: "Twenty-five years ago, dating, I believe, from this very month, Hankow was opened with 'great expectations' to foreign trade. Its history has been one of a few successes and many bitter disappointments, and the semi-jubilee we are celebrating at this time gives little promise of better things to come."[101]

Part of the reason for these disappointments can be found in the lay of the land at the Yangtze-Han confluence. As Governor-general Kuan-wen discouragingly remarked in his report of the first visit to Hankow by foreign ships: "Its natural configuration has given Hupeh the popular name 'swamp country' [*tse-kuo*]. The Yangtze and Han are indeed the source of its prosperity, but every late summer and fall their flow is so great that they swell out of all control. With the arrival of winter and spring they silt up so much that the larger boats find it difficult to get through."[102] The fact that virtually no ocean-going ship could reach the town in these low-water winter months was a considerable handicap to Hankow as a terminus for direct overseas trade. Moreover, although ships of the 5,000-ton class could usually make their way to Hankow from the sea, the city's natural harbor was ill-suited to accommodate them. It was small, shallow, and unsheltered, and in addition to the frequent and powerful freshets described by Kuan-wen, in summer there was a continuous five-knot current at dockside.[103] These natural conditions made the frustration of foreign hopes to a degree inevitable. As T. H. Chu reflected in the 1930's:

> From the inception of Hankow as a treaty port, alien merchants began to arrive, numerous native products very quickly accumulated, and the port consequently became a market for direct exportation. Later on, however, its location being far in the interior, Hankow came to be mainly a centre for the gathering and distributing of imported as well as native commodities. Direct trade has thus been declining whereas the transit trade has shown a considerable increase, revealing conspicuously the nature of the port as a transit one.[104]

Thus from the first Hankow was far better suited by both location and physical configuration to transshipment, by which it had come to prominence in the Ming and Ch'ing domestic trade, than to the role into which foreign "pioneers of commerce" envisioned forcing it.

Human and social factors, as well as geography, combined to limit the transformation Western merchants could effect in the commerce of Hankow. Although trade with the West (or with Western agents) became a major adjunct to the port's existing trade, in accommodating it the domestic trade simply expanded to include new participants. These participants were non-Chinese and their ultimate markets were located overseas, but in the Hankow trade people from different cultural backgrounds had always converged to negotiate transactions in the interests of diverse and distant producers and consumers.

The historian P'eng Yü-hsin, although he argues for a different conclusion, presents evidence that supports the view that the West simply "plugged in" to an existing system of trade at Hankow. P'eng's research in local sources shows that the Chinese goods most sought after by foreigners at Hankow, such as tea, hides, tung oil, hemp, iron ore, and coal, already had large markets before the Westerners arrived. Moreover, the local Chinese firms that dealt with the foreigner were not for the most part new or transplanted organizations, but grew directly out of existing commercial houses, which broadened their operations to deal with the West. This was as true of imports as exports, since many Hankow shops that formerly retailed native products soon switched over to include or specialize in marketing foreign goods.[105] P'eng's seven-link chain in the marketing of tung oil culminated in a foreign buyer; by such networks not only were Western traders isolated from the greater portion of the production and marketing process, but Chinese parties to the trade were likewise isolated both from the personal influence of the foreigners and from any significant awareness that a shift to a foreign market may have occurred.

British trade reports and other contemporary sources also indicate that the West simply plugged into an existing trade. Western merchants demanded the opening of Hankow less for the opportunity to purchase tea and other native products than to procure better access to the "China Market" as an outlet for manufactured goods. To a modest extent their anticipations were fulfilled, and foreign imports were purchased in some volume by consumers in the Middle Yangtze region. But Western merchants who had hoped to market their goods at the Yangtze ports themselves met with little but disappointment. As early as 1867, the British consul reported that "old established [British] China firms, who have gone to the expense of establishing branches in this port," found the import trade taken out of their hands by small-scale native commission agents, operating with virtually no overhead.[106] In the following years, the litany of complaints continued. In 1874 the British consul reported that "the trade in Manchester goods has passed into the hands of Chinese almost entirely, in consequence of the steady efforts of the native traders to get control of the business supported by the facilities afforded them by the banks and merchants in Shanghai."[107] In 1885: "There is really no market here for foreign goods [carried by Western merchants themselves], metals and opium perhaps excepted. All piece goods are bought in Shanghai and carried here on Native account."[108]

The Western goods traded at Hankow in the early 1860's were for the most part destined not for the Middle Yangtze region but for transshipment to regions farther inland. Even this trade was far less than Western merchants had anticipated, and later in the decade it too evaporated as Szechwan and Shansi merchants increasingly bought their goods directly at Shanghai, transporting them across China themselves.[109]

Although historians have tended to overestimate the early foreign trade at Hankow on the basis of trade figures, contemporary reporters seem to have been more aware of the limitations of these data. In the first place, as British Consul Alabaster stressed in his comments on the 1879 report, all imported items passing through the local Maritime Customs office were recorded as "foreign trade," even though most were in Chinese hands long before reaching the port.[110] Second, often a "foreign" merchant was an illusion. Chinese merchants transporting goods between Hankow and points farther inland had to pay duty at the various likin stations along the way, whereas Western merchants shipping along the same route were not subject to duty. The theory behind this was that while the goods remained in foreign hands they had not yet been imported into China (or, alternatively, had already been exported) and thus were exempt from purely domestic taxation. Consequently, it became common practice for Chinese businessmen to set up bogus "foreign firms" (*yang-hang*), in which a Western front man was registered as principal owner when in fact he was merely a salaried clerk employed for the sole purpose of signing Transit Pass (*yang-p'iao*) applications. Many of the busiest *yang-hang* of the city were in fact fully Chinese operations, to which "some enterprising milkman" of foreign origin had lent his name.[111] According to British Consul Caine, as early as 1869 this system alone maintained *any* foreign involvement in the import trade of Hankow,[112] and it was used extensively for exports as well.

Thus between the Chinese merchants' tendency to bypass Hankow and purchase foreign goods at Shanghai and their manipulation of the Transit Pass system, Westerners remained isolated from most of the commercial activity of the port. In the early years, this isolation was further intensified by the situation in the transport trade. Of the nearly 1,500 commercial vessels nominally in foreign employ calling at Hankow in 1862, virtually all were owned and manned solely by Chinese.[113] Although the general trade of Hankow continued to operate at tremendous levels, Western participation was quickly narrowed from the position of dominance the China Hands had once envisioned to focus on one large (but on the Chinese side by no means overwhelming) facet of that trade: the export of tea. As the Maritime Customs commissioner at the port conceded in his summary for 1876, "We must acknowledge that, with the exception of the exportation of tea, the trade of the port—foreign importations from Shanghai and Native exports—has entirely passed into the hands of the native merchants."[114]

Thus before 1890 the introduction of direct foreign trade at Hankow did not have a major effect on native control of the city's commerce; that is, foreigners did not take the trade in either domestic or imported goods significantly out of the hands of Chinese merchants. There are, however, three other areas in which the opening of the port might have had an important effect: the financing of the trade, the relative composition of commodities within it, and its technology (particularly in the area of transport). As for finance, the so-called "modern bank," organized according to Western models, was introduced early and was to be the wave of the future. Nevertheless, as Chapter 5 will show, in our period commercial finance remained overwhelmingly in the hands of institutions owned by Chinese and operated along inherited Chinese lines.

The balance of commodities in the Hankow marketplace, on the other hand, was altered significantly, as tea for the first time rose to prominence among the items of trade. This affected both the structure of the Hankow commercial elite and the lives of peasant producers in the city's regional hinterland. (The tea trade—probably the greatest single area of foreign influence during these years—will be discussed in Chapter 4.) In transport technology, the West also induced important, though complex, changes. Let us look at these in more detail.

Although the introduction of the steamship had an almost immediate effect on the Hankow trade, in this area too early Western hopes were frustrated. Those who sought the opening of the port had originally intended that British steamers make London and Hankow their termini, but it quickly became apparent that ships suited to the long ocean voyage around the Horn were ill-fitted for the last leg of their projected journey, up the Yangtze. Consequently, most ocean steamers stopped at Shanghai, and either river steamers or native craft were used for the Shanghai-Hankow leg. A British reporter at Shanghai noted in 1871 that: "This used to be the case more exclusively than it is now. Generally two or three ships have gone up at the beginning of the season and taken direct freights from Hankow to London. But the opening of the Suez Canal has increased the tendency to direct shipments."[115] The growth of direct trade that the canal encouraged remained modest, however, and the same reporter noted that the nine steamers on the London-Hankow run that year had managed to carry only about one-quarter of the total tea export, the remainder going to Shanghai for transshipment. A decade later little progress had been made, and only around 1883–84 did direct overseas steamer runs begin in earnest.[116] Even then, as we have noted, freights in foreign hands were largely restricted to export tea; steamers outbound from London frequently were forced to carry cargoes for Australia or other markets before heading to Hankow to pick up return shipments.

This brings us to the far larger steamship trade between Hankow and Shanghai, which was inaugurated upon the opening of the port and reached significant proportions almost immediately. Although foreign merchants failed to establish themselves as major parties to the Hankow trade, they did succeed in becoming major carriers of merchandise. K. C. Liu has covered this subject admirably and thoroughly,[117] so I will concentrate on the single question of how great an impact foreign steamships in Chinese waters had on the existing trade and shipping patterns of Hankow.

Apparently that influence was significant but not shattering. Early British writers, noting the rapidity with which steamships took hold on the Hankow-Shanghai route, believed they had discovered the panacea for the river trade. Frederick Bruce, for example, concluded in the spring of 1864 that "owing to the violence of the winds and the rapidity of the current in certain places, the application of steam to navigation was required before the Yangtze could be made available as a highway for transport,"[118] a remarkable statement in view of the enormous Hukwang-Kiangnan grain trade that the river had been bearing for centuries. A dramatic reduction in native cargoes on foreign steamers that very year revealed the extent of Bruce's naiveté and pointed to an entirely different cause for the steamer's early and transitory dominance of river traffic. As K. C. Liu suggests, the introduction of the steamship broke the Yangtze blockade that had been imposed throughout the 1850's and early 1860's by the Taiping occupation of Nanking. However, when Nanking fell to imperial troops in 1864, the junk trade in domestic merchandise quickly reasserted itself and won back, by its low cost, much of the freight that had been transported by foreign steamer.[119]

Steamships subsequently supplanted the chartered lorchas that Western merchants had relied upon for Hankow-Shanghai runs in the early years of the treaty port. In the domestic trade as well, the steamers' greater speed increasingly recommended them to shippers of perishable goods. But the great majority of native traffic on the lower Yangtze continued to travel by junk.[120] Furthermore, until well into the 1880's all other water routes serving Hankow (including the upper Yangtze and the Han) remained impassable to steam vessels. In these waters even Western merchants continued to rely primarily on hired native craft through the end of the century.[121]

As the trade (and the population) of Hankow continued to grow in the post-Taiping decades, the domestic junk traffic increased along with it. British Consul Patrick Hughes summarized these developments in 1877: "Steam navigation injuriously affects lorchas but has little influence on junks. In fact the river junks are rather benefited than otherwise, as they are employed in the increasing quantity of imported goods, and in the conveyance to the steamers of native produce, some of which, but for the existence of a rapid means of communication, would never find a market."[122] Thus the steamship did not displace but rather intensified the traditional domestic junk trade of Hankow. Longtime resident Griffith John put the average number of native craft calling there annually during the 1860's at about twenty-five thousand; by 1905 a Japanese reporter estimated the number to be between seventy and eighty thousand.[123]

One significant aspect of the introduction of the steamship to Chinese waters was the stimulus it provided to native imitation, one of the rather few documented cases of technological transfer in these years. Just as Chinese merchants quickly arrogated to themselves the distribution and marketing of foreign produce in China, so before long they competed effectively in freight shipment. In 1871 the "officially supervised–merchant operated" China Merchants' Steam Navigation Company set up its first branch office in Hankow, with the stated purpose of devoting itself primarily to tribute-grain shipments, but professing interest in merchant goods as well. Its early history in Hankow was one of rapid and steady success. In 1877 it was able to buy out the Shanghai Steam Navigation Company (a subsidiary of the American firm Russell and Company), and in 1883 it invested 45,000 taels in a larger, modern pier and attached tea warehouse in the city. During these years the Chinese firm was consistently able to lure native traffic away from its foreign competitors.[124] Moreover, it was the Chinese, rather than any foreign firm, who first successfully extended steam navigation beyond the Yangtze into the interior. Acting without the government support given to the China Merchants' Company, a Hankow merchant named Wu Hsin-chiu (in the 1890's?) established a small steamship run up the Han River to Hsien-t'ao, and his success soon invited the competition of the rival merchant Yao K'uan-ch'ing.[125]

Thus, although the steamship modified trade flows around Hankow and stimulated the port's existing trade, Chinese merchants progressively asserted control over steam navigation, as they had over other aspects of the distribution system. In the process, Westerners were forced into a relatively isolated position at Hankow, in which they remained until the Treaty of Shimonoseki permitted the widespread establishment of foreign factories in the city.

In conclusion, to put in focus the foreign trade and its overall effect on Hankow, let us look at the thesis, argued in most detail by Rhoads Murphey, that after mid-century Hankow and other major Chinese cities were increasingly involved in trade with one another, rather than with secondary urban centers or with the countryside. The obvious example is the Shanghai-Hankow trade. Hankow Maritime Customs commissioner Francis White, blind to all indigenous trade at the port, reported in 1877 that "Shanghai is the depot from which nearly all goods are received by Hankow, and to which nearly all goods are sent, either for consumption or transit."[126] On the evidence of such statements, Chinese historians such as P'eng Yü-hsin have portrayed Hankow in the century following the Opium War as merely an "inner treasury" to be drawn upon at will by Shanghai in its conduct of the overseas trade.[127] Murphey gives a global perspective to this argument:

> In China three levels of the concentration of urban functions began to appear. Shanghai and Hong Kong were central places and strongly dominant ports for foreign trade for the country as a whole, analogous to London, New York, Buenos Aires, Calcutta, or Bombay. At the second level Tientsin, Hankow, and Canton played the same kind of role for north, central, and south China respectively. . . . The third level, smaller regional or provincial service centers, was represented by places such as Changsha, Chungking, or Foochow, all of them also part of the treaty port system. . . . The growth of commercial nodes at these three levels was a symptom of increasing commercialization and exchange beyond traditional levels, and one which in some respects bypassed or superseded traditional centers and lower-order systems.[128]

Ironically, Murphey's conclusions (especially regarding the bypassing of lower-order systems) seem more valid than the assumptions behind them. In particular, his assumption that in China transoceanic trade was more compelling than "traditional" domestic networks of exchange does not appear accurate for the period before the Sino-Japanese War. Neither do the events of this period seem to justify the conclusion that there was at this time an irregular increase in the already high level of commercialization in China.

There is considerable merit in the argument that trade was increasingly concentrated between regional metropolises, but the view of Hankow as chiefly an appendage of Shanghai is misleading. Even while trade with the West, and with Shanghai for eventual export, commanded a larger share of Hankow's commercial energies, the domestic trade remained throughout our period (and arguably much later as well) the principal focus of the great commercial emporium of the Middle Yangtze. Moreover, the trade with Shanghai continued to include many elements of the old domestic exchange with Kiangnan. With each of its other service areas, as with Kiangnan, Hankow did tend to confine its trade increasingly to the major regional city. However, although the Western trade (and in particular the introduction of the steamship) no doubt accelerated this trend, it was more directly a function of the long-term development of the indigenous commercial network. Just as in earlier centuries exchange with Hankow's Hunan hinterland had increasingly concentrated on trade with Hsiang-t'an, in the nineteenth century Hsiang-t'an began to be bypassed in favor of the larger and more central Changsha.[129]

Correspondingly, we have seen that Hankow played a severely restricted role as a marketing center for its local hinterland. A minor revival of this function seems to have taken place in the 1850's, in the wake of the area's devastation by the Taipings. But as Hankow's links with the regional and interregional trade were reestablished, it once again tended to transcend its local surroundings, and the Western trade simply accelerated that trend. These developments had repercussions beyond the purely commercial concerns that have been the focus of this chapter: they also helped create a more cosmopolitan urban society.

To get a better picture of Hankow's role in the national economy, and of the implications of this role for local society, one must look in detail at the city's trade in specific commodities. I have chosen salt and tea, two of the foremost local items of exchange throughout the Ch'ing, as the subjects of the following two chapters. In fact, trade in these two commodities was so important in the life of the town that an examination of them seems a necessary prelude to subsequent discussions of urban society. Holding these later discussions as my goal, I will avoid as much as possible questions of pricing or levels of trade, concentrating instead on social implications.

Study of the salt and tea trades in conjunction is especially useful, since the two commodities were the province of very different segments of local society. Although the tea trade did serve a sizable domestic market, it alone among the city's trades was primarily an item of foreign exchange. Salt, on the other hand, remained throughout these years solely a domestic affair. The similarities and differences in the organizational histories of the two trades thus offer one more clue about the influence of the West on the direction of change in nineteenth-century Chinese urban society.

CHAPTER THREE

The Salt Trade

In his 1871 *Travels of a Pioneer of Commerce*, Thomas Cooper described an evening's stroll on the Yangtze:

> After dinner I walked along the bank of the river towards Hankow, and as it was night attracted no attention. Hundreds of junks, moored in tiers out from the shore, each heavily laden with salt, showed what an enormous trade exists between the coast and Hankow. I gathered from a custom-house watcher, whom we encountered in our walk, that upwards of fifteen thousand salt-laden junks arrive at Hankow every year, each carrying an average of 2300 piculs, equivalent to 166 tons, making up the enormous total of two and a half million tons.[1]

Whether or not the customs attendant's estimates were accurate (we have little means of judging such figures for domestic commerce), salt accounted for a huge percentage of the total trade of Hankow. In China as in Europe, the importance of salt as a dietary requirement and a food preservative, as well as its limited natural availability, made it a major item of interregional trade long before the "commercial revolution" brought about a comparable circulation of other dietary staples. The Wuhan area had long hosted a salt depot of the first importance.

T'ang and Sung dynasty Nan-shih, the Wuchang suburb whose commercial position approximated that of Ch'ing Hankow, was already known as an enclave of wealthy interregional salt traders. By the late Ming they were a force in Hankow; however, they were wiped out in the devastations of the rebel leader Chang Hsien-chung. The salt merchants regained their prominence only gradually, but by the end of the eighteenth century they dominated once more the social and cultural life of the port. One local historian even labeled the period of Hankow history from the late Ch'ien-lung through the Taiping Rebellion "the era of the salt merchants." In these years salt ranked either first or second (to grain) in the total value of commodities traded at the port, and in the 1840's Governor-general Yü-t'ai put the average number of salt boats in Wuhan harbors at between one and two thousand at any time. Salt's relative importance in the trade of Hankow declined greatly over the latter half of the century, yet by 1907 it was still estimated at an annual value of four to five million taels.[2] The changing procedures for handling this trade thus provide an important perspective on the commercial life of the port, and an insight into the economic basis of one of the city's key elite groups.

The Kang *and* P'iao *Systems*

A study of the salt trade of Hankow should begin with a brief overview of the Ch'ing salt administration as it affected the city. The Liang-Huai salt district, centered at Yangchow, Kiangsu, was the largest of the areas into which the government salt monopoly was divided. Liang-Huai comprised two subdistricts: Huai-pei (essentially the province of Anhwei) and Huai-nan (covering Hupeh, Hunan, and western Kiangsi). Hankow throughout most of the Ch'ing was designated the central depot (*an*, *k'ou-an*) for the Huai-nan region, as Nanchang was for Huai-pei. In theory this meant that all salt consumed in that area would first be shipped in bulk, under strict government license, from Yangchow to Hankow, where upon payment of duty it would be repackaged into smaller units and resold for distribution to retail areas. Even if the bulk salt passed directly through its ultimate destination en route up the Yangtze, it was required to travel first to Hankow to be dutied and repackaged. The marketing of salt from other production and distribution areas, such as Szechwan, was normally illegal in the Huai-nan subdistrict.

The merchants who shipped bulk salt up the Yangtze were known generically as *yün-shang* (transport merchants), whereas those who purchased repackaged salt at the depot for further distribution were referred to as *shui-fan* (river peddlers). The smaller-scale merchants in turn resold the salt to retail shops (*tien-p'u*) in local areas. During most of the Ch'ing, *yün-shang* transporting government salt to Hankow or Nanchang operated under a legal system known alternately as the *kang-fa* or *yin-fa*. Under this system the number of authorized *yün-shang* in the entire Liang-Huai district was limited to some two hundred individuals, who were virtually accorded the status of government officials. As holders of hereditary *kang* privileges, these merchants in essence held enfeoffed title to a particular salt distribution route; since there was a rigid quota for the annual salt shipment to each county within the district, often a single merchant delivered a county's entire annual entitlement of salt.

One can easily imagine the abuses to which this system gave rise. The net result was a consumer price tag on government salt that made smuggled salt very attractive, and often the only means for a householder to afford this essential commodity. Eventually, as Thomas Metzger has recounted, in 1832–33 Liang-Kiang Governor-general (and concurrently Liang-Huai Salt Commissioner) T'ao Chu decided to experiment with completely abolishing the two-century-old *kang-fa* in the Huai-pei portion of his jurisdiction. T'ao formulated a new program, which he designated the *p'iao-fa* (ticket system). Like a *kang* merchant, the purchaser of a *p'iao* was formally entitled to ship each year a portion of the quota of Huai salt for a specific retail destination. However, in Metzger's words: "The main point of the ticket system was to attract small investors, or, more accurately, to allow the many eager small investors to enter the trade. Thus, while the average merchant with a monopoly under the *yin* system had to ship some 12,000 *yin*, the ticket system allowed merchants to ship as little as ten *yin*."[3]

The new system succeeded quite well in Huai-pei, but for some reason T'ao Chu refrained from instituting it in the Huai-nan subdistrict, centered on Hankow. This was left to his successor, the well-known early anti-Taiping general Lu Chien-ying. In switching Huai-nan to the *p'iao-fa* in 1849, Lu was motivated primarily by the same concerns that had prompted T'ao Chu's actions in Huai-pei: to counteract the corruption and "wastage" at the ports of distribution (chiefly Hankow) that made official salt unable to compete in price on the local market with smuggled salt. Lu felt that the new system would give his yamen at Nanking increased control over the entire salt-distribution network by eliminating the independent power of the large *kang* merchants. The immediate stimulus for his action, however, was the destruction by fire of more than four hundred government salt boats tied up together at Hankow. Since this was but the latest of several recent disastrous losses by fire or flood at the port, Lu felt it prudent both to decrease the size of individual bulk shipments to Hankow and to revitalize security procedures in the local salt office there.[4]

Whether Lu Chien-ying's reforms in the Huai-nan subdistrict would have had the long-term success of T'ao Chu's in Huai-pei became a moot question when four years later the Taiping armies cut the Yangtze River link between the Liang-Huai factories and Hukwang. Merchants who had recently purchased their Huai-nan transport licenses abandoned upriver shipments altogether, and as a later Maritime Customs official reported, "the result was that these *p'iao*, originally worth many thousands of taels, could be picked up for a few hundreds."[5] Still, the population needed salt, and so Hukwang Governor-general Chang Liang-chi requested and received imperial permission to legalize the importation of Szechwan salt via routes that bypassed Hankow. Chang's goal, of course, was to tap at least a portion of the inevitable smuggling trade for governmental purposes, but not until three years later, in 1856, was his successor, Kuan-wen, able to set up customs stations at I-ch'ang and Sha-shih, and thereby recover some salt revenue to help provision troops.[6]

By 1860 the situation had been reversed. Rebels in Szechwan had interrupted the flow of salt to Hukwang, which sent local retail prices skyrocketing, whereas the lower Yangtze had been reopened by the new provincial navies, and Hankow was held securely by imperial troops. The time was ripe for restoring the *p'iao* system; the problem was how to entice the salt merchants to return. Kuan-wen therefore initiated an experimental "sales management bureau" (*tu-hsiao chü*) in the city. Two local merchants, expectant officeholders, were bonded and presented with passage documents bearing the governor-general's personal seal. On this authority they were empowered to solicit capital from local sources and purchase salt at the Liang-Huai factories for transport to Hankow, where a government salt office would collect duty on the salt, to be turned over to the provincial administration for the exclusive purpose of providing troop rations. Quarterly reports were to be submitted via the Hupeh salt taotai to the Board of Revenue and to Hupeh Governor Hu Lin-i.[7]

This interim system operated to general satisfaction until early 1863, when Liang-Kiang Governor-general Tseng Kuo-fan decided that the Yangtze had been sufficiently repacified to allow formal reconstruction of the entire Liang-Huai distribution network. Tseng incorporated many elements of Kuan-wen's Hukwang system into his own new comprehensive code, which remained the basic document governing Liang-Huai operations throughout the remainder of the century. According to Tseng's plan, the Hankow office would be elevated to the status of general superintendency (*tu-hsiao tsung-chü*), with jurisdiction over several sub-bureaus throughout Hukwang and responsibility for overseeing salt sales, setting prices, collecting duty, and preventing smuggling. Every year 160,000 *yin* of salt (at 600 catties per *yin*) were to be shipped to Hupeh, divided into four seasonal shipments (*yün*) of 40,000 *yin* each. Comparable shipments were ordered for Hunan, likewise to pass through the Hankow depot.

The *p'iao* system was formally reinstituted, although now each *p'iao* (now also called *yin-p'iao*) authorized its bearer to ship annually the rather larger standard quantity of 500 *yin*. Detailed routes were prescribed for the delivery of salt to each county in the Huai-nan subdistrict. E. H. Parker described the system as it operated in 1873:

> Having purchased his five hundred *yin* of salt [at Yangchow] the merchant pays the tax upon the whole at the rate of about twenty cash the catty, and takes out a certificate which he must exhibit at all the barriers he passes in his journey up the river. Some of the merchants convey salt to Hankow, others to Kewkiang [for distribution to western Kiangsi], others again past Hankow to Hunan marts, and many also to marts lower down the Yangtze. A merchant can only dispose of salt at his own mart; that is a Hankow merchant holding a license to convey salt to Hankow can only dispose of it there.[8]

A total of 1,000 *p'iao* were offered for sale to cover salt destined for Huai-nan: 300 for destinations in Hupeh, and the remainder for Hunan and western Kiangsi. Despite the restrictions he set on the total number of *p'iao* to be issued, Tseng made clear that at the outset he would accept any and all applicants, since his immediate goals were the quick reinvigoration of the system and the rapid generation of revenue from ticket sales. Only practice was to determine which of the original purchasers merited permanent recognition as government salt merchants.[9]

Salt Smuggling in the Hankow District

Salt smuggling was the most persistent of the problems that both inspired and undermined the neat administrative systems outlined above. Contemporaries divided smuggling within the district governed by Hankow into two types: (1) *wai-szu*, the transport of salt from production areas other than Liang-Huai into the district for sale, and (2) *nei-szu*, the transport and sale of Huai salt through clandestine channels. Smuggling of the latter type was usually carried on through the port of Hankow, whereas that of the former was generally designed to avoid the city, and thus more efficiently serve the needs of the counties on the periphery of the Huai-nan district.

Wai-szu. Although it bypassed Hankow, salt smuggled into Hukwang from Szechwan and Canton directly affected salt operations at the port, both because it competed with the Hankow depot's trade and because Hankow officials and merchants were charged with controlling such irregularities. Szechwan salt generally entered Hukwang down the Yangtze via Ching-chou and I-ch'ang, supplying much of Hupeh and parts of Hunan; Kwangtung salt traveled into Hunan via the Hsiang River valley and the port of Heng-chou. Part of the problem was simply the inaccessibility of these peripheral areas for salt traveling the authorized route; the Liang-Huai merchants themselves freely admitted even in the system's heyday that they were loath to make these runs because the expenses entailed made them unprofitable.[10]

Smuggling from both Szechwan and Canton intensified considerably over the first half of the nineteenth century, prompting Lin Tse-hsü in the 1830's to declare eradicating this trade one of the chief priorities of his tenure as Hukwang governor-general. By 1849 the problem had become so acute that the Hupeh salt taotai wrote, "This year legally transported salt barely amounted to a single [*yin*] . . . , and our local salt treasury is consequently empty."[11] Seen in this light, the formal legitimation of non-Huai imports four years later appears to be not merely a step dictated by Taiping military actions, but a tacit official acknowledgment of the state of decay into which control over the Hukwang market had fallen even in peacetime.

The period of official sanction further secured the market for non-Huai salt in Hupeh and Hunan. Consequently, when Tseng Kuo-fan drew up his revised 1863 Liang-Huai code, he chose not to prohibit directly the importation of Cantonese salt to Hunan or of Szechwan salt to Hupeh. Instead he attempted a compromise solution by which he hoped to guarantee the bulk of the salt revenues from these provinces for his own Liang-Huai administration, while allowing non-Huai salt to satisfy any market demand that his own merchants might prove unable to meet. To accomplish this, he and Hukwang Governor-general Kuan-wen concocted a scheme whereby certain salt traders from Kwangtung and Szechwan would be permitted to enter the Huai-nan district under license from the depot authorities at Hankow. However, to ensure that Huai salt would retain the lion's share of the market, the governors of Hupeh and Hunan were ordered to set up control stations at specified points of entry from Szechwan and Kwangtung (Ching-chou and Heng-chou, respectively), and there collect a surcharge (*yen-li*) on incoming salt eight *li* per *yin* higher than that collected on Huai salt entering the provinces. (A *li* equals one-thousandth of a tael.) This, it was hoped, would make Huai salt competitive in price and simultaneously bring all parties some tax revenues from the non-Huai product. The proceeds of this eight-*li* surcharge were to be divided between the governors of the Hukwang provinces and Tseng's own Liang-Huai administration, as compensation for infringement on its proper territorial rights. Two years later, a similar stratagem was adopted to legalize and tax importations into Hupeh of salt from Shensi.[12]

Although Tseng's plan did succeed in guaranteeing all parties a share of the revenue from Cantonese, Szechwan, and Shensi imports, it failed in its larger goal, to recapture most of the central China market for Huai salt. In Hunan, Cantonese salt continued to undersell the Huai product, and imports from Szechwan (still illegal in Hunan) flourished. In Hupeh, a scant year after the adoption of Tseng's new plan, the provincial salt taotai was compelled to request further reductions in the entry duty for Huai salt in order for it to remain at all competitive with that from

Szechwan and Shensi. Indeed, the market for Szechwan salt in Hupeh became so great that in 1867 Governor-general T'an Yen-hsiang decided to set up a provincial Szechwan salt bureau at Hankow, under the supervision of the Hankow taotai (not the Hupeh salt taotai, whose offices were at Wuchang, and whose reporting superiors were the Liang-Huai administrators at Nanking). Finally, in 1872 Tseng Kuo-fan was persuaded to cut his losses, and he memorialized the throne requesting that five Hupeh prefectures and one independent department "temporarily" be ceded to the Szechwan salt district, leaving only the four prefectures immediately surrounding Wuhan under Liang-Huai jurisdiction. When, five years later, Liang-Huai Commissioner Shen Pao-chen sought to rescind this temporary cession, Hukwang Governor-general Li Han-chang persuaded the court that this was economically infeasible. Thus, although the Huai salt merchants of Hankow regained a considerable degree of prosperity in the decades after the Taiping Rebellion, the scope of their activities was continually diminished as the administration pragmatically adapted to market realities.[13]

Nei-szu. The illicit trade in Huai salt similarly allowed of no lasting solution. An 1877 article in the Shanghai newspaper *Shen-pao* recounted the history of reforms at Hankow intended to combat this nagging problem and concluded that none had worked; internal smuggling continued to be an ever-more-profitable enterprise.[14] Metzger notes of T'ao Chu's 1832 reforms in Huai-pei that "it may almost be said that the ticket system was explicitly designed to stop smuggling by attracting local smugglers into the legal trade."[15] The same could be said of Lu Chien-ying's parallel efforts in Huai-nan. Yet professional smugglers continued their prosperous business, and there is evidence that in later years they were joined by maverick Western traders.[16] The chief culprits were neither of these groups, however, but the formally licensed Huai salt merchants themselves. Boats carrying government salt to Hankow regularly brought a quantity of contraband salt over and above their authorized cargoes. This surplus was not declared for duty, but was simply offered to the highest bidder.

At least once, in 1831, this type of activity prompted investigation and intervention by Hupeh provincial officials. At that time Governor Yang Tse-tseng estimated that over three hundred thousand *yin* of salt passed illegally through Hankow each year as unreported overage alone. The excess salt was acquired at the downriver factories, where merchants were offered an under-the-table discount on their bulk purchase, with an additional quantity of salt included to raise the total purchase price to that expected by the authorities for the original quantity.

The overage was marketed in Hankow harbor aboard the myriad small punts that plied among the large salt boats at anchor there. As a result, the contraband salt never got as far as the officially inspected markets onshore. Black marketeering at Hankow was of course doubly injurious to government interests: not only did salt traded in this way avoid payment of duty, but more importantly, the illegal trade undercut the price of legal salt and disrupted the orderliness of the Hankow salt market. A great deal of official attention and expense was lavished on maintaining this order. Consequently, at this time the administration was willing to sponsor a cumbersome dragnet to defend it, involving an elaborate registration and reporting procedure for salt boats, the neighborhood vigilance of *pao-chia* functionaries from Hankow and Wuchang, and the establishment of a harbor patrol fleet manned by local salt-administration officials.[17]

Endemic smuggling and black marketeering on such a scale indicated a fundamental flaw in the system. The illegal trade continued to thrive because, despite constant official efforts to keep the price of government salt competitive, it was consistently overpriced. In part this was the natural consequence of the circuitous paths it was required by law to travel en route to the consumer, and of the several changes of hands it was made to undergo. As a result, officials in consumer areas frequently complained of an ultimate retail price more than double the bulk price paid at Hankow.[18] Yet by far the greatest escalation in price occurred before the *shui-fan* made their purchases at the port, in consequence of the morass of administrative exactions and private embezzlement, price manipulation and featherbedding, that the Hankow salt trade supported. In 1849 Lu Chien-ying echoed an oft-repeated but valid official formula: to eliminate smuggling the retail price of salt must be lowered. To lower this price, excessive price differentials between salt entering and leaving Hankow must first be narrowed. To accomplish this narrowing, the expenditures of the Hankow merchants must be kept under close and constant scrutiny.[19]

It would be wrong to characterize the Hankow salt market as hopelessly corrupt. It supplied the funds necessary to keep the salt-distribution system running even as smoothly as it did. Moreover, it financed in large part the social welfare machinery upon which the urban poor (and at times their rural counterparts) depended for their very survival. However, the market was also a source of enormous profits, legal and otherwise, for a key segment of the city's elite, and in consequence it largely underwrote the cultural life of the town.

The Hankow Salt Market before the Taiping Occupation

The salt trade is one of the few areas in which it is possible to conceive of the three Wuhan cities as a single locality. Contemporaries used "Hankow," never "Wuchang" or "Hanyang," to designate the salt depot of the central Yangtze, but just as frequently the market was referred to by its functional title, "Hukwang depot" (O-an or Ch'u-an). This was more apt, for although Hankow was the center of the trade, the entire Wuhan area participated in it. The salt merchants' headquarters, major warehouses, and residences were all on the Hankow side, but the office of the Hupeh salt taotai, whose role in the trade was central, was located at Wuchang. Salt boats could be found tied up throughout the area, but in the early part of the century their major anchorage was at a cove near Hanyang city. When this silted up they shifted to the Wuchang side, and after the Taiping hiatus Hankow became the favored mooring.

By the first half of the nineteenth century, the salt market at Hankow was in the hands of an extremely large professional establishment that had become solidly entrenched over the course of preceding generations. This establishment spanned all the socioeconomic strata of the town, but its key element was the transport merchants, the wealthy holders of hereditary *kang* privileges who brought salt up the Yangtze to the Hankow depot. The approximately two hundred transport merchants of the Liang-Huai district were organized into a handful of large commercial firms (*yen-chia*), which were structured along lines of family and local origin, and which maintained branch headquarters at each of the major depots where they traded. About ten such firms maintained sales offices (*mai-tien*) at Hankow, each headed by a supervising agent (*yüeh-tai*), and each owning or renting permanent anchorages in Wuhan harbors.[20]

When salt-laden boats arrived from downriver, they were directed by depot authorities to tie up at these anchorages in groups of ten, known as *pang*. The *pang* were deemed necessary for protection against pirates and heavy weather, and were also utilized by depot officials as units of collective responsibility to prevent smuggling by masters of individual vessels.[21] In accordance with a practice known as *cheng-lun* (sequential ordering) or *sui-tao sui-mai* (sales in order of arrival), as each boat or group of boats reached Hankow it was assigned a number that determined the sequence in which its cargo could be unloaded and sold. This practice was designed to preserve an orderly market, and, as we have seen, it had parallels in many private-sector trades. Often weeks passed before a boat's turn arrived, however, and competitive or impatient merchants frequently undercut the market price in order to sell quickly and free their boats for other cargoes.

As Saeki Tomi, Ho Ping-ti, and others have shown, the transport merchants of the Liang-Huai salt district were both economically and politically one of the most influential groups in late imperial China. Economically they were probably without peer, since they not only held the most lucrative commercial monopoly in the empire, but also invested the capital accumulated there in the transport of other commodities. (We should remember that the salt trade of Hankow was entirely unidirectional, and constituted but half of the largest single exchange relationship in late imperial China: the grain-for-salt exchange between Hukwang and Kiangnan.) Because of the Liang-Huai merchants' legendary wealth, the Ch'ien-lung Emperor was able to wring from them contributions of several million taels on each of his southern tours.[22]

The political influence of the Liang-Huai merchants was based not only on this power of the purse, but also on their status as quasi-governmental officials (*i-shang-i-kuan*). Although the merchants purchased their salt outright at Yangchow and resold it for a profit at Hankow, these transactions were formally viewed as little more than internal accounting procedures between agencies of the imperial administration, and until the salt left the Hankow depot in the hands of the *shui-fan* it was considered to be government property (*kuan-yen*). Similarly, the warehouses and other facilities of the Hankow salt market, which were in fact the collective property of the transport merchants, were officially held to lie in the public domain, as were the funds covering the depot's operating budget.[23]

Overall responsibility for the Hankow salt trade was shared by two men, the Hupeh provincial salt taotai (*yen tao*) and the "head merchant" (*tsung-shang*). The former was a regular bureaucratic official whose appointment by the Board of Revenue (generally on the recommendation of the Liang-Huai salt commissioner at Nanking) was subject to the Ch'ing law of avoidance. He supervised all salt matters in the Huai-nan district, not simply those at the Hankow depot, but his most pressing concern was the collection at Hankow of the regular salt duty (*kuo-k'o*) on shipments from downriver. The head merchant, on the other hand, was selected by the transport merchants from among themselves. Because his duties were more circumscribed, he exercised more immediate control over the operations of the Hankow depot, arbitrating conflicts between other merchants and representing the salt merchants as a whole before the taotai, the local and provincial administrations, and the Liang-Huai authorities at Nanking.[24] Although he was ostensibly under the supervision of the salt taotai, the head merchant exercised a tremendous degree of independent power because of the financial resources he controlled. According to one story, for example, when an early-nineteenth-century censor memorialized the throne about corrupt practices at the Hankow depot, the head merchant went directly to Peking and by means of a judicious bribe quashed the proposed inquiry at the top.[25]

The day-to-day management of salt transactions at Hankow was the responsibility of a specialized class of "depot merchants" (*an-shang*) residing at the port. They maintained an orderly market, provided for the storage of bulk salt and its repackaging into smaller units (*pao*) for sale to the *shui-fan*, collected government duty to forward to the taotai, guarded against smuggling within depot precincts, and managed local operating funds (*pan-kung-fei*)—the source of their own salaries. The legal basis of the depot merchants' authority lay in the formal commissions (*chih-chao*) they were granted by the salt taotai; in practice, they were chosen by the transport merchants, who "invariably selected their relatives and friends" for these supposedly regulatory posts.[26]

Relations between the quasi-official transport merchants and their bureaucratic superiors thus were generally quite cozy throughout the eighteenth century and the early nineteenth. Conflicts between state and merchant did arise, however. Of the many alleged abuses by merchants that reached the ears of reform-minded administrators in the Liang-Huai home office, none was more vexing than merchant abuse of the salt depot treasury (*yün-ts'ang*) at Hankow. Income for the Hankow treasury was derived from a per-unit assessment levied by the depot merchants on all salt traded in the city. This was separate from the regular duty, which was likewise collected on a per-unit basis and whose entire proceeds were forwarded via the salt taotai and the Liang-Huai commissioner to the Board of Revenue for application to central-government budgetary needs.[27] The depot treasury, on the other hand, was intended to cover the operational expenses of the Hankow salt market, and it was controlled by the local head merchant. Liang-Huai authorities looked on with increasing distress as these local funds began to approach and eventually exceeded the annual totals of regular salt duty collected at the Hankow station.*

A particular point of contention was the *hsia-fei*, or "coffer funds," defined by Ho Ping-ti as "a group of expenses incurred in entertaining officials and sundry contributions to local administration, which was

*Of course, disbursements from the depot treasury also underlay the Hankow merchants' clout in local and provincial politics. Thus the reform efforts of Liang-Huai officials in Kiangnan often look like regional conflicts over fiscal resources with official administrators of the central Yangtze.

paid out of the common merchant treasury."[28] The *hsia-fei* at Hankow was essentially a budgetary entry within the accounting procedures of the merchant-managed depot treasury, conveying much the same meaning as the English "slush fund."[29] Legitimate expenses covered by the Hankow salt merchants' *hsia-fei* included various charitable and public-spirited donations. Detailed discussion of this type of activity lies outside our present topic, but some idea of its scope may briefly be given.

Projects in Hanyang county or in the city of Hankow itself received most of the local contributions made collectively by Hankow salt merchants. *Hsia-fei* funds could be tapped either on a routine basis or by means of a single large donation in a crisis. Examples of the former were the salt merchants' monthly contribution to the Hanyang orphanage, dating from the Yung-cheng reign (1723–35), and their triennial payment to the county fund that provided transportation for local candidates to the metropolitan examinations in Peking.[30] Typical crisis expenditures occurred in 1801, when a donation from this fund enabled the local government to quell a major rice riot; in 1814, when a similar contribution helped feed an influx of refugees from the famine-stricken Han River valley; and in 1831, when a series of contributions financed flood relief efforts throughout the province.[31] Such outlays from the *hsia-fei* fund must be distinguished from the additional contributions made individually at such times by Hankow salt merchants as private citizens.

Downriver Liang-Huai authorities no doubt mildly resented such local philanthropy insofar as it conflicted with their own interests in the Hankow depot, but they were indignant at various other "miscellaneous expenses" for which the *hsia-fei* acted as cover. These included bribes to local officials, lavish expenditures on entertainment, padding the payroll with sinecures for friends and relatives, and direct embezzlement by fund custodians. In Ch'ing bureaucratic terminology, the management of *hsia-fei* funds seemed a clear-cut case of *chung-pao*, or "gorging at the middle." This meant that the profits from the Huai-nan trade neither accrued to the government nor were reflected in lower prices paid by local retailers or consumers, but were disproportionately withdrawn at the midpoint of the distribution network by the large wholesale merchants of Hankow.[32]

The earliest indication of home-office dissatisfaction with the management of collective funds at Hankow seems to have been a 1764 campaign by Liang-Huai Salt Commissioner Kao Heng. According to the commissioner's report, the *hsia-fei* at Hankow had been instituted in response to local merchants' need to offer *yang-lien* (monetary gifts to guarantee fiscal integrity) to avaricious local officials, but had thereafter come to serve as an excuse for merchant abuses of the sort just described. There was, he said, a conflict between the ordinary transport merchants and their elected representatives, that is, the head merchant and the managers of the *hsia-fei* funds (the *hsia-shang*). He described the outright theft of collective merchant capital (*shang-pen*) by these fund controllers, as well as their practice of investing collective funds in privately profitable ventures.[33] In conceiving of the problem in this fashion, he was in line with the general trend of mid-eighteenth-century commercial policies, initiated in the Yung-cheng Emperor's reforms, which stressed the need to protect rank-and-file merchants from illegal expropriations by their more centrally placed colleagues (see the discussion of Hupeh Governor Yen Ssu-sheng's 1745 brokerage reforms in Chapter 6, below). Kao Heng's solution was to order that all salt duty and assessments for depot overhead be paid directly to the Hupeh salt taotai by the "shipment overseer" (*yün-szu*) of each incoming fleet of salt boats, a policy that he expected would eliminate the need for the head merchant and collective funds altogether. Whatever *yang-lien* payments to local officials or profit-generating investments were necessary to ensure the smooth operation of the depot might thereafter be left in the hands of a formally accountable bureaucratic functionary, the taotai.

Kao Heng's attempt to reassert bureaucratic control at the local level must have foundered on the rock of merchant opposition, for a quarter century later the familiar head merchant and *hsia-fei* not only still existed but had become such a notorious center of fiscal abuse that in 1789 the throne ordered Liang-Huai Commissioner Ch'üan Teh to investigate the matter personally and draw up detailed regulations for managing collective funds at the port.[34] By this time the grounds of debate had shifted: the cause of official concern was no longer exploitation of the transport merchants by their chosen headmen, but the fact that these headmen were failing to exercise any regulatory control whatsoever over their charges. Whether because of personal interest or simple ineffectiveness, Ch'üan proved the wrong man to call the merchants into line. He determined that the Hankow depot had a reasonable need for a *hsia-fei* fund of between five and six hundred thousand taels per annum, and therefore in effect directed the *raising* of the permissible surcharge on Hankow salt transactions from six *ch'ien* per *yin* to eight. (A *ch'ien* equals one-tenth of a tael.) During the next twelve years, Ch'üan took no action as this increased surcharge allowed collective funds at Hankow to soar. In 1799, over eight hundred thousand taels were brought in to the *hsia-fei* fund, and the following year the figure topped one million taels.

Around the turn of the nineteenth century, Ch'üan Teh was succeeded by Chi-shan, a very different sort of commissioner. Chi-shan's suspicions of the Hankow merchant establishment were encouraged by the Grand Council, which tersely noted that the era of wholesale corruption associated with the ascendancy of Ho-shen (the nefarious favorite of the Ch'ien-lung Emperor) had ended, and that the Hankow office had better find some excuse other than official "squeeze" to justify its inflated budget. The new commissioner thereupon went in person to Wuhan to examine the books and call the responsible parties onto the carpet.

His investigation revealed that the Hankow salt merchants did have legitimate expenses that justified increased revenue. He noted that many outlays from their treasury genuinely "contributed toward public needs" (*yin-kung t'i-yung*), for example, by underwriting new and expanded programs of civil construction and relief work. Moreover, during this time of White Lotus disturbances the Hankow salt merchants collectively had not only hired an increased security force for their own warehouses and fleets, but had also assumed the chief financial burden of a newly organized system of "local braves" (*hsiang-yung*) for the defense of the city as a whole.[35]

Chi-shan's concern, however, was not philanthropy but salt policy. Although he applauded the salt merchants' public spirit, he also found that they had used these legitimate expenses as a cover for private enrichment. After hearing months of legal and fiscal testimony, he wrung from the leading depot merchants of Hankow a confession that they had managed collective finances largely for their own benefit, indulging in extravagant entertainments and engaging in particularistic (*ch'ing-mien*) hiring of superfluous personnel. The commissioner's reports reveal a desire to balance several goals: a guaranteed level of government revenue from salt, a fair price for the consumer, and the elimination of merchant corruption. The four-point program he enunciated called for: (1) the absolute limitation of the merchant-collected surcharge at Hankow to the rate of eight *ch'ien* per *yin* legally established by Ch'üan Teh, which Chi-shan discovered to have been greatly exceeded in recent years, (2) the required reporting of all requests for support tendered by local officials at Wuhan, (3) the keeping of more detailed account books by the head merchants, to be turned in monthly for official inspection, and (4) close regulation by the Hupeh salt taotai of the collective assets of the Hankow merchants.

Chi-shan took one further action. As noted above, salt boats were supposed to unload and sell their cargoes according to the order of their arrival in the city; however, in the early 1790's the number of incoming shipments had become so great that this system was regularly circumvented. In the intense competition to sell, prices were discounted, and government revenue was seriously threatened. Moreover, in their haste to sell merchants had become liberal in granting credit to the *shui-fan*, and in the process many *kang*-holding transport merchants had overextended themselves to the point of bankruptcy. Liang-Huai Commissioner Ch'üan Teh had come to their rescue with a set of protective regulations called the Statutes of Attachment and Sequence (*feng-lun chih li*), under which local salt authorities were actually to impound cargoes of salt as they arrived at the port and then dispose of them in strict sequential order. This system proved beneficial beyond all expectation to the big merchants, not only by eliminating cutthroat discounting but by allowing them to raise the fixed price of salt on the Hankow market. Chi-shan found these new regulations to have been largely responsible for the suddenly increased prosperity of the Hankow merchants, and therefore the indirect cause of their notorious *hsia-fei* abuses. Consequently, after extensive interviews on local conditions at the depot, in 1803 he successfully memorialized the throne requesting that the statutes be abolished and a more loosely competitive market revived.[36]

Despite all official efforts to control the excess profits of the Hankow salt merchants, however, local sources consistently identify the Chia-ch'ing and Tao-kuang reigns as the golden age of this group's prosperity. By the late 1830's sequential sale of salt was once more tightly enforced, and local *hsia-fei* extravagance again attracted the attention of the court. The local surcharge on salt transactions had by this time risen from the Ch'ien-lung rate of six *ch'ien* per *yin* to fourteen *ch'ien*, and the annual *hsia-fei* income had risen to more than two million taels. This was fully twice as much as the total government salt revenue from the Hankow depot. Accounting procedures for the *hsia-fei* were virtually nonexistent. As T'ao Chu reported, the power of the Hankow head merchants both over their colleagues and vis-à-vis the local authorities was virtually unsupervised, and hence their opportunities for private enrichment were unlimited.[37] At his suggestion, the court ordered Hukwang Governor-general Lu-shen to tighten surveillance over accumulated *hsia-fei* funds at the depot. Lu-shen's investigations further revealed the uncontrolled nature of the Hankow salt market, and he concluded that a great percentage of the trade there went unreported, whereas even the portion that was officially noted was profitable chiefly to private interests. He devised a program of on-the-scene supervision by the magistrates of Hanyang and Chiang-hsia counties, and ordered a field transfer of the nearby Ta-yeh county magistrate to the newly created post of general inspector of salt duty (*tsung-k'a*) for the Wuhan salt-boat anchorages.[38]

Once again, however, the effectiveness of the reform proved short-lived. A local gentry diatribe, written on the eve of Lu Chien-ying's 1849 general overhaul of the Huai-nan system, offers this remarkable picture of the Hankow market in decay:

> The profits from *kang* salt go neither to the government nor to the people, but are monopolized by the merchants. The profits that they are unable to hoard for themselves are divided among officials' private secretaries [*mu-pin*], retainers [*men-k'o*], and the like. Most of the transport fees ostensibly paid to boatmen and shipping brokers must in fact be kicked back in the form of bribes to the salt merchants' household henchmen [*shang-chai p'u-i*], who make the actual awards of shipping contracts. Even the maidservants in merchant households must be paid monthly gratuities.
>
> Salt boats at Hankow are arranged at the jetty so that they may sell their salt in order of arrival. . . . However, in some cases the merchants sell their salt illegally beforehand. Then, before their proper sequential turn arrives, they make up the shortage by buying smuggled salt. This practice is known as "overfilling the dumpling steamer" [*kuo-lung cheng-kao*]. If a boat's sequential number is about to be called and the merchant has been unable to procure enough smuggled salt to make up for what he has already sold illegally, he will file a false report of water spoilage, or even deliberately sink his own boat in the harbor. This is known as *fang-sheng* [the Buddhist practice of freeing birds or small animals in order to gain religious merit].

The writer concludes by urging reform in the Huai-nan region, on the model of T'ao Chu's successful efforts in Huai-pei, which he interprets as a wholesale liberation from accumulated legal and parochial encumbrances. Following T'ao Chu's reforms, he writes, "whenever a man of wealth took his capital to the salt bureau to purchase *p'iao*, no matter from which province he came, or how many or how few *p'iao* he wished to buy, he simply received his contracted amount of salt to be delivered to the agreed-upon destination. . . . By this means salt matters were completely reformed."[39]

In contrast to this depiction of the Hankow salt merchants as sleek profiteers, however, we have the contemporaneous report of Hupeh Salt Taotai Hsieh Yüan. His report suggests that the merchants were in financial trouble, and that they themselves initiated the replacement of the *kang* by the *p'iao* in the Huai-nan zone. According to Hsieh, the merchants felt they had been forced into corrupt practices by tremendous declines in profits, brought about by the growing incidence of smuggling of competitive non-Huai salt and by increased overhead at the Hankow depot. Taotai Hsieh derided all previous attempts at reform, concluding that "the merchants in each case sought to better their own position, whereas the officials simply sought the path of least resistance." Perpetuation of the *kang* system at this point, he argued, would lead both to the bankruptcy of the already impoverished and dispirited merchants and to a total collapse of government revenue from the Huai-nan salt route.[40]

Liang-Huai Commissioner Lu Chien-ying seems to have viewed Hsieh's report with considerable skepticism. Although he did shortly transfer Huai-nan from the *kang* to the *p'iao* system, in the memorial in which he reported doing so he contended that the progressive identification of the Hupeh salt taotai's office with merchant interests had rendered it useless as a regulatory mechanism. He agreed, however, that overhead at the Hankow depot had reached unmanageable proportions. His own investigations revealed that the depot surcharge on Hankow salt had risen from the four *ch'ien* per *yin* mandated by T'ao Chu in 1832 to an actual total in the late 1840's of from twenty to thirty *ch'ien*. This ballooning slush fund was being used primarily to finance an ever-expanding sub-bureaucracy at the port, as friends and relatives were added to the payroll in the guise of antismuggling personnel. Lu tersely noted that the largest single dispenser of suspect appointments was none other than the salt taotai's office itself.[41]

Clearly, Lu's own goal in shifting the Huai-nan zone over to the ticket system was to sweep away as much as possible of this vast patronage network. In this effort he seems to have been more successful than any of his predecessors. Under the *p'iao* system salt purchased at the factory was immediately assigned a county of ultimate destination, rather than simply being included in a Hupeh or Hunan provincial quota, and this, combined with smaller units of purchase, often made unloading and repackaging at Hankow unnecessary. Moreover, the official duty on salt transport was now paid in advance at the time of purchase, and so financial dealings at the Hankow station were sometimes eliminated altogether. As a subsequent Hanyang local historian remarked, "Hankow became no longer a necessary juncture for the salt trade."[42]

The Hankow Salt Market after the Taiping Rebellion

The salt trade at Hankow never completely recovered from its interruption during the Taiping occupation. Under the solicitous care of such Reconstruction officials as Kuan-wen, Hu Lin-i, and Tseng Kuo-fan, the volume of salt exchanged at the port again reached major proportions, and salt taxes collected there were a valuable source of government revenue throughout the remainder of the dynasty. But the legendary prosperity of the Chia-ch'ing and Tao-kuang salt merchants was never regained. Tseng's reorganized administration for the Huai-nan district was in general a continuation of Lu Chien-ying's *p'iao* system, but it differed in one major respect. Tseng formally redesignated Hankow the principal depot for the zone, and his new regulations stipulated that all salt destined for Hukwang must pass through the port for official inspection. Yet the effect of this decision was greatly diminished by the realities of salt smuggling in the Middle Yangtze region. As we have seen, the portion of the Hukwang market formally assigned to Huai salt shrank steadily in the 1860's and 1870's until it comprised no more than a handful of prefectures. Moreover, the volume of salt shipped declined on a per-area basis as well; a local writer complained in 1867 that at that time the annual quota of Huai salt for all of Hupeh province was less than the prerebellion quota for Hanyang county alone.[43] The effect of this trend on local administrative revenues and on the relative power of salt merchants within the Hankow community was significant.

Tseng Kuo-fan could afford to adopt a protective policy toward the Hankow market because the Taiping occupation had accomplished what a century of salt commissioners could not: it had evaporated the *hsia-fei* treasuries and completely dismantled the vast patronage-based salt establishment at the port. The Hankow salt trade that took shape in the later nineteenth century bore a superficial resemblance to its progenitor, but in several crucial aspects it was greatly changed.

Merchants. The task of conveying salt from the Liang-Huai factories to Hankow now fell to a new group of some six hundred merchants, holders of the "new tickets" (*hsin-p'iao*) issued after 1863 by Tseng Kuo-fan. A small number of these franchisees were direct descendants of the Hankow *kang* merchants (E. H. Parker noted in 1873 that transport rights had in some cases "been held by the same person or the same family for scores or even . . . hundreds of years").[44] Yet the majority of post-Taiping "*p'iao* merchants" (*p'iao-shang*) were neither former *kang* merchants nor original holders of the *p'iao* issued by Lu Chien-ying in 1849. As a Western reporter noted:

> After the stamping out of the Rebellion . . . it was found that many of these [1849] *p'iao* had been lost or destroyed or their owners had been killed. In restoring the Huai administration, and more with a view to raise some funds, new *p'iao* were issued in exchange for every old one on the payment of Tls. 400 to Tls. 600, and for sale at Tls. 1200; in other words, the salt merchants were called upon to pay forced contributions to the exchequer depleted by years of anarchy. To the many *p'iao* lost or destroyed must be added those which their owners had perforce to allow to lapse owing to their inability to pay the fee demanded. It may, therefore, be safely assumed that of the present *p'iao* but few were acquired by exchange for old ones existing prior to the Rebellion.

Thus by 1900 it could be said that "for the majority of merchants . . . tenure of *p'iao* dates back only to the end of the Rebellion."[45]

Most of the post-Taiping salt merchants operating in the Huai-nan subdistrict resided in Hankow, where they constituted a class of nouveaux riches. This was reflected in the growing market for the *p'iao* themselves. In reorganizing the Liang-Huai trade in 1863, Tseng Kuo-fan had chosen to peddle these transport privileges to any and all takers, specifying that *hsin-p'iao* would be available to anyone able to meet the modest purchase price, "no matter whether official, gentryman, merchant, or wealthy commoner." Thus Tseng attracted speculators from all parts of the empire to his new corps of *p'iao* merchants.[46] The initial investment required a certain amount of ready capital, which was difficult to come by after years of turmoil and devastation, but it was soon apparent that those willing to gamble early on the stability of Tseng's salt administration had "acquired their warrants at a very low price indeed."[47]

The *p'iao* issued by Tseng Kuo-fan were valid in perpetuity and their number was strictly controlled. The number of licenses sold in 1863 was not augmented until the early 1890's, when the need to finance the impending war with Japan forced the administration to offer a new issue for sale. Of the original licenses, some were held by several merchants in combination, some were controlled by one man alone, and others were held several to a single individual. At any given time, about three hundred *p'iao* holders or co-holders delivered salt for Hupeh, and a comparable number delivered Hunan salt via Hankow.

P'iao were not legally transferable except with government consent, to an approved merchant. Nevertheless, an active market in them was carried on, in much the same way as trading privileges on a contemporary stock or commodity exchange are bought and sold. Officials soon found cause for alarm in the poorly regulated, open speculation conducted in *hsin-p'iao* at Hankow. A typical speculator was Chang Tzu-hsiu, a Hunanese one-time lower official (by purchase) who had been stripped of his rank for misconduct in commercial matters. In 1882 Chang, despite his unsavory record, managed to have his name placed on the list of authorized *p'iao* recipients, purchased 89 *p'iao* by means of a 580,000-tael loan contracted in haste (and allegedly with some coercion) from a Hankow native bank, and immediately resold them for a handsome profit.[48] In part because of such machinations, the value of *p'iao* shot up dramatically, from the original 1863 issue price of 1,200 taels to 8,000 taels just twenty years later, and to 10,000 taels by the century's end.[49]

The freedom with which trading rights changed hands shows how little a monopoly the post-Taiping salt gabelle actually was. The openness of the market was further enhanced by *p'iao* holders' practice of leasing out their privileges, either on a semipermanent basis or for intervals as short as a single shipment between Yangchow and Hankow. The going rate for such rentals in the later decades of the century was about 2,000 taels per shipment. Increasingly, Huai salt was transported by any enterprising merchant who wished to lease the option, and the *p'iao* licensees of 1863 quickly developed into a new class of purely commercial capitalists, able to deal either in the commodity itself or in options on that commodity by renting out their transport privileges. If they chose the latter course, they could command a yearly fee, at no cost or risk to themselves, of 8,000 taels (four quarterly shipments at 2,000 taels apiece), or almost seven times their original capital outlay of 1,200 taels.

However, despite the financial windfall indicated by the appreciation in the value of *p'iao*, these later transport merchants never approached the political or even economic power of their predecessors under the *kang* system. Although both groups constituted a privileged elite, the later merchants were greater in number and smaller in individual scale than the earlier group. Furthermore, the later merchants were less able to manipulate the trade for their own advantage, since the postrebellion system was designed to avoid earlier difficulties in controlling Hankow depot merchants by limiting the role of transport merchants at the port.

The smaller economic scale of the post-Taiping transport merchants was reflected in their Hankow warehouses. Formerly salt warehouses had been collectively owned and maintained by *hsia-fei* funds, but now they were usually leased from a class of professional urban landlords.[50] Unlike the earlier *kang* merchants, moreover, the *p'iao* holders seldom owned their own fleets. Instead, they contracted with independent boat owners (*ch'uan-hu*), who then transported the salt to Hankow. Many of these boat owners no doubt specialized in the salt trade, but they were not restricted to it and customarily sold their services to the highest bidder, regardless of cargo.[51] The British firm Hogg Brothers and Company, which in 1866 subcontracted for a bulk salt shipment, left this account of the procedure:

> We obtained passes from the Salt Commissioners to purchase at the Government depot near Chinkiang so many thousand peculs [*sic*] of salt for sale at Hankow. Our Chinese agent took the passes, made out in the name of the Chaou Fang Hong (that is, our Hong), paid our money at Chinkiang for the salt, and obtained passes from the proper Chinese officer to pass the various customs houses on the way to Hankow. The salt was shipped in Chinese boats under the inspection of the Chinese officials and the hatches sealed by them.[52]

Hogg's description of the sale of their salt at Hankow indicates that in many respects the prescribed routine was strictly and efficiently carried out at the port:

> Arrived at Hankow the salt junks proceeded to a spot pointed out by the proper Chinese officer appointed there to superintend salt sales. The salt remained there stored awaiting sale in its turn, that is, the government only allows sales to be made from the junks in the order of their arrival. The government officer fixes the price at which the salt shall be sold upon the arrival of the before named turn and the said officer receives the money paid for the salt as sold, and as clearances are made, hands the proceeds over to our compradore for our account.

Those who purchased salt at Hankow were either retailers for the immediate area (*p'u-fan*) or local traders reshipping the salt to other Hukwang counties (*shui-fan*, *yen-fan-tzu*). The latter held local monopolies for their particular counties, which they obtained on a short-term basis from the Liang-Huai commissioner by posting a bond guaranteeing ability to meet the local likin charges and willingness to abide by salt policies and price regulations. Although local traders made regular trips to the provincial depot to purchase their stock, they normally lived in and operated out of small commercial centers in the region and had comparatively little connection with the society of Hankow's large salt merchants or of the city generally.

Taxation. In promulgating his 1863 Liang-Huai code, which remained in effect throughout the dynasty, Tseng Kuo-fan decreed that all Huai salt destined for Hupeh be brought ashore at the Hankow depot, weighed and repackaged into smaller units by depot officials, and then sold by the *p'iao* holder to the local distributors. Salt destined for Hunan was likewise to pass through Hankow for inspection, but it was to be weighed, repackaged, and sold at a smaller depot at Changsha. In establishing these procedures Tseng removed the Hankow depot's key pre-Taiping function of collecting the imperial salt duty (*kuo-k'o*); under his new system such duty was to be paid in advance at the time of purchase from the downriver salt factory.* At the same time, however, wholly new provincial taxes on salt, the Hupeh and Hunan salt likins (*O-li* and *Hsiang-li*), were instituted, in effect replacing the informal commissions that these provinces had formerly deducted in collecting the imperial duty. (The institution of a provincial likin reflected, of course, the rise in provincial fiscal autonomy at this time.) The Hupeh salt likin was originally set at 4.2 taels per *yin*, and the Hunan at 1.15 taels per *yin*, but over the course of the late 1860's they were reduced to 1.8 and 0.85 taels, respectively. The likin for Hupeh was collected at Hankow and for-

*A supplemental duty known as the "overland duty" (*lu-k'o*), designed to tax shipment of salt between the Hankow depot and the local areas, was collected in Hupeh until 1868, when provincial authorities succeeded in having it abolished. Their efforts were seen as a gesture of support for local salt merchants and undoubtedly resulted from collective lobbying by the merchant community of Hankow. (See Li Han-chang, memorial of T'ung-chih 7/1, and Kuo Po-yin, memorial of T'ung-chih 7/6, both in *HPTC*, 51.23.)

warded via the salt taotai to the Provincial Likin Bureau, where it was added to likin collected on other commodities. The Hunan salt likin was collected at Changsha, and the proceeds split between local authorities and those in Hankow. Salt likin revenues, like those from likin generally, were applied to the maintenance of regional antirebel armies and to subsequent "reconstruction" (*shan-hou*) projects in the two provinces.[53]

Government Supervision: Brokers. In post-Taiping Hankow, the day-to-day duties of weighing and repackaging the salt, collecting likin assessments, and overseeing sales to local traders fell to a new class of functionaries known as *yen-hang*. As local Maritime Customs Commissioner Robert DeLuca reported, the *yen-hang* of Hankow "are not merchants at all in the ordinary sense, but salt brokers. They do not lay in a supply of salt for sale to the public, but act as middlemen between the head office and the real salt dealers, who are the *p'u-fan* and *shui-fan*."[54] Thus the *yen-hang* were the functional equivalent of the pre-Taiping depot merchants, the *an-shang*. Their status within the trade was considerably different, however, and their advent signified a major transformation in the character of the trade as a whole.

The changeover from the *kang* to the *p'iao* system, and especially to the post-Taiping *p'iao* system as conceived by Kuan-wen, Hu Lin-i, and Tseng Kuo-fan, was in essence a transfer of the Huai-nan salt-distribution network from the public to the private sector. The unique status of the pre-1849 *kang* merchants as quasi-officials made policing of the Hankow market's daily operations appear superfluous. These duties fell to the depot merchants, who, as we have seen, were nominated by the *kang* merchants from among themselves, in appointments rubber-stamped by the Hupeh salt taotai. The post-Taiping *p'iao* merchants were, in contrast, not quasi-officials but simply private businessmen. As such they appeared to require a new type of formal official supervision. Under the governorship of Hu Lin-i, and at the suggestion of Hu's private secretary for fiscal affairs, Wang Chia-pi, the model for this supervision was found in the government-licensed brokers (*ya-hang*) who operated in most private-sector trades. In mid-1856, in the wake of his general overhaul of the brokerage licensing system in Hupeh (see Chapter 6), Hu requested that the Board of Revenue bring the functionaries in charge of salt transactions at Hankow under the brokerage licensing requirements to which their counterparts in other major trades were subject. Following the board's approval, Hu issued orders that market managers not only of the Hankow depot but of all secondary salt distribution centers throughout the province be required to apply to his specially appointed agents for brokerage licenses identical to those used in other trades.[55] By this single stroke, the private *p'iao* merchants were brought under the control of a separate class of government appointees whose status and powers were qualitatively superior to their own, and the Hankow salt trade lost its unique character as a government monopoly, to become indistinguishable in practice from the other trades of the city.

The institution of salt brokers at Hankow was retained by Tseng Kuo-fan in his 1863 reconstruction of the Liang-Huai system. In the half century thereafter, the number of salt brokerage firms at the depot ranged between ten and thirteen. According to Tseng's regulations, brokers within these firms were to be registered with the Hankow depot authorities by name, age, and native place, and the firms themselves were to enter into a mutual security bond (*hu-pao*) whereby financial responsibility for any impropriety would be shared equally by all *yen-hang* of the port. In 1873, E. H. Parker described the brokers' routine activities:

> When the [*p'iao*] merchant has arrived with his cargo of salt at Hankow, he stores it in his own warehouse, until some firm of . . . *yen-hang* . . . appears to take over the consignments. The merchant's salt is then marked and numbered, after which it is passed from the hands of the *yen-hang*, strictly in its turn, into the hands of the *yen-fan-tzu*, or local salt distributors. . . . The *yen-fan-tzu* has to pay at once the price . . . together with the local likin into the hands of the *yen-hang*. The latter deduct the local likin . . . and hand over the balance to the General Superintendency, which takes due note of it and passes it on to the importing merchants.[56]

The salt brokers were required to submit periodic reports on their activities and on the state of the Hankow market to the Hupeh governor, the Liang-Huai commissioner at Nanking, and the Board of Revenue.

Government Supervision: Taotai and Superintendent. Despite their exercise of official powers, the *yen-hang* were really merchants, of course, and like brokers in other trades they were recruited primarily from the merchant community of Hankow. In his initial effort to resuscitate the shipment of Huai salt to Hukwang, Governor-general Kuan-wen had envisioned a fully "merchant-run" (*shang-pan*) salt depot at Hankow, with *yen-hang* franchisees exercising full control, subject only to his own regional administration. (As we shall see in Chapter 6, this policy was in line with Kuan-wen and Hu Lin-i's overall commercial philosophy and the reconstruction program they instituted in the late 1850's.) However, when a few years later Tseng Kuo-fan sought a more comprehensive revitalization of the Huai-nan subdistrict, the concept of broker-merchant self-regulation took second place to the desire for greater bureaucratic control. Therefore the *yen-hang* were relegated to routine management of Hankow depot operations, and Tseng installed above them a superintendent (*ta-yüan*) as the official in charge of his new Hankow General Office for Superintendency of Salt Sales in Hupeh. This was a wholly new post. In the old days, as we have seen, overall control of the Hankow depot had been exercised by a head merchant, loosely responsible to the Hupeh salt taotai but in effect an independent power elected by the merchants themselves. Thus it can be seen that in the immediate post-Taiping years, although the salt trade as a whole was moving more unambiguously into the private sector, a simultaneous effort was being made to bureaucratize more effectively the administration's overseeing of the trade.[57]

There is, of course, some danger in overstressing this bureaucratization, as a comparison of the new post of superintendent and the continuing one of salt taotai makes clear. The administration had originally conceived of the salt taotai as responsible to the Board of Revenue via the Liang-Huai commissioner, but in the early nineteenth century these taotais had been increasingly dominated by the salt merchants. In the post-Taiping decades, however, the salt taotai came to represent almost completely the interests of the Hukwang governor-general and the Hupeh governor, essentially in collecting the provincial salt likin. Collection of likin on salt, as on other commodities, was managed by a newly created organ known as the Hupeh Provincial Bureau for Salt, Tea, Brokerage, and Likin Matters, of which the salt taotai was a standing member. The taotai continued as before to be regularly appointed by the central government at Peking, although in practice taotais were increasingly nominated by Hupeh officials.* The new superintendent, on the other hand, was personally appointed by the Liang-Huai commissioner and was responsible to him alone. It seems that the superintendent was selected from among the gentry members of Tseng's private secretariat (*mu-fu*), a talent pool theoretically as distinct from the central administration's preferment list as it was from the ranks of the Hankow salt merchants.

The mutual exclusivity of these talent pools is open to question, however. One example of possible overlap is T'ien Wei-han, who served a term as superintendent at Hankow in the 1860's or 1870's.[58] Originally a native of Shang-wu county, Chekiang, T'ien had come to Hankow as a salt merchant in the pre-Taiping years and eventually became a registered native of the city. When Hankow fell to the rebels, he fled with his family back to Chekiang, and when that area too came under attack he organized and led a merchant-militia (*t'uan-lien*) defense system there. It was almost certainly in this capacity that he first came to the attention

*In practice, the office of salt taotai was usually a collateral post held by the Wuchang taotai or, less frequently, by the Hankow taotai. (*1867 HC*, prefatory list of current officials, p. 1; *HPTC*, ch. 115. See also Table 8, p. 202.)

of Tseng Kuo-fan. Returning to Hankow early in the Reconstruction period, he maintained his official contacts and his public spirit, as well as his concern with matters of trade. Subsequently he was selected by Tseng's Liang-Huai office to draw up and promulgate the local salt ordinances that were incorporated into the new district-wide code. T'ien is said to have labored on this project for twenty years, which would seem to indicate that the local power of such officially connected merchants continued at least into the early 1880's.

What room, then, was left for post-Taiping Hankow salt brokers and other leading merchants to build up their own power independent of these newly established regulatory organs, the General Superintendency and the Hupeh Bureau? Was T'ien Wei-han an isolated instance, and had he divested himself of his merchant identity in entering upon a career of government service? What sequel was there to the tale of collective merchant funds and expenditures that had so vexed officials in the first half of the century?

No sooner had the trade been reestablished at Hankow than the familiar official-merchant cat-and-mouse game resumed, but on slightly different terms. Tseng Kuo-fan's 1863 salt reforms included specific provisions governing the "investigation of salt brokers" at the Hankow depot. Brokerage houses were to be brought under the direct supervision of the newly installed superintendent, who was charged with keeping detailed records of their behavior. The list of the chief offenses that Tseng anticipated can help identify the points at which the brokers' self-interest might come into conflict with the interests of other groups in the Hankow marketplace. First, by systematically delaying delivery of the duty that they collected on transactions, the brokers might (like their predecessors the depot merchants) acquire a source of investment capital that rightfully belonged to the administration. Second, they might "encroach upon guest [merchant] capital," that is, demand illicit payments from *p'iao*-holding transport merchants in exchange for the privilege of discharging salt out of sequence or at other than the assigned price. Finally, brokers might manipulate the market price by dealing on their own account, a practice considered detrimental to the retail merchants who purchased their stock at the port.[59]

Almost immediately Tseng's fears proved grounded. Tu Wen-lan, the first superintendent of the Hankow depot, quickly found himself confronted by a "conspiracy" among the Hankow brokers to forestall duty payments (*t'o-ch'ien*) and to allow transport merchants, anxious to employ their capital elsewhere, to undercut the fixed price. After only a few months, Tu petitioned for stronger powers in dealing with the brokers, and for permission to institute a stricter licensing system of his own.[60]

Four years later the problem of price manipulation by brokers at Hankow came to a head, and the superintendent had to take disciplinary action in order to hold down the price of Huai salt at subordinate Hupeh distribution points.[61] The brokers, however, seemed to accommodate their manipulations to each of the counter-efforts undertaken by the local and Nanking authorities.* In 1911, E. H. Parker summed up his forty years' experience in and about the port by acknowledging that "salt can easily be got at and cornered at . . . Hankow, whether it comes from Sz-Ch'wan or from the sea."[62]

The problem of collective funds and spending, however, seems to have concerned no one in these years, and the term *hsia-fei* seems to have passed from the vocabulary of the Hankow depot after the time of Lu Chien-ying. Several factors may have contributed to this development, the most important perhaps being the establishment of the salt likin, which allowed provincial and local governments at Wuhan a routine means of deriving a share of local salt revenues to replace the irregular exactions of earlier times. Moreover, the growth of institutionalized public service in the private sector (the system of *shan-t'ang*, or benevolent halls) provided a channel for salt merchants to contribute to the community as individuals, rather than as a collective body. Finally, the development of a formal guild structure in the salt trade, similar to those employed in other local trades, provided a more orthodox cover for the accumulation of collective merchant capital.

Merchant Organization in the Salt Trade

In searching for the origins of structured merchant organization in the Hankow salt trade, one is struck by the administration's persistent desire to impose order, despite its fear of the power of an independently organized merchant elite. Bonding (*pao-chieh*) was common in Chinese business practice from very early times, and the need for it was particularly pressing in the salt trade, in which the administration had an unusual interest. Mutual responsibility (*hu-pao*) groups were at various times enforced within that trade, with the aim not only of combating criminal activity but of distributing liability for financial loss stemming from any reason whatever.[63] We have seen, for example, that at least as early as the Tao-kuang reign salt-laden boats coming to Hankow were

*The compiler of the 1867 Hanyang county gazetteer identified the policy requiring that all salt destined for Hupeh consumers be resold at Hankow as the source of the problem of merchant graft. He noted that the policy stemmed from the desire of a "sympathetic" government to allow substantial opportunities for private profit, but added that this sympathy should be reciprocated by scrupulously honest behavior from the merchants. (*1867 HC*, 8.44.)

herded by government officials into *pang* (from this use of the word to refer to boats lashed together at anchor, the more general usage usually translated as "guild" was probably derived). In such cases, although the original impetus to collective organization may have been government mandate, it was the demonstrated utility of such organization to merchants that ensured its survival.

Pang of this sort were more directly related to the transport trade in general than to the salt trade in particular, but parallel organizational structures appeared at various times and levels within the salt market at Hankow. The word *yün*, literally "transport," for example, was also used to refer to a large-scale organization with a clear hierarchical structure headed by a "shipment overseer" (*yün-szu*) and designed to oversee the shipping of an entire quarterly quota of salt. Whereas this sort of organization was temporary and task-oriented, similarly structured groups of a more permanent character may likewise be identified in the pre-Taiping trade. Fujii Hiroshi, for example, has suggested that the term *kang* itself often denoted a guildlike syndicate of merchants.[64] Although a *kang* warrant was held in the name of a single individual, a group of merchants, most often united by bonds of kinship or local origin, usually banded together to finance—and profit from—the enormous transactions the *kang* system entailed.

Although these separate, ascriptively bound groups retained their identity, in the eighteenth century and the early part of the nineteenth they were subsumed under the head merchant, who arbitrated internal disputes and represented the salt merchants collectively in dealing with the outside world. Moreover, he was (like the *pang* and *yün* headmen) authorized by the state to guarantee the proper conduct of merchants and to enforce collective financial responsibility. Because the Hankow salt market in these years was regarded as part of the public, not the private, sector, all real property and tangible assets in the trade, such as warehouses and piers, were considered public property and so were managed corporately by the head merchant as the other merchants' elected representative. (Such matters as hiring warehousemen and engaging security forces also were under his care.)

The point at which collective activities and responsibilities spawned a formal organization is not clearly revealed in the available sources. However, as early as 1764 the Huai-nan salt merchants were said to have established a *kung-so* (guild organization) at Hankow under the leadership of an elected "controller" (*ch'uan-szu*). This controller was charged with quasi-official powers similar to those of the head merchant, and in fact the two were probably the same person.[65] But the use of *kung-so*, rather than *chü* (bureau) or other terms more generally applied to the

Hankow depot administration, suggests that this organization was established by the merchants for the collective pursuit of their private interests, as distinguished from those of the official salt administration. The campaign carried on at about this time by Liang-Huai Commissioner Kao Heng to reassert control over the Hankow merchants makes this conjecture the more likely.

By the beginning of the Tao-kuang reign (1821), the Hankow salt merchants had constructed a number of temple complexes in the town, which served in effect as corporate headquarters. One of these, which probably dated from the preceding century, was the Temple of the Great King (Ta-wang miao). This temple had been built principally as a place of collective worship, but large, open discussions of matters relating to the trade were also held there. As befitted the meeting place of the city's leading commercial elite, it was famous for its size and imposing appearance.[66] Across town was the Temple of the Heavenly City (T'ien-tu yen), which was formally designated the *kung-so* (guildhall) of the city's salt trade. Less a place of business than the Temple of the Great King, this temple provided elegant quarters for transient *kang* merchants visiting Hankow and was used as a cool and fashionable retreat for their colleagues who resided in the city year round. Here were held the extravagant feasts, unrivaled elsewhere in the great emporium, that so irked a succession of Liang-Huai commissioners. An informal poetry society composed of wealthy and cultured salt traders met regularly in the temple's precincts.

Almost certainly the "salt merchants" included in the pre-Taiping *kung-so* were only the *kang*-holding transport merchants and their delegates who managed the Hankow depot. *Shui-fan* handling internal distribution within Hukwang and local retailers were excluded from this elite. The exclusive group comprising the guild had good reason to pool their interests, for not only were they regularly subjected to official interference, exaction, and investigation, but they viewed their interests as at odds with those of the other parties involved in the local salt market. We may recall that in 1803 a suddenly overstocked market enabled the *shui-fan* buying salt in the city to seek extensions of credit that proved ruinous to many *kang* merchants, as well as to bargain for substantial discounts from the established price.[67] The *kang* holders could rely only on their own (uncertain) solidarity to combat the competitiveness that had broken down the market stability upon which their position of advantage depended. As revealed by Hukwang Governor-general Lu-shen's 1831 investigations, the transport merchants found their interests to be at odds not only with the administration and with the *shui-fan*, but with their own employees as well. The widespread practice of "internal smuggling" (*nei-szu*), which was then causing concern in Peking, was attributed by the merchants to a pervasive network of "merchant assistants" (*shang-huo*) and "merchant servants" (*shang-szu*), who conspired to defraud both their employers and the government tax collectors by operating a black market at Hankow in smuggled Huai salt. As a result, the provincial authorities found that "the licensed merchants are losing their capital and their power is daily withering away."[68] Here was yet another reason for a strong, united trade association.

The virtual extinction of the Hankow salt trade during the Taiping Rebellion dissolved this guild structure, just as its temple headquarters was burnt to the ground. The post-Taiping trade, as we have noted, was conducted almost completely by new personnel, but a revived salt guild did not trail the market's recovery by very long. The new organization shared two traits with its predecessors that distinguished it from the many other guilds in the city: it was structured specifically to override the varying ethnic and geographic origins of its members, and it remained restricted to the merchant elite.

Thus very few of the thousands of merchants, boatmen, and porters involved in the late Ch'ing salt trade at Hankow were represented by the city's salt guild (although most no doubt belonged to guilds of their own). Although the salt guild controlled the trade at every level, its membership was drawn from two groups, the salt brokers and the transport merchants. The salt brokers had ample reason to combine their interests, since the administration held them collectively responsible for each other's conduct and financial solvency. The initiative for the formation of the post-Taiping guild came not from the brokers, however, but from the *p'iao*-holding transport merchants. A local historian noted that "ever since the Liang-Huai district changed over from the *kang* to the *p'iao* system, various merchants engaged in transporting salt had come to sell their cargoes at the Hupeh depot. A majority of them decided that since they came from widely scattered areas, they ought to unite to protect their mutual interests."[69]

The operations of the resulting Hankow Salt Guild (Huai-yen kung-so) were managed by a headman known as the *yüeh-shang*, who was elected each month by the members. Continuity was provided by a semipermanent manager (*t'ung-shih*), who was charged with handling general guild administration and details of guildhall housekeeping. The guild was financed by a ten-tael levy collected by the brokers on all salt transactions at the depot (apparently the successor to the pre-Taiping *hsia-fei* assessment), and when the construction of a formal guildhall complex was undertaken in the late 1880's, an additional per-catty levy was superimposed.[70] A primary function of the *kung-so* was to articulate merchant interests vis-à-vis the General Superintendency, and thus almost daily negotiations were carried on between the guild's headman and the superintendent or his staff. These negotiations periodically succeeded in achieving official acquiescence in merchant demands, such as a modification of likin-collection procedures in 1872.[71]

Conclusion: The Salt Trade and Local Society

In the century or so before the Taiping Rebellion, the salt merchants constituted the financially and culturally dominant stratum in local society. These merchants as a group exercised enormous influence through their collective treasury, disbursements from which were used to provide famine relief, to finance local defense, and increasingly to underwrite regular local philanthropic activities. The implicit political power that this collective wealth gave the salt merchants was augmented considerably around the turn of the nineteenth century, when the White Lotus Rebellion debilitated the central administration, and merchants were forced to assume a larger share of local government and its costs. In retrospect, we can identify in this period of simultaneous merchant prosperity and administrative fiscal distress the beginnings of a new pattern of private (i.e., nonbureaucratic) initiative in the management of urban public affairs. Throughout the pre-Taiping period, the Hankow merchants' formal superiors in the Liang-Huai administration fought a generally losing battle to bring their independent power under control.

The Taiping closure of the Huai-nan trade brought a wholesale shake-up of the Hankow salt establishment. All reports indicate that the new class of salt shippers that entered the trade in the early Reconstruction years evolved over the course of the next half century into a secure and privileged elite, but they were a more diverse group than their prerebellion counterparts. On the one hand, the specific invitations to purchase salt transport licenses issued by Kuan-wen and Tseng Kuo-fan to local gentry and brevet-rank holders brought into the trade men whose existing power had come from noncommercial pursuits: landholding, examination success, and command of anti-Taiping militia. On the other hand, various newly risen commercial forces, such as Cantonese and Ningpoese traders with extensive foreign contacts (for example, the Hogg Brothers' compradore), also gained entry into this traditional preserve of scholar-merchants from Hui-chou and Shansi.

Both pre- and post-Taiping decades were marked by a dramatic loss of bureaucratic control over the conduct of the trade. This is seen, for example, in the continuing shrinkage of the Huai-nan subdistrict, the growing percentage of the trade within the district that went unreported, and the state's acknowledged inability to control the activities of its own post-Taiping salt brokers.

One deliberate response of the state in recognition of its waning control over the central China salt "monopoly" was to foster what I would term a privatization of the trade. With the inauguration of the *p'iao* system in 1849, the bulk transport merchants of Huai-nan ceased to be seen as government personnel, subject to the normal administrative sanctions of their superiors. In a very real sense, the trade had become less "feudal" with the abolition of the quasi-official enfeoffments that *kang* privileges represented. As historians in the People's Republic have demonstrated, comparable processes of privatization (or the eclipse of *kuan-pan* by *min-pan* enterprises) were underway throughout all of Chinese commerce and industry from the late seventeenth century through the mid-nineteenth. Areas affected by this process included the salt wells of Szechwan, the coal pits of the Peking area, the copper mines of Yunnan, and the pottery kilns of Ching-te-chen.[72]

Despite the installation of new government officials (the Hankow depot superintendent) and quasi-officials (the salt brokers) as checks on the anticipated venality of private merchants, the post-Taiping salt traders continued to have a major say in running their own affairs. Within the administration, persons like T'ien Wei-han, who belonged both to the merchant community and to the network of new government functionaries that had come to prominence through the anti-Taiping militia, probably served to further merchant interests. A more effective and lasting guarantee of merchant input into the making of salt policy was the alliance of salt merchants and brokers under the aegis of the newly formed Hankow Salt Guild. By presenting a united front to the superintendency in regular negotiations, the merchants and brokers were able to score some notable successes, such as modifications in likin-collection policy.

Although the Salt Guild could effectively articulate merchant interests vis-à-vis the state, it was powerless to protect the new salt merchant elite from the general trend toward social and economic pluralism in post-Taiping Hankow. The leaders within the trade no longer held a position of clear dominance over the financial and cultural life of the port as a whole, as had their prerebellion counterparts. Rather, they had to share this position with controlling figures in other trades. Moreover, the post-Taiping salt elite was itself more heterogeneous and comprised capitalists of considerably smaller scale. Participation in the Hankow salt trade during the second half of the nineteenth century was open to any private merchant who could afford to rent a *p'iao*, either individually or through a syndicate, on a long-term or a per-shipment basis. The government had installed a level of regulatory agencies, tax-collection bureaus, and brokers between itself and these merchants, and the merchants had responded with an essentially private trade organization to negotiate their interests vis-à-vis the state. In many respects, the world of the post-Taiping Hankow salt trade had come to look very like the familiar Western conception of preindustrial, urban, commercial capitalist society.

CHAPTER FOUR

The Tea Trade

For most Western students of Chinese history, the mention of Hankow immediately calls to mind the trade in "China Tea." The naive notions of Hankow's overnight rise ex nihilo to a major trading port in the 1860's, discussed in Chapter 1, no doubt derived largely from their authors' similar identification of Hankow with its role in the Sino-British trade. This identification, it might be added, may be an extension of the Western reporters' own viewpoint: were it not for the tea trade, virtually none of them would ever have set foot in the town. In Western eyes, tea was Hankow's sole reason for being.

The reality, of course, was otherwise. An investigation of annual gross values of trade at the port conducted by the Japanese consul in 1907 revealed that tea ranked only fourth among items of trade (behind such domestically marketed commodities as vegetable oil, rice, and miscellaneous grains).[1] Well into the present century it was the domestic trade, in which tea played a far more modest role than in foreign commerce, that gave the city its major importance. Although the centrality of the tea trade to Hankow must not be overestimated, neither can there be any question of its significance in the life of the town, socially as well as economically, in the second half of the nineteenth century. It was a trade of enormous proportions, and to the extent that the West did have an impact on the city, it did so principally through the local tea market. Above all, tea changed the nature of Hankow's relationship with its regional hinterland and altered the composition of the city's elite.

The Overseas Trade in Historical Context

Although tea began a meteoric rise in relative position among the commodities exchanged at Hankow upon the opening of the port, it had been an important trade item there for centuries. Little is yet known about China's domestic tea trade, but there is evidence that the Wuhan area marketed tea for domestic distribution as early as the T'ang dynasty.[2] By at least the mid-Ming, according to Fujii Hiroshi, a national market existed in this Chinese dietary staple.[3] During this period Ch'ien-t'ang county, Chekiang, and Hsiu-ning county, in the Hui-chou area of Anhwei, were among the empire's foremost tea producers, and men from these counties were among the wealthiest and most active merchants in China. Immediately upon its founding Hankow assumed a role in the national distribution of Lower Yangtze teas, but it achieved central importance in the trade only in the late seventeenth and eighteenth centuries, when, according to one recent estimate, overall domestic circulation of tea approximately tripled.[4] The chief beneficiaries of the rise in demand were the tea-producing areas of central China—Hunan and southern Hupeh—and Hankow's role in the domestic trade changed accordingly from transshipment point to regional collection center. It is probably no coincidence that in this period merchants from Ch'ien-t'ang and Hsiu-ning began to find their way to the city in greater numbers, no doubt in the hope of establishing themselves within the growing trade in central China tea.[5]

Hankow retained its importance as a center for the domestic trade well into the twentieth century, but from very early times the city had begun to concentrate upon exporting tea to a foreign market—north to Mongolia and Siberia. An appreciation of the scale of this Asiatic trade is essential to a true perspective on the more celebrated overseas trade that subsequently developed. Long before the teas of central China had captured a significant domestic market, they formed the major component of China's trade with her neighbors to the north. The famous tea-for-horses exchange with the Mongols, first officially inaugurated in the Ching-te reign of the Sung (1004–7) and consigned to the border market town of Chang-chia-k'ou, drew entirely upon Hukwang teas collected and shipped via the Wuhan cities. Curtailed for military reasons in the late Ming, the trade was reopened by the K'ang-hsi Emperor in 1696, and it rapidly attained unprecedented levels. Before the hiatus the trade had been a state monopoly, but in Ch'ing times it was formally transferred to private hands—especially the great Mongol commercial house of Ta-sheng-k'uei, headquartered at Ulan Bator. Mongol merchants thus established themselves not only at Hankow, but in its up-country satellite markets as well.[6]

By at least the sixteenth century, the export of Hukwang tea via Hankow to Mongolia had been joined by a parallel trade to Asiatic Russia. Tea shipments normally traveled on Chinese boats up the Han as far as northern Shensi, whence they proceeded overland through Kansu and Tsinghai to Siberia. Although no figures are available, this trade is said to have been large, and to have grown rapidly during the K'ang-hsi reign, when the tsarist government invested considerable sums in constructing Siberian roads for its facilitation. A second major period of growth in the early nineteenth century resulted from a sudden rise in the Russian demand. One Soviet scholar finds that the volume of tea passing through the central market of Kiakhta increased by 600 percent between 1802 and 1845.[7] Thereafter, tea, traveling primarily via Hankow, came to constitute about 95 percent of the total exports from China to Russia.

The Russian trade continued to thrive after the opening of Hankow as a treaty port. In 1880, for example, an estimated fifteen hundred tons of tea was shipped along the age-old route up the Han River to Siberia.* Russian merchants had been active in the city long before 1861, and after Western residence there was formally permitted by treaty they came to constitute a sizable percentage of the foreign community. The Russians usually dealt with local Hanyang and Wuchang merchants, who both negotiated the foreigners' purchase of tea and marketed their Russian-made woolens. Then the Russians shipped their tea north through Hankow-based Shansi transport brokers with whom they had done business for generations. By the early 1860's the Russians had set up a processing plant in the city, at which tea destined for Siberia was compressed into bricks, making it more adaptable to the overland portions of the journey. The original Hankow brick-tea factory was powered by manual labor, but in 1873 the Russians dismantled a steam-driven factory that they had constructed a decade earlier in the tea country at Ch'ung-yang and rebuilt it within the Hankow British concession. In 1875, 1878, and 1893 they set up additional plants in the city, with the result that the Siberian trade continued to grow—in the words of an envious British consul, "by leaps and bounds."[8]

It was in the context of the flourishing domestic and Asiatic trades that the overseas tea trade to Europe and North America grew up in the nineteenth century. A few pioneer tea producers in Hunan and southern Hupeh probably had begun to produce for the European market before the Opium War, but their product was shipped up the Hsiang River di-

*Only brick tea bound for Siberia, which was normally of inferior quality, continued to follow this route after the opening of Hankow. Tea of the first quality destined for European Russia generally was shipped by sea to Odessa, after 1869 via the Suez Canal. Some tea for the Russian market was also purchased in London, after having been shipped there by British merchants. In 1891, following a visit to Hankow by the Russian Crown Prince, the tsarist court decided to discontinue all overland tea shipments and to supply Asiatic Russia instead by shipments down the Yangtze to Shanghai, and thence by sea to Vladivostok. For the volume of trade on the overland route in 1880, see Parker, *China*, p. 149. For other routes and later developments, see Gill, pp. 47–48; Chao-li-ch'ao Tea Factory, p. 12; *Present Day Impressions*, pp. 476–78, 484–85, 488.

rectly to the port of export, Canton, and thus Hankow played no part in its collection.[9] After 1842, when the bulk of the overseas trade was moved to Shanghai, upriver tea-producing areas were gradually tied into the Hankow market, where their crops were collected for shipment down the Yangtze. Although the importance of central-China tea and of the Hankow marketplace was sufficiently developed by the 1850's to suggest to Western merchants the desirability of direct trade at the port, the available evidence indicates that only after the opening of Hankow did teas from Hukwang begin to capture a really significant share of the overseas market. In a very few years thereafter, British tea purchases at Hankow grew from nothing into a major trade, which quickly became the primary rationale for Sino-Western contact at the port. As an early British consul reported, "The growth of the export trade [at Hankow] from 1861 to 1863 was principally owing to the increase in the export of tea."[10] Chinese and British trading partners, often after testing the possibilities of trade at other Yangtze ports, quickly decided that at Hankow the export-tea crop of central China might best be collected and transferred to Western hands.

The Opening of the Hankow Tea Market, 1861

The inauguration of the export trade in Chinese tea at Hankow found Chinese and British merchants, as well as the local representatives of their respective governments, all groping for an institutional form through which the new trade might be smoothly and profitably conducted. Since Hankow was opened as the direct result of a war prompted largely by questions of protocol and diplomatic recognition, British officials were as anxious that this new form not impinge on their national dignity or preserve the humiliating and repressive systems they had fought against as they were that the anticipated trade prove a source of profit to their own nationals. Chinese officials, on the other hand, held conceptions of fair trade that differed greatly from those of the British. Moreover, in this period of prolonged domestic strife, their overriding concern was that the Hankow tea market provide enough government revenue to finance at least the military preparations needed for the port's security. The resulting confrontation in the summer of 1861 reveals a great deal about the customary practice of business in Hankow and about the diplomacy of imperialism on the local level.[11]

The tea tax (*ch'a-shui*) in Hupeh province had been instituted in 1855 by Governor Hu Lin-i as part of a broad package of commercial exactions intended to defray the costs of his regional anti-Taiping army. In addition to the likin, or transit tax on general cargoes, Hu declared taxes on cotton and silk cloth, timber, and tea. The tea tax, managed out of a special office at the up-country market of Yang-lou-tung in Hupeh's P'u-ch'i county, incorporated three types of assessment: on production (*yeh-li*), on refining (*hang-li*), and on transport to market (*hsiang-li*). At Hankow, where the tea was sold in bulk, it was subject to one further exaction (*pao-ch'a li-chin*), collected by the port's likin administrators. This complex fiscal apparatus had been set up originally to tax tea produced for the domestic market, but by 1859—in the wake of the Treaty of Tientsin—Hu Lin-i had ordered his subordinates to reevaluate collection procedures with an eye to tapping the anticipated direct tea trade with Europeans at Hankow.[12]

Upon the arrival of Western merchants in early 1861, local authorities acted quickly to bring the foreign tea trade under their fiscal umbrella. The first move to institute formal control came from the Hupeh Provincial Bureau for Salt, Tea, Brokerage, and Likin Matters, the omnicompetent economic supervisory agency set up by Hu Lin-i and administered by a committee of provincial officials of taotai rank. This bureau, whose activities in the salt trade have already been described, was primarily concerned with collecting revenue, but it was also charged with maintaining trade institutions that would be profitable to merchants, stable, and easy for the local administration to oversee. Because the bureau was an agent of the provincial government, its interests did not necessarily coincide with those of either the domestic customs or the Imperial Maritime Customs, both of which provided revenue for the central, rather than the regional, administration.

On 27 May 1861 the Hanyang prefect, acting under instructions from the Hupeh Bureau, issued a proclamation to all Chinese merchants "ordering all Tea brought to Hankow to be deposited in a recognized Hong for sale therefrom," with the primary purpose of facilitating the collection of likin on the exported tea. British Consul Arthur Gingell immediately protested this action to Hankow Taotai Cheng Lan, the local Chinese official formally responsible for managing relations with foreigners. Gingell declared that this sort of "system of monopoly Hongs, and requiring merchants to deal with them," was an infraction of the 1842 Treaty of Nanking.[13] The taotai responded, correctly but somewhat lamely, that as he was not currently a member of the Hupeh Bureau, which had instigated the action, and as several of the bureau's members were superior in official rank, there was little he could do to dissuade them from their course. In fact, the bureau had chosen to act via the Hanyang prefect's office instead of the taotai's precisely because it saw this matter as a wholly domestic one.

In the meantime, the Hupeh Bureau proceeded to draw up a set of regulations to formalize the arrangement it had in mind. To this end it called a conference of local Hankow officials, leading Chinese merchants, and the Hankow compradores of all the major foreign firms engaged in the tea trade. These parties arrived at a general agreement, but the fairness of their claim to represent all the interests involved is (and was) called into question by the facts that (1) neither the British consul nor his Chinese counterpart, the taotai, had been notified of the conference, and (2) none of the compradores had informed his foreign employer of what he was agreeing to in the employer's name. The bureau justified these omissions on the grounds that regulation of the trade was purely an internal, provincial matter, and that the intended institutional arrangement would be merely an extension of customary Chinese business practice not readily understandable to the foreigners, whose interests would not be so much affected that they need be informed. Although all parties to the negotiations managed to secure some profit from the final arrangement, it is unlikely that in calling this council the Hupeh Bureau had the deliberate goal of duping the foreigners.

On 29 June the bureau promulgated its new regulations, and directed the Hanyang prefect to serve notice on several foreign firms that were conducting business in a manner contrary to the new rules. The regulations stated that all teas brought to Hankow for export must be sold through a single Chinese firm known as the Hsieh-hsing kung, referred to in English-language sources as the "Hee Hing Company" or, more often, the "Black Tea Hong." This firm was to be responsible for standardizing weights and measures and otherwise maintaining an orderly local market in tea, and for collecting a 3-percent duty on all transactions, which would be divided according to the following schedule:[14]

1.2%	to the Likin Board, as a "subscription to the military expenses"
0.6	to foreign compradores, "for their trouble"
1.2	to the Black Tea Hong, as its commission
3.0%	

Consul Gingell immediately rallied the British merchant community at Hankow to resist what he viewed as a reversion to the abominated Cohong system,* and on 1 July he complained in a personal letter to

*Between about 1760 and 1842, the tea trade at Canton had been regulated by the Cohong, a group of merchant brokers who served as middlemen between Western traders and the Chinese Imperial Household Department, or "Hoppo." The Cohong was the descendant of a group of brokerage firms that had operated locally since Ming times, performing the same role in the foreign trade as other *ya-hang* did in domestic commerce. Both the Canton Cohong and the Hankow Black Tea Hong were government-franchised brokerage firms granted exclusive powers to regulate the local market and collect com-

Governor-general Kuan-wen. A spirited three-way correspondence ensued among the consul, the governor-general, and the Hankow taotai (called in by Kuan-wen to placate Gingell), resulting in a pledge by the taotai on 14 July that all monopolistic practices in the trade would be forbidden. Nevertheless, since Chinese and British conceptions of the problem and of terms like "monopoly" differed greatly, an understanding of this sort could exist only on paper, as subsequent developments demonstrated.

The Chinese view of the arrangements is explained in a letter sent by the taotai to Gingell on 2 July, which seems never to have been fully or accurately translated for the consul, who could not read Chinese.[15] This letter reveals clearly that the new regulations were intended merely to place the new export trade in the context of long-standing business practices at Hankow, as modified in response to post-Taiping reconstruction. In the late 1850's a Hankow mercantile firm operated by one Yao Hsieh-hsing had been granted a license (*pu-t'ieh*) to serve as a broker in the local domestic tea trade by the Hankow issuing office set up by the Board of Revenue. Whether Yao's firm was the only one so authorized is not stated; probably it was not. When foreign buyers arrived in the spring of 1861, the Hupeh Bureau (which, it should be remembered, had been established to oversee domestic commerce before foreign trade at Hankow was even contemplated) received a petition from Yao's "Black Tea Hong" requesting that, in exchange for guaranteed delivery of a 1.2 percent likin on all transactions it managed, it be granted sole brokerage jurisdiction over all tea sold for export at the port. Apparently any similar petitions that may have been received from competing firms did not offer as high a return or as strong a guarantee, and the bureau granted Yao's request. In relating this history to Gingell, the Hankow taotai argued that the Black Tea Hong was simply a broker, like any other broker, and thus the proposed system was quite different from the monopolistic sales practices that had characterized the trade at Canton.

Gingell seems never to have grasped this point, and he continued to view the Black Tea Hong as a large tea *dealer* granted a monopoly to sell to the foreigners tea it had purchased on its own account. (The key word "broker" never appears in the consul's descriptions of the affair.) In fact, the Hong was never a principal in the trade, and its profits were limited to an agent's commission (*hang-yung-ch'ien*) similar to that of brokers in

---

mercial taxes. Two factors did, however, distinguish the Canton system (after 1760) from either the Hankow system or the usual pattern of Chinese brokerage. First, brokers in Canton had an unusual degree of control over the personal lives of foreign merchants. Second, in the Canton trade the Chinese seller, the Hoppo, was indeed a monopoly. (See John K. Fairbank, *Trade and Diplomacy on the China Coast* [Cambridge, 1953], pp. 50–51.)

other trades in which both buyer and seller were Chinese. It was not a "monopoly" in the sense that private Chinese tea dealers were required to sell their merchandise to it for sale to the foreigners; rather, they were required to sell through it, in much the same way as commodities exchanges are conducted through licensed brokers in the West. The requirement that private traders deposit their goods with a central market manager for regulated, even sequential, sales was standard practice, as we have seen in the government-controlled salt trade and in private, guild-controlled trades as well.

The dust had hardly settled after the first confrontation when, on 19 August, the Hanyang prefect made a second attempt to restrict the export of tea to the agency of a single broker by ordering all Chinese dealers to dispose of their product through the Black Tea Hong. Apparently in an effort to mollify the British, he this time specified that all likin and commission charges be deducted from the Chinese seller's side only. Consul Gingell was not appeased, however, and he responded by initiating a new round of heated correspondence. The issue made no progress toward resolution, and throughout 1861 both native and foreign tea merchants continued to trade as they saw fit.

Meanwhile, at Kuan-wen's direction the officers of the Hupeh Bureau continued to monitor the activities of the Hankow export-tea market throughout this first, experimental season. In October they submitted their report, along with proposals for a permanent institutional framework for the trade. Their recommendations, endorsed and forwarded to the throne by Kuan-wen, centered on the following three points:

1. Foreign merchants and their Chinese agents (*ku-huo*) should be prohibited from personally visiting up-country tea markets to purchase crops. The bureau argued that allowing them to do so would signify that not only the stipulated treaty ports, but these up-country markets were in effect open to foreign trade.

2. All tea sold for export at Hankow should be required to pass through a government-licensed brokerage firm or firms (*kuan-hang*).

3. In order to ensure that provincial transit taxes on tea could be effectively collected, Hankow should be designated the official port of export for tea from central China, and thus a branch of the fledgling Imperial Maritime Customs Service should be opened at the port to collect duties on the spot, rather than at Shanghai as had been suggested by the chief customs administrator, Robert Hart.[16]

Charged by the throne with deciding the fate of these requests, the Tsungli yamen found that article nine of the Treaty of Tientsin specifically forbade local officials to establish prohibitions on up-country commercial travel. Over the expressed disapproval of Robert Hart, it acceded to the Hupeh Governor-general's request that a Maritime Customs office be opened at Hankow. However, it offered no guidelines whatsoever on the matter of requiring that all tea from central China be sold via a government-licensed broker or brokers at Hankow—the key issue of the Black Tea Hong controversy.[17] Apparently, this was to be determined by local authorities and local practice.

Ultimately, the Black Tea Hong incident proved less of a crisis than the impassioned correspondence of Consul Gingell would indicate. There is, in fact, little evidence that the consul ever succeeded in drumming up much support from the local British merchants, once their first flush of outrage at the independent action of their own compradores (in signing the agreement with local officials) had subsided. The controversy, which had been fanned by British officials largely over issues of international law, died down when the actual performance of the tea market proved satisfactory to all its direct participants. The British had won acknowledgment of their right to travel up-country (although in fact they exercised it only rarely, as we shall see), whereas the opening of the Hankow branch of the Maritime Customs, before the 1862 tea season, resolved the problem of taxation to the satisfaction of both central and provincial Chinese administrations, and eventually of Consul Gingell as well.[18]

Moreover, government-licensed brokers became a permanent feature of the Hankow tea trade. In later years several brokerage houses rather than the single Black Tea Hong performed this function, but as long as the brokers remained simply mediators in the trade rather than principals, their number had little effect on the freedom of the market. In fact, the price of tea at Hankow floated freely, determined by supply and demand, and not once during the sometimes stormy history of the trade did foreign merchants accuse Chinese market managers of fixing prices. Thus in the first confrontation at Hankow between Chinese and Western commercial philosophies, Chinese practice generally proved the more viable. This set the pattern for future leadership of the local trade by native merchants.

The Structure of the Hankow Tea Trade, 1861–89

The Hankow tea trade was a seasonal affair. Two, or occasionally three, crops of tea found their way to the port for sale each year, the first arriving in late May or early June and the others following at intervals of about two months. Many of the leading figures in the trade—such as the foreign buyers and tea tasters, as well as Chinese merchants, brokers, and bankers—spent most of the year away from the city, and several accounts tell of the excitement generated by their annual arrival. The tea season was virtually the only time the British Concession had any life to it at all. In the city itself, all the lodging houses were packed with Chinese teamen who "swarmed like bees." The streets were filled to overflowing, and many sedan-chair bearers and carriage-rental firms survived the year on business done in these few months alone.[19]

The majority of the foreign buyers and their staffs felt little identification with Hankow, since they lived for most of the year in the more amenable confines of the International Settlement at Shanghai. At its greatest, the Western community involved in the Hankow tea trade numbered some seventy to eighty men (excluding Russians involved solely in the overland trade to Siberia).[20] They remained at Hankow for as little as a few weeks, and many left even before the smaller second and third crops hit the seller's block. Their ships usually arrived at the port bearing cargoes of British merchandise such as cotton textiles, and intense competition ensued to be the first to unload and dispose of this inbound cargo, then leave with a hold full of tea. This rivalry often precluded any cooperation among the foreign merchants, not only putting them at a disadvantage collectively, but leading to strains on the tea market as a whole.

Because the Western tea merchants did not reside at Hankow, they were more dependent upon their Chinese staffs there than was usual elsewhere in the Sino-foreign trade. Foreign tea merchants, as we have seen, were accorded the right to visit up-country tea markets to make purchases. Few ever did so, however. Some of the more substantial foreign firms contracted their own networks of Chinese (chiefly Cantonese) agents to make up-country purchases,[21] but most chose instead to rely upon collection networks operated by the large Chinese tea dealers and brokers of Hankow. Negotiations with these dealers and brokers, with Chinese-run credit institutions, and with purchasers for import cargoes were all managed for the Western merchants by their Chinese agents. The degree of independence enjoyed by these agents has already been indicated by their autonomous actions in the 1861 dispute over the Black Tea Hong. As a result, compradores involved in the Hankow tea trade became one of the most powerful social groups in the city, and indeed in all of China; many of them eventually graduated into important commercial and administrative posts both in Hankow and elsewhere.[22]

A few large houses with long-term interests in the China trade, such as Jardine, Matheson and Company and the American firm Augustine Heard and Company, provided some stability to the foreign position in the Hankow tea market, but most of the buyers at the port were commercial adventurers with remarkably little understanding of the market or sense of the risks they ran. These firms came and went, frequently overextending their credit in their haste to buy. The June 1867 comments of Jardine's Hankow buyer about one intemperate trader, Mackeller and Company, reveal considerable bitterness at such rashness: "I am utterly at a loss to understand how they are going to pay for all the tea they have bought, as I know that nearly all the [Chinese] teamen have been paid by orders due some days hence. They have been the utter ruin of this market, which would have been very much lower than this but for the reckless way in which they have been buying."[23] Bankruptcy was frequently the result, as it was for Mackeller that very year.[24]

Many foreign tea merchants at Hankow were as unscrupulous as they were irresponsible, and they engaged in any number of deceptive business practices. British consular and Maritime Customs officials, who were usually close personal friends of the foreign traders, nevertheless often felt obliged to concede this point. Consul Chalconer Alabaster, for example, wrote his home government in 1882 that "it is said that the weights vary in nearly every [foreign] warehouse, and although it is strongly denied by some of those interested, there is no doubt that they do in many."[25]

In general, then, most Westerners in the tea trade at Hankow were noteworthy for the shortness of their vision. They had little interest in the stability of the trade and would sacrifice business ethics, proper credit management, and all regard for a stable market price in the hope of a quick profit. Their resulting disunity was apparent to Chinese and foreign observers alike.[26] At least into the mid-1880's, Chinese tea merchants were able to exploit this disunity, both to sustain a higher price than their product might otherwise have commanded and to dictate the terms of the trading process. As we shall see, the stabilizing factor in the Hankow tea market was consistently its Chinese participants.

The Chinese side of the Hankow tea trade comprised a complex hierarchy of middlemen and agents that kept the tea producer at several removes from his ultimate market, the foreign buyer. This hierarchy was analogous to the other marketing systems for commercialized agriculture that characterized the domestic trade of late imperial China, but it had unique features as well.[27]

Nineteen recognized "tea districts" spanned the five or six provinces from which tea was transported to Hankow for export. Tea was grown in these districts, not under a plantation system, but by small, independent peasant households (*ch'a-hu*). Many surviving sources document the rapidity with which small proprietors in these areas altered their patterns of land use to capitalize on the new foreign demand for tea. For example, the Yang-lou-tung region of southern Hupeh shifted dramatically from producing green tea for the domestic market to producing black tea for export to Western Europe.[28] Similarly, after 1861 Liu-yang county in Hunan quite suddenly abandoned its primary traditional crop, hemp, for tea cultivation.[29]

In most areas, the *ch'a-hu* were loosely organized under the leadership of a "mountain headman" (*shan-t'ou*), an independent, small-scale rural capitalist who formed the lowest link in a collection network that reached to Hankow and beyond.[30] The *shan-t'ou* apprised local producers of shifts in market demand and supervised the picking, drying, and initial firing of the tea. He then arranged its sale to an itinerant buyer known as a *ch'a-k'o* (literally, "tea-guest," the equivalent of the *k'o-shang*, or "guest merchant," in other trades). Several hundred *ch'a-k'o* fed the Hankow market each year. Many were independent entrepreneurs, but most were either employees or contract agents of larger Chinese tea dealers. In either case, the *ch'a-k'o* rarely sold directly to Western buyers, and in fact were prohibited from doing so by an 1872 proclamation of the Hankow taotai designed to ensure good market order.[31]

The "tea dealers," "tea merchants," or "teamen" known to the West were therefore not the *ch'a-k'o* but the proprietors of the large tea dealerships (*ch'a-chuang*, *ch'a-hao*) that employed these itinerant merchants or bought from them. Some *ch'a-chuang* were located at central market towns in or near the tea country; others were headquartered in Hankow itself.[32] In the best of times, well over two hundred *ch'a-chuang* were active in the Hankow marketplace, but the number varied considerably with market and financial conditions. In one particularly difficult three-month period in 1877, for example, over fifty such firms were said to have failed.[33] A few of the *ch'a-chuang* active in the export trade after 1861 were old firms originally set up by local merchants to serve the domestic or Asiatic trade. Most, however, were newly founded or taken over and expanded by non-native merchants: Cantonese and Ningpoese in the overseas trade or Shansi men in the ever-expanding Russian trade. Over the course of the nineteenth century, many of the former had simply moved their operations to follow the center of the Sino-foreign tea trade, from Canton to Shanghai and thence to Hankow or one of its up-country satellite markets (such as Yang-lou-tung, which grew in the 1870's from a small market town to a major commercial center of thirty thousand people). Some Hankow *ch'a-chuang* proprietors, such as T'ang Lung-mao, formerly Heard's compradore at Foochow, had acquired their capital and contacts in foreign employ. During this influx of outside merchants, the indigenous *ch'a-chuang* of Hupeh and Hunan were not forced out of business so much as absorbed, or brought into some sort of subordinate partnership by the larger firms of non-natives.[34]

Recent Chinese writers have tended to stress the evil effects of this "takeover" by non-native tea dealers on the regional economy of central China, but in fact it was merely one instance of the internal commercial colonization that characterized much of the trade of late imperial China. Starting in at least the sixteenth century, long before the foreign trade became significant, merchants from one region had pioneered the extraction or cultivation of a single, highly profitable commodity within an area of the country separate from their own and subsequently monopolized its production. The medicinal herbs and timber trades discussed in Chapter 8 are two examples, and the export-tea trade of central China was little different in this regard.

In the years after 1861, many non-native tea dealers moved their homes along with their businesses to Hankow, but the majority continued to live in Canton or Shanghai during the off-season. They arrived at Hankow in March or April and set up collection depots either at their Hankow offices or at centrally located outposts to receive tea from the *ch'a-k'o*. At the facilities of the *ch'a-chuang* the tea received the distinctive character it was to bear all the way to the British or American consumer's table, and in this respect the export-tea trade differed from most domestic trades. Although the tea trade's structure of rural producers, itinerant collectors, and dealers was similar to that of other trades, the Hankow tea dealer was more than a collection agent. The *ch'a-chuang* assembled the various local teas brought in by the *ch'a-k'o*, sifted them and picked them over, refired them, and blended them into a distinctive finished product to which the dealer affixed his chop. Inasmuch as these activities represented direct intervention in the production process by commercial capitalists, they marked a major step forward in the passage from a simple circulation economy to industrial capitalism.[35]

The *ch'a-chuang* prepared one or more sample chests of its product and forwarded them to a Hankow tea broker (*ch'a-chan*) for offering to foreign buyers. These large tea brokers, the successors of the Black Tea Hong of 1861, were the kingpins of the export-tea trade. At the trade's height, from the mid-1860's to the early years of the twentieth century, there were between ten and twenty *ch'a-chan* in the city, serving both the domestic and the export markets. Whereas the domestic tea brokers were often natives of central China, the more powerful export brokers were invariably non-natives, from Shansi, Ningpo, and especially Canton. These huge export agents set up shop in Hankow only during the few months when foreign buyers were in the city.

Except for the fact that they dealt with foreigners or their agents, the Hankow tea brokers were little different from the brokers in wholly domestic trades. They owned warehouses (*chan*—the ubiquitous "godowns" of treaty-port parlance) to store tea while it was being offered for sale, provided lodging for itinerant merchants, supervised weights and measures, and ensured the continuity of market price. After accepting a sample chest offered by a *ch'a-chuang*, a broker usually divided it up for inspection by several prospective buyers. When a bid had been received and a unit price agreed upon based on the quality of the sample, the parties to the transaction or their agents were brought together at the broker's warehouse to weigh the total lot and calculate the final price. The broker then deducted taxes and his own commission, and undertook delivery of the bulk merchandise to the buyer.

The Hankow broker thus "represented" (*tai*) both Chinese and Western merchants, and often managed all the dealings of both parties to the transaction. In other words, a single broker might have as clients Western firms that went to him for all their purchases, and Chinese tea dealers who marketed through him their entire chop. On the buyer's side, sometimes the broker and the Western merchant had established their relationship decades earlier, in the days of the tea trade at Shanghai or even Canton; both broker and buyer at Hankow were likely to be branch managers of Shanghai-based firms.[36] On the seller's side, many Hankow brokers controlled a stable of *ch'a-chuang* with whom they maintained close personal ties and for whom they constituted the only link with the foreign market. This was particularly true, of course, when the *ch'a-chuang*'s own facilities were not located in Hankow. A good example is provided by several family-run tea dealerships located in a single Hupeh county, which shared permanent representation by a Hankow broker.[37] Thus, although the broker formally neither bought nor sold, he no doubt appeared to many on both sides to be their customary trading partner at Hankow. His position was one of considerable power.

The network of business linkages that extended from *ch'a-chan* to *ch'a-chuang* to *ch'a-k'o* to *shan-t'ou* to peasant cultivator was strengthened by the manner in which the trade was financed. Tea transactions at the broker's warehouse were increasingly conducted on credit. In addition, a chain of continuing credit relationships was maintained, and it perpetuated the dependence of businessmen further down the production scale upon those more highly (or centrally) placed. The foreign buyer, for example, regularly advanced funds for operating expenses both to Hankow brokers and to individual tea merchants. The brokers in turn extended loans to *ch'a-chuang* in order to guarantee a steady influx of tea during the marketing season. Similar capital advances, or "prepurchases" (*yü-mai*) of promised merchandise, were extended down the line of production and collection to the peasant householder in order to finance initial cultivation of the tea crop.[38]

Like the entry of non-native merchants into the central China tea market, this system of capital advances has frequently been condemned by historians as perpetuating ties of "feudal" dependency that exploited peasant producers and small businessmen and inhibited their self-reliant development into a capitalist entrepreneurial class. To an extent, the validity of this view seems beyond question. Nevertheless, as recent writers have pointed out, the system was also "progressive" insofar as it facilitated a gradual movement of native financial interests into direct participation in the processes of production.[39] The evidence from Hankow does not support the contention that this network of financial and personal dependence led inevitably to exploitation of the small man. To some extent the paternalistic economic policies of the Ch'ing administration provided judicial recourse against such eventualities; as Chapter 6 will show, in several known cases officials specifically upheld the rights of subordinate parties in the tea trade vis-à-vis the brokers. However, it was by collective action, rather than by formal government appeal, that smaller-scale Hankow tea merchants most displayed their political and economic muscle.

Collective Organization in the Tea Trade

As a result of such celebrated incidents as its 1883 boycott of Western buyers, the Hankow Tea Guild has come to be remembered as an instrument for collective action against the West. Yet the Guild's utility was far broader. It pleaded merchant interests before, and wrested concessions from, the local administration; it curbed the disruptive activities of maverick Chinese businessmen (at the same time, Jardine was forced to sit helplessly by as maverick foreigners jeopardized Western interests); and, most importantly, it maintained a smooth working relationship between the two major Chinese participants in the trade, the brokers and the merchants.

P'eng Yü-hsin has argued forcefully that the hundreds of teamen active in the export trade of Hankow were at the mercy of the larger yet fewer brokers and warehouse owners, since competition between the former made them vulnerable to manipulation by the latter.[40] Shigeta Atsushi, in the mainstream of Japanese scholarship on late imperial commerce, echoes P'eng's views, identifying the Hankow tea brokers as among the middlemen (Japanese: *tonya*) that held a stranglehold on most trades, to the detriment of both rural producer and small merchant.[41] In fact, however, most independent teamen in Hankow felt benefited by the brokers' strict control over the trade, and the Hankow Tea Guild, which the teamen themselves created, constantly pressed for the tightening of such controls.

The precise origins of the Tea Guild, like those of most Hankow economic organizations, cannot be identified with certainty. The hundred or more tea dealers who came to Hankow to trade with the West in 1861 either were already part of collective organizations based on home area or province, or formed such groups shortly after their arrival. Membership in these organizations was by firm, not by individual merchant, and thus, although membership criteria included local origin (*t'ung-hsiang*) as well as trade (*t'ung-yeh*), the groups were clearly intended to be professional rather than social organizations.[42] In some cases, the local tea guilds belonged to larger provincial clubs that were not restricted to a single trade.[43] In the 1860's there were six tea guilds (*pang*) in Hankow, each constituted along provincial lines. At some point thereafter, they acknowledged their collective interests by amalgamating into a single Hankow Tea Guild (Han-k'ou ch'a-yeh kung-so). Yet the component organizations never forfeited their individual identities, and well into the twentieth century the umbrella organization was referred to both formally and informally as the "Six Guilds" (Liu-pang).

Surprisingly, we cannot even identify with certainty the six provinces associated with the six tea guilds of Hankow. In none of its surviving communications does the Six Guilds organization offer this information, and the reports of outside observers conflict. The earliest report I have seen, dating from 1888, lists the six as Hupeh, Hunan, Kiangsi, Kwangtung, Shansi, and Anhwei. In 1936 T. H. Chu repeated this listing, but two years later the well-informed Negishi Tadashi substituted Fukien and Kiangnan for Shansi and Anhwei.[44] My suspicion is that in time merchants from more than six provinces may have come to participate in the overall guild structure, although its name remained the same, and this discrepancy between name and substance may have led to the confusion among later scholars. As we shall see in Chapter 8, growth tended to take place within existing guild organizations, and thus new merchants might have joined with those of another province rather than form their own separate association.

The exact point at which the Six Guilds amalgamated, and the immediate motive for doing so, cannot be precisely ascertained. In his autobiography, Hsü Jun, compradore at Shanghai for the British tea firm Dent and Company, provided the following brief account, dated 1868:

In this year the tea guild [*kung-so*] was founded at Shanghai. I requested that Mr. Yü Tzu-mei oversee the initial rental of quarters on Stone Street, extending back to the Old Sluicegate. . . . A tea guild was also set up at Hankow. Sheng Heng-shan, Chang Yin-pin, and others were publicly selected from among the various tea merchants of Hunan, Hupeh, Kiangsi, and Kwangtung to collaborate with the officers of the Shanghai guild in regulating the trade.[45]

Hsü's dating of the establishment of the Hankow guild, however, is called into question by a dispatch of the British consul from the preceding year that cites a proclamation issued by a unified "Tea Guild" of the city.[46] Other sources suggest a date later than 1868 for the founding. As with many organizations of this type, the truth may be that an ad hoc association of leading Hankow tea merchants had functioned for some time as spokesman for the trade, with the tacit or explicit consent of its other participants, and only later was the organization formalized by drafting codified regulations, registering with the local administration, and renting or constructing a permanent meeting place. By 1871, however, all of this had been accomplished.

Although Hsü Jun's account may not reliably date the founding of the Hankow Tea Guild, he reveals several likely conditions of its establishment. First, the Hankow Guild closely coordinated its activities with those of the corresponding guild at Shanghai, and Hsü and other Shanghai luminaries may have taken part in its founding. This suggestion is not supported elsewhere, and the Hankow Tea Guild subsequently displayed such independence of action that it seems unlikely to have been manipulated by a downriver parent organization. Nevertheless, Chinese commercial intelligence networks were quite as developed as Western ones, and a close relationship between the tea guilds of two major cities would have been in keeping both with the linked structure of traditional Chinese commerce and with the increasing tendency for the major urban centers—particularly the mercantile elite of those centers—to trade chiefly with one another.

Second, Hsü tells us that the chief founder of the Hankow organization was Sheng Heng-shan, who, like Hsü, was an employee of Dent and Company: their chief Hankow compradore. This suggests that compradores were often among the leaders of the Chinese business community, but need not imply undue foreign influence in the local guild organization. In fact, it reinforces the impression of the independence and self-interest of compradores created by the 1861 Black Tea Hong incident, and perhaps also suggests that they saw themselves as *Chinese* entrepreneurs more than has heretofore been granted. The Hankow Tea Guild was an organization of Chinese, for Chinese, and in its founding Sheng no doubt acted primarily as a private merchant. The second founding member identified by Hsü, Chang Yin-pin (Chang Te-ming), was apparently never in foreign employ. He, rather than Sheng, became the acknowledged leader of the guild over the next twenty years, when Western merchants were one of the chief targets of guild activity.

It was in fact against foreign merchants that the combined Hankow Tea Guild directed its first collective action. The occasion was the 1867 failure of Mackeller and Company, which through reckless mismanagement was forced to close its doors leaving outstanding debts of over three hundred thousand taels to Chinese creditors, besides a somewhat lesser amount owed to Western firms at the port. The relatively light penalties inflicted upon Mackeller's managers by the British consul under British bankruptcy law generated considerable animosity among the Chinese mercantile community, and an atmosphere of suspicion tainted the Hankow marketplace for years thereafter.

When Mackeller failed, the taotai (strongly supported by the Hukwang governor-general) adamantly backed the demands of Chinese merchants for full and immediate payment, whereas British Consul Walter Medhurst insisted on Western bankruptcy proceedings. The Westerners had so little experience of the Chinese merchants' capability for collective organization that Medhurst was convinced only official pressure lay behind any mercantile agitation. He wrote in August that:

> The mutual trade of the Chinese and foreign merchants flows on as if Mackeller and Co.'s bankruptcy, and the subsequent matters springing out of that failure, were totally forgotten. The Native merchants entertain profound faith—in my opinion, much too profound—in the integrity and honesty of Foreign merchants, and no official or proclamation is able to remove that confidence.[47]

Whatever the truth of Medhurst's statement about Chinese faith in foreign respect for law, the merchants were prepared to hedge this faith with pragmatic measures. At the very moment that Medhurst was writing, two foreign firms (Alfred Wilkinson and Company and Jerdein and Company) were under a complete boycott imposed by the fledgling Tea Guild, an action taken independently of the taotai to protest the two firms' having reached private settlements with the bankrupt Mackeller, which liquidated outstanding debts to themselves while Chinese merchants still awaited payment.[48]

Yet Western merchants were not the only targets of the Tea Guild's activities. A good example of its role in articulating the interests of the trade versus the local administration is its campaign, waged jointly with the Salt Guild, for procedures that would make it unnecessary for merchants traveling up-country to buy tea (or sell salt) to carry large quantities of silver for payments at local likin stations. The two guilds argued that not only could this specie be lost in the sudden storms for which Hupeh was noted, but it made the merchants easy prey for the bandits who roamed the tea-growing hill country. By 1872 the two guilds had convinced the Hupeh Bureau to inaugurate a series of notes (*li-p'iao*) that merchants could purchase at the Hankow customs station and then surrender in lieu of cash at the various checkpoints they passed on their inland rounds. Ten years later, a new and more streamlined series of these notes was issued, after further pressure from the Tea Guild.[49]

As the Hankow Tea Guild gained power and prestige in the early 1880's, it began to apply pressure on the administration for direct tax relief. This relief might be administered in the roundabout ways familiar in Chinese fiscal practice, for example, the concession that 50 catties of tea would pass likin barriers charged only for 48, "to allow for the tea drying and losing its weight on the way to the Port." Relief might also take the form of direct tax cuts; in 1886 the guild successfully petitioned for a 5-percent reduction in the special defense levy to which tea merchants were subject, and the following year it negotiated a further cut of 15 percent in this assessment.[50]

Thus the guild employed its collective weight to protect the credit rights of individual members (in its boycott of Wilkinson and Jerdein) and to exact specific concessions from the local administration. The chief thrust of its activities in the city, however, was its constant struggle to maintain stability and standardization in the trade. One is struck by the remarkable objectivity demonstrated throughout this struggle; in most cases the guild alone among the participants in the Hankow tea trade took the long view and sacrificed immediate gain to maintain a stable marketplace. Its actions in the 1870's and 1880's display two general characteristics: (1) *legalism*, or a desire to codify mutually-agreed-upon rules of conduct in the trade, and (2) an adaptive *rationalism*, which, for example, prompted it to adopt the Western pound as a more precise unit for weighing tea. As P'eng Tse-i has pointed out, both the general anomic tendencies in Reconstruction society and the specific shock of the sudden and enforced expansion of Western trade had created an atmosphere of greater competitiveness and commercial disorder than that of earlier periods. In the tea trade in particular, a class of maverick and opportunistic native merchants had arisen, and their disregard for quality control threatened the profits of all.[51] It was against them that the tactical maneuvers of the Hankow Tea Guild were principally directed, although the fact that many Western merchants were able to capitalize on the presence of maverick Chinese traders and therefore encouraged their activities lent to the guild's regulatory measures an aura of competition with the West. To an extent, then, the Tea Guild did act to inhibit the freedom of the marketplace, but there is no evidence that it sought either to fix the market price of tea directly or to restrict participation in the trade to a select group of charter participants. Despite the guild's struggles for regulation, apparently its members were quite comfortable with an open market—even when, in the bleak years of the late 1880's, it operated to their detriment.

The most persistent problem commanding guild attention throughout these decades was that of conformity between sample and bulk in the teas offered for sale at Hankow. We have noted that the various *ch'a-chuang* normally forwarded sample chests of tea to their broker's warehouses for inspection by potential buyers. When a buyer tendered an offer, a unit price was arrived at on the basis of the sample tea, and when the bulk arrived it was weighed at the warehouse and the total purchase price computed. According to the available sources, during the first years of the Hankow trade problems of discrepancy between sample and bulk seldom arose, but as the number of mercantile houses in the trade grew, competition increased, and the less-established Chinese firms sought ways to increase their margins of profit. The practice thus arose of following up a high-quality sample chest with a bulk shipment that was either generally inferior or adulterated with lesser teas or extraneous matter. When this was discovered, the purchaser would demand a renegotiation of the unit price before the final bulk price was computed. After 1870, adulteration became so common (one source estimates it occurred in 30 percent of all transactions) that Western merchants customarily first agreed upon a unit price based upon the sample inspected, then demanded a discount at the time of weighing, regardless of the quality of the bulk shipment. As a result, the efforts of the tea brokers to uphold a stable price contingent solely upon market conditions were undermined.[52]

The Tea Guild first attempted to counter this trend in June 1872, when the leaders of the Six Guilds called a meeting of all member merchants to draw up a set of regulations that would eliminate what they felt to be the root of the problem.[53] Chief among these regulations was a provision that tea dealers would no longer be permitted to send an advance sample for their brokers to offer to Western buyers. Instead, a merchant would be required to wait until his total shipment had been delivered to the broker's warehouse, and only then would a sample chest be selected at random from the bulk offering. The selection of this sample would be made, not by the seller, but by an agent of the Tea Guild specifically appointed for the purpose. A second regulation, designed to alleviate foreign suspicions, called for the inspection and random sampling of the merchandise at the time of weighing and final purchase, to be carried out jointly by a member of the purchasing firm and an agent (*ching-shou*) in the employ of the broker. To discourage foreign buyers from reneging on the contracted sale price because of subsequent market fluctuations, the guild further specified that delivery and payment be completed within three days following the bulk weighing and inspection of the merchandise.

The guild, which represented only the tea dealers (*ch'a-chuang*) of the city, submitted the proposed new code to a meeting of the tea brokers (*ch'a-chan*), who enthusiastically approved its provisions. These men, by virtue of their semiofficial position as government licensees, then forwarded the regulations in a petition to the Hankow taotai, recommending that they be given the force of law. This the taotai did, adding a further regulation that no tea be surreptitiously exchanged at Hanyang city or change hands anywhere but at the approved warehouses of central Hankow.[54]

The new regulations were now "on the record" (*tsai-an*), and thus were legally binding in the city. The guild, moreover, was able through the taotai to enlist formal official support for their enforcement—for example, by having likin stations throughout the province actively forbid the passage of sample tea chests separate from bulk shipments.[55] In addition, the guild was able to draw upon the taotai's assistance to revise procedures in areas outside its immediate jurisdiction. For example, the guild had no direct control over teas coming into the city from the downriver port of Kiukiang, and samples of these were frequently offered for sale at Hankow while the bulk was still in the Kiukiang area. In order to standardize operations, the guild petitioned the Hankow taotai to coordinate procedures with his Kiukiang counterpart, and in the following year the latter official issued an order that no sample chests be sent to Hankow until the bulk of the shipment had at least been registered at the Kiukiang customs house and customs fees fully paid for its shipment upriver, in order to discourage the later substitution of inferior teas. The Hankow teamen professed themselves not fully satisfied with this arrangement but conceded that they had been at least partially successful in enforcing their controls outside Hupeh province.[56]

As with so many other attempts at reform in late imperial China, either private commercial or official, an initial program designed to correct the root of a problem led only to a continuing process of give and take, of systemic breakdown and ensuing efforts to tighten the network of control. As early as 1874 it was apparent that the sample-chest question would be no exception to the rule. Within two years after the new regulations had been enacted, a drastic decline in the actual price of tea at the port was attributed to a recurrence of the old discounting abuses. Consequently, the Hankow brokers petitioned the taotai to reproclaim his support for the guild's regulations.[57] By 1879 the problem had reached such proportions that the brokers felt compelled to suspend trading temporarily while they attended to one specific abuse that endangered market functions. Because of the language barrier, the largely English-speaking buyers had found it necessary to employ compradores, and the Chinese merchants and brokers, to engage agents. These middlemen had great opportunities for *chung-pao*, the familiar phenomenon of siphoning off profits at the middle. In its 1872 code the Tea Guild had taken note of this danger and requested closer supervision of the agents' activities by brokers and local customs authorities. Now, seven years later, the problem was even worse. It had become common practice for the brokers' agents, when completing a transaction and accepting payment, to offer a last-minute discount below the agreed-upon price, based on supposed discrepancies between sample and bulk, at considerable private profit to the agent and the compradore. In May 1879, therefore, the tea brokers of Hankow closed the market and withdrew for a private caucus, which resulted in a decision to eliminate completely their use of hired agents. They resolved that in the future all negotiations with foreign buyers would be conducted by a partner (*chan-huo*) of the brokerage firm involved.[58]

All these measures were directed against the undesirable practices of Chinese participants in the trade. As the Tea Guild gathered strength and confidence, however, it began to solve the same problems by another means: imposing controls on Western buyers who capitalized upon renegade Chinese. In October 1876 the guild took the first step in this direction by meeting at the close of the year's tea season to draw up a comprehensive set of regulations governing all details of the transaction, and again it requested that the Hankow taotai proclaim these regulations law. This time, however, they asked that he forward copies of the applicable regulations to the foreign consuls in the city, along with a statement of guild members' grievances at what they considered to be unscrupulous behavior by Western traders. The following excerpt from the document reveals the Tea Guild's cynicism at Western professions of support for a fair and rational market:

> The tea trade has been conducted with foreigners at this port since 1861. At that time all transactions were made in ready cash, and if disputes arose they were resolved in open discussion, without lingering suspicion. . . . As soon as the weighing process was completed, payment would be made in silver. . . . From this time on the trade began to grow in both scale and profitability. . . . As market conditions changed, most foreign merchants remained upright men and ad-

hered to the old system. There were some among them, however, who schemed to take the easy way around. In some cases they waited several days after the tea had arrived at the warehouse before allowing it to be weighed, and even after the weighing we sometimes had to wait as long as half a month before receiving payment. The foreign merchants could then claim that the tea they had received did not accord with the sample, using this as a pretext to demand a cut in the price. . . . Although the taotai's proclamation of 1872 corrected this situation to some extent, it has unavoidably had less and less effect as time has passed. . . . We humbly note that when Chinese merchants purchase goods from Western merchants, payment must be made to the foreign firm before the goods are weighed or shipped, whereas with tea the merchandise is delivered up for weighing before any payment has been received. If the foreign consuls truly regarded Chinese merchants as the equals of Western merchants, this difference would not exist.[59]

In the regulations that accompanied this statement, the guild attempted to establish procedures that would once again force all controversies to be resolved openly instead of by private accommodation. They stipulated that when a foreign buyer claimed discrepancy between sample and bulk, he might no longer settle the dispute by accepting a discount. Rather, the guild would suspend all trading while an immediate formal inquiry was held. Should either the Chinese merchant or broker be found guilty of duplicity, he would be subject to a heavy fine, payable into public coffers. At the same time, the guild demanded that Western traders comply with several other new provisions. First, weighing was to be more strictly supervised, and more than one chest was to be tested before short-weighting could be claimed. Second, the three-day limit imposed in 1872 for completion of payment following delivery of the tea was reaffirmed. Here the Chinese had a trump, which they now chose to play. Foreign vessels leaving Hankow laden with tea had to pass several riverine likin stations en route to the coast. Since their cargoes at this point had officially been exported, they were no longer subject to likin charges; however, this could be proved only by surrendering at these checkpoints special Transit Passes, which were issued at the point of export, Hankow. The guild now requested that the Hankow taotai withhold these passes until payment in full at the contracted price had been received. The taotai endorsed these proposals and communicated them to the foreign consuls.

The reaction of British Consul Patrick Hughes was predictable. Although he conceded that "the extraordinary state of Exchange" may have caused the Chinese merchants "some inconvenience," he refused to acknowledge the seriousness of the problem, complaining instead that the new regulations "contain in their details . . . much that is objectionable both in form and matter." He forwarded his copy of them to the British Chamber of Commerce, which upon Hughes's strong encouragement "declined to entertain them in their present form at all."[60] The 1876 season had long been concluded, however, and so the issue was shelved rather than resolved.

For the next few years business was conducted without a major confrontation. Apparently the foreign merchants successfully avoided the issue, and the Chinese seemed willing, for the time being, to continue to rely upon private compulsion to guarantee prompt and fair payment. In the early 1880's, however, the issue resurfaced, evoking a considerably greater emotional response than in the late 1870's. The result was one of the earliest and most widely reported organized economic sanctions taken against the West in late imperial China.

The Tea Boycott of 1883 and Its Aftermath

By 1882 the tea market of Hankow had thoroughly deteriorated. Though the practice of privately issuing sample chests had been strictly forbidden, it was still commonplace, as were discrepancies in quality between sample and bulk. The granting of discounts and extra quantities of tea to compensate for such variances had become so regular a practice that the putative market price had little real meaning. The atmosphere of mutual recrimination had grown intense, as was noted by the Western commissioner of the local Maritime Customs office:

> Foreign buyers charged Chinese sellers with practising all sorts of deception regarding quality, manner of packing, and so on. The Chinese, on the other hand, declared that they were bullied by buyers into giving greater weight than they were paid for. The truth, as usual, lay near the mean with—in the opinion of most whom I have spoken to on the subject—a tendency to favor the Chinese, who were generally conceded to have some grievance.[61]

To make matters worse, the tea warehouses of Hankow had become notorious for the inconsistency of the scales used in bulk weighing, a condition most observers attributed to tampering by Western buyers. Thus, at the close of the 1882 season, the state of the market was so bad that when the Chinese merchants announced they were ready to take matters into their own hands, they found support in surprising quarters. As the year ended, British Consul Alabaster wrote:

> It is a matter of congratulation that the variable weights at present used will probably be reduced to uniformity in the course of the coming season. . . . The Native Tea Guilds have issued a notice that to remedy the subject of complaint they propose appointing a public weigher whose services will be compulsory whenever there is a dispute. Whether this will succeed is open to question . . . but uniformity of weights is certainly desirable, and either other measures will be taken to secure that the weights are just or some compromise in the shape of a fixed allowance will be arrived at.[62]

As the opening of the 1883 season neared, excitement ran high in both the Chinese and foreign business communities of the port. Local tensions were exacerbated by an attempted secret society uprising, which had only very recently panicked the Wuhan cities. At the start of the tea season, Hankow was still under martial law and unsure of its future. Perhaps the Tea Guild's readiness to suspend trade was owing in some measure to apprehension at this breakdown in local security; alternatively, it may have been emboldened by the presence of Chinese soldiers in the city.[63] Amid this turmoil, just before the season was to open the guild held a plenary meeting under the chairmanship of Chang Yin-pin, which culminated in the drafting of a new set of regulations. The tea brokers, though they remained outside the Six Guilds structure, were invited to participate in this discussion. During the first week in May the draft regulations were issued in circular form to the Western tea buyers and simultaneously sent via a petition for ratification by the Hankow taotai.

Chief among the new regulations, and the cause of most subsequent antagonism, was the guild's demand for an impartial arbitrator (*kung-cheng jen*), who was to be "publicly selected" and whose decision would be binding in all matters of dispute between buyer and seller.[64] The guild was prepared to accept a foreigner in this capacity, provided he be "open-minded, disinterested, of upright and steady disposition, and a man regarded with trust by both Chinese and Western merchants." Second, provisions for standardized and supervised weighing of tea were established. The regulations noted that when Western merchants had first arrived at Hankow, it was intended that a standard unit of weight, the Western pound, be employed in all tea transactions. Subsequently diverse standards had arisen, which the guild (perhaps overcharitably) ascribed to the varying provincial origins of the teamen and brokers. Now, however, use of the Western pound was to be strictly enforced. Whenever a bulk transaction took place, whether at a Chinese or a foreign warehouse, a public weighing was to be held under the direct supervision of an officer of the guild. Each chest of tea would be weighed, and the foreign buyer compensated according to a fixed schedule for every chest that fell short of the contracted specifications. The weight of the chest and of the packing material would be closely scrutinized.

The 1872 regulations forbidding advance or privately circulated samples and calling for selection of the sample by a guild officer were reaffirmed in the strongest possible language. The statement on the subject suggests a resemblance between the forms of market management the guild and the brokers desired for the tea trade and those employed in the government-supervised salt market. Bulk shipments would be handled in order of their arrival at Hankow, and samples would be offered on the market according to strict sequential precedence. In the tea trade, however, this would not have eliminated competition, since samples of tea varied in character and quality, and consequently commanded differing prices.

Finally, the new code promised punishment to any Chinese businessman found guilty of subverting its regulations. If the offender was a tea dealer, he would be arraigned on charges brought by the members of his own provincial guild and tried before an open meeting of the combined Six Guilds. If the guilty party was a broker, and therefore outside the Tea Guild, the guild would press charges against him in a petition to his licensing agency, the local administration.

In general, the regulations of 1883 were a rational application of inherited Chinese business practice to the Sino-foreign trade. In insisting upon the foreign pound for all transactions, the guild simultaneously performed the normal function of Chinese commercial organizations by enforcing standards within the trade (exhibiting a far greater devotion to uniformity than did their Western trading partners) and demonstrated a cosmopolitan receptivity to foreign improvements. Similarly, the impartial arbitrator was a feature of the rational marketplace long known in Chinese commerce,[65] and yet again, the guild was willing to accept a foreigner in this post. They left selection of this official to the Hankow British Chamber of Commerce, which designated the British tea merchant Thomas Rothwell.[66]

In terms of both guarantees of impartiality and concession to foreign interests, the new regulations gave Western merchants little cause for complaint. The Maritime Customs commissioner described the foreign reaction: "On the whole, no one seriously contested the fairness of the prepared rules, nor objected to the arbitrator individually, but there was a strong feeling of opposition on the foreign side to being made party to a bargain which they had nothing to do with the making of."[67] Shortly after receiving the guild's circular, the foreign merchants called a meeting at the Hankow Club in the British Concession to deliberate upon a unified response. Even when faced with a perceived challenge, however, Western merchants were unlikely to achieve solidarity. Only once before, in 1879, had the foreign merchants agreed upon anything (a resolution that individual firms not sign purchase contracts before the market formally opened). Even then, however, a British journalist had wryly noted the agreement's singularity, and expressed skepticism about its durability.[68] Thus no one was surprised when the 1883 meeting "was not very well attended and did not therefore fully represent the trade."[69] The only fruit of this effort was a memorandum to the guild requesting further regulations, particularly one reinforcing the earlier ban on sample chests being precipitously sent up from Kiukiang. The guild dutifully responded that it would see what it could do.

On Saturday, 12 May, the guild issued the first sample chests to prospective buyers, and by the time bidding opened on the following Monday, the Western merchants had had ample time to reconsider their response. At the opening of trade, several foreign buyers loudly protested the unilateral imposition of the regulations, and one British firm, Dodwell and Company, refused to bid at all under the new system. Trading was then suspended by the Chinese brokers, and Chinese and Western merchants withdrew to plot their strategies. The Tea Guild was convinced that Dodwell had deliberately waited until samples had been issued before making its theatrical exit. The British firm, however, had a "crack steamer" waiting in the harbor to take on tea, and thus the guild felt its best tactical move would be to withdraw samples from Dodwell and boycott any further trade with that firm, to which all Chinese tea dealers agreed. The Western buyers' response was threefold: they determined to refuse en bloc any bidding on the samples previously offered until the boycott on Dodwell was lifted; they deliberated on a set of counterproposals to the guild's new code; and they deputed the British consul, Chalconer Alabaster, to take their case before the Hankow taotai.

Late the same day, 14 May, Alabaster fired off a note to Taotai Yün Yen-ch'i protesting the "illegality" of the new regulations under the treaties. The consul claimed that the boycott of Dodwell and Company had resulted in "substantial losses" for that firm and said that since by treaty commerce was open to all, such a boycott constituted restraint of trade. He demanded that Dodwell be compensated for each day of business lost. Taotai Yün by this time had studied the guild's new regulations, and he replied that he found them to be "just and fair" and in violation of no treaty. He therefore told Alabaster that he had ratified the new code of regulations and expected Western merchants to abide by them.

Nevertheless, the taotai summoned Tea Guild Chairman Chang Yin-pin to his yamen to clarify the guild's position. Chang supported the new regulations by claiming that it was high time the weights used in tea transactions be standardized and that insistence on this point was "a principle precisely opposite to restraint [of trade]." Moreover, he added with some irony, how could compensation for Dodwell's losses be computed when the firm had not tendered an offer to buy?

The taotai's reply brought forth an ultimatum from Alabaster, saying that if Chang were not suitably punished the consul would appeal directly to the provincial authorities in Wuchang. Yün Yen-ch'i complied by once again calling in Chang, who reiterated the logic of the Six Guilds' actions and the alleged deviousness of Dodwell's reaction. Chang suggested that the proper channel for Western protest would have been a communication addressed to the Tea Guild, and he concluded that if any compensation were due, it was to the Chinese merchants who were being hurt by the Western buyers' refusal to bid on their teas. Taotai Yün then responded that he felt the guild's actions eminently reasonable, and laid the blame for the current impasse on the Westerners. He noted that his own responsibility was to pursue the truth of the matter, rather than to side indiscriminately with the Chinese, but that in the present context they were clearly in the right. Let the British consul go over his head, if he so desired.[70]

As it turned out, both taotai and consul were saved further argument by a more natural resolution of the conflict. While Alabaster was protesting the new regulations on principles of international illegality, the counterproposals generated by the Western merchants' meeting of 14 May had turned out to differ from the Chinese regulations only on such issues as rounding off the weights of tea chests to the nearest pound or half pound. The Chinese guild received the Western proposals politely, then responded that since their own rules had already been promulgated to itinerant merchants in the interior, there was no alternative but to let them stand for the current season. They promised, however, that the following year they would give serious consideration to Western suggestions. This exchange prompted the *North-China Herald* to comment, "Hence the question of weighing may be regarded as settled upon the terms proposed by the Tea Guild."[71]

In the mutual attempt at a boycott, "the inability of the foreigners to combine together became at once apparent."[72] The Russian tea buyers, who had not participated in the Western withdrawal from the market, immediately picked up the best of the offered teas. Seeing this, other buyers quickly broke ranks, and a brisk trade ensued. The farce reached its climax when Dodwell itself gave in:

> This firm was left to settle its difficulties with the Guild single-handed. I believe they wrote the Guild explaining that their compradore in telling teamen they would not weigh their teas upon Guild terms, did so without their authority, and that further correspondence followed, after which the taboo was withdrawn and our settlement resumed its normal conditions during a tea season.[73]

The tea boycott of 1883 was not unique in modern Chinese history; it was but one instance of a type of collective action that was regularly employed in domestic commerce and in the late nineteenth century occasionally was used successfully in the foreign trade.[74] It was neither a "popular movement" nor a "political strike," and was thus unlike subsequent nationalistic boycotts or labor union activity. The Tea Guild had little intention of directing an attack at Western merchants—in fact, it was the latter who actually precipitated the stoppage of trade. Still further from Hankow teamen's minds was any thought of combating foreign imperialism or economic encroachment; the tea dealers were quite comfortable in their role as prime beneficiaries of the foreign trade. Moreover, the boycott was purely an elite action. The tea merchants of Hankow were not yet a self-conscious bourgeoisie armed with revolutionary ideals. Rather, they had evolved from the traditional gentry-merchants who had dominated Chinese domestic commerce since the Ming, and many were heirs to family businesses centuries old. Yet they proved themselves capable of a form of collective action to achieve economic ends that would before long become a potent political weapon.

Although the 1883 boycott was an economic and not a political act, it was undertaken to defend a principle—one that Western merchants at the port professed to share but honored inconsistently at best. This was the principle of the rational and open marketplace in which all parties might profit subject only to the restrictions of market value. At the same time, the boycott represented the culmination of a fifteen-year campaign for quality control; if the Chinese tea merchants were to offer a desirable product at a reliable profit, its quality and unit quantity must both be standardized. Thus the guild consistently sought to eliminate such practices as adulteration and short-weighting, so that prices and profits might be based more predictably upon the market value of their commodity.

The Hankow Tea Guild emerged from the 1883 affair a more powerful organization than it had entered it. At the beginning of the 1884 season, "almost all [foreign] tea firms" jointly submitted a protest to the British Chamber of Commerce, complaining that this organization, without having first consulted all interested parties, had signed a contract with the Tea Guild to appoint an arbitrator in compliance with the new regulations. The protest, however, came too late. An arbitrator had already been appointed, and his appointment, along with the regulations that required it, stood.[75] Thereafter, one foreign merchant each year served in rotation in this post. He was nominated by the British, but was subject to the rules established by the Tea Guild. At the start of the season, the guild annually issued under Chairman Chang's signature an abstract of these rules in Chinese and English, along with a notice announcing the name of that year's arbitrator. In 1888 British Consul

Clement Allen reflected that: "The noticeable point is that the Guild dictates its terms to the European merchant, and does so without the least attempt to soften its expressions, or to consult his wishes or opinion, while the merchant, on his side, accepts the position and submits meekly. Speaking confidentially, I fear that the malpractices of some of our own people are responsible for the undesirable state of things."[76] The following year Allen reported simply that "the rules of the Tea Guild . . . are still in force, and seem to work without friction."[77]

The arbitrator functioned extremely well. Only once, it appears, was his authority seriously challenged in a dispute over weights. In 1886 the British firm Welsh and Company refused to allow the Chinese broker to call in this official, and as a result the Tea Guild met and "perfectly voluntarily" voted to boycott Welsh. British Consul Charles Gardner was called in to mediate, and he advised Welsh to capitulate, after which the matter was amicably settled and the boycott lifted. As Gardner reported of the arbitrator, "The system has worked I consider to the advantage of both Foreign and Chinese dealers."[78]

Thus the Tea Guild remained, in the words of the *North-China Herald*, "almost omnipotent" in Hankow.[79] In 1889 it completed construction of a magnificent new headquarters in the city and at the same time issued a declaration of its continuing purpose, to "exercise exclusive management over . . . the tea trade with the various nations of the West."[80] The guildhall was opened in the customary fashion with a series of feasts and Chinese opera performances, to which were invited not only the leading merchants and officials of the city but leaders of the foreign community as well, thus fittingly symbolizing the guild's prestige among Chinese and foreigners alike.[81] The Tea Guild was attuned to foreign influences—so attuned, in fact, that in 1893 it began publication of Hankow's first lasting Chinese-language newspaper, the *Hanpao*.[82] At the same time, the position the guild occupied within the domestic commercial tradition is pointed up by its rivalry with the local Salt Guild, which functioned wholly within the domestic economic system. The Tea Guild's new guildhall expressed this rivalry, for it was constructed within months of the Salt Guild's, and the two buildings were given names identical save for the words "tea" and "salt."[83]

Yet the prestige of the Tea Guild, in both native and foreign circles, proved no defense against a new threat from an entirely different quarter. It has been suggested, in fact, that the construction of its new guildhall was less an act of celebration than a last-ditch effort to provide a visible symbol of unity in the face of the most severe test the guild had yet confronted—the challenge of international competition.[84]

The Crisis of the Hankow Tea Trade

From about the beginning of the Kuang-hsü reign, the Hankow tea market began to operate under conditions of increasing economic stress. We have already seen some of the manifestations of this growing pressure in a greater impetus to solidarity among the Chinese merchants and in increasing conflict with their Western trading partners. The threat of foreign competition also brought to the fore the issue of quality control, and this heightened the potential for friction between the merchant-capitalists at Hankow and other elements within the production and collection hierarchy. Ultimately, the crisis of the tea trade also created hostility between the Hankow merchant community as a whole and the imperial administration.

The vicissitudes of the Hankow tea trade in the decades after it reached its maturity (about 1864) are difficult to chronicle, since the figures that exist are neither based on consistent indicators nor necessarily reliable. As British Consul Chalconer Alabaster noted, elaborate systems of discounting, as well as the widespread use of "the baker's dozen and publisher's shilling," deliberately obscured the true volume of trade.[85] At best the reports, frequently contradictory, give only a general picture.

Figures culled by K. C. Liu from Maritime Customs reports show that the total volume of tea carried annually from Hankow to Shanghai by foreign steamer (that is, the majority of that exported from Hankow) fluctuated within rather narrow limits between 1864 and 1874, with a net overall increase of slightly more than 5 percent. Intermittent descriptions from these years confirm the picture of a stable, modestly growing trade.[86] In the late 1870's, however, the Hankow market began to show signs of depression. Consequently, Chinese merchants began to ship larger quantities of Middle Yangtze tea directly to Shanghai for sale and export, and the Hankow market was threatened with obsolescence. However, this attempt at cost-cutting rationalization was blocked by the concerted efforts of native property holders in Hankow and of "shipowners and other interested persons in England."[87]

During the 1880's fluctuations in the trade became more erratic and less favorable. Occasional seasons, such as 1881, 1882, and 1888, yielded abundant, high-quality crops that stimulated the level of mercantile activity and with it the optimism of participants and observers.[88] Over the course of the decade, the total *volume* of exports from Hankow grew modestly; yet the *profits* of Chinese merchants and growers declined. In 1885 Hukwang Governor-general Pien Pao-ti reported that teas that

TABLE 7
Chinese, Indian, and Ceylonese Teas as Percentages of Total British Tea Imports, 1866–1903

Year	China	India	Ceylon	Total
1866	96%	4%	0%	100%
1885	61	37	2	100
1886	57	40	3	100
1887	47	47	6	100
1903	10	60	30	100

SOURCES: For 1885–87, FO, *Commercial Reports*, 1887, "Hankow," cited in Yao, ed., 2: 1211; for 1866 and 1903, Moulder, p. 138.

several years earlier had commanded 50 to 60 taels per hundred catties on the Hankow market now averaged only 18 to 22 taels for the first crop, 13 to 14 taels for the second crop, and 6 to 9 taels for the third crop. Figures cited in other contemporary sources confirm this dramatic price collapse.[89] The decline took a heavy toll: tea dealerships, quick to spring up in favorable years, folded with increasing frequency. Governor-general Pien noted, for example, that in the major satellite market Yang-lou-tung their number had dropped from 80 to 28 within a few years.

According to most accounts, it was in 1887 that the problems besetting the trade first assumed disastrous proportions. Observers noted despair among Chinese merchants in general and an alarming number of suicides among the less secure petty traders. Hankow's Maritime Customs commissioner commented in his annual report: "People say the crisis in the China Tea trade, long impending, has come at last. This year it looked very like it. There was no rush to buy. Though tea poured in quickly, it went out slowly."[90] In that year, the Hupeh Bureau and the Maritime Customs Service both launched investigations of the causes of the crisis.

The immediate cause was hardly a secret: the tea of central China was increasingly unable to compete for the British market with that produced by British India and, lately, by Ceylon. Whereas total tea exports from Hankow doubled between 1866 and 1886, exports from India increased fourteenfold during that time.[91] Table 7 shows clearly the Chinese losses to South Asian competition, both over the long term and during the key period of 1885–87.

The losses to foreign competition were recognized by all at the time. The real question was: Why was the tea of central China unable to hold the British market? One answer, suggested by some contemporaries and favored by "conspiracy" theorists in recent years, was that foreign buyers (both British and Russian) had suddenly discovered that by concerted action they could artificially depress the market price because of competition among the ever-multiplying Chinese sellers at Hankow.[92] This view does much to remove suspicions of monopolization or price fixing by the Chinese Tea Guild, but it hardly squares with what we have seen of foreign behavior in the 1883 boycott and its aftermath.

A related argument advanced at the time was that Hankow prices were being undermined by the offering of second- and third-crop teas, which were markedly inferior in quality to those of the first crop and drew correspondingly lower prices. During the crisis year of 1887, the Hankow Tea Guild acted decisively to alleviate this problem. In a truly remarkable demonstration of the guild's ability to command unity even in times of severe financial strain, its members jointly resolved to refrain from offering secondary crops at all, in an effort to uphold the price of the first crop, upon which all sellers placed their chief hopes.[93] It appears that this resolve held, and may have brought a brief reprieve in the steady decline of profits. Nevertheless, it was not the basic cure that the crisis demanded. As we have seen, the prices of first-crop teas had been dropping so steeply that the availability of secondary crops could only marginally have been a factor.

A more plausible reason for the loss of the British market was found by the Hankow Maritime Customs' Chinese investigators: a decline in the quality of the Chinese product. Maritime Customs assigned some of the blame for this to flagging quality-control checks by merchants, but suggested that the heart of the problem lay in the system of production. Chinese tea was cultivated by poor, small-scale peasant households rather than large, capitalist plantations, as in India. Thus the Chinese producer simply could not afford to fertilize his land adequately, and it became more depleted with each year of continuous use. Moreover, he could not afford to replace the tea bushes periodically, a step necessary to maintain the steady quality of the leaves. These problems were compounded by further damage attributable to labor shortages. To be at its best, the tea had to be picked quickly, at the moment of peak ripeness. Chinese peasant households could not always afford the extra hired labor necessary for this rapid harvesting and were usually forced to take the time needed to pick the crop using only family labor. As tea prices at Hankow declined, the producers' ability to hire labor was further constrained, which resulted in further deterioration of the crop, which resulted in still lower prices.[94]

The investigations of the Hupeh Bureau confirmed the overall shortage of capital throughout the production, collection, and processing system—a capital shortage in part created by the system's diffuse structure.[95] Not only did this structure contribute to a decline in the quality of the product, but because the tea changed hands several times before final sale at Hankow, it was subject to a series of markups that made its price tag less attractive to the foreign buyer than that of competitive offerings.[96] In general, the elaborate network of collection agents and middlemen that had worked so well in Chinese domestic commerce for centuries proved clumsy and unresponsive when faced with the new phenomenon of extrasystemic competition.

Thus the Tea Guild was faced with a market situation it could not control. Despite its dominance in the Hankow marketplace, it lacked the leverage to restructure the entire system of production and thus to remedy the weaknesses revealed by both Chinese and foreign investigations. Instead of addressing the root of the problem, the guild sought to alleviate the exactions that ate into its members' profits most directly—the government taxes on tea production, transport, and sales. For years Hankow tea merchants had sought to reduce the percentage of their returns that found its way into state coffers. In the 1870's, the favorite tactic was simple evasion, using the Transit Pass system described in Chapter 2. In this maneuver, Chinese merchants falsely claimed to be employees of a foreign firm in order to obtain passes that exempted them from taxes on transit between up-country markets and Hankow. For years this evasion was so widespread in the tea trade that it kept down the real burden of taxation. In the mid-1880's, however, just when the trade as a whole was in decline, the Maritime Customs began to combat this practice more successfully.[97] Thereafter, merchants turned to direct pressure on the Chinese administration by the Tea Guild in their quest for tax relief. As we have already seen, the guild did have a number of modest successes in this area.

In November 1887, however, Tea Guild Chairman Chang Yin-pin submitted a memorandum to provincial and Maritime Customs authorities that described the decline of the trade in the bleakest of terms. To a modern reader, the guild's memorandum sounds angry, defensive, and indeed almost pathetic, reflecting Hankow tea dealers' growing desperation in a market that continued to deteriorate despite their greatest efforts to shore it up. In this document, the guild acknowledged the inroads made by Indian tea but denied that the Chinese product was inferior in quality. Instead, it assigned blame solely to the untenable price markups needed to offset taxes payable at each stage of production and collection.[98]

Most Hupeh provincial officials were sympathetic to the guild's line of argument. In the mid-1880's, for example, Provincial Treasurer K'uai Te-piao and Governor-general Pien Pao-ti several times vehemently resisted the central government's attempts to raise tea taxes.[99] In 1890, provincial authorities even secured from the Board of Revenue permission to reduce these assessments significantly, "as soon as an alternative source of revenue is found to meet expenses." Through the end of the dynasty, however, no such alternative was found, and no wholesale tax cut was ever effected.[100] The frustrations of the Hankow tea merchants, arising out of a decline in trade that proceeded unchecked into the twentieth century, and which stemmed in fact from a variety of causes, were thus increasingly vented against a single target: the claims made on their profits by the imperial state.

Conclusion: The Tea Trade and Local Society

The superimposition upon domestic commerce of a direct overseas tea trade with Western Europe had a limited but significant effect on the structure of local society at Hankow. Since in the process tea rose from a modest to a commanding position among commodities traded at the port, the prosperity and prestige of all those associated with it rose accordingly. This was particularly striking, since new arrivals from Canton and Ningpo (both by way of Shanghai) made up the controlling interests in the tea trade, serving as brokers and staffing the major dealerships. They joined and to some degree displaced commercial elites of longer standing at the port. The influence of this new elite in Hankow, however, was not shared by the foreigners themselves, who were insulated from local society and were kept by the perpetuation of indigenous business practices and by their own predilections from any major policymaking role in the trade.

Within the trade, the Chinese participants provided a much greater stabilizing influence than did the British, and they maintained a solicitous interest in the long-term health of the market. They thus were consistently the champions of a Weberian "economic rationality" at Hankow. Although Western traders paid lip service to such rational principles as standardization of weights and measures, quality control, and a fair and impartial bankruptcy procedure, in practice they often abandoned these principles in the interest of a quick profit. It was the Chinese (at first the administration, and subsequently the leading tea dealers) who repeatedly initiated measures designed to maintain a fair, stable, and rational market. These measures were largely derived from business practices in other, wholly domestic trades. Their workability ensured their acceptance in the Sino-foreign trade, but it did not necessarily imply cost-effectiveness or the capacity to respond to foreign competition. When confronted by such competition, the diffuse structure characteristic of Chinese domestic commerce proved a liability rather than an asset.

In the process of enforcing acceptance of their own market procedures, Hankow tea merchants achieved a considerable degree of solidarity. This solidarity could not stem the decline of the trade as a whole, but it did serve to bring under control the irresponsible actions of maverick Chinese merchants. Freewheeling competition and speculation were not unique to the tea trade, but were common in many areas of Hankow commerce and society in the immediate post-Taiping decades. They derived in part, of course, from the new prospects for gain opened up by the sudden introduction of direct foreign trade at the port. More basically, I would argue, they stemmed from the disruption of established commercial society during the Taiping interregnum. In the mid-1870's and throughout the 1880's, however, forces of control within the local tea trade succeeded in bringing this freewheeling competition within bounds, to the general benefit of the economy and society. This development, too, had parallels in other trades, as our study of the credit market in the following chapter will show.

The tea merchants' solidarity allowed effective collective action, such as the boycotts and pressure tactics of the Tea Guild. These instruments proved useful not only against recalcitrant foreigners, but against the Chinese administration as well—for example, in achieving tax reduction. Although in our period these tactics were not used for explicitly political purposes, the capability for such application was clearly coming into being. The guild's incipient interest in political matters was demonstrated by its founding of a newspaper in the early 1890's. Coupled with its simmering resentment of the Ch'ing administration over fiscal issues, this new politicization was to make of the Tea Guild a potential vehicle for revolutionary action in the early twentieth century.

CHAPTER FIVE

Credit and Finance in Hankow

IN A MUCH-CRITICIZED but influential study, Gideon Sjoberg argued that "preindustrial cities" in all cultures were dominated by kinship groups and voluntary associations. This he attributed in large measure to the need for such groups to act as credit institutions. More formal credit facilities were lacking, he believed, because of both a shortage of available collateral in urban areas and the prevalence of "elite attitudes" among the cities' moneyed classes.[1] Studies of late imperial Chinese cities, however, have increasingly made clear that although they were indeed "preindustrial," at least the leading commercial centers did not conform to Sjoberg's generalizations.[2] Although both ascriptive and associative groups did play important financial roles, professional credit organizations serving a more general business clientele existed alongside.

In nineteenth-century Hankow, merchants both large and small had remarkably easy access to credit and capital. Provided one could produce a guarantor (*pao-jen*), a seemingly easy task, monetary advances were readily forthcoming from merchants anxious to stimulate sales or money shops eager to put their deposits to work. Reports further suggest that a guarantor needed remarkably little in the way of personal substance—we are told, for instance, that the wife of a porter generated a second income for her family by serving as a professional guarantor and negotiator of consumer credit in her neighborhood.[3]

Investors in Hankow were able to float almost casually from one commodity to another as opportunity presented. Many made a killing; others went bankrupt. The latter had the choice of simply fleeing creditors or going underground until they saw a chance to start afresh. This was less true at the start of the century than at its midpoint, but certainly it had become characteristic of Hankow well before the Taiping hiatus. The two decades after the opening of the port saw it at its most freewheeling, and only around 1880 did stabilizing influences begin to have an effect.

Financial Institutions

At one end of the spectrum in the Hankow money market were the pawnshops, the traditional usurers who supplied much of the private credit in the agrarian sector. Families of pawnbrokers operated in the city throughout the century, and the county pawnbrokers' guild had its headquarters there. Some wealthy urban merchants diversified their interests by setting up pawnshops in the surrounding countryside, capitalized from the profits of their trade in the city; other, urban pawnshops were established by retired officials essentially as trust funds for their accumulated estates. Yet, whether because they were unable to compete with the interest rates offered by banks (as Yang Lien-sheng suggests) or simply because they were inappropriate to the financial needs of a major commercial center, pawnshops appear to have commanded a very small percentage of Hankow's credit market.[4]

At the other extreme, the most advanced type of financial institution in the city was the *yin-hang*, or "modern bank." As elsewhere in China, these were first established in Hankow by foreigners, the earliest being founded in 1863 by the British firm Masney and Company.[5] One Chinese historian, P'eng Yü-hsin, has argued that foreign control of these banks gave Western merchants an unfair advantage over their Chinese trading partners and led ultimately to Westerners' gaining complete control over the local marketplace.[6] Contemporary sources, however, note that until well into the 1880's neither foreign banks nor foreign currencies had garnered sufficient local respect to play any significant role in the trade of the port.[7] When foreign-style banking finally began to win favor, particularly in the tea trade, the Chinese business community was not slow to respond. By 1891 the Hankow Tea Guild had put together a consortium of native banks to form what was probably the first native-owned "modern bank" in China.[8]

Between these two extremes lay the several varieties of Chinese bank that in our period dominated the financial world of the port. These have been described well in English-language studies; thus we need review their role in Hankow only briefly. The "northern" or "Shansi" banks (*p'iao-hao, p'iao-chuang*) originally specialized in the transfer of funds from one area of the country to another and in conversion between local currencies. Augustus Margary described this function in his report of the preparations made in Hankow for his ill-fated 1874 journey to Yunnan:

> The 31st, 1st, and 2nd were taken up in bargaining for and procuring a boat, hiring servants, and concluding financial arrangements, which at first threatened to become exceedingly troublesome. But an order was at length obtained on a Shen Si [*sic*] branch bank which had been set up in Yun Nan. . . . The banker who supplied me with this order had the civility to call, and proved to be a man of great consequence and ability. He informed me that the government of Yun Nan was also supplied with funds through his bank. Along with the order, a tally of brass was given to me, which was to be presented at the bank in Yun-Nan Fu to serve as the standard of payment. And four per cent discount was the rate charged for the accommodation.[9]

As in Margary's case, Shansi banks usually paid no interest on deposits, but instead frequently charged depositors for their services. Their appeal lay primarily in their reputation for absolute security. Consequently, as Margary was informed, by the nineteenth century they had come to be employed less by private merchants than as a repository of the funds of other banks and, increasingly, by the central and provincial governments. In the process they had acquired a quasi-official character.

The several large Shansi banks of Hankow refrained almost entirely from competing among themselves. The local community of Shansi bankers was small and interlocked by personal ties, but its social and economic influence was far out of proportion to its numbers.[10] The Shansi bankers retained their influence into the 1890's, when the advent of a modern postal system usurped their basic function, the remittance of funds. For much of the century, however, the banks had engaged in local lending as a sideline, and in the twentieth century they were able to fall back upon this activity for a while after their major business was lost.[11] The bills of exchange issued by local Shansi banks, payable to bearer upon demand, circulated freely as currency in both the domestic and foreign trades of the port.[12]

The "southern" or "native" banks of Hankow, known in Chinese as *ch'ien-p'u*, *ch'ien-chuang*, or *ch'ien-tien*, were a different creature from their Shansi counterparts. Contrary to widespread belief, they developed indigenously, before the major introduction of Western influence. According to a well-documented recent study, the first native bank at Shanghai was established by local coal merchants in the mid-eighteenth century as a repository for their pooled surplus capital. By the 1790's, well over a hundred native banks were recorded in that city.[13] Although the opening of the port to foreign trade in 1842 stimulated their proliferation, the banks' early development can probably best be attributed to the overall monetization of China's domestic economy, which had been progressing steadily since the late Ming. In the rise of native banks, Hankow lagged somewhat behind Shanghai, yet there too they were fairly well established before the opening of the port to foreign trade.[14]

The chief local antecedents of these banks seem to have been the open-air moneychanging tables (*ch'ien-cho*) that in the eighteenth century and early in the nineteenth lined the streets of the city in great numbers. By the eve of the Taiping invasion, these humbler operations already were vanishing from the scene, as more sophisticated financial institutions took their place.[15] As successive waves of merchants and capitalists migrated to Hankow throughout the century, each group brought its own techniques of financial management. Through a process of mutual emulation and assimilation, a sophisticated and more or less uniform type of native bank gradually evolved in the city.

Some writers have sought to distinguish between *ch'ien-p'u* ("money shops," "exchange shops") and other institutions known most generally as *ch'ien-chuang* ("money banking shops," "traditional native banks"). Whereas the former are identified as simply money changers, the latter are credited with a wide range of banking functions, including accepting deposits, commercial lending, and issuing private banknotes.[16] In Hankow such variations in terminology were not necessarily revealing. In the first half of the nineteenth century, native banks were usually called *yin-hao*, whereas in the post-Taiping period this term was almost completely replaced by *ch'ien-chuang*.[17] There is no evidence that the two terms connoted a significant variance in function. In the later period the terms *ch'ien-p'u* and *ch'ien-tien* were also common, but again no clear distinction among types of bank can be observed. *Ch'ien-p'u* probably denoted a smaller-scale operation with a clientele restricted to local retailers, whereas the other terms suggested bankers to the wholesale trade, but all three were used to refer to a type of institution that both made loans and issued notes. Clearly, however, this general category included banks of many different sizes, oriented to many different clienteles.[18]

Native banking in Hankow was a mobile profession. Despite repeated failures, a period of favorable prospects in overall market activity might see a spate of new foundings. In a single two-month period of 1878, for example, in one several-block stretch of the city alone about a dozen banks opened their doors.[19] Over a hundred native banks were reported in Hankow in the first half of the nineteenth century, and by 1891 the total may have exceeded five hundred.[20] According to one reporter, "They are crowded along the streets and alleys as close together as the scales of a fish"; frequently an otherwise unremarkable side street might host several banks in a row.[21] Such an overabundance produced a financial situation both highly competitive and frequently chaotic.

In describing the empire-wide proliferation of Ningpo and Shaohsing native banks during the 1850's, Nishizato Yoshiyuki noted that these banks primarily (if not exclusively) served the community of Ningpo merchants within the commercial centers in which they were established. He concluded that this gave the Ningpoese a decided advantage over merchants of other local origins, especially in the foreign trade as the treaty ports were opened, since, unlike his competitors, a Ningpoese had a ready source of credit wherever he went.[22] The overall impression left by reports of native banks in Hankow, however, is that the majority were not restricted in their clientele and were considerably less parochial than Nishizato suggests. Of course, networks of personal relationships made it easier for a merchant to obtain credit from a banker of the same local origin, and most banks invested most heavily in enterprises run by fellow-provincials.[23] An early-twentieth-century source notes that some of the larger native banks of Hankow remained oriented toward the provincial guild to which they belonged, although the majority were not so aligned.[24] In some instances, banks appear to have been capitalized and backed by leagues of fellow-provincials. (In one famous case, a failed bank's debts were covered in large part by a subscription taken up within the city's Cantonese Guild.)[25] Hunanese merchants operated an interlocked chain of banks at various points along the Hsiang-t'an–Hankow trade route, as did Szechwan merchants between Hankow and Chungking.[26] However, the smaller banks, which constituted the majority of those in the city, tended to serve a local-origin group far less than the urban neighborhood in which they were located; thus the businesses along many streets were linked financially by a network of credit centered on a bank in their midst.[27]

A local correspondent commented in 1887 that: "The native banks occupy the position of leadership in commerce. Even more so is a bank's managing agent [*ching-shou*] the leader of its various employees. Consequently his responsibility is great."[28] What sort of men were the proprietors and managers of these native banks in Hankow? At the upper end of the scale were those who had close official connections or themselves held low official rank. A great many held purchased gentry status. Some, perhaps the majority, of Hankow's native bankers were merchants, whose banking activities were a subsidiary means of capitalizing their other commercial projects. Wang Li-ta, a purchased-ninth-rank official whose local origin is unclear, seems to have been representative of this class. Wang made his fortune as the owner of a large porcelain dealership in Hankow, a business valued in 1869 at close to six thousand taels (including inventory). With the profits, he had entered the burgeoning field of urban real-estate development, and he eventually owned and rented out a block of eight residential buildings in Hankow as well as a shop in Hanyang city, together worth an additional 2,800 taels. In 1863 he opened the Chi-t'ai-yang bank in Hankow, which issued banknotes in exchange for deposits of silver; these he reinvested in his porcelain operations. Wang's banknotes circulated widely, particularly in the Sino-foreign opium trade at the port.[29] Similarly, the Hsü family from Ningpo was involved in various commercial enterprises at Hankow in the 1860's. The Hsüs had close dealings with foreign merchants, acting partly as compradores and partly as independent dealers, chiefly in the cotton and opium trades. They also owned several pawnshops in the surrounding countryside, managed by fellow Ningpoese. One leading Hsü, a purchased-ninth-rank official named Hsü Chi-t'ang, eventually opened a bank in Hankow as a family sideline and began to issue notes.[30]

Many Hankow bankers, especially those with ties to nonbanking trades, were linked into a broader network of native banks in the leading commercial centers of China. A well-known example was the Fang lineage of Chen-hai county, Ningpo. Starting from modest beginnings in the sugar and silk trades during the early eighteenth century, the Fangs expanded from their native town into Shanghai, where they soon plunged into the booming Sino-foreign tea trade. Around 1830 they opened their first bank in Shanghai. By mid-century they had set up a bank in Hankow, which was linked by direct family ownership to others in Shanghai, Ningpo, Hangchow, and other major cities.[31]

The existence of such large, intercity banking networks indicates that by the later nineteenth century Chinese native bankers had been at least partially successful in creating an integrated and responsive national money market. Thus financial managers could select particularly flourishing regions of the country for concentrated investment and avoid others at times of local or regional threat. This mobility could adversely affect a local economy. In 1877, for example, "the principal Native Banks withdrew their capital" from Hankow because they feared that the current Shensi-Shansi famine would jeopardize investments in the trade of the city. The effect on local merchants was, we are told, "disastrous."[32]

The linkage of banking and nonbanking establishments by common capitalization and management, seen in all three of our examples, was a greater potential hazard to the local economy, since it increased vulnerability to the overextension of credit that plagued the Hankow marketplace. Both Wang Li-ta and the Hsü family were ultimately undone by this. Only five years after Wang expanded into the world of finance, his bank found itself unable to redeem a large number of its notes, and he was forced to forfeit both his porcelain business and his property holdings in consequence. Hsü Chi-t'ang's bank similarly proved the undoing of his family, at least in Hankow, for when he defaulted on notes issued to a Western merchant's Chinese compradore, the entire family enterprise was seized in recompense. Whereas Wang's and Hsü's local prominence prompted them to stay and defend their banks' failures, a more usual response in similar circumstances was simply to abscond. If even the native banks backed by such formidable commercial enterprises could founder, it is hardly surprising that lesser banks were even less secure.

Credit and Indebtedness

In 1874 a local Chinese journalist filed this report:

> Hankow is the hub of land and river traffic and the point at which resident and traveling merchants from both north and south China congregate. In the more than two hundred years of the present dynasty, the number of such "guest merchants" has steadily increased, so that today it cannot readily be ascertained. Until the Hsien-feng reign, payment for transactions in every commodity was routinely made in cash, and consequently over the years very few merchants failed because of indebtedness.
>
> Such, however, is no longer the case. . . . If we ask why this is so, we find that it is because notes issued by local banks may be taken in exchange at any market and at shops of whatever size. In a short time the guest merchants accumulate debts that they cannot repay, and as many as 80 to 90 percent of them eventually find themselves in financial difficulty. Ultimately they must forfeit their personal possessions in order to repay their business debts. There is no end to the degeneration in such market practices.[33]

The reporter seems to have allowed his sense of drama to exaggerate the contrast between current conditions and those of the good old days (a rhetorical technique not uncommon in Chinese journalistic style). As we have seen, credit institutions played an important role in Hankow by the early nineteenth century. However, there is no reason to doubt that a major increase in the use of credit occurred at about mid-century. It is important to note that at Hankow, as elsewhere, this development took place prior to and independent of the arrival of the West.*

The native banks of Hankow participated in the overall expansion of credit by accumulating funds in return for the more convenient and portable banknotes and then lending these funds to mercantile firms. Notes were issued in denominations pegged to weights of silver (*yin-p'iao*) or to copper cash (*ch'ien-p'iao*) and were payable either to the issuee alone or, more frequently, to any bearer (*p'ing-p'iao*). They might be is-

*Nishizato (1: 14) dates the shift toward general acceptance of credit in commercial transactions at lower Yangtze ports before the opening of these ports in 1842. Tu similarly finds that before the Opium War the cotton, wheat, and bean trades of Shanghai all routinely relied upon bank-issued credit instruments in clearing their transactions.

sued with a specific period of maturity (*ch'i-p'iao*) or be payable at any time upon demand. Examples of the latter type were the "flower notes" (*hua-p'iao*) issued by various banks in denominations of one thousand cash, which in the 1870's became a common form of currency throughout the Wuhan cities.[34] After the opening of the port, notes issued by Hankow native banks very quickly became acceptable for transactions in the Sino-Western trade.[35] Moreover, they were used by the government to pay troops; consequently the demobilization of a military unit in the region could lead to a run on a Hankow bank by homeward-bound soldiers who held its notes.[36]

The major means of extending loans to merchants was a procedure for overdraft credit known as the *kuo-chang* system, which allowed a commercial depositor to receive banknotes in excess of his cash deposits, the balance to be cleared periodically by the bank. Native banks located in the wholesale markets and the major shopping streets of Hankow stood ready to provide a virtually unlimited supply of notes to their regular customers, and often a mercantile house would operate on credit extended simultaneously from half a dozen or more native banks. Larger and more established businesses also borrowed from one or more Shansi banks in the city and from native banks located in the other major commercial ports of China.[37] Being impatient to put their capital to work, most native banks of Hankow kept specie or cash on hand totaling only a small percentage of their notes currently in circulation.[38] Thus not only did banks issue more notes than they had assets (these were known locally as *k'ung-p'iao*, or "empty notes"), but even banks with substantial assets generally had insufficient cash reserves to meet unanticipated demands for payment.*

Credit in Hankow was not the exclusive province of financial institutions, but was also exchanged between commercial firms that had regular dealings with one another, either through frequent transactions or as separately accountable branches of a single parent firm. After 1861 this practice was extended to include credit offered by or to Western merchants. The problems to which this could give rise have already been seen in the bankruptcy of the British tea dealer Mackeller and Company, noted in the previous chapter. In general, credit between merchants was a rather sticky affair. In 1882, for example, when a debt collector employed by a Hankow merchant was dispatched to clear accounts owed by a nearby fruit dealership, the fruit dealer committed su-

*An inflationary expansion of the money supply by issuing banknotes unbacked by specie is, of course, not necessarily an evil in an expanding commercial economy. What was perilous in Hankow was rather the absence of a central bank or similar control mechanism for the money supply.

icide. A local correspondent was moved to remark, "We can see from this how sensitive a matter is the settlement of debts!"[39]

The great ease of borrowing in Hankow, as well as in other major commercial centers, led in the second half of the nineteenth century to widespread speculation on credit. The extent of this practice alarmed contemporary observers; one reporter noted that even quite wealthy and long-established mercantile houses not infrequently failed because they had contracted too many debts.[40] Increasingly, the response of either a merchant-speculator or a banker-financier who found himself unable to meet financial commitments was to stealthily close shop and disappear in the dark of night. Countless such flights are documented for Hankow, and they must have numbered in the hundreds or even thousands between 1860 and 1890. In many cases, although not most, foreign merchants found themselves among the creditors of a bank or merchant house that had evaporated overnight.[41] Creditors and debtors were engaged in a city-wide cat-and-mouse game to collect and avoid payment. Investors in native banks often attempted to disguise their interests in a bank in order to escape repercussions in case it failed, or to conceal their other holdings from potential creditors by such means as registering their real property under an alias. For their part, creditors often attempted to pass suspect banknotes off onto their Western trading partners, if only in the expectation that, should the issuing institution fail, the Western creditor would be able to bring his consul's authority to bear in his quest for payment.

The most unscrupulous bank managers managed to peddle a large issue of new notes on the very eve of their default, in order to finance their flight.[42] Another common practice was for creditors to try to foresee an impending failure and to make closing deals in exchange for their silence. A dealer in Szechwan goods, for example, suddenly closed his doors at midnight one summer evening in 1881, packed his most valuable assets in chests, and disappeared, leaving only the posted notice "Out of Business." He was shortly discovered to have been in debt to several banks and other merchants for a total of over ten thousand taels. Certain of his creditors had advance warning and had made closing deals, but one of them, the proprietor of a native bank who was dependent upon the dealer's repayment to meet his own debts, was too late to claim his proper share, and so himself absconded the same night.[43]

The fate of this native bank's proprietor illustrates the "domino effect" the failure of an important business might have. A bankrupt merchant house might bring down with it any number of banks upon whose loans it had been financing its operations; a bank's sudden evaporation could in turn cause the collapse of commodity dealers who relied upon its notes. The most disastrous failures of all involved the many chains of native banks within the city, linked to each other either in a formal network of ownership or by interlocking credit relationships. The collapse of one of these banks, brought about perhaps by the defaulting of a dealership it underwrote, frequently brought about the failure of the entire chain, and in turn endangered the merchant houses each of the banks supported.[44]

As a result of widespread speculation on credit, interlocking credit relationships, and the relative ease with which a failed merchant or bank could avoid payment, reversals in the local market that might otherwise have been minor could have a disastrous effect on the whole business community of Hankow. One such reversal occurred in the winter of 1874–75. At its bleakest point, a local correspondent reported the interrelated closing of a silk dealership, a cotton dealership, and half a dozen native banks, noting that ten other banks and twenty or more dealers in a wide variety of merchandise were thereby placed in immediate danger of failing.[45] The disappointing tea season of 1877 was another period of market weakness, with "many establishments of long standing having had to succumb under their heavy reverses, dragging with them in their fall several native banks that had advanced money freely on teas."[46] Poor economic conditions continued throughout the following winter, and by the time business picked up again in the spring, many other native banks had gone under.[47] One local Chinese reporter analyzed the setbacks of the year as follows: "In all of the many trades of Hankow, credit is easy to obtain. Thus the number of merchants bringing commodities into the town is large, and in all the marketplaces the stock on hand accumulates rapidly. Turnover in inventory is insufficient, and this causes an even further rise in the level of indebtedness."[48] Clearly, some sort of action was required to curb the irresponsibility of credit managers, and both public and private authorities eventually attempted such regulation.

Regulation and Organization in the Hankow Financial World

In her fine study of native banks in nineteenth-century Ningpo and Shanghai, Susan Mann Jones concludes that "the *ch'ien chuang* in traditional China were remarkably free of the governmental controls that served to protect and sustain comparably sophisticated banking systems in other cultures."[49] It is certainly true that Hankow, like the rest of China, had no specific regulatory agency to oversee its banking establishment and probably did not even possess a formal legal code governing behavior in the financial world. The local administration operated under severe constraints in its attempts to regulate native banking in Hankow, as it did in the lower Yangtze ports described by Jones. Yet officials in Shanghai seem to have adopted a laissez-faire policy more readily than did those at Hankow. According to Nishizato, no effort was made to control speculation on credit in Shanghai until the local magistrate issued proclamations prohibiting such activity in 1887 and 1889. Neither effort had a significant effect.[50] In Hankow the attempt came almost two decades earlier, and if the results were not wholly satisfactory, neither were the controls cavalierly ignored by the business community of the port.

Local and provincial officials in Wuhan had long paid close attention to the activities of financial institutions. For example, the pawnshops of Hankow had come under strict government control in the Chia-ch'ing period, when Governor-general Pai Wen-min fixed their monthly interest charges at 2 percent during the winter months and 3 percent at other times. Pai's ordinance remained in force at least through the end of the nineteenth century.[51] The regulation of local currency was similarly an area of government attention, not only in the consistent battle the administration waged against counterfeiting, but also in the policy it set to determine which of China's innumerable local currencies would be accepted in Hankow shops and markets.*

Local officials attempted to exercise control over credit and indebtedness in several ways. The least ambitious and longest established was the prosecution of defaulters. Contrary to the frequent assumption that the late imperial state exerted little effort to enforce commercial liability, local officials in Hankow (in particular the office of the Hanyang county magistrate) played a consistent and conscientious role in guaranteeing the repayment of debts. Foreign merchants utilized their privileged access to the Hankow taotai to enlist official cooperation in pressing for payment, but local sources make clear that Chinese merchants had similar recourse to the magistrate's yamen for such purposes. One 1874 estimate claimed (possibly with exaggeration) that fully 90 percent of all legal cases brought before the Hanyang magistrate by petition concerned failure to meet credit obligations.[52]

Local records supply abundant evidence of the administration's availability as a recourse for commercial creditors. One of the more interesting cases involved a massive fraud hatched by four local merchants:

*Examples of administrative policy on currency are the regulation of "commercial copper" by Governor Yen Ssu-sheng in 1739 and the 1877 prohibition of "small cash" by Hanyang Magistrate Ts'ai Ping-jung (*SP*, Kuang-hsü 3/4/23). The administration also maintained two valuation offices (*kung-ku chü*) in nineteenth-century Hankow to test the purity of the silver in monetary use (Ts'ai, vol. 6, no. 1–2, p. 78).

Cheng Wei-kuang and Lu Shih-ch'eng, both from Canton; Ts'ai Ming-hsien, from Shaohsing; and Li Tung-yuan, from Wuchang. Lu, who was involved in many Hankow business ventures, both independent and compradorial, conceived a plan whereby Cheng and Ts'ai would set up a tea and tobacco dealership, financed by totally unbacked promissory notes issued by Li. Contracts and purchase orders signed by Cheng were to be "guaranteed" by Ts'ai and Li. When the entire paper empire collapsed, Cheng was hauled before the taotai by his Chinese creditors (the fact that he also owed a considerable amount to Western trading partners eventually brought the incident to the Tsungli yamen's attention). The taotai energetically pursued the investigation of all four conspirators, not only to compel them to fulfill their financial obligations, but also "to protect Hankow merchants in general from this sort of operation."[53]

One business failure that seems to have involved no such fraudulent intent was that of a certain Ta, a Kiangnan native who had moved to Hankow after his home area was devastated by the Taipings. Between the late 1850's and the late 1870's he slowly built up a chain of foodstuffs dealerships in the city and became one of its leading citizens. However, the dominolike collapse of several native banks handling his accounts forced Ta into default in 1877, and he was dragged before the Hanyang magistrate. Despite both his apparent innocence of deliberate wrongdoing and his respected social standing, he was sentenced to a thousand strokes of the bamboo. During the beating he died; perceiving this, the magistrate ordered the punishment temporarily halted and the defendant carried off "to rest somewhere," while he himself withdrew to his inner quarters to avoid further unpleasantness.[54]

A third case involved the Cheng-yuan bank, run by Yeh Hsin-yü, in which was deposited a portion of the funds of the Hankow salt depot. When the Nien threatened the city in 1865, Yeh fled to the countryside, taking his bank's assets with him, and in the process he allegedly sustained considerable losses. After order was restored, the salt depot superintendency filed suit at the county yamen for prompt return of its deposits. Magistrate Li Chen-lin several times imposed repayment deadlines on Yeh, who each time proved unable to produce more than a fraction of the amount due. Ultimately, Li ordered Yeh beaten to death for his crime of "flagrant mismanagement of property."[55]

In light of such draconian punishments, it is hardly surprising that Hankow businessmen in default so frequently chose to abscond rather than face legal proceedings—and consequently we may perhaps attribute the chaotic state of credit in this period less to official negligence than to excessive official zeal. If a defaulter fled, the official hearing the case usually passed on the debt to his debtors, or to his agents or relatives. If a commercial firm failed, the native bank handling its finances became liable for its outstanding debts.[56] The local administration's attitude in cases of default was a matter of formal public record. In response to an alarming rise in the rate of business failures, in July 1877 the Hanyang prefect and magistrate jointly proclaimed that they intended "to root out one by one the accumulated abuses surrounding these irresponsible declarations of bankruptcy," chiefly by having government functionaries seize all a bankrupt's personal possessions until all outstanding claims were settled. This hard-line measure apparently was widely supported by Hankow merchants and immediately reduced the rate of default.[57] Moreover, the local administration not only enforced payment after an enterprise had already failed, but at times officials closed banks that were rumored to be in trouble or banned the circulation of banknotes issued by institutions suspected of insolvency.[58]

Of course, none of these measures struck at the roots of the problem, namely, the ease with which commercial paper could be issued without regard for cash reserves and an uncritical readiness to grant credit in order to encourage commercial transactions. Government efforts were, however, also directed at these areas, with "periodic success" (as one 1881 source noted).[59] The first attempt may have come as early as 1865. Richard Halkett, then assistant Maritime Customs commissioner at the port, reported that:

> Compradores were found to have been speculating to a ruinous extent, chiefly with their employers' capital, and the prices they had nominally given to obtain goods at long credits, and the sacrifices they made in order to raise funds, vitally damaged the legitimate trader. It became absolutely necessary to do away with the credit system, of which, it was fully proved, the Compradores reaped the entire benefit, and the consequence was a temporary cessation of trade during the latter part of the year.[60]

Whether the action Halkett described was taken by Chinese or Western merchants, by the Maritime Customs office, or by the local authorities is left unclear. Whatever consequences resulted, they clearly did not include the "doing away with the credit system" Halkett desired. Probably it was the local administration that halted trade in 1865, for in March 1871 the *North-China Daily News* briefly reported an incident in Hankow that may have marked a repetition of the earlier action: "Some difficulty between the Taotai and the native banks seems to impede operations, by checking the necessary advances. This dispute, however, is verging on a settlement, and a large [foreign tea] trade is looked for."[61] For the 1871 dispute, as for that of 1865, our data are insufficient to reveal fully the nature of the controversy. It is clear, however, that already the local authorities had found the native banks of Hankow in such poor control of the local credit market that they had intervened directly and had declared a moratorium on lending.

However, the financial institutions of Hankow had not neglected to make some effort at collective self-regulation. Throughout the first half of the nineteenth century, this regulation was exerted by a variety of *pang* (guilds), organizations that were constituted along lines of common provincial origin as well as common occupation, a practice that made sense in light of the fact that the various banks with a common home province were likely to be connected by interlocked investments, if not by direct common ownership. One such *pang* linked the Shansi banks; a Japanese source described it as the most highly capitalized and most respected Hankow guild of the period.[62] Others represented the native banks operated by local Hupeh men and by natives of Chekiang (Ningpo and Shaohsing), Anhwei, and Kiangsi.

In 1866 came the first formal effort at collaboration between the Hupeh, Chekiang, and Anhwei groups, and in 1871 the three were joined by the Kiangsi bankers to establish the Hankow Financial Guild (Han-k'ou ch'ien-yeh kung-so), whose stated purpose was to control the money market of the city.[63] The component *pang* within this organization seem to have retained their individual identities, for as late as the Republican period the guild was known informally as the "three *pang*" or "four *pang*."[64] It seems likely that these two unification drives were undertaken specifically in response to the administration's 1865 and 1871 attempts to discipline the trade, in order both to develop an alternative program for improving the local credit situation and to forestall direct government supervision. We have no sources to confirm this motivation, however.

The Shansi bankers' *pang* did not join with the others, since the functions and interests of the institutions it governed were different from those of the native banks at this time. Much later, however, the Financial Guild reorganized itself into two separate organizations based upon functional specialty: one comprised the smaller native banks, concerned primarily with currency exchange, and the other was limited to larger institutions that were chiefly in the business of issuing notes. The Shansi bankers' *pang* then affiliated with the latter organization.[65] Although this restructuring seems to have taken place around the turn of the twentieth century, it shows how the functions of the various types of banks were beginning to be redefined toward the end of the period that concerns us here.

The most basic function of the bankers' *pang* in the post-Taiping decades was to control currency and its rate of exchange. Setting and policing the silver standard for Hankow was the jurisdiction of the Shansi *pang*,[66] and through its efforts the Hankow tael remained as consistently uniform as it did. The weight and purity of the tael varied from locality to locality. Whereas in most major commercial centers the guilds controlling the trade in each commodity retained the right to establish separate taels, in Hankow the power of the Shansi bankers was so great that they succeeded in limiting the number of taels to two: one for domestic and one for foreign transactions.[67] The exchange rate of silver and the various copper currencies in use at the port was set, after 1871, by a daily meeting of the Financial Guild and was then communicated to member banks before the opening of each day's business.[68]

A second major function of the guild was to serve as a tribunal for the resolution of conflicts involving its members. Sometimes the local administration referred a financial dispute to the guild's authority, as the Hanyang magistrate did in 1872 when he ordered the guild's chairman to arbitrate a conflict between a native bank and a local compradore.[69] Other cases could be resolved before they reached the official level. In 1877, for example, a man brought a banknote into a famous native bank of the city and demanded payment. The note seemed counterfeit, but since it was for a large amount and the bearer was a highly decorated military official, the bank's proprietor took the matter to the guild, which decided to pass it on to the Hanyang magistrate. The note's bearer, however, sensed an impending threat to his honor and through the mediation of a mutual acquaintance offered to throw a lavish banquet for the guild, in exchange for its not bringing the matter before the authorities. His offer was readily accepted.[70]

Besides these basic policing functions, the Financial Guild aimed to control more generally the abuses of credit current at the time of its founding. Although both responsible bankers and the local administration considered this regulatory effort to be in their own interests, the two groups had differing approaches to solving the problem. (I have suggested that the initial clash between the two was probably the stimulus to the establishment of the formal guild.) By 1874, when the guild had had three years in which to consolidate its powers, the time was ripe for a more definitive confrontation.

This confrontation was precipitated by the arrival in March of a new Hanyang magistrate, surnamed Yao, who determined to make solving the credit problems of Hankow a major task of his administration.[71] Yao was astonished at the high rate of business failure in the city, and particularly by the many default cases his yamen had handled in recent years. Consequently, even before taking over the seals of his office, he called in the leaders of the Financial Guild and told them that he intended to prohibit totally the circulation of banknotes in Hankow. Upon assuming office he had regulations drawn up and posted throughout the city requiring that all commercial transactions be conducted in hard currency. The immediate response of the guild was defiance. Several of the city's leading native bankers deliberated on a course of action and decided to issue jointly a new series of notes, collectively flouting the regulations. Acting quickly, however, Magistrate Yao seized the bulk of the new issue, and he seemed briefly to have won the day.

However, Yao's unsubtle attempt to reverse the direction of commercial development in late imperial China had little chance of permanent success. As one Chinese reporter commented, such a unilateral effort by the administration to dictate wholesale changes in the financial structure of the city was considered highly irregular, and although Yao's goals were excellent, popular opinion recognized a more complex economic reality than did the new magistrate. Without exception, businessmen found the new rules unworkable. Hankow shops of all sizes were forced to carry impractical quantities of cash on hand, and they quickly began to express their impatience. Almost at once Yao was forced to rescind his prohibition on the smaller denominations of cash notes, in his words, "for the convenience of the common people." His proscription of the larger, silver notes lasted slightly longer, but he soon discovered that the major reason for this was that he had arrived during the slackest period of the annual trade cycle. When the wholesale market in most commodities (including the export market in tea) opened the following month, the need for credit instruments on a major scale became immediately apparent. The precise directions from which pressure was brought to bear on the magistrate are not revealed, but in early April Yao once again called in the Financial Guild leaders, this time to inform them that he had approved the issue of new notes. (Probably the guild itself had much to do with this decision.) Almost immediately banknotes and credit notices of all kinds resumed their former level of circulation.

After this ill-fated foray into direct regulation, the local administration left supervision of credit largely to the ever-stronger Financial Guild. The guild responded by tightening its control over the credit market. Almost certainly one of its first steps was to announce that member banks would not honor banknotes issued by nonmembers, which in effect drove nonguild credit instruments from the Hankow marketplace.[72] It then turned to procedures for overseeing its member institutions. In order to operate a native bank in the city, a prospective proprietor was required to have on file with the guild a "joint security bond" (*lien-ming pao-cheng*) bearing the signatures of at least five other guild members as guarantors; only then would the guild endorse his petition to the Hanyang magistrate for formal approval to issue credit. Moreover, the guild required each member to keep on deposit with itself a "security account" (*pao-cheng yin*) of at least four hundred taels. It should be stressed that this sum was not prohibitively large, even for prospective bankers of only modest capitalization (late-nineteenth-century Hankow native banks varied in assets from about two thousand to over one hundred thousand taels), but it obviously served to discourage operations at the lower end of the scale, for which this bond represented a larger percentage of total assets. The guild paid a modest annual interest on security accounts, which by regulation was to be distributed 10 percent to a bank's manager, 10 percent to its other employees, and 80 percent to its investors.[73] By requiring security accounts from its members, the Financial Guild essentially solved the chronic problem of the Hankow credit market, namely, the inadequacy of cash reserves.

Because of the Financial Guild's increased control, although individual native banks might still fail, the domino effect of failures in linked banks and commercial firms was largely checked in the 1880's. The banks also had higher profits and greater security, which were widely attributed to the new spirit of cooperation evidenced within the transcendent Financial Guild.[74] An early-twentieth-century local history identified the guild as "the general organ for financial administration in the *chen*," suggesting that by this time it was popularly conceived as a quasi-public institution.[75] Whereas the Financial Guild of Shanghai was essentially an exclusive organization set up by and for sojourning bankers from Shaohsing and Ningpo,[76] after 1871 its Hankow counterpart was deliberately inclusive and attempted to incorporate all provincial groups significantly represented among the native bankers of the city. This may be one reason why the periodic crises of credit that plagued Shanghai in the 1880's and thereafter seem in large measure to have been weathered in Hankow by the mid-1870's.

For the financial world as for virtually every area of Hankow life, the decade of the 1890's marked a major turning point, however. According to figures cited by Su Yün-feng, the number of native banks, which at the start of the decade exceeded five hundred, dropped to one hundred by 1898 and to a mere 56 by 1915. The foreign-style "modern banks," which in 1891 had numbered only four (having declined from a high of 40 in the early, experimental treaty-port years), multiplied to take their place.[77] The native banks had proved able to maintain their preeminence as underwriters of both the domestic and the foreign trade of the port, but industrial capitalism drove them out.

Conclusion: Credit, Commerce, and Society

The financial world of Hankow underwent major changes over the course of the nineteenth century. In response to the increasing monetization of the overall economy and the intensification of interregional trade, relatively primitive institutions such as moneychanging tables and pawnshops had begun to be displaced well before the Taiping hiatus. Beginning in the 1820's and 1830's, new types of financial institutions were developed to provide businessmen with the easier and more fluid access to capital they required, through such innovative services as bills of exchange, deposit banking, book transfers of funds between depositors, overdraft credit, and (the most modern feature of all) negotiable and transferable credit instruments.[78] In the process, such institutions both expanded the money supply (hence stimulated trade) and contributed to the creation of an integrated national financial system incorporating all the major commercial centers of the empire.

Locally, the greatest proliferation of credit institutions coincided with the period of most unrestricted commercial competition, the 1860's and early 1870's. The result was an anarchic credit market, which threatened all parties to the trade. The bureaucratic administration responded, not by negligence, but by a zealous enforcement of debt obligations and by periodic attempts at a basic regulation (and once the outright prohibition) of credit. Neither policy proved effective, but the combination of a deteriorating credit market and the unwelcome prospect of direct government intervention did spur private efforts at regulation. The result was a new and powerful organization, the Hankow Financial Guild. The guild seems not to have excluded any aspirant to the trade on the basis of a low level of capitalization, provided that he vow to conform to guild-imposed standards of responsibility and keep on deposit with the guild a minimum security account. In enacting the latter provision, the guild launched an extremely significant innovation in Chinese financial management: it assumed the basic function of a central bank. By the 1880's, then, the Hankow Financial Guild had achieved a level of stability in the local credit market adequate to the needs of the great interregional and foreign trade, and perhaps greater than that attained at Shanghai or other commercial centers.

The Financial Guild's significance for Hankow society as a whole was not limited to the rationality and control it imposed in money, banking, and credit. It represented a new type of guild organization, which attempted to bring together all participants in a trade or profession regardless of local origin. Hankow's bankers were in the vanguard of this trend, whose more general implications will be considered in Part II of this study. The breadth of representation that this new structure afforded the guild, along with the increasing respect accorded it by the local administration, was an important step in the process of privatization of economic—and eventually also social—policymaking power in the city.

CHAPTER SIX

The State and Commerce

THE PRECEDING chapters have suggested that during our period a process of privatization was under way in the commercial life of Hankow. In the salt trade, this amounted to a de facto abrogation of direct state proprietorship; in other trades, it meant more simply the state's farming out of regulatory authority to participants in the trades. Officials continued to take an interest in commerce, both domestic and foreign (for purposes of revenue, private enrichment, and even the benefit of the populace they governed), but increasingly they restricted their own roles to formulating general policy (usually in consultation with the appropriate guild), appointing overseers (the increasingly prevalent brokers), prosecuting flagrant offenders (as in the enforcement of credit obligations), and, of course, reaping what the administration considered its fair share of the profits. However, the linkages between state and commerce, and between official and merchant, were complex ones. In this chapter, we will explore them in greater detail, showing the influence of these interconnections on both administrative policy and the way that policy was enacted.

Existing scholarship on late imperial commercial policy may be roughly divided into four general approaches, which I would dub the "repression," "neglect," "collusion," and "stimulation" theses. The first approach, which until recently dominated Western literature on the subject, sees the Ch'ing bureaucracy as actively hostile to trade. Although evidence for this view may be found in the physiocratic fulminations of various social critics among the Ch'ing gentry, the approach probably grew out of the frustrations of nineteenth-century Western merchants in China, who tended to view all official restrictions on their activities as deriving from a reactionary, anticommercial bias. These early impressions were reinforced by the "scientific" findings of Weber and his contemporaries on pervasive "traditionalist" habits of thought in Chinese society and, more recently, by Western theories about general "preindustrial" cultural traits.[1] Repression theorists argue that the ruling bureaucracy, fearing alternative sources of political power, consistently sought "to restrict the growth of merchant capital by promptly declaring any important profitable enterprise a state monopoly" and that "the merchant class was not treated with courtesy by the government officials and had no access to them."[2] A corresponding line of thought, which until recently marked most mainland Chinese scholarship, argues that the commercialization that took place in the late Ming was possible only in an era of eroding bureaucratic controls, and that the restoration of strong government under the Manchus ushered in a period of virtual refeudalization, which allowed the resurgence of gentry-landlords and kept down incipient commercial-capitalist forces.[3]

The "neglect" thesis shares the view that the Ch'ing administration was no great friend of merchants and trade, but postulates a government policy of aloofness or indifference. The pioneering scholar and sometime Maritime Customs official H. B. Morse offered a classic statement of this view when he characterized the imperial government as no more than a "taxing and policing agent," which refrained from almost any interference in the conduct of trade. A more recent restatement is Frances Moulder's conclusion that "the major difference between the Chinese and the European old regimes seems to be not that the Chinese government was able to *suppress* commerce and industry, whereas the European governments were not, but that the Chinese simply failed to *promote* commerce and industry as the European governments did."[4] In Morse's view, under this policy of aloofness the state abandoned consumers and small merchants to the self-interested dictates of a few powerful commercial capitalists and the guild organizations they controlled. He is seconded by the Japanese scholar Imahori Seiji, who has argued that China's "feudal" commercial system, dominated by large capitalists through local communal ties (*kyōdōtai*), was the direct consequence of the laissez-faire policy adopted by the state.[5]

The repression and neglect theses are not mutually exclusive, but have frequently been applied in tandem to the Ch'ing administration. An excellent example is the study of the Ch'ing statutory code (*Ta Ch'ing lü-li*) done at Harvard by F. L. Dawson in 1948. Dawson concluded his analysis of commercial policy:

> In its formal aspect, this system of laws reacted to the detriment of the merchant class in two ways:
>
> a) *positively*, by setting up a system of monopoly controls over trade, which were associated with various other forms of bureaucratic restriction on private enterprises and implemented by a formidable system of collective responsibilities.

b) *negatively*, by failing to make any adequate provision for property rights, contractual relationships, or a definition of corporate activity.[6]

Like the two approaches noted so far, the "collusion" approach is harshly critical of the Ch'ing administration. This view, propounded chiefly by a large and influential segment of Japanese scholarship, argues that the rapacious Ch'ing government both conspired with and exploited mercantile forces for reasons of administrative expediency and personal venality. The collusion thesis owes something to Marx and much to the theories of pioneering Japanese sinologist Naitō Konan, who saw post-Sung China as characterized by an increasing accumulation of state power. Thus Hatano Yoshihiro, for instance, has argued that in late imperial times the "despotic system of absolute power," or "absolutism" (*zettaishugi*), allowed the bureaucracy great opportunities for financial aggrandizement but prevented others from accumulating capital except as a special privilege bestowed by the officials, who fostered the growth of a money economy and commercialization for their own ends. From the Ch'ien-lung period on—that is, before the major Western impact—the wealth that officials had accumulated was gradually turned into commercial capital. The officials, landlords, and large merchants as a class thus were parasites on the peasants, handicraft workers, and small merchants.[7]

Collusion between state and commercial capital is stressed even more strongly by Saeki Tomi, whose pioneering work on the salt monopoly led him to conclude that the Ch'ing, far more than previous dynasties, used large, interregional merchants to underwrite administrative control mechanisms on both national and local levels. In a recent article, Saeki draws an explicit comparison with Europe: "In Europe, autocratic rule developed with the financing of urban merchants, and the merchants received political patronage from the autocratic rulers [in exchange]. In this context of mutual profit and mutual assistance, the system of autocratic rule generally took shape." Saeki argues that a similar form of absolutism characterized the Ch'ing and that large, urban-based merchants paid the bills for (and in part brought to power) the alien Manchu regime, in exchange for a freer hand to exploit the market.[8]

The last approach, the "stimulation" thesis, is rooted in Chinese and Japanese scholarship of the 1950's, but in recent years has begun to achieve currency in both East and West. Proponents of this view suggest that the late imperial administration actively sought to nourish commercial activity, both to increase state revenues and out of a paternalistic belief that a high level of trade was a prerequisite of a prosperous and well-functioning economy. For example, Fujii Hiroshi traced the late

Ming commercial boom to the promulgation of the *k'ai-chung-fa*, which he identified as a program to open the northwest frontiers under which the court deliberately encouraged the circulation of goods and merchants throughout China. Teng T'o tied the mercantile expansion of the sixteenth and seventeenth centuries to government programs for monetizing the economy and encouraging local economic incentive. Recent Chinese writers such as P'eng Tse-i and Wei Ch'ing-yüan have linked the unprecedented economic prosperity of the mid-Ch'ing to deliberate legal reforms enacted by the early Manchu rulers.[9] These scholars, and many of their American counterparts, have pointed to the conscious liberalization of state economic controls as the primary means used to stimulate the economy. Ramon Myers, who has probably gone the farthest in this direction, has depicted the quantitative growth of the late imperial commercial economy as in large part precisely a response to the long-term government policy of transferring mercantile functions from the public to the private sector.[10]

As is doubtless clear by now, I feel that the evidence from nineteenth-century Hankow supports the stimulation thesis—although this is not to say that the repression, neglect, or collusion approaches are altogether invalid, since the Ch'ing administration's role in commerce was complex and at times even contradictory. Our evidence also supports the observations of recent English-language studies that have demonstrated the paternalist* control the Ch'ing sought to exert over the circulation of commodities: for example, by regulating the price of grain, encouraging or requiring guarantors in wholesale transactions, and instituting criminal punishments for economic activities deemed contrary to the public interest.[11] Thus in Hankow we find that the provincial administration purchased rice on the wholesale market in order to dump it on the retail market in times of high demand and rising prices, that it legally required guarantors to underwrite major firms and transactions, and that it enforced such policing devices as five- and ten-man mutual responsibility groups (*hu-pao, hsiang-pao*) among itinerant merchants.[12] As we shall see, however, paternalist policies should not be confused with repressive ones. Indeed, to the extent that these policies took priority in official minds (they did not always do so), they were

*My use of "paternalist" to describe these policies derives from the work of European historians, especially E. P. Thompson, *The Making of the English Working Class* (New York, 1966), pp. 197–98. Such policies in Ch'ing China have been admirably summarized by Moulder (pp. 48, 62–66) under the term "provisioning"—a label that I reject as specifying too narrowly their overall intent, which was to protect popular livelihoods (including commercial-related livelihoods), as well as food supply, and so ultimately to maintain social stability.

often designed to facilitate rather than to restrict the circulation of commodities.

Why did the Ch'ing state seek to stimulate commerce? Most directly, it did so because of its reliance on trade as a source of revenue. Too often, Western scholars have underestimated that reliance. In 1954, for example, Rhoads Murphey wrote that whereas merchants in late imperial China were heavily dependent on the state (e.g., for the maintenance of waterways), the fact that government income was derived almost solely from agricultural sources freed the state from any reciprocal reliance on the commercial classes.[13] Discussing such mid-nineteenth-century fiscal reforms as the introduction of the likin, Mary Wright in 1957 cautioned her readers not to infer too much, since to late Ch'ing bureaucrats "the very idea of developing commerce into an important source of revenue was unthinkable."[14] However, our study of Hankow commerce (as well as other current research) leads inescapably to the opposite conclusion. In 1864, for example, Governor-general Kuan-wen testified that close to 70 percent of total government revenue in Hupeh and Hunan provinces was derived from commercial sources. For the empire as a whole, Wang Yeh-chien has estimated that whereas in 1753 some 74 percent of revenue at all administrative levels was provided by the land tax, by 1908 this had fallen to 35 percent, with the difference made up chiefly by commercial taxes.[15] Clearly, by the late Ch'ing the Chinese state relied heavily upon commercial exactions. Its officials, aware of this fact, shaped their policies accordingly.

The extraction of government revenue from commerce at Hankow was accomplished in three general ways: (1) by taxing the transport of merchandise, using the domestic customs, the Imperial Maritime Customs, and the likin transit tax; (2) by taxing major wholesale transactions, using government-licensed commodities brokers; and (3) by a variety of irregular and indirect channels.

Transport Taxes

The Hupeh provincial gazetteer informs us that the domestic customs (*ch'ang-kuan*) were collected in that province as a tax on cargo-carrying boats, rather than on their cargo.[16] The Wuchang Customshouse, which was responsible for collecting customs in the Wuhan area, was established in 1664. Various official reports from the early nineteenth century testify that in those years it was still an important source of revenue for local and provincial governments.[17] After the Taiping hiatus, in early 1857, Hukwang Governor-general Kuan-wen and Hupeh Governor Hu Lin-i reconstituted the domestic customs as a network of eleven substations spread across the three counties of Chiang-hsia (Wuchang city), Hanyang, and Huang-p'i. Four of these eleven stations—the most remunerative—guarded the approaches to Hankow *chen*. Government income from this new system averaged between 1,000 and 1,800 taels per month, much of which was retained in local administrative coffers.[18]

The Maritime Customs (*hai-kuan*) was a later addition, and coexisted with the domestic customs at Hankow after its inception there in 1861. When the Chinese Imperial Maritime Customs was established, Inspector General Robert Hart and his superiors in the Tsungli yamen had decided to tax all international trade emanating from the Yangtze valley at Shanghai. Several months after the opening of Hankow, however, in a memorial to the throne Kuan-wen stated that the absence of a Maritime Customs office there was allowing native merchants to evade local transit dues (*tzu-k'ou-shui*). Consequently, the court approved the establishment of the Hankow Customs, or Chiang-Han kuan, under the joint management of a foreign commissioner and a Chinese superintendent. The latter post was assigned to the Hankow taotai as a collateral duty, and after 1862 the Hanyang prefect served collaterally as assistant superintendent. The Hankow Customs came to comprise a head office in Hankow proper, branch offices in the British Concession and in Hanyang city, and a far-reaching network of customs barriers (*k'a*) to collect transit dues. The customs revenues, which quickly became very large, were shared in varying proportions by the local, provincial, and central administrations.[19]

In contrast to customs, the likin was levied on goods rather than on vessels. Likin was not directly connected with the central imperial administration, and this feature differentiated it from all previous commercial taxes (at least all legitimate ones). It was levied by and for the provincial governments, initially to cover the cost of their independent military forces engaged in suppressing the Taiping Rebellion. Likin evolved directly out of the provincial governments' traditional practice of soliciting merchant contributions to meet extraordinary regional expenses, and was justified at first as a routinized means of collecting these contributions. Indeed, throughout its history likin was never formally referred to as a "tax" (*shui*, *k'o*, etc.), but instead was termed a "contribution" or "subscription" (*chüan*, *chüan-shu*). In practice it was an extremely complex system of commercial exaction, involving a number of subcategories. For example, in Hupeh the general commodities likin (*huo-li*) was supplemented by specific taxes on salt (*yen-li*) and tea (*ch'a-li*) collected by and for the province in addition to the duties on these goods (*yen-k'o* and *ch'a-k'o*) collected on behalf of the central government. There were also more localized impositions on retail trade and on production.

The collection of likin in Hupeh province was first formalized in 1855 by Hu Lin-i, following the precedent introduced in 1853 by Lei I-hsien in Kiangsu and subsequently approved by the Ch'ing court.[20] Hu's system was greatly influenced by Wang Chia-pi, a Hupeh native and *chin-shih* of 1844, who had devised the system while employed as a private secretary to Lei I-hsien and who transferred to Hu Lin-i's personal staff upon Lei's retirement in 1854. Immediately after recapturing the Wuhan area in December 1856, Hu set up a major collection station at the Hankow piers, and it soon became so busy that a second station was established elsewhere along the waterfront. Six others were installed at various locations in Hanyang county within the following year. The original Hankow station eventually assumed overall responsibility for branch stations throughout the province.

The Hupeh provincial government very quickly became dependent upon its magnificent likin revenues, which allowed Hu Lin-i to proceed with remarkable speed in the full pacification of the province and then to lead his troops in campaigns of military assistance to the lower Yangtze region. The tax continued to be critically important long after the Taipings had been crushed, indeed throughout the remainder of the dynasty. Governor Tseng Kuo-ch'üan, for example, noted in 1866 that "likin is the single most profitable source of Hupeh provincial revenue"; more than two decades later Hukwang Governor-general Ch'en Ming-chin credited likin collections from the Hankow stations with "paramount importance in underwriting our military expenses."[21] In 1884 the Hankow branch alone yielded some 274,300 strings of copper cash.[22]

With the great success of likin as a revenue-generating device came an inevitable broadening in the application of its proceeds. As we have seen, the tax was initially justified solely as a source of emergency military provisions (*chün-hsiang*), and although the court ultimately bowed to pressure in authorizing its use for postrebellion reconstruction as well, both in theory and in practice likin remained above all a source of military revenue for the provinces in which it was collected. However, extraprovincial officials could hardly fail to seek opportunities of cashing in on the bonanza that likin collection in Hupeh, especially in Hankow, proved to be. In 1868, for example, Liang-Kiang Governor-general Tseng Kuo-fan and Yangtze Naval Commander P'eng Yü-lin successfully memorialized the throne requesting that 160,000 taels be diverted annually from the receipts of the Hankow station to help maintain the overall Yangtze fleet.[23] Officials of the home province, moreover, increasingly put likin revenue to uses other than those for which it was intended; for example, in 1870 Hukwang Governor-general Li Hung-chang diverted 50,000 taels of Hankow revenue to province-wide flood relief and dike repairs.[24] Although likin was supposed to be the domain of the provincial government, local authorities at Hankow also found ways to exploit it for their own needs. In 1884 the Hanyang prefect succeeded in attaching a 10 percent surcharge to likin collections at both the Hankow and Parrot Island stations, claiming that the proceeds would be for "the exclusive purpose" of carrying out needed harbor repairs. In order to do so, however, he was forced by provincial authorities to agree to turn over all revenues from this surtax in excess of ten thousand strings of cash per year to the treasury of the provincial salt taotai, whence they would be distributed to support Hupeh educational institutions. It turned out—as all officials involved in the gambit must have anticipated—that the average annual yield from the "river construction surtax" was four times the ten thousand strings of cash. Thus the educational system of the province, that most sacred of Confucian sacred cows, came to be underwritten heavily if not primarily by commercial taxes at Hankow.[25]

Another inevitable corollary to the richness of Hankow's fiscal base was corruption in tax collection. As E. H. Parker observed, "The trade position of Hankow is so magnificent that it can easily stand a 'squeeze.' " Yet Parker went on to lament the level this corruption had reached in Hupeh and the province's notoriety for "the greatest peculation in likin matters."[26] Hu Lin-i's correspondence reveals that he was fully aware of this potential for graft and consequently selected men of proven loyalty to staff the original likin collection bureaus. His initial choices as provincial likin administrator, Hu Chao-ch'un, and as head of the Hankow office, Wu Ch'uan-hao, are good examples. Both came from old, prominent Hankow families and were holders of higher examination degrees (Hu a *chin-shih* of 1835 and Wu a *chü-jen* of 1846). Both had played important roles in local anti-Taiping resistance by spreading propaganda, organizing noncooperation with rebel officials occupying Wuhan, and soliciting financial contributions to loyalist forces. Although neither was a merchant, both had long-standing contacts with the Hankow commercial establishment (Hu's father, for example, made his living preparing merchants' sons for the civil service examinations), and both had a high reputation for financial competence and integrity.[27]

Hu Lin-i could judge his subordinates by their behavior during the Taiping crisis, but subsequent Hupeh administrators were less successful in their choice of appointees. In the later nineteenth century, the performance of the Hankow likin office steadily deteriorated, despite brief rectification campaigns undertaken by incoming governors and governors-general. The low point came while T'ang Hsün-pang, an expectant prefect, was bureau manager. T'ang's "extremely vile" reputation among the local business community prompted Governor-general Pien Pao-ti to summarily dismiss him in 1883 and to strip him of official rank; subsequently, it was discovered that T'ang had been pocketing fully half the Hankow bureau's receipts.[28] Yet in a bureaucratic system routinely lubricated by "squeeze," T'ang's offenses differed from those of his colleagues more in degree than in kind—the Hankow taotai himself was said to hold "the most lucrative government office in the province."[29]

To a detached observer like Parker the commercial economy of Hankow appeared capable of bearing such escalating corruption without undue strain, but to the individual merchant whose prosperity was by no means secure official venality became an increasing source of irritation. This is clearly revealed in the growing frequency and intensity of attacks on Hankow likin abuses that appeared in the merchant-oriented Shanghai newspaper *Shen-pao*.[30] Even had the likin system remained relatively uncorrupt, the tax itself would have served as a source of increasing tension between local merchants and officials. Manipulation aside, merchant complaints about the system centered on: (1) mushrooming rates and surcharges, (2) time-consuming and clumsy collection procedures, and (3) the progressively smaller voice allowed merchant representatives in making collection policy.

At the outset, Hu Lin-i and his deputies sought to avoid such frictions, and Hu Chao-ch'un's success in getting provincial collections underway was widely attributed to his policy of regularly consulting leading Hankow merchants whenever procedural questions arose.[31] But this rapport did not long survive the system's first generation of overseers. In 1880, for example, the Hankow Likin Bureau, without consulting merchants, issued supplementary regulations designed to counter the evasion of dues by vessels entering the harbor. The new rules proved extremely unwieldy, and this prompted an outraged letter from one Hankow trader, which was printed on the front page of *Shen-pao*.[32] He cited the unmanageability of the new system and lambasted local officials for favoring immediate administrative revenue over the smooth conduct of a trade that had proven consistently profitable to both the state and merchants. By requiring newly arrived vessels to make numerous stops along the Hankow waterfront to fill out a multiplicity of tax declarations, local administrators were violating the cardinal principles of healthy merchant-state relations: "In the enactment of regulations, one should strive for simplicity and convenience, rather than vexatiousness and the imposition of impediments to trade. In enforcement, one should seek methods that are comprehensive and refined, rather than those based on petty grasping."

Hankow merchants vented their displeasure with perceived likin excesses in several ways. First, increasing numbers sought to evade payment. This had prompted the revised regulations of 1880 and also lay at the heart of the prolonged controversy over Transit Passes in the tea trade. According to Governor-general Pien Pao-ti, in the decades following the introduction of these passes in 1875, more and more merchants, of ever more humble scale, fraudulently used them to avoid paying likin. Pien linked this increase to the growing burden the tax posed.[33] A more sophisticated form of evasion, systematically practiced by merchants and guilds of many trades, was gradually and surreptitiously to increase the size of a standard bulk unit of merchandise upon which the likin was computed. This practice, of course, necessitated paying ever greater gratuities to likin inspectors, who were not blind to what was going on, and so fed the cycle of corruption and higher taxes that had prompted it in the first place.[34]

A second form of merchant resistance was to bring organized pressure to bear on the authorities. In preceding chapters we have noted successful efforts of the salt and tea guilds both to streamline collection procedures and to reduce likin assessments. In 1868, broader merchant pressure persuaded Hupeh authorities to suspend altogether the imposition of likin duty on overland shipments to and from Hankow, leaving only that on the much larger river trade.[35]

Despite these isolated victories, the complaints of Hankow merchants were often ignored. Their hostility toward the growing system of taxes, surcharges, and exactions to which they were subjected in the post-Taiping decades is clearly expressed in such documents as the Hankow Tea Guild's memorandum of 1887 (see Chapter 4) and the 1880 letter to *Shen-pao* discussed above. Implicit in the former document and explicit in the latter is a contrast between the shortsighted and acquisitive officials of the day and not only Chinese officials immediately after the rebellion, but also broadminded officials of the foreign powers. By the 1880's, then, we can detect signs of the merchant-state estrangement that was to have such far-reaching consequences for the fate of the Ch'ing.

Government Brokers: Revenue and Control

At Hankow, as throughout the empire, government-licensed brokers (*ya-hang*) were a time-tested means of overseeing the commercial economy. Our previous discussions have concentrated on the brokers' role as intermediaries between buyer and seller, but their position vis-à-vis the administration was no less significant. With the fall of the T'ang, the controlled-market system that had been building since early imperial times was largely swept away, and the Sung reunification inaugurated a period of merchant "emancipation" (to use Lien-sheng Yang's term) under more relaxed and indirect government control mechanisms. One such mechanism was the requirement that a government-licensed middleman, or broker, be present at all wholesale transactions in a number of key commodities. The brokerage system was continued and refined by successive dynasties through the Ch'ing, which saw it at its most developed. Under the *Statutes and Precedents of the Ch'ing Dynasty* (*Ta Ch'ing lü-li*), a restricted number of brokerage licenses (*ya-t'ieh*) were issued by the Board of Revenue, upon the recommendation of provincial officials, assigning brokers to each marketing center of appreciable size and defining their jurisdictions by locality and by commodity. According to Ch'ü Chih-sheng, brokers were assigned in sixteen trades, including fourteen agricultural commodities and two handicraft products, cotton and silk cloth. Brokers were also mandated in arranging overland and riverine transport and in recruiting contract labor. It was illegal to conduct any wholesale transaction in these trades without a government broker as witness and mediator.[36]

The basic function a broker served in his quasi-official role was to maintain an orderly market in his commodity. Most important, he was to safeguard a market-determined price (*shih-chia*), one not upheld by monopoly supports but floating freely between the parameters of bid and offer. (Clearly, the Ch'ing government *was* concerned with providing such "rational" market guarantees.) The broker was endowed with various police powers to prevent commercial or common criminal misdeeds by the merchants under his care. He was charged with keeping a register of names, local origins, items of trade, and trade routes covered by these merchants. Moreover, he drew up formal contracts for and kept a record of all transactions, noting the names of all parties, quantities traded, and price, which he submitted to local authorities and the Board of Revenue for periodic inspection.

But the broker's official function was twofold: he not only allowed indirect state control over the marketplace, but he provided government revenue. It is clear that in certain times and at certain places during the Ch'ing, brokers collected direct commercial taxes; in the era of rapid expansion of the Chinese state beginning with the early-twentieth-century *hsin-cheng* reforms this became universally so.[37] In our period, however, the fiscal role of brokers at Hankow (and probably elsewhere) remained indirect. That is, the broker paid the state a brokerage tax (*ya-shui*), comprising a large initial purchase price for his license and a smaller fee paid at each annual renewal. Merchant transactions bore the burden of this imposition indirectly, since the commission the state authorized the broker to collect on such deals (*ya-ch'ien*, *hang-yung-ch'ien*) went in part to offset the broker's outlay for his license. (As we have seen in Chapter 2, the broker's income was also augmented by such collateral functions as renting out lodging and warehouse space, as well as by dealing on his own account in the commodity he regulated.)

Inevitably, tension developed among (1) the state's need to exploit the brokerage system for commercial revenues, (2) its desire to maintain control over the trade, and (3) the need to control the brokers themselves. Both in the K'ang-hsi Emperor's initial promulgation of Ch'ing brokerage laws in 1686 and, more forcefully, in Yung-cheng's 1733 brokerage reforms, this third concern was paramount. Both edicts emphasized limiting the total number of licenses issued. This decision was made not, it should be stressed, in an effort to restrict the growth of trade, but out of an economic logic that argued for holding down the excessive proliferation of middlemen in order to prevent undue harassment of merchants (*lei-shang*) and thus allow the freest possible circulation of goods. The spirit of these early Ch'ing policies reveals the state's willingness, even in an age of agrarian expansion, to sacrifice potential revenues from commerce for a greater degree of control over its agents.[38]

By the mid-eighteenth century, brokerage houses at Hankow numbered in the hundreds. Both the range of trades in which Hankow brokers operated and the brokers' sheer numbers prevented any single broker or group of brokers from gaining a stranglehold on local commercial life (a frequent complaint in smaller commercial centers), but as an institution and a class they had enormous power. The unique features of the Hankow marketplace augmented this power. For instance, in the interregional emporium it was much more common than in lesser markets for buyer and seller to deal through agents, so that often only the broker knew the identity of both principals in a transaction. Further leverage accrued to Hankow brokers because of the uncommonly large warehouses and inventories they controlled. In addition, the wide-ranging functions assigned to brokers by local ordinances gave them control over all aspects of the trade. They were responsible for: (1) inspecting sample merchandise, arbitrating unit price, calculating total sale price, and converting this price into silver; (2) bringing together agents of the buyer and seller, guaranteeing both agents' and principals' fidelity, and supervising the payment of agents' fees; and (3) overseeing delivery of goods and inspecting the bulk shipment for possible qualitative or quantitative discrepancies.[39]

In the first half of the nineteenth century, the policy instituted under the early Ch'ien-lung reforms of Hupeh Governor Yen Ssu-sheng governed the selection and appointment of the omnicognizant Hankow brokers. Yen had been concerned by the number of marginally solvent individuals operating as brokers in the city at the time of his arrival in 1745, and so he ordered that all brokers be guaranteed by an additional person of recognized wealth and community standing. Before a broker could be licensed, this guarantor was required to sign a written bond and take a verbal oath before the Hanyang magistrate. The governor vowed to cashier any magistrate who was lax in supervising these procedures and to revoke the license of any existing broker who failed to meet standards of personal substance and mercantile confidence. Moreover, Yen decreed that if a broker's private fortunes declined significantly after his appointment, he might be regarded as unfit for his duties and his license withdrawn for reissue to a more qualified candidate.[40] Yen's Hupeh policies, like Yung-cheng's central reforms (in whose wake they followed), thus placed control over brokers and, by extension, maintenance of market order above the generation of government revenue.

With the Taiping ravage of Hupeh and that province's gradual reconquest by Hu Lin-i, this emphasis changed. In 1855–56, although he was not yet in possession of the Wuhan cities, Hu devised a package of brokerage reforms that came to serve as a model for the empire as a whole and essentially remained in force through the end of the dynasty.[41] The net effect of these reforms was to greatly relax government restrictions both on the number of brokers and on the criteria for their selection. These policies reflected a revised, crisis-generated economic reasoning in which middlemen were seen less as impediments than as lubricants to the circulation of goods (a view probably not unrelated to a more sophisticated understanding of the commercial division of labor). More important, the reforms represented a new ordering of priorities, which set commercial revenue ahead of state control over trade.

Hu Lin-i observed that in the devastation of Hupeh by the rebels, especially the three times Hankow was lost and recaptured, many licensed brokers had died or disappeared, and the credentials of many of those who remained had been destroyed. He viewed this as a fortuitous means to solve his own most pressing problem: raising funds to provision his troops. Hu therefore memorialized the throne, requesting permission to exceed the Board of Revenue quotas in effect since 1733 by issuing two thousand new brokerage licenses (*hsin-t'ieh*) in Hupeh. Although licensed brokers who could produce their old credentials were eligible for new licenses at a considerable discount, after a fixed period all old licenses were to be void, and only holders of Hu's new issue would be permitted to conduct business in the province. The price of the new licenses varied according to a schedule grading the potential profitability of each post and, as in the past, comprised a substantial initial cost and a yearly renewal fee thereafter. Most important, from Hu's point of view, was the throne's concession that the revenue from the sale of these new licenses would not be sent directly to the Board of Revenue as in the past, but instead would be applied to the expenses of Hu's regional military command (*chün-ying*). Considerable evidence (including the wording of licenses issued in Hupeh and elsewhere throughout the remainder of the dynasty) indicates that Peking never recovered direct control over this source of revenue. Thus in the process of Hu's reforms a degree of fiscal autonomy passed permanently from the central to the provincial level.[42]

Important as this change proved to be for the history of the Ch'ing, more significant for local social history was the relaxation of appointment criteria that accompanied Hu Lin-i's new brokerage policies. The old guard had been broken; although certain of them did resume brokerage in Hankow, the majority never returned. Thus both to revive the trade as quickly as possible and to generate immediate revenue, Hu was anxious to "broadly encourage" the purchase of his new licenses. The former stringent requirements for a guarantor and for the investigation of a brokerage candidate's wealth and reputation were dropped, and at least during the period of military emergency, anyone who could afford the license became eligible to operate as a broker.

To achieve this liberalization, Hu was required to memorialize the throne specifically for permission to waive the old imperial prohibition on issuing broker's licenses to holders of gentry degrees or brevet official ranks. Because Hu Lin-i both cherished an implicit faith in the virtue of a local Confucian scholar-elite and recognized the sociopolitical value of trade, such a merger of gentry and commercial roles was to him a natural one. Moreover, as Hu argued in his memorial, in practice the distinction had long been ignored. In recent decades brokers in Hupeh had been in the habit of acquiring gentry status by purchase, whereas legitimate degree holders purchased brokerage licenses under assumed names. Hu contended that the old law was therefore neither enforceable nor desirable. After considerable hesitation, the throne acceded to the governor's request, and Hu's revision seems to have remained in force thereafter.[43]

Hu Lin-i added another provision, which served to stabilize and perpetuate the new commercial elite in Hankow and elsewhere in Hupeh: a right of inheritance. As Hu was aware, brokerage in Hankow had for centuries been the preserve of a large but constant number of elite merchant families. Thus his new regulation allowing an heir to take over his family's brokerage upon paying a fee equal to half the original license's price was but a legal articulation of what had formerly been accepted practice. Nevertheless, as a formal regulation it was unprecedented.[44] In fact, Hu's new policy did allow the self-perpetuation of family brokerages at Hankow. As late as 1920 the county gazetteer recorded that in every local trade the market was still dominated by ten to twenty "old houses that were originally granted brokerage licenses by the Board of Revenue" under Hu Lin-i's 1856 reforms.[45]

This brings us back to the question of control. Paradoxically, the increase in the number of state-licensed commercial agents that the new policies authorized did not represent greater government intervention in trade. By allowing more brokers in the Hankow marketplace, Hu diluted their status as quasi-officials and decreased state control over their activities; by relaxing restrictions on brokerage appointments, he was in essence turning over control of the market to natural economic elites, in most cases to the leading merchants themselves. The increase in the number of brokerage licenses meant in practice that many trades of Hankow not previously governed by brokers now came under their regulation. For example, nonofficial broker-warehousers (*ching-chi*) had long served as middlemen in the medicinal herbs trade, but only after Hu Lin-i's reforms were these men granted formal government licenses, and with them the legal right to regulate other types of merchants engaged in their trade.[46] With the formal granting of hereditary privileges, these powers became entrenched.

Dozens of houses served as brokers in each of the major trades of Hankow, and Hu's upping of the license quotas increased their number. Yet, as Hu noted, it was common both before and after his reforms for many of these houses to be linked by family ties. He recognized the danger of monopoly inherent in such practices, but resolved in his open-market sale of licenses to make no effort to discourage it. Hu justified his action by a trade-off common in Ch'ing commercial administration in other areas: the hazards of too-intimate ties among brokers in a given trade would be offset by the greater ease with which the state could then impose principles of collective responsibility, in revenue collection and in general conduct.[47]

Throughout the Ch'ing, the administration viewed collaboration among Hankow brokers of the same trade with guarded approval: collaboration was encouraged as a means of stabilizing the market, but demanded constant official vigilance against restraint of trade. As early as the 1678 regulatory code of the Hankow Rice Brokers' Guild, market managers in the major commodities had combined, with official blessing, to regulate collectively all aspects of exchange. As the subsequent history of the Hankow rice trade reveals, this collective enterprise proved both satisfactory to the local administration and very profitable to the brokers.[48]

Attempts at collective control of the market by brokers in a given trade became more frequent over the years. Some two centuries after the 1678 rice brokers' code, a more ambitious effort was undertaken by Hankow's vegetable-oil brokers. Hu Lin-i's reforms had made the oil brokers responsible for drawing up and enforcing standing regulations for trade in their commodity. In the late 1870's the oil market suffered several reverses, which forced an increasing number of large broker-dealers to sell off their inventories below cost in order to meet immediate financial obligations. Consequently, in 1880 the major brokers called a meeting at which they resolved to abandon their standing policy of "always allowing the price to follow the market, as agreed upon by buyer and seller, and never attempting to fix the market price." Instead, they proposed the enforcement of minimum price supports. They each put up a bond, which would be forfeited by any broker found guilty of approving a transaction that undercut the minimum price.[49] Unfortunately, it is not recorded whether local officials approved this measure; they may have done so on a temporary basis, to assist a stricken trade. Clearly, however, the apologetic phrasing of the brokers' request, as well as their decision to stop short of actually fixing the price of oil on the Hankow market, indicates an awareness of official opposition to such efforts.

Local and provincial officials were alert to the dangers of excessive collaboration among the brokers of Hankow, particularly when, as in the oil trade, brokers were also major dealers in the trades they managed. As early as 1745 Governor Yen Ssu-sheng announced his determination to combat "monopolistic partnerships" among brokers, and a century later Governor-general Yü-t'ai reported to the throne his vigilance against "monopolization to inflate the market price" by Hankow brokers.[50] Yet over the course of the late imperial period, and especially in the nineteenth century, there was a trend toward relaxing state controls on the marketplace. This was not the result of powerful merchant interests asserting themselves at the expense of a feeble or corrupt administration; rather, it was evidence of the increasingly pragmatic stance on commercial matters taken by central, provincial, and local Hankow authorities. Most officials knew the importance of commerce to all segments of the area's population and were willing to take all reasonable measures to bolster the trade. Gradually such measures came to be identified, by both officials and merchants, with the liberalization of certain state controls.

At the same time, the administration was unwilling to countenance exceptionally venal behavior or strong-arm tactics by its licensed agents in the Hankow marketplace. It consistently sought not only to protect consumers from artificially inflated prices in necessary commodities, but also to shield smaller merchants from broker intimidation or fraud. One bullying tactic against which the government maintained its guard was the appropriation of capital left on account by traveling merchants with their brokers at the port. Yen Ssu-sheng, for instance, records a running battle against Hankow brokers who demanded excessive deposits from their clients, invested these on their own account, and proved reluctant to return them.[51]

After the Taiping Rebellion, local administrative zeal in protecting Chinese merchants from their brokers seems not to have abated. Detailed regulations prohibiting fraudulent activities and specifying punishments for each type of violation were drawn up by Hu Lin-i personally and were printed on the brokers' licenses issued by Hupeh for the Board of Revenue.[52] These regulations were enforced; for example, in 1874 one leading tea broker of the city was successfully arraigned before the taotai on fraud charges brought by one of his Chinese clients, and when the British firm Welsh and Company challenged the authority of the Tea Guild's chosen arbitrator (see Chapter 4), the Chinese broker claimed to have called the arbitrator in to protect himself from similar charges of fraud.[53]

We have seen, then, that since there was no clearly enunciated imperial policy on the internal regulation of trades, the officials governing Hankow evolved their own consensus. This was characterized by the gradual devolution of control upon brokers (increasingly privatized) and guilds. At the same time, however, officials retained the prerogative to intervene directly when necessary (as they did in the tea trade in 1861 and the banking trade in the late 1870's) and to serve as last recourse for aggrieved parties, such as creditors, consumers, and small merchants. In other words, the administration attempted to balance its increasing liberalization with a minimal degree of economic paternalism.

Other Channels of Commercial Revenue

Apart from taxing commercial transport and wholesale transactions, the provincial and local administrations had a large repertoire of other means for extracting revenue from the Hankow trade. Like taxation, these means were used with increasing regularity over the course of the nineteenth century. They included: (1) seigniorage, (2) direct state proprietorship of commercial ventures, (3) investment of state funds in private enterprises, (4) merchant contributions, and (5) commercial borrowing.

Seigniorage. Throughout the eighteenth and nineteenth centuries, the provincial government gained revenue from a local smelting and coinage operation first set up by Hupeh Governor Yen Ssu-sheng in 1744. Yen took advantage of the unusually high copper : silver exchange rate that resulted from the continual flooding of the Hankow market with "commercial copper" (*shang-t'ung*) and the impatience of the larger local merchants to convert their capital into silver as quickly as possible. Buying this copper at a discount, the government was able to remint it locally at par to meet its payrolls, especially that of the provincial garrison at Ching-chou. So successful was this operation that several times additional furnaces were added to the fifteen originally constructed.[54]

State Proprietorship. As a major trading center, Hankow was a central locus of the commercial enterprises in which the Chinese state was directly involved. Most important of these was the salt monopoly, which, as we have seen, was becoming a private trade in the course of the nineteenth century. Yet the state also owned an increasing number of more localized ventures, especially financial institutions—for example, the three "Haikwan" (customs) banks of the city.[55] These banks had a peculiar status: private entrepreneurs (often officials acting in a private capacity) put up most of the capital and took most of the profits, whereas the state took a smaller share in exchange for declaring them formal government entities. In essence the Haikwan banks were an early manifestation of the *kuan-tu shang-pan* (official supervision and merchant management) system, subsequently applied to Western-style industrial enterprises at Wuhan and elsewhere. The Hankow Haikwan banks had been set up under the auspices of the taotai when the local Maritime Customs office was established, in order to collect and store customs revenue for the state. However, they also issued government-backed notes and engaged in a variety of other financial dealings of a quasi-official nature. In addition to the Haikwan banks, a number of other financial institutions of the city, including several pawnshops, were at least partially government sponsored.[56]

State Investment. Many historians assert that the Ch'ing put state funds to work through investment in privately owned and managed businesses more than did any previous Chinese ruling house. In Chapter 5 we noted that by the nineteenth century government funds were deposited in, then reinvested by, Shansi banks. In Hankow, government funds were also deposited in native banks; after mid-century, for example, provincial funds were continuously invested in the privately owned Shan-hou-sheng and Cheng-yüan banks.[57]

Aside from bank deposits, the government invested its funds in commerce by a system known as *fa-shang sheng-hsi* (issuing funds to merchants for the generation of profits). Local administrations throughout China regularly used this device to finance the maintenance of public works and other continuing local expenses, and the county and prefectural administrations governing Hankow were no exception. Authorities at Hanyang preferred to entrust such funds to a guild (such as that of the pawnbrokers) rather than to individual business houses, so that the guild's members could be made collectively responsible for reinvesting this capital and dividing the profit between themselves and the state.[58]

State investment, like state proprietorship, was more commonly associated with financial than with mercantile enterprises; however, from the mid-eighteenth century until the Taiping hiatus the Hukwang Governor-general's yamen maintained a sizable account on deposit with the Hankow salt merchants (a portion of their *hsia-fei* fund), upon which a monthly dividend of 1.5 percent was collected, to be applied to public services in the Wuhan cities.[59] The county government, moreover, occasionally acquired and developed commercial properties at Hankow for rental to private merchants.[60]

Merchant Contributions. The administration also derived support from the Hankow trade by soliciting contributions (*chüan-shu*) from wealthy local merchants—in effect, a primitive form of progressive income tax. Such solicitations can be divided into three types: (1) those connected with the dispensation of gentry degrees or official ranks (*chüan-na*), (2) those designed to tide over immediate financial crises, and (3) those of a more routine nature. The first variety were traditionally embodied in official "sales drives" (*shou-chüan, shih-li*) declared by the court at Peking to meet specific central government fiscal needs (in theory short-term). From the outbreak of the White Lotus Rebellion in northern and western Hupeh through the end of the dynasty, the merchant community of Hankow was a particular target of such drives. A special office set up in Wuchang primarily to tap this community collected 4,056,430 taels from the sale of degrees between 1800 and 1845, with the proceeds divided between the provincial command and the central government. A separate sale of brevet official ranks in Wuhan netted 32,687 taels in 1807 alone.[61] In 1857, Governor Hu Lin-i secured "extraordinary" permission for the province of Hupeh to begin selling official ranks to meet its own needs, with the proceeds to be used to provision Hu's troops. Soon after setting up a provincial head office for this purpose in Wuchang, he added a branch in Hankow in order to spare local merchants a journey across the river. In the late 1850's, when rice was still scarce, payment for these ranks was demanded in grain; but as grain prices dropped and the "extraordinary" sale took on an air of permanency, payment was accepted in cash. Between 1869 and 1871, Hu Lin-i's successors reported taking in half a million taels through this operation.[62]

The second type of merchant contribution promised no such quid pro quo as a gentry degree or official rank, nor was it always voluntary. Before Hu Lin-i's innovation of 1857, whenever a provincial or local administration faced immediate financial need, it resorted, not to the sale of ranks, but to a subscription drive initiated among prosperous local merchants. When a great flood inundated both the Yangtze and the Han river valleys in 1831, for example, the provincial government levied a subscription on the salt merchants of Hankow, which over a three-year period yielded 150,000 taels to help meet the costs of relief and dike repair (estimated at 290,000 taels total).[63] According to the testimony of one Hupeh administrator of the 1880's, such enforced contributions were a regular feature of post-Taiping commercial life in the province.[64] Prosperous Hankow merchants also engaged in more genuinely voluntary giving, out of a desire to assert themselves in community leadership. For its part, the administration appreciated such public spirit, remembering the names of generous merchants and keeping track of their networks of solicitation from less forthcoming colleagues. One leading Hankow rice dealer of the 1840's was known to officials by the code name "the Orange," presumably because he could so readily be squeezed![65]

But in times of financial stress, voluntary contributions tended to evaporate. At the height of the Taiping devastations, when Hu Lin-i sought to raise a subscription from the brokers of Hankow (then temporarily in government hands), he could arouse little response. Even after receiving a court edict "exhorting" their support, many brokers still chose to close their businesses or plead a decline in profits rather than contribute.[66] For this reason, Hu initiated the third variety of solicitation, a routine, legally mandated percentage contribution (or, more accurately, a supplemental commercial tax). The likin began as a solicitation of this type, but it was not unique. Around 1880, for instance, an imposition known as the "one-percent port contribution" (*chiu-chiu shang-pu chüan*) was levied on all merchandise traded at Hankow, and similar exactions on specific trades and markets were added in the following years.[67]

Government Borrowing. Although not, strictly speaking, a form of revenue, loans from private businesses were a final way in which the administration sought commercial support. There is some evidence that borrowing was already common in the first half of the century, but not until the post-Taiping decades did the Hupeh provincial administration become chronically reliant on this type of assistance. Both Chinese and foreign firms lent money to the government. In 1866, for example, a local Chinese merchant made a huge loan to the province at an interest rate of about 16 percent per annum. The following year, the Hankow agent of Jardine, Matheson and Company made a two-month loan of 50,000 taels at 1.75 percent per month to enable Hupeh to meet its monthly payroll. In 1883, Governor-general Pien Pao-ti reported that the province was hopelessly in debt to the foreign merchants of Hankow.[68]

As borrowing became more common, the provincial administration began to seek more sophisticated methods of soliciting credit. Thus, to help pay its assessed share of assistance to Tso Tsung-t'ang's 1867 northwest campaigns, Hupeh organized a 70,000-tael bond issue yielding 1.25 percent per month, backed by the revenues of the Hankow Maritime Customs office. Some twelve years later these bonds (and their sequels) were still being paid off.[69] In 1884 provincial authorities even contemplated floating an issue of common stock (*chao-chi ku-fen*) among merchants in order to capitalize a proposed provincial munitions factory.[70] It is probably against the background of this evolving body of precedents that the financing of self-strengthening industrialization in Wuhan, begun by Chang Chih-tung in 1890, can best be viewed.

The Emergence of a Provincial Commercial Policy

In consequence of the complex web of fiscal reliance by the state upon commerce, as well as official recognition of the importance of the trade to the livelihood of all strata of the population, the attitude of the provincial and local administrations toward the commercial world of Hankow could hardly have been adversarial. As the state gradually shifted from dependence on agriculture to financing from commercial revenue, commercially central Hupeh province became increasingly important within the financial structure of the empire as a whole, as did Hankow within Hupeh. Bureaucrats were keenly aware of this fact, and over the years developed a policy of "sympathy" (*t'i-hsi*) for the Hankow commercial establishment and support for trade.

Hupeh authorities' encouragement of the Hankow trade is first clearly evident during the mid-eighteenth-century tenures of two major "statecraft" governors, Yen Ssu-sheng and Ch'en Hung-mou; acknowledging the value of commercial activity and utilizing commercial institutions to achieve state goals was an important part of both men's programs.* The correspondence of Lin Tse-hsü and other Hupeh administrators in the first half of the nineteenth century reveals that most of them were likewise free of the agrarian bias with which their class has often been charged. Instead, they recognized "the critical importance of the trade" and acted accordingly. When Lin sensed a depression in local commerce, for instance, he conducted a detailed investigation of prices and volumes of trade at Hankow, based on personal interviews with major merchants.[71] The continuing river-construction work on the Han during these years, as Morita Akira has pointed out, was frequently detrimental to local agricultural interests even while it facilitated transport of goods to and from Hankow; provincial officials were fully conscious of this conflict yet continued to support the projects.[72] The pro-commerce stance of provincial administrators extended to the foreign trade as well. The official correspondence of Kuan-wen and Hu Lin-i, for example, demonstrates that they welcomed the commercial prospects offered by the opening of Hankow, even while they braced themselves for the diplomatic and public security problems it was certain to cause.[73]

Many, if not all, local administrators at the port held similar views. As a pre-Taiping visitor remarked, "The large merchant houses and the officials are most accommodating to one another."[74] Hanyang county and prefectural officials expended great efforts to maintain public security, "in order to make Hankow prosperous for the merchants of the various provinces, and its markets peaceful sites for the conduct of foreign trade."[75] The office of the taotai, in particular, was staffed by men of strong commercial leanings. One Western visitor, granted an interview with Taotai Cheng Lan in the early 1860's, came away with the

*The basic beliefs and programs associated with the Ch'ing "statecraft" (*ching-shih*) movement are as yet imperfectly understood. The best concise description I have seen is in Hao Chang, *Liang Ch'i-ch'ao and Intellectual Transition in China* (Cambridge, Mass., 1971), pp. 26–34. According to Chang, the movement "was characterized by an almost exclusive concern with the organizational and managerial issues" involved in practical administration, and a merger of "the Legalist goals of wealth and power" with "the political premises of the traditional Confucian state." Ch'en Hung-mou (Hupeh governor, 1746–48) and Yen Ssu-sheng (Hupeh governor, 1739, 1744–45) were regarded in the nineteenth century as examplars of statecraft policymaking, and thus numerous writings of each were included in the *Huang-ch'ao ching-shih wen-pien* (Collected essays on statecraft in the Ch'ing dynasty), edited by Wei Yüan and Ho Ch'ang-ling, 1826. Specific Hankow policies of Ch'en and Yen are discussed elsewhere in this study.

impression that "he appeared very desirous of mixing himself up in commercial matters, volunteering information as to price, resources of the country, etc., etc., and inquiring the value of all importable commodities."[76]

The Chinese businessmen of the port appreciated the value of sympathetic officials. Thus, for example, when word arrived in 1889 of the imminent posting to Wuhan of the progressive Chang Chih-tung, the British consul reported that "the price of land in the native town has risen as if by magic."[77] In a variety of ways this appreciation translated itself into active demonstrations of support. One traditional means for doing so was chosen by the merchant community when Taotai Ho Wei-chien left office in 1882; declaring that they "could not forget his virtue and benevolence," merchants took up a collection to install in the yamen plaques and banners in his honor.[78]

Thus the procommercial orientation of provincial and local officials at Wuhan extended back at least to the "high Ch'ing." Yet without question a qualitative change in the intensity of administrative patronage of trade began in the black days of the 1850's, under the governorship of Hu Lin-i. Although Hu was by all accounts a solid Confucian fundamentalist, he balanced Confucian views with an incipient mercantilist developmental strategy, in such formulations as:

> The cultivators remain the roots and the merchants the branches and leaves. . . . However, I consider that the merchants' "pursuit of the branches" in seeking personal profit and increase of their own fortunes is equally of benefit to the cultivators, who likewise by industriousness seek to maximize their own profits and minimize their losses. By the process of one part yielding one part [i.e., by commercial investment], the roots themselves are multiplied.

A healthy commercial economy appeared to Hu to be a prerequisite to a secure and pacified realm. The situation in recaptured Wuhan was far from this ideal: "Within four years Wuchang has fallen three times and Hanyang four times. The state treasuries are bankrupt and the people destitute. The provinces of the southeast have surely suffered great distress, but their plight is nothing compared with that of the Wuhan cities." Such conditions justified radical innovations, or what Hu himself described as a "thorough reform experiment designed to stimulate commerce" (*chao-shang pien-t'ung shih-pan*).[79]

In coordination with his like-minded colleague, Hukwang Governor-general Kuan-wen, Hu initiated a series of pragmatic and politically risky measures intended to demonstrate "sympathy" and offer "encouragement" to existing and potential mercantile forces in the area. Hu's measures included throwing open brokerage to members of the gentry and all other interested men of means and dramatically easing restrictions on brokers' relocating or enlarging their operations; similarly, Kuan-wen invited all comers to partake of the fruits of the liberalized post-Taiping salt administration. Their total package, incorporating reforms in the salt and tea trades, brokerage, and the commercial tax structure—virtually the entire spectrum of the state's formal interest in commercial matters—proved remarkably successful in reviving trade at Hankow and throughout the province. As anticipated, it also brought about an immediate recovery of government revenue from (and to a limited extent control over) commerce.[80] In the long run, these successes were achieved at some cost to bureaucratic power, as many longstanding restrictions on commercial activity were permanently abrogated; however, this loss merely accelerated the trend toward privatization that had been underway for centuries in Chinese commerce.

To implement his new commercial policies, between 1855 and 1858 Hu Lin-i gradually developed an integrated administrative apparatus to oversee regional trade. Evolving directly out of his wartime network of quartermaster's depots, this apparatus consisted of branch bureaus (*chü*) in each commercially significant local area of Hupeh. As we have seen, Hu had initially set up local bureaus to collect likin, sell brokerage licenses, solicit contributions, and so on. Gradually the various bureaus in each locality were merged into a single, multifunctional bureau responsible for all revenue from commercial sources, as well as for the patronage of local trade and local commercial interests. Each local bureau was headed by a "gentry deputy" (*shen-yüan, wei-shen*) and staffed by "upright gentry" (*kung-cheng shih-shen*) drawn from the locality itself. All such personnel, however, were selected and periodically evaluated at the provincial level, and indeed the whole structure was clearly oriented toward provincial, not local, rule.[81] This combination of management by indigenous local elites and the use of regional resources to solve regional problems was characteristic of the modified "*feng-chien*" political philosophy Hu brought to his task.* In promulgating the new system, Hu consistently voiced *feng-chien* sentiments in specifying his intent to circumvent the lower levels of the bureaucratic hierarchy, the county and prefectural yamens, with their proliferation of sub-bureaucratic hirelings and the excessive opportunities for corruption that this cre-

*At its simplest, the *feng-chien* (feudal) tradition in Chinese political thought advocated a much higher degree of local autonomy within the imperial state and the replacement of administration by extralocal bureaucratic functionaries with that by natural local elites. See Lien-sheng Yang, "Ming Local Administration," in Charles O. Hucker, ed., *Chinese Government in Ming Times: Seven Studies* (New York, 1969), pp. 1–10, and Philip A. Kuhn, "Local Self-Government under the Republic: Problems of Control, Autonomy, and Mobilization," in Frederic Wakeman, Jr., and Carolyn Grant, eds., *Conflict and Control in Late Imperial China* (Berkeley, 1976), esp. pp. 261–68.

ated. His goal was to protect the interests both of the state (i.e., his provincial administration) and of producers (both cultivators and merchants) from the siphoning off of surplus at this parasitic middle level.

As the cornerstone of his new commercial administrative apparatus, Hu devised a central control board at the provincial capital. This organization, the Hupeh Provincial Bureau for Salt, Tea, Brokerage, and Likin Matters, for the first time integrated all facets of a provincial government's interests in trade. It remained a vital organization in Hupeh through the end of the century, when it began to be superseded by new-style agencies created in conjunction with the late Ch'ing reforms.

The Hupeh Bureau had a large staff of handpicked gentry managers, holders of brevet and expectant official ranks dispensed and withdrawn by the governor; this staff handled the collection of receipts from the branch bureaus. In addition, and of more significance for late imperial administrative history, the bureau's board of directors included the provincial treasurer, the provincial judge, the provincial grain taotai (often held as a collateral appointment by the provincial judge), the Wuchang taotai (collaterally the provincial salt taotai), and after 1861 the Hankow taotai (collaterally superintendent of Maritime Customs).[82]

The durability of this provincial economic brain trust and the strength of the ties between its members are revealed by the continuity of its personnel between the time of Hu Lin-i and that of Chang Chih-tung some four decades later. (See the sample career patterns outlined in Table 8.) Moreover, at least one Hupeh Bureau board member succeeded to the governorship (Provincial Treasurer Ho Ching in 1867). Clearly, the bureau comprised an elite corps of bureaucrats with extensive and deliberately cultivated expertise in commerce, international trade, and provincial finance. Clearly, too, these men had the opportunity to forge many personal ties with the business world of Hankow.

The functions of this innovative administrative body included coordinating overall commercial policy, and provincial executives regularly convened its directors to deliberate major economic decisions. Governor-general Li Han-chang called them together in 1878, for example, to discuss the commercial implications of constructing a floodgate some eighty miles down the Yangtze from Wuchang.[83] Yet both the Hupeh Bureau and its subordinate offices remained concerned above all with revenue. They were specifically charged by Hu Lin-i and his successors with the delicate task of collecting the maximum revenue while imposing the minimum burden on merchants and the circulation of goods. Thus, for instance, as virtually his first act upon assuming the governorship in 1866 Tseng Kuo-ch'üan sent notices to the Hupeh Bureau and each of its branches emphasizing the need to maintain the "support of

TABLE 8
Leading Members of the Hupeh Bureau, 1858–93

Member	Office	Year of initial appointment
Cheng Lan	I-ch'ang taotai	1858
	Hankow taotai	1861
	Wuchang taotai/salt taotai	1867
	Hankow taotai	1869
Ho Wei-chien	Hupeh Military Supply Bureau head	1866
	Wuchang taotai/salt taotai	1868
	grain taotai	1874
	provincial judge	1875
	Hankow taotai	1876 (held until 1882)
K'uai Te-piao	Wuchang taotai/salt taotai	1875
	provincial judge/grain taotai	1880
	provincial treasurer	1883 (held until 1888)
Yün Yen-ch'i[a]	grain taotai	1877
	provincial judge	1879
	Hankow taotai	1882
Yün Tsu-i[a]	Wuchang taotai/salt taotai	1881
	Wuchang taotai/salt taotai (reappointed)	1887
	provincial judge/grain taotai	1890
	Hankow taotai	1893

SOURCE: *Hu-pei t'ung-chih*, ch. 115, augmented by other reports.
[a]Yün Yen-ch'i and Yün Tsu-i were probably related, especially since they claimed a common native place, Yang-hu county, Kiangsu.

public opinion" and the "love and respect of merchants." In 1883 Governor-general Pien Pao-ti similarly stressed the paramount importance of keeping the faith of commercial taxpayers. The Hupeh Bureau itself declared in an 1882 proclamation that "it is the aim of this office to accommodate merchants to the utmost."[84]

Hupeh had need to accommodate and protect its merchants, for its extraordinary success in tapping its sources of commercial revenue was routinely exploited to support military operations elsewhere in China.[85] As time went on, the demands of other provinces for assistance became increasingly onerous. In 1876, for example, Governor Weng T'ung-chüeh reported making regular monthly contributions from the provincial treasury to support the military forces of the Ch'ing court (30,000 taels) and of Kansu province (40,000 taels), Anhwei province (50,000 taels), Shensi province (20,000 taels), Kweichow province (20,000 taels), and Yunnan province (10,000 taels), as well as one-time payments of 150,000 taels for "North China maritime defense" and

200,000 taels for Tso Tsung-t'ang's Sinkiang campaigns.[86] Hupeh's fiscal resources were further strained by heavily financing the defense of the southeast coast during the Sino-French War of 1883–84.[87]

Beginning in the late 1870's, with the advice of the Hupeh Bureau and especially its most consistently outspoken member, K'uai Te-piao, Hupeh officials began steadfastly refusing additional outside claims upon the province's commercial resources. In each case they cited protection and support of native merchants as the reason for their denial. In 1878, when Board of War President Yüan Pao-heng requested an increase in Hupeh's salt likin, with the proceeds to be applied to relief efforts in Honan, Hukwang Governor-general Li Han-chang (at K'uai's urging) refused on the grounds that salt merchants' profits were already strained.[88] In 1884 Governor-general Pien Pao-ti resisted a further diversion of Hupeh likin receipts to Fukien defense efforts, arguing that "as military crises have become more prolonged, and one tax or subscription has followed another, [the merchants] have approached the limits of their ability to pay." The same year, Pien defeated a central government scheme to increase tea taxation at Hankow, claiming that "the collection of abundant commercial taxes depends primarily upon showing a considerate attitude toward the merchants."[89] In 1886, on the basis of a report prepared by K'uai and the Hupeh Bureau, Governor T'an Chün-p'ei fought a court proposal to raise brokerage-license fees because of the adverse effect this would have on recruitment of capable men and therefore on the smooth circulation of merchandise. As T'an reasoned, "When merchants see the price of licenses go up, it is not surprising that they hesitate to buy. Licenses should be sought voluntarily by merchants, not forced upon them by officials."[90]

In one sense, Hupeh administrators and the Hupeh Bureau were simply resorting to a common tactic of late imperial provincial officials in attempting to protect regional fiscal resources from outside milking by pleading "sympathy for commerce." But in the 1880's something more was clearly at work. One detects in the arguments of Hupeh officials of those years a special urgency, based on a sophisticated understanding of the contemporary commercial situation. By this time it had become clear to K'uai Te-piao and his bureau colleagues that the post-Taiping commercial boom centered on Hankow had begun to lose its momentum, and that consequently any significant increase in commercial taxation was likely to prove counterproductive, forcing merchants into either systematic tax evasion or bankruptcy. Taking note of the decline in overall market activity, they concluded that "commercial vigor has truly shrunk to an unhealthy level"; seeing the increased frequency of native-bank failures, they argued that "the commercial situation has become stagnant and indebtedness overextended."[91] In the mid-1880's, aware of the threat posed by international competition, the Hupeh Bureau launched its own full-scale investigation of the critically endangered Hankow tea trade.[92] And clearly implied in its reports of the period is the notion that a tax cut might be required to stimulate regional commerce.

In the end, of course, the needed stimulus came from another source altogether: the grafting of Western-style industrialization onto the commercial economy of Hankow and central China. It is interesting to observe how, in this process, provincial management of industry was similarly grafted onto the existing structure of commercial management. In 1886, for example, when Governor T'an Chün-p'ei sought to develop a systematic program for exploiting copper deposits in Hupeh's Ching-shan county, he began by setting up a Provincial Mining Bureau (*tsung-chü*) at Hankow, modeled on the Hupeh Bureau. Six years later, when laying the plans for his self-strengthening cloth mills at Wuchang, Chang Chih-tung set up the Hupeh Provincial Textile Bureau (Hu-pei sheng chih-pu chü), naming Grain Taotai and longtime Hupeh Bureau Director Yün Tsu-i to be its manager. Even the Hankow Chamber of Commerce (Han-k'ou shang-wu chü), set up by Chang in response to a reform edict of 1898, can be seen as an institutional offspring of the Hupeh Bureau—in its management by two expectant taotais, its financing from Hupeh brokerage-license receipts, and its dedication to "the encouragement and stimulation of industry and trade."[93] Viewed from this perspective, the self-strengthening efforts of the late nineteenth century were in many regards less a response to an external shock than the product of an evolving domestic tradition of state patronage of business.

Merchant and Bureaucrat: The Convergence of Private Interests

The preceding survey of formal government interest in and policy toward the trade of Hankow tells but part of the story. In order to fully appreciate the relationship between state and commerce at the port, we must take into account the overlap of private interests between individuals in the commercial and government sectors. In a variety of ways, these interests drew closer together over the course of the nineteenth century. Although throughout Chinese history the twain had managed occasionally to meet, in the late Ch'ing more and more merchants became officials and officials, merchants.

The Hankow trade was too lucrative for many bureaucrats to refrain from private commercial investment. In the early decades of the nineteenth century, the ideal place for their money was the salt trade; in light of the quasi-official status of the salt merchants, legitimate bureaucrats might participate in that trade without excessively tarnishing their reputations. Salt, moreover, was both highly profitable and relatively secure; all that trade in it required was a few connections and a rather large initial outlay of capital. Thus it invited men like Huang Ch'eng-chi, a Hui-chou native and *chin-shih* of 1797, whose official career culminated in the governorship of Kwangsi. Huang had periodically held posts in the Wuhan cities, and he retired around 1820 to become one of the leading salt merchants of Hankow.[94]

After mid-century, as the salt trade became both more privatized and more risky, bureaucrats invested more frequently in financial institutions. As elsewhere in China, in Wuhan pawnshops had always been underwritten largely by retired officials, men who had already made their fortunes and were looking for a relatively secure investment.[95] But as the new area of native banking began to present greater opportunities for profit over the course of the nineteenth century, it too attracted private investment by officials, for example Wang Wen-shao, who while lieutenant-governor of Hunan became sole proprietor and backer of a Hankow native bank managed by two fellow Hangchow natives. Similarly, a former district magistrate surnamed Chang, while serving as salt comptroller at Wuhu in the 1870's, became a founding partner of a Hankow bank. Chang was a close friend and protégé of his immediate superior in the salt administration, Hupeh Salt Taotai K'uai Te-piao, and he was subsequently accused of using this connection to misrepresent his bank as being a formal government organ.[96]

The duplicity with which officials made private investments is strikingly illustrated by the career of Sheng Shih-feng, the collapse of whose Sheng-yu-t'ai bank in 1868 precipitated a major scandal.[97] Sheng had served as a circuit intendant and as a provincial judge, and at the time of his Hankow escapades was a junior member of the Board of Punishments. As it developed, however, for some years he had been both an independent merchant at Hankow under the assumed name Huang Heng-shan and a Hankow compradore for Dent and Company under the chop "Ahone." Despite his denials, it was eventually confirmed that he was in fact the chief investor behind the Sheng-yu-t'ai bank, and it was widely rumored that his friend and sometime patron, former governor-general Kuan-wen, was also an investor. For any number of reasons, officials acting as private entrepreneurs in Hankow preferred to conceal their investments—Sheng, for instance, was also discovered to own two local pawnshops registered in the name of his six-year-old son.

Officials whose personal wealth remained untainted by trade (if such existed) might still have an interest in commerce through their kinsmen. The preference of Chinese elite families for dividing their offspring among careers in officialdom, estate management, and trade is well known; perhaps the most celebrated example in modern China is the Yeh lineage of Hankow. The Yeh family fortune, which derived from, and for more than two centuries centered on, the nationally known Yeh-k'ai-t'ai medicine store at the port, allowed them to sire dozens of successful examination candidates and more than a few high officials—notably Yeh Ming-ch'en of Arrow War notoriety.[98] Family bonds between merchants and officials were especially marked in the post-Taiping timber trade, headquartered at Parrot Island in Hanyang harbor and dominated by Hunanese. Among the leading timber merchants were relatives of Tseng Kuo-fan and Tso Tsung-t'ang, and both these officials took an active interest in the market's activity (see Chapter 8). A particularly crass, though perhaps apocryphal, story is told about the forced entry into this market in the 1870's of a guild of merchants from Hupeh's Ta-yeh county. The Ta-yeh Guild appealed to their county's native son Ho Feng-shih, then serving as governor of Kiangsi, to pressure Hankow authorities to admit them to the timber trade. This Ho agreed to do, but only on the condition that his own relatives be admitted to the guild, formerly the exclusive preserve of three other surname groups.[99]

Merchants were also granted official patronage for reasons other than kinship ties. As with Ho Feng-shih, common native place also played a role. Because of their common home county, Tso Tsung-t'ang repeatedly protected Chang Tzu-mu and his son Chang Ch'ung-shu, commercial adventurers who frequently ran afoul of local Hankow authorities.[100] When Lin Tse-hsü was Hupeh Treasurer in 1831, he frequently crossed the river from his Wuchang yamen to visit fellow Fukienese merchants in Hankow. As a reform-minded official, Lin was careful to keep such contact on his own terms and within the bounds of seemliness. Consequently one of his first official acts was to issue orders restricting merchant access to his chambers, notifying his secretaries that "if some merchant presents his calling card or writes a letter with devious intent, that merchant is to be immediately handed over to the proper authority for punishment."[101]

Interpenetration of merchant and official roles was by no means a one-way street, and over the course of the Ch'ing more and more prominent and not-so-prominent Hankow merchants came to possess brevet official ranks (*chih-hsien*). Most often these men were simply *chih-yüan* or *tso-tsa*, that is, holders of the lowest, auxiliary ranks; the more successful might aspire to the title of "expectant" (*hou-pu*, *hou-ch'üeh*) magistrate, prefect, or taotai. The exact percentage of all Hankow merchants who held ranks at any time is difficult to determine, but impressionistic evidence suggests that by the second half of the nineteenth century more than half of the city's brokers and major wholesale dealers had such status. For example, most of the numerous Hankow businessmen whose activities were for one reason or another reported to the Tsungli yamen held official rank.

There were certainly ample opportunities for merchants to acquire such rank. We have earlier discussed the sale of both ranks and gentry degrees held at Wuhan throughout the century, under the central and later the provincial government's *chüan-na* program. According to the system's leading student, Hsü Ta-ling, not only did the imperial court after mid-century abandon all restraint in the number of such ranks it dispensed, but their prices also fell steadily as the court became more desperate for funds. For a man already possessing the lowest degree (which could easily be purchased), an expectant taotai's rank would have cost 18,040 taels in 1798; the same rank would have cost 11,808 taels in 1851, and only 5,904 taels in 1889.[102] By that time this most exalted of expectant ranks lay easily within the reach of even a modestly prosperous Hankow merchant.

Besides public esteem, another incentive for seeking ranks was that official status exempted one from ordinary criminal punishments. In the freewheeling commercial world of postrebellion Hankow, brevet ranks were, if anything, even more sought after by commercial opportunists than by their more substantial colleagues. Each of the four men involved in the 1865 credit fraud discussed in the preceding chapter held official rank, as did the Changs mentioned above. A great deal of the official correspondence from Hankow and Hupeh records the efforts of local and provincial officials to strip such unsavory characters of their ranks, so that they might be bound by ordinary criminal codes.

Especially in the post-Taiping period, official ranks were routinely purchased by merchant guild leaders, so that they might deal with local administrators on a more equal footing. The story is told that one such official-merchant, a leader of the Medicine Guild named Wan Hsing, called upon Chang Chih-tung shortly after the latter's arrival in 1889. Chang examined Wan's calling card, looked up at the merchant in front of him, and said with a chuckle, "By all means go out and show this distinguished magistrate in!"[103]

Brevet and expectant official posts were one thing, of course, and real, serving offices (*shih-kuan*, *shih-chih*) another. Yet appointments of substance could occasionally be bought. The Ch'ing court sought to minimize this practice, but in extreme need yielded to fiscal demands.

In the first six months of Hu Lin-i's grain-contribution drive at Wuhan, for example, the court authorized him to dispense ten actual official posts. There are scattered mentions of such sales at Hankow throughout the century, although the delicacy with which they are reported makes clear that this was a subject of some embarrassment for all parties.[104]

Were lower-level posts within Hankow itself open to recruits from the city's merchant elite? The Hankow submagistracies of Li-Chih and Jen-I were regular bureaucratic appointments; yet the county gazetteer's list of the successive holders of these posts, although it gives their home provinces (revealing that the posts were subject to the law of avoidance), uncharacteristically omits mention of any regular examination degrees. Might some of these men have been longtime sojourning merchants who had graduated into the local bureaucracy? Submagistrates' unusually long terms of office may indicate that they had put down roots in the city, possibly even before their appointments. In the 1860's, for example, Chou Tsuan-wen served six years as Jen-I submagistrate, then shifted to the Li-Chih post for three years more.[105] One early-nineteenth-century submagistrate, Hu Chan-men, hailed from Hangchow—the hometown of many merchants—and held no gentry degree. For "military merit" (*chün-kung*), which usually signified a financial contribution to imperial troops, he was awarded the Hsin-t'an submagistracy in southern Hanyang county and then shifted to the Jen-I post in Hankow.[106] Conceivably, Hu may have been a wealthy Hankow salt merchant who was rewarded with a local office for a well-timed contribution to the anti-White Lotus campaigns then critically draining Hupeh administrative treasuries.

Whether or not regular administrative posts like submagistracies were in fact open to Hankow's commercial elite, there remained a wide variety of powerful and lucrative quasi-official positions into which entry by strictly local, irregular paths was customary. These included patronage appointments in the local salt, likin, brokerage, and contribution-solicitation offices. Liu Jen-shan, for example, served simultaneously as manager of Hankow's Medicinal Herbs Guild and head of the bureau that issued brokerage licenses. In the later nineteenth century, prominent merchants commonly served simultaneously as likin-collection administrators. With conscientious service, such men could expect an eventual award of an expectant magistracy or prefectureship from grateful official superiors.[107]

By all the means we have catalogued, then, the interests and at times even the functions of merchant and bureaucrat were becoming closer in late Ch'ing Hankow. The hoary principle of "delimitation" (*hsien-chih*) of official-gentry and merchant roles, a hallmark of late imperial commercial policy still frequently endorsed in print by Hu Lin-i and his successors, was in practice increasingly compromised. The acronym *chih-shang* (official-merchant), like *shen-shang* (gentry-merchant), could be used to describe an ever-broader segment of the Hankow elite.

Conclusion: Collusion or Conflict?

Given the complex reliance of the Chinese state upon revenue from commerce at Hankow, the emergence of a coordinated provincial policy and policy-implementation apparatus designed to bolster trade and the state's revenue from it, and the overlap of private interests of individual merchants and bureaucrats, might the evidence from Hankow not endorse arguments for the "absolutist" collusion of imperial state and commercial capital? Our answer must be no, for a number of reasons.

First, neither the late imperial administration nor the commercial world of Hankow was monolithic; rather, each contained several competing levels. To cite an obvious example, the Hupeh provincial policies outlined above were implemented at the expense of both the central and the county administrations, which in the process lost not only revenue but prestige. To the extent that the provincial government succeeded in establishing itself as the merchant's friend, popular confidence in and esteem for other levels of government were bound to suffer by comparison. Moreover, given an increasingly differentiated hierarchy of commercial interests, no government could either satisfy all merchant elements or afford consistently to back one stratum against all others.

Second, although the goals of merchants and administrators may have overlapped, their order of priorities was different. Merchants sought profits first, and only secondarily the social stability that permitted them to operate unhindered. The state sought social harmony and order, but also to maximize the revenue that allowed it to fulfill its ever more complex and expensive tasks. Although the state's interest in stimulating trade led it to relax its controls, its need to preserve social stability forced it simultaneously to pursue more paternalistic economic policies. The latter policies could not please everyone; at worst, like Magistrate Yao's ill-considered prohibition on commercial credit, they pleased no one.

Finally, although it led the state to encourage mercantile activity, commercial taxation was a double-edged sword. More than anything else, the ever-increasing burden of commercial taxes strained merchant-state relations at Hankow. We have seen repeated evidence of the hostility of Hankow merchants toward the system of taxes, surcharges, and ad hoc exactions to which they were increasingly subjected in the later nineteenth century. In our period, this hostility appeared most strikingly in the 1887 memorandum of the Hankow Tea Guild. At this early date, grievances might be so clearly articulated only during a commercial crisis, and then only by the segment of the mercantile world most influenced by foreign ideas. But in the final days of the imperial state, as taxation intensified and foreign influence spread, such tension would come to affect the loyalties of the entire Hankow merchant community.

PART TWO

URBAN SOCIAL ORGANIZATION

CHAPTER SEVEN

Local Origin in an Immigrant City

IT HAS BECOME axiomatic that China's vast territory, combined with weak central administrative integration, produced a society atomized into local subcultures. The size of these subcultures varied greatly. Furthermore, they nested one within another: a Swatow man, for example, was secondarily but importantly both a Cantonese and a southerner. Local groups were determined by such features as a common home-area marketing system, shared social customs, and (perhaps most important outside the home region) the peculiarities of local speech.

Recent research, including that presented here, leads to the conclusion that although geographically determined subethnic distinctions presented no insurmountable barrier to interregional trade and exchange, they constituted the most important distinguishing feature between individual Chinese in the late imperial period.[1] In contrast, kinship and surname groups were of major importance primarily for the elite and were less significant in some areas of the country than in others. Religious differences, with the exception of the Moslem minority, were less compelling in a society with a strong tradition of eclecticism and syncretism. Class, calling, and status were all less permanent than subethnic heritage, particularly in a commercial, urban setting. The standard format followed in gazetteer biographies, with its opening statement of name, style (*hao*), and native place before any other information, reflects the paramount importance of local origin in defining personal identity.

In Ming and Ch'ing China, there was nevertheless a remarkably high level of geographic mobility. Lawrence Crissman, in a provocative and influential article, has sought to demonstrate the relevance of research on overseas Chinese urban communities to the study of late imperial cities, on the grounds that both were formed by similar migrations.[2] In both domestic and overseas cities, Crissman points out, the Chinese population divided into ethnic (or subethnic) "segmentary groups" based on native place. He notes that "individuals and groups in the population of a Chinese city were more or less foreign depending on the distance and differences between their home area and the host locality. . . . All these 'foreigners' were divided into many ethnic communities usually on the basis of geographic origin and occupation."[3] Thus subethnic distinctions played a significant role in determining marriage patterns, neighborhoods, and the constituency of voluntary associations.

In major cities, at least, subethnic distinctions were reinforced by commercial specialization. This specialization went beyond marketing the products of one's home area, for specific local-origin groups sought to become expert in producing and distributing certain types of goods or providing certain services. In Hankow the correlation between trade and native place was evident even to unsophisticated observers: a Western reporter in the 1860's remarked, for example, that "the chief dealers in Opium are Cantonese, those in Cotton and Silk Piece Goods Chekiang people, the Crockery and Medicine trade is done by Kiangse merchants, [and] the Tobacconists are all Fukien men."[4]

Of all late imperial urban centers, Hankow probably best exemplified the "immigrant city" depicted by Crissman. In this, of course, it was atypical. Other major commercial centers, such as Canton, Nanking, and Tientsin, attracted new arrivals, but these cities were the products of a slower, more organic growth. Hankow's late founding, coupled with the commercial importance of its location, produced a vacuum that was filled by abnormally rapid and intensive immigration. Not only did the city's role in the national market attract major traders from distant areas of the country, but in the late Ming and early Ch'ing the Wuhan area was simply unable to supply enough people from all the socioeconomic strata needed to populate the newborn trading center. As a result, if localities like Hui-chou and Shaohsing were important "talent-exporting areas,"[5] Hankow was among the chief "talent-importing areas" in the empire. It was perhaps rivaled only by Chungking, whose decimation in the seventeenth century by the "butcher of Szechwan," Chang Hsien-chung, created a similar vacuum, and by Shanghai, whose phenomenal growth after attaining treaty-port status was replicated nowhere else in the country.[6]

Three Types of Urban Relocation

The ratio of immigrants at Hankow to the original inhabitants of the area (those sharing the linguistic and cultural peculiarities of Hanyang county) cannot be precisely determined, but it appears to have been startlingly high. An 1850 Chinese commentator described one neighborhood that could claim no native residents (*t'u-chu*) of its own; 90 percent of its population at the time was made up of sojourners, 10 percent of registered natives who had all immigrated within the past generation or two.[7] Although this is an extreme example, it may not be completely unrepresentative. In 1813 a *pao-chia* enrollment of the city turned up approximately 50 percent registered natives and 50 percent natives of other areas; not only were the former likely to have included many recent immigrants, but the total number of enrollees was far smaller than the actual population of the city, with those not enrolled more likely to have been transient non-natives.[8] A century later, the *Brief Gazetteer of Hankow* (*Han-k'ou hsiao-chih*) noted that only one-tenth of the population could be considered by cultural and linguistic criteria to be natives of the place.[9] Additional evidence that immigrants made up most of the Hankow population is provided by the male-female ratio. The 1912 census revealed a population 64 percent male, half a percent higher than the ratio for the national capital and very much higher than that of most contemporary American cities, where the numbers of males and females were usually about equal.[10] Descriptions of Hankow from the mid-nineteenth century suggest that this male-female ratio of nearly two to one held true for those years as well. Oliphant, for example, remarked in 1858 that "Hankow, being simply a mercantile emporium, comprises in its population a much larger proportion of males to females than is to be found in Chinese cities generally. This is easily accounted for by the fact of so many of its inhabitants being merely visitors."[11]

In order to elaborate upon Oliphant's "easy" explanation, one must look more analytically at the city's non-native population. Persons who relocated to Hankow over the course of the late imperial period can be classified into three relatively distinct groups, based upon patterns of relocation. I will label these patterns "migration," "urbanization," and "sojourning."

Migration. Although interregional migration in early periods of Chinese history (for example, the culture's southern expansion during the T'ang and Sung) has long been studied, its importance in late imperial times has only recently begun to capture scholarly attention. Migration occurred in all periods. Although such other factors as deliberate colonization were occasionally involved, most migrants were displaced persons, with or without their families, who had been forced by either natural or military disaster to abandon their native places. The *liu-min* (vagabonds) regularly mentioned in Chinese sources were such migrants, of course, although the term usually involved negative connotations that I do not mean to invoke here. Many, although not all, mi-

TABLE 9
Characteristics of "Migration" Relocation

Category	Characteristic	← Nearly all	← Most	Equal	→ Most	→ Nearly all	Opposite characteristic
Intended term of relocation	temporary					x	permanent
Return to native place	seasonal					x	irregular or never
Household status on arrival	male alone			x			family group
Former residence	rural		x				urban or semiurban
Employment status	menial		x				professional
Motive for relocation	displacement		x				advancement

grants came from rural areas and found only menial employment in the city. For all migrants relocation was intended to be permanent, and few ever returned to their native places. (For a tabulation of the characteristics of migration relocation, see Table 9.)[12]

Migration to Hankow was a continuing phenomenon, but it accelerated in times of widespread distress. Three major military disturbances, in particular, sent waves of migrants into the Wuhan area and to Hankow: the rise of the Ming, the peasant wars accompanying the Ming fall, and the Taiping Rebellion. At all three times, the primary direction of migration was westward, as population flowed into the Middle Yangtze region from the Lower Yangtze. The largest of the three migrations was probably that of the late Ming, of which Wei Yüan (1794–1856) wrote:

> At the end of the Ming dynasty, the bandit leader Chang Hsien-chung nearly exterminated the population of Szechwan, severely decimated the population of Hupei and Hunan, but brought relatively little harm to the population of Kiangsi. Consequently, after the pacification of the country people of Kiangsi began to migrate to Hupei and Hunan and people of Hupei and Hunan began to migrate to Szechwan. There was a popular saying that [people of] Kiangsi filled up Hupei and Hunan and [people of] Hupei filled up Szechwan.[13]

Our best sources on patterns of migration to the Wuhan area are clan and lineage genealogies, although these genealogies represent only families that prospered in their new surroundings, and thus are not fully representative of the Middle Yangtze's migrant population as a whole. I have been able to consult eight of these dealing with kinship groups based in Hanyang county and five for groups in adjoining counties, all for lineages that had some members active at Hankow.[14]

Of the thirteen families, all but one had migrated to the Wuhan area from the Lower Yangtze region, seven from Kiangsi and five from Kiangnan; the remaining family hailed originally from Hupeh's own Ma-ch'eng county. Eight of the thirteen had migrated during the Yüan-Ming transition, three in the mid-Ming, and two during the Ming-Ch'ing transition. One might suspect that those who migrated during the Ming founding were fleeing the peasant rebellions of that era, and four of these families (including three from Kiangsi's particularly hard-hit Chi-an prefecture) did make that claim. A greater number, however, seem to have been allied with the victors in the dynastic struggle; five of the thirteen families were established in the Wuhan area by early Ming officials posted to the region, who upon retirement opened up or reclaimed rich tracts of agricultural land in the vicinity. (Four of these founders were original supporters of Ming T'ai-tzu; the fifth served in Wuhan in the 1460's.) Only one of the thirteen clans (that from Hupeh) claimed to have fled the late Ming peasant wars. Since the rebel leader Chang Hsien-chung both despoiled Ma-ch'eng and recruited many of his troops there, this family's founder may have been either a landlord forced to flee by Chang or a rebel recruit who settled elsewhere once Chang's rebellion collapsed.[15] Because families that produced genealogies tended to have been established in a region for centuries, these histories do not reflect the third major wave of migration, that of the Taiping period. Other sources, however, testify to this last wave of migrants; the merchant Ta family of Kiangnan, for example, was displaced by the rebels in the 1850's and relocated to Hankow.[16]

Overall, then, although most migrants were rural, the westward migrations, especially at times of great upheaval, involved persons of all socioeconomic strata from both rural and urban backgrounds. Although most settled in rural areas of the Middle Yangtze, their descendants or branches often established themselves in Hankow or other cities of the region. Thus throughout most of the nineteenth century, the majority of permanent, multigenerational Hankow residents probably were descendants of participants in one of these large-scale population movements.

Urbanization. The second variety of relocation to Hankow was urbanization, defined for our purposes as the drawing off by the city of persons from its hinterland on a relatively permanent basis. It was to this phenomenon that British Consul Gingell referred when he reported in 1863 that: "Hankow still continues to steadily increase in magnitude and busy life. Large numbers of Chinese of different grades are flocking to the place . . . in search of employment which they readily find."[17] The hinterland from which this population was attracted was a more narrowly defined version of the Middle Yangtze macroregion: central and eastern Hupeh, northern and central Hunan, and southwestern Honan.[18] By far the greatest percentage, however, came from nearby rural Hupeh counties.

To some degree, persons drawn to Hankow from its hinterland had been displaced from their old home area. Beyond the pressure of a growing population, both recurring flood (in the Han River valley) and famine (in the arid plains of Honan), as well as post-Taiping demobilizations of government troops, stimulated urbanization in the later nineteenth century. But, as with urbanization movements in other societies, the main motive of most immigrants was to find employment in the booming economy of the port. Almost all such employment opportunities were menial, as unskilled laborers or peddlers.[19] Many immigrants both from nearby counties and from Hunan joined the rapidly expanding corps of longshoremen and dockworkers, a segment of Hankow society that was to become extraordinarily volatile in the early twentieth century.[20] Of greater immediate concern to the city's more prosperous residents was the urbanization-related swelling of Hankow's marginal population. As the author of the 1884 county gazetteer lamented, "Ever since the 1820's the rich and flourishing market activity of Hankow has brought to the town large numbers of vagabonds who survive as beggars."[21] Less stable still were the prostitutes, gamblers, and petty criminals, whose numbers multiplied after 1870. The rise of these déclassé elements had significant consequences for Hankow's later history, since they contributed to the growing incidence and perception of social disorder.[22]

Many refugees left the city after a brief period, but most urbanization immigrants came to stay. For most the option to return to the village remained open and was exercised in times of crisis. During Taiping raids, for example, many Hankow dwellers "fled and returned to [their] villages"; but even they were described as "residents" (*chü-min*) rather than transients.[23] The Hankow population was subject to seasonal fluctuations when lower-class residents with nearby native places returned to their villages in peak agricultural seasons.[24] In general, however, this was a matter of periodic return to the rural locale rather than periodic visits to the city in slack farming seasons, as can be seen from the fact that many, even among Hankow's lowliest occupational groups, either brought their families along or set up households in the city.[25] (For a tabulation of the characteristics of urbanization immigrants, see Table 10.)

Unlike the periodic migrations into Hankow, urbanization was a

TABLE 10

Characteristics of "Urbanization" Relocation

Category	Characteristic	← Nearly all	← Most	Equal	→ Most	→ Nearly all	Opposite characteristic
Intended term of relocation	temporary					x	permanent
Return to native place	seasonal			x			irregular or never
Household status on arrival	male alone		x				family group
Former residence	rural	x					urban or semiurban
Employment status	menial	x					professional
Motive for relocation	displacement				x		advancement

continuous and accelerating process. Thus it is to relocation of this type that the general population growth of the city in the eighteenth and nineteenth centuries can largely be attributed. The 1884 gazetteer quoted above states that this urbanization began several decades before the Taiping disaster; with allowances for the massive exodus and repopulation brought about by the rebellion, the process was a cumulative one. The Protestant missionary Robert Wilson wrote in 1862 that "during my three months' stay here last year it was easily perceptible that the place was filling up," and ten years later a missionary doctor reported that "throughout the city there are spaces covered with the huts of recent settlers."[26] In his 1871 report on health at Hankow, the same doctor commented that all but two of the 57 lepers he surveyed had recently come from agrarian regions outside the city.[27]

This mid-nineteenth-century urbanization, which took place before the introduction of significant factory industry, resembles the preindustrial urban growth in eighteenth-century London and Paris, and, as in those cities, it probably helped establish the preconditions for subsequent industrialization.[28] Nevertheless, the most intensive urbanization at Hankow came after, not before, industrialization. In the mid-1860's a British consul, noting the contrast between Hankow and Shanghai, remarked that "fortunately for China, nothing has supervened to convert Hankow into a city of refuge for two provinces."[29] As the 1870's and 1880's were to show, his expression of relief was a bit premature. But it was only with the forced-draft, and largely foreign-capitalized, industrialization of the 1890's that the happy contrast of Hankow with Shanghai as a magnet for regional rural drain lost all validity.

TABLE 11

Characteristics of "Sojourning" Relocation

Category	Characteristic	← Nearly all	← Most	Equal	→ Most	→ Nearly all	Opposite characteristic
Intended term of relocation	temporary	x					permanent
Return to native place	seasonal			x			irregular or never
Household status on arrival	male alone			x			family group
Former residence	rural				x		urban or semiurban
Employment status	menial					x	professional
Motive for relocation	displacement					x	advancement

Sojourning. Relocations of both the migration and the urbanization types were moves of at least intended permanence. In this regard, both can be contrasted with the third type of relocation, usually termed "sojourning." The essence of this type is that it was seen formally as a temporary relocation. (In actuality, sojourning in Hankow could be either short-term, long-term, or permanent.) It, rather than the other types of residence, has long been held to be the defining characteristic of the late imperial Chinese urban population: Max Weber remarked that in China "the 'city' was . . . never the 'home town,' but typically a place away from home for the majority of its inhabitants."[30] Moreover, Chinese sources from the Ch'ing consistently employ terminology that supports this conception: individuals and groups of individuals are described as "lodging" (*yü*), "sojourning" (*ch'iao-yü*), or "being stationed" (*chu*) in the city.[31] (See Table 11 for an outline of the characteristics of sojourning.)

As central to sojourning in Hankow as temporary residence was an individual's reason for being in the town. A sojourner came to the city specifically to advance his career and fortunes. Skinner's work on this class in modern Chinese history is founded on that recognition: "The simple fact is that aside from the peasantry large numbers of men in traditional China pursued their occupational calling away from home; they were sojourners, and the local systems and central places where they sojourned were typically more urban than the native places where they still maintained their residence."[32] These were upwardly mobile individuals, although not always men of substance (probably most apprentices in Hankow mercantile firms were sojourners), and they had moved to the central emporium both for economic opportunity and to escape personal and behavioral constraints imposed in their home areas. However, unlike hinterland immigrants, who merely sought employment of any sort, sojourners were careerists. Furthermore, although their places of origin were often, as Skinner suggests, less urban than Hankow, perhaps the majority came from local systems, such as Hui-chou, Canton, or Ningpo, that were at least semiurban in character. Sojourners were not, for the most part, country bumpkins.

Most Hankow sojourners engaged in commercial activity. We may divide them into two groups corresponding to the paired opposites in the Chinese conventional phrase "resident and traveling merchants" (*ku-shang*). The latter group included both the itinerant "guest merchants" (*k'o-shang*), who varied greatly in scale and capitalization, and the small, independent boatmen operating within the trade. These men were transients. For many of them Hankow was merely one stop along their routes (although usually a terminus), although for others, such as those in the tea trade, it constituted a seasonal home base. These sojourners resided at Hankow only intermittently, but at any given time they made up a considerable percentage of the city's population. A longtime resident estimated that in the postrebellion period the boat crews that visited the town each year totaled 165,000 persons (six or seven per boat).[33] Assuming an average docking of about one week over an eight-month trading season, this suggests that an average of about ten thousand boatmen were in the city at any given time.

The number of *k'o-shang* was also very large. Computing on the basis of the salt trade, in which there were six hundred transport merchants employing eleven thousand junk masters and crews in these years, we arrive at a ratio of one itinerant merchant to every 18.2 boatmen.[34] Applying this to the figure for total boatmen, allowing for the fact that merchants in the salt trade had considerably above-average capitalization (and hence presumably employed a greater number of boatmen) and adding in the merchants who brought their goods overland, we can estimate that ten to twenty thousand itinerant merchants called at Hankow during each trading season. These *k'o-shang* no doubt were accompanied by a greater number of porters and personal servants. In all, at any given time during the eight-month trading season the city probably hosted between twenty and thirty thousand short-term commercial transients. Although these estimates are inexact, they conform to overall impressions of nineteenth-century Hankow society.

The *k'o-shang* were a major feature of the city's life. Those who did not dwell upon boats in the harbor found their lodging at inns (*fan-yin-tien*), at temples (*yen-miao*), at their home area's *landsmannschaft* (*hui-*

kuan), or at the combination warehouse and hostel (*k'o-hang* or *k'o-chan*) run by local brokers in their commodity.[35] As the 1818 gazetteer noted, "In the town of Hankow the merchant population all rent their living quarters. They are one place in the morning, and gone that very night."[36]

The other half of our contrasting pair, the sedentary "resident merchants," were somewhat more stable. In Hankow this group included the depot merchants of the salt trade, brokers in most commodities, the proprietors and staffs of large and small wholesale dealerships, and retailers of all descriptions. Although these merchants, like their transient colleagues, were non-natives (Hankow, as we have noted, remained dominated commercially by outside groups), they were local residents for much longer periods. For some of them Hankow remained an outpost. Participants in the tea trade, for example, were frequently merely branch managers who returned to their home commercial headquarters in Kwangtung or the Lower Yangtze during the off-season. (Thus Griffith John noted of the merchants in his sermon audiences that "many of them come and go annually.")[37] Others, however, were more permanent inhabitants of the city.

Long-term sedentary merchants of modest means usually lived in their shops. The more affluent either rented luxurious apartments (*yü-kuan*) or rented, purchased, or built the mansions (*t'ing-kuan*) to which whole areas of the town were given over.[38] It is impossible to gauge with any accuracy what percentage of the population of nineteenth-century Hankow these men comprised, but their total number reached the tens and conceivably the hundreds of thousands. Moreover, there was no impediment to their having wives and children at Hankow, and local sources frequently refer to such sojourners living in stable family situations in the city.

Sedentary merchants often lived in Hankow for very long periods of time. The 1822 *Hankow Compendium* (*Han-k'ou ts'ung-t'an*) lists dozens of such merchants, all from the elite and many from the salt trade, who sojourned for upwards of ten years; many of them permanently relocated to Hankow and established branches of their families there.[39] The histories of several prominent local families provide evidence of similar relocations in earlier times. The Yeh lineage of Hanyang county, which produced the ill-fated Yeh Ming-ch'en of Arrow War notoriety, was an offshoot of a venerable mercantile family with ancestral residences and continuing relations in such potent commercial areas as Hsiu-ning county in Hui-chou prefecture, Anhwei, and P'iao-shui county in the Yangchow area of Kiangsu. The founder of the Hanyang Yehs had sojourned at Hankow in 1650 as the proprietor of a medicine dealership, and by intermarriage with local women the family gradually developed indigenous roots in the city.[40] As late as 1865, the British consul reported the arrival of many wealthy sojourning merchants "who have come to take up their permanent residence at the port," indicating that in the post-Taiping period as well the temporary status of sojourners in Hankow could be merely a matter of convention.[41]

To summarize, most Hankow residents at any time during the nineteenth century were, in Crissman's words, "more or less foreign" to that locality. Those with the deepest local roots were descendants of migrants during the Ming and early Ch'ing; others had migrated later during the Taiping upheavals. From the earliest days of Hankow these were joined by a continual flow of sojourners, whose numbers fluctuated somewhat with the state of the trade but in general seem to have remained fairly stable. Of this group, some stayed only briefly, some remained for longer periods, and some lived in Hankow permanently. As a group they comprised a substantial minority of the Hankow population. Finally, in the nineteenth century came a steadily accelerating stream of immigrants from the surrounding countryside, some of whom returned to their villages during crises and in peak agricultural seasons, but most of whom became more or less permanent urbanites. All three of these groups to some degree remembered their "foreign" home areas, and together they greatly outnumbered the small group in Hankow who claimed a long-standing native pedigree from Hanyang county. The degree to which these outsiders remembered their home areas, and the degree to which those who relocated to Hankow subsequently became "Hankow men," is a subject to which we will return.

Hankow's Subethnic Composition

Where did the population of nineteenth-century Hankow come from? The immediate answer is, of course, from all parts of China. As the K'ang-hsi poet Cha Shen-hsing had written:

> From every famous, far-flung border town
> One by one they answer to its call.[42]

The compiler of the 1818 county gazetteer conventionally described Hankow as "the crossroads of merchants from seven provinces," and a half century later Griffith John listed twelve provinces whose natives regularly attended his local sermons.[43] We have seen in Chapter 2 that men from every part of China came to Hankow to market the produce of their home areas; however, the city hosted in unusually high concentrations natives of a number of key areas. The first of these was the Middle Yangtze region, in which the city was situated; other areas gained prominence, not by geographic proximity, but as leading talent exporters. Men from these areas frequently had succeeded in wresting the trade in other areas' goods from native merchants and had become the agents marketing those goods at the great central-China emporium.

The Middle Yangtze. Natives of this region dwelling in Hankow may be divided into five groups: (1) those native to the city or to Hanyang county, (2) those from Wuchang and its hinterland, (3) those from what may be termed Hankow's "urbanization periphery," (4) those from other leading commercial systems of south-central Hupeh, and (5) those from Hunan.[44]

We have already seen that by contemporary criteria Hankow natives were a rare breed—by one estimate no more than 10 percent of the city's population. To judge from the trade associations they formed, the majority of these seem to have been skilled or semiskilled artisans (carpenters, masons, shoemakers) or small-scale retailers (butchers, millers, grocers, teashop proprietors).[45] A small percentage of the national commercial elite that traded at Hankow was made up of local men, although in general the city hosted merchants from elsewhere in China rather than producing its own. Similarly, Hankow natives made up but a small minority of the region's indigenous literati.[46] Of greater significance were the dozen or so Hanyang-county lineages that managed to retain wealth and prominence for centuries during the Ming and Ch'ing. Most of these were based in rural areas, especially in the fertile southern section of the county known as Han-nan, but to varying degrees they came to participate in commerce at Hankow, in some cases forming family branches in the city itself. Not surprisingly, many wealthy local lineages that refrained from participating in the Hankow trade during the years of our study became involved in commerce and industry there during the self-strengthening era after 1890.[47]

As we have seen, the natural barrier of the Yangtze prevented Wuchang city from forming close socioeconomic ties to Hankow throughout most of the Ch'ing. In the late nineteenth century, however, the provincial capital and its surrounding county (Chiang-hsia) began to send a small but growing contingent of gentry-merchants and skilled laborers across the river to the regional metropolis.[48] An earlier and closer tie linked Hankow and several tea-producing counties of Wuchang prefecture. Mountainous Ch'ung-yang and T'ung-shan counties, near the Kiangsi border, and P'u-ch'i county, adjacent to Hunan, had attracted Shansi merchants in Russian employ throughout late imperial times, and eventually tea dealers from these counties came to sojourn in Hankow to conduct their trade. Another Wuchang county, Hsien-ning, was one of the wealthiest in central China, owing both to its tea crop and to the national reputation of its cotton cloth since the early eighteenth century. Hsien-ning merchants and workers of all economic levels helped market these products at Hankow. In light of both its prosperity and its proximity, it is not surprising that Hsien-ning at the turn of the twentieth century produced the first chairman of the Hankow Chamber of Commerce.[49]

By at least the second half of the nineteenth century, however, the majority of the Hupeh natives at Hankow hailed from a ring of predominantly rural counties surrounding the Wuhan cities, an area I have called Hankow's urbanization periphery. The counties included Huang-p'i, Hsiao-kan, and Han-ch'uan of Hanyang prefecture, and (to a lesser extent) Wuchang prefecture's Chia-yü. Huang-p'i natives were the most numerous—eventually, perhaps, the most numerous of any single local-origin group at Hankow. They had conducted local trade at Hankow since the town's founding, and by the nineteenth century were active as artisans and petty traders (*hsiao-mao*), not only in the county's specialty, copperware, but in a wide variety of other goods. Huang-p'i and these other counties had also traditionally supplied the bulk of Hankow's menial labor force—laborers, porters, dockworkers—and their numbers increased dramatically during the surge of preindustrial urbanization of the 1870's and 1880's. The revival of commerce after the Taiping Rebellion, as well as the reconstruction and expansion of the city, drew many men from the surrounding countryside to serve as regular and casual laborers in the construction trades. Ultimately, natives of these counties came to comprise the core of Hankow's unemployed and marginal population.[50]

Merchants from two other economic systems of south-central Hupeh were also prominent at Hankow. These were the "Huang-pang" and "Han-pang," the two groups that dominated the trade of the Han River valley. The Huang-pang was headquartered at Huang-chou (Huang-kang), and its members were said to have migrated originally from Kiangsi, many via Hupeh's Ma-ch'eng county; the Han-pang centered on Mien-yang department's Hsien-t'ao *chen*. At Hankow, both groups occupied a comfortable niche in the lower commercial elite, a level or two below the national elite of great interregional traders.[51]

The majority of the Hunanese in Hankow were drawn from the Hsiang River valley, which linked the city to southeast China. Most hailed from the riverine marketing systems of Changsha, Hsiang-t'an, Heng-chou, and Pao-ch'ing. Hunanese tended to make up neither the extreme upper stratum of Hankow society nor the extreme lower one.

Many were directly involved in the transport business, as shipping brokers (*ch'uan-hang*) or independent boat owners and operators (*ch'uan-hu*) under contract to these brokers.[52] Hunanese were also active as wholesale dealers, but were poorly represented among the great interregional traders of the port. For example, Hunan's single largest bulk export, its rice shipments to Kiangnan, was usually financed by merchants from Lower Yangtze trading systems from the time shipments reached their regional collection points at Changsha and Hsiang-t'an through changes of hands and vessel at Hankow to lower Yangtze depots such as Nanking.[53] Similarly, Hunanese made up perhaps the majority of the collection agents and wholesale dealers in the tea trade at Hankow, but they never penetrated the ranks of the trade's kingpins, the warehouse owners and brokers.[54] One trade the Hunanese truly controlled was the timber and bamboo trade of Parrot Island, and it was from this springboard, aided by the patronage of several post-Taiping national leaders of Hunanese origin, that the Hunanese vaulted into prominence at Hankow in the last decades of the century.

As a group, natives of the Middle Yangtze macroregion probably made up slightly more than half of the Hankow population throughout the middle and late Ch'ing. Although other groups were also growing in size, the process of preindustrial urbanization, especially in the post-Taiping decades, increased the Middle Yangtze's numerical dominance. Economic and social dominance, however, consistently belonged to others.

Hui-chou Prefecture, Anhwei. This prefecture, also known as Hsin-an, was probably the premier talent-exporting area of China between the fifteenth century and the early nineteenth, producing officials, literary figures, and, above all, merchants. The pivotal role played by these men in the rise of the late imperial circulation economy has been brilliantly analyzed by Fujii Hiroshi and Shigeta Atsushi.[55] Beginning in the mid-Ming, merchants primarily of the three Hsin-an counties Hsiu-ning, She-hsien, and Wu-yüan began to pursue aggressively the possibilities of interregional trade in items of daily consumption, experimenting with new business methods and new markets, and eventually bypassing almost completely their own fairly desolate home area and its specialties (timber and wood products) for trade in rice, salt, tea, cotton, silk, and other commodities for which a large national demand could be developed. As early as the sixteenth century they had also begun to test the market for Western imports, which they obtained from smugglers along the Fukien coast.

By the beginning of the K'ang-hsi reign, Hui-chou natives had come to Hankow in significant numbers, and over the course of that period their numbers at the port skyrocketed. A source from 1704 boasts that over half of Hankow's "many shops and ten thousand houses of business" were owned and operated by Hui-chou natives.[56] A report from the Yung-cheng reign merely notes their numbers as "especially large."[57] Although increased competition from other provincial groups during the eighteenth century probably brought about some decline in their relative dominance of the Hankow trade, their absolute numbers in the town continued to grow well into the Tao-kuang period, and they probably remained the largest single contingent of merchants there until the Taiping hiatus.

Most Hui-chou men in Hankow were involved in either the salt or the tea trade, although some did deal in other commodities.[58] Tea was the less important of the two; Shigeta informs us that most Hui-chou merchants preferred to ship their teas to Shanghai. Those who did trade at Hankow were merely dealers in the tea-marketing hierarchy, and like the Hunanese seem to have been excluded from the exalted ranks of the brokers in the trade.[59] Salt, however, was a different matter. This trade was chiefly responsible for the increasing number of Hui-chou merchants in the city, and although they did not have the market entirely to themselves, they made up the largest percentage of the fabulously wealthy Hankow depot merchants and Huai-nan *kang* franchisees.

Such sources as Hanyang gazetteer biographies, Hui-chou Guild records, and above all Fan K'ai's 1822 *Hankow Compendium* provide rich accounts of the lives of these men.[60] Between the late seventeenth century and the first half of the nineteenth, they constituted the dominant economic and taste-making group in the city; both fully conscious and very proud of this fact, they strove deliberately to "influence and transform" local social modes and mores.[61] Many prominent She-hsien and Hsiu-ning families were active in the city over the entire period, either living continuously in Hankow or returning in successive generations for extended periods of residence. They manifested their position and power by literati tastes and behavior, leadership of local philanthropic activities, and movement into (not necessarily local) gentry and official roles.

Although it is reasonable to suppose that some Hui-chou merchants brought apprentices with them to Hankow, there is no evidence that artisans, boatmen, laborers, or other humbler workers from that area relocated to Hankow. Thus the Hui-chou population at Hankow seems to have been socially top-heavy. As the nature of the city (and of Chinese commerce generally) changed during the nineteenth century, particularly after the Taiping Rebellion, Hui-chou influence dramatically declined. Although some wealthy Hui-chou merchants were still to be seen, they increasingly gave way to newer commercial powers. By

1911, a publication of the Hankow Chamber of Commerce could omit any mention of them in discussing the leading local-origin groups in the city's trade, and a commercial guidebook of 1918 identified Hui-chou men at Hankow as simply "teashop proprietors and restaurateurs."[62]

Shansi and Shensi Provinces. Beginning in the later reigns of the Ming, the chief rivals of the Hui-chou merchants for the position of dominance in the domestic commerce of all of China were men from Shansi and (to a lesser extent) Shensi provinces. The process by which this group achieved its ascendancy was a complex one, which is discussed in detail by such scholars as Saeki Tomi and Terada Takanobu.[63] Contemporaries commonly said that Hui-chou men controlled the commerce of south China and Shansi-Shensi men that of the north.[64] Although this was not strictly true, it provides one rationale for the groups' having met in almost equal strength at Hankow. By at least the seventeenth century, merchants from the two northwest provinces were present in the city in substantial numbers, and their numbers continued to grow throughout the Ch'ing. A construction project undertaken by the Shansi-Shensi community was able in the 1870's to elicit donations from 1,159 houses of business operated by fellow provincials.[65] By at least this time, they were one of the largest local-origin groups at the port.

A large percentage of the Shansi and Shensi natives sojourning at Hankow hailed from areas in the lower valley of Shansi's chief river, the Fen. These areas included the important city T'ai-yüan and several counties of Fen-chou prefecture (Fen-chou, Wen-hsi, P'ing-yao) in southwestern Shansi, as well as the neighboring Shensi county P'u-ch'eng. Although the two provinces sent many lower-status elements, such as Han River boatmen and overland porters, to the city, they were best known locally as a spawning ground of great and prosperous merchants. These merchants were involved in the trade in more than a score of items, including the hides and animal products for which their home on the outskirts of inner Asia was celebrated and the famous Fen-chou wine.[66] They were also able, however, to take control of the port's trade in the produce of other areas. The department of Chün-chou in Hsiang-yang prefecture of northwestern Hupeh, for example, was well known for its tobacco crop, but this crop was marketed in Hankow solely by Shansi and Shensi men.[67] Chün-chou lay on the Han River along the much-traveled Shensi-Hankow route, and it is likely that tobacco production there was capitalized and overseen by the northern merchants plying this route. Similarly, Shansi and Shensi merchants sold at Hankow heavy woolens that they imported from Asiatic Russia.[68]

Shansi and Shensi merchants had in the early Ch'ing obtained a foothold in the Liang-Huai salt administration (due in part to a relatively cozy relationship with the new Manchu rulers of China), and this had done much to promote their interests nationally. They seem to have operated in the Huai-pei subdistrict more frequently than in the Huai-nan district, centered on Hankow, but some—for example, Wang Wenning of P'u-ch'eng—did achieve positions of power in the local salt market.[69] We have already seen the significant role played by northern merchants in the tea trade of the port; in the 1870's at least 23 Shansi dealerships were engaged in bringing in and processing tea from Hunan and Hupeh growing districts.[70] Shansi and Shensi merchants also served as factors, brokers, and compradores, especially in the Russian tea trade. Finally, the most important single vocation of northern men was managing the Shansi banking system. Although the Shansi banks began to decline in the late nineteenth century, they remained potent commercial forces in Hankow well beyond the close of our period.

Aided no doubt by their diverse interests, and particularly by their stake in the burgeoning tea trade, the Shansi-Shensi merchants of Hankow managed to maintain their local prominence despite new competition, even while their Hui-chou colleagues faded. Although the northern community seems to have exited en masse at the arrival of the Taipings, the northerners subsequently reestablished themselves, and they achieved their period of greatest glory in the years thereafter, when foreign consular reports spoke with awe of the local economic clout of "the rich Shan-se merchants."[71] Yet unlike the Hui-chou merchants in their prime, the northern men never exerted a social influence in Hankow commensurate with their economic power. Instead, they chose to live prudent and frugal lives within a uniquely close-knit, inward-turning subethnic community.

Kwangtung Province. Although today we tend to associate Cantonese merchants with foreign trade and the treaty ports, they had played an important role in the domestic trade of China since at least the early Ch'ing. As far as the Middle Yangtze region and beyond, Cantonese marketed the tropical foodstuffs and ironware for which their province became nationally known, returning with grain and other commodities. Thus they had established themselves in the cities of the Hsiang valley and in Hankow by at the latest the Yung-cheng reign. Under the Canton system, Kwangtung merchants also became the chief managers for the domestic distribution of foreign imports, not the least of which was opium. Although opium was never numbered among Hankow's leading items of trade, by at least the 1830's the local wholesale market in the drug supported several large warehouses and highly capitalized dealerships operated by Cantonese. Control of the local opium trade remained in the hands of southerners through the end of the century.[72]

As is well known, the opening of the northern ports in 1842 and of the Yangtze in 1861 spelled the decline of the trade at Canton but not of the Cantonese merchants themselves. Because of their long experience with their Western trading partners, Cantonese accompanied the foreigners as compradores when other ports were opened. In Hankow, an 1860's guidebook for prospective Western arrivals warned, for example, that the foreign merchants of the city were "entirely dependent upon their Cantonese and Ningpoese compradores."[73] Of the two, the Cantonese were dominant, largely because they had specialized in tea, the focus of the port's foreign trade. All six of the Hankow compradores from our period whose provincial origin Yen-p'ing Hao could ascertain in his recent study were Cantonese.[74] Moreover, most of the leading tea sellers were also from Kwangtung, including several of the largest dealers and the majority of the brokers and warehouse owners. By the early twentieth century, and probably well before, the Cantonese at Hankow clearly controlled all aspects of the foreign trade. As this trade grew in importance in the life of the port, they accordingly displaced traditional local-origin groups within the city's economic and social elite.[75]

Unlike the traditionally powerful groups, the Cantonese community at Hankow (including primarily but not exclusively natives of the four delta counties surrounding Canton city) was not concentrated principally within the upper strata of local society. Many southerners came to the city as domestic servants in foreign or Chinese employ; a larger number were dockhands or warehouse employees.[76] On a somewhat higher social plane were the independent food purveyors to the foreign community or those responsible for constructing the British Concession.[77] Eventually the southerners' imported skills made them indispensable in the life of the city, not only as industrial entrepreneurs, but also as skilled laborers in the construction, operation, and maintenance of new public works and utilities.[78] It was by bringing in this large, wealthy, and skilled community of southerners, I believe, that the opening of the treaty port did most to redirect the social history of Hankow in our period.

Ningpo and Shaohsing Prefectures, Chekiang. The rise to prominence in Hankow of natives of the Yangtze-delta prefectures Ningpo and Shaohsing was almost exclusively a nineteenth-century phenomenon.[79] Although both areas had had some earlier experience in marketing their local specialties (notably wine from Shaohsing and marine delicacies from Ningpo), only in the Chia-ch'ing period did their merchants begin to develop into a national commercial force. Initially their ascendancy was based on technical innovations in capital financing (in developing native banks), but it was the combination of these innovations and an association with Western merchants after 1842 that really catapulted them to national prominence. In Hankow the Ningpo Guild was founded at the comparatively late date of 1780; by the beginning of the twentieth century (by which time it had amalgamated with the Shaohsing contingent), it was generally acknowledged to be the supreme commercial power in the city.[80]

Ning-Shao merchants established themselves at Hankow on a dual basis: the native banking system and the lower Yangtze River trade. Both of these continued to be important well beyond the period covered in this study. We have already discussed the native banks of Hankow, among which Ning-Shao men assumed a guiding role.[81] The river trade between Hankow and downriver ports continued into the twentieth century to be carried largely aboard medium-sized lorchas (*chiu-chung*) owned or chartered by Ningpoese. The most important of the many commodities carried in this fashion were cotton and silk textiles, in which the Ningpo men at Hankow had come to specialize;[82] they also carried marine products and tung oil upriver, and timber, cereals, and beans downriver. A few Ning-Shao people had also infiltrated the Huainan salt trade; T'ien Wei-han, the former *kang* merchant appointed by Hu Lin-i to draw up local salt ordinances in the post-Taiping period, was a native of Shaohsing.[83] The breakup of the old salt monopoly accomplished under Hu's reforms probably allowed a larger number of Ning-Shao merchants to enter the trade and to partake of the profits once controlled by Hui-chou and other older merchant groups.

Like the Cantonese, the Ningpoese served as compradores in Hankow, and like them they used the advent of Western trade to advance their position in native commercial circles; for example, Ch'ien Yen, a native of Ningpo's Tz'u-ch'i county and a major tea broker and warehouse owner in Hankow, moved his original operation upriver from Shanghai upon the opening of Hankow.[84] Ningpo men shared with Cantonese control of the tea and other export trades well into the twentieth century. Curiously, however, although Ning-Shao natives became the most powerful force in the trade of the city as a whole, in the foreign trade they remained second to the southerners. Some sense of this can be gathered from the puzzlement expressed by Heard and Company's Hankow agent in 1866, who noted that despite the Cantonese dominance of local compradorial roles,

> what would best suit the house requirements here is a Ning Po Compradore, who would possess a decided advantage both in procuring freight and selling imports. The trading people here are . . . from Ningpo or from districts much better inclined towards Ningpo men than Cantonese, and the ease and success with which the only two Ning Po Compradores in the place have met has been

very marked, and with a Ning Po Compradore it would be much easier to do business in wax, tobacco, etc.[85]

The rapidly expanding Cantonese position at Hankow, although it had venerable roots, was due almost completely to association with Western merchants. The Ning-Shao traders, in contrast, although they had greatly profited from their Western contacts both at home and in Shanghai, owed their preeminence at Hankow less to the foreign trade than to a more indigenous process of change: the increasing development and diversification of the Yangtze River trade throughout the nineteenth century and the great strides taken in financial management under the Ning-Shao banking network. When the next great transformation in the sources of economic power at Hankow occurred around the turn of the century, Ning-Shao men seem to have been better able to assume positions of leadership: among the first Chinese privately owned modern industries in Hankow were a late Ch'ing paper mill and a match factory set up by Ningpo men, and the first vice-chairman of the Hankow Chamber of Commerce was a native of Shaohsing.[86]

Secondary Talent-Exporting Areas. Apart from Hui-chou, Ningpo, and Shaohsing, the four Lower Yangtze provinces as a whole supplied a large percentage of Hankow's commercial population. Much of this population, of course, arrived either in westward migrations or in the course of marketing local specialties at the port. The influx of such men had led to the creation of over a dozen local-origin associations representing various Yangtze areas, most dating from the seventeenth century or early in the eighteenth. A few such areas, however, produced like Hui-chou a surplus of professional sojourners who could be found in a variety of key commercial roles in Hankow. Particularly in evidence were natives of Ch'ien-t'ang county (Hangchow) in Chekiang; Chiang-tu, Chen-chiang, and Sung-chiang counties in Kiangsu; Nan-chang and Nan-feng counties and I-ning department of Kiangsi; and T'ung-ch'eng county (Anking) and T'ai-p'ing prefecture in Anhwei. Most of those claiming Chiang-tu (Yangchow) as their home were salt merchants, often hailing originally from other Lower Yangtze localities (for decades the richest of all Hankow salt merchants were the Pao family, from the town of Tan-t'u in Chen-chiang). Other Lower Yangtze sojourners included transport brokers, craftsmen, native bankers, merchants, and merchant-literati. Many of these men speculated in several commodities simultaneously, and in treaty-port days many formed joint partnerships with Western traders from Shanghai, whom they represented in the city.[87]

Moslems. The ethnicity of only one group in Hankow, the Moslems, was not primarily a function of local origin. The Moslems, a comparatively small but tightly knit segment of the society, were mostly well-to-do dealers in mutton products and in specialty pastries.[88]

Home-District Registration and Ties to Native Place

What was the real content of a Hankow resident's attachment to his ascribed native place (modern Chinese: *lao-chia*)? Since there was no "average" Hankow resident, the answer depended upon particular local origin, social status, and occupation; thus the best we can do here is to explore some of the factors that affected a Hankow resident's ties to his extra-Hankow "home."

Nostalgia for one's acknowledged place of origin was both an instinct and an institution in late imperial society. Many associations, such as those we will discuss in Chapter 8, were formed with at least the partial purpose of promulgating remembrance of the home area.[89] This remembrance often operated in ways that can appear arbitrary to us. The nationally prominent Yeh clan of P'iao-shui county, Kiangsu, for example, had members residing in widely scattered areas of the empire. All of them acknowledged P'iao-shui as their "native district" (*pen-i*), although by the clan's own testimony it had a long history before any Yeh ever set foot in that county, and by the eighteenth century a great many members, such as those comprising the Hankow branch, had for many generations neither been formally registered there nor even seen the district.[90]

In some cases, as with the Hankow Yehs, the native-place tie was reinforced by a continuing line of relatives in the native district. Similarly, Wang Ch'uan-i and his family, whom the Hanyang gazetteer tells us were by local standards "Hankow people," maintained close ties with kinfolk at their former family home in Chekiang.[91] Those whose business in Hankow was merely seasonal, of course, maintained far closer family ties outside the port.

To an extent these kinship ties, even among permanent Hankow residents, were financially reinforced. Susan Mann Jones has argued that a major goal of such groups as the Hui-chou or Ningpo merchants when seeking expanded markets was "ensuring that some of this money [the profits of trade] would be fed back into the local system from which the trade was drawn."[92] The Fang clan was a notable example: a large percentage of the profits from Fang dealerships and banks in Hankow was funneled back to Ningpo.[93] Likewise, the Meng clan, whose "Ching-hsiang" retail chain dealt in such products as silk, cotton, tea, and glassware, had outlets in many major cities as early as the seventeenth century. Their three large Hankow emporia in operation during the second half of the nineteenth century channeled funds back into the family estate in central Shantung.[94] This sort of activity no doubt increased significantly during the treaty-port period, as the foreign sector of the Hankow trade became permeated with Shanghai-based firms, frequently operated by families with home areas elsewhere in the Yangtze-delta region or in Kwangtung. Certainly, economic feedback into the native district was an important part of sojourning during the late imperial period. My general argument here, however, will be that this sort of activity has been overestimated. How, to take a ready example, can we reconcile the view that sojourning was basically extractive with the widely reported physical splendors of such sojourner-dominated localities as Yangchow and Hankow?

A better index of attachment to native place than either contact with relatives or remission of funds is the frequency of returns "home" by those pursuing callings in the city. Not surprisingly, the available data indicate that patterns of return varied greatly. Among lower-status groups such as laborers from nearby counties and boatmen from Hunan, many tended to return in peak agricultural seasons, although they retained permanent residence in the city.[95] Many more affluent merchants, particularly those whose trades were seasonal, returned to their more distant home provinces when the markets closed for the year. Others, though year-round Hankow residents, might make frequent visits to relatives in their native districts.[96] Natural or military disaster might force residents to flee Hankow or prompt them to help a threatened home area. T'ien Wei-han, for example, though both legally and actually a resident of Hankow, returned to his native Chekiang for several years to organize local militia resistance to the Taipings.[97]

Frequently, periods of alternate abode in the home area and at Hankow served as a prelude to the permanent transfer of a family's residence to the port. Chu Hung-shu, for example, was the son of a merchant who conducted his trade at Hankow but returned periodically to his family in Hui-chou. The father died while away from home, and Chu soon thereafter made a permanent move to Hankow to see to his father's burial and to carry on the family business.[98] Yeh Hung-liang likewise split his time between his medicine business at Hankow and his family home in Kiangsu. He fathered two sons by his wife in the home province, then one (Yeh Ch'eng-chüan) by a concubine at his place of sojourn. After his death, his estate was equally divided among the three sons. The elder two both failed financially, whereas Ch'eng-chüan prospered. Eventually his brothers joined him at Hankow, and the three jointly established the Yeh lineage there.[99] A variation on this pattern can be seen in the Wang family of Hui-chou's Hsiu-ning county, which for centuries ran a commercial empire at Hankow, including operations for importing and processing foodstuffs, dry goods emporia, and dyeing shops. After founding the family's fortune at the port, around 1700 Wang Shih-liang and his Hankow-born wife turned management over to an agent and retired to Hui-chou. Some two decades after Shih-liang's death, his grandson Wang Kuo-chu moved permanently to Hankow and resumed direct family management of the business empire. Although the Wangs continued to prosper and to proliferate at the port and took an active role in local public-service activities, they did not sever ties to their home county to the same extent as did the Yehs. Thus even in the Republican period, we find one head of the Wangs' Hankow businesses retiring to Hui-chou.[100] Clearly, individual immigrant and sojourner merchants at Hankow had a broad and a complex range of attitudes toward their native places.

The best single test of such attitudes is probably choice of burial site. For example, Chu Hung-shu formally expressed his determination to become a Hankow man by having his father's remains interred at the city. Similarly, Yeh lineages throughout China acknowledged a certain mountainside in P'iao-shui county as their family cemetery, yet Yeh Ch'eng-chüan in founding the Hankow line symbolized both his new native status and his recognition of his old home by having himself buried in Hanyang county, facing in the direction of P'iao-shui.[101] The Lao clan, in their wanderings from Chekiang through Hunan to eventual residence in Hankow, acknowledged their displaced condition (and undoubtedly their poverty) by having their dead formally buried at whatever point their migration had brought them; when they consciously became the "Laos of Hankow," they set aside a permanent gravesite in the town.[102] Local-origin associations in the city offered assistance in returning their sojourning members' remains home and encouraged this manifestation of native-place remembrance.[103] But for those too impoverished to afford shipment of remains or for those whose ties to the host locality had become sufficiently strong for them to choose burial there, these associations maintained communal cemeteries (*i-chung*), where a sojourner might rest among fellow provincials within the locality in which he had lived and worked.[104]

The question of local identity and attachment to native place is complicated by the legal requirement, enforced under the Ch'ing as under earlier dynasties, of maintaining "registration" (*chi*) in a particular locality. The 1870 edition of the *Ch'ing Statutes* begins its section on this topic with the pronouncement that "all classes of households are obligated to register" and proceeds to catalog offenses and punishments for negligent officials and registration personnel and for various types of registration fraud.[105] Although the statutes never fully elucidate the basic concept of registration, certain elements of that concept can be deduced from its comments. First, the statutes express the belief that failure to maintain careful registration records will necessarily lead to "upheaval and chaos" throughout the empire; clearly the primary fear is that the state will lose its ability to account for individuals. Second, registration served as the counterpart of Western birth certificates—it provided a legal name for use in all future contact with the state, such as tax payment, litigation, and examination candidacy. Third, the registration procedure was designed in some measure to deter occupational and class mobility, since registration entailed assigning such classifications as "soldier," "civilian commoner" (*min*), "artisan," and "hereditary servant."

One thing, however, the registration process was clearly not intended to do. Although the process was to be managed by the county magistrate and an individual was to carry his county registration with him as an identifying feature, the system was not designed to deter geographic mobility. No criteria or procedures are specified within the statutes for changing one's county of registration, but the terms "former registration" (*pen-chi*), "original registration" (*yüan-chi*), and "immigrant registration" (*ju-chi*), frequently employed there, make clear that geographic movement was foreseen. Moreover, specific procedures are provided for dividing households (*fen-i ts'ai-ch'an*) and establishing new, geographically separate units.[106]

In the corpus of legal proclamations and precedents of Hanyang county, the procedures for changing registration had become explicit. First, a candidate for change of registration into the district was required to be a taxpaying landowner in the county for a period of twenty years or the descendant of such a landowner. Local ordinances make clear that the landowning requirement could be satisfied by owning an urban house or shop instead of cultivated fields. Second, the candidate had to produce a written bond of good character and to swear before the county magistrate that he would "tremblingly obey" all the regulations of the county. Finally, a monetary contribution was demanded, the amount to be determined by the assignment of the candidate's household to one of three grades of wealth.[107] These conditions would seem to have presented a formidable obstacle for those aspiring to change registration into Hanyang county, but throughout the nineteenth century a combination of official unconcern and ignorance of local precedent, subadministrative corruption, and deception by registration candidates had rendered the procedure far less rigorous and made the prospects for changing registration considerably brighter for most immigrants.

Although, as we have noted, registered natives of Hanyang county continued to comprise only a small fraction of the actual Hankow population, their absolute numbers rose over the course of the nineteenth century. In the neighborhood with only 10 percent registered natives noted by Yeh Tiao-yüan in 1850, all the "locals" had deregistered (*lo-chi*) from other areas in recent generations.[108] In the post-Taiping years we are told that the frequency with which households changed their registration to Hanyang increased steadily.[109] However, although in-registrants no doubt outnumbered out-registrants, the percentage of local natives within the Hankow population probably declined. This was because, although immigration to the city took place across the entire socioeconomic spectrum, change of registration was confined largely to the elite or near-elite. Only they could afford the financial exactions demanded for the procedure, and as we shall see, they had the most to gain from the process.

The district of one's registration had no necessary correlation to the locality in which one was born, established one's family, and raised one's children. Since the unit of registration was the household, as Skinner points out, "the son born to a sojourner inherited his father's native place along with his surname."[110] For this reason, the fact that an individual was formally designated a native of some other locality did not indicate that he was other than Hankow born and bred. On the other hand, county of registration could not be equated with genuinely acknowledged ethnic origin, which was often more meaningfully signified by "former registration" or "original registration," concepts that had no legal import. Thus, of the eighty or more sojourners whom Fan K'ai wrote about in 1822, between one-fourth and one-third had changed their formal registration to Hankow, although they retained an ethnic attachment to some other area.[111] For example, reregistrants Wu Shih-ch'ao and Fang Hui-ko were identified locally as "Hankow natives, originally registered at She-hsien." In fact the matter could be even more complicated. Cheng Hao-t'ing, who sojourned at Hankow for many years in the early nineteenth century, bore registration from Huo-ch'iu county in Anhwei, yet continued to be identified as a She-hsien man. And the Yeh clan upon its establishment in Hanyang was known, despite its registration and clan headquarters at P'iao-shui, Kiangsu, through former registration in Hsiu-ning county in Anhwei.[112]

The fact that changing registration did not necessarily erase previous local identification seems to have stimulated reregistration; for example, Wang Wen-i, the early Ch'ing founder of the Hui-chou local-origin association at Hankow, was fully able (perhaps better able) to lead his home area's sojourning community as a registered native of Hankow. Throughout the Ch'ing, leading figures in the Hui-chou association seem to have been allowed to reregister at Hankow, even though "registration in the six counties" of Hui-chou was among the association's stated membership criteria. This was possible because all members continued to be identified for social (as opposed to legal) purposes by their Hui-chou county of "original registration."[113]

If registration was a direct function of neither ethnic identity, place of birth, nor actual permanent residence, what motivated someone to change or to maintain his home district? I would argue that registration in the middle and late Ch'ing, at least among elite groups and those having aspirations to upward mobility, was a means to an end; specifically, it was seen as a function of educational opportunity. Over the course of the eighteenth and nineteenth centuries, a definite correlation can be observed between sojourning merchants who chose to change their registration to Hankow and those whose descendants became officials, degree-holding gentry, or otherwise successful scholars and literati of the area. Local scholarly notables such as Yüan Sun-kai, Fang Hui-ko, Hung Ch'in-yu, Hsiang Ta-teh, Hsiang Ta-fu, Sun Shih-lou, Ting Jen-ching, Ting P'ing-yüan, Wu Chang-keng, Wu Shao-po, and Wu Shih-ch'ao all had in common the fact that their fathers or grandfathers had come to Hankow as commercial sojourners and had subsequently changed their registration to Hanyang county.[114] The Hanyang Yeh clan, which produced so many scholars and officials throughout the Ch'ing, was descended from a merchant-literatus who had switched his registry to Hankow under the Ming. Although this trend primarily involved merchants who aspired to regular gentry status, it involved existing officials and gentry as well. Thus at least two descendants of Wang Lan, who changed his registration from Soochow after relinquishing his post as Hankow's Jen-I submagistrate in 1784, became successful and famous local scholars.[115] Clearly, as a local correspondent commented in 1875, "being registered in Hanyang county is seen as a shortcut to personal advancement."[116]

Three aspects of educational opportunity depended upon place of registration: entrance into local schools, county stipends for local scholars, and candidacy for the locally administered civil service examinations. The last was the most crucial. To take the county- and provincial-level examinations in any given place, a candidate was required to be a registered native of that area. However, by at least the Wan-li reign of the Ming, the imperial government, recognizing the increase in interregional trade, had begun to allow a small number of sojourning merchants to establish "supplementary registration" (*fu-chi*) or "commercial registration" (*shang-chi*) in their counties of sojourn, thereby making their dependants eligible to sit for special "supplementary-registration examinations" (*fu-chi ying-shih*) for the lowest gentry degree.[117] Whether this practice survived into the late Ch'ing is unclear; in any case, this limited dispensation could not satisfy the aspirations of the ever-growing number of interregional traders engaged in commercial activities away from home.

More important, in order for natives of such talent-rich areas as Hui-chou and Yangchow to fit into the local quotas for taking and passing exams, it was almost necessary for them to sit for the examinations outside their native places. This meant establishing registration elsewhere, logically in the county where a merchant conducted his trade. This fact is reflected in Ho Ping-ti's finding that in the 1827 Hui-chou gazetteer's list of the prefecture's native sons who had attained the *chin-shih* degree, a total of 377 had obtained the degree under residential registration elsewhere, nearly three times the number who had received it under the home area's own quota.[118] Many of these men, as well as the natives of other achievement-oriented localities, sat for their examinations at Hanyang county, which produced only a modest number of scholars of its own. Thus Wu Chang-keng (the son of a Hui-chou native) and Hung Ju-k'uei (whose father hailed from Shensi) sat for and achieved the *chü-jen* degree as Hankow registrants. Hanyang Magistrate Ch'iu Hsing-shu, reckoning in 1818 that the number of local examination candidates had more than doubled over the preceding forty years, attributed the phenomenon chiefly to sojourning merchants who had successfully filed to change registration for precisely this purpose.[119]

Securing admission into local educational institutions was another reason for establishing local registration. The administration-supported county school (*hsien-hsüeh*) admitted only a small number of students, and their positions were hotly sought after. Sojourning merchants, through their guilds, usually set up private schools to educate their own children. However, the imperial government also made certain provisions in this regard. To educate the sons of government salt merchants, the Ming had introduced a system of special "salt-transport schools" (*yün-hsüeh*) in cities, such as Hankow, that hosted major salt depots. Finding this system too cumbersome, the Ch'ing replaced it with a procedure whereby a quota of the sons of non–locally registered salt (and other) merchants might be admitted to the county schools of certain areas that regularly hosted large numbers of sojourners.[120] The county school of Hanyang, consequently, had positions for eight specially selected "merchant students" (*shang-hsüeh*) at any given time. When in 1851 Lu Chien-ying abolished the monopolistic *kang* system in the Huai-nan district, the county raised this quota to ten on the reasonable presumption that a larger number of qualified candidates would thereafter be seeking such positions.[121] Yet the number of sojourners' sons seeking entrance to the local schools was far in excess of the quota allowed, and for many merchants change of registration to Hanyang county was the obvious solution.

The competition was even keener for the position of "stipended scholar" (*shih-hsi*) of the county. Hanyang county provided about a dozen of these stipends, which were intended to cover the living expenses of promising scholars from the time they received their *sheng-yüan* degree until they attained a higher degree or, as was often the case, for life. These sinecures were awarded only to fully registered residents of the county, but many recipients, including Ting Jen-ching and Wu Chang-keng, were sons or grandsons of reregistered sojourners.[122]

As might be expected, competition for educational opportunity spawned many abuses in the registration machinery of Hanyang county. Most of these abuses centered on registration falsification, particularly the practice of maintaining simultaneous registration in two different counties. When a merchant filed to change his registration to Hankow, the procedure was supposed to cancel automatically his registration in his former county. However, Hanyang authorities often neglected to notify officials of the former county that a filing had taken place. This of course greatly benefited the registrant, since he and his descendants could then choose between two counties' educational opportunities, as well as sit for examinations in both localities, thereby doubling the chances of success. This situation precipitated a famous local legal case in 1794, concerning Hung T'an, whose father, Hung Tzu-chien, had been a Hui-chou salt merchant stationed at Hankow for more than forty years, during which time he had adopted Hanyang county registration but had not allowed his Hui-chou registration to lapse. Hung T'an had become a student in the Hanyang county school, but when he took and passed the local *sheng-yüan* examination, a jealous competitor exposed his dual registration. As a result, provincial authorities stripped Hung of his honors, impeached the Hanyang magistrate for his negligence, and inaugurated procedures whereby changes of registration to any Hupeh county would require the direct approval of the governor, whose personal responsibility it would be to notify authorities in the former home area.[123]

Inevitably, however, this precautionary measure fell by the wayside, and in 1875 abuses in the registration system again erupted in a scandal of major proportions. In this year several local *sheng-yüan*, headed by Li Ping-lin, petitioned the Hanyang prefect and magistrate, requesting that the two officials investigate the widespread practice of falsified and dual registration. Drawing the officials' attention to Hung T'an's case (which the petitioners seem only recently to have discovered), claiming that abuses had been multiplying in recent years, and demanding the promulgation of new and strictly enforced regulations for changing registration, the local scholars concluded that "we believe that only in this way can the selection of talent be broadened and at the same time our own locality be properly protected and nurtured."[124]

The two officials did conduct an investigation.[125] They found that family connections were often used to allow candidates to sit for local examinations under false registration; specifically, mercantile families that had legitimately established registration in Hanyang county frequently imported nephews, cousins, and other relations from other areas of China and, claiming them as sons, entered them in the presumably less competitive Hanyang *sheng-yüan* examinations. (This suggests the fascinating thesis that nationally prominent mercantile families may have systematically established locally registered branches at various commercial centers throughout China and routinely shuttled their heirs back and forth between local examinations, thus multiplying their chances for success.) Moreover, the officials found that a considerable number of outside merchant families had managed to secure local registration without having satisfied the twenty-year residency requirement, by claiming descent from an established local family with whom they shared a common surname but had no blood ties. This practice had become increasingly widespread during recent decades, in the wake of the Taiping devastation. As might have been anticipated, the prefect and magistrate, like the gentry petitioners, blamed all these abuses on the venality of local yamen functionaries. For a "merit fee" (*kung-te ch'ien*) of several dozen taels, they found, the clerks serving in the Temple of the God of Literature (Wen-ch'ang tien) had been falsifying examination and scholastic eligibility based on local registration requirements. (The officials did not mention, but a knowledgeable observer subsequently pointed out, that record tampering on the scale alleged would not have been possible without at least the county director of studies and several local literati also having been on the take.)[126] In consequence of their investigation, the two officials reasserted their support for the former strict procedures for changing registration, including the twenty-year residency requirement, and pledged to take measures to eliminate any opportunity for bypassing these rules.

A final twist to the story, however, reveals that times were indeed changing. When the Hanyang incident was publicized in the Shanghai newspaper *Shen-pao*, an anonymous writer who claimed firsthand familiarity with the situation in Hankow as well as with analogous conditions in Hangchow and Soochow immediately responded with a front-page letter of comment.[127] Although the author concurred with the Hanyang gentry and officials in deploring subadministrative corruption, in his opinion the matter could not so easily be reduced to questions of clerical or even official impecuniousness. The problem was really one of fundamental social change. At the root of the Hanyang incident was the stubborn insistence of local authorities and the indigenous elite on maintaining the twenty-year residency requirement. Not only could this rule no longer be enforced in the wake of the Taiping devastations, but it was undesirable, since it did not accord with contemporary increased geographic mobility. Although the letter's writer did not suggest the complete abolition of the registration system, such notions were in the wind—and in fact had been mentioned by the Hanyang petitioners (who strongly opposed such proposals).

From the 1875 incident and the continuing conflict over the registration process in Hanyang, we can see it was no accident that the first of several statutes incorporated into the *Ch'ing Statutes* under home-district registration provided punishments for the offense of sitting for examinations under false registration: registration was primarily important as a function of the educational and examination system. For the upwardly mobile, careerist types who congregated at Hankow, registration was purely a matter of convenience; even then, for many it was a "confused and indistinguishable" attribute,[128] with no more significance to their conception of themselves than a social security number in present-day Western society.

If county of home-district registration was merely an artificial attribute selected for pragmatic reasons, the same cannot be said for native place as an emotional construct. As we have seen, native place and locality of registration were very often not the same, and the two elicited different types and degrees of attachment. For some Hankow residents, the native place was a true home, to which they returned after retirement or (like many Hunanese managers in the timber trade) after accumulating sufficient capital to invest in rural real estate.[129] Others did not cherish the prospect of return but might still feel strong native-place ties, reinforced by relations with living kinfolk or occasional visits "home." For many others, however, native place—like district of registration—was less a tangible reality than simply a residual suffix to their signatures. A host of factors determined the strength of native-place ties, including the native place's proximity, the density of its social fabric, the role of native products in a line of business, and inherent geographic and climatic appeal (Hunan's lush Hsiang River valley, for example, provided a stronger inducement to return than did Anhwei's rugged Hui-chou prefecture). For all sojourners and immigrants, however, even those with the most tenuous ties to the native place itself, native identity played a large role in determining range of associations within the host city.

Local Origin as an Ordering Principle in Hankow Society

Whatever the strength of an individual resident's ties with his acknowledged native place, he was likely to feel drawn to "compatriots" (*t'ung-hsiang-jen*) at Hankow. There was a genuine bond of sentiment between those who shared cultural, linguistic, and religious peculiarities, as is clear from the ability of local-origin associations (*t'ung-hsiang-hui*) to command continuing devotion and participation.[130] (These associations will be dealt with in detail in the chapters that follow.) Emotional ties, more than any practical considerations, probably lay behind the tendency of inns in Hankow to cater to visitors from one particular area and led to the formation of ethnically dominated neighborhoods within the city.[131] Beyond these sentimental bonds, however, lay a wide range of utilitarian concerns. The accident of common home area could provide a convenient excuse for linkage when linkage was useful, just as a web of business contracts or other obligations could cement sentimental ethnic attachments.

Let us look first at native-place ties in noncommercial realms. At the most basic level, compatriot appeals could be used to provide friendly muscle in violent disputes; when threatened in a barroom argument, for example, a Hankow fireworks dealer was rescued by two compatriot soldiers who, although strangers to the dealer, took abuse of a fellow provincial as a personal affront and beat up his antagonists.[132] Another area of assistance was litigation; thus the officer whose attempt to pass bogus banknotes was recounted in Chapter 5 was extricated from his legal difficulties after prevailing upon a "multi-talented" Huang-p'i compatriot to mediate with the Financial Guild on his behalf.[133] Economic aid was also dispensed along lines of common origin. One manifestation of this was the expectation that men of wealth and local stature would serve as guarantors for the financial contracts of newly arrived compatriots. Feng I-lin, a well-known Cantonese compradore arraigned before the Hankow taotai for systematically embezzling his Western employer's accounts, based his defense on the argument that he needed the money to cover enormous sums forfeited as a guarantor for bankrupt fellow provincials. Feng claimed he was a target for solicitation by every Cantonese adventurer at the port.[134] Finally, political aid was advanced to compatriots by local officials, who were not exempt from such appeals. A Hankow timber dealer, for example, succeeded in temporarily obtaining suppression of the Dragon Boat Festival (which had led to thefts from his stockyard by aspiring boat builders) through a common-origin tie with the naval commandant of the port.[135] Political patronage also functioned in the awarding of appointments; thus the Hupeh salt taotai's yamen was routinely staffed by compatriots of the incumbent official.[136]

The major role of local origin in the organization of late imperial commerce is axiomatic in current scholarship, and study of the Hankow trade offers ample support for this assumption. Native-place ties frequently cemented commercial groups, from guilds of wholesale merchants to such grass-roots units as fleets and boat crews, work gangs of porters and longshoremen, construction crews, and warehouse staffs.[137] Compatriot ties were often the basis for recruiting employees. For example, when Wang Shih-liang's descendants tired of managing their commercial empire at Hankow, they entrusted it to a Hui-chou compatriot, Cheng Chin-fu.[138] Just as Shansi banking houses virtually held hostage in the home area dependants of their managerial staffs elsewhere, so at Hankow warehouse owners from Hunan, Honan, and Szechwan guaranteed the good faith of their up-country purchasing agents by employing or housing their dependents.[139] Recruitment for menial employment as well was often along compatriot lines. Tsungli yamen archives tell of a stockboy in a Russian brick-tea plant in the 1870's who was introduced and guaranteed by a compatriot tea dealer from Hsien-ning county.[140] Similarly, Lu Yü-shan, a Kiangsi native who had migrated to Hupeh's Ch'ung-yang county, found employment there in an up-country tea refinery. After he was transferred in 1878 to the tea dealer's Hankow office, Lu prevailed upon a compatriot foreman in the Russian tea factory to find him better employment there. The hazards involved in such recruitment were revealed, however, when the Russians discovered both Lu and the foreman to be leaders of a ring that was systematically pilfering bricks of tea from the factory.[141]

The interregional trade networks built up by certain local-origin groups were reflected in the linkage and interdependence of clusters of businesses within Hankow. Local specialization in products and services, if nothing else, assured that this would be so; thus seven tea dealerships of Hsien-ning county were linked by ties with a common Hankow broker, who specialized in marketing their county's product.[142] Another sort of linkage was provided by the extension of credit between compatriot firms, whether or not they dealt in related commodities. A Sung-chiang native named Shen Chen, for instance, wishing to enter into partnership with a British merchant and unable to come up with his share of the capital, succeeded in borrowing 850 taels from an unrelated firm also run by Sung-chiang men.[143] For this reason, the failure of a Hankow native bank often led to the collapse of several commercial houses run by compatriots of the bank's proprietor.[144] Business partnerships and interlocking managements were likewise often determined by native-place ties. A Hsü family and a Wang family of common Hui-chou origin, for example, were linked in a complex network of commercial enterprises in Hankow, which included cotton dealerships, opium warehouses, native banks, and pawnshops in the surrounding countryside.[145]

Such particularistic commercial relationships led Weber and his heirs to categorize late imperial Chinese commerce as essentially prerational, and they have also been emphasized by Japanese scholars (both Marxist and non-Marxist), who tend to identify them as "feudal." The theory of *kyōdōtai* (roughly equivalent to the German *gemeinschaft*), especially as developed in the work of Imahori Seiji, stresses sojourner merchants' use of local-origin ties to tyrannically dominate a host locality and the power a few commercial capitalist bosses exercised over both their compatriots and the host population as a whole.[146] Imahori's conception of *kyōdōtai* has been criticized in Japan, and few other historians see the influence of native-place ties on Chinese commerce as quite so malignant. Nevertheless, most Japanese and Western authorities have agreed on both the prevalence of common-origin ties throughout late imperial commerce and their negative effect on China's economic and social development.[147]

I wish to stress, however, the extent to which organization along bonds of common origin was violated in the commercial world of nineteenth-century Hankow. An entrepôt of Hankow's magnitude and economic responsiveness could simply not have operated effectively had it been so thoroughly prisoner to parochial ties. In fact, it was not. As we have seen in our study of individual trades, city-wide interlocking of compatriot businesses of the sort posited by Nishizato Yoshiyuki for Ningpoese sojourner communities did not exist at the great emporium of the Middle Yangtze. Although compatriot ties frequently determined the formation of partnerships, these ties often played no part whatsoever within a business. Legal cases in the archives of the Tsungli yamen repeatedly describe commercial ventures jointly undertaken by merchants of diverse local origin; a firm set up by Wuchang, Shaohsing, and Kwangtung natives and one established by Wuchang, Szechwan, Kweichow, and Kiangsi men are representative.[148] Even Hankow merchants whose business partners were all from the same native place regularly traded with or subcontracted jobs from noncompatriots. Menial labor for the trade might also be recruited along nonparticularist lines. The Board of Punishments archives, for example, record an independent junk master from Hunan's Yüan-ling county engaged in carrying tobacco from Ku-ch'eng, Shensi, to market at Hankow who chose to sign his crew on as needed in the free labor markets at his various ports of call rather than bring them along from home; in 1820, his three-man crew hailed variously from Lin-hsiang (Hunan), Ching-shan (Hupeh), and Hsing-an (Shensi).[149]

In late imperial China, Hankow was the meeting ground par excellence for entrepreneurial types from all parts of the empire, and both its location and its freewheeling markets fostered a transcendence of parochial ties. Demographic factors also contributed to this cosmopolitanism; despite periods of numerical dominance by such groups as the Huichou merchants, neither the native population nor any single sojourner community was consistently able to monopolize commercial opportunity at the port. Although this diversity existed before the Taiping hiatus, it was even more characteristic of the increasingly pluralistic society of the postrebellion decades.

Let us look briefly at the ways in which local-origin subcommunities within Hankow interacted. When presented to a Chinese at Hankow, usually one could tell at once to which ethnic group he belonged, or at least whether he belonged to a group other than one's own. Besides spoken accent or dialect, physical appearance revealed ethnic identity. In 1858 even Laurence Oliphant, a non-Chinese, first-time visitor to the port, could note the intermingling of men from all parts of the empire, whose origins were clearly betrayed by their facial features and local costumes.[150] A Chinese visitor, Yeh Tiao-yüan, has left us a vivid description of one segment of the Hankow population: he was struck by the Shansi men, popularly called "old westerners" (*lao-hsi*), as they strolled about the city in their native dress of long sheepskin coats and heavy, thick-soled shoes.[151]

Despite the existence of ethnic neighborhoods (which sometimes, notably among Shansi men, were virtual ghettoes with an internally enforced isolation policy),[152] most Hankow residents had regular and intensive contact with people of differing local origins. This was the case not only in business matters, but also in such leisure haunts as teahouses, wineshops, and opium dens. Nor was the persistence of regional speech patterns a serious impediment to at least basic communication between Chinese of differing local backgrounds. Griffith John, who began to preach in Hankow in the early 1860's, reported that although natives of all parts of China attended his street sermons, "to most our speech

[Mandarin] was quite intelligible."[153] The Hankow dialect, which served as the lingua franca of this commercial crossroads, was (and is) a conglomerate speech, whose simplicity made it easy to learn and maximized the elements it shared with the home speech of any sojourning merchant.[154]

Interaction between local-origin groups at Hankow occasionally led to overt subethnic conflict. This might stem either from antipathy between certain groups or from competition for economic opportunity. Confrontations of the latter sort could become particularly violent when they involved informal guilds, work gangs, fleets of junks, or other ethnically homogeneous task organizations.[155] Not surprisingly, the most basic and lingering ethnic animosities at the port were directed against the persons perceived to be the most "foreign." As Heard and Company's local agent discovered in his dealings with compradores, even though the most "native" people at Hankow were from central China, the Lower Yangtze Ningpoese were received with ease and familiarity in local circles. Sojourners from culturally more distant areas, such as Shansi and Kwangtung, were among those with the strongest sense of group solidarity. Among Shansi people, this cohesiveness was typically accompanied by prudence and a preference for a low social profile; in contrast, the more flamboyant Cantonese regularly released subethnic tension in cathartic social celebrations such as the fifth lunar month's Dragon Boat Festival.[156]

Nevertheless, local-origin-based feuds or vendettas of the sort common in southeast China or in Taiwan were unknown in Hankow. In general, ethnic confrontations remained brief, contained, spontaneous, and easily resolved. The prevailing mood of the city was cosmopolitan, and the conflicts it engendered were primarily economic rather than ethnic.

Native Identity, Locational Identity, and Social Change

The great majority of the Hankow population in the nineteenth century, as in earlier periods, was made up of persons who were in some measure "outsiders." In this chapter we have explored the factors that brought these persons to the port, the subethnic composition of the city, the strength of attachment to acknowledged place of origin, and the sense of camaraderie among persons sharing a common native place. Before moving on to discuss associations based on subethnic ties, let us examine briefly the degree to which immigrants and sojourners at Hankow thought of themselves as citizens of that locality.

In terms of functional participation, at least, the city's leading sojourner merchants represented themselves as fully integrated members of a Hankow community. Gazetteer biographies and other contemporary sources laud many non-natives for local philanthropy: financing water-control and other construction projects; lodging the homeless in the wake of flood, famine, or military devastation; establishing free lifeboat services, orphanages, schools, medical services, and firefighting facilities; and participating in the "benevolent halls" (*shan-t'ang*) that coordinated such services.[157] The Republican-period gazetteer includes a special section devoted to some of the most openhanded of these sojourner philanthropists. The ever-present threat of flood and fire, as well as that of social disruption, undoubtedly inspired many of their activities; yet a real sense of community service often seems also to have been at work—for example, the gazetteers occasionally describe wealthy merchants in salt and other trades whose personal fortunes were dramatically diminished by overgenerous giving.[158]

Military crises provide further proof that sojourning merchants identified with local interests. When Hankow was attacked by the White Lotus, the Taiping, and the Nien, many non-native merchants, rather than flee to their home areas, took charge of urban militia units and other defense measures, sometimes paying for their allegiance with their lives.[159] In a later security crisis of the 1880's, the sojourning merchants, who had more invested in Hankow than did native workers and local petty traders, were as a group the last to remain in the city to see to its defense.[160]

In professional matters as well, locally active businessmen may have identified their interests with affairs at the port more directly than with the doings of the home office to which they were subordinate. Our earlier discussion of the salt trade revealed that salt merchants at Hankow cooperated with local authorities in preference to those at the distant Liang-Huai headquarters; the recurring merchant/administration conflicts were invariably initiated by the Nanking-based salt authorities, whereas officials at Wuhan were either fiscally dependent upon the merchants, in collusion with them, or unwilling to risk alienating these pillars of the Hankow community. For their part, the merchants, though they invariably hailed from other provinces, preferred to devote a larger share of the profits of the trade to the locality in which they worked, lived, and raised their families than to the broader, ill-defined imperial purposes supposedly served by the Lower Yangtze administrative coffers.

Ho Ping-ti, writing specifically of Hankow, and Tou Chi-liang, writing of the analogous Chungking, similarly argue that sojourners' sentiment and sense of personal identity were deflected toward the host locality. Ho claims that "merchants of various provinces and localities who managed businesses at Hankow for extended periods inevitably tended to develop close ties to the indigenous Hankow society."[161] Tou describes the process as the expansion of the perceived group interests of local-origin-based subcommunities (*hsiang-t'u*) to merge gradually in a composite community spirit (*she-ch'ü*) in the host locality as a whole.[162]

Sojourners at Hankow expressed their acculturation by adopting such personal styles (*hao*) as Sun Ch'u-ch'ih ("the ponds of Hupeh"), Hsü Lin-han ("near to Hankow" or "near to the Han River"), and Wang Hui-han ("joined with Hankow").[163] As a more tangible manifestation of assimilation, sojourners often took wives or concubines from among the native population or other guest communities.[164] As we have seen, many of them, whether or not they changed their registration to Hanyang, established genealogical lines at the port. Some families, such as several Wang lineages from Hui-chou, can be traced at Hankow for centuries, even though they remained by their own choosing "sojourners." Often the children of such lines never saw their ascribed native places and instead grew up and spent their lives in the merchant-literati circles of the host city. Over generations many may have fallen upon less prosperous times and begun to merge with Hankow's nonelite population. Yet even then they might retain some identifying features and consciousness of the old home district.

The long-held Western view of Chinese cities exemplified by the ideal type constructed by Max Weber no doubt had its origins in contemporary reports that a large percentage of the urban population was composed of immigrants and sojourners who retained this consciousness of a distant native place. Through a process of speculative extrapolation that took no account of variances in city type or of temporal change, Weber concluded that Chinese urban dwellers felt no effective identification with the locality in which they resided. This view was elaborated by subsequent social scientists, who even comparatively recently have emphasized an unofficial "law of avoidance" in Chinese society, which allowed rapacious, upwardly mobile types virtually unrestricted leeway in the war of all against all that constituted the city. For example, the development of a responsible urban consciousness favorable to "modernization" in Japan, attributed to "the permanent exodus of [merchants and artisans] along with *bushi* from the village," has been contrasted favorably with China, "where gentry, merchants, and artisans often made money in cities and then returned to consume it in village residences."[165] Thus the Chinese city has been contradictorily seen as at once liberating its sojourner population from the moral constraints of kinship and village attachments and remaining fragmented into particularistic subcommunities based upon these very "sib" and local-origin ties.

As their attitudes toward registration show, late imperial urban residents could take a coldly pragmatic view of their supposedly magical attachments to native place. The histories of many Hankow families support Skinner's conjecture that "within the span of a few generations [of urban residence] native place must be seen as an ascribed characteristic."[166] A corresponding growth of identification with the host locality was reflected in patterns of philanthropy and public service; nevertheless, most non-native Hankow residents maintained ties to their home areas, at least for such utilitarian purposes as access to employment opportunities and physical or financial aid from their compatriots in the city.

The result has been succinctly described by the political scientists Robert Melson and Howard Wolpe, in an article based on studies of a wide range of cultures; they conclude that "communal transformation entails the multiplication rather than the substitution of social identities."[167] There is thus no reason to assume that the identification of a Chinese urban dweller with his native place—what may be termed his "native identity"—in any way precluded the development of a conception of himself as a full member of the community to which he had immigrated or in which he sojourned—what I would term his "locational identity." Thus a Hui-chou native at Hankow could easily develop a locational identity as a "Hankow man" (*Han-k'ou jen*) without necessarily relinquishing a native identity with his home village and local socioeconomic system in Hui-chou. (Indeed, in the legal realm of home-district registration such multiple identities were precisely what many Hankow sojourners surreptitiously tried to achieve.) The development of this locational identity facilitated the emergence of what Philip Curtin has termed "locational solidarity," a sense of common cause among urban residents, which, as we shall see, became increasingly manifest at Hankow over the course of the nineteenth century.[168]

Finally, we should take particular note of Melson and Wolpe's assignment of identity multiplication to periods of "communal transformation" and "social mobilization." The interaction of diverse, self-conscious subethnic populations seems characteristic of commercially oriented urban centers in many cultures, particularly at times of major social change. For example, the developing Indonesian town studied by Clifford Geertz in the early 1950's hosted many "highly professional small businessmen [who] formed well-integrated, regionally-based groups tending to specialize in a certain branch of trade."[169] Medieval

London was likewise dominated by a class of provincial-born merchants, who maintained ties to their rural homelands while participating in the creation of a powerful commercial metropolis and fighting fiercely for the revolutionary political prerogatives of their common host locality.[170] As we will see in the chapters to follow, this multiplication of personal identities and the mixture of competition and cooperation among subethnic groups to which it gave rise were major factors in the process of social mobilization that characterized nineteenth-century Hankow.

CHAPTER EIGHT

Guild Structure

In nineteenth-century Hankow, the most important element directing both social and economic life was not the local administration, gentry cliques, kinship groups, or powerful individual magnates, but a form of association referred to most often in Western writings as the "guild." The power of guilds in Hankow was almost palpable; in 1888, a veteran British diplomat, for example, described one guild headquarters as "in my opinion one of the finest modern buildings in China."[1] The multistory guildhalls, with their brightly tiled exteriors, easily dominated the cityscape. Apart from physical splendor, the guilds' power was reflected in their numbers and in the number of their members. Probably more than half of the city's adult male population was affiliated with some type of guild, many perhaps with more than one. The Republican-period gazetteer records well over a hundred guilds in the city, a number we know to be an underestimate.[2] And individual guilds could have thousands of members.

Guilds were secondary economic organizations. They were secondary inasmuch as they transcended the primary social group of nuclear family (*chia*, *hu*), as well as the primary economic group of business firm (*hao*, or likewise *chia* or *hu*). Regardless of their variation in membership criteria and wide range of functions, guilds were basically economic in orientation. Membership was voluntary rather than ascribed. Although compulsions to join could be applied (and were), the decision to join was ultimately a matter of choice; ascribed characteristics such as local origin often played a role in determining eligibility, but these characteristics did not mean automatic guild membership. There were other voluntary associations in Hankow (such as benevolent halls and neighborhood groups) that were not guilds. These differed, however, in that they were not essentially economic organizations.

A guild in Hankow could define its membership criteria along three possible lines: (1) common type of work (*t'ung-yeh*), (2) common geographic origin (*t'ung-hsiang*), or (3) common position within the production or marketing hierarchy—what we may roughly call "economic class." Each guild drew the parameters for its membership along one or a combination of these lines, setting narrow or broad limits as it saw fit. This selection process, and its changes during the nineteenth century, will be the focus of this chapter.

Generally speaking, in our period type of work and geographic origin were much more significant than was economic class in determining the composition and structure of Hankow guilds. That is, guilds were vertically rather than horizontally constructed. For this reason I have chosen to avoid directly discussing the class dimension in the present study. It will suffice to note that guilds composed, say, of capitalists or workers in a given trade did slowly begin to appear in the last quarter of the nineteenth century, but by 1889 they as yet made up only a minute percentage of all Hankow guilds.

As for type of work, historians have frequently distinguished between commercial guilds (*shang-pang*) and artisan or craft guilds (*kung-pang*), and these analytic categories would have been familiar to residents of nineteenth-century Hankow. Yet this general distinction was less significant in determining guild constituency than was the specific commodity in whose trade or processing a guild specialized. Perhaps more than elsewhere, Hankow guilds involved in marketing a product were also involved in processing it (such as refining tea or smelting metals), and this diminished the importance of the distinction between *shang-pang* and *kung-pang*.

Similarly, guilds based solely or in part on geographic origin are sometimes categorized simply by their members' relation to the host locality, as either "native guilds" (*pen-pang*) or "sojourner guilds" (*k'o-pang*).[3] Once again, however, at Hankow this distinction was blunted, since almost all merchants and artisans there hailed originally from elsewhere in China, and their origins were extremely diverse. Thus in dealing with guild formation in Hankow we can bypass the grosser distinction between *pen-pang* and *k'o-pang* to concentrate on the specific catchment areas of local-origin groups.

Guild Nomenclature and Formal Status

A confusing variety of terms was used in Hankow to refer to guild or guildlike organizations. Although at times such terms were applied with precision, they were at other times used quite broadly. In fact, at Hankow distinctions in guild nomenclature were hazier than at other major commercial centers, a fact regularly lamented by local reporters.[4]

This haziness, I believe, indicates the wide range of organizations Hankow residents saw as similar, as well as organizational flexibility.

Hang (as in yin-hang, or "modern bank"). Katō Shigeshi and Shiba Yoshinobu have demonstrated that after the collapse of the T'ang market system, *hang*, which originally referred to a row of shops in the same trade, gradually came to refer throughout China to "something more nearly approaching an autonomous trade association," relatively free from government control.[5] By the Ch'ing this usage too had largely passed from currency. In Hankow *hang* was used most frequently to refer to a single (usually wholesale) business house or to the entire trade in a given commodity, as in references to the *pa-ta-hang*, or "eight great trades," of the city. More specifically, *hang* was used as an abbreviated form of *ya-hang*, or "brokerage house." Nevertheless, the term was still occasionally employed, either alone or in the compound *ch'i-hang* (trade combine), to refer to a guildlike organization.

Pang. This word, with its more modern alternate *pang-hui*, is the one most frequently identified with the English "guild." Many writers have interpreted the term quite loosely and applied it to a variety of economic organizations; others, like Jean Chesneaux, have read it narrowly, to signify a group of uniform (low) economic class and common local origin: "A pang simply consisted of several score, or at the most several hundred, unskilled workers who had clubbed together in order to find employment and to escape from the feeling of isolation resulting from barriers of language or dialect."[6] In fact, the term was used broadly in late imperial China to refer to a variety of different groupings.[7] One of its most common uses in Hankow was to refer to groups of boatmen united by local origin, place of anchorage in the city, and often task assignment. This usage appears to be closest to the derivation of the word's meaning "guild," having long been applied in the grain-tribute system to a convoy of boats tied up together for protection from the elements and from pirates, and by extension to the mutual-protection associations of the boatmen. Probably most of the boatmen's *pang* in Hankow were ad hoc groups, although some had connections with more formal local-origin clubs and at least one (the Honan provincial boatmen's *pang*) eventually established a permanent meeting hall.[8] Applied more generally, in Hankow the term seems most often to have referred to an occupational group that had no permanent home, or if it did, to that group as distinguished from its real property holdings (even then, it was often used interchangeably with others such as *hui-kuan* and *kung-so*).[9] Lacking a proper hall, such groups either met in local teahouses or temples (which might or might not be recognized as their special domain) or affiliated with larger groups that owned their own halls.

The term *pang* was applied to hundreds of groups in Hankow, both lower-class groups such as coolies and beggars and more exalted clubs like those of bankers and tea dealers. Many but not all were based on common local origin.

Kung-so. Meaning literally "public hall," *kung-so* was used to refer to the premises owned and occupied by guild associations. It also referred to the organizations themselves, but apparently only to organizations that possessed their own halls. Thus, when the Honan boatmen's *pang* bought its hall, both hall and *pang* became *kung-so*. Generally speaking, *kung-so* were organized along lines of trade rather than local origin, but in Hankow this distinction was only partially reliable. The very different translations of this term by the pioneering scholars Morse and MacGowan as "craft guild" and "trade union," respectively, indicate a fundamental ambiguity in the nature of the institution and the constituency it might represent.[10]

Hui-kuan. Like *kung-so*, *hui-kuan* referred both to a building and to the organization that occupied it. *Hui-kuan* were permanently housed local-origin associations. Neither the translation "religious fraternity" supplied by Morse nor "chamber of commerce," chosen by MacGowan, is fully appropriate, but taken together they give some idea of the range of functions of such organizations. *Hui-kuan* were not, strictly speaking, trade organizations, but as the following pages will show, they were nearly impossible to isolate from them in practice.

Other Terms. Local-origin and trade associations in Hankow were often given official titles that belied their true functions. Among these were *shu-yüan* (academy), borne by the guilds of Hui-chou and Ningpo-Shaohsing. The Hui-chou club was formally known as the Tzu-yang shu-yüan, commemorating in its name the site near Soochow where Chu Hsi had established an academy. Probably as a deliberate response, the later Ning-Shao club adopted the name (Wang) Yang-ming shu-yüan. Both institutions in fact operated schools, but *shu-yüan* referred, not specifically to these academies, but to the guilds' overall corporate structure, within whose framework the academies played only a small part. Various terms meaning "temple" (*miao*, *tien*, *yen*) were adopted by other guild organizations, whose principal activities were commercial rather than religious.

The curious phenomenon of giving guilds honorific or potentially misleading names is related to the problem of their formal constitution and, more specifically, their legal status. One of the founders of the Hui-chou club, Wu Chi-lung, wrote in the seventeenth century that "all provincial groups at Hankow adopt the title 'ancestral temple' as a pretext for founding their *hui-kuan*,"[11] thereby implying a covert aspect to such organizations. Genuine misgivings prompted merchants at Hankow to avoid giving their associations more pragmatic names, but equally valid public-relations reasons were probably at work as well. Worship of a deity or commemoration of a cultural hero like Chu Hsi or Wang Yang-ming provided a prestigious front for economic activity, which was thereby made less vulnerable to official or popular opinion.

This chapter will concentrate on groups that had a relatively formal character and were recognized by local officials and popular opinion as the proper spokesmen for a particular interest group within urban society. This restriction is narrower than it may at first appear. Several recent writers have argued that informal or ad hoc associations played a more significant social and economic role in late imperial urban China than the written record can reveal, and research on Hankow tends to support their claims. Informal *pang*—including work gangs, secret-society chapters, and true guild or proto-guild structures—far outnumbered their formal organizational offspring. Amitai Etzioni provides a useful definition of "organization" that can help to distinguish the latter:

> Organizations are social units (or human groupings) deliberately constructed and reconstructed to seek specific goals. . . . Organizations are characterized by: (1) divisions of labor, power, and communication responsibilities, divisions which are not random or traditionally patterned, but deliberately planned to enhance the realization of specific goals; (2) the presence of one or more power centers which control the concerted efforts of the organization and direct them toward its goals; these power centers also must review continuously the organization's performance and re-pattern its structure, where necessary, to increase its efficiency; (3) substitution of personnel, i.e., unsatisfactory persons can be removed and others assigned their tasks.[12]

To these prerequisites of deliberate goal seeking and well-articulated internal structure, I would add another (implicit in Etzioni's definition and explicit in those of other theorists), namely, a commitment to at least a relatively permanent group structure and goals. By these criteria, economic associations in Hankow shaded from those that fully met each of these requirements off toward the more numerous spontaneous and impermanent groupings.

I would identify three signals which marked a trade or local-origin association's transition to formal organizational status in the Ch'ing: (1) ownership or long-term rental of a hall to serve exclusively as the meeting place and business office of the organization, (2) the drawing up and public promulgation of a code of regulations governing organization members, and (3) some sort of agreement with the local administration providing legal recognition of the organization's right to exist. The first two were essentially internal matters, requiring merely a consensus to remain in existence permanently and (for the first step) the decision to contribute or otherwise raise the necessary funds.[13] The third step, of course, required not only an internal resolution but also the acquiescence of the local authorities.

In the West, late imperial guilds have conventionally been viewed as a legal anomaly. In the words of one writer, "The guilds were never within the law; they grew up outside the law; and as associations they neither recognized the law nor claimed its protection."[14] With regard to codified law, this view seems to have some justification. My reading in various statute and precedent collections of the Ch'ing central government has turned up no regulations governing trade and local-origin associations or providing for their registration with either central or local authorities.[15] Yet such groups regularly applied to local and regional officials to have their corporate existence made a matter of public account; for example, when the leaders of the Hui-chou community in Hankow decided at the end of the seventeenth century to formally establish their local-origin association, they petitioned both the Hanyang prefect and the Hupeh governor for approval.[16] Similarly, in the treaty-port period, the Hankow Tea Guild was formally instituted only after having solicited the permission of the taotai and having its founding officially put "on the record" (*tsai-an*).

Just what did *tsai-an* signify to the administration? Official recognition did not involve a change in a guild's fiscal status; no state charters of incorporation were issued, nor was a corporate tax collected. However, by granting recognition the administration acknowledged a guild's right to exist and to operate according to its stated bylaws. Although the licensing of guilds was not legally required, officials were commanded by statute to be vigilant against the "monopolistic formation of a cartel" (*pa-k'ai tsung-hang*),[17] and granting or withholding recognition was a useful means of signifying that a guild did or did not meet official expectations in this regard. On the whole, Hankow officials adopted a lenient attitude toward sanctioning and formally recognizing local commercial organizations. As one correspondent noted: "Each trade has its own *pang*, also referred to as *hui-kuan*. Not only do these deliberate upon regulations and the correction of prevalent abuses in the trade, but they promote cordiality and friendliness and foster local sentiment. Thus the authorities generally do not prohibit them."[18] Yet there are reports of recognition being withheld because of the monopolistic potential of an organization.

Obvious advantages accrued to a trade or local-origin association from official recognition. Administrative recognition gave the organization legitimacy in dealing with its constituents, as well as with external forces: competitors, litigants, contractual partners, and the general population. By applying his seal (*ch'ien-yin*) to the guild's code of regulations, an official gave them the force of law. Thus the Tea Guild's regulations included:

> *Item.* These regulations have been submitted to the Hankow taotai, and are now a matter of official record [*li-an*]. If there is a tea broker who does not obey such established law [*ch'eng-fa*] or deliberately subverts these regulations, in addition to suppressing all trade between him and our component guilds, we will request by petition of the guild that he be officially prosecuted.[19]

In Part I we have seen the ways in which this authority was used by the Salt and Financial guilds, as well as by the Tea Guild, in the regulation of trade and in confrontations with native and foreign contestants for markets and funds.[20] In noncommercial matters an organization could call upon official recognition to defend its collective property against such endemic urban problems as encroachment, blocking of access, and zoning violations.[21] It was these advantages, no doubt more than any administrative compulsion, that induced Hankow guilds to petition for official approval.

Anonymity, of course, also had its benefits. More important, for many small trade and local-origin groups gaining recognition was not worth the effort. Even such a formidable association as the Hui-chou local-origin club existed informally for 27 years before deciding to register with the authorities.[22] Likewise, it appears that none of the six provincial tea *pang* that made up the Hankow Tea Guild had ever individually petitioned for recognition.

Thus guilds in Hankow fell generally into one of two classes. The difference in legal status between the two was not legality versus illegality or orthodoxy versus heterodoxy, but rather explicit official sanction versus its absence. Although some nonsanctioned groups (such as those of boatmen) did shade at times into illegal or heterodox activity, usually the government sought to suppress this activity rather than the groups themselves. All *kung-so*, most *hui-kuan*, and certain *pang* seem to have been sanctioned, whereas *hsiang-hui* (incense-burning societies), most *pang*, and guildlike secret societies, whether or not they were proscribed, were nonsanctioned. The difference rested in the degree to which the administration could exert indirect control over the group, and the corresponding degree to which the group could make use of official patronage.

Local-Origin Associations

Although isolated *hui-kuan* may have existed in China as early as the beginning of the fifteenth century, the institution is generally considered to have been a product of the Ming Wan-li reign and to have undergone its major formative development during the K'ang-hsi period of the Ch'ing. At this time a variety of related organizational forms, such as loosely structured compatriot societies and guest hostels with strong regional biases, began to conform systematically to a standard type.[23] Some such organizations may have existed at Hankow during the late Ming and not survived the devastations of the Manchu conquest; however, the earliest *hui-kuan* foundings on record date from the second half of the seventeenth century, when several of the city's largest and most powerful clubs came into being. By the nineteenth century an estimated 40 percent of all *hui-kuan* in China were located in Hupeh, and the number at Hankow was second only to that at the imperial capital.[24] These clubs were drawn from a broad geographic area; in 1892 the local Maritime Customs commissioner reported eleven provinces represented by local *hui-kuan*, many by several organizations.[25]

Goals. Several general factors influenced the formation of *hui-kuan* in late imperial China. Chief among them, stressed as paramount by most Japanese and many Western writers on the subject, was commerce. Merchants traveling to a city in search of new markets set up organizations there to represent the interests of their home area. Ho Ping-ti, although acknowledging the role of interregional commercial expansion, has argued for the primacy of two other factors: travel to take civil service examinations and widespread migration during the formative period of the *hui-kuan* as an institution.[26] The first can have played little part at Hankow, since Wuchang (the site of the Hupeh and Hukwang examinations) had its own local-origin clubs. Migration, discussed in the preceding chapter, played a major role in the founding of *hui-kuan* throughout Hupeh province, and no doubt to a lesser degree in Hankow itself. Nevertheless, the basic impetus to the formation of all local-origin clubs at that city was, incontestably, trade.

Among the earliest and most lavish of Hankow's local-origin halls were those set up along the shores of Back Lake, behind the town, and along the canal that formed the city's landward boundary. These lodges were established by resident sojourners at Hankow explicitly to accommodate compatriot itinerant merchants bringing their wares to the great market along the overland trade routes terminating in that neigh-

TABLE 12

Goals Stated at the Founding of Hankow Local-Origin Guilds, pre-1889

Goal	No. of times stated
Ethnic goals	
Maintain native-place sentiment (*hsiang-ch'ing*)	2
Maintain home registration (*wei-ch'ih pen-chi*)	3
Worship home-area deities (*chi-shen*)	1
TOTAL	6
Commercial goals	
Manage collective commercial activities (*ying-yeh*)	4
Control collective commercial activities (*chu-ch'üan yeh*)	1
Protect and promote members' commercial activities (*wei-ch'ih shang-yeh*)	4
Study commercial developments (*yen-chiu shang-yeh*)	3
Enforce commercial regulations (*wei-ch'ih pang-kuei*)	1
Promote collective profit (*wei-ch'ih kung-i*)	3
TOTAL	16
Other goals	
Discuss collective affairs (*i-shih*)	2
Construct and manage collective property (*t'i-ch'uang shih-yeh*)	1
Engage in philanthropic activities (*tz'u-shan shih-yeh*)	2
TOTAL	5

SOURCE: *1920 HC*, 5.22–34.

borhood.[27] Many venerable institutions of this sort, which were legitimately local-origin clubs, nevertheless acknowledged the fact that their goals were primarily commercial. The Fukien *hui-kuan*, founded in the K'ang-hsi period, thus identified its aims as "the regulation of commerce and the promotion of charitable works," and the Kiangsi *hui-kuan* of about the same vintage promulgated a founding code of regulations that dealt almost solely with commercial matters.[28]

A fuller idea of the goals of the city's *hui-kuan* can be gathered from the extensive materials on Hankow guildhalls presented in the Republican-period county gazetteer.[29] Its list of organizational foundings reveals that of all the guildlike structures established in Hankow before 1889, slightly more than half (45) included a local-origin requirement among their criteria for membership.[30] Twenty-one of these local-origin clubs, however, stated at their founding one or several major organizational goals, and these goals (which are broken down in Table 12) reveal that the organizations were not simple defensive brotherhoods. Rather, the majority were fundamentally and avowedly economic in orientation.

Membership. Some scholars have assumed that secondary economic organizations in late imperial cities remained rather small, yet this is not borne out by at least the major local-origin clubs of Hankow and other commercial centers. A recent study, for example, has indicated that the Swatow *hui-kuan* at Shanghai in the late 1870's claimed twenty to thirty thousand members.[31] Figures that can be derived for similar groups at Hankow (largely on the basis of lists of contributors to group projects) suggest that numbers there were somewhat lower, yet still formidable. The Shansi-Shensi club, a large, but probably not the largest, group in the city, can be assigned a membership of well over a thousand in the 1870's and 1880's, and the Kwangtung *hui-kuan* in the same period seems to have had at least five hundred members.[32] Even groups with more narrowly restrictive membership criteria, like the guild of Shansi bankers, might have more than a hundred.[33]

The question of *hui-kuan* size is complicated by the problem of the nature of membership in such organizations. Was the unit of membership the individual or the business firm? There is considerable evidence that in the great local-origin clubs of Hankow it was the latter. A legal case of 1883 refers to a tea firm as "belonging to the Changsha Guild," and another source refers to the native banks of the city as each belonging, qua bank, to their respective provincial organizations.[34] Most significantly, the records of the great Shansi-Shensi Guild nearly always refer to guild members not by personal name but by a standard three-character firm name, or *hao*. Moreover, the guild customarily referred to its members as "the various firms" (*ko-hao*).[35] Such indications led Niida Noboru to conclude that only "managers representing their business firms" were admitted to *hui-kuan* membership.[36] But whether a firm's entire staff or only the manager belonged, membership by firm clearly reveals that such Hankow local-origin associations were very different from the havens for displaced souls one might otherwise take them to be. At the other end of the scale, however, were the more numerous small-scale local-origin clubs in the city, within which individual membership was no doubt the norm.[37]

How exclusive was guild membership? Although many Hankow residents no doubt belonged to only one group, this was not necessarily or universally so. For example, none of the six regulatory codes of local-origin and trade associations I have examined in full included clauses prohibiting members from simultaneously belonging to other guilds (although they might prohibit members from engaging in other trades).[38] If a local-origin club was not trade specific, it seems likely that its members would simultaneously belong to the trade guilds governing their occupations; in the latter part of the century, for example, Hankow native banks belonged both to their respective provincial guild and to the transcendent bankers' guild. An individual could also belong to one guild (probably on the basis of local origin) in a private capacity and another (probably trade) through his house of business. Moreover, where the home areas represented by local-origin associations overlapped, people seem to have had the option of joining any or all groups for which native place qualified them.

Catchment Areas. With few exceptions, local-origin clubs chose regular administrative units or groups thereof as their designated home areas, although the size of these home areas varied greatly. The breakdown in Table 13 of the constituencies of 45 local-origin clubs from our period shows that counties (either singly or in groups) were the favored units of *hui-kuan* organization.[39] One explanation for this is that such units were more likely to be specialized also in terms of trade, and so certain counties (such as Huang-p'i, in Hupeh) were represented in Hankow by more than one *hui-kuan*. More generally, catchment area can be related to a rough correlation between the size of the unit represented and its distance from the host city. For example, most of the single counties represented were located nearby in Hupeh (e.g., Huang-p'i) or elsewhere within the Middle Yangtze region. The groups of counties tended to lie farther afield, most often in the highly commercialized Lower Yangtze region. These included Hui-chou, Shaohsing, and Ningpo prefectures, but also lesser-known and less administratively unified areas. The provincial or multi-provincial groups came from even greater distances (Fukien, Shantung, Yunnan-Kweichow). Such groupings derived in part from the greater ease with which cultural differences between local areas within an area represented could be submerged in the face of more pronounced differences between the constituents as a whole and the natives of the host area. As the history of the Shansi-Shensi *hui-kuan* noted, its two provinces had competed more often than they had cooperated; it was only when Shansi and Shensi people found themselves in an equally foreign environment, such as Hankow, that they were able to band together.[40]

A further explanation for the correlation between size and distance would take into account the routes followed by the trade: the farther afield from which a merchant group came, the more likely it was to accumulate natural allies along the way. Skinner rightly notes that whereas the constituencies of local-origin groups were almost always expressed in terms of administrative units, "nevertheless, available evidence suggests that the relevant catchment areas were typically market-

TABLE 13
Catchment Areas of Hankow Local-Origin Guilds at Their Founding, 1644–1889

Unit of representation	Number
Less than one county	2
One county	14
Several counties or one prefecture	19
Several prefectures	1
One province	5
Two provinces	2
No geographic unit (Moslem associations)	2
TOTAL	45

SOURCE: *1920 HC*, 5.22–34.

ing or trading systems at one level or another within the marketing hierarchy."[41] Thus the many Hankow local-origin clubs representing several counties with no administrative connection at the prefectural level and the one association made up of six Kiangsi prefectures with no administrative link were held together by the commercial interdependence of the individual administrative units; for example, one local-origin club incorporated five Hunan counties of varying prefectures, all of which were located along the Hsiang River valley trade route.

Such commercial interdependence could support a combined local-origin club even when its lower-level administrative units were distributed across the boundaries of higher-level units, like the province. Skinner cites the Su-Hu kung-so at Hankow (founded in 1891, and so not included in our sample), which represented both Soochow prefecture in Kiangsu and Hu-chou prefecture in Chekiang.[42] Another example was the Chung-chou hui-kuan, which at its founding comprised four counties straddling the Hopei-Honan border. In one instance, even national borders were transcended: by the end of the nineteenth century the Kwangtung *hui-kuan* at Hankow also incorporated a "Hongkong guild."[43] Thus, in contrast to the organs of local areas like Hui-chou and Shaohsing, where basic ethnic loyalties were at work, many local-origin guilds at Hankow seem to have been founded merely on a pragmatic solidarity based upon networks of commercial extraction and distribution.

The awkward tendency to define local-origin associations in terms of administrative units when in fact very different sorts of units were being represented goes far toward explaining the frequent overlapping or nesting of catchment areas—why, for example, *hui-kuan* representing many local systems within a province like Kiangsu (e.g., the Chin-t'ing hui-kuan, Yüan-ning hui-kuan, and Shang-yüan hui-kuan) could co-exist in the city with a separate organization representing all of Kiangsu province. In an extreme case, a native of the marketing community of Chin-t'ing, in Wu-hsien, Soochow prefecture, Kiangsu province, might affiliate in Hankow either with his own narrowly defined Chin-t'ing *hui-kuan*, with the Soochow Guild, with the Kiangsu provincial *hui-kuan*, or presumably with any combination of the three. The magnitude of the economic system with which his occupation most strongly identified him probably determined his decision. Many local-origin groups were restricted by trade as well as by locality, and this too led to overlapping of catchment areas. Hanyang's neighboring Huang-p'i county, for example, had four separate, occupationally specific clubs at Hankow.

Simplex and Multiplex Guilds. In examining guild structure, we may usefully distinguish between "simplex" and "multiplex" guilds. Simplex guilds were internally undifferentiated. They might be smaller informal groups (*pang*) or larger formal organizations (*hui-kuan*, *kung-so*, etc.); they could be formed along lines of common trade, of common local origin, or of the two in conjunction. In contrast, multiplex guilds were internally differentiated. That is, they were larger umbrella organizations incorporating two or more simplex components. They were almost always formal organizations, but could be united by either local-origin or common-trade ties. For the moment, let us concentrate on multiplex local-origin guilds.

Hankow hosted several such associations that incorporated components with trade specializations; for example, the Szechwan *hui-kuan* comprised the Szechwanese medicinal-herbs *pang* and the Szechwanese boatmen's *pang*.[44] Other multiplex *hui-kuan* at the port contained local-origin *pang* with more restrictive catchment areas than that of the parent organization; for example, the Shantung provincial club was subdivided into components representing individual counties or prefectures within that province. (Contemporaries felt that the components of the Shantung club clustered into two major factions, those that followed the sea route between Shantung and Hankow, and those that traveled overland—an illustration of the significance of trade routes in determining guild structure.)[45] Some of the largest multiplex *hui-kuan* of the city had components of various types. The Shansi-Shensi club's 23 member *pang*, for example, included groups based on local origin, common trade, and a combination of the two.[46]

The degree to which simplex components of multiplex *hui-kuan* were able to maintain their own organizational integrity varied. Usually, however, they had both a ritual means to preserve their identity (worship of their own patron deities) and a functional necessity for doing so (especially trade groups that regulated exchange in their commodity). Subunit integrity was usually reflected in the physical layout of the *hui-kuan* premises. The Ling-nan (Kwangtung) club was thus divided into four halls, or lodges: the Yüeh-k'uei t'ang, Feng-ch'eng t'ang, Yü-shan t'ang, and Ku-kang t'ang, housing respectively the four counties Nan-hai, Shun-te, P'an-yü, and Hsin-hui.[47] Numerous side chapels within the Shansi-Shensi guildhall complex served similar functions for its member *pang*; however, in an extreme illustration of component independence, the Shansi tea guild (*hung-ch'a pang*), though a member in full standing of the multiplex provincial club, maintained its own private meeting hall at some distance from the parent guildhall.[48] We may recall that this Shansi tea *pang* was one of the "Six Guilds" incorporated into the Hankow Tea Guild in the 1870's. Thus a simplex group based on both common trade and common origin evidently could affiliate with two distinct multiplex groups, sharing ties of local origin with one and ties of trade with the other. Such associational patterns, then, seem to have been more marriages of convenience than the result of some deeply rooted and "magical" parochialism.

External Ties. What ties existed between local-origin associations in a host city such as Hankow and the home areas they represented? *Hui-kuan* had a stake in fostering individual sojourners' ties to their native place, no matter how devoid of real personal sentiment these had become, inasmuch as these ties served as the essential normative element of group cohesion. Thus, for example, groups referred to their members as all "registered natives" of the home area when, as we have seen, current registration in that area was often not a requirement for membership. The ideal of ultimate return to the home area was likewise an important integrating feature; thus the Kiangsi club had inscribed in large characters over its main portal "To die in Kiangsi!" (*szu tsai Hsi-chiang*).[49] *Hui-kuan* like that of Hui-chou operated cemeteries, which were ostensibly temporary resting places for remains until they could be shipped home for final reburial; there is little evidence, however, that this last step was regularly accomplished (whereas sojourners in Hankow were often permanently buried there).[50]

Organizations of sojourning merchants in Hankow sometimes remitted funds to the home area, especially in crises; for example, during the prolonged drought and famine that afflicted northwest China in the late 1870's, the Shansi-Shensi club remitted large sums home for various relief projects. However, this step required a special decision by the club's managers, and the money remitted was not taken from a fund permanently established for such purposes, but rather was temporarily diverted from funds collected for a building project in Hankow that coincided with the Shansi drought.[51] None of the *hui-kuan* budgetary records that survive reveal a standing fund for remissions to the home area, nor do any *hui-kuan* regulatory codes incorporate procedures for doing so.

Some Hankow *hui-kuan*, as we have noted, represented groups of merchants that were thrown together, not by the exigencies of local-product specialization nor by the accident of common location along well-traveled trade routes, but rather by a genuine and strongly cultivated corporate identity. Such groups in Hankow included the four that chiefly supplied the leaders of the town's commerce and society: those of Hui-chou, Shansi-Shensi, Kwangtung, and Ningpo-Shaohsing. Among these groups, the chief extra-Hankow loyalty was arguably not to the home area per se, but rather to the network of similar organizations distributed throughout the major commercial cities of China. These networks were reinforced by a tendency of merchants within the group to belong to chains of commercial houses with branches in each major city where the home area's *hui-kuan* existed. Skinner has noted the utility of such links between guilds for transmitting commercial intelligence. Specifically, he claims that "couriers carried market and price information from the Hui-chou guild in Nanking to the Hui-chou guild in Hankow."[52] The publication of trade-route guides by members of these groups provides further evidence that they were used to transmit intelligence. Such *hui-kuan* networks had conceivably become abstracted of any real allegiance to the home areas they claimed to represent.

Although there is evidence that the major *hui-kuan* at Hankow cooperated with others representing the same home area in other localities, there is nothing to confirm that they were formally joined into an integrated, intercity organization. We know, for example, that the Ling-nan (Kwangtung) hui-kuan in Hankow was rebuilt and expanded in 1744 on the floor plan of an older Ling-nan club at Hsiang-t'an, another major commercial city along the regular Kwangtung-Hukwang trade route.[53] Moreover, as P'eng Tse-i has suggested, more than convention probably lay behind the fact that provincial associations often chose the same name for their *hui-kuan* at various cities throughout the empire: Kwangtung was always represented by the "Ling-nan hui-kuan," Kiangsi by the "Wan-shou kung," and Fukien usually (but not at Hankow) by the "T'ien-hou kung."[54] Yet in the voluminous surviving documentation from the Hankow clubs representing Hui-chou and Shansi-Shensi, two local-origin areas with numerous *hui-kuan* distributed throughout China, there is no mention even of the existence of other units, let alone of any organizational relationship with them. Consequently, the evidence from Hankow seems to support Gary Hamilton's contention that "the overwhelming majority of regional associations were independently organized in each location without organizational connections with associations established elsewhere. In other words, *hui-kuan* were strictly local organizations, even though their organizers were non-locals."[55] As we shall see, usually the strongest temptation (one increasing with time) was to affiliate with organizations located within the same host city but representing other home areas, rather than with organizations located elsewhere but representing the same home area.

Thus the evidence from Hankow tends to belie the emphasis of Japanese scholars such as Imahori Seiji on the closed and generally reactionary nature of local-origin associations in late imperial urban society.[56] More convincing for Hankow is the argument of Ho Ping-ti, developed largely in response to this Japanese scholarship, that "contrary to the impressions of previous writers on the subject that the prevalence of *hui-kuan* reflected the existence of unusually strong local particularism in China and has hence hindered China's modernization, . . . the institution of *hui-kuan* has in fact facilitated interregional and social integration."[57] More generally, I would see *hui-kuan* as one form of the "communal association" common to developing societies, occupying a halfway house between the parochial and the cosmopolitan.[58] As such, in late imperial cities like Hankow, *hui-kuan* seem on balance to have been a progressive force in local society.

Trade Associations

In the earliest type of common-trade organization at Hankow, both common local origin and common trade served simultaneously as criteria for membership. This form of organization was a natural development in a marketplace in which most commodities of trade were local specialties. Chapter 2 has shown how true this was for raw products such as sugar, hemp, beans, and coal; for handicrafts and processed goods, local areas were even more likely to hold a virtual monopoly over both production and distribution. Although many guilds in Hankow dealt in silks, for example, the variety of silk produced in Kiangsu and Chekiang was so distinctive that it constituted a separate item of trade, monopolized by merchants of these two provinces.[59] Hence it is not necessary to attribute the fact that the Hankow guild supervising the market in this product was restricted to Kiangsu and Chekiang natives to any unusual degree of traditionalistic parochialism.

Despite the sound logic behind linking common-trade and local-origin membership requirements, by our period there had come into existence in Hankow another variety of trade organization for which no native-origin requirements were stated. The Scalemakers' Guild, for example, boasted in its regulations that since its founding in the late eighteenth century, "masters and journeymen of various firms from all parts of the empire have come to Hankow and thereby fallen under our organization's auspices."[60] Although it represented a later development than the trade guilds based also on local origin, the geographically heterogeneous trade guild had appeared by the early Ch'ing. Probably the first such guild in Hankow—perhaps the first in all China—was the powerful Rice Market Guild (Mi-shih kung-so), which convened in 1678 to draw up a code of regulations to submit to the local administration for approval. The code's preamble began:

> We who manage the rice market at Hankow are engaged in the brokerage of grain. If we had no hall in which to gather for collective discussions, we would be unable to decide upon our trade's regulations. Moreover, our points of view would differ and our weights and measures would not be uniform. This would be inconsistent with our responsibilities, inasmuch as rice is the staple item in the human diet. If our weights and measures were not uniform, how would it be possible to display our records for public inspection or to safeguard at all times our professional good faith? Consequently, all of us who share this common trade have gathered together to devise a standardized business practice and to reaffirm periodically our guild regulations.[61]

Although they couched their proposals in terms calculated to win the hearts of local officials (the sacred position of rice and public scrutiny of their operations), the Hankow rice brokers were in fact embarking upon a revolutionary undertaking, one that local administrators charged with preventing the "monopolistic formation of a cartel" routinely guarded against. As the Chinese historian Teng T'o pointed out, their success in winning bureaucratic approval for the founding of a single, private, inclusive organization to manage the entire trade in the most basic of commodities at its largest market in the empire was nothing short of a landmark in China's socioeconomic history, indicating the emergence of the self-conscious power of the "urban class" (*shih-min*).[62] In Hankow, the Rice Market Guild's precedent in transcending local particularism was followed by many other trade associations. By 1889, virtually half of all permanently housed guilds in the city (including *hui-kuan*) had no local-origin restrictions on membership.[63]

Included among the trade organizations of Hankow were groups of both the simplex and multiplex types. The simplex variety, that is, guilds that were internally undifferentiated, might either combine common trade and local origin (as did the Kiangsu-Chekiang silk dealers), or integrate members of diverse geographic origins into a single body (such as the Scalemakers' Guild and the Rice Market Guild). In multiplex trade organizations, on the other hand, common trade served to unite component *pang* with more restrictive membership criteria.

In general, three factors seem to have played a role in differentiating simplex components within a multiplex trade guild. The first and least common was jurisdiction within the host locality; the Woodworkers' Guild (Mu-tso kung-so), for example, included a "civil guild" (*wen-pang*) for craftsmen active at Hankow and Hanyang and a "military guild" (*wu-pang*) for those at Wuchang.[64] The second was specialization within the trade; for example, the Copper Guild was subdivided into a *ta-hang* dealing in water pipes and a *hsiao-hang* selling copper jewelry.[65] The third and most common was subdivision by local origin; the Hankow Tea Guild, formed in the 1870's to incorporate six provincial *pang* of tea dealers, was an example. This third pattern also pertained in the multiplex guilds of the timber and medicinal herbs trades, the subjects of the following case studies.

Guilds of the Timber Trade. The timber and bamboo market at Wuhan grew from modest beginnings to become the most important of its kind in China.[66] The trade in wood products (*mu-ts'ai*) began like many others as a trade in luxury goods. Since the late Ming, merchants from Kiangsi had marketed their native cotton cloth throughout the empire, using Hankow as their central entrepôt. One area to which the sale of this cloth took them was the Miao River valley of Kweichow, where they discovered timber of rare and unusual quality. In the early Ch'ing, Kiangsi merchant boats thus began to make their return runs from Kweichow laden with cargoes of this wood, which they disposed of at Hankow.

Only in the early nineteenth century, however, did the city become a significant center for the trade in bamboo and timber of more pedestrian quality, which merchants from Hunan were starting to import from their home districts. A bulk trade in cheaper wood became much more feasible after the appearance in 1769 and later gradual silting up of a long sandbank, soon known as Parrot Island, off the shore of Hanyang city. Mooring and unloading large, timber-bearing barges proved much easier at this location than at Hankow proper, and by the 1840's Parrot Island had been established as the principal site of China's largest interregional timber market. Even so, the greatest period of market growth came only after the Ch'ing reconquest of Wuhan from the Taipings. Government forces then began construction of a great fleet of antirebel river gunboats, for which they relied almost exclusively on lumber purchased at Wuhan. Shortly thereafter, the lifting of the eighteenth-century ban on overseas navigation by Chinese subjects inspired the large-scale construction of seagoing junks. This, plus the accelerated opening of mines and self-strengthening industries, created an unprecedented demand for the timber of Parrot Island.

The history of the Wuhan timber trade was marked by conflict, occasionally violent, among three major clusters of guilds. The first to arrive were two guilds of Kiangsi merchants, the "Kiangsi *pang*" (with headquarters at the Lin-chiang hui-kuan, in Hankow) and the "Huang-pang," made up of merchants of Kiangsi origin who had migrated to eastern Hupeh's Huang-chou prefecture. These two guilds dominated the Hankow timber trade until the mid-nineteenth century, when Hankow proper was eclipsed by the satellite market on Parrot Island. Unfortunately for the Kiangsi men, Hunanese merchants had gotten to the island first, and by the time its advantages as a mooring had become clear, the Hunanese had secured a de facto monopoly on its long, sandy beachhead and the straits separating it from the Hanyang shore. Faced with a competition having both a better market facility and a home base in the production area, the Kiangsi and Huang-chou guilds were rapidly driven out of the timber trade, and after the Taiping hiatus they did not renew their claim on the Hankow marketplace.

The second group of merchants to enter the trade were the "Han-pang" (or "Pei-pang," from Hupei), which represented portions of the Han River valley. These merchants were subordinate in the trade and generally served as local agents for the Kiangsi and Huang-chou merchants. However, they survived the collapse of these groups and managed in the long run to increase their importance in the market.

The third group, the Hunanese, began to arrive only in the early part of the nineteenth century. As a whole, Hunan merchants were popularly known as the "Nan-pang"; in fact, they were divided into eighteen independent and autonomous *pang*, each representing a discrete locality within the home province and each dealing in a type of wood native to its home area. The catchment areas of these eighteen *pang* all fell within the five major timber-producing prefectures of Changsha, Heng-chou, Pao-ch'ing, Ch'ang-te, and Ch'en-chou. Yet not administrative units but transport routes determined the patterns of federation of these simplex *pang* into multiplex trade associations: the eighteen *pang* were clustered into two major multiplex alliances based on the waterways they traversed en route to Wuhan. One of these was known as the "Tung-hu" group because its component *pang* all followed a route passing to the east of Tung-t'ing Lake; it comprised merchants from the drainage systems of the Hsiang, Tzu, and Lei rivers. In administrative terms, it incorporated basically the prefectures of Changsha, Heng-chou, and Pao-ch'ing. The second group was called "Hsi-hu," since its members all followed a route to the west of Tung-t'ing Lake. It represented the Yüan River valley and comprised the prefectures of Ch'ang-te and Ch'en-chou (see Map 4).*

When the Hunanese timber *pang* sought to formalize their organizational status in Wuhan by erecting proper guildhalls, they drew upon alliances of convenience bearing even less relation to administrative districting. In the Tao-kuang reign, before Parrot Island had silted in firmly enough to allow major construction, four such guildhalls were built on the facing mainland shore, outside Hanyang city. These four were (1) the An-I hui-kuan, representing An-hua and I-yang counties of Pao-ch'ing prefecture, (2) the Ch'i-yang hui-kuan, representing the single county of that name, (3) the Ch'en-Kuei hui-kuan, representing Ch'en-hsien and Kuei-yang counties of Heng-chou prefecture, and (4) the Wu-liang tien, representing the remainder of Heng-chou as well as all of Changsha prefecture. Again, a glance at the map suggests that riverine transport routes underlay these alliances.

With the reopening of the timber market after the Taiping hiatus and the intervening buildup of Parrot Island, more than twenty Hunanese *hui-kuan* were constructed on the island itself. Most of these represented either individual timber *pang* or small groups of *pang*, but there were also larger Tung-hu and Hsi-hu *hui-kuan*. A single, overarching Liang-hu hui-kuan was constructed by the entire Hunanese timber-merchant community around 1865, uniting the Tung-hu and Hsi-hu groups. This unified organ grew in importance in subsequent decades, reconstructing and enlarging its premises in 1875 and again in the early 1890's.

As the Wuhan timber market continued to expand in the post-Taiping period, merchants of Hupeh's Han-pang sought to reassert their former claim to a share of the trade. In the early 1870's they filed suit at the prefectural yamen to break the Hunanese monopoly over the moorings at Parrot Island. Hanyang Prefect Fan Kuo-t'ai saw this as a native guild suing a sojourner guild, and argued that since Parrot Island was part of Hanyang county and the Han-pang included, at least in part, merchants from that county, all or most of the trade ought to be turned over to them. He further imposed a financial penalty on the Hunanese for hav-

*This phenomenon lends strong support to Skinner's assertions about the primacy of river-drainage systems in the formation of communal and regional bonds in late imperial China. A further example can be found in the internal structure of the timber-merchant associations from Pao-ch'ing prefecture. There were two *pang* from Pao-ch'ing at Parrot Island, known as the Ta-ho (large river) and the Hsiao-ho (small river) guilds. The former was composed of merchants from Shao-yang county and the latter of those from Hsin-hua county, but neither exclusively so. For both, the relevant territorial unit was the river valley, which cut across county lines.

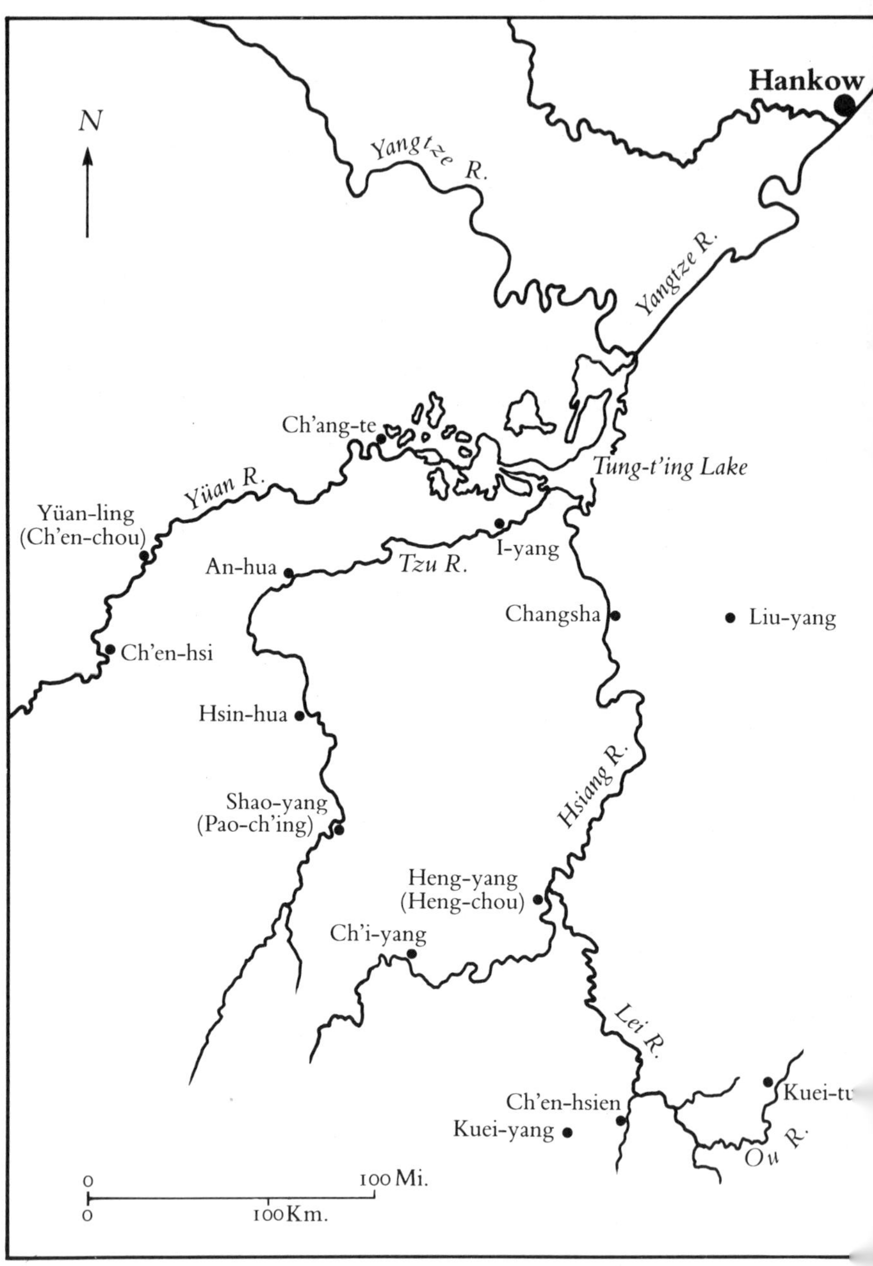

Map 4 Hunanese timber-production centers.

ing so long excluded local merchants from the trade. The Hunanese refused to yield, and fierce brawling erupted between the two groups, which according to some accounts spread downriver to Hupeh and Hunan communities at Chinkiang and Nanking.

The Hunanese timber merchants then appealed to their two nationally prominent fellow-provincials Tseng Kuo-fan and Tso Tsung-t'ang (both of whom had relatives in the timber trade). At Tseng's request, the Hupeh governor intervened to overturn Prefect Fan's decision and effect a compromise. Timber dealerships and transport commissions were to remain in the hands of the Hunanese, but timber brokerage was to be given over solely to the Han-pang. After this settlement, Hupeh merchants began to apply for brokerage licenses (*ya-t'ieh*) and set up firms on Parrot Island.

As the embodiment of this conciliation, Tseng and Tso interceded to bring about the admission of Han-pang merchants into the previously all-Hunanese Liang-hu hui-kuan, whose name "Two *hu*" was now conveniently reinterpreted to signify Hunan and Hupeh, rather than Tung-hu and Hsi-hu. Thus the Liang-hu hui-kuan became in effect the first wholly inclusive trade organization for the Wuhan timber market. Tseng and Tso attempted to soothe the animosities generated by their enforced relaxation of the guild's membership criteria by making lavish donations to the guildhall's 1875 reconstruction project. The Hunan-Hupeh alliance thereafter suffered some shaky moments, but remained in force through the end of the Ch'ing.

Guilds of the Medicinal Herbs Trade. Whereas the timber market at Wuhan was an early-Ch'ing creation, the medicinal herbs trade went back at least to the early Ming, before the Han River's change in course brought modern Hankow into being.[67] In these years the medicine market was located in Hanyang city's commercial suburb Nan-shih, where a number of local-origin medicine *pang* divided the market by each specializing in several local varieties of drugs. The most prosperous and influential of these *pang* were those representing Szechwan, Kiangsi, Shensi's Han-chung county, and Huai-ch'ing prefecture of Honan. Each was but one component of a local-origin *hui-kuan* (due to the crucial importance of the medicine trade in these early years, their role in such groups was usually a major one), but no overarching trade association for the market existed.

After the river shifted in the late Ming, the Szechwanese medicine guild was the first to perceive the potential of what is now Hankow as a site for warehouses and market activities. From the time of its relocation, the Szechwan *pang* fought a long and ultimately unsuccessful campaign to monopolize moorings for medicinal herbs boats in the town; it was defeated by the fact that Hankow, unlike Parrot Island, expanded to accommodate new arrivals. Thus in 1689 Huai-ch'ing merchants built the Huai-ch'ing hui-kuan, alternately known as the Yao-wang miao (Medicine God Temple). Soon after came the Kiangsi *pang*, which together with the cloth and timber guilds from that province built the magnificent Wan-shou kung, or Kiangsi *hui-kuan*. Then came a Chekiang-Ningpo contingent, and finally the Han-chung *pang*. Each later arrival staked out an area of pier and warehouse space in virgin territory on the Han and Yangtze downriver from their established competitors.

Whereas wharfage and real estate in Hankow were relatively elastic during these years, up-country herb-cultivation areas soon reached their limits of expansion. Thus the medicine guilds of Hankow first came into serious conflict over the issue of territorial collection rights. Each local-origin guild of medicine dealers and brokers at Hankow had its own network of rural producers and collection agents, and each claimed exclusive rights over certain regions. The Kiangsi merchants, for example, held customary rights not only over their home province, but also over herb-cultivation areas in Hunan, an economic colonization of the sort described in Chapter 2. We should note that this colonization was commodity specific; that is, although Hunanese merchants vigorously excluded Kiangsi men from collecting timber in their native province, they appear to have made no similar claim to medicinal herbs. Indeed, one wonders whether the relatively speedy and graceful withdrawal of the Kiangsi merchants from the Wuhan timber market might not have been effected in return for a tacit granting of drug-collection rights in Hunan, and we are left with a tantalizing glimpse of an intricately interlocked system of commodity-specific domestic economic colonies overlaying the commercial map of late imperial China.

Although conflict over collection rights had probably flared up at Hankow earlier, the real problems started only during the post-Taiping reconstruction. In the new atmosphere of commercial freedom, fraught not only with opportunity but with the potential for market anarchy, it was the Kiangsi guild that first broke ranks and launched an unprecedented campaign to pry the Yü-chou production area of Honan away from the Huai-ch'ing guild, and the Sian area away from the Han-chung guild. Cultivators and local merchants in these areas seem to have responded to competitive bidding not with loyalty to their old patrons but with delight. The Huai-ch'ing and Han-chung guilds at Hankow thus felt compelled to counterattack.

The weapon they chose will be familiar from our study of the Sino-foreign tea trade: the boycott. The details of this affair are not clear, but the Huai-ch'ing and Han-chung guilds seem to have jointly determined to withhold their own local medicines from Kiangsi buyers at Hankow, and these buyers in turn put pressure on their colleagues who imported drugs to Hankow to halt penetration of the production areas under dispute. In fact, the Huai-ch'ing and Han-chung merchants were able to exact an indemnity (*ti-sou*) from the offending guild to cover losses suffered.

The boycott provided the final stimulus to a movement, which had been underway for some time, to set up a trade-wide guild with strict powers of regulation and arbitration. Since the advent of Hu Lin-i's reformed brokerage system a certain amount of order had been imposed upon the trade (e.g., in quality control), but government-licensed brokers could not eliminate cutthroat competition like the Kiangsi invasion. Moreover, members of the trade declared themselves not fully confident of the integrity of all those who had managed to procure brokerage licenses. In addition, they wanted to standardize the locally determined practices of each group of brokers and the local-origin guilds of medicine dealers they served.

Thus, before the start of the trading season in April 1870, the leaders of all medicine *pang* active at Hankow held a banquet at the Yao-wang miao (the temple of the trade's patron deity, owned and operated by the Huai-ch'ing *hui-kuan*) and together drafted a detailed regulatory code (*hang-kuei*) for the trade as a whole. In addition to a statement of general principles, they drew up a schedule (which survives) of 34 major medicines traded at Hankow, grouped according to local origin. Each item on the schedule was followed by eleven columns of standards to govern its trade, which were to be enforced upon all dealers at the port. These standards included the type of container (e.g., "wooden chest") in which the drug was to be marketed, the approximate weight of the unit of sale and the percentage of discrepancy to be allowed, and the fineness of the silver to be used in payment. The schedule further specified the percentage of the agreed-upon unit price to be paid by the buyer, received by the seller, taken as commission by the broker, allowed as a discount for late delivery, and so forth.

The adoption of this regulatory code did not signify the formal creation of a trade-wide medicinal herbs *kung-so*. Each provincial medicine *pang* instead continued to exist as an independent entity, and usually also as a component of its respective multiplex provincial *hui-kuan*. I have nowhere found a record that the medicinal herbs trade as a whole ever constructed a guildhall or solicited contributions for such a purpose. Nevertheless, after the adoption of the code, the trade as a whole increasingly assumed other trappings of formal organization. For three years after the inaugural 1870 meeting, the leaders of all provincial *pang* in the trade met annually at the Yao-wang miao. In 1874 they transferred the site of this meeting to a more neutral hillside temple on the outskirts of Hanyang. At their yearly convocation the trade's leaders would propitiate the Medicine God, deliberate over emendations to their regulatory code and to the detailed schedule of weights, measures, and price guidelines, and elect a "chief of affairs" (*shou-shih*) to serve for that year as the trade's formal representative in contacts with the local administration and in routine dealings with the leaders of other trades.

In both the timber and the medicinal herbs trades, then, trade-wide regulations were adopted and at least an ad hoc inclusive trade organization established in the second half of the nineteenth century. In the beginning, in both trades various provincial *pang* first established production, collection, and distribution networks; then an institutionalized means of resolving the clashes inevitable at each point of contact between these networks was imposed from above. In both trades, such innovations followed upon the Taiping interruption of trade and Hu Lin-i's post-Taiping brokerage reforms; the arrival of the West does not seem to have had a direct influence in either case.

Trends in Structural Change

In a major theoretical article on "Social Structure and Organizations," sociologist Arthur Stinchcombe argued:

> An examination of the history of almost any type of organization shows that there are great spurts of foundation of organizations of the type, followed by periods of relatively slower growth, perhaps to be followed by new spurts, generally of a fundamentally different kind of organization in the same field. . . . Our interest in these spurts derives from the fact that organizations formed at one time typically have a different social structure from those formed at another time.[68]

In other words, although certain types of organizations (Stinchcombe uses the example of American college fraternities) may have a long history, there is an observable correlation between the time within that history when an organization of that type is established and the structure and orientation of that particular organization. This is so largely because changing external social conditions both allow and demand new kinds of organizations, which tend to be founded within the framework of existing general types conceived of as stable.

In its list of "Hankow's *hui-kuan* and *kung-so*," the 1920 county gazetteer includes 179 disparate organizations that contemporaries felt belonged to a single general type, which we call the "guild." Yet over time the structure chosen for these groups changed, as Stinchcombe would predict. This change occurred along four general lines.

TABLE 14

Membership Criteria of Hankow Guilds at Their Founding, 1644–1920

Date of founding	Membership criteria: Common origin only	Common origin plus common trade	Common trade only	Total
1644–1722	5	7	3	15
1723–95	8	2	3	13
1796–1856	5	1	7	13
1857–89	2	7	29	38
1890–1920	2	8	22	32
TOTAL	22	25	64	111[a]

SOURCE: *1920 HC*, 5.22–34.

[a]This total represents all groups included in the *1920 HC* list for which both membership criteria and approximate date of founding can be established. See note 30.

Changing Membership Criteria in Newly Founded Organizations. A breakdown by date of founding and membership criteria for all guilds in the 1920 list for which such information is available appears in Table 14. Organizations founded solely on principles of common occupation or trade made up a decided minority (21 percent) of all guild foundings in the seventeenth and eighteenth centuries, a slight majority (54 percent) in the first half of the nineteenth century, and a considerable majority (76 percent) between the recapture of the city from the Taipings and the local advent of industrialization. Moreover, the three decades from 1890 to 1920 (the year of the gazetteer's publication) show a similar large majority (69 percent) of guild foundings to be along lines of trade alone, confirming that the direction of change in our period was no temporary aberration, but was in accordance with longer-range trends.

Despite the small size of our sample and the difficulties with its composition (see note 29, above), the figures argue convincingly that common trade tended to displace common local origin as a determinant of membership in secondary economic organizations. The trend would be even more striking but for a modest renaissance in the founding of guilds based on both common origin and common trade in the post-Taiping period. These were largely single-product, single-county guilds drawn from immediately contiguous central Hupeh counties, and they had probably been on the scene before the rebellion but had gone unrecorded because they lacked a formal guildhall.

The trend in Hankow takes on broader significance when compared with findings from Shanghai compiled by the Japanese scholar Ōtani Takashi. Table 15 gives his collation by reign period of the foundings of *hui-kuan* (which we take to signify local-origin groups) and *kung-so* (common-trade groups). In Shanghai, as in Hankow, common-trade

TABLE 15

Foundings of Shanghai Guilds in the Ch'ing Period

Reign	*Hui-kuan*	*Kung-so*	Total
K'ang-hsi	0	1	1
Ch'ien-lung	4	4	8
Chia-ch'ing	3	2	5
Tao-kuang	2	5	7
Hsien-feng	0	4	4
T'ung-chih	3	8	11
Kuang-hsü	11	18	29
TOTAL	23	42	65

SOURCE: Ōtani Takashi, "Shang-hai te t'ung-hsiang t'uan-t'i yü t'ung-yeh t'uan-t'i," cited in Fu, p. 39.

foundings overtook common-origin foundings in the early nineteenth century, to become the great majority in the post-Taiping years. Other scholars have noticed a similar phenomenon throughout China during this period. Tou Chi-liang (studying Chungking) and Ho Ping-ti (studying various localities) have argued that the trend toward occupationally based guilds derived largely from the withering of parochial attachments in the Chinese urban milieu. Ho concludes that "generally speaking, no matter how deep were the sentiments of local origin at the outset, the economic advantage of common-trade association was sooner or later able to overcome them."[69] The conclusions of the present study in general support those of Professor Ho; however, a more mundane reason might also be advanced for the growing popularity of trade-based organizations—the growing identification of individual merchant houses with particular trades. The research of Shigeta, Fujii, and other scholars suggests that among Chinese commercial houses specialization by commodity was only a gradual development, which accelerated in the Kuang-hsü period.[70] This surely contributed to the growing preference for common-trade organizations. Whether due to deparochialization or to functional specialization, the movement to common-trade guilds may be interpreted as an instance of Weberian "rationalization." As we have seen, regardless of membership criteria virtually all Hankow guilds were overtly economic in orientation; the common-trade format was clearly better suited to the calculated pursuit of individual members' profits.

The Relaxation of Membership Criteria Within Existing Organizations. A small but significant number of Hankow guilds founded in the seventeenth and eighteenth centuries had by the end of the nineteenth broadened their scope by relaxing one or more of their membership requirements. A common way of doing this was to expand catchment area; for example, the Ling-nan hui-kuan, which in the K'ang-hsi period had represented only four counties of Kuang-chou prefecture, subsequently came to represent all of Kwangtung. This breakdown of narrow local ties (abetted no doubt by the foreignness of the host city to men from such distant regions of China) accords with the trend toward deparochialization noted above.

A second way of relaxing membership criteria cannot be explained in this fashion. It involved opening groups formerly based on common trade and common origin to merchants of other trades but not to those of other local origins, thus retaining the parochial basis of group solidarity while abandoning the occupational specificity. The Tan-Huai hui-kuan, for example, originally represented only straw-hat dealers from four Honan and Hopeh counties but later came to admit any merchants hailing from these areas. This sort of expansion is probably best explained by the movement of the merchants in the original group into other commodities of exchange—for the Tan-Huai merchants, into the trade in imported opium.

A final way of relaxing membership criteria combined both of the above types; that is, a group based on common trade and common origin with a narrowly defined catchment area would successively or simultaneously drop barriers to membership for men of other trades and for natives of contiguous home areas. The Kiangsu *hui-kuan* of Hankow, for example, was originally set up in the K'ang-hsi period as the organ of red-paper dealers from a single county but eventually came to represent all Kiangsu natives, in whatever trade.

The second and third ways of relaxing admissions represent a form of deparochialization inasmuch as they constituted a breakdown of the most narrow local sentiment as an organizational rationale. They do not, however, support the view that local origin per se could not survive as an organizational principle.

The Formation of Multiplex Trade Organizations. Multiplex guild structures, in which a parent organization incorporated several more specialized components, were formed with increasing frequency in Ch'ing Hankow. Often smaller units based on both common trade and local origin banded together to manage the trade in a given commodity. The resulting organization was usually known as the "——— trade *kung-so.*" Two alternatives were open to smaller groups founding a larger trade association along these lines. They might merge into the larger group, thereby formally dispensing with their individual group identities; the result would be not a true multiplex group but rather an integrated trade organization with no residual local-origin restrictions. This pattern, apparently, was followed in the 1678 founding of the Rice

TABLE 16

Multiplex Common-Trade Guilds Founded in Hankow, 1796–1889

Organization	Date of founding
Peking-Goods Guild (Ching-huo kung-so)	1858
Noodle Dealers' Guild (Mien-pang kung-so)	1862
Grain Dealers' Guild (Liang-hang kung-so)	1862–74
Paper Dealers' Guild (Chih-yeh kung-so)	1868
Native Bankers' Guild (Ch'ien-yeh kung-so)	1871
Leather Goods Guild (P'i-huo kung-so)	1877
Oil Dealers' Guild (Yu-yeh kung-so)	1878
Woolens Dealers' Guild (Chien-jung kung-so)	1887
Salt Guild (Yün-shang kung-so)	1889
Tea Guild (Ch'a-yeh kung-so)	1889

SOURCE: *1920 HC*, 5.27–30.

Market Guild.[71] More commonly, the component groups simply federated into a larger organization while retaining individual integrity. Arguably such multiplex organizations retained a parochial character inasmuch as they represented a confederation of local-origin guilds; in practice, however, I believe that once the collective *kung-so* had been established, local-origin restrictions became increasingly vestigial. We have seen, for instance, that the Hankow Financial Guild, which was initially formed by three local-origin bankers' *pang*, soon afterwards allowed (or perhaps even demanded) the assimilation of a fourth provincial bankers' group. Similarly the Hankow Tea Guild, set up by six provincial tea guilds, seems to have included natives of at least eight provinces even while it continued to be known informally as the "Six Guilds."[72] The formation of trade-wide *kung-so* by merger and by federation therefore seems to have yielded roughly similar results.

The composite *kung-so* designed to regulate all aspects of a single trade in the city made its first appearance quite early in Hankow, with the seventeenth-century Rice Market Guild and perhaps one or two similar organizations. Nevertheless, only after the final recapture of the city from the Taipings and the subsequent reconstruction of regional trade did the single-trade *kung-so* become the prevalent form of local commercial organization. The pioneer effort in this period seems to have been the Ching-huo kung-so, an 1858 organization established, we are told, through "contributions of the various guilds dealing in Peking handicrafts throughout Hankow."[73] The founding of similar organizations to govern other trades followed in rapid succession (see Table 16). A dozen or so like organizations for which founding dates cannot be ascertained, such as the Gauze Dealers' Guild (Sha-yeh kung-so), Cotton

Dealers' Guild (Pu-yeh kung-so), Copper Dealers' Guild (T'ung-yeh kung-so) and Lime Dealers' Guild (Shih-kao kung-so) do not appear in the table but were probably also set up during this era.[74]

We can see, therefore, that not only was a new institutional form gaining dominance in these years, but guild nomenclature was being standardized, replacing the previous plethora of titles. Not only did the post-Taiping trend toward single-trade, multiplex guilds begin before the opening of Hankow as a treaty port, but most of the early guilds of this type dealt in products (e.g., Peking goods, noodles, grain, and paper) for which there was never an overseas market. They represented a wholly indigenous innovation, which, like the trend in new guild foundings, can justly be interpreted as a movement away from reliance on parochial ties.

The Formation of Multiplex Local-Origin Organizations. A simultaneous but very different movement, however, confounds a simple "rationalization" model of organizational evolution in Hankow: this was the trend toward large multiplex *hui-kuan* united by local origin alone. Although organizations of this type had existed in Hankow much earlier, increasing numbers were formed in the second half of the nineteenth century.

Most often, multiplex *hui-kuan* were formed when local-origin guilds representing smaller geographic units within the same home province or region federated into a larger organization representing the province or region as a whole. One example was the Shansi-Shensi club, which had a long history in pre-Taiping Hankow, but had been disbanded during the rebel occupation. In the reconstruction years, former component *pang* had reestablished themselves independently in the city, and only in the 1880's did they resolve to refederate on their former model. The result was a guild of broader scope and greater size than its predecessor.[75] Some other provincial or regional groups that, unlike the Shansi and Shensi men, had no earlier history of organizational unity also federated at Hankow. The long-standing guilds of Hui-chou and T'ai-p'ing prefectures, for example, in the late nineteenth century combined to establish an all-Anhwei provincial *hui-kuan*. The Ningpo guild absorbed the Nanking contingent and then federated with the Shaohsing guild to form the Ning-Shao *hui-kuan*. Likewise, due to their "relationship having become extremely close," the Fukien and Kiangsi *hui-kuan* joined in setting up a multiplex organ to represent both provinces.[76] By the last years of the Ch'ing, a local commentator reported that local-origin representation at Hankow had become almost exclusively the domain of ten or so regional-level organizations, which had gradually subsumed the once-numerous smaller groups (*hsiao t'uan-t'i*).[77]

The direction and the timing of this trend both raise questions and suggest generalizations about the nature of Hankow society. For example, in his classic study of Chungking, Tou Chi-liang found that the more common pattern giving rise to large multiplex *hui-kuan* was the reverse of that in Hankow: a provincial-level club would be set up first, and only gradually would it become internally differentiated into component *pang* with more restrictive catchment areas.[78] The difference between Chungking and Hankow in this regard may have been a function of the nature of immigration to the two cities. In Chungking, where broad waves of migration were the principal cause of population growth, old provincial identities may have provided the earliest bond in organization building, and only thereafter did smaller geographic units become sufficiently well represented to support individual component guilds of their own. In contrast, at Hankow, where most non-native subethnic groups were not migrants but bands of sojourning merchants or tradesmen, identification with a local production area or marketing system probably preceded broader provincial ties.

The Chinese historian Tu Li, studying Shanghai guilds of 1736–1839, notes a process of internal differentiation (*fen-hua*) in larger provincial clubs analogous to that found in Chungking by Tou Chi-liang. He associates this with a movement toward division of labor (*fen-kung*), which he adduces as evidence of protocapitalist trends in pre–Opium War Chinese society.[79] Negishi Tadashi, on the other hand, found the general trend in Shanghai to lie in the opposite direction—smaller *pang* federated into larger multiplex groups, as at Hankow.[80] However, Negishi's evidence is drawn largely from the post-Taiping period. This allows a possible reconciliation with Tu Li's findings, which would posit a trend toward internal differentiation or even fragmentation of previously undifferentiated groups in the late eighteenth century and early in the nineteenth, followed by the reverse process of merger and federation—a general strengthening of collective ties—after the 1850's. Tu Li himself seems to suggest the possibility of such a two-stage process by identifying the trend toward differentiation as a "special characteristic" of the period he is studying. The two-stage model for Shanghai could also apply to Hankow, where the trend toward federation into large, multiplex *hui-kuan* was likewise especially pronounced in the post-Taiping decades.

Why was this so? On the basis of his study of Shanghai, Negishi suggests that the post-Taiping trend toward formation of provincial-level clubs was related to the overall late Ch'ing promotion of the province as a unit of identity and loyalty at the expense of smaller units and of the empire as a whole.[81] This may to some degree be true of Hankow, yet it cannot explain the overall trend. Such amalgamations as those of merchants from Shansi and Shensi, or from Fukien and Kiangsi, seem to have been determined not by the administrative unit of the province, but by trade flows. As I will suggest shortly, therefore, the post-Taiping trend toward federation into larger local-origin organizations—simultaneous with that toward federation into larger trade organizations—may best be traced to factors specific to the local urban society.

Structural Change and Organizational Growth

There were four major trends in structural change within Hankow economic organizations during the nineteenth century: (1) common trade tended to replace local origin as the favored membership criterion in newly founded guilds; (2) membership criteria were relaxed in existing guilds, along lines both of local origin and of trade; (3) federation into multiplex trade organizations occurred with increasing frequency; and (4) federation into multiplex local-origin organizations likewise became more frequent. Taken together, these trends suggest several general conclusions about the direction of change in Hankow commercial society.

First, a process of deparochialization was clearly underway. Even where common trade did not directly replace local origin as the determinant of guild constituency, often a more narrowly defined local catchment area gave way to a broader one. To some extent, this provides evidence of an indigenous process of "rationalization"—progress along a path Weber identified within the European past but denied in China. The earlier conduct of business in Hankow was not in any real sense "irrational," nor had the activities of Chinese businessmen ever been oriented toward anything other than the deliberate maximization of their opportunities for profit; but the displacement of local origin by common trade as a criterion for guild membership clearly derived from the utilitarian concerns of the marketplace. The accumulated experience of Chinese interregional traders, which resulted in such refinements as increased cooperation among merchant groups following the same trade routes, clearly recommended to businessmen the virtues of trade-wide organization. Formation of such groups was also aided, of course, by prolonged residence in the host city. As we have seen in the preceding chapter, this residence regularly led to a more pragmatic view of native place and an easing of parochial attachments.

Second, ascriptive ties (in this case those of local origin) retained their utility within this atmosphere of general organizational rationalization. Parallels in other cultures, where social scientists have noted the utility of such ties in "social mobilization" (as conceived by Karl Deutsch) can perhaps explain this apparent paradox.[82] Particularly useful is the work of Lloyd and Suzanne Rudolph on the role played by caste associations in nineteenth- and twentieth-century India.[83] These caste associations, I would suggest, were a rough functional equivalent of the local-origin associations in nineteenth-century Hankow. Both could be defined as "semi-ascriptive" organizations, inasmuch as both were voluntary associations that were based upon ascribed personal characteristics. Both represented a fairly wide segment of the society, integrated their members into the larger sociopolitical process, articulated interests vis-à-vis similar groups and the state, and were an effective instrument of independent community action.

Third, underlying all four trends was a basic tendency toward organizational growth. Whether such growth was accomplished by discarding local-origin ties or by deliberately utilizing them, I would argue that it was a "rational" goal adopted in the members' personal and financial interests on the basis of their accumulated experience in the late imperial marketplace. Moreover, whether this growth resulted from expanding existing group boundaries or federating with other related groups, it reflected the erosion of the narrowest parochial ties under the influence of shared experience in the cosmopolitan host city. Again the Indian caste associations provide a parallel in their tendency to federate into organizations such as the "Mukkulator," analyzed by the Rudolphs:

> The bases of Mukkulator social and political identity remain ascriptive social and cultural communities within specific geographical locations, but just as the caste association attenuated the importance of these factors by upgrading and extending the *jati* [informal ascriptive caste groups, analogous to the Chinese local-origin *pang*], so the federation of caste associations has further attenuated their importance by the addition of choice. . . . By further blurring the distinction between natural and voluntary association and ascription and choice, the caste federation seems to break down the dichotomy between tradition and modernity.[84]

On the basis of available research on a wide range of cultures, Melson and Wolpe formulate as a general postulate that: "In an atmosphere of social mobilization . . . communal groups will tend to fuse or expand their traditional boundaries to include groups and individuals with whom they can identify and who might prove useful allies. . . . Accompanying communal fusion and expansion is the deparochialization of traditional group ties and perspectives."[85] The expansion of Hankow guilds in the latter part of the Ch'ing supports this thesis. Guilds discovered such "useful allies" in neighboring groups with whom they shared a trade, a native place within a common higher-level administrative unit or economic region, or a trade route. In Chapter 9 we shall observe a further process of expansion and alliance, based solely upon shared presence in the host locality—perhaps the ultimate compromise of sojourner mentality and ascribed native-place ties. The entire process of expansion represented a gradual shift from an exclusive organizational orientation to an inclusive one.

The Timing of Structural Innovations

Although some of the trends we have observed were more gradual (notably the displacement of local origin by trade as a membership requirement in newly founded guilds), true to Stinchcombe's prediction, both the number of guild foundings and the major innovations in guild structure tended to concentrate in spurts. The first came in the several decades following the Ch'ing conquest, when many of the venerable Hankow guilds got their start. The second and more pronounced occurred in the second half of the nineteenth century. What stimulated this second period of innovation and growth?

I have already suggested that the concept of social mobilization can describe this period in local history. In applying the term, however, we must strip from it certain of the connotations it sometimes carries. The social mobilization underway in Hankow between about 1855 and 1889 was not primarily of the Western-imitative, "developmental" sort. Rather, it resulted from a combination of the general social energies unleashed when the Taiping Rebellion disrupted the norms and restrictions that had long guided local social and commercial behavior, and a movement directed both to reconstruct the social fabric and to harness or control those very energies. The process of social mobilization at work after 1890 unquestionably did embody some elements that might be described as "catch-up modernization"; however, these must be seen, not as initiating this mobilization, but rather as joining and to some degree deflecting a process that had been underway for some time.

In the immediate post-Taiping decades, several factors encouraged trade-inclusive organizations and deparochialization in general. One of these was undeniably the advent of direct foreign trade. The desire of all Chinese participants in this trade to present a united front to their Western trading partners was the principal stated reason for the formation of at least one such group—the Hankow Tea Guild.[86] However, confrontation with the West can have been a factor in only a few cases, since Hankow's direct foreign trade during these years remained largely a one-product affair.

A second factor was the inauguration in the late 1850's of Hu Lin-i's revised brokerage regulations. We noted in Chapter 6 that Governor Hu's new system not only called for many more brokers at Hankow (as throughout the province), but also instituted these government-licensed market managers in trades for which they had not previously been required. In most cases, this meant an enforced standardization of weights, measures, and market procedures on a trade-wide basis, where previously local-origin merchant groups had been left to manage their own portion of the trade according to individual custom. Closely related to this expansion of the brokerage system was the state's assignment of collective financial responsibility to the brokers or leading merchants in each trade; an example was the administration's 1867 mandate declaring all Hankow salt brokers "mutually liable for each other's dues and debts."[87] Both enforced standardization and trade-wide mutual liability promoted merchant organization on a comparable basis, transcending local origin. In the salt, timber, and medicinal-herbs trades, the reforms had just this effect.

A third factor was the new willingness of the provincial and local administrations to intervene directly in the marketplace and to impinge upon the guilds' traditional prerogative to manage their own affairs. This willingness no doubt derived in part from the revised tax structure that Hu Lin-i and Kuan-wen had introduced, primarily in order to support a large provincial standing army. As we have seen, this new tax structure relied on commercial sources of revenue more than had been so before the Taiping interregnum. The government had, moreover, developed an unprecedentedly refined and centralized machinery, the Hupeh Bureau, to effectively oversee and coordinate its expanded interests in the marketplace. The new administrative initiative eventually forced Hankow merchants in many trades to regroup into more explicitly trade-regulatory organizations to demonstrate to the administration that the state need not assume so direct a role. Thus the initial attempt by the Hupeh Bureau to set down detailed procedures for the conduct of the export-tea trade, resulting in the "Black Tea Hong" affair, brought about the unification of the six provincial tea *pang* into first an informal, then a formal organization exercising control over the entire trade. Even more strikingly, the local administration's move to control the city's credit market in the early 1870's was the immediate stimulus for the federation of three provincial bankers' *pang* into the 1871 Hankow Financial Guild.

The fourth and most influential factor inspiring the shift to common-trade membership criteria (and prompting state intervention) was the unprecedented level of competition and the resulting disorder in the post-Taiping Hankow marketplace. Breaches of quality control (adulteration and short-weighting) in the tea trade, reckless issuance of credit and assumption of debt in the financial market, and invasion of customarily restricted production areas in the medicine trade all contributed directly to the establishment of inclusive trade-regulatory organizations in the 1870's. For the small producer and the consumer, some aspects of the imposition of trade-wide controls probably proved beneficial and others injurious, but for the Hankow commercial establishment these controls proved almost uniformly a blessing. Their ultimate effects on the urban society were, I would argue, essentially progressive.

This fourth factor, the freewheeling atmosphere of Hankow's post-Taiping society and economy, was also a basic stimulus to organizational growth—along both local-origin and common-trade lines. A pervasive cultural malaise can be detected in Hankow during the last years of the Taiping Rebellion, when the city had been recovered from the rebels but still felt insecure, and in the reconstruction years that followed. Much of the old commercial and social order was felt to be gone, replaced by the crass opportunism associated with a new breed of relatively unsocialized commercial entrepreneurs. A real and acutely felt rise in crime and vagrancy also accompanied the rapid urbanization of these decades. As the Shansi-Shensi Guild stated in the preamble to its newly revised and expanded regulatory code, "In recent times the ways of the world have been declining day by day, and the hearts of men have become increasingly unsteady."[88] The remedy the guild offered for this social and commercial anomie was an enlarged and highly supervised organizational structure. No doubt similar feelings lay behind the rapid increase in guild foundings in these years, many of which, I am convinced, represent associations that predated the rebellion but now felt a new need to formalize their organizational status by acquiring a proper meeting hall (made much more affordable by plummeting urban real estate values after the rebel occupation) and by registering with the local authorities.

Of course, the stimulus for this new spurt of formal-organization building did not come only from a perception of threat. Postrebellion Hankow also provided unprecedented opportunities for groups that could effectively and efficiently mobilize manpower and capital. In market development, real estate management, and the administration of public services (with the access to local power that this entailed), the Taiping occupation had left a vacuum that in Hankow the guilds were best prepared to fill, but which required a streamlining and expansion of organizational structure. As the Shansi-Shensi men stated in discussing their post-Taiping collective financial management, "The hearts of the men from our two provinces are as one; with this unity comes firmness of resolve, and with this resolve comes the ability to persevere for long periods with no slackening in the management of our interests."[89] To comprehend these interests more fully, we turn in the next chapter to a survey of the functions of Hankow guilds.

CHAPTER NINE

Guild Functions

During the Ch'ing, especially in the second half of the nineteenth century, Hankow guilds progressively broadened their institutional horizons by expanding group boundaries and selectively relaxing membership criteria. In the process, their functions gradually diversified and multiplied. We turn in this chapter to the roles guilds played in four major areas, which were of course neither discrete nor necessarily exhaustive of all guild activities: (1) cultural functions, such as worship and sponsorship of theatrical performances, which served to cultivate group consciousness, (2) commercial functions, or regulation of trade and pursuit of members' professional interests in the local marketplace, (3) corporate functions, the financial activities needed to maintain the organization, and (4) community-service functions, including both those provided to guild members alone and those for the urban population as a whole.

Cultural Functions

Historians and social scientists are becoming increasingly aware that "rational" economic ends can be pursued only in real situations and that these situations are infused with priorities, goals, and taboos that are culturally defined. The suggestion that guilds in Ch'ing Hankow were moving toward economic "rationalization" must likewise be tempered by this awareness, especially since in Hankow the group identity of all guilds was bound up with their function as transmitters of a cultural tradition, including its religion and ideology.

In any social milieu, especially one fraught with hazards and uncertainty, religious belief can be a valuable tool in economic association building. Guilds in all cultures have made use of this fact. But whereas in Europe the religious function of guilds was often divorced from the commercial organization per se and vested instead in a roughly overlapping "fraternity" of the faithful,[1] all Hankow guilds to a greater or lesser extent were themselves religious brotherhoods. Before a proper guildhall could be constructed, a guild usually met in one of the town's many temples, and after its completion the guildhall might be known by some title (*miao*, *tien*, or *yen*) usually reserved for religious sanctuaries. The gods enshrined there were often associated with the guild's home area. Shansi-Shensi merchants, for example, set up temples for the worship of Kuan Yü (the Three Kingdoms hero, who was the special patron of men from the northwest) wherever they sojourned;[2] the central building of their Hankow guildhall compound was thus the "Temple to Lord Kuan." Patron deities often fit into the same hierarchical nesting arrangement as did ethnic identities and guild structure. The large, multiplex Kwangtung provincial club, for example, convened in the central sanctuary (*miao*) of its compound in order to worship the provincial benefactor, after which the four county-based *pang* that made up the larger club would disperse to side chapels (*t'ang*) to worship each county's local patron.[3] There was a similar arrangement in the even larger multiplex Shansi-Shensi Guild (as is reflected in the guildhall's floor plan, Figure 2).

Not only guilds based upon local-origin ties had this religious function. Each trade, even when carried on by men from various parts of the empire, had its proper patron deity or deities, and trade-wide incense-burning societies were convened to propitiate these deities at the start of each trading session.[4] The Coal Boatmen's Guild, for example, could take as its central stated purpose securing the protection and favor of the trade's private gods.[5]

Ritual observances were an important part of guild activities. In addition to regular worship, most guilds held large sacrifices in the spring and autumn of the year. (The cost of these ceremonies comprised a major percentage of an organization's annual operating expenses.) Guild regulatory codes suggest that these events were treated with great seriousness and devotion. The Shansi-Shensi Guild, for example, had rules providing for the ritual cleaning and purification of its entire precincts before the semiannual observance, for the proper maintenance of priestly vestments, and for the procurement and storage of incense and other items; the Hui-chou club devoted a lengthy chapter of its organizational history to the proper conduct of these rituals.[6] Not only did ritual and worship serve to help integrate a guild, but they seem to have satisfied the spiritual needs of individual guild members. As Weber's analysis of the Protestant ethic makes clear, worldly pragmatism does not preclude genuine religious faith, and the two may even reinforce each other. In this respect, the empire-wide trade diasporas of groups like the Shansi-Shensi or Hui-chou merchants may have been roughly analogous to those of Jewish merchants in Europe, Gujarati merchants on the Indian subcontinent, and Islamic merchants in sub-Saharan Africa; in each case the hazards and travails of commerce probably strengthened rather than eroded belief in a patron deity.[7]

Inasmuch as group identity was closely bound up with worship of a specific patron, conspicuous devotion to that deity was a form of self-assertion. This in part underlay competition in the splendor of guild headquarters, especially in central halls of worship. In the stone tablet commemorating the construction of its Kuan Yü temple, for instance, the Shansi-Shensi Guild noted that the temple's magnificence was intended to display the superior power of the guild's divine patron to merchant groups from other parts of the empire.[8] Public displays like the "lantern festival" (*teng-hui*) financed by the Hunan Timber Guild on Parrot Island in 1876 likewise combined faith and self-proclamation. Since business in the timber trade had tripled in the preceding several years, the guild decided to sponsor this street festival to "thank the gods and entertain the local populace." People from the entire Wuhan area thronged to participate in the singing and dancing and to witness the spectacular five- by sixty-foot dragon-shaped lantern constructed by the Hunanese merchants.[9] A similar event was sponsored by the flourishing Kwangtung Guild two years later, when more than five hundred members contributed funds for a special observance of the mid-autumn festival open to all residents of the city.[10]

Earlier writers have often noted that such festivals represented a public "burning off" of profits potentially viewed as excessive, but clearly both a genuine need for religious propitiation and ethnic or occupational identity were also at work. Guilds throughout China regularly put on public performances of operas or plays with particular significance for the patron deities of their home areas or trades, and all of the more famous Hankow guildhalls had a prominent central theatrical stage (see Figure 2). Performances also served to celebrate particular guild achievements. As we have seen, the thriving Tea Guild opened its newly completed guildhall in 1889 with a series of stately dramatic performances to which local Chinese and foreign notables were ceremoniously invited.[11] In contrast, after twenty years of construction, the Shansi-Shensi complex opened with a great public theatrical event that drew mobs of people from all social strata. The crowd was packed like sardines into the spacious courtyards of the guildhall, and many were injured in the chaotic shoving that ensued.[12]

Less often, guilds embraced an ethical ideology rather than a devotional one. The Hui-chou club, perhaps the best example, included in its

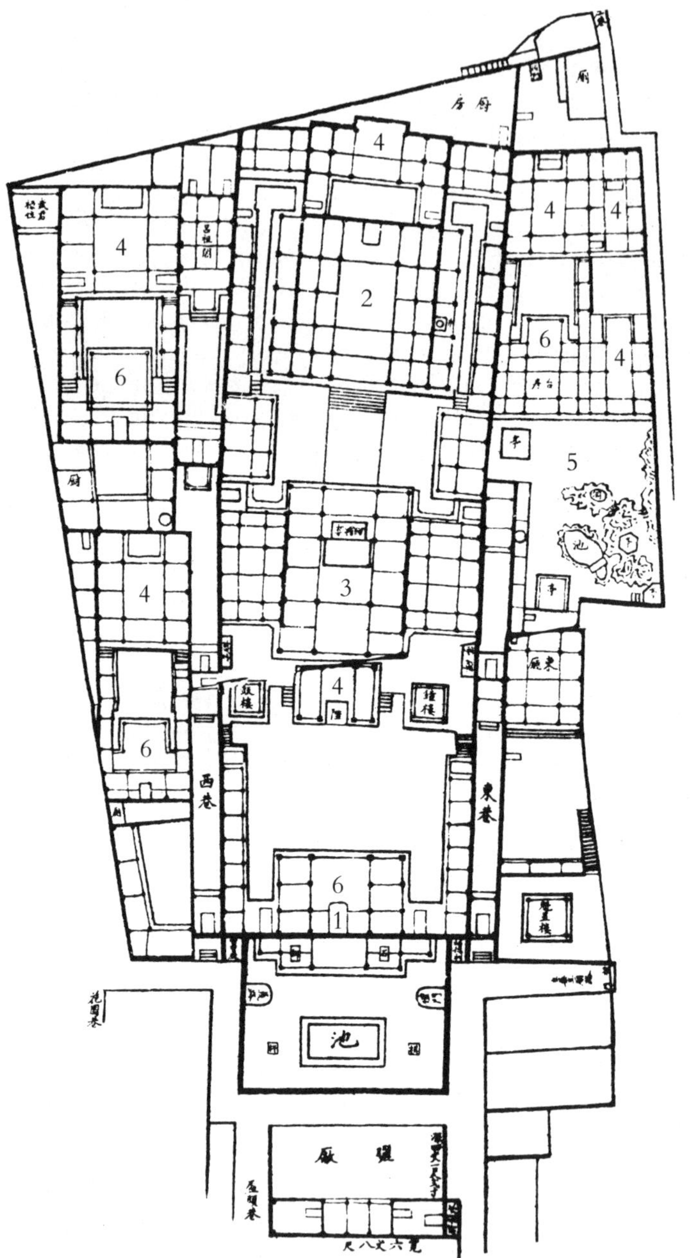

Fig. 2 Floor plan of the Shansi-Shensi Guildhall complex, ca. 1889. (Source: *SSHK*.)

1. Main gate.
2. Spring and Autumn Hall.
3. Temple to Kuan Yü.
4. Subordinate temples.
5. Pleasure garden.
6. Theatrical stages.

guild history a chapter tracing the *tao-t'ung* (transmission of the True Way) from Confucius through Hui-chou's local cultural hero Chu Hsi down to the guild itself.[13] This pedigree reinforced group identity and gave Hui-chou men a sense of superiority to other merchants in the city. As the guild proclaimed, "Many of the famous places of the north and south, and along the Yangtze and the Han, have established guildhalls here, but only we Hsin-an men have given ours the title *shu-yüan* [academy]. This is because of the great importance we attach to the fact that our native place was the home of Chu Hsi."[14] In subsequent years, this strategy was imitated by several other groups, including not only the Shaohsing club (which named its guildhall after Chu Hsi's chief rival in the Neo-Confucian pantheon, Wang Yang-ming) but also such strictly trade-based groups as the grain dealers, who dubbed their guildhall the Ling-hsiao shu-yüan—the Preeminent Academy.[15]

Schools were an integral part of many guild organizations, serving to prepare the sons of sojourning merchants (who were unable because of local registration quotas to gain entry into the county school) for the state civil service examinations. The Hui-chou Guild gazetteer, for example, included a full chapter on academy operations.[16] We will have more to say on educational functions in discussing the guilds' role in community service; here we need only note the ideological focus and moral facade such schools gave the overall guild establishment, for in late imperial China education was in itself an important ethical good. For the same reason, the Hui-chou Guild compound also contained a prominent formal lecture hall (*chiang-t'ang*), within which member merchants would periodically assemble to hear explications of the Tao.[17] Yet neither the regulatory code of the Hui-chou Guild nor that of any other trade or local-origin organization in the city contained a single injunction governing the personal moral conduct of its members, beyond the pragmatically derived and contextually defined rules of trade.

These strands of religiosity, gentry pretensions, and self-conscious celebration of native place were nowhere better illustrated than in the layout of the nineteenth-century Kiangsi Guildhall. The compound, one of the most splendid in Hankow, housed three major temples, all covered in glittering ceramic tile imported from the home province. Within the central courtyard stood a pavilion dominated by an ornate lantern, where guildsmen in leisure hours could sip tea and compose poetry. The pavilion was flanked by two goldfish ponds, each lined with precious weathered rocks from the bed of Soochow's Lake T'ai. In the rear of the compound stood a Buddhist treasure hall, housing paintings and calligraphy by a famous priest from the Ch'an monastery atop

Kiangsi's Mount Liang. The main gates of the inner and outer compounds were surmounted by two large opera stages.[18]

Merchant groups' stance as the self-proclaimed guardians of a cultural tradition while engaging in a profession regularly if not uniformly disparaged by that tradition demanded of many a self-conscious apologia. The Hui-chou men, for example, protested that commerce was far from their preferred calling, but that, given the scarcity of arable land in their home area, what choice had they but to accept this baser means of livelihood?[19] A similar, long-standing alibi formed part of the mythos of Shansi merchants wherever they sojourned.[20] This uneasy self-consciousness seems to have been fading, however, over the course of the nineteenth century, particularly in the post-Taiping years. Significantly, in the second half of the century multiplex, occupationally based guild organizations increasingly preferred the secular, matter-of-fact title *kung-so* (public office) to such ideologically inspired names as "academy" or "temple." Perhaps a moralistic cloak to smooth relations between outside capitalists and lower-class local natives was felt to be less necessary in the more hybrid city of post-Taiping years; certainly there was a general trend toward the secularization of local commerce and society at that time, and more-Confucianized groups (from Hui-chou, Kiangsi, and Shansi) were being displaced by less-Confucianized commercial forces (from Ningpo and Kwangtung).[21]

I would not argue that the process of secularization or that of deparochialization in general was ever complete in the late imperial period; for example, the late-founded, non–ethnic-restrictive Salt Guild of the 1880's chose to meet (and presumably to worship) in a temple while awaiting the construction of its own guildhall. In general, a complex web of cultural assumptions underlay the regulations, organizational behavior, and business conduct of the entire spectrum of commercial guilds. Yet a certain liberalization of these assumptions does seem to have taken place in the post-Taiping years, paralleling the structural changes we have already observed. This is best suggested, perhaps, by the Tea Guild's willingness to select a Western merchant as its "impartial arbitrator"—making him in effect an officer of the guild, although not formally a guild member. A selection process based on such pragmatic, universalist criteria would probably not have been possible in an earlier period.

Commercial Functions

The collective supervision and fostering of commerce was the principal rationale of virtually all formal guild organizations in Hankow, and a guild's most basic purpose was to integrate its members' business interests. If the guild was not occupationally homogeneous, this might entail promoting guild members' professional use of each other's services, for example, by bringing together native bankers and potential clients who shared a local-origin tie. Guild leaders were always available to mediate contractual dealings and to resolve commercial conflicts between members.[22] Similarly, they mediated dealings between member businesses and members of other guilds. (Deals that involved cooperation in the pursuit of mutual profit might be sealed by a theatrical performance commissioned jointly by the two guilds.)[23] Leaders of two guilds might also confer to resolve conflicts between individual members of their clubs, as when officials of two *hui-kuan* met to resolve disputes between boatmen over anchorage rights.[24]

Guilds also provided facilities to be used in the course of members' commercial undertakings. Most offered dormitory accommodations for itinerant merchants of their home area or trade, and sometimes the guilds themselves were the offspring of local-origin or trade-restrictive hostels. Many larger establishments, like the T'ai-p'ing Guildhall, also served as warehouses or stockyards for members' goods.[25] The pooled capital of guilds was used to acquire commercial waterfront properties. Piers were constructed not only by the largest and wealthiest guilds but also by smaller groups engaged in river transport, such as the boatmen's guild of P'ing-hsiang and Li-ling counties on the Kiangsi-Hunan border.[26] In fact, the construction and collective ownership of piers often seems to have been the chief impetus for guild establishment. Guilds were thus an important vehicle for capital accumulation. The most basic application of these funds was to finance facilities for commercial purposes, but, as we shall see, such facilities were not the only guild investments.

Guilds rather than the local or central administration were the basic instruments for regulating commerce. The establishment and maintenance of standard weights and measures, for example, was the recognized purview of the individual guild governing trade in each commodity; as early as 1678 the Rice Market Guild announced that "when any colleague acts as a wholesale rice broker for an itinerant merchant in the transaction of his business, the weights and measures employed in the transaction must first be submitted to the guild for approval, rather than adopted on an individual basis."[27] The administration encouraged and supported the guilds' initiatives, and in some cases (like the Financial Guild's establishment of the local silver standard and bimetal exchange rate) these activities were viewed as semigovernmental.[28]

Guilds specified procedures for their members in the recruitment and training of employees and in the conduct of business. As late as the turn of the twentieth century the local Japanese consul, describing procedures for commercial transactions, remarked that Hankow possessed no set codes of business conduct other than those independently established by individual guilds.[29] Guilds determined the opening and close of the annual trading season, the size of each shop or firm, sales and delivery procedures, means of contractual documentation, and related matters.[30] The Tea Guild's ultimately successful attempt to lay down the rules for conduct of the Sino-foreign export trade at the port was thus merely an extension of established guild prerogative.

Since most guilds were considered constructive forces for upholding the social order, local authorities actively supported both their internal regulation and their arbitration (*tu-t'ung*) of commercial disputes between members and outsiders.[31] Yet this atmosphere of cooperation did not preclude tensions and disputes between guild and administration. On the one hand, we have seen how guilds could function as pressure groups to wrest specific concessions from the state; on the other, the authorities could take action against guilds that they felt were not fulfilling their social obligations, specifically by acting in overt restraint of trade.

Local officials were wary of two basic forms of guild monopolization: tampering with the market price and too narrowly restricting admission to the trade. The administration, committed to maintaining the highest possible level of commodity circulation, sought in general to guarantee that the fluctuating market price (*shih-chia*) remained free from manipulation. Although guilds quite naturally were interested in commanding the highest possible price for their merchandise, the concerns of guild and administration did not necessarily conflict on this score, because the administration recognized the need of some level of price controls to provide market stability, hence the basis for a socially responsible guild. A guild could bolster prices indirectly, as the Tea Guild did in 1887 by resolving not to sell second-crop teas. A more direct tactic was to reduce competition by enforcing sequential priority. This practice allowed a floating market price to be determined by bargaining between a single buyer and a single seller, but denied the buyer the option of accepting a lower offer by a competitive seller. Many guilds enforced such a sequential system, and the administration not only approved the practice but imitated it in the Hankow salt market.[32] Guilds that did not see a need for such elaborate market controls simply specified, as the bronzeware dealers did in 1879, that members should not undercut other members in the process of bargaining with a buyer.[33] Only rarely did a guild set a minimum price, as the tung-oil dealers did in 1880. This bold step could be undertaken only with special permission from the local administration, which was granted only under exceptional circumstances.[34]

Most Hankow guilds were willing and even anxious to admit all candidates who satisfied their occupational or local-origin requirements for membership. In fact, most demanded that all new arrivals join the guild, as is seen in the Kiangsi Guild's regulation that: "Whoever [among potentially qualified members] newly arrives in Hankow to do business must join the guild within one year. If he delays one month [over this time] action will be taken against him by the guild."[35] Although guilds sometimes sought to discourage excessive competition by charging higher membership fees to later arrivals than to charter members,[36] most were more concerned to encompass all prospective tradesmen than to restrict the trade to given individuals. In terms of membership, then, they were "protectionist" rather than "monopolistic." On the other hand, guilds were actively concerned with keeping control of the trade firmly in their own hands. For example, the Bronzeware Guild insisted in its 1879 regulations that bronze pipes in Hankow be produced and sold only in shops belonging to and designated by the guild, and the Scalemakers' Guild stipulated that member artisans were not to practice their trade at any site not specifically authorized by the organization.[37]

Local authorities generally approved of this restrictiveness. The limits of their approval, however, are demonstrated by an incident reported in *Shen-pao* in January 1880.[38] The article reports the attempt of the professional itinerant fish peddlers of Hankow to form a guildlike "trade combine" (*ch'i-hang*), headquartered in the T'ao-sheng Temple in a back alley of the town. The peddlers collected money from among themselves and held a two-day feast, highlighted by theatrical performances in honor of their patron, the God of the Underworld. They drew up a code of regulations, one of which called for the maintenance of a register (*pu-chi*) of all fishmongers authorized by the combine. The guild was not exclusionist; in order to register, an individual was required only to pledge to respect the agreed-upon regulations and to pay the modest (but not insignificant) fee of five strings of cash to the common treasury. However, all unregistered individuals would thereafter be prohibited from bringing fish to peddle in Hankow markets. Because these rules and procedures closely resembled those adopted by many other guilds of the city, the group no doubt anticipated support from the local authorities for their actions. The officials, however, took a broader perspective. In the winter agricultural slack season, many suburban "poor people with nowhere to turn" (*wu-k'ao ch'iung-min*) depended for their subsistence upon occasionally bringing fish into the city markets to sell. The attempt of the fulltime fishmongers to deprive them of this recourse would thus not only increase the misery of the surrounding countryside, but might also spark fighting in the volatile urban marketplaces. Accordingly the authorities, although expressing apparently genuine regrets at having to interfere, could not allow the guild's prohibition of the sale of fish by nonregistrants. They did not, however, dissolve the fledgling guild or void its other regulations and procedures.

The state's paternalist policy in regard to restraint of trade thus involved a trade-off familiar from other contexts.[39] Increased guild restrictiveness meant both a lesser need for the administration to directly regulate the marketplace (a function that in the later imperial period it was no longer inclined or able to perform) and a greater potential for enforcing the collective responsibility of leaders within the trade. On the other hand, greater guild power and restrictiveness could antagonize those excluded from the trade, inhibit the necessary (and taxable) flow of goods, and endanger the freely floating market price, upon which the authorities based their hope of ensuring adequate supplies of goods for the consumer and adequate employment for those involved in production and distribution. Guilds and officials thus arrived at a mutual accommodation, which was defined with precision only in specific situations, such as that presented by the fish peddlers in 1880.

Although guild restrictions on open competition were increasingly articulated in the post-Taiping years, these were neither a new development nor (despite the suspicions of Western merchants)[40] one directed specifically against the foreigner. Although it is probably true, as Ch'üan Han-sheng has argued, that many Chinese guilds did tend in the last quarter of the nineteenth century to devote more energy to combating the economic challenge of the West,[41] in Hankow the direct target of increased guild controls was rather the perceived rise in irresponsible business conduct, which jeopardized both quality control and market order. The cause of this rise (in the contemporary view, as well as my own) was not the arrival of the West per se, but more generally the anomistic tendencies of post-Taiping commercial society, to which the advent of the Western trade was but a single contributing factor.

In an influential study based in part on data from Hankow, the Chinese historian P'eng Tse-i reached similar conclusions regarding the causes for the reinvigoration of post-Taiping guilds. In the process, however, P'eng draws inferences that run counter to those of the present study. For P'eng, guilds were "traditional monopolistic instruments of feudal government control" over trade and the economy. The reassertion of imperial control in the post-Taiping period, he argued, led to the large-scale refounding of guilds and a steady growth in their aggregate power. At the same time, the revival and marked growth of trade in these years led to increasing competition, which the guild system attempted with some success to stifle. In addition to generally increased competitiveness, in P'eng's view guilds faced two more specific obstacles: (1) the introduction of Western ideas of "free trade," and (2) the rise of an indigenous Chinese capitalism. According to P'eng, Chinese guilds were fundamentally at odds with this burgeoning capitalism; they remained essentially a force for the assertion of commercial controls, and thus as Chinese society evolved from feudalism to capitalism and semicolonialism, they became merely an urban "feudal remnant," although for many years one of real power.[42]

P'eng's characterization of Chinese guilds as "feudal" (a view implicitly shared by Weber and Western developmental theorists) seems an inappropriate dismissal, at least for our period. Hankow guilds were neither anticapitalist nor overly monopolistic; furthermore, our discussion of the 1883 tea boycott has revealed that to view them as fundamentally opposed to the Western notion of "free trade" misses the basic point of this confrontation.

Chinese writers, and Western writers influenced by them, have seen the reactionary or "feudal" nature of late Ch'ing guilds as most evident in their confrontation with the newly emerging, more "capitalist" Chambers of Commerce.[43] On the other hand, Japanese scholars, including Imahori and others with a cynical view of late Ch'ing commerce, have seen the organizational innovations of the early twentieth century as a direct outcome of the guilds' own development.[44] Our study of Hankow guilds before 1890 seems to support the latter view. If it is hard to visualize Confucianized commercial elites such as those dominating the Hui-chou Guild as spearheading the foundation of such westernized groups as the Hankow Municipal Chamber of Commerce, it is far less difficult to see the continuity of twentieth-century groups with the more cosmopolitan, innovative, and financially sophisticated merchants of Canton and Ningpo, who by the 1860's had begun to dominate the economy of the port. In the hands of such men, the late imperial guild proved a remarkably adaptable organizational vehicle.

Corporate Functions

The corporate activities of trade and local-origin associations in Hankow, originally a peripheral concern to finance relatively small ritual and operational costs, often became in time more and more central to an organization's goal structure as they yielded a substantial body of assets in which guild members became essentially shareholders. I do not here use the term "corporate" with any technical strictness: by "corporate functions," I mean merely to distinguish a sphere of guild activity encompassing the collective financial dealings of a group on its own account, separate from commercial management for its members.[45]

The regulatory code of the Hankow Coal Boatmen's Guild states as that group's major annual expenses "staging the guild's theatrical performances, worshiping our deities, paying the monthly wages of our employees, and performing public charitable acts."[46] This is a fair summary of the operational budget of more humble Hankow guilds; it excludes only the costs of maintaining real property, which increasingly concerned the city's larger groups. Most guilds claimed ritual expenditures, covering routine worship as well as the great semiannual sacrifices with their attendant theatrical productions, as their single largest annual expense.[47] The Hui-chou Guild, for example, recorded that in 1806 it spent over a thousand taels on its spring and autumn sacrifices, which, combined with the additional hundred taels it spent on incense and paper consumed in routine worship, comprised nearly two-thirds of its large annual budget.[48] For the Shansi-Shensi Guild, toward the end of the century ritual costs made up a smaller percentage but were still the largest single item in the operating budget. In both groups, overhead and routine operating costs for guild premises were a considerably smaller chunk. Lantern oil burned to light guildhall precincts took the largest slice—close to one hundred taels for the Hui-chou group. In contrast, almost nothing was required for the salaries of menial workers such as gatekeepers, caretakers, and night watchmen; for example, the seven gatekeepers employed by the Hui-chou Guild received a combined annual salary of less than one tael! In both groups a somewhat larger amount (84 taels for the Hui-chou Guild) paid the salaries of guild-sponsored firefighters and maintained fire-fighting equipment. Finally, although both clubs had spacious premises and owned a good deal of urban land apart from their headquarters, for both the tax paid on all real estate holdings was minuscule. For the Hui-chou guild it totaled less than two taels per annum, or only about 0.1 percent of yearly operating expenses.

The annual budgets recorded by both of these groups exclude two items of expenditure that we know to have concerned them, which must have been accounted separately. One was philanthropic activities, a subject to be treated in the next section. The other was irregular expenses incurred in the construction, purchase, development, and renovation of real estate. The construction projects that took first priority for many groups involved transport facilities, such as the piers, warehouses, and stockyards already noted. However, the greatest construction project of all was the guildhall itself.

Constructing a hall was a project of considerable magnitude and great emotional significance. As we have seen, the decision to construct a permanent meeting place was a major point in the transition from an informal association like a work gang or drinking club to a formal and respected organization. Consequently, the guildhall was designed not only to be functional but also to serve as a monument to the glory of the group. Local-origin guilds competed to make their own hall "the most glittering and beautiful" in the city.[49] Thus the Kiangsi Guildhall had dazzling tile facades and the Shaohsing Hall its celebrated pillars of jade-like polished stone. Typically, the Hui-chou men felt that their guildhall "should surpass all others,"[50] and the Shansi-Shensi group remarked that: "It is said of Hankow that all the provincial temples there compete to be the most resplendent and awesome. Why should the Shansi-Shensi guildhall alone be of modest scale?"[51] Guildhall complexes at times grew to include many structures spread across several blocks of the city. Trade-based groups tended to be somewhat less ostentatious, but the construction of a major guildhall such as those of the salt or tea merchants was also a great undertaking accompanied by much fanfare and festivity.[52]

What sources of revenue were available to Hankow guilds to offset these regular and irregular outlays of funds? Their most basic income was derived from the entrance fee paid by members. The very first regulation drawn up by the early Ch'ing Rice Market Guild stated that "when each colleague enters the guild he must pay an entrance fee of fifteen taels,"[53] and the Kiangsi Guild, reflecting the more modest economic level of its constituents, required that "whoever arrives in Hankow to become a shopkeeper must pay a guild entrance fee of four hundred cash."[54] This income was supplemented by one-time fees, such as the two hundred cash the Kiangsi club assessed its members for opening a branch shop, the five hundred cash it charged for hiring a new apprentice, and the additional five hundred cash assessed for granting that apprentice membership in the guild. The Scalemakers' Guild charged its members a full thousand cash for taking on new employees.[55] The rules of this group also illustrate the fines levied on uncooperative members: one thousand cash was charged for breaking any guild regulation and an equal amount for failing to report a violation by a fellow member.

In addition to these one-time fees and fines, many guilds collected regular monthly or annual dues.[56] Especially in common-trade organizations, the amount of such assessments was likely to be determined by the volume of business transacted by individual members; the Rice

Market Guild, for example, demanded 0.8 percent of its members' annual gross receipts. Sometimes a guild imposed a regular commission on transactions in its commodity rather than awaiting a year-end contribution. The Tea Guild, for instance, levied a charge of 1.6 percent (on large lots) or 0.4–0.5 percent (on smaller lots) on "all teas sold in the Hankow market."[57] Similarly, the Coal Boatmen's Guild stated that: "Anyone transporting coal from the government coal-boat office [*ch'uan-chü*], no matter what sort of boat is used for its transport, must pay a fee of one cash [*wen*] per picul [*tan*, about 133½ lbs.]. . . . Any boat anchoring in the harbor, after reporting to the government office, must register also with this guild in order to verify the number of *tan* it is carrying."[58] These guild assessments, frequently known as "likin" (long before the institution of the tax by that name), were often not part of the guild's standing regulations, but rather were determined by group vote in order to cover the costs of a specific project, usually to capitalize construction. The salt merchants, for example, levied a charge of ten taels per bulk shipment in order to finance the building of their guildhall.[59]

The assets of a *hui-kuan* (less often of trade organizations) were from time to time augmented by voluntary contributions from individual members, either unsolicited or in response to a specific subscription drive. Usually such gifts were in cash, though they occasionally took the form of real property either granted outright or transferred to guild ownership in return for a nominal payment.[60] Most often contributions were requested in connection with a specific building project, although as a cynical visitor to Hankow at mid-century remarked: "When soliciting funds there is no need to have a good reason in order to rake in generous donations. It is because of this that all the guildhalls and temples have become so richly endowed."[61]

If surcharges on members' business transactions and subscription drives for contributions were generally imposed in order to finance guildhall construction, they seem seldom to have been lifted when such construction was complete. A 1906 Maritime Customs report on the Hankow Salt Guild, for example, indicates that the guild's levy of ten taels per shipment, initially imposed in order to cover the costs of guildhall construction, was still in effect almost two decades after the hall had been finished.[62] As collective assets increased, the corporate aspects of the city's more successful guilds became increasingly central to their organizational character. In contrast to early groups like the Rice Market Guild and to smaller groups in the later period for whom levies on members' business primarily underwrote the guild's modest operating expenses, by the nineteenth century the major guilds of Hankow had begun to utilize this revenue-raising device specifically to accumulate capital. Such groups soon could finance their entire annual budget solely out of the interest from their capital investments. Consequently they came to develop detailed procedures for managing guild capital and income.

Guilds made capital investments of two general kinds. One, which seems to have become increasingly popular after the Taiping interregnum, was investment in business enterprises, particularly financial ones. Occasional reports of local authorities forcing guilds to stand behind failing credit institutions (for example, the Shaohsing Guild for pawnshops and the Kwangtung Guild for native banks)[63] suggest that the guilds were major investors in these shops or banks. Later, in 1891 the Tea Guild backed Hankow's first Chinese-owned modern bank—an investment that demonstrates a guild's willingness to invest in profit-making ventures outside its own direct purview.[64] Unfortunately, few materials on this type of investment have survived.

The second and more common type of investment was in real property—outside the guild's own precincts and specifically to generate income. Such real estate could be already developed, developed by the guild, or left undeveloped. Occasionally it could be cultivated land, but the surviving documentation attests that even this was almost always urban. Virtually since their inception, guilds had invested in urban land; however, such investment intensified beginning in the late eighteenth century to become very widespread in the second half of the nineteenth.[65] Thus the guilds, as corporate groups, became increasingly important as urban landlords. Moreover, the remarkable lack of guild investment in rural agricultural land both reinforces the impression of Hankow's detachment from its rural surroundings and casts doubt on general postulations of the extractive role of late imperial cities vis-à-vis their hinterlands. Fortunately, considerable documentation on real estate investment is available; it figures prominently, for example, in the records of the Hui-chou and Shansi-Shensi guilds.

The Tzu-yang Academy (Hui-chou Guild). During the early Ch'ing, the Hui-chou merchant community at Hankow was headquartered and partially lodged at two small temples located in an idyllic suburban setting on the landward side of the city. The prosperity and increasing size of this group in the late K'ang-hsi period urged a greater visibility, however, and in 1694 three leaders of the compatriot association called a meeting of the group's 24 most influential members to deliberate on plans for a grand Chu Hsi academy (and guildhall), to be located in the middle of town and to take as its centerpiece an elaborate meeting hall to be known as the "Respect the Way Lodge." One of these leaders, Wu

Chi-lung, was asked to draft a "Letter to My Compatriots," soliciting contributions for the project. The response, apparently voluntary, provided sufficient funds to cover the cost of the building. Four project managers and 24 associate managers were selected by the fraternity as a whole; the three men who had convened the original meeting were among the former. The group acquired four *mu* of land (slightly more than half an acre) in a downtown area of Hsün-li ward, within a neighborhood already heavily populated by Hui-chou men. Several prominent group members, voluntarily but apparently with some hesitation, sold their houses to the group and moved into temporary quarters elsewhere in order to vacate the proposed guildhall site. The final complex, comprising some one hundred separate chambers and constructed at a cost approaching ten thousand taels, was completed in 1704, eleven years after the plan had originally been conceived. Among its attractions were accommodations for some members and a great ceremonial gate upon which was mounted a stage for theatrical performances. The project was a massive undertaking, which reflected the dominant position of the Hui-chou community in salt and in other leading trades.[66]

In the eighteenth century, the corporate property and assets of the academy grew. The guild built an adjoining West Hall in 1717, a large lecture hall in 1721, a dormitory for transient compatriot merchants in 1743, and several subsidiary chapels in 1775; several times throughout the century it also expanded lodging and library facilities. Although the guild also purchased and developed for collective use property in other sections of town (for example, a small temple on the shores of Back Lake), most of its holdings were in or around the sprawling complex, popularly known as "Hui-chou ward" (Hsin-an fang), which dominated one portion of the city's central district. At some time in the early part of the century, the whole area was enclosed by a wall.

The Hui-chou complex stretched transversely across the city's major traffic arteries, which paralleled the Han River. The guildhall's central hall was north of Chung chieh (Center Street) and faced south toward the Han. Across the street, running southward as far as Hankow's principal thoroughfare, Cheng chieh (Main Street), was a street enclosed at either end by ceremonial gates and joined along the way by several radiating alleys. This street had been built largely by the guild and was lined by its properties, but during daylight hours it was open to the public and constituted one of the most bustling shopping areas of Hankow. Known originally as Hsin-an Alley (*hsiang*), the street soon outgrew this designation and became known as Hsin-an Street (*chieh*), one of the few transverse thoroughfares given this name. In 1775 Hsin-an Street was completely reconstructed by the guild as a "major highway" (*k'ang-*

ch'ü). Across Main Street, Hsin-an Street was again begun by a gate and continued its course south to the riverbank, where in 1734 the guild had constructed one of the major pier complexes in the city, known as Hsin-an ma-t'ou, or Hsin ma-t'ou. Although intended primarily for guild members, the pier was described as a "public wharf" (*i-pu*) and may have been open for general use upon payment of rental and service charges.

In addition to the pier, in these years the Hui-chou men engaged in several other projects deliberately intended for the public good, including a major public road, a school, and a public ferry. (These activities will be discussed more fully in the following section.) The guild had also accumulated many rental properties, the income from which was used to underwrite its continuous building projects. These properties were generally commercial, and although guild members were given preference in renting them, guild membership was apparently not a necessary condition of lease: the primary goal was corporate profit. A document of 1734 describes an example of such rental holdings, a single block containing sixteen shophouses, two kitchens, and a larger hall or warehouse. The guild valued this block at one thousand taels—whereas its annual rent was 360 taels. Thus, even in the early eighteenth century investment in such property seems to have repaid capital outlay in something less than three years, indicating the immense opportunities open to groups that could generate significant capital for investment.[67]

In 1788 the academy and many other holdings were badly damaged by flood. After several attempts at piecemeal repair, a plenary meeting was convened in 1796, and the guild decided to undertake a mammoth reconstruction of the entire complex. Accomplished between 1798 and 1805, this reconstruction affected all parts of the academy, as well as most of the guild's rental holdings. Special attention was lavished on the roads within and around the compound, some of which, it was claimed, were transformed from "winding, twisted, stagnant, muddy, and foul-smelling" puddles into broad, paved thoroughfares. As for the shops that lined these streets, "the bamboo huts of old, which were crowded together like the teeth of a dog, can now be seen to form a straight, even line."[68] Several related projects, like establishing fire-fighting companies and acquiring and clearing a suburban burial site, were accomplished at the same time. The group celebrated the completion of the project in 1806 by publishing its own gazetteer.

How was this undertaking financed and managed? The 1796 plenary meeting of the guild delegated responsibility to one of the current general managers of the organization, Wang Heng-shih, who was to be assisted by 26 specially designated project managers. Almost immediately

Wang ran into problems with the other members. Several expressed doubt that the guild's present capital was sufficient to see such grand plans through to completion. To be forced to give up the project halfway, they argued, would be to dishonor their forebears in the organization. In particular, it seems, they feared that it might eventually be necessary to borrow from outside sources. Wang rebuked them for their timidity and issued a general call for contributions. Two years later the guild decided that a sufficient amount had been collected, and the project was begun. The managers reportedly exercised great care to check the economic feasibility of each step before it was commenced.

The skepticism, however, proved to have been well founded. Shortly after the project was begun, funds had to be diverted to hire a paramilitary defense force when White Lotus rebels threatened the city; moreover, expenses in general tended to exceed initial estimates. By 1804 the project was close to four thousand taels in arrears, and when a related street renovation estimated at a cost of eleven thousand taels was proposed, the guild found itself in need of more than fifteen thousand taels in order to go on building. By this time rental incomes were substantial, but they could not produce so large a sum in short order. Consequently, the guild for the first time voted to levy a "likin" charge on all commercial transactions by member merchants to cover future lacks, and in addition took up a strikingly innovative subscription to supply the fifteen-thousand-tael deficit.

The new subscription was a bond issue floated among the guild's membership. One hundred and fifty bonds (*ch'ou*) were printed up at one hundred taels per bond, to total the fifteen-thousand-tael deficit. These were issued to members, apparently after some arm-twisting, according to the assessed financial capability of each individual. Each bond was to be paid off by the guild over a ten-year period in annual installments of sixteen taels, thus yielding a total interest payment (*tzu-chin*) to the bondholder of 60 taels, or 6 percent per annum. The feasibility of this bond flotation was calculated precisely. At the time of issue the surplus of total rental income over guild operational expenses was averaging between 2,000 and 2,300 taels per year; however, it was anticipated that the income generated by the projects completed via the bond issue would raise the annual surplus to 2,400 taels, the amount required to repay the borrowed capital plus interest (16 taels per bond × 150 bonds = 2,400 taels). Any additional surplus revenue accrued over the ten-year course of repayment, plus all surplus revenue after the repayment had been completed, would be reinvested in property development, with profits to go to the guild's entire membership.[69]

By the beginning of the nineteenth century, the Hui-chou Guild had accumulated a staggering amount of real estate. In order to safeguard the guild's title to these properties, its managers decided to petition the Hanyang prefect:

> Over the years, the Hui-chou scholar-merchant guild has bought up various properties and market buildings. Our managers in yearly succession assume control over the collection of rental fees, which are used to meet the expenses of our spring and autumn sacrifices. Between the seventh year of K'ang-hsi [1668] and the sixtieth year of Ch'ien-lung [1795] we have purchased collective property for which we now hold a total of 67 title deeds [*ch'i-yüeh*]. Our only fear is that in the years to come, since these deeds are so numerous and so frequently passed from one custodian to another, they may be lost or scattered, and we would then have no record upon which to base our claim of ownership.
>
> Thus we have collected these deeds and recorded them in a single register, and we request that you officially seal them and proclaim them, so that they will become a matter of formal public record. Moreover, we beseech you to permit them to be engraved in stone, so that there will be no fear of their becoming lost. Thereupon we guest people will be forever the recipients of your great kindness.[70]

The prefect agreed to this, and ordered that a copy of the register be retained at his yamen as an authoritative source to resolve any future litigation.

Fortunately, the guild's 1806 gazetteer reprints the texts of all 67 deeds, which reveal a great deal not only about the Hui-chou Guild's holdings, but also about the concept of urban property during the Ch'ing.[71] The property that they represent shows clearly the capital-investment potential of large Hankow guilds by the early 1800's. In addition to the various properties the guild occupied and used itself (which involve but 5 of the 67 deeds), the Hui-chou organization rented out: (1) two large blocks along Hsin-an Street, incorporating 36 shophouses; (2) 31 "foundationless [*wu-chi*] properties," including shops and residences constructed of tile, earth, bamboo, and rushes, in the immediate neighborhood of the academy and Hsin-an Street;[72] (3) ten shops on the Hsin-an pier; (4) a large, enclosed market on Hou chieh (Back Street), elsewhere in Hsün-li ward; (5) a large, enclosed market on Main Street, not far from Hsin-an Street; (6) a row of shophouses along Hsiung-chia Alley, in Ta-chih ward; (7) eight additional, extensively developed properties scattered throughout Hankow proper; (8) a large and important block of shophouses and residences across the river in the county seat, Hanyang city; and (9) many smaller holdings, including urban garden plots and some rural paddy fields and wheatfields. Most of these properties had been purchased out of capital funds, and many had been developed by the guild itself as investments. They were managed by specially elected officers of the guild known as *szu-shih* (overseers), who were replaced annually following an audit of their accounts by the guild's general managerial board.[73]

One acquisition-of-title document printed in the gazetteer sheds light on the conduct of land transactions by such groups and provides evidence of cooperation between guilds, a subject to which we shall return. This document is a "Certificate of Exchange" drawn up jointly in 1804 by the Hui-chou Guild and the Che-Ning (Ningpo) Guild:

> It is here recorded: We natives of these two regions, gathered together in Hankow, have both founded *hui-kuan* to worship our former worthies and honor our native-place ties. In its new reconstruction, the Che-Ning Guild is hampered by the narrowness of its site and hence cannot expand to the desired dimensions. Behind the Temple of the Triple Origin lies a vacant property owned by the Hsin-an Academy, upon which the Ningpo Guild might expand. Since no reliable market exists by which to estimate a value so that the land might be purchased, the Ningpo men have decided to request the intercession of a go-between [*chü-chien*], through whom they have approached the Hsin-an Academy about the property. The latter graciously convened for a private deliberation [*meng-i*], at which it agreed to the proposal presented.
>
> The Che-Ning Guild has long owned one residence and one shop in front of the Nanking guildhall. They have further recently acquired from the Cheng family three shops located in Hsün-li ward. By the signing of this contract [*ch'i-chü*], these properties are ceded to the Hsin-an Academy to be used as rental properties, in exchange for which the Hsin-an Academy will cede a portion of the vacant land southwest of the front wall of the Temple of the Triple Origin, four *chang* deep and three *chang* wide [approximately forty by thirty feet] . . . and will transfer it to the Che-Ning Guild. The latter may never expand beyond the temple wall, and the rest of this vacant land remains the property of the Hsin-an Academy.[74]

The document was signed by three Managers of the Che-Ning Guild and four of the Hui-chou Guild, as well as by twelve other members of the two clubs as witnesses. Although the Hui-chou Guild seems to have driven a rather hard bargain, the incident demonstrates that other expansive guilds, like that of Ningpo, engaged in both major reconstruction and real estate investment during this period.

The Hui-chou Guild left a detailed statement of its corporate finances for the year 1806,[75] a statement that reveals the profitability of collective enterprise in a prosperous and growing commercial city. All income listed in this statement is from rental properties—that is, the guild seems to have run no business directly and not to have invested in commercial enterprises per se. Total income for the year was listed as 4,404 taels. (Elsewhere, the average annual income from rents is placed at over 4,300 taels, so this year's revenue was not exceptional.)[76] In 1806 the total income from rural property owned and rented out by the group was only six taels, indicating not only the small percentage of the guild's total capital that was invested in this type of land, but also probably why so little was thus invested. In contrast, the amount of rental income derived from the two rows of shops along Hsin-an Street (an area probably equal to or less than the total rural holdings in square footage) was 2,249 taels. Rural investment simply could not compete with urban property in profitability, particularly when an investor could afford to develop the property attractively.

Balanced against this gross income were the guild's total annual operating expenses, which for 1806 were 1,830 taels, or only about 42 percent of the gross revenues listed. Where did the remaining 58 percent go? The accounts indicate that an unspecified but substantial portion went for the "repair and new acquisition of various shops," that is, for reinvestment in profit-making ventures.[77] The remainder was applied to paying off the bonds issued in 1804.

After 1806, our information on the Hui-chou Guild is fragmentary. A book-length travelogue on Hankow printed in 1822 indicates that at this time Hui-chou natives were still both socially and economically the dominant local-origin community,[78] but after the Taiping interregnum and the subsequent changes in the salt trade, the Hui-chou merchants seem to have declined, and they are no longer mentioned among the leading commercial powers of the port. Despite its commercial decline, however, the Hui-chou Guild retained one major source of income in the city, which protected its position of local power: ownership of land. The Hui-chou contingent became, in a sense, "old money." There are few sources to indicate how well the guild kept its property intact after the Taiping occupation. Most of the value of the developed property was certainly lost when the rebels razed the city, and in the process no doubt some land titles were thrown into question. It is my general impression, however, that corporately held property remained more secure than did individually held titles to land. (By the turn of the nineteenth century, as we have seen, the guild had registered with the magistrate and engraved in stone the claims to all its holdings.) In the post-Taiping years, then, the Hui-chou group may have evolved into a corporate body of urban landlords.

At least the Hsin-an Street area, fronting the guildhall complex, was reconstructed in the postrebellion years in magnificent fashion. By the 1870's it was again described as "one of the most bustling places in Hankow" and an extremely prosperous marketplace.[79] The shops that lined this street, all still owned and leased out by the guild, were high-rent operations dealing in luxury goods like jade and silks. In the reconstruction years, Hsin-an Street was specifically cited as a model by individual and corporate entrepreneurs (for example, the Kiangsi Guild) who wished to develop commercial blocks along the same lines.[80] The most famous such emulation was undertaken by an almost equally venerable institution of the city, the Shansi-Shensi Guild.

The Shansi-Shensi Guild. The joint local-origin guild of Shansi and Shensi natives in Hankow constructed its first formal guildhall, the Spring and Autumn Hall (Ch'un-ch'iu lou), in 1683, a decade before the Hui-chou merchants. Although the guildhall's purpose was avowedly to provide a place for commercial deliberations, its layout was ritually determined. The forwardmost temple of the walled compound faced onto a courtyard, entered through a formidable main gate; a grand theatrical stage was mounted on the gate, facing inward. In 1719, the patronage of a compatriot local official contributed to the hall's first major repair.[81]

Over the course of the eighteenth and nineteenth centuries, the Shansi-Shensi Guild acquired a veritable empire within the city. It purchased land back of the town and set up a subsidiary "Hall for the Comfort of Travelers" (I-lü kung-so), which offered compatriot merchants such services as lodging, health care, and burial. Furthermore, it converted an area of former "waste land" directly behind the central guildhall compound into a series of streets for pedestrian access, and around the turn of the nineteenth century constructed two stone bridges to facilitate communication across the frequently flooded back street of the town. These streets and bridges were completely overhauled in the 1830's. In this vicinity too was the Pao-lin Temple, originally the headquarters of the Shansi Cloth Guild, which eventually merged with the larger provincial organization. In time the Shansi-Shensi club came to possess most of the property stretching from its central compound, near the Hui-chou Guild in the middle of the city, to the landward edge of town where the Pao-lin Temple was located. Using "subsidiary capital," the guild gradually purchased this entire area, which came to be known popularly as the "Shansi-Shensi district" (*Shan-Shen-li*). Although some of this property was designated for collective use, much of it was developed specifically to generate rental income, usually but not always from renting to guild members.[82]

Along with most of the town, the Shansi Guildhall and all of the group's collective holdings were destroyed by the Taipings in 1854, and for more than a decade after the town was recaptured most of the site that had once been occupied by the splendid Shansi-Shensi hall remained covered with ruins and overgrown with weeds. In the interim, smaller components of the former multiplex guild began to reestablish themselves separately, most operating out of rented quarters in temples, teahouses, and so forth. Some, however, began piecemeal efforts to resurrect portions of the former collective guildhall. In 1863, for example, the Shansi tobacco *pang* began to reconstruct the small Kuan Yü temple at the front of the guildhall compound, and a few years later the Shansi medicinal-herbs *pang* commenced work on a subordinate chapel of the complex, the Temple of the Five Sages.[83] In these years, there was no overarching Shansi-Shensi Guild to undertake a general reconstruction project covering the complex as a whole.

In 1870 the powerful Shansi bankers' *pang*, having at length convinced itself of Hankow's new military security and commercial revitalization, called a convocation of the 26 simplex guilds of Shansi or Shensi natives then existing in the city and with extravagant appeals to regional pride proposed a joint reconstruction of the former guildhall complex. Work on the project began in 1875 and went on for the better part of twenty years. By 1881 the centerpiece of the complex, the monumental Spring and Autumn Hall, had been completed and was formally inaugurated with a gala theatrical performance and open house. The central complex was constructed in an almost purely Chinese style, but with the aid of Western blueprints (furnished, incidentally, by a member of the Hui-chou Guild), and it was acclaimed by both Western and Chinese architectural critics. Though located several blocks inland, this central complex was clearly visible from the Han River and constituted a principal feature of the city's skyline. It included not only the guild's major collective meeting halls and temples, but also numerous smaller attached chapels (dedicated to the God of Literature, the Heavenly Mother, the Seven Sages, various Buddhas, and so on) used for the specialized worship and conduct of business of the *hui-kuan*'s component guilds (see Figures 2 and 3).[84]

The reconstruction project did not end with the completion of the central guildhall complex, and the guild turned thereafter to repairing all attached and outlying structures and roadways used by the guildsmen. Prominent among these was the primary access road leading to the guildhall complex (Kuan-ti Temple Alley), which was reconstructed in apparent imitation of the Hui-chou Guild's Hsin-an Street and like that street was fronted by an imposing gate and temple. At this time the guild finally acquired its own pier, the Ma-wang miao, which made up for its considerable remove from the guildhall complex by its proximity to the new foreign concession area and the China Merchants' Steam Navigation Company's new modern steamship facilities.[85]

How was this massive project financed and managed? According to the commemorative tablets engraved to celebrate the completion of the Spring and Autumn Hall, the initial proposal made by the bankers' *pang* was met (as in the Hui-chou Guild) by considerable skepticism. Not

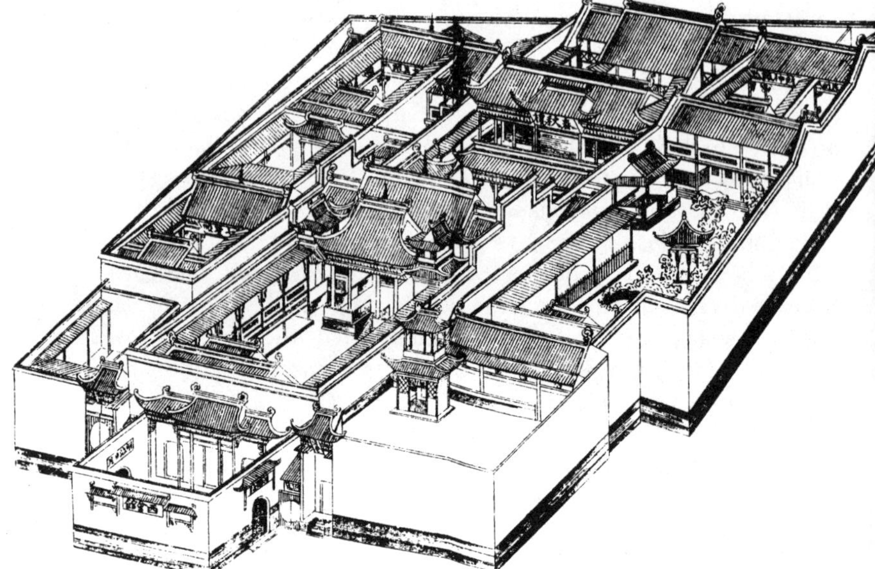

Fig. 3 The Shansi-Shensi Guildhall compound, ca. 1889. (Source: *SSHK*.)

only did guildsmen fear that such a project could not be financed through to completion, but some doubted whether the Hankow of 1870 demonstrated either the military security or the commercial prospects to warrant such an undertaking. The proponents of the plan won votes of approval from the various other guilds "one by one."[86] Two leaders of the bankers' *pang* who had been most vocal in supporting the project were designated project managers. These men, Wu Yu-ch'ing and Chao Shu-chih, were distinct from the annually rotating managers of the reconstituted multiplex guild as a whole. The project managers were similarly to be replaced annually, but Wu Yu-ch'ing was also appointed overall "general manager" (*tsung-tung*) for the entire project, a post that he held for twenty years, during which he devoted an exceptional amount of concern and energy to the undertaking.

At the original conference of 1870, the guild hoped to finance the reconstruction project solely through voluntary contributions by members. A letter of solicitation was circulated for this purpose, containing such sentiments as: "A great building cannot stand upon a single pillar. Consequently, with this notice we advise our colleagues of the great project that we are planning, so that they can give such assistance as they can freely afford. We want to collect a little bit from everyone, and so to accumulate a large amount, in the same way that fur from under the forelegs of many foxes is collected to make a fox coat."[87] The Shansi-Shensi foxes were not to be so easily fleeced, however, and within the year hopes of financing the project wholly by donations had faded. Thus in the autumn of 1871 a second conference was convened, which approved a proposal that all goods sold by Shansi or Shensi natives in the city be subject to a surcharge to be applied to "collective assistance and charitable works," that is, the reconstruction project. A detailed list of the duty to be paid on each of 24 commodities traded (for example, "it is decided by consent that every *pao* of safflower be assessed three cash") was collectively drawn up and issued at the start of the next trading season.[88]

This policy had considerably more success than the appeal for funds, and over the ensuing twenty years a total of 249,066 taels was collected in this way. Some 1,159 contributors were identified, a few by personal name, the majority by firm name (*hao*), and a few by groups of firms (for example, "the collective cotton *hao* of T'ai-yüan and Fen-chou"). As with the Hui-chou project, however, the managers' ambitions eventually outran their resources, and the final bill for the reconstruction project came to 271,461 taels, leaving a deficit of more than twenty thousand taels.[89] (Part of this overrun was caused by the guild managers' diverting some of the project's income to relief for the home provinces during the severe famine in northwest China in 1877–78.) Fortunately, before this the project managers had spent their money wisely, and by this time the Shansi-Shensi Guild was deriving considerable income from other sources, namely, rental properties in which money for redevelopment had been continuously invested.

Since so few Shansi-Shensi men had remained in Hankow during the Taiping occupation and since they had been relatively slow to return, in the post-Taiping years the guild had some difficulty in demonstrating title to its once-extensive rental real estate and in dislodging squatters. Several of the guild's "old-timers" (*lao-ch'eng*) consequently dredged up surviving deeds and sifted through other evidence of ownership in order to present a comprehensive claim to the Hanyang magistrate. At least partially because of their prominence (and perhaps also their ability to extend gratuities), they were able to recover "almost all" of the guild's prerebellion holdings.[90]

The properties thus recovered were both developed and extended in the reconstruction years. Most dramatic, perhaps, was the transformation of Kuan-ti Temple Alley, the central access street to the guildhall complex. Although most of this area had formerly been occupied by guild members, as a corporate body the guild owned less than half of the property along the street. In the latter part of the nineteenth century, the guild seems to have made an effort to acquire all of this land as its own. For example, a bill of sale survives transferring some properties along the street from an individual guild member to the group for 100,000 cash.[91] At the same time, the guild spent considerable sums redeveloping the street, with the result that it eventually became a major marketplace for the city as a whole.

The guild also acquired and developed property in the "Shansi-Shensi district" northeast of the guildhall complex and at scattered sites throughout the town: for example, it purchased a row of three shophouses in 1877 for one million cash; a single shop in 1892 for 255,000 cash; another in 1894 for 55,000 cash; and yet another in 1895 for 60,000 cash. According to one account from the mid-1890's, the guild's rental properties included: 26 developed properties in Kuan-ti Temple Alley; seventeen developed properties in the area northeast of the guildhall complex; two developed properties to the southeast of the complex; three developed properties in Narrow Street (Chia chieh), Hsün-li ward; four developed properties outside the city; two vegetable-gardening fields along the lakefront behind the city.[92] As the rental-property register of the guild proclaimed, "Our endowment was founded in the past, has been added to in the present, and will continue to be enlarged in the future." This corporate expansion was clearly seen as a necessary corollary of group solidarity and power.[93]

Management of these considerable investments required steadily increasing attention. The reconstituted guild's regulatory code included several items related to their accounting, which can be summarized:

1. Managers (*ching-ying*, subordinate to the guild's general managers, or *shou-shih*) were to be appointed annually to keep records of all income from and disbursements for collective property, including shops, residences, garden plots, and undeveloped lands.

2. Men were not to lodge in any of the guild properties, whether within or without the central complex, without paying suitable rent to the group. If the managers exacted private rental fees, they would be punished.

3. Rent on properties was to be paid on an annual basis. Moneys derived from them were to be maintained in one of two accounts, the *lao-hsia* and the *hsin-hsia*. Each was to be held in the custody of a comptroller (*szu-hsia*) and audited annually.

4. Whenever repairs were carried out on any rental property owned by the guild, that property's value was to be reassessed. If an increase in rent was found to be appropriate, it was to be collected by the guild as a whole. No private initiative by the managers in regard to rental prop-

erties, with consequent adding of rent surcharges accruing to the profit of a manager, was to be permitted.

5. To the two general managers heretofore responsible for all guild operations were added four additional general managers charged specifically with overseeing the rapidly expanding guild assets and the income derived from them. Whereas the original general managers were drawn from all the component *pang* in rotation, these four new officers were to be drawn only from the Shansi bankers' *pang*. Each year, on the eighth day of the fourth month, all six top officers were to be replaced, and a complete audit of all guild assets was to be conducted.[94]

Aside from the rise of bankers to dominance within the guild seen in the fifth of these regulations, the new rules demonstrate a successive addition of specialized officers to administer the guild's financial dealings—a reflection of its increasingly corporate orientation.

As the guild's "Record of the Continuing Acquisition of Property" boasts, in the last decades of our period the combined rental income from property investments regularly exceeded total operating expenses for the year.[95] This is borne out by the guild's financial statement for 1895, which was reproduced in its gazetteer, published the following year.[96] The total declared income for 1895, all from rental properties, was listed as 964.3 taels silver, plus 828,900 copper cash. Operating expenses for the year totaled 110 taels silver, plus 2,033,600 copper cash. If we calculate silver : copper conversion at the officially stipulated rate of 1:1,000, the guild appears to have had a deficit for the year of 351 taels. However, this ideal conversion rate undoubtedly did not apply. In attempting to determine the actual conversion rate in late-nineteenth-century cities, Frank King, for example, found rates of 1:1,500 common and at least one rate (Tamsui, Taiwan, 1882) of approximately 1:2,000.[97] Frederic Wakeman notes that by 1838 the average exchange rate throughout the empire was something like 1:1,650.[98] If the Shansi-Shensi budget is calculated at the conservative silver : copper rate of 1:1,500, the guild would have had a modest surplus of 51 taels; at a rate of 1:2,000 it would have had a more substantial annual surplus of 251 taels. Almost certainly the actual situation was nearer to, or more favorable than, this last estimate, especially since none of these calculations takes into account the likelihood that the guild imposed a different conversion rate for rent collection and expenditures, in each case favoring itself (it was managed, after all, by professional bankers). A surplus revenue over expenditures for the year of 251 taels, if taken as typical for these years, would have amounted to a surplus profit on total revenues for the corporation of a handsome 19 percent per annum.

The Hui-chou and Shansi-Shensi guilds were among the largest in nineteenth-century Hankow, but there is no reason to suspect that in the style or the scope of their corporate activities they were unique. At least in the post-Taiping period, they were rivaled or even surpassed in local prestige and power by guilds representing Kwangtung, Ningpo-Shaohsing, Kiangsi, and Fukien merchants, and by non–local-origin guilds representing the rice, salt, tea, and native-banking trades; most of these groups, and smaller ones as well, also acquired and developed real property in the town. Shimizu Taiji, writing in 1928, noted that throughout China guilds not only owned many urban shops, but were sometimes corporate proprietors, hiring salaried managers and clerks to operate shops in the guild's name.[99] I have uncovered no evidence of this in Hankow before the 1890's; either it was unreported or it represents a later development in the trend for guilds to gradually evolve from protectionist brotherhoods into (at least in effect) capital corporations.

Guild investment in urban property was especially profitable during the post-Taiping reconstruction. Because of deaths, emigration, and the destruction of title claims during the Taiping interregnum (all of which seem to have affected corporate groups less than individuals), land in Hankow during the late 1850's and the 1860's was very cheap. Urban land ownership seems thus to have become concentrated, as organizations, such as guilds, that could quickly amass capital (by subscription, "likin," etc.) bought up and developed large tracts of the town. The financial wisdom of such action soon became apparent. In 1892, the Maritime Customs commissioner at the port said of the price of land in the postrebellion years: "Land in the Native town is becoming increasingly expensive. Immediately after the Taiping Rebellion land could be purchased easily and cheaply; but the rise in price has been steady, and the Chinese assert that the market value of land in Hankow has now reached the same point as before the rebellion."[100] In consequence, guild corporate activities, originally intended as peripherally supportive of its commercial or fraternal roles, became increasingly central to the group's orientation, and if a guild's commercial position declined while its corporate profits grew, such activities might even become its major focus (as seems to have happened with the Hui-chou Guild).

Groups that had invested wisely, like the Hui-chou and Shansi-Shensi guilds, in their mature period had a regular and increasing surplus of investment income. Much of this surplus was reinvested, as the Shansi-Shensi managers resolutely pledged to do. The 1804 Hui-chou bond issue shows, however, that a portion could also be earmarked to repay investments made by individual members in the corporate group, as well as to distribute some of the corporate profits among these investors.

To summarize, then, over the course of the Ch'ing the larger guilds of Hankow became increasingly involved in corporate investments in the city and evolved sophisticated mechanisms to manage their finances. The system embodied the basic requisites for economic "rationality" prescribed by Weber and his heirs: detailed capital accounting, replaceable managerial personnel, and contractual instruments (in the form of title deeds, bills of sale, and rental agreements) guaranteed by the local administration. The system, moreover, included both profit-making opportunities for investors and a built-in program of capital reinvestment, both in the acquisition of new properties and in value-enhancing improvements made to current holdings.

The major "modern" element missing from this system was, of course, industrial production. There appears to be little reason, however, to think that investment in industry could not have been subsequently incorporated into the complex financial machinery at guilds' disposal. In fact, by founding a modern bank in the 1890's, at least one Hankow guild, the Tea Guild, seems to have taken this step. The establishment of a bank provided one link by which capital accumulated through the traditional mechanisms of old-style guild corporations might be channeled into financing Hankow's early industrialization.

Community-Service Functions

By "community-service functions" I refer to philanthropic activities in which the guild as a corporate body engaged. In the nineteenth century, these activities were directed both inward toward the membership alone and outward toward the wider communities within which the guild was situated. Guild charity was not the only source of public service in Hankow; however, the guilds' role in local philanthropy was a central one.

Philanthropic works (*shan-chü*) were at times cited as a rationale for guild formation (see Table 12, p. 260). This was particularly true of local-origin guilds, which were designed not only to promote a home area's commercial interests but also to provide support for its natives during sojourns in the city; however, similar aims were also espoused by guilds with no local-origin restriction, such as the Coal Boatmen's Guild, which claimed as a chief goal "the performance of public charitable acts."[101] Here, as in many late imperial contexts, "public" (*kung*) meant first and foremost "collective." That is to say, the philanthropic activities of Hankow guilds derived from (and in many cases remained restricted to) self-nurturance. In Hankow this self-nurturance began with providing coffins and burial sites, but could include such other activities as providing food and clothing for destitute guild members.[102]

From caring for guild members to performing charitable works for the urban neighborhood within which the guild was located was a small but significant step. Local guilds first institutionalized charitable activities on a neighborhood basis in the 1820's, when the first "benevolent hall" (*shan-t'ang*) of the city was set up by the (then informal) salt merchants' guild to provide food for the neighborhood's poor.[103] It was imitated by a handful of other commercial groups in the 1830's and 1840's but became a regular feature of city life only in the post-Taiping decades, when close to one hundred benevolent halls sprang up in the town. Despite their general association throughout China with gentry philanthropy, in Hankow, as in other major commercial centers, these institutions were more frequently financed by merchants, often as an offshoot of a guild.[104]

Other neighborhood-centered philanthropy undertaken by Hankow guilds derived from their role as local property holders. Out of concern for their real estate holdings, long before the establishment of benevolent halls the guilds had begun to assume responsibility in such areas as civil construction and fire fighting. In the eighteenth century, for instance, the Hui-chou guild widened, straightened, and resurfaced the "public thoroughfare" (*i-lu*) passing in front of its guildhall complex, so that for the first time the street was able to accommodate cartage traffic; its leaders noted with satisfaction the general applause this project received from outside the guild. In about 1800 the group bought and demolished a nearby building to open up an alley so that carriers could supply the entire community with well water without leaving puddles to hinder ordinary traffic.[105] An important bridge spanning a rivulet running through the city was built for public use by the Kiangsu Guild in the early nineteenth century;[106] similarly, in the eighteenth century the Shansi-Shensi Guild constructed two stone bridges near its premises to be used for access and egress on the frequent occasions when the Yü-tai Canal overflowed its banks. These were reconstructed in 1834 and again late in the century. Although the guild no doubt profited from the bridges, it represented them as the result of its "sympathy" for the flood-stricken quarter and claimed their rebuilding as a "public work" (*i-chü*) to benefit both "community residents and passersby" (*chü-min hsing-jen*).[107]

Fire fighting was another neighborhood service undertaken by guilds as an outgrowth of concern for their corporate holdings. Guilds often donated the land for fire lanes (*huo-lu*, *huo-tao*) designed to prevent the spread of flames and to provide both access for fire fighters and escape routes for residents; guilds also financed the clearing and construction of these lanes.[108] In maintaining them, the guild acted as the neighborhood's patron and its intermediary with the local administration. When the Shansi-Shensi Guild successfully petitioned local officials to prohibit encroachment on one such lane, for example, the guild claimed to represent not only its own members but all neighborhood residents (*p'i-lien*).[109] Guilds also maintained fire-fighting units: the water-pumping engines (*shui-lung*) and the detachments (*shui-hui*) that manned them. Dozens of such detachments were financed and directed by Hankow guilds, including those established by the Hui-chou Guild in about 1801, by the Grain Dealers' Guild in the 1860's, and by the Shansi-Shensi Guild in 1880.[110] The first and last of these teams employed respectively 44 and 46 full-time firemen.

Beyond the local neighborhood, guilds increasingly tended to extend their patronage to the city as a whole. In 1806, for example, the Hui-chou Guild established a public ferry (*i-tu*) across the Han River.[111] Various groups also set up "public schools" (*i-hsüeh*). Although both these and the academies that gave their names to the corporate bodies of several merchant groups were established primarily to educate the children of guild members, some admitted outsiders as students, and in such cases the sponsoring guild was happy to claim credit as a benefactor of the urban community as a whole. As the Hui-chou club proclaimed of its school, "Since none of the people of any place within Hankow's four wards is denied its benefits . . . the guild's merit for reforming men's hearts and conduct is not limited to men hailing from the six counties [of Hui-chou prefecture] alone."[112] Significantly, the guild identified the school's service area as "Hankow's four wards," rather than the county or the Wuhan area as a whole—an indication that the *chen*, although not administratively discrete, was a unit of conscious identification and informal self-administration for its inhabitants.

Probably the most important public service undertaken by guilds in the name of the entire city was municipal defense. Around 1799, for example, the White Lotus rebels threatened Hankow. When they had captured the important county seat of Hsiao-kan, less than one hundred *li* (about thirty miles) away, "Hankow residents turned green with terror." However, the Hui-chou Guild, under the leadership of Wang Heng-shih, began to organize self-defense forces and conspicuously continued the construction of its huge guildhall complex, an undertaking that in such unsteady times set an example of stability to the rest of the town. Wang himself played a major role in keeping the urban population calm until the arrival of the imperial armies charged with its defense, and the guild thus developed a reputation for providing local leadership in times of crisis.[113] During the Taiping debacle half a century later, the town as a whole proved less defensible. Twice the rebel armies took it with little local resistance, but when in August 1853 Hupeh Governor Ch'ang Ta-ch'un chose to make a disastrously unsuccessful stand there against a third assault, his chief support and organizational assistance came from several of the city's guilds.[114] Similar guild-led defense activities were reported during various Nien-rebel threats in the 1860's and 1870's. Clearly, the major guilds of Hankow represented those who had the most to defend in the city, both in accumulated real property and inventory, and in continuing opportunities for profit. They also possessed the best-organized apparatus for leading a defense. At least by the post-Taiping period, this combination of motivation and organization had led guilds to support peace-keeping forces on a semipermanent basis as a defense against internal as well as external sources of disorder. In the closing decades of the nineteenth century, these forces evolved into standing private armies known as "merchant militia" (*shang-t'uan*), which were to play a large role locally in the chaotic last years of the dynasty.[115]

Certain modern writers, such as Imahori Seiji, have taken a dim view of the philanthropy of Ch'ing guilds. They argue that although such activities were claimed to benefit the "public" (*kung-kung*), in fact the narrower interests of the guild itself determined the selection of projects, while conspicuous spending encouraged the "superiority feelings" of guild members.[116] Some contemporary observers in Hankow expressed similar cynicism. The 1850 visitor Yeh Tiao-yüan remarked somewhat cryptically that: "Each guild donates several thousand silver [taels], but if market prices rise they reverse themselves. This is a fine way to receive 'secret merit,' since the recipients are none other than the donors."[117] Although Yeh noted that he referred to alleged charitable activities, he provided no other context or specific referent.

Undoubtedly both profit and self-interest motivated some varieties of public giving by Hankow guilds. On the other hand, in many cases utilitarian explanations seem insufficient. During the famine in northwest China in 1877–78, for example, not only did the local Shansi-Shensi Guild divert large amounts of both corporate and individual members' incomes to relief for the home area, but according to a commendatory proclamation issued by the Hupeh provincial treasurer, "the various guilds . . . of Hanyang and Hankow have continually been contributing funds, totaling altogether 7,620 taels. . . . This is truly a voluntary act of charity, which exhibits no particularism in the selection of its recipients." The proclamation specifically identified fourteen occupational guilds of Hankow as large donors, including those of the salt, vegetable oil, and grocery trades.[118]

Clearly, then, Confucian public-mindedness influenced at least some guild charity. Relief in the 1877–78 famine was exceptional, however, because it was designed to benefit a needy area outside the city; most guild philanthropy revealed a desire to assume a leadership role within the host community, whether in a guild's local neighborhood or in the city as a whole. As Tou Chi-liang has argued, the expansion of guild community-service activity reveals a shift in Ch'ing economic organizations away from emphasis on parochial group interests (*hsiang-t'u*) to an identification with the interests of the host community as a whole (*she-ch'ü*).[119] Tou noted that this movement was at times prompted by official pressure (as with the anti-Taiping defenses at Hankow or the frequent levies on the salt merchants' collective treasuries to underwrite the local administration's public projects), but that guilds also argued community needs before the administration (as in anti-encroachment campaigns). In most cases, however, guilds took action on their own initiative in response to perceived community needs shared by guild members and their nonguild neighbors.[120] At Hankow, such public service seems to have been reinforced rather than hindered by guilds' pursuit of their more narrow corporate ends, particularly acquiring and developing real property both in the immediate neighborhood of a guildhall and scattered elsewhere throughout the city. Such profit-making ventures increasingly ensured that even guilds ostensibly oriented to distant home localities would develop strong roots, and hence interests, in Hankow.

From the perspective of the city rather than the guild, these developments reveal the first stages in the evolution of municipal government. Skinner has described the process in these terms:

> One can, I think, discern two lines of development toward citywide leadership structures that coordinated urban services. One grew out of merchant associations, the other out of gentry institutions (though . . . the two were never wholly independent and became increasingly intertwined during the nineteenth century). On the merchant side, the first significant development was the extension into the public realm of services initially provided by guilds and native-place associations for their members alone.[121]

In order to reflect their broadened community identification and more fully assert their role in city-wide leadership, however, Hankow guilds had to transcend their (already expanded) group boundaries. This was accomplished by constructing a network of interguild linkages and alliances, a process that is the subject of our final chapter.

CHAPTER TEN

Guilds and Local Power

ORGANIZATIONAL GROWTH and multiplying functions also meant increased local power for Hankow guilds. Before evaluating the guilds' aggregate power and the degree to which it reflected urban autonomy, this chapter will address the distribution of power within guilds, cooperation among them, and their relations with the local representatives of the central administration.

The Distribution of Power Within Hankow Guilds

As the Fukien Guild declared at the time of its founding, the guilds of Hankow were designed to function as "self-governing and autonomous public associations" (*tzu-chih tzu-li chih kung-t'uan*).[1] That is to say, power over guild policy and operational decisions was to belong entirely to the group and to be vested in its membership as a whole. Of necessity, however, day-to-day decisions were regularly made not by plenary vote but by a smaller number of guild officers deputed to act in the guild's name. These officers usually but not always served in a group rather than singly.

In occupationally defined guilds these officers were frequently referred to as "supervisors of affairs" (*tung-shih*), or, less often, as "chiefs of affairs" (*shou-shih*).[2] In multiplex trade guilds the heads of component local-origin *pang* shared decision-making power within the umbrella organization, but one generally stood out as primus inter pares, often on a relatively permanent basis. Thus, although the Tea Guild was led by the supervisors of the Six Guilds, known by English-speaking contemporaries as its "managers," for several decades guild correspondence and proclamations were signed by a single man, Chang Yin-pin, who was a cofounder of the group and styled himself (in English) its "chairman."[3] The Salt Guild every year elected twelve of its members to rotate monthly as operational supervisors and share joint responsibility for overall management during the entire year. As in the Tea Guild, however, a single officer was permanently designated chief in charge.[4]

In large local-origin guilds the pattern of leadership was often more complex. Shimizu Taiji, writing in the Republican era of China as a whole, claimed that such groups customarily selected four supervisors per year; each served for one quarter, but the four shared overall responsibility throughout the year. Usually they were augmented by twelve "assistant managers" (*fu-tung-shih*), who each assumed one month's duty.[5] Japanese reporters at Hankow at the beginning of the twentieth century found that locally there were two levels of guild managers, the supervisors of affairs and a subordinate class known as "overseers" (*szu-shih*); one-year and one-month terms of office were equally common for both, with no necessary correlation between seniority and tenure of office.[6] From local sources we know that the Kiangsi, Ningpo, and Hui-chou guilds at Hankow were indeed managed by officers known as *tung-shih*, who served in groups (of three in the Ningpo Guild, four in that of Hui-chou), apparently for one-year terms.[7] The Hui-chou Guild also had two sorts of subordinate guild officials: (1) separately appointed managers for the club's collective property (*szu-shih*), who served on an annual basis, and (2) intermittent project managers for specific collective enterprises (*chu-shih*), whose terms coincided with the life of the project.[8]

The Shansi-Shensi Guild, a sprawling, multiplex affair, had an even more complex managerial arrangement. Each of its component *pang* had its own manager, known as "head gentryman" (*shou-shih*, with a different second character from "chief of affairs"), and together these men constituted a governing board for the overall organization, known as the "Shansi-Shensi *hui-kuan* head gentrymen of the ten [in reality considerably more than ten] *pang*" (*Shan-Shen hui-kuan shih-pang shou-shih*).[9] Two members of this group were selected each year to serve as "headmen" (*shou-jen*), who handled "all collective business, no matter whether large or small" and pledged "to serve faithfully and impartially the interests of all members." Financial affairs were managed by subordinate officials known as *ching-kuan*, who were also replaced annually.[10] Special projects, such as the renovation of the guildhall premises, were supervised by a single "general manager" (*tsung-tung*), who served for the life of the project and was assisted by several annually replaced project *tung-shih*.[11]

Clearly, then, the managerial configuration institutionalized by the regulatory codes of at least the larger trade and local-origin guilds of Hankow fully satisfied the leadership criteria for "formal organizations" identified by organization theorists such as Amitai Etzioni. The guilds had not only "one or more power centers which control the concerted efforts of the organization and direct them toward its goals," but a highly articulated, bureaucratic substitution of personnel.[12] Formally, at least, they were not governed by a patrimonial elite. But to what extent did these formal systems reflect genuine input by rank-and-file members?[13]

In every known case, the officers of Hankow guilds were elected by a vote of the full membership at a plenary meeting, usually annual. Project managers were likewise elected by the membership as a whole, at meetings called specifically for this purpose. Leaders so chosen were described as having been "publicly" or "openly" selected (*kung-t'ui*).[14] Probably most nominees were selected in advance by a small coterie of leading members, but invariably the entire membership at least sat through a formal election and thereby granted collective legitimation to the selection process. In this regard, Hankow guilds were clearly the repositories of a native democratic tradition.

But did an elite stratum within the guild monopolize elected office and real power? Formally, there was no such monopolization; none of the surviving regulatory codes for Ch'ing Hankow prescribes a separate category of membership corresponding, say, to the "liveried" members of preindustrial English guilds, who were exclusively eligible to hold office and make policy. (Probably for this reason, an early British observer of Chinese guilds described them as "more democratic" than their European counterparts.)[15] In practice, however, four factors seem to have influenced selection for guild office: (1) gentry status, (2) position as a licensed broker, (3) personal wealth and business success, and (4) family connections.

Gentry Status. Gentry status enabled guild leaders to articulate guild interests to local officials more effectively, and thus gentry credentials were probably an implied requirement for managerial positions in most of the larger local guilds. The Shansi-Shensi Guild, for instance, described its leaders as "literati-merchants" (*shih-shang*).[16] In practice, this was not a very restrictive prerequisite, since most larger guilds probably had many gentry members, whether by purchase or examination, to choose among. In the major guilds, it would seem, gentry status was a necessary but hardly a sufficient qualification for a position of leadership.

Brokerage Status. Chinese and Japanese scholars have commonly assumed that brokers were prominent in guild decision-making structures, and there were sound practical reasons for this to have been so.[17] Brokers were responsible to the authorities for regulating the market and collecting commercial taxes, as well as for ensuring the good conduct of all participants in the trade. Since the guild was a convenient instrument for satisfying these requirements, the merging of brokerage and guild leadership would seem logical. On the other hand, however, there were intrinsic conflicts of interest between brokers and dealers in a trade, and this probably engendered rank-and-file resistance to broker domination.

In fact, there are few if any reported instances of brokers monopolizing power within Hankow guilds. More commonly, it seems, when brokers participated in a guild at all they tended to form a separate organization. The pioneer Rice Market Guild of the late seventeenth century, for example, was made up exclusively of brokers, and in the timber trade separate simplex guilds of Hupeh brokers and Hunanese dealers were linked at a higher level in the multiplex Liang-hu hui-kuan. The nineteenth-century Tea Guild, on the other hand, excluded brokers from membership, although it cooperated with them and solicited their concurrence on important policy decisions; the Medicinal Herbs Guild was formed by dealers in specific reaction to Hu Lin-i's imposition of licensed brokers in that trade (although it is not recorded whether or not brokers were formally excluded from membership). Many smaller guilds, of course, managed trades in finished handicraft products, such as paper, shoes, and clothing, for which licensed brokers simply did not exist.

In a recent, suggestive study, the Shanghai historian Tu Li has posited a gradual shift over the course of the Ch'ing from "feudal guilds" (*feng-chien hang-hui*) monopolized or dominated by brokers as an instrument of bureaucratic extraction, to a later form in which private merchants gained equal representation with brokers, to guilds for nonbroker merchants alone. Tu associates this trend with growing capital accumulation by private merchant-entrepreneurs, and ultimately with what he views as the incipient transformation to capitalism in Chinese commercial society.[18] Hankow guilds do not provide the clear evidence for this model that Shanghai guilds appear to, yet, as we have seen, the direction of change in Hankow does seem to have been in a roughly similar direction—that of privatization.

Personal Wealth and Business Success. An assumption even more broadly shared among Chinese and Japanese scholars has been that wealthy guild members could exploit the organization's resources for private gain. Katō Shigeshi, for example, wrote (apparently as an article of faith) that "the member merchants of a *hang* did not always work together for their common benefit, but it was more likely that the richer merchants of a *hang* tyrannized over the poorer members and made a monopoly for their own benefit."[19] Imahori Seiji noted that since capital was usually equivalent to local power, wealthy capitalists could seize upon the fact that guilds needed their support vis-à-vis the local authorities to manipulate the guild for their own purposes and to bring smaller, less resourceful groups under the guild's (and hence their own) patronage.[20] Many writers have held, moreover, that since wealthy interests bore much of the cost of guild financing, they expected a proportionate share of the power and benefits in return.

Some evidence from Hankow supports, at least on the surface, each of these contentions, but as a whole the sources do not necessarily bear out their authors' common assumption of the plutocratic nature of late imperial guilds. Yeh Tiao-yüan, with customary cynical ambiguity, wrote in 1850 that wealthier merchants were able to create bonds of dependency among fellow guild members by their apparent generosity in financing the organizations, but that this generosity was illusory and was usually withdrawn in times of real need.[21] More concrete evidence is provided by the Shansi-Shensi Guild's 1888 decision to augment its two annually rotating "head gentrymen," drawn from the entire membership, with four more to be selected only from the *hui-kuan*'s most affluent component, the Shansi bankers' guild.[22] To all appearances, however, this was a popular decision arrived at by consensus of the entire 26 member *pang* of the *hui-kuan*. As Tou Chi-liang points out, for the rank and file of Chinese guilds personal wealth and professional success constituted the best evidence of the financial capability needed to manage the collective accounts.[23] The Shansi-Shensi Guild stated that the bankers were added to the management team for precisely this reason; as we have seen, the rapid appreciation of the *hui-kuan*'s assets at this time may have justified such a step.

Family Ties. The final potential requisite for guild leadership was the result less of a rational search for qualified managerial talent than of a residual particularism in Ch'ing socioeconomic behavior: it was the tendency, stressed by scholars who identify late imperial commerce as "feudal" in character, for certain lineages to dominate guild leadership from one generation to the next. Again, Tou Chi-liang provides the most charitable explanation for this phenomenon in his observation that where a guild was initially capitalized by a heavy assessment on charter members, there was often an implicit understanding that their descendants would receive preferential consideration for future leadership positions.[24]

The breakdown in Table 17 of major construction projects undertaken by the Hui-chou Guild over the course of the eighteenth century suggests that kinship groups did dominate leadership positions in Hankow guilds. Although men of twenty different surnames appear among

TABLE 17
Managers of Hui-chou Guildhall Construction Projects, by Surname, 1704–1801

Project and completion date	Total managers	Surname Wang	Surname Wu	Surname Yü	Wang-Wu-Yü total	Percentage of total managers
Initial construction, 1704	24	6	3	6	15	63%
Pier construction, 1734	12	2	6	0	8	67
Street construction, 1775	33	11	5	5	21	64
General reconstruction, 1801	26	6	3	7	16	62
TOTAL	95	25	17	18	60	63%

SOURCE: *TYSY*, 8.43–44.

the 95 leaders credited for the four projects, almost two-thirds of them (63 percent) have the three most prevalent surnames in the list. Precisely how many of these Wangs (with water radical), Wus, and Yüs were related cannot at this point be determined, but it seems likely that multigenerational lineage domination did occur. More clear-cut, though less encompassing, evidence comes from the same guild in the nineteenth century: Yü Shih-chiung, a merchant from Hsiu-ning county who arrived at Hankow in the 1840's and held the Hui-chou Guild's highest office, general manager, was succeeded in this post by his son Yü Neng-p'ei and grandson Yü Sheng-chu.[25]

Some writers have argued that kinship domination of guild office holding declined significantly over the course of the Ch'ing;[26] despite the evidence cited above, it seems at least possible that this was occurring in nineteenth-century Hankow. The structural changes described in Chapter 8—the shift from local-origin to inclusive common-trade organization and the enlargement of catchment areas in many remaining local-origin groups—would have worked against family domination. Instead, personal wealth and business success, guaranteed access to responsible officials, and leadership talent probably came to recommend a leader to his constituency. Clearly not family pedigree but the ability to make tough decisions and to enforce solidarity upon recalcitrant members, as well as access to the taotai and the foreign Maritime

Customs commissioner, kept Chang Yin-pin atop the Tea Guild in the post-Taiping decades. Reportedly, the Hui-chou Guild's Yü Neng-p'ei was respected by his compatriots not primarily as Yü Shih-chiung's son, but rather for "his ability to obtain a consensus among members in matters relating to the advancement of trade" and his skill at fundraising.[27] More typical perhaps was Wang Heng-shih, selected as general overseer of the Hui-chou guildhall reconstruction of 1801. Well into his seventies at the time, Wang was chosen by his peers because he was a community "elder" (*weng*) and, significantly, because "he had spent his entire life in the marketplace [*shih*] and was thus extraordinarily able in the management of affairs."[28]

Once a guild's leaders had been "openly selected," major decisions involving the interests of the membership were still made, in virtually every case I have found, not by these leaders alone but by a specially convened deliberative body. At times this body comprised only a somewhat expanded leadership group within the guild; for example, the decision of the Tea Guild in 1887 to halt the sale of second-crop teas, the decision of the Shansi-Shensi Guild to divert guild funds to relief for the home provinces during the famine of 1878, and the same guild's 1880 decision to expand greatly its local fire-fighting operations were all made by such groups.[29] More often, however, important decisions were arrived at by means of a special plenary meeting of the membership. These meetings, known as *hui-i* or *kung-i*, are frequently mentioned in the sources on Hankow guilds. Like the general-election meetings, these "public deliberations" could no doubt be orchestrated by the guild's more important members, but there are reports of lively debates that could be resolved only by vote of the assembly (as in the Hui-chou Guild's meetings in preparation for its guildhall reconstruction). Plenary meetings seem to have been required in order to reach decisions on such matters as issuing new codes of guild regulations, undertaking major capital projects, and adopting new methods of collective finance.[30] They were also regularly convened to deliberate on sanctions against members violating guild rules or action to be taken against an outsider.[31] One such meeting precipitated the Tea Guild's 1886 boycott of the British firm Welsh and Company for its refusal to submit to binding arbitration in a dispute over weights.[32]

To what extent, then, did the leaders of Hankow guilds exploit or oppress their constituents? Legal charges brought, often successfully, by members of occupational guilds against brokers and other entrenched interests in the trade provide counter-evidence to H. B. Morse's claim that since merchants were not "burghers" as well as "guildsmen," the "law does not give the individual any adequate protection against coercion by the collective guild."[33] Similarly, the specific and repeated injunctions in Hankow guild regulatory codes (particularly in the later period) against misuses of authority and collective property by guild officials (for example, renting out guild premises or investing guild funds for private profit) indicate not only that such abuses were a problem, but that guilds were dedicated to taking action against them. When actual violations came to light, the offending guild officer immediately became a pariah.*

In none of the surviving sources on Hankow guilds—including local legal cases and letters to newspapers—is blanket criticism directed at guild leaders, from within or without, for oppressive or high-handed treatment of fellow guildsmen. In Hankow, at least, the guild system seems to have worked to the general satisfaction of all involved. Viewed another way, although guild leadership gave significant additional power to a commercial capitalist like Chang Yin-pin, this power was different from, and more conditional than, power based on personal attributes such as wealth, gentry status, or family ties. Even the most autocratic and long-serving guild leaders of Hankow were to a considerable degree the servants of their constituencies.

To sum up, the power distribution in Hankow guilds resembled the arrangements identified by Robert Dahl in the segmented political constituencies of a contemporary American city. Leadership within each group was concentrated in the hands of what Dahl called a "political stratum"—the members who, whether by inclination or because marked out by the attributes we have discussed, were politically more active than the rest. The key characteristics of this political stratum in Hankow, moreover, corresponded to those found in the American city: (1) it was not a "closed" or "static" group; (2) it did not constitute "a homogeneous class" with well-defined class interests pursued independently of the broader membership; and (3) it was both responsive and responsible to its overall constituency.[34]

*Several regulations on this subject appear, e.g., in the Shansi-Shensi code, *SSHK*, 2.9–11. One case of misuse of guild office involved Cheng Chin-fu of the Anhwei Guild, who in 1909 was discovered to have invested over a thousand taels of collective funds on his own account. The formal disciplinary action taken against Cheng included dismissal from guild office; more tellingly, he was ostracized by his Anhwei compatriots at Hankow. (See WMCIA, "Wang-yü-hsia.") Another case involved Wu Jung-hsüan, a manager of the Medicinal Herbs Guild who in the 1890's was impeached for overcollecting guild assessments on members' transactions in order to finance repair of a local temple in memory of his deceased mother. (See WMCIA, "Yao-ts'ai.")

Interguild Linkages and Guild Confederations

Throughout medieval and modern China, urban guilds seem to have been moved to cooperate more often than to compete. Katō Shigeshi, writing of Sung guildsmen, concluded that "even if they were not of the same *hang* [guild], the fact remains that as long as they were merchants belonging to some *hang* or other of the same city, they made much of their membership in a *hang*, and tried to help each other for their mutual benefit."[35] In nineteenth-century Hankow, guilds cooperated both in matters of trade (as the Tea Guild and Salt Guild lobbied for reductions in the likin tax) and in corporate activities (as the Hui-chou and Ningpo guilds exchanged real estate). At some time early in the century, in many urban localities this cooperative spirit led to the creation of more or less formal city-wide guild alliances.

The springboard for investigation of this development was Tou Chi-liang's discovery that for much of the nineteenth century the most important *hui-kuan* of Chungking acted, not independently, but in a confederation known as the "Eight Provinces" (Pa-sheng). According to Tou, this group had gradually coalesced during the Tao-kuang reign, when with increasing frequency the leaders (*hui-shou*) of the various guilds set up ad hoc conferences to resolve conflicts or confront common problems. Gradually the guild leaders regularized these assemblies, and at some time in the 1840's they jointly elected from among their number two full-time "general managers" (*tsung-li shou-shih*) and procured a permanent office in the center of town. The group's arbitration and decision-making powers were thereafter recognized de facto by the local authorities, and eventually it came to exercise a wide range of governing powers over the city as a whole. The high point in these powers came when Shih Ta-k'ai's Taiping forces attacked the city and the Eight Provinces, by taking responsibility for defense, social welfare, education, and other popular needs, assumed (in Tou's words) "the status of central government." After the immediate threat receded the confederation relinquished its most extensive powers, but it continued to play a primary role in providing local leadership throughout the century (for example, it independently ransomed the city from French reprisals after an 1862 attack on a Catholic church by a local mob).[36]

Japanese scholars such as Negishi Tadashi and Imahori Seiji have also commented on the Chungking Eight Provinces organization.[37] Imahori identified it as one of the "guild-merchant" (from the German *Mark Genossenschaft*) organizations that he found characteristic of Chinese urban society and cited similar developments in cities of Hunan, Kwangtung, and Taiwan. In such guild confederations, he saw the institutional precedent of the twentieth-century chambers of commerce. Unlike Tou Chi-liang, Imahori viewed these confederations as repressive rather than representative, and he saw their rise as a stage in the growing subjection of the cities to the power of pooled commercial capital.

Evidence from other commercial centers reveals that city-wide guild alliances were not uncommon and that they were increasingly the instrument merchants used in attempting to influence economic policy. As early as 1857, for example, the headmen of the "Thirteen Guilds" (comprising merchants of Szechwan, Shansi, Shensi, Hui-chou, Ningpo, Huang-chou, Fukien, Honan, Hanyang, Wuchang, Kiangsi, and Chin-ling) at Sha-shih, in western Hupeh, united in an unsuccessful effort to block Hu Lin-i's imposition of likin collections at the port. Through the early twentieth century, they continued to meet regularly at a permanent meeting hall, with one of their number serving as "chairman" to articulate the guilds' joint interests to local officials.[38]

Recent studies in English have highlighted the potential of guild confederations in the late Ch'ing to unite for more overtly political purposes. Edward Rhoads, for example, has identified the coalescence of the formal "Seventy-two Guilds" at Canton in 1899 as a deliberate break with the separate guilds' apolitical traditions and an effort to mobilize merchant reaction to the conservative coup at court that had aborted the Hundred Days' Reforms.[39] More provocatively, Mark Elvin has argued that a similar city-wide guild alliance was the direct antecedent of the first modern municipal government in China, that of Shanghai in 1905.[40] Synthesizing such researches, G. William Skinner has pondered the likelihood of an early "informally instituted mode of 'municipal' governance" in late imperial China:

> One is led to wonder if citywide leadership structures might not be intermittent in nature, with . . . periods of heightened activity and mobilization in response to exceptional threats or opportunities—that would periodically breathe life into otherwise latent political forms?
>
> Guild confederations . . . may have appeared in China only when they were specifically encouraged by bureaucratic officials, but this does not mean that informal arrangements amounting in effect to a sub-rosa municipal government were necessarily absent from commercial cities.[41]

The history of guild linkages in Hankow seems to support such a conceptualization. There is evidence that throughout the nineteenth century religious observances cemented organizationally discrete groups of merchants; for example, the incense-burning societies brought together at the start of each commercial season all participants in a trade, regardless of guild affiliation, to worship the trade's patron deity and deliberate on the ground rules for the market that year.[42] Five diverse trade guilds headquartered at one or another of Hankow's several Thunder God temples (*Lei-tsu tien*) may likewise have been linked by religious observances: they were the Beanthread Dealers' Guild, the Wineshop Proprietors' Guild, the Salt Guild (before its 1889 construction of an independent guildhall), and the Uptown (*shang-pu*) and Midtown (*chung-pu*) Grain Weighers' Guilds.[43] The last two organizations, at least, seem to have been in some way connected; all five may have had informal ties based on devotion to a common patron deity and perhaps strengthened by an interconnected priesthood.

Of far more consequence were semiformal guild alliances that had already sprung up before the Taiping occupation. The first of these was known as the "Upper Eight Trades" (*shang-pa-hang*) and united several of the most lucrative commercial trades of the city: copper and lead dealers, piece-goods dealers, medicinal herbs dealers, paper dealers, Shansi bankers, pawnbrokers, vegetable-oil dealers, and dealers in miscellaneous commodities (*tsa-huo*). A second alliance, known as the "Lower Eight Trades" (*hsia-pa-hang*), represented the major varieties of handicraft workshops (*tso-fang*) of the town. Leaders of the former group met regularly at the Shen Family Temple (Shen-chia miao), and those of the latter met at the Temple of Threefold Obligation (San-i tien), both ostensibly for collective worship but, as a contemporary commentator noted, to coordinate commercial activities as well.[44] Apart from the basic fact of their existence, however, our knowledge of these two early trade confederations of Hankow is very scanty.

For the post-Taiping years we are in a somewhat better position. There is no indication that the Lower Eight Trades was revived following the rebel occupation and razing of the town, although this may simply reflect a gap in surviving sources. The Upper Eight Trades, however, survived under the new title "Eight Great Guilds" (*pa-ta-hang*, *pa-ta-pang*) and continued to meet regularly at the Shen Family Temple. Although the number "eight" was retained as a link with the past, the revived confederation evidently represented a greater number of the major wholesale trades of the city, including such newly prominent groups as the tea dealers and the native bankers.[45] The Eight Great Guilds was apparently not a rank-and-file organization but a board of governors, drawn from the managers of the guilds it represented. At the top was a single manager-in-chief (*lao-tsung*), selected by the board. For many years during the 1870's and 1880's this post was held by Liu Tzu-t'ao (native place unknown), an examination *chü-jen* and former county magistrate who had retired to a second career in Hankow commerce as proprietor of the Liu-t'ien-pao Medicinal Herbs Dealership.[46] The Eight

Great Guilds, as we shall see, took on an ever-greater range of quasi-governmental functions within the city.

In addition to being allied at the top by a governing board of their respective managers, the major wholesale guilds of Hankow became linked in the post-Taiping decades by coordination among their functionally specific subsidiary operations in welfare and public security. Guild activities in these areas included, as we have seen in Chapter 9, regular sponsorship of benevolent halls. Beginning in about the 1870's, these halls were routinely coordinated in the officially declared annual "winter defense" (*tung-fang*), in which they systematically dispensed food and carried out other relief measures in order to tide the urban population over the slack season and thereby ensure social tranquillity. Although the fullest coordination among local benevolent halls was not achieved until some years after our period—with the establishment in 1908 of the Hankow Philanthropic Society (Han-k'ou tz'u-shan-hui), a modern, multi-faceted community-service organization founded jointly by the city's benevolent-hall managers—the movement toward consolidation can be discerned earlier.[47]

Coordination of fire-fighting societies (*shui-hui, lung-chü*) likewise linked their parent guilds. Of necessity, over the course of the nineteenth century these units, whether sponsored by guilds directly, by their offshoot benevolent halls, or by nonguild gentry associations, came to function as a city-wide network dividing territorial jurisdiction and frequently operating together to fight larger fires.[48] Moreover, in crises the fire-fighting detachments came to serve another purpose that required close coordination: they acted as privately financed paramilitary forces. During the abortive secret-society uprising in 1883, a municipal network of fire-fighting detachments was devised under the auspices of the Eight Great Guilds to maintain calm and prevent looting while government forces hunted down the leaders of the planned rebellion.[49] Immediately afterwards, the guilds of the city began to remove police functions from their fire-fighting detachments and vest them instead in guild-run merchant militia (*shang-t'uan*), which were more closely coordinated than their forerunners. These militia were the town's chief public-security organs through the end of the dynasty. In 1910, they followed the example of the benevolent halls by uniting into a single, city-wide organization, the Hankow Militia Alliance (Han-k'ou ko-t'uan lien-ho-hui).[50]

Eventually, the linkages between guilds became fully formal and officially recognized. First, in 1898 the most prominent guilds of Hankow were united in the Hankow Chamber of Commerce (*shang-wu chü*), established under the patronage of Chang Chih-tung in response to an imperial edict issued during the Hundred Days' Reform. Definitive evidence is lacking, but local sources suggest that in Hankow implementing this order meant granting formal government legitimation to the existing Eight Great Guilds leadership structure, with the imposition of two official-merchants (expectant taotais Wang Ping-en and Ch'eng I-lo) as the organization's "general directors" (*tsung-li*).[51] Later, in the complete disorder brought about by revolution and imperial counterattack in 1911, the entire spectrum of Hankow guilds formed an inclusive city-wide confederation, the All-Hankow Guild Alliance (Ko hui-kuan kung-so lien-ho-hui). The stated reason for this decisive action was "the recognition that in view of the widespread looting and plundering . . . we could not delay in making preparations and exhausting our energies in the pursuit of public peace and security."[52] Like the action of the Chungking Eight Provinces during the Taiping crisis half a century earlier, this represented an almost complete assumption of governmental powers by a confederation of private commercial groups that had become responsive to and responsible for the wider urban community. Unlike the Chungking Eight Provinces or Hankow's own earlier Eight Great Guilds, both of which involved merely the most powerful guilds of the city, the All-Hankow Guild Alliance included over a hundred member organizations of all types, sizes, and social strata. Their collective action at this time of dynastic collapse revealed them as the true repository, at least for the moment, of legitimate governmental authority in Hankow.

The Administration's Role in the Rise of Guild Power

That in 1911 the guilds of Hankow collectively stepped forward to fill the power vacuum left by the collapse of the imperial administration at the local level might be taken to imply that the bureaucracy, while it remained an active force, had sought with some success to suppress as competitive the power of guilds and guild alliances. The formation of the first Hankow Chamber of Commerce at official instigation, however, argues otherwise, as does the pattern of official patronage of guild organizations that had emerged in Hankow during the late imperial period.

Guilds, of course, actively courted official patronage. For this purpose they devised honorific titles such as "guild patriarch" (*hui-shou lao-yeh*) to bestow upon high-placed, nonmember benefactors who could offer them privileged access to local and provincial authorities (Hu Lin-i's kinsman Hu I-tieh held this title in the Hunan Timber Guild for several years).[53] Officials themselves could and did become members of local-origin clubs that offered fellowship to any compatriot residing in Hankow or its environs—an area that conveniently included the provincial capital. The well-known correlation between commercial and examination success for a given local area ensured that major Hankow local-origin guilds would frequently find compatriots in official posts nearby. In the eighteenth century, for example, a Hanyang prefect of Hui-chou origin was regularly the guest of honor at social gatherings in the Hui-chou guildhall of Hankow, and the club's history boasts of many other local and metropolitan officials of Hui-chou origin feted there over the years.[54]

Like other sojourners, officials felt a need to worship their home area's special deities, and Hankow guilds were quick to exploit the potential access to office this afforded them. The Hui-chou Guild boasted of many "great officials" who had worshipped regularly in the guild's sanctuaries during their tenures at Wuhan.[55] Lin Tse-hsü, a Fukien native serving as governor-general of Hukwang, entered in his diary at New Year's of 1838, "Went to the Fukien Guildhall at Hankow in order to burn incense at its Heavenly Mother [T'ien-hou] shrine."[56] Two months later he recorded another visit in greater detail:

> Today being the birthday of the Heavenly Mother, I went to the Fukien Guildhall at Hankow in order to take charge of the sacrificial observances there. Last month the manager [*szu-shih*] of our local-origin club requested that I [compose a fitting inscription and] have a ceremonial tablet constructed. . . . Yesterday I sent one of my runners ahead to the guildhall at Hankow to have the tablet mounted; this morning at the break of dawn I crossed the Yangtze to sacrifice and worship in person.[57]

Guilds profited from these assiduously cultivated official connections in several ways. Not least, of course, was gaining approval for their commercial initiatives. When pursuit of their business interests ran counter to the wishes of the local administration, groups like the Hunan Timber Guild were able to enlist powerful official patrons such as Tseng Kuo-fan and Tso Tsung-t'ang to intervene on their behalf. (Just as the Fukien Guild courted Lin Tse-hsü's patronage by requesting a tablet bearing his inscription, the Timber Guild later in the century solicited and displayed samples of calligraphy by such prominent Hunanese as P'eng Yü-lin and Liu K'un-i.) Moreover, official benefactors were a major source of capital for a guild's corporate projects. Hupeh Governor Chang Lien-teng, for example, a native of Shansi, contributed heavily to the repair of the Shansi-Shensi guildhall in 1719.[58] Patronage could also come from compatriot officials in quite distant posts; for example, provincial directors of education in Yunnan and Kwangsi made major contributions to the Hui-chou Guild's construction project of 1798–1805.[59]

Apart from direct financial aid, official support was manifested in legal injunctions favoring guild corporate interests. Many references in the records of the Hui-chou Guild attest to that group's frequent use of publicly proclaimed official protection of its collective assets: prohibiting encroachment by squatters on guild-owned or adjacent property; guaranteeing its title to land and developed properties; excluding undesirable porterage traffic, such as night-soil carriers, from its environs; and zoning street-hawkers and peddlers away from its residential holdings.[60] The Shansi-Shensi club's history reveals that it was similarly adept at procuring official protection for its holdings and activities.[61] Most striking, perhaps, was the local administration's outright confiscation in the late 1870's of the Ma-wang miao (a temple with attached pier facilities, mule stables, and market buildings) from the ownership and operation of a group of allegedly corrupt (and potentially seditious?) Taoist priests and its subsequent award of this valuable property to the Shansi-Shensi Guild, on the grounds that the guild's members used the facilities most heavily and that it would manage the complex in greater accord with the public interest.[62]

From the officials' point of view, good relations with Hankow guilds proved useful for a number of purposes. Guilds were checks on the commercial and social behavior of their members; in 1869, for example, the leaders of the Kwangtung Guild were called in by Hankow Submagistrate Chou Tsuan-wen and charged with investigating the property holdings of one of the guild's financially irresponsible members.[63] Local officials also appreciated the guilds' utility in time of local crisis, as when guilds helped to feed influxes of rural refugees from floods or other disasters. More generally, the guilds' eagerness to engage in Confucian philanthropic activities was acknowledged as a major contribution to the social stability of the city.

We have seen throughout this study that in Hankow, at least, guilds and other private forces had begun as early as the turn of the nineteenth century to assume social regulatory and welfare functions that the local and provincial administrations, impoverished and weakened first by the fierce White Lotus campaigns in Hupeh province and thereafter by continuing rural unrest in upland areas, were no longer able to provide. Over the course of the century, particularly in the uneasy yet dynamic post-Taiping decades, these functions expanded to encompass many that no authority had ever provided, but which were increasingly demanded by the new and more complex urban society of the time. In both traditional and innovative social services, the administration bestowed its blessing upon the "self-reliant" initiatives of the local urban population and its indigenous economic leadership. Hankow officials' annual proclamation of the essentially privately managed "winter defense" and their willing reliance upon guild-sponsored networks of fire fighters and militia to keep the peace during crises gave ample evidence of this blessing.

In their dealings with the Eight Great Guilds—the organization that by its claim to inclusiveness might seem to have presented the greatest overt challenge to the administration's monopoly of political authority—officials grasped eagerly at the chance to trade an ever-greater share of local power for local self-management. In the wake of the attempted 1883 uprising, for example, virtually the first act of Hankow Subprefect Chang Ou-fang was to convene a meeting of the Eight Great Guilds' leaders at their headquarters (the Shen Family Temple) and turn over day-to-day police functions to them.[64] At least from that time on, the Hankow taotai met twice monthly with important "gentry-merchants," specifically the Eight Guilds' leaders, to deliberate matters of local policy. These meetings were held on the first day of the lunar month at the Shen Family Temple and on the fifteenth at the Temple of the Four Officials (Ssu-kuan miao).[65] For much of the second half of the nineteenth century, moreover, the Eight Great Guilds was utilized as a tax agent, charged by the local administration with collecting the "one-percent port contribution."[66] On at least one occasion, in 1891, the Eight Guilds' fiscal and public security duties were linked when the organization was put in charge of managing the finances of a locally constructed and operated river-patrol fleet for Hankow and its environs.[67] It is hardly a surprise, then, that when asked to form a city-wide merchants' association in 1898, local officials should merely give more formal recognition to an organization on which they already relied.

To sum up, it is probably valid to view the expansion of guild structures and spheres of activity over the course of the nineteenth century as a privatization of local power that served as a prelude to China's twentieth-century political "disintegration." Alternatively, however, it can be seen as the genesis of a more effective and "modern" urban governmental apparatus under the very encouragement and patronage of the declining imperial order.

Guilds and Urban Autonomy

This and the preceding chapters have shown that in Hankow (1) guild concerns and authority extended well beyond the governance of a guild's own membership and trade, (2) guild linkages and confederations existed throughout much of the nineteenth century, (3) these confederations increasingly took actions that assumed the interests of the city as a whole to be their own, and (4) this was done with the blessing and support of the local administration. How do these findings fit into the existing corpus of scholarship on the place of guilds in late imperial politics and society? Immediately, we can see that judgments such as "The merchants' guild was not powerful enough to have a voice in matters concerning the common good of the community, still less in the governing process,"[68] which were long central to Western thinking on the subject, were premature. Similarly, Max Weber's argument that the powers of the Chinese guild "involved only special competencies of particular associations in particular questions of concrete group interest"[69] seriously underestimated the functions of such organizations. But what implications does our revised picture of the role of guilds have for the late imperial city as a whole, particularly for the issue of urban autonomy?

Urban autonomy exists when three separate criteria are met. First, a city must be recognized as a discrete political unit. In Ch'ing administrative law this criterion was never met by Hankow, or perhaps by any city other than the imperial capital. The *chen* did not become a "special municipality," independent of its hinterland, until well into the Republican period. Nevertheless, since the early Ch'ing, Hankow had been a discrete administrative unit at the subprefectural and subcounty levels. Moreover, over the course of the nineteenth century guild confederations and coordinated philanthropic and security networks (for example, the security patrols managed by the Eight Great Guilds in 1883) had taken as their explicit jurisdictions the well-defined contours of the *chen*. By the end of the century, in the eyes of both administration and populace Hankow was clearly a municipal entity.

The second prerequisite for urban autonomy is a self-conscious resident population, or, in Weber's term, an "urban community." The Weberian tradition staunchly denied this attribute to Chinese urban places, and for Weber "citizenship" (equated not with voting rights but with membership in "a joint community of burghers") never became in imperial China "a specific quality of the urbanite."[70] Yet we have seen evidence that long-time Hankow residents from whatever native place did develop a "locational identity" as inhabitants of the city and a "locational solidarity" with fellow urbanites, a process encouraged by the expansion of guild boundaries and the alliance of such groups on a citywide scale. As Mark Elvin has concluded:

The guild confederations of the nineteenth century were not organizations of powerful outsiders. Nor were they organizations defending purely merchant against "gentry" interests. They symbolized the consolidation of power of a new urban élite based at least as much on commerce as on landholding. Businessmen in late traditional China were not members of a disadvantaged caste, but were respected and influential citizens.[71]

The final prerequisite for urban autonomy is the formal granting by an external authority of the right of self-determination to the urban population. Again, such a grant never appeared, nor really could appear, in Ch'ing statute. Imahori Seiji, one of the first scholars to discover the existence of guild confederations in Chinese cities, pointed out that although in Europe such organizations succeeded in extracting municipal charters from feudal sovereigns, the failure of their Chinese counterparts to do likewise virtually guaranteed that urban autonomy (*shiminteki na jichi*) would not be possible in China.[72] However, the specific powers that European medievalists like Pirenne associated with this autonomy—the power to enact and enforce commercial legislation, jurisdiction over the finance and maintenance of public works, the authority to raise and control militia, and so on—all to a considerable extent devolved upon guilds and guild federations in Hankow. Also, increasingly the exercise of these powers was coterminous with the boundaries of the municipality.

In nineteenth-century Hankow, it seems, there was an unusually wide gap between de jure and de facto systems of political authority. Thus a substantial degree of de facto autonomy had emerged, with real power balanced between officials and the leaders of local society; over the course of the century the balance shifted very much toward the latter. This discrepancy between formally claimed and informally exercised power was not unique to Hankow but, as anthropologists like Eric Wolf have pointed out, is a common phenomenon in the local-level politics of complex societies:

> The formal framework of economic and political power exists alongside or intermingled with various other kinds of informal structure which are interstitial, supplementary, and parallel to it. . . . Sometimes such informal groupings cling to the formal structure like barnacles to a rusty ship. At other times, informal social relations are responsible for the metabolic processes required to keep the formal institution operating, as in the case of armies locked in combat. In still other cases, we discover that the formal table of organization is elegant indeed, but fails to work, unless informal mechanisms are found for its direct contravention.

This situation does not imply that the formal structure itself is either meaningless or powerless; as Wolf notes, "The informal structures of which I have spoken are supplementary to the system; they operate and exist by means of its existence, which is logically, if not temporally, prior to them."[73] Such a conceptualization nicely describes the complex balance of administrative power and guild power in nineteenth-century Hankow.

Conclusion

NINETEENTH-CENTURY Chinese society was not stagnant, listlessly awaiting the shock of foreign irritants against which to react or foreign models to emulate. When it came, that shock was real. In Hankow, it was first severely felt in the 1890's, and the resulting changes in all aspects of the city's life were enormous. But during the preceding century, Hankow society had also been changing, along a course dictated by the internal logic of China's own socioeconomic development. Nearly all the specific changes identified in this study can be explained independent of the arrival of the West; to the extent that the Western presence was felt in the city after the opening of the port in 1861 (and perhaps even before that year), for the most part it simply reinforced these ongoing trends.

The changes suggested in this study can be summarized under four headings: commerce, personal identity, social structure, and social organization. In commerce, the state's financial dependence on trade grew steadily. As state expenditures rose out of proportion to agrarian revenues, the central administration increasingly looked for support to the interregional trade centered on the Middle Yangtze, regional administrators looked to Hankow local officials, and these in turn relied upon Hankow merchants. Somewhat paradoxically, this growing fiscal dependence was accompanied by a dramatic relaxation of state controls on commerce (or, in the salt trade, by the abrogation of direct state proprietorship). I have suggested that this was part of a long-term trend toward the privatization of many sectors of the Chinese economy, which had begun by at least the seventeenth century. That trend, however, accelerated under the mid-nineteenth-century Hupeh administrations of Hu Lin-i, Kuan-wen, and their successors, who consistently chose to sacrifice control over commerce for its stimulation in their quest for greater revenues. Hu's innovations in the brokerage licensing system offer a striking, but hardly isolated, example of this pattern. Virtually across the board, merchant self-regulation superseded direct state control in the trades of Hankow.

The results were twofold. Hankow merchants were allowed to pursue, free from legal encumbrances and usually with state encouragement, the rationalization of business practices that had been underway for some time, including greater use of contractual instruments and guarantees, new forms of partnership and capital accumulation, and, especially, expanded banking and credit facilities. At the same time, the urban merchants' economic independence—particularly as exercised by their collective self-regulatory organs—gave them considerable leverage in noneconomic areas.

With respect to personal identity, geographic mobility in Ch'ing (particularly post-Taiping) China led to a multiplication of local identities for certain segments of the population. Primary, parochial attachments to native place were attenuated among immigrants to Hankow and, perhaps more surprisingly, among self-proclaimed sojourners there as well. This phenomenon facilitated the rise of a specifically urban consciousness and the emergence of a true "urban class" (*shih-min*) of the sort found by Teng T'o as early as the eighteenth century yet denied by Max Weber well into the twentieth. The set of attitudes that spawned this class is probably nowhere more clearly expressed than in the Hui-chou Guild's 1801 selection of Wang Heng-shih to manage its construction project on the grounds that Wang "had spent his entire life in the marketplace [*shih*] and was thus extraordinarily able in the management of affairs." The identity as "Hankow men" developed by long-term residents was gradually translated into a sense of locational solidarity and an impetus to communal self-nurturance demonstrated, for example, in the popularly financed and managed construction of a city wall in the 1860's. Despite Weber's denials, then, not only an urban class but also an urban community was emerging in nineteenth-century Chinese cities.

This urban class at Hankow was far from homogeneous. Although economic opportunities had never really been monopolized by a single group, the depopulation and commercial hiatus brought by the Taiping occupation precipitated a wholesale restructuring of the commercial order at the port. As Hu Lin-i observed, the leading merchant firms and families after the imperial recapture of the city were only rarely those prominent in the prerebellion era. More significantly, commercial power became more diversified, as Hunanese with fellow-provincial official patrons or ties to former comrades from Tseng Kuo-fan's regional anti-Taiping Hsiang Army, Ningpoese with advanced financial management techniques, and finally Cantonese with Western skills and connections muscled their way into a commercial elite once dominated by more culturally conservative Hui-chou and Shansi natives. In trade, dealers and brokers in tea, timber, cotton, vegetable oil, and a host of other commodities could now aspire to equal standing with the aristocratic salt and grain merchants of pre-Taiping years. Moreover, the pervasive trend toward socioeconomic pluralism was evident at nonelite levels as well, as the easy credit market of the 1860's and 1870's allowed commercial adventurers of all backgrounds and levels of capitalization to get in on the ground floor of the city's economic recovery.

Two additional trends in Hankow's social structure should be noted, although I have not dealt with them directly in the present study. First was the growth of a chronically underemployed urban lower class, which, along with stresses arising from the greater commercial openness of the post-Taiping decades, helped create an increasing local perception of social disorder. Second, and related, was the beginning of self-conscious class differentiation within the urban population.[1] In the 1870's and 1880's this second trend was noticeable but minor; in the wake of the forced-draft industrialization of the 1890's and 1900's, it would rapidly become more pronounced.

In social organization, the most striking change was the growth of Hankow guilds, not only in control over their respective trades, but also in size, corporate assets, and range of functions. In terms of membership, this meant a shift from an orientation toward exclusiveness to an ever-greater inclusiveness. In community service, guild initiatives increasingly focused on the city as a whole. Perhaps this city-wide focus first appeared during the White Lotus threat around the turn of the nineteenth century, when the Hankow salt merchants independently, and contrary to the interests of their administrative superiors at Nanking, chose to divert funds from their collective treasury to create a force of local braves for the defense of the entire city. But the expanding scope of guild activities and presumed jurisdictions, as well as the impetus to joint action and organization, was especially pronounced in the atmosphere of social mobilization that characterized the post-Taiping era. In large part this mobilization was seen as a necessary response to the commercial and social anomie of the period. Recourse to private organization-building in times of perceived social breakdown was not unprecedented in Chinese history (Hilary Beattie, for example, has recently shown how formal clan structures in rural Anhwei were created as a deliberate response to uncertainty about the effectiveness of state control in the first decades of Ch'ing rule);[2] what was unusual in late-nineteenth-century Hankow was the urban location and merchant sponsorship of such activity.

The result for Hankow was the rise of a guild-centered, sub-rosa municipal government apparatus, which reached full development only in the political crisis of 1911. By the last decades of the nineteenth century, a de facto power-sharing arrangement had come into being in Hankow, in which the role of the bureaucratic administration had been dramatically reduced in relation to the totality of governmental and semigovernmental activities actually carried out in the city. If, as Ira Lapidus has pointed out, urban autonomy and imposed imperial rule may be conceived not as mutually exclusive alternatives but as the poles of a continuum,[3] then despite the formidable-looking bureaucracy in late Ch'ing Hankow, the city's position along this continuum was already somewhat closer to the pole of autonomy. This reflected a gradual popularization of political functions that paralleled (though it lagged behind) the privatization of economic power.

In Hankow, at least, this popularization was a political counterpart to the socioeconomic pluralism of the post-Taiping city. Robert Dahl has defined a pluralistic political system as one "dominated by many different sets of leaders, each having access to a different combination of political resources."[4] Such a system need not be egalitarian—Dahl contends, in fact, that the American city he studied is itself far from egalitarian. Nor does the application of the pluralistic model seem limited to societies possessing representative democratic institutions. The key is rather a multiplicity of power bases, whose possessors are to a considerable extent responsible to their constituencies and at the same time play a significant role in the governance of the system as a whole. By such a definition, the Hankow of the Eight Great Guilds can best be seen less as subject to the tyranny of an absolutist state or a feudal agrarian elite than as a relatively self-contained, pluralistic political system.

It would be foolish to push this analogy to contemporary American cities too far, yet it also seems wrong to fault Chinese cities for failing to possess the particular manifestations of urban autonomy that appeared in the medieval European commune. Our failure to perceive in a given historical context the indicators we deem progressive may suggest simply that those indicators are specific to the Western path of development, or that we have too narrowly defined them in the first place. Likewise, processes that we identify as "rationalization" or "modernization" can take place only within cultural situations that each have their own peculiarities. In late imperial China, one such peculiarity was the nature of the state. The state's monopoly of ideological orthodoxy (by consensus of the elite), combined with an extremely low level of effective governmental penetration of the society, meant that for substantive urban autonomy to be achieved it was unnecessary, indeed undesirable, to provoke legalistic confrontations—by demanding municipal charters, for example. Rather, in the interstices of the imperial system there was ample leeway for local self-reliance, urban as well as rural.

Weber and his heirs have assumed that urban autonomy was a necessary precondition for the development of a "modern" society. If this assumption is correct (and it has not been challenged in the course of this study), then my argument that substantial urban autonomy had been achieved in nineteenth-century China would suggest two possible alternatives. Either (1) China would, if left to itself, ultimately have developed into an industrial capitalist society comparable to that of the West, or (2) if China would not have so developed, the reason must be sought in causes other than the failure of its cities to mature to the point where they might have fulfilled their required catalytic role. The fact that China's indigenous cultural development was decisively deflected by Western intervention in the 1890's and after, of course, rendered both of these alternatives merely hypothetical.

One final process of change was also underway in nineteenth-century Hankow. The growth of a specifically urban consciousness, the beginnings of self-conscious class differentiation, the increase in collective merchant self-regulation in economic matters, and the increasing assumption by merchants of governmental or quasi-governmental responsibilities in noneconomic affairs all clearly contributed to the embourgeoisement of the city's broad, dominant stratum. This incipient bourgeoisie was being molded within a milieu that was essentially preindustrial and in which the influence of the West was as yet only minor. Yet this milieu was extremely cosmopolitan in a strictly Chinese sense, inasmuch as it united in one densely crowded, intensely urban setting the most diverse subethnic types. The potential for psychological and cultural transformation inherent in such conditions has been repeatedly emphasized by classical Western urbanists from Georg Simmel to Robert Redfield.[5] Moreover, both participation in a developing national market and growing access to local and provincial officials in matters of policy formulation (via, for example, the Hupeh Bureau) were gradually politicizing Hankow merchants. In their growing irritation with government tax policies, as well as the apparent inefficacy with which commercial tax revenues were spent, merchants became more and more alienated from the imperial regime. By the last years of our study these latent antagonisms were still far from bearing fruit; nevertheless, a Protestant missionary at Hankow could write home in 1886:

> Although it is to be feared that the authorities of the present day no more believe in an intelligent and thoughtful democracy than those of the past, yet the people

are undoubtedly making progress in various directions, and there are undoubted signs of life around us. The most recent unsatisfactory conflict with France started many a strange question in the minds of the thinking population. . . . That there is a desire for some kind of change is evident.[6]

In 1911 China's youthful bourgeoisie, in the Wuhan cities and elsewhere, threw its support behind revolutionary administrations with remarkable rapidity. Indeed, several merchants active at Hankow during the last years of our study, in wholly domestic as well as compradorial trades, were among the most prominent initial supporters of the Republican cause.[7] Certainly this response was in large measure conditioned by the tremendous changes on the national and international scenes that clustered around the turn of the century, but it also owed much to a long-term process of change in Chinese urban society.

Reference Matter

Notes

Complete authors' names, titles, and publication data for works referred to below can be found in the Bibliography, pp. 397–409. The following abbreviations appear in the notes:

1818 HC: *Han-yang hsien-chih*, 1818.
1867 HC: *Han-yang hsien-chih*, 1867.
1884 HS: *Han-yang hsien-shih*, 1884.
1920 HC: *Hsia-k'ou hsien-chih*, 1920.
BPP: Great Britain, House of Commons, *British Parliamentary Papers*.
CCJP: *Ch'ang-chiang jih-pao*.
CPA: Ch'ing Palace Archives.
CPIWSM: *Chou-pan i-wu shih-mo*.
DUSCH: United States Consulate at Hankow, *Despatches from United States Consuls in Hankow, 1861–1906*.
FO: Great Britain, Foreign Office, Archives.
HPCSOJ: Tsungli yamen, Archives. "Hu-pei chiao-she O-jen i-wei-chieh ko-an."
HPTC: *Hu-pei t'ung-chih*.
HPTCCY: "Hu-pei t'ung-chih chih-yü."
HPYJCS: Tsungli yamen, Archives. "Hu-pei Ying-jen chiao-she."
HYFC: *Han-yang fu-chih*.
IGC: Inspectorate General of Customs.
IWL: *I-wen-lu*.
JMA: Jardine, Matheson and Company, Archives.
LMS: London Missionary Society, Archives.
MCA: Ming-Ch'ing Archives.
NCDN: *North-China Daily News*.
NCH: *North-China Herald*.
SP: *Shen-pao*.
SSHK: *Han-k'ou Shan-Shen-hsi hui-kuan chih*.
TLYM: Tsungli yamen, Archives.
TYSY: *Han-k'ou Tzu-yang shu-yüan chih-lüeh*.
USNA: United States National Archives, Washington.
WMCIA: Wuhan Municipal Commercial and Industrial Alliance.

Introduction

1. Pirenne, *Medieval Cities*. More recent treatments of the subject that contest certain elements of Pirenne's thesis, although they support his general scheme,

are Rörig, *Medieval Town* (assembled from work done in the 1930's and 1940's), and Waley, *Italian City-Republics*.

2. On the relationship of Pirenne's ideas to those of Weber, see Don Martindale's "Prefatory Remarks" in Weber, *The City*, pp. 49–56.

3. Pirenne, pp. 74–75.

4. Weber, *The City*, pp. 80–81.

5. Pirenne, pp. 170–71.

6. Weber, *The City*, pp. 111–12.

7. See esp. Pirenne, pp. 192–98; Weber, *The City*, pp. 91–96. More sober assessments of this phenomenon appear in Rörig, p. 28, and Waley, pp. 38–39.

8. On democracy, see Weber, *The City*, chap. 5. On the emerging concept of a public sector, see Hans Rosenberg, *Bureaucracy, Aristocracy, and Autocracy: The Prussian Experience, 1660–1815* (Cambridge, Mass., 1958). Rosenberg (p. 6) credits the medieval communes with devising "the rudiments of a modern system of public administration, public taxation, public finance, public credit, public works, and public utilities."

9. Weber, *The City*, p. 212. See also Pirenne, p. 118.

10. Eberhard, "Data," p. 254. See also Pirenne, pp. 154–56.

11. Weber, *Religion of China*, p. 16.

12. Weber, *The City*, p. 68; *idem*, *Religion of China*, p. 13.

13. Weber, *Religion of China*, p. 16.

14. Weber, *The City*, p. 77.

15. *Ibid.*, p. 82; Weber, *Religion of China*, p. 91.

16. Weber, *Religion of China*, p. 93; see also *idem*, *The City*, pp. 119–20.

17. Weber, *Religion of China*, p. 91.

18. Weber, *The City*, p. 81.

19. Weber, *Religion of China*, p. 90.

20. *Ibid.*, p. 102.

21. Weber, *The City*, p. 88.

22. Weber, *Religion of China*, p. 241.

23. Weber, *The City*, p. 83.

24. *Ibid.*, p. 97.

25. *Ibid.*, pp. 81, 104.

26. Weber, *Religion of China*, p. 16.

27. Levy and Shih, esp. pt. 1, pp. 6, 9; Feuerwerker, esp. pp. 23, 144, 243.

28. I refer specifically to: Balazs, "Villes" and *Civilization*; Eberhard, "Data," *Social Mobility*, and *Settlement and Social Change*; and Murphey, "City as a Center of Change." Related themes are sounded, among other places, in Dawson, "Law and the Merchant," and Trewartha, "Chinese Cities." Fei Hsiao-tung incorporates several Weberian assumptions concerning the Chinese city (e.g., the primacy of its "garrison" role) into his somewhat different arguments; see Fei, chap. 5.

29. Eberhard, *Settlement and Social Change*, p. 45.

30. Balazs, "Villes," p. 239. Cf. Murphey, "City as a Center of Change," p. 354.

31. Balazs, "Villes," p. 239; Eberhard, "Data," p. 266; Eberhard, *Settlement and Social Change*, p. 52; Murphey, "City as a Center of Change," pp. 357–58; Trewartha, p. 81.

32. Murphey, *Treaty Ports*, p. 57; Fei, p. 98.

33. Balazs, *Civilization*, p. 78. Cf. Dawson, p. 56. Eberhard, it should be noted, does see a "bourgeois culture" developing after the eleventh century, but emphasizes that this had no political correlative (*Social Mobility*, p. 268).

34. Balazs, *Civilization*, p. 78; Eberhard, "Data," pp. 264–67.

35. Eberhard, "Data," pp. 264–67.

36. Trewartha, p. 82.

37. Eberhard, for example, explicitly identifies the "pre-industrial" city of his study with the "classical city" of the T'ang ("Data," p. 261).

38. Shiba, *Commerce and Society*; see also his "Urbanization." Shiba's analysis of Sung cities of course draws upon earlier research, especially that of Katō Shigeshi and E. A. Kracke. A later work, somewhat less influential but more detailed on urban conditions, is Ma, *Commercial Development and Urban Change.*

39. An early analysis of this change is Fujii, "Shin'an shōnin"; see esp. no. 1, pp. 1–44.

40. Skinner, "Marketing."

41. Mote, "Transformation of Nanking." The concept of a "rural-urban continuum" is now common in Western urbanology.

42. Elvin, *Pattern*, chap. 12; Skinner, "Marketing," pt. 2; Skinner, "Introduction: Urban Development in Imperial China" and "Regional Urbanization in Nineteenth-Century China," both in *idem*, ed., *City in Late Imperial China*, pp. 3–32, 211–49.

43. Rozman, *Urban Networks*; Murphey, *Outsiders*, esp. pp. 177–79.

44. Skinner, "Cities and the Hierarchy of Local Systems," in *idem*, ed., *City in Late Imperial China*, pp. 275–352.

45. Elvin, "Gentry Democracy"; *idem*, "Market Towns."

46. Shiba, "Chūgoku toshi," p. 187. As Shiba notes, the Weberian heritage has been at least as strong in Japanese studies of Chinese cities as it has been in the West. A prime example is the influential work of Imahori Seiji; Imahori himself acknowledges his debt to Weber in *Kōzō*, p. 303.

47. DeGlopper, "Social Structure," p. 633.

48. Murphey, *Shanghai*; David D. Buck, *Urban Change in China* (Milwaukee, 1977); Kenneth Lieberthal, *Revolution and Tradition in Tientsin, 1949–52* (Stanford, 1980).

49. DeGlopper, "Social Structure"; *idem*, "Religion and Ritual in Lukang," in Arthur P. Wolf, ed., *Religion and Ritual in Chinese Society* (Stanford, 1974); *idem*, "Doing Business in Lukang," in W. E. Willmott, ed., *Economic Organization in Chinese Society* (Stanford, 1972); Elvin, "Market Towns"; *idem*, "The Administration of Shanghai, 1905–1914," in Elvin and Skinner; *idem*, "The Mixed Court of the International Settlement of Shanghai (until 1911)," *Papers on China*, 17 (1963), pp. 131–59. For partial results of the Ningpo Project, see Jones, "Finance in Ningpo"; *idem*, "Ningpo *Pang*"; Shiba, "Ningpo and Its Hinterland"; and James Cole, "Shaohsing: Studies in Ch'ing Social History," Ph.D. diss., Stanford Univ., 1975.

50. Geertz, *Peddlers and Princes*; Lapidus, *Muslim Cities*. Among the many studies of individual European cities are Daniel Waley, *Medieval Orvieto* (Cambridge, 1952), and George Rudé, *Hanoverian London, 1714–1808* (London, 1971).

51. Susan Mann Jones and Philip A. Kuhn, "Dynastic Decline and the Roots of Rebellion," in Fairbank, p. 144.

52. Pao, 34.10.

53. Tōa dōbunkai, vols. 11 and 12. See also Su, *Hsien-tai-hua*, pp. 121–24.

54. Allen to Walsham, 22 June 1888, FO 228/864; Su, *Hsien-tai-hua*, p. 279.

55. Esherick, p. 5. See also Chang P'eng-fei, *Han-k'ou mao-i chih*, and Chapter 2 of the present book.

56. The latter figure included 1,495 Europeans and 1,502 Japanese (*Present Day Impressions*). See also Chapter 1.

57. On the development of new urban land in the 1890's and 1900's, see Ts'ai I-ch'ing, vol. 6, no. 3; Su, *Hsien-tai-hua*, pp. 523–26; Esherick, p. 120.

Chapter One: Hankow in the Nineteenth Century

1. The lower length of the Han River, between Hsiang-yang and Hankow, is also known as the Hsiang River, though written with a different character from that used for the more famous Hsiang River of Hunan. See Fan, 1.9, and Morita, *Suirishi*, p. 84.

2. On the strategic importance of the Wuhan area, see Hu Lin-i, *I-chi* (1875), 14.2–3.

3. Hu Chao-ch'un, "Ts'un-wen t'ang wen-chi," *I-shu*, 2.7.

4. Information on Hankow's climate is drawn from newspaper accounts, including *SP*, Kuang-hsü 3, 12th month, 10th day, Kuang-hsü 5, 12th month, 22d day, Kuang-hsü 7, 11th month, 3d day; *NCDN*, 29 January 1869, 18 November 1871, 25 January 1878; as well as from personal observation. Hereafter, Chinese dates will be abbreviated in the format "Kuang-hsü 3/12/10."

5. Du Halde, 1: 99.

6. Oliphant, p. 574.

7. Williams, *Middle Kingdom*, p. 144; also Wolseley, p. 382.

8. Williams, *Middle Kingdom*, p. 144.

9. Hill, *Twenty-five Years*, p. 11; Thompson, p. 73.

10. Baldus to Etienne, 3 August 1835, *Annales*, 10: 75.

11. *BPP 1861*, 66, p. 340. In the nineteenth century, the chief commercial area of Wuchang was a sandbank south of the city known as Chin-sha Island. Before the Taiping hiatus it had served as a major anchorage for salt boats, but this function was discontinued after the rebel occupation. Chin-sha Island retained its role as the center of the provincial grain tribute collection, but increasing commutation of tribute payments beginning in the 1850's diminished its importance in this sphere as well. HPTCCY, *ts'e* 5; Li Shao-ling, pp. 20–21. See also Chapter 2, below.

12. Du Halde, 1: 99.

13. Oliphant, p. 571.

14. *BPP 1861*, 66, p. 340. On Hanyang's role in local commerce, see Chapter 2, below.

15. "Chiao-t'ung chih," in Hsü Huan-t'ou, ed., p. 4. See also Gill, p. 46.

16. Chang Chih-tung, memorial of Kuang-hsü 24, *Cheng-shu*, 12.21.

17. Fan, 2.1; Green, p. 230.

18. Wu Chung-fou, *Shang-ku pien-lan* (Guide for merchants), cited in Shigeta, "Konan beishichō," p. 485.

19. Walter E. Weyl, "The Chicago of China," *Harpers Magazine*, 18 October 1918.

20. *BPP 1861*, 66, pp. 340, 342.

21. John to London Headquarters, 18 September 1861, box 11.3.E, LMS.

22. Hill, *Hoopeh*, p. 1.

23. Bishop, p. 72.

24. Du Halde, 1: 99; Elgin, p. 298.

25. K. C. Hsiao, p. 559; a British intelligence report from the late 1840's cited by Hsiao notes that at that time, even in such a major city as Nanking 80 percent of the land within the city walls was cultivated farmland.

26. *Ta Ch'ing i-t'ung-chih*, cited in Liu Wen-tao, 1.1.4; Ch'en Hung-mou, 25.1.

27. *1818 HC*, 7.20–21. See also *SP*, Kuang-hsü 6/1/8, and numerous other local accounts.

28. Wolseley, p. 385.

29. Cornaby, pp. 39–40.

30. Huc, 2: 142.

31. Williams, "Topography of Hupeh," p. 101.

32. Hu Chao-ch'un, "Ts'un-wen t'ang shih-chi," *I-shu*, 12.4, 13.4.

33. Oliphant, p. 559.

34. Cornaby, p. 40.

35. *NCH*, 3 June 1887.

36. Yeh, 1.2; *TYSY*, 8.58–59; Mayers et al., p. 445; Mizuno, p. 56.

37. Green, p. 130.

38. *NCDN*, 27 December 1871.

39. A Japanese estimate for 1905, cited in Lewis, p. 6. See also P'an Lei, 11.26; Fan, 2.1; Yeh, 6.7; *Annales*, 10: 75.

40. Wolseley, p. 390.

41. Fan, 6.1.

42. Cornaby, p. 39. A poem by one Lu Hsiao-yin describes the dazzling sights of the lanterns and sounds of the hawkers at Hankow's night market, as well as the "smells of jasmine and fragrant lotus filling the street"; HPTCCY, *ts'e* 6.

43. Green, p. 131.

44. Cornaby, p. 39.

45. Shiba, *Commerce and Society*, p. 67.

46. *1920 HC*, 12.1. This island of sand had completely eroded by late Ming times. It was not the same as the identically named sandbank that surfaced at the Hanyang shore around 1769 and came to serve as the headquarters of the area's timber market, described in Chapter 8, below. See P'an Hsin-tsao, p. 39; *Ying-wu-chou hsiao-chih*.

47. Fan, 1.16 and 3.1; Shiba, *Commerce and Society*, p. 128; Ma, p. 59; Wang Pao-hsin, 1.5.

48. Fan, 3.1; Smith, p. 6.

49. *1920 HC*, 12.1; Wang Pao-hsin 1.1–12; P'an Hsin-tsao, p. 62; Tōa dōbun-kai chōsa hensambu, 11.456. On Hanyang's South Market, see WMCIA, "Yao-ts'ai."

50. Hu Chao-ch'un, "Ts'un-wen t'ang wen-chi," *I-shu*, 2.7; Chang Shou-po, p. 1; Chin, p. 66.

51. Authorities differ on the exact year in which this shift occurred. The year 1497 is given in the earliest source I have myself seen, *HYFC*, 12.3. Most other sources, however, place the event sometime in the 1460's. See Fan, 1.14; *1920 HC*, 12.2; Oxenham, p. 283; *Kuang-hsü Hu-pei yü-ti chi*, 5.21; P'an Hsin-tsao, pp. 28–30; Chin, p. 65.

52. T'ang I-yen, "Feng-shui yün" (On geomancy), reprinted in Fan, 1.14. The "upper bank" in T'ang's account seems to refer to Hankow's Han River shoreline, and the "lower bank" to its Yangtze shoreline. On the early population of Hankow, see also *1920 HC*, 12.2; Ts'ai, vol. 5, no. 6, p. 35.

53. *HYFC*, 12.3–6; Wang Pao-hsin, 1.5, 1.8; Liu Wen-tao, 1.1.4.

54. "Tsai Yü-tai-ho te ku-tao shang" (On the old course of the Yü-tai canal), *CCJP*, undated; "Ch'ieh-shuo Ch'iao-k'ou te ch'iao" (More about the bridges

of Ch'iao-k'ou), *CCJP*, 24 August 1980; Ts'ai, vol. 5, no. 6, p. 35, and vol. 5, no. 8, p. 34.

55. Wei Chin-feng, "Tzu-chung chi" (The Tzu-chung record), reprinted in Fan, ch. 4, especially 4.3–4 and 4.15. Also Fan, 1.12; P'an Lei, 11.26; *HYFC*, 12.3; Ts'ai, vol. 5, no. 7, p. 24.

56. Hsiung Po-lung, cited in *1867 HC*, 27.66; Liu Wen-tao, 1.1.4. See also *TYSY*, 1.8; P'an Hsin-tsao, p. 62.

57. *1920 HC*, 4.57.

58. The status of the "four great *chen*" as administrative "curiosities" is discussed by Frederick Mote, who views them as rare exceptions to the rule that in late imperial China, "administrative" and "economic" cities were indistinguishable (Mote, pp. 106–10).

59. Skinner, "Cities and the Hierarchy of Local Systems," in Skinner, ed., *City in Late Imperial China*, p. 314.

60. Hung, 31.1–8.

61. Examples are the initial establishment of harbor lifeboat services, the 1863 decision to construct a Hankow wall, and a major scandal in the local educational system. See, respectively, IGC, *Lifeboats*, Chinese enclosures, p. 30; "Hupei Han-k'ou Ying-kuo tzu-ti an," TLYM; Medhurst to Alcock, 6 February 1868, FO 228/456; *SP*, Kuang-hsü 1/10/16. After 1862, the prefect served collaterally as assistant superintendent of Maritime Customs at Hankow (Kuan-wen, memorial of T'ung-chih 1, "Ts'ai-cheng," MCA).

62. *Li-tai chih-kuan piao*, 53.1497.

63. *1867 HC*, 8.33–34, 12.2; *1920 HC*, 1.19, 5.11; Chin, p. 67; P'an Hsin-tsao, p. 62. On the activities of the subprefect, see, e.g., *SP*, Kuang-hsü 4/9/23, Kuang-hsü 4/11/17, Kuang-hsü 9/5/3. On the activities of the assistant subprefect, see Post Records, U.S. Consulate, Hankow, USNA.

64. See Chapter 5, below; also Rowe, "Urban Control," esp. pp. 101–2.

65. *SP*, Kuang-hsü 3/7/23; see also *1920 HC*, 5.11.

66. *Li-tai chih-kuan piao*, 54.1515.

67. Hung, 31.8. On submagistrates generally, see K. C. Hsiao, p. 5.

68. *1867 HC*, 14.54–60; see also Chapter 6, below.

69. *1920 HC*, 12.1; Chin, p. 67.

70. *1884 HS*, 1.1.

71. Fan, 1.13.

72. *1867 HC*, 8.34; Yeh, 5.6. Ts'ai I-ch'ing states (no. 5.8, pp. 34–35) that they were also notoriously well-paid, receiving regular "presents" from merchants within their jurisdictions. (Ts'ai I-ch'ing was the pen name of Ts'ai Fu-ch'ing, a turn-of-the-century Hankow merchant and chairman of the Hankow Chamber of Commerce at the time of the 1911 Revolution.)

73. *SP*, Kuang-hsü 9/5/3; Fan, 5.16; report of Li Han-chang, Kuang-hsü 4/2/20, HPYJCS; report of Li Han-chang, Kuang-hsü 3/10/28, HPCSOJ; Yeh, 1.1.

74. Caine to Wade, 4 May 1870, FO 228/494.

75. Lin, *Jih-chi*, p. 276.

76. Kuan-wen, memorials of Hsien-feng 11/4/16 and Hsien-feng 11/10/4, CPA; *1867 HC*, 12.1–2 (source of citation); Gingell to Bruce, 12 June 1861, FO 228/313; FO 682/1797.

77. In late 1861 the taotai was given the collateral post of superintendent of the Hankow Maritime Customs Office. On the various categories of taotais in the Ch'ing political structure, see Oda Yorozu, *Shinkoku gyōseihō* (Guide to

Chinese official titles) (Taipei, 1905), pt. 1.b, pp. 45–50, and H. S. Brunnert and V. V. Hagelstrom, *Present Day Political Organization of China* (Taipei, 1971), entries 833, 842, and 844.

78. Skinner, "Cities and the Hierarchy of Local Systems," in Skinner, ed., *City in Late Imperial China*, pp. 333–34.

79. Johnson to U.S. Embassy, Peking, 9 April 1883, Post Records, U.S. Consulate, Hankow, USNA. As one British consul noted, civil cases involving foreigners were also "always referred in the first instance to the Intendent of the circuit, who gives instructions to his subordinates to investigate them and report thereon" (Gardner to O'Conor, 10 February 1886, FO 228/831).

80. *SP*, Kuang-hsü 2/12/19, Kuang-hsü 4/10/8, and Kuang-hsü 8/3/28. On the Hupeh Bureau and the taotai's role in it, see also Chapters 4 and 6, below.

81. *1867 HC*, 12.5 and 14b.5–12; *1920 HC*, 4.38–47 and 5.11.

82. For the *li-chin chü*, see *SP*, Kuang-hsü 8/3/28 and *HPTC*, 1.1373. For the *pao-chia chü*, see *SP*, Kuang-hsü 5/9/19 and Rowe, "Rebellion and Its Enemies," pp. 92–94. For the *tien-pao chü*, see Su, *Hsien-tai-hua*, p. 445. For the *chao-shang chü*, see *SP*, Kuang-hsü 7/10/17. For the *pao-kung chü*, see "Hu-pei Han-k'ou Ying-jen tzu-ti an," TLYM. For the *Chin-chüan chü*, see *SP*, Kuang-hsü 4/10/4. For the *ho-po so*, see *SP*, Kuang-hsü 7/intercalary/5.

83. For the *hsün-szu wei-yüan*, see *SP*, Kuang-hsü 9/5/3. For the *yang-chieh wei-yüan*, see Gardner to O'Conor, 10 February 1886, FO 228/831. Ch'en Ch'eng-tse is mentioned in Allen to Walsham, 14 June 1888 and 1 September 1888, both FO 228/864.

84. See, for example, Yeh, 5.6; *SP*, Kuang-hsü 1/10/18, Kuang-hsü 3/7/23, and Kuang-hsü 8/12/5; IGC, *Tea*, p. 24.

85. See, for example, the biography of Hanyang Magistrate Sun Fu-hai, *1920 HC*, 4.58, and the discussion of Hu Lin-i's brokerage reforms in Chapter 6.

86. Philip A. Kuhn, "Local Self-Government under the Republic: Problems of Control, Autonomy, and Mobilization," in Frederic Wakeman, Jr., and Carolyn Grant, eds., *Conflict and Control in Late Imperial China* (Berkeley, 1975), p. 264 and *passim*.

87. For details, see Chang Chih-tung, memorial of Kuang-hsü 24, *Cheng-shu*, 12.21.

88. P'an Hsin-tsao, p. 67; Chin, p. 67. A similar formation of discrete municipal governments in major commercial and industrial cities took place some half century earlier in Meiji Japan and has been credited with an important role in that nation's rapid industrial development after the 1880's; see Yazaki, p. 289ff. What effect such a move might have had in nineteenth-century China is an interesting question.

89. "Shang-yeh chih," in Hsü, ed., p. 14. See also Oliphant, p. 566.

90. *1818 HC*, 12.9 and 12.19; *1920 HC*, 3.1. For a detailed discussion of *pao-chia* activities in Hankow, see Rowe, "Urban Control."

91. A series of registers held at the MCA and studied by James Lee, entitled *Hu-pei-sheng min-hu-k'ou shu-mu tsung-ts'e*, provide population figures for Hanyang county that roughly accord with those of the *pao-chia* enrollment figures recorded in the county gazetteers. According to these registers, the population of the county increased rapidly from 393,492 in 1803 to 463,669 in 1843, when the series ends. In my view, these figures are as underreported as the *pao-chia* enrollments. I wish to thank Dr. Lee for sharing this information with me.

92. *1818 HC*, 12.10 and 12.19.

93. Kuo Wen-hao, cited in Wang Pao-hsin, 1.8; Yen Ssu-sheng, cited in Su, Third year's report, p. 81; *TYSY*, 8.26.

94. The average household size for Hanyang county, as reflected in the population registers cited in note 93 above, was just under five persons.

95. *1818 HC*, preface, p. 2.

96. Emrys Jones, *Towns and Cities* (London, 1966), p. 32.

97. Hu Lin-i, *I-chi* (1875), 8.15.

98. Elgin, p. 293.

99. *NCH*, 8 January 1859.

100. *Times*, 13 May 1861.

101. Wilson to London office, 5 March 1862, LMS.

102. Gingell to Bruce, 10 March 1863, *BPP 1864*, 64, no. 3302, p. 40.

103. Gingell, "Report on Trade at Hankow," *BPP 1863*, 73, no. 3104, p. 133; MacPherson to Hart, 31 January 1865, *BPP 1866*, 71, no. 3587, p. 109; FO, *Diplomatic and Consular Reports*, 1888, p. 14; IGC, *Decennial Reports, 1892*, p. 179.

104. Elvin, *Pattern*, p. 178.

105. Murphey continues, "Before 1850 Hankow itself was only a moderate sized town." (Murphey, "City as a Center of Change," p. 354.) Today, Professor Murphey would probably not endorse the extreme position reflected in this earlier statement. However, as recently as 1977 he wrote that "the foreign stimulus . . . was the primary cause of the rapid growth of Shanghai, Tientsin, and Hankow" (*Outsiders*, p. 134).

106. In 1817, for instance, Governor Chang Ying-han reported discovering in Hankow a secret Roman Catholic cell with caches of Bibles and other Christian literature (memorial of Chia-ch'ing 22, 12th month, 25th day, "Nung-min yün-tung," MCA). See also Fan, 4.21–23. Fan, writing in 1822, shows familiarity with details of Christian thought and practice.

107. *Lettres édifiantes*, 9: 497 and 11: 514.

108. De Couteux, letter of February 1730, *Lettres édifiantes*, 11: 483–84.

109. De Couteux, letter of 1730, *Lettres édifiantes*, 11: 512; Loppin to Radominski, 1737, *Lettres édifiantes*, 12: 355–56; des Robert to Brisson, 1741, *Lettres édifiantes*, 12: 381.

110. *Lettres édifiantes*, 12: 186ff describes these persecutions in detail. The numerical estimate is from Latourette, p. 166.

111. Eight Chinese Christians to Torette, 1831, *Annales*, 10: 66–69; Baldus to Etienne, 3 August 1835, *Annales*, 10: 69–78; Rizolati to Association for the Propagation of the Faith, 28 October 1840, 19 January 1841, 15 May 1842, 25 November 1842, 20 October 1845, 15 April 1850, 18 February 1852, and 28 January 1853, *Annales*, vols. 13–18, 23–25; Latourette, pp. 232–33.

112. Blakiston, p. 69; see also Thompson, p. 170.

113. Tōa dōbunkai, 11.315–16. See also Chapter 4, below.

114. Su, *Hsien-tai-hua*, p. 95.

115. FO, *Diplomatic and Consular Reports*, 1888, p. 14.

116. Bowers, p. 269; Medhurst to Alcock, 3 March 1866, FO 17/456. A complete list of foreign firms in Hankow, with their Chinese names, appears in *China Directory, 1874*.

117. Alabaster, "Report on Trade, 1879," FO 17/838.

118. Francis White, "Hankow," in IGC, *Reports on Trade*, 1881, p. 10.

119. Gingell, "Report on Trade at Hankow," 30 June 1862, *BPP 1863*, 73, no. 3104, p. 133; Bowers, p. 270.

120. Williams to U.S. Embassy, Peking, 1 April 1862, Post Records, U.S. Consulate, Hankow, USNA.

121. *BPP 1866*, 71, no. 3587, p. 122.

122. Wilson to London office, 22 December 1862, LMS; Gingell to Bruce, 12 January 1863, FO 228/351.

123. A. G. Reid, "Report on the Health of Hankow," *Customs Gazette*, 11 (1871): 45, in *DUSCH*.

124. Little, *Yangtze Gorges*, p. 17; IGC, *Decennial Reports, 1892*, p. 167.

125. Tōa dōbunkai chōsa hensambu, p. 709; *NCH*, 8 June 1866.

126. See LMS archives, *passim*; also MacGillivray, pp. 5, 89. Detailed information on missionary activities in treaty-port Hankow appears in Su, *Hsien-tai-hua*, pp. 98–106.

127. *SP*, Kuang-hsü 12/12/15.

128. Kokuryūkai, ch. 23. See also Marius Jansen, *The Japanese and Sun Yat-sen* (Cambridge, Mass., 1954), pp. 49–50.

129. Mayers, p. 445.

130. Gingell to Bruce, 28 December 1862, *BPP 1864*, 63, no. 3295, p. 134. Dean, "Sino-British Diplomacy," pp. 71–96, provides an excellent, detailed account of the acquisition of the concession site. See also Su, *Hsien-tai-hua*, pp. 96–97.

131. Cheng to Caine, 22 January 1870, translated in Caine to Wade, 4 May 1870, FO 228/494.

132. Probably the first Chinese shop established within the British Concession was that of Yao Chang-chieh, a prominent bronzeware dealer, in 1913; *Yao-shih tsung-p'u*, 14.1.39.

133. Green, p. 96. A somewhat harsher assessment is offered in Hsiao Chih-chih, "Han-k'ou tsu-chieh," pp. 77–80.

134. Richard Halkett, "Report from Hankow," IGC, *Reports on Trade*, 1865, p. 42.

135. Allen to Walsham, 22 June 1888, FO 228/864.

136. *SP*, Kuang-hsü 4/8/29. On foreign industry in Hankow before 1890, see P'eng Yü-hsin, "Yang-hang," p. 26; Su, *Hsien-tai-hua*, pp. 119–21. Dockworkers at foreign-owned piers probably outnumbered Chinese laborers in foreign factories during these years, inasmuch as a British pier had been constructed at Hankow in 1876 and a Russian pier as early as 1865. But as Hsiao Chih-chih has concluded, neither foreign-owned piers nor the "coolie problem" they generated became significant until around 1895 ("Ma-t'ou kung-jen," p. 3).

137. John, p. 201.

138. A Hankow Mixed Court (Hui-shen-kung-t'ang) was established in 1868 to adjudicate such conflicts (*1920 HC*, 10.7).

139. Henri Cordier, *Bibliotheca Sinica* (New York, 1968), 3: 2276.

140. Green, pp. 230–31; A. Novion, "Report on Hankow," IGC, *Reports on Trade*, 1876, p. 22.

141. Ts'ai, vol. 6, no. 3, p. 42. See also "Liu-chia-miao chin-hsi" (Liu-chia Temple, past and present), *CCJP*, 9 October 1979; "Chiang-an ti-ch'u te yu-lai" (The origins of Chiang-an ward), *CCJP*, no date; P'i Ming-hsiu, p. 60; Esherick, pp. 86–87, 103.

142. IGC, *Decennial Report, 1892*, p. 179.

143. Murphey, *Outsiders*, p. 225.

144. Cornaby, p. 10.

Chapter Two: The Trade of Hankow

1. Fujii, esp. no. 1, pp. 3–34.

2. Huc, 1: 129.

3. *Ibid.*, p. 141.

4. Wu Chung-fu, *Shang-ku pien-lan* (Guide for merchants), cited in Shigeta, "Konan beishichō," p. 485.

5. Skinner, "Cities and the Hierarchy of Local Systems," in Skinner, ed., *City in Late Imperial China*, esp. pp. 286–87. The eight levels in Skinner's terminology are: central metropolis, regional metropolis, regional city, greater city, local city, central market town, intermediate market town, and standard market town.

6. Skinner, "Regional Urbanization in Nineteenth-Century China," in Skinner, ed., *City in Late Imperial China*, pp. 212–15 and *passim*.

7. The history of the Hankow rice trade has been documented by Japanese scholars. See Nakamura, "Kokō bei no ryūtsū"; Kitamura, "Shōnin shichō"; Fujii, esp. no. 1, pp. 25–26; Shigeta, "Konan beishichō," esp. p. 437. See also Ch'üan, "Mi-liao mao-i"; Ch'üan and Kraus, *Rice Markets and Trade.*

8. Ch'üan, "Mi-liao mao-i," p. 77.

9. Cited in Saeki, *Ensei*, p. 307.

10. Hankow's rice supply is discussed by firsthand observers in *Hsien-chuang-i-kung nien-p'u*, p. 74; Huc, 2: 297; Mizuno, p. 445. See also Abe, esp. pp. 467, 502; Shigeta, "Konan beishichō," p. 436.

11. Fujii, no. 1, p. 26; Su, *Hsien-tai-hua*, pp. 24–25. Evelyn Rawski's account of rice collection in Hunan highlights Hankow's isolation from its hinterland in the matter of grain supply. Rice grown in rural Hunan passed from the producer through several different hands before reaching a local collection point such as Hsiang-t'an. Then, when Hankow rice dealers came to make their purchases, indigenous "compradores" were required to bridge the cultural gap between buyer and seller. See Rawski, pp. 104–7.

12. Nakamura, p. 60ff; Kitamura, p. 8.

13. See, e.g., Yeh, 1.15; *SP*, Kuang-hsü 2/4/22. Part of the explanation for the apparent decline in the Hunan-Kiangnan rice trade may have been the rise in direct Szechwan-Kiangnan rice shipments beginning around the turn of the nineteenth century. See biography of Li Hsiang-hsing, HPTCCY, ch. 6.

14. HPTCCY, ch. 6.

15. Mizuno, pp. 290–91. Food grains other than rice made up an additional 18 million taels of the annual trade at Hankow.

16. Wang Pao-hsin, 1.17.

17. Mizuno, pp. 290–91.

18. Chang Shou-po, p. 25.

19. Mizuno, p. 290. Fuller information on the Hankow oil trade appears in *SP*, Kuang-hsü 6/8/13; Ts'ui-jung Liu, pp. 74–90; Su, *Hsien-tai-hua*, p. 32.

20. Ts'ai, vol. 6, no. 1–2, p. 78; "Wu-Han ch'eng-chen ho-t'u"; Su, *Hsien-tai-hua*, pp. 29–30, 37; Ts'ui-jung Liu, pp. 93–115; Mizuno, pp. 498–515; P'eng Tse-i, *Shou-kung-yeh shih tzu-liao*, 2: 241–44; interview with P'an Hsin-tsao, Wuhan, 1981. For details on Hankow's trade relations with other major Hupeh markets (Sha-shih, I-ch'ang, Hsiang-yang, Lao-ho-k'ou), see Su, *Hsien-tai-hua*, pp. 23–54.

21. Parker, *China*, p. 148. On the marketing of beans, see Ts'ui-jung Liu, pp. 35–40.

22. Elgin to Malmesbury, 5 January 1859, FO 405/3; P'eng Tse-i, *Shou-kung-yeh shih tzu-liao*, 2: 163; Saeki, "Chūgoku kinsei ni okeru dokusai kunshu no keizai seisatsu" (The economic policies of China's autocratic rulers in the modern period), in Saeki, *Chūgokushi kenkyū*, 2: 62; Wolseley, p. 389.

23. Evidence on the use of these trade routes appears in such sources as Yeh, *Han-k'ou chu-chih*; TLYM; FO; and *SP*. Useful secondary accounts include Kitamura, pp. 5, 14ff; Fujii, no. 1, pp. 26 and 32; Chang Kuo-hui, p. 94; Morita, *Suirishi*, p. 138; Morita, "Shōku henran," *passim*; Nishizato, no. 1, p. 8; Murphey, *Shanghai*, pp. 94, 98–99; Lewis, pp. 6–7. Rozman, p. 131, provides a list of fifteen "major long-distance transportation routes in China," for five of which Hankow was a principal terminus.

24. *NCDN*, 1 September 1869.

25. Francis White, "Report from Hankow," in IGC, *Reports on Trade*, 1877, p. 21.

26. Morita, *Suirishi*, esp. pp. 99, 138.

27. See for example *SP*, Kuang-hsü 4/6/20.

28. Skinner, "Regional Urbanization in Nineteenth-Century China," in Skinner, ed., *City in Late Imperial China*, p. 217. See also pp. 248–49; Skinner, "Introduction: Urban Development in Imperial China," in *City in Late Imperial China*, p. 24n; Skinner, "Mobility Strategies," p. 330; Moulder, pp. 32–35.

29. P'eng Tse-i, "Shou-kung-yeh te fa-chan," pp. 54–57; Hou, p. 280; Wei and Lu, p. 35. This recent trend in Chinese scholarship develops arguments for the eighteenth-century emergence of a national market first advanced in the late 1950's. See, for example, the recently translated articles by Yang I, "The Land System of the Early Ch'ing Dynasty" (1958), and by Liu Yung-ch'eng, "The Handicraft Guilds of Soochow during the Ch'ing Dynasty" (1959), both in *Chinese Studies in History*, Fall-Winter 1981–82, esp. pp. 105, 140–41.

30. P'eng Tse-i, "Shou-kung-yeh te fa-chan," p. 54.

31. *Ibid.*, p. 56. The temptation is strong to associate this phenomenon with that described in Michael Hechter, *Internal Colonialism: The Celtic Fringe in British National Development, 1536–1966* (Berkeley, 1975). In China, however, the colonization process seems not to have been so thoroughgoing or the consequences for the colonized area so negative. This was largely because in China, as the examples cited show, internal colonization was largely confined to extracting a single commodity from a more or less diversified agrarian economy.

32. Numerous examples of investors shifting between commodities appear in sources on Hankow; see, for example, the biography of Li Hsiang-hsing, HPTCCY, ch. 6. On shifts of commercial capital between regions, see Patrick Hughes, "Report on Trade at Hankow, 1877," FO 17/1788, and Chapter 5, below.

33. Skinner, "Mobility Strategies," p. 331.

34. *SP*, Kuang-hsü 9/7/21; *1920 HC*, 5.24–25; Ts'ai, vol. 6, no. 1–2, p. 78; "Huang-p'i chieh" (Huang-p'i Street), *CCJP*, 21 July 1964.

35. Wang Feng-sheng, 2.20–21; *Liu-shih tsung-p'u* (1924); *Feng-shih tsung-p'u*.

36. *Kuang-hsü Hu-pei yü-ti chi*, 5.22–23.

37. *Han-yang hsien-chih* (Gazetteer of Hanyang county), 1748 ed., cited in Fujii, no. 1, p. 15; *1818 HC*, 7.22; Fan, 1.17; Elgin to Malmesbury, 5 January 1859, FO 405/3.

38. *SP*, Kuang-hsü 6/7/5.

39. Hu Chao-ch'un, "Tsun-wen-t'ang shih-chi," *I-shu*, p. 6.

40. *Liu-shih tsung-p'u* (1932), ch. 2; *Han-yang Yao-shih ts'u-p'u*, ch. 2 and 3; *Yao-shih tsung-p'u*, 6.10.

41. *1818 HC*, 7.21; *SP*, Kuang-hsü 5/11/11.

42. Fan, 2.1; *SP*, Kuang-hsü 5/7/12; Chang Shou-po, p. 20; "Tsai Yü-tai ho te ku-tao shang" (On the old course of the Yü-tai canal), *CCJP*, n. d.

43. Fan, 2.26; *SP*, Kuang-hsü 4/1/21 and Kuang-hsü 8/6/18; "Han-k'ou te Liu-tu ch'iao" (The Liu-tu Bridge neighborhood of Hankow), *CCJP*, 23 August 1962. Other produce markets on Hankow's periphery are reported in Wang Pao-hsin, 3.47; Liu Wen-tao, 1.1.5.

44. Tai Chün-yüan, memorial of Chia-ch'ing 25/3/3, "Hsing-k'o t'i-pen," MCA.

45. Murphey, *Outsiders*, p. 8.

46. Skinner, "Marketing," esp. pt. 2, p. 212; Skinner, "Mobility Strategies," p. 328. For an urbanologist's view, see Sjoberg, p. 91.

47. In one recorded case, for example, an independent boat operator suddenly backed out on a contracted shipment of Western merchandise in order to take a more lucrative salt contract; report of Kuang-hsü 13/5, HPYJCS.

48. WMCIA, "Wang-yü-hsia."

49. WMCIA, "Yao-ts'ai hang-yeh."

50. P'eng Yü-hsin, "Yang-hang," p. 29.

51. Medhurst to Alcock, 23 January 1867, FO 17/482.

52. Good examples are Hatano, *Kindai kōgyōshi*; Yokoyama, *Kindaika no keizai kōzō*; and Fu, *Shang-jen chi shang-yeh tzu-pen*.

53. Myers, p. 85.

54. The following general breakdown is based on primary data culled from TLYM; MCA; *SP* reports; Yeh, *Han-k'ou chu-chih*; Mizuno, *Kankō*; and Nishin bōeki kenkyūjo. Relevant secondary sources include Feng, "Ya-shui hsing-chih chih yen-pien"; P'eng Yü-hsin, "Yang-hang"; Negishi, *Baiban seido*; McElderry, pp. 23–25; and Shiba, "Ningpo," pp. 410–14. My understanding of the structure of late imperial commerce owes a great deal to conversations with Professor Susan Mann Jones.

55. Mayers et al., p. 445. A discussion of the operations of a group of Hankow brokers, those in the rice trade, appears in Abe, p. 502.

56. Report of Hukwang Governor-general Kuan-wen, T'ung-chih 6/1/29, "Hu-pei Che-chiang Feng-t'ien Fa-Ying-Mei-O chiao-she," TLYM. Nieh is designated a *mai-pan* (compradore) in the original.

57. Chinese People's Bank, pp. 730–31; *Yao-shih tsung-p'u*, ch. 6; *SP*, Kuang-hsü 7/intercalary/6. On *chuang* capitalization, see Nishin bōeki kenkyūjo, 1: 972.

58. Alabaster to Wade, 7 July 1880, FO 228/651.

59. *SP*, T'ung-chih 13/11/9.

60. Fujii, no. 3, pp. 78–79.

61. Hankow agent Richard Dudley to Shanghai office, 20 May 1861, JMA.

62. WMCIA, "Wang-yü-hsia."

63. These reports of the Hankow taotai appear in TLYM. For more detail on partnerships between men of diverse local origin, see Chapter 7, below.

64. Weber, *Social and Economic Organization*, p. 191ff. Unfortunately, I have uncovered no account books from nineteenth-century Hankow; a number from Peking, however, are discussed in Robert P. Gardella, "Commercial Bookkeeping in Ch'ing China and the West: A Preliminary Assessment," *Ch'ing-shih*

wen-t'i, 4, no. 7 (1982): 56–72. On the significance of innovations in bookkeeping, see also DeRoover, *Money, Banking, and Credit*.

65. Imahori, "Goka no kindaika," pp. 1–8. On the earlier history of Chinese partnerships, see Shiba, *Commerce and Society*, p. 199ff.

66. "Ts'ung Wan-li tao Ch'ien-lung" (From Wan-li to Ch'ien-lung), in Teng, esp. pp. 221–24.

67. Yeh, 5.3.

68. IGC, *Reports on Trade*, 1865, p. 40.

69. "Chinese Partnerships."

70. Levy and Shih, 1: 6 and *passim*.

71. Report of Hukwang Governor-general Li Han-chang, Kuang-hsü 6/8/28, HPYJCS.

72. Yü-t'ai, memorial of Tao-kuang 21/11/28, CPA.

73. On the seasonal management of Hankow markets, see *SP*, Kuang-hsü 2/2/18 and Kuang-hsü 2/2/28; Mizuno, p. 291.

74. Weber, *Religion of China*, p. 102; Sjoberg, pp. 200–207.

75. For Hankow harbor regulations, see: *HPTC*, 50.14–16; *SP*, Kuang-hsü 6/6/17 and Kuang-hsü 3/10/2; Mizuno, p. 296. Augustus Margary provided an excellent description of one sort of Chinese business contract in discussing the preparations undertaken at Hankow for his ill-fated 1874 journey to Kweichow: "A regular Chinese form of agreement was drawn up by the boat owner and handed over to me. The main conditions were that he would convey me to Chen-yuan Fu in Kwei Chou for the sum of 110,000 cash, which was to be paid in several installments along the way, starting with a pre-payment of 60,000 cash at Hankow. The sum was to include everything and to free me from all those incidental appeals on behalf of the crew which so frequently spring up *en route* to delay and annoy the traveller." (Margary, p. 2.) For examples of other forms of contract in Ch'ing commerce, see Teng, pp. 201–3, and Fu-mei Chang Chen and Ramon Myers, "Customary Law and the Economic Growth of China During the Ch'ing Period." *Ch'ing-shih wen-t'i* 3, no. 10 (1978): 4–27.

76. Weber, *From Max Weber*, p. 331.

77. Little, *Far East*, p. 94.

78. *NCH*, 12 August 1854.

79. P'eng Yü-hsin, "Yang-hang," p. 24.

80. Chang P'eng-fei, ed., *Mao-i chih*; see also Esherick, p. 5; Cheng Yu-kuei, *Foreign Trade and Industrial Development of China* (Washington, 1956), pp. 22–23.

81. *1867 HC*, 8.43.

82. Hu Chao-ch'un, "Tsun-wen-t'ang shih-chi," *I-shu*, 11.8–9.

83. Hu Lin-i, *I-chi* (1866), 8.15.

84. Lord Elgin, for example, noted during his 1859 inspection of the city that "although it has suffered grievously from the rebellion . . . a good deal of business is even now doing there" (Elgin to Malmesbury, 5 January 1859, FO 405/3). Rapid rebuilding accompanied the revival of trade; a member of the British preopening reconnaissance team was gratified to discover, amidst stacks of new lumber on all sides, "houses and shops springing up daily from the piles of ruins about" (Wolseley, p. 383). For other comments on the city's recovery, see Chapter 1, above.

85. Hu Lin-i, *I-chi* (1866), 8.15. On the turnover of salt merchants, see IGC, *Salt*, p. 63.

86. Report of Hankow Consul Gingell, 30 June 1862, *BPP 1863*, 73, no. 3104, p. 133.

87. IGC, *Decennial Reports, 1892*, p. 179.

88. Fan, 2.27.

89. Chinese People's Bank, p. 731. See also P'eng Yü-hsin, "Yang-hang," p. 22.

90. "Correspondence Respecting the Opening of the Yangtze-Kiang to Foreign Trade," *BPP 1861*, 66, p. 342; Blakiston, p. 65.

91. Huc, 2: 127.

92. Report of A. MacPherson, 31 January 1865, *BPP 1866*, 71, p. 108.

93. Oliphant, p. 563.

94. Murphey, *Outsiders*, p. 197.

95. "Customs Regulations," Hankow, dated 7 May 1874, in IGC, *Customs Rules and Regulations*, pp. 61–63 (English) and 64–66 (Chinese); report of H. E. Hobson, 19 February 1869, in IGC, *Reports on Privileges Conceded*, pp. 18–19.

96. Except where noted, the following summary has been compiled from reports of Hankow Maritime Customs officials and British and American consuls, and from *SP*.

97. *BPP 1866*, 71, p. 121.

98. Medhurst to Alcock, 12 February 1866, FO 17/456; Mayers, p. 444.

99. *SP*, Kuang-hsü 9/12/1.

100. Gardner to O'Conor, 9 January 1886, FO 229/831.

101. *NCH*, 29 May 1885.

102. Kuan-wen, memorial of Hsien-feng 8/11/9, CPA.

103. Murphey, *Shanghai*, p. 97.

104. Chu, p. 197.

105. P'eng Yü-hsin, "Yang-hang," esp. pp. 26–28. P'eng's evidence likewise supports Murphey's recent conclusion that the major effect of the foreign trade was simply "diverting into external channels slightly increased supplies of goods which had previously been circulated more domestically" (*Outsiders*, p. 177).

106. Medhurst to Alcock, 23 January 1867, FO 17/482.

107. Alabaster, "Report on Trade for 1874," FO 17/732.

108. R. E. Bredon, "Hankow," in IGC, *Reports on Trade*, 1885, p. 75. A Chinese report on the same phenomenon is found in *SP*, Kuang-hsü 2/3/13. Similar stories were heard in other treaty ports. The most revealing statement of all, perhaps, is that of Tientsin Customs Commissioner Thomas Dick in 1867: "The mere operation of buying goods in their own country is one for which the Chinese have always been considered thoroughly qualified. It was merely a temporary condition of affairs under which, for a year or two, Foreign imports were sold through secondary foreign agents at secondary ports. As soon as the Chinese merchants became accustomed to the matter of doing business with foreign vessels, they returned to their own practice of making their purchases at the headquarters of the import trade—Shanghai." (IGC, *Reports on Trade*, 1867, p. 21, cited in K. C. Liu, pp. 109–10.)

109. *NCH*, 1 September 1869.

110. Alabaster, "Report on Trade, 1879," FO 17/838.

111. *NCH*, 12 November 1884. Among the numerous other reports of this common activity are Kuan-wen, memorial of Hsien-feng 11/9, *HPTC*, 50.12–13; Alabaster to Fraser, 19 April 1880, and Alabaster to Wade, 7 July 1880, both FO 228/651.

112. Caine to Alcock, 29 July 1869, FO 17/506.

113. Gingell to Bruce, 10 March 1863, *BPP 1864*, 62, no. 3302, p. 40.

114. A. Novion, "Report from Hankow," in IGC, *Reports on Trade*, 1876, p. 21.

115. Anonymous letter dated 21 December 1871, *Times*, 9 February 1872.

116. See R. E. Bredon's Hankow reports in IGC, *Reports on Trade*, 1882, p. 74, and 1885, p. 75.

117. K. C. Liu, *Steamship Rivalry*. See especially Liu's tables charting the growth and fluctuations of the Hankow-Shanghai steamer trade, 1861–74, on pp. 42, 66, 107, and 150.

118. Bruce to Russell, 7 June 1864, *BPP 1865*, 53, p. 11.

119. K. C. Liu, pp. 13–14, 67–68.

120. *Times*, 9 February 1872; MacPherson to Hart, 31 January 1865, *BPP 1866*, 71, p. 116.

121. The activities of one Chinese shipping agency serving primarily Western clients are described in the report of the Hankow taotai, Kuang-hsü 13/5, HPYJCS.

122. Hughes, "Report on Trade at Hankow," 1877, FO 17/788.

123. John, p. 90; Lewis, p. 6.

124. *1920 HC*, 9.1; Hughes to Fraser, 10 March 1877, FO 228/590; Hsü Jun, p. 32; A. Novion, "Hankow," in IGC, *Reports on Trade*, 1876, p. 21.

125. "Chiao-t'ung chih," in Hsü Huan-t'ou, ed., p. 4.

126. IGC, *Reports on Trade*, 1877, p. 9.

127. P'eng Yü-hsin, "Yang-hang," p. 24.

128. Murphey, *Outsiders*, p. 178.

129. Rawski, p. 107; Lewis, p. 7. According to Lewis, the population of Hsiang-t'an declined by 50 percent over the course of the nineteenth century because of that city's eclipse by the regional city Changsha.

Chapter Three: The Salt Trade

1. Cooper, p. 21. Major sources utilized in the following reconstruction of the Hankow salt trade include *Liang-Huai yen-fa chih*; relevant memorials of Hupeh provincial officials; *HPTC*; E. H. Parker, "Salt," a report included in Hughes to Wade, 12 May 1873, FO 228/525; and IGC, *Salt*. The most comprehensive secondary work on the Ch'ing salt trade has been done by Saeki Tomi; see both his monograph *Ensei* and a number of articles appearing in his collection *Chūgokushi kenkyū*. Two English-language studies that deal specifically with areas other than Hankow but are of use are Ho, "Salt Merchants," and Metzger, "T'ao Chu's Reform."

2. Fan, 3.1; Ts'ai, vol. 5, no. 10, p. 40; *Hsien-chuang-i-kung nien-p'u*, p. 54; Mizuno, pp. 290–91.

3. Metzger, "T'ao Chu's Reform," p. 23. Matthews defines *yin* as "a load of eight bags of salt, weighing 6¾ piculs net."

4. Lu, 5.1–6, 5.11–19; *1867 HC*, 8.43; *SP*, Kuang-hsü 3/7/1; Saeki, "Shindai Dōkōchō ni okeru Kaikan ensei no kaikaku" (The reform of the Huai-nan salt administration in the Ch'ing Tao-kuang reign), *Chūgokushi kenkyū*, 2: 636 and *passim*. On the 1849 fire, see: *HPTC*, 51.14; Li Shao-ling, pp. 20–21.

5. Alec W. Cross, "Report on Hunan," in IGC, *Salt*, p. 63.

6. Kuan-wen, memorial of Hsien-feng 6, *HPTC*, 51.18–19.

7. Kuan-wen, memorial of Hsien-feng 11/5/20, CPA; *Liang-Huai yen-fa chih*, 73.1; *HPTC*, 51.20.

8. Parker, "Salt," FO 228/525.

9. *HPTC*, 51.20–21; IGC, *Salt*, pp. 64, 88.

10. Lu-shen and Yang Tse-tseng, memorial of Tao-kuang 11, in Wang Yün-wu, ed., 1.232–35; *HPTC*, 51.13.

11. Lin, *Cheng-shu*, p. 411; Hsieh Yüan, report of Tao-kuang 29, *HPTC*, 51.14.

12. *Liang-Huai yen-fa chih*, 71.9–10; Kuan-wen, memorials of T'ung-chih 3/4 and T'ung-chih 4/7, *HPTC*, 51.21–22. The relative taxation of Huai and Szechwan salt in Hupeh continued to be a focus of government attention for decades; see Li Han-chang, memorial of Kuang-hsü 4/4/10, in Li Han-chang, unpaginated; Pien Pao-ti and P'eng Tzu-hsien, memorials of Kuang-hsü 9/10 and Kuang-hsü 10/4, in Pien, 5.25–27 and 7.26–27. The legalization of Shensi salt in Hupeh was rescinded in 1868; see Kuo Po-yin, memorial of T'ung-chih 7/8, *HPTC*, 51.23.

13. *Liang-Huai yen-fa chih*, 73.10; IGC, *Salt*, p. 63; T'an Yen-hsiang, memorial of T'ung-chih 6/4, *HPTC*, 51.22–23; Tseng Kuo-fan and Li Han-chang, memorial of T'ung-chih 11, in Wang Yün-wu, ed., 5: 2349–51; Li Han-chang, memorial of Kuang-hsü 2, in Li Han-chang, ch. 7. By 1889, Hupeh province was deriving nearly eight times as much tax revenue from legal Szechwan salt imports as from Huai salt (Su, *Hsien-tai-hua*, p. 214).

14. *SP*, Kuang-hsü 3/7/1.

15. Metzger, "T'ao Chu's Reform," p. 39; Saeki, *Chūgokushi kenkyū*, 2: 636, 639.

16. Kuan-wen, report to Tsungli yamen, T'ung-chih 4/1/20, HPYJCS.

17. Lu-shen and Yang Tse-tseng, memorial of Tao-kuang 11, in Wang Yün-wu, ed., 1: 232–35.

18. Lin, *Cheng-shu*, p. 411; Saeki, *Ensei*, p. 55.

19. Lu, 5.1.

20. Fan, 3.16; Chi-shan, memorial of Chia-ch'ing 7/5/18, CPA.

21. Lu-shen and Yang Tse-tseng, memorial of Tao-kuang 11, in Wang Yün-wu, ed., 1: 232–35.

22. The grain-for-salt exchange is documented in Kitamura, p. 3; Fujii, no. 1, p. 23 and no. 3, p. 94; Saeki, *Ensei*, p. 153; Saeki, *Chūgokushi kenkyū*, 2: 62. Sometimes a role in the grain trade preceded rather than followed trading in salt. For example, Li Hsiang-hsing, an early-nineteenth-century Hankow salt merchant described as "the wealthiest man in all Hukwang," initially made his fortune as a pioneer of direct rice shipments from Szechwan to Kiangnan. (HPTCCY, ch. 6.) On the Ch'ien-lung "contributions," see Teng T'o, "Lun *Hung-lou-meng* te she-hui pei-ching ho li-shih i-i" (On the social background and historical significance of *The Dream of the Red Chamber*), in Teng, p. 183.

23. The phrase *i-shang-i-kuan* ("both merchants and officials") is used to describe Liang-Huai merchants in Hou, p. 282. To judge from Hou, this is a Ch'ing usage, but I have not found independent confirmation. On warehouses, see: IGC, *Salt*, p. 96. On collective funds, see: Chi-shan, memorial of Chia-ch'ing 7/5/18, CPA; Pao, 34.9–11.

24. Fujii equates the salt depot head merchant with the more general late imperial institution of "libationer" (*chi-chiu*), a headman elected by all the merchants in a trade in a given locality. He notes that when local official policy toward the trade was being formulated or official control tightened, officials might demand a major say in the selection of this headman. In this respect, Fujii

sees the head merchant as the true heir of the T'ang *hang-t'ou*, or market official. (Fujii, no. 3, pp. 87–88.)

25. Ts'ai, vol. 5, no. 11–12, p. 59.

26. Chi-shan, memorial of Chia-ch'ing 7/5/18, CPA. On the duties of the *an-shang*, see also *1818 HC*, 11.1; Wang Chia-p'i, *ts'e* 3; Saeki, *Chūgokushi kenkyū*, 2: 639.

27. Wang Chia-p'i, *ts'e* 3.

28. Ho, "Salt Merchants," p. 142. A fuller description of the *hsia-fei* appears in Saeki, *Ensei*, esp. pp. 219–20. According to Saeki, the *hsia-fei* at Hankow was first instituted during the Ch'ien-lung reign.

29. The term *hsia-fei* was also used more widely in Ch'ing government accounting to refer to any miscellaneous expense fund. Governor-general Yü-t'ai, for instance, uses it in a discussion of the general accounting system of his Hukwang administration (memorial of Tao-kuang 21/11/28, CPA).

30. *1818 HC*, 17.9; *1867 HC*, 10.26–27.

31. *1920 HC*, 15.6; *1867 HC*, 10.27; Wang Feng-sheng, 1.1.

32. Lu, 5.2.

33. Kao Heng, memorial of Ch'ien-lung 29, *HPTC*, 51.13. Ho Ping-ti stresses this conflict of interests between head merchant and transport merchants, stating that the *hsia-fei* "was handled exclusively by a few merchant treasurers . . . who were either head merchants or their trusted agents," that it "was never strictly audited," and that the burden of paying it "was inevitably shifted to the entire group of transport merchants" ("Salt Merchants," p. 143).

34. Chi-shan, memorial of Chia-ch'ing 7/5/18, CPA.

35. *Ibid.*; Chi-shan and Wu Hsiung-kuang, memorial of Chia-ch'ing 7/9/5, CPA.

36. Chi-shan and Wu Hsiung-kuang, memorial of Chia-ch'ing 7/9/5, CPA.

37. T'ao Chu, cited in Saeki, *Ensei*, pp. 244–45.

38. Lu-shen and Yang Tse-tseng, memorial of Tao-kuang 11, in Wang Yün-wu, ed., 1: 232–35.

39. Anonymous, "Chin-hu lang-mo" (Wasted ink from a golden inkwell), HPTCCY, ch. 6.

40. *HPTC*, 51.14.

41. Saeki, *Chūgokushi kenkyū*, 2: 639.

42. *1867 HC*, 8.43.

43. *Ibid.*, p. 44.

44. Parker, "Salt," FO 228/525.

45. IGC, *Salt*, pp. 63, 81.

46. *Liang-Huai yen-fa chih*, 71.9; *1920 HC*, 5.29–30.

47. IGC, *Salt*, p. 81.

48. Pien Pao-ti, memorial of Kuang-hsü 8/12, in Pien, 4.1–3.

49. IGC, *Salt*, p. 64.

50. *Ibid.*, p. 91.

51. Reports of the Hankow taotai dated Kuang-hsü 3/3/7 and Kuang-hsü 13/5, HPYJCS.

52. Hogg Bros. and Co. to Medhurst, 28 April 1866, FO 228/416. Because Hogg Bros. was a foreign firm, its activity in the salt trade was illegal under Chinese law.

53. Li Hung-chang, memorial of T'ung-chih 11, "Ts'ai-cheng," MCA; Pien Pao-ti, memorial of Kuang-hsü 10/3, Pien, 7.10–11. See also Tseng Kuo-ch'üan, memorial of T'ung-chih 5/8, *HPTC*, 50.27. In fact, Hupeh came to rely more heavily on taxation of Szechwan than of Huai salt, largely because

Szechwan provincial officials were empowered to collect not only likin but also the regular duty, an increasing percentage of which they diverted to the province's own financial needs. Ultimately, these "national" revenues were officially redirected to underwrite provincial self-strengthening industrialization in the Wuhan cities. (See Li Han-chang, memorial of Kuang-hsü 2, Li Han-chang, ch. 7; Kennedy, p. 171.)

54. IGC, *Salt*, p. 103.

55. Hu Lin-i, letter to Board of Revenue, letter to Hupeh salt taotai, and public proclamation, all ca. Hsien-feng 6/6 or 6/7, all in draft copy in Wang's hand in Wang Chia-p'i, *ts'e* 3.

56. Parker, "Salt," FO 228/525.

57. *Liang-Huai yen-fa chih*, 71.7; Gingell to Bruce, 12 June 1861, FO 228/313; Parker, "Salt," FO 228/525. An extreme view of the "bureaucratization" of these years is expressed in Ts'ai, vol. 5, no. 11–12, p. 59.

58. T'ien's biography appears in *1920 HC*, 13.13.

59. *Liang-Huai yen-fa chih*, 71.10.

60. *Ibid.*, 73.9–11.

61. *Ibid.*, 74.11.

62. Parker, *China*, p. 235.

63. Lu-shen and Yang Tse-tseng, memorial of Tao-kuang 11, in Wang Yün-wu, ed., 1: 232–35.

64. Fujii, no. 4, p. 121.

65. *HPTC*, 51.13.

66. Fan, 2.13, 2.16, 2.37.

67. Chi-shan and Wu Hsiung-kuang, memorial of Chia-ch'ing 7/9/5, CPA.

68. Lu-shen and Yang Tse-tseng, memorial of Tao-kuang 11, in Wang Yün-wu, ed., 1: 232–35.

69. *1920 HC*, 5.29.

70. IGC, *Salt*, pp. 102, 111; P'eng Tse-i, "Hang-hui," p. 79; *1920 HC*, 5.30.

71. *NCH*, 22 June 1872; see also Chapter 4, below.

72. See, respectively, P'eng Tse-i, "Shou-kung-yeh te fa-chan," p. 45; Teng, p. 195; Wei and Lu, pp. 19–20; Hou, p. 277.

Chapter Four: The Tea Trade

1. Mizuno, pp. 290–91. By 1907 the value of the tea trade relative to the trades in other commodities at Hankow had declined somewhat from its heyday in the 1860's and 1870's, but I believe this ranking is approximately valid for the earlier period as well.

2. Chao-li-ch'iao Tea Factory, p. 4, cites the *Hsin T'ang shu* (New T'ang History) to this effect; see also Li Shao-ling, p. 46.

3. Fujii, no. 1, pp. 22–23.

4. P'eng Tse-i, "Shou-kung-yeh te fa-chan," p. 53; see also Fujii, no. 1, p. 26.

5. For example, the Yeh clan, which had roots in both these areas, established a branch lineage in Hanyang county in the 1650's; see *Yeh-shih tsung-p'u* and Chapter 7, below.

6. Chao-li-ch'iao Tea Factory, pp. 4–8. The account given in this source is drawn from the archives of the Ta-sheng-k'uei commercial house, held by the Mongolian Autonomous Region Archives.

7. *Ibid.*, p. 9; Tōa dōbunkai, 11: 315–16; M. I. Sladkovskii, *History of Economic Relations Between Russia and China* (Jerusalem, 1966), p. 71.

8. FO, *Diplomatic and Consular Reports*, 1888, p. 10. See also reports of Hupeh

Governor Kuo Po-yin, T'ung-chih 7/12/15; Hukwang Governor-general Li Han-chang, T'ung-chih 8/7/5 and T'ung-chih 10/1/24, all HPYJCS; IGC, *Reports on Trade*, 1875, p. 101; Mizuno, p. 422.

9. This claim is made in Chao-li-ch'iao Tea Factory, p. 5. Yet Hatano Yoshihiro, in a comprehensive listing of teas purchased by Europeans under the Canton system, identifies none from either Hunan or Hupeh (Hatano, pp. 94–97). One can probably conclude that their volume was quite small relative to that of teas from southeast China.

10. *BPP 1866*, 71, p. 111; see also *BPP 1865*, 53, p. 73.

11. Sources on this dispute include two dispatches from British Hankow Consul Arthur Gingell to British Chargé at Peking Frederick Bruce, dated 3 July and 2 September 1861, both FO 228/313, which summarize numerous local communications or include transcripts in both English and Chinese. An account of this episode appears in Dean, *China and Great Britain*, pp. 56–58. I have referred to Dean's version, but feel that his interpretation of these events solely in the context of diplomatic history presents an inadequate picture of the forces and institutions actually involved.

12. *HPTC*, 50.41–43; Hu Lin-i, letter to Tan Shao-ts'un, Hsien-feng 9/7/15, Hu Lin-i, *I-chi* (1875), 65.10.

13. Gingell to Bruce, 3 July 1861, FO 228/313. Unfortunately, the Chinese originals of neither this proclamation by the Hankow prefect nor subsequent orders issued by the Hupeh Bureau have been preserved.

14. *Ibid.* Quotations are from Gingell's report, and do not necessarily accurately translate the original document.

15. Hankow Taotai Cheng to Gingell, dated Hsien-feng 11/6/7, Chinese enclosure in Gingell to Bruce, 3 July 1861, FO 228/313.

16. Kuan-wen, memorial of Hsien-feng 11/9, *CPIWSM*, T'ung-chih reign, 2.4–8. See also the differently worded memorial of Kuan-wen on this subject, dated Hsien-feng 11, *HPTC*, 50.12–13.

17. Prince Kung et al., memorial of Hsien-feng 11/9, *CPIWSM*, T'ung-chih reign, 2.33–35. The Tsungli yamen formally endorsed the right of Western merchants and/or their agents to make up-country purchasing trips in article four of its "Five Regulations for Trade at the Yangtze Ports," issued in late 1861 (*CPIWSM*, T'ung-chih reign, 2.25–26).

18. Gingell to Bruce, 12 January 1863; Gingell to Hankow Taotai Cheng, enclosed in Gingell to Bruce, 27 June 1863. Both FO 228/351.

19. "Shang-yeh chih," in Hsü Huan-t'ou, ed., p. 14; FO, *Commercial Reports*, 1888, p. 14.

20. IGC, *Reports on Trade*, 1881, p. 10.

21. Entry of 21 March 1867, Hankow to Shanghai Private Letter Book (C55/1), JMA; Gingell to Bruce, 27 June 1863, FO 228/351.

22. Evidence of the dependence of foreign merchants upon their Hankow compradores is furnished in reports of the investigation surrounding Mackeller and Co.'s bankruptcy, by T'an Yen-hsiang, T'ung-chih 6/5/12, and Li Han-chang, T'ung-chih 6/8/8, HPYJCS. One Hankow compradore later active in government service was Liu Shao-tsung (Seating), Heard's chief tea buyer at the port and subsequently head of the Hankow office of the China Merchants' Steam Navigation Co. See Hao, p. 113.

23. Entry of 22 June 1867, Hankow to Shanghai Private Letter Book (C55/1), JMA.

24. FO 228/436, *passim*; Caine to Alcock, 25 January 1869, FO 228/476.

25. Alabaster, "Report on Trade, 1882," FO 228/934.

26. See, for example, *SP*, T'ung-chih 11/5/10; *NCDN*, 20 May 1879.

27. Sources drawn upon in the following description of the tea collection network include accounts in Chinese and Western newspapers; Tsungli yamen and British Foreign Office archives; Imperial Maritime Customs publications, especially IGC, *Tea, 1888*; and miscellaneous documents included in Yao, *Tzu-liao*. Major secondary sources include Chu, *Tea Trade*, and Shigeta, "Kishu shōnin."

28. Pien Pao-ti, memorial of late Kuang-hsü 10 or early Kuang-hsü 11, Pien, 5.45–48; Chao-li-ch'iao Tea Factory, p. 5. The provincial origins of the teas traded at Hankow are recorded in Mizuno, p. 289.

29. T'an Ssu-t'ung, "Liu-yang ma-li shu" (Essay on the advantages of hemp cultivation for Liu-yang county), 1897, excerpted in Yao, 3: 1472.

30. The role of the *shan-t'ou* in the central China tea trade approximated that of the *pao-t'ou* (labor boss) in the production and rural processing of cotton in the lower Yangtze region, as described in Yokoyama, pt. 2.

31. *SP*, T'ung-chih 12/4/13.

32. Some *ch'a-chuang* had several locations; e.g., the firm run by the Hunanese Hsiao P'iao-chen had its head office in Hsiang-t'an but maintained a permanent branch in Hankow. (Report of Li Han-chang, T'ung-chih 10/1/24, HPYJCS.)

33. *SP*, Kuang-hsü 3/6/2; *NCDN*, 18 April 1871.

34. Pien, 5.46; Chao-li-ch'iao Tea Factory, pp. 6–7; Shigeta, "Kishu shōnin," p. 602; Hao, p. 170.

35. This observation was made in the mid-1960's by Shigeta ("Kishu shōnin," p. 603), and again recently as part of a broad revisionist interpretation of the Ch'ing economy by P'eng Tse-i ("Shou-kung-yeh te fa-chan," p. 56). This phenomenon in early modern China seems to invite comparison with the processes of "protoindustrialization" that have been studied by historians of early modern Europe.

36. One example was the Ningpoese broker Ch'ien Yen; see report of Li Han-chang, T'ung-chih 10/1/24, HPYJCS.

37. Report of Pien Pao-ti, Kuang-hsü 9/10/21, HPYJCS.

38. Entry of 21 March 1867, Hankow to Shanghai Private Letter Book (C55/1), JMA; report of Pien Pao-ti, Kuang-hsü 9/10/21, HPYJCS; Shigeta, "Kishu shōnin," p. 610.

39. P'eng Tse-i, "Shou-kung-yeh te fa-chan," p. 56. Commercial credit was extended not only from Western patrons to Chinese clients, but the other way around as well; see the discussion of Mackeller and Company's bankruptcy, below.

40. P'eng Yü-hsin, "Yang-hang," p. 29.

41. Shigeta, "Kishu shōnin," pp. 610–13.

42. For an example, see report of Pien Pao-ti, Kuang-hsü 9/10/21, HPYJCS.

43. For instance, in the Tao-kuang period the tea guild of Anhwei province was a component of the overall provincial organization of Anhwei natives at Hankow. See Niida, p. 503.

44. Allen to Walsham, 12 May 1888, FO 228/864; Chu, p. 237; Negishi, *Shina no girudo*, pp. 82, 226.

45. Hsü Jun, p. 14. See also Hao, p. 189.

46. Medhurst to Alcock, 19 August 1867, FO 228/436.

47. *Ibid.*
48. FO 228/436.
49. *NCH*, 22 June 1872; *SP*, Kuang-hsü 8/3/28.
50. IGC, *Tea, 1888*, pp. 24, 49.
51. P'eng Tse-i, "Hang-hui," p. 81.
52. *NCDN*, 2 September 1872, notes that Western buyers generally attributed these discrepancies to poor handling during shipment to Hankow from up-country refining centers.
53. *SP*, T'ung-chih 11/5/22.
54. *Ibid.*
55. *SP*, T'ung-chih 12/4/13.
56. *Ibid.*
57. *SP*, T'ung-chih 13/4/8.
58. *SP*, Kuang-hsü 5/4/12.
59. *SP*, Kuang-hsü 2/10/1.
60. Hughes to Wade, 31 October 1876, FO 228/569.
61. R. E. Bredon, in IGC, *Reports on Trade*, 1883, p. 77. Sources employed in this account of the 1883 tea boycott include Chinese- and English-language newspaper accounts; report of Hukwang Governor-general Pien Pao-ti, Kuang-hsü 9/10/21, HPYJCS; report of R. E. Bredon, IGC, *Reports on Trade*, 1883; and report of British Consul Chalconer Alabaster, FO, *Commercial Reports*, 1883. Although the boycott is mentioned in passing in numerous secondary sources, none contains a satisfactory account of the incident. The fullest accounts (still very brief) appear in Morse, *Trade and Administration*, and P'eng Tse-i, "Hang-hui," which largely follows Morse.
62. Alabaster, "Report on Trade, 1882," FO 17/934.
63. At least one newspaper account draws a connection, although a vague one, between the two events: *SP*, Kuang-hsü 9/4/14. I have described the uprising plot in Rowe, "Rebellion and Its Enemies."
64. A slightly abridged version of the guild's 1883 regulations appeared in *SP*, Kuang-hsü 9/4/3. Complete and identical texts of the regulations, in their final form as ratified by the Hankow taotai, may be found in Tōa dōbunkai, 2: 672–74, and in Ch'üan, *Hang-hui*, pp. 182–85. In the summary of the code presented here, only articles dealing specifically with the conduct of trade are discussed. Those dealing with the internal functioning of the guild will be treated in Chapter 9.
65. See, for example, Fujii, no. 3, p. 87ff.
66. IGC, *Reports on Trade*, 1883, p. 77.
67. *Ibid.*
68. *NCDN*, 20 May 1879.
69. *NCH*, 18 May 1883.
70. Report of Pien Pao-ti, Kuang-hsü 9/10/21, HPYJCS.
71. *NCH*, 15 June 1883.
72. FO, *Commercial Reports*, 1883, p. 80.
73. *NCH*, 15 June 1883.
74. An early-twentieth-century writer (anonymous, but probably H. B. Morse) remarked, "In the few cases in which [Chinese guilds] have come into conflict with foreign traders, the latter have always been brought to their knees, as the guilds have suspended trade, closed ports, and raised riots at will in order to support their regulations" (*Present Day Impressions*, p. 218). For the use of the collective boycott in domestic commerce, see the discussion of the medicinal herbs trade in Chapter 8, below.
75. *NCH*, 25 April 1884.

76. Allen to Walsham, 12 May 1888, FO 228/864.
77. Allen to Walsham, 1 June 1889, FO 228/878.
78. Gardner to Walsham, 25 August 1886, FO 228/831.
79. *NCH*, 11 June 1886.
80. *1920 HC*, 5.30.
81. Allen to Walsham, 2 September 1889, FO 228/878.
82. The Wuhan Municipal Library holds an incomplete run of this newspaper, including several very early issues. The paper's masthead identifies it as a publication of the Hankow Tea Guild.
83. *1920 HC*, 5.30.
84. P'eng Tse-i, "Hang-hui," p. 97.
85. Alabaster, "Report on Trade, 1882," FO 17/934. For a more recent and thorough critique of these statistics, see the chapter "What Do the Trade Figures Mean?," in Murphey, *Outsiders*.
86. K. C. Liu, pp. 66, 150, 197; *SP*, T'ung-chih 12/4/15, T'ung-chih 12/5/4.
87. *NCDN*, 11 June 1877; Francis W. White, "Hankow," in IGC, *Reports on Trade*, 1881, p. 7. The quotation is from White, describing events of "about five years ago."
88. *IWL*, 23 July 1881 and 6 May 1882; FO, *Diplomatic and Consular Reports*, 1888, p. 14.
89. Pien Pao-ti, memorial of Kuang-hsü 11, Pien, 5.45–48. See also Hankow Maritime Customs Superintendent P'ei Shih-k'ai, report of Kuang-hsü 13/11/3, excerpted in Yao, 3: 1473.
90. IGC, *Reports on Trade*, 1887, p. 79; see also *NCH*, 3 June 1887.
91. *Present Day Impressions*, p. 205.
92. Pien, 5.45–48; *IWL*, 6 May 1882; Chao-li-ch'iao Tea Factory, p. 11.
93. *SP*, Kuang-hsü 13/4/30; *NCH*, 27 May 1887 and 3 June 1887.
94. P'ei Shih-k'ai, reports of Kuang-hsü 13/10/14 and Kuang-hsü 13/11/3, excerpted in Yao, 2: 1209–10, 3: 1473; IGC, *Tea, 1888*, p. 27.
95. Pien, 5.45–48, 6.3–5. In 1891, Governor-general Chang Chih-tung ordered yet another investigation of the deteriorating tea trade, probably also to be conducted by the Hupeh Bureau. Like earlier investigations, it laid the blame on the poor quality of the Chinese product, resulting from structural weaknesses in the production and marketing systems. See Su, *Hsien-tai-hua*, p. 397.
96. See Ch'en K'uei-lung, memorial of Kuang-hsü 34, *HPTC*, 50.41–43.
97. IGC, *Tea, 1888*, p. 24.
98. "Han-k'ou ch'a-yeh kung-so cheng-pao ch'a-shih ch'ing-hsing chi-lüeh" (Abridged report of the Hankow Tea Guild on conditions in the tea market), in IGC, *Tea, 1888*, pp. xxiv–xxv. A rather free translation appears in the same volume, pp. 48–49.
99. Pien, 5.45–48, 6.3–5.
100. Ch'en K'uei-lung, memorial of Kuang-hsü 34, *HPTC*, 50.43.

Chapter Five: Credit and Finance in Hankow

1. Sjoberg, p. 214.
2. Among these are three studies of Ningpo and the Ningpoese bankers: Nishizato, "Nimbo shōnin"; Jones, "Finance in Ningpo"; and Jones, "Ningpo *Pang*." See also Yang, *Money and Credit*, and McElderry, *Old-Style Banks*. Sjoberg's generalizations are belied in Europe as well; see, for example, DeRoover,

Money, Banking, and Credit. I am grateful to Thomas Rawski for bringing DeRoover's work to my attention.

3. *SP*, Kuang-hsü 5/7/26.

4. Yeh, 1.6; *1884 HS*, "Kung-k'uan-pu," pp. 3–4; *1920 HC*, 15.16–17; report of Li Han-chang, T'ung-chih 6/8/8, HPYJCS; WMCIA, "Tien-tang-yeh"; Yang, *Money and Credit*, p. 100.

5. Su, *Hsien-tai-hua*, p. 113.

6. P'eng Yü-hsin, "Yang-hang," p. 23.

7. IGC, *Decennial Reports, 1892*, p. 177.

8. Su, "Chin-tai-hua," First Year's Report, p. 122. I conjecture that this was the first Chinese-owned modern bank in China because the earliest listed in Yang's *Money and Credit* (p. 87) dates from 1897.

9. Margary, pp. 1–2.

10. According to one insider's account, all but two of the nineteen *p'iao-hao* of late Ch'ing Hankow were owned and run by men from the Fen River area of Shansi. The two exceptions were owned by natives of Hunan and of Hupeh, but the latter, at least, had a Shansi manager. (WMCIA, "P'iao-hao.")

11. Nishin bōeki kenkyūjo, 1: 133; Tōa dōbunkai, 6: 608. Chang Kuo-hui, p. 95, dates the decline of the Shansi banks at Hankow from the wholesale takeover of the city's economy by Shanghai interests that he perceives in the 1860's, but I believe his entire argument to be greatly overstated.

12. Hughes to Fraser, 4 October 1877, FO 228/590. The role of the Shansi bankers in Ch'ing China seems analogous to that of the Italian "merchant-bankers" (or "exchange bankers") in medieval Europe. See DeRoover, pt. 1.

13. Tu, "Shang-hai hang-hui hsing-chih"; see also Nishizato, pt. 1.

14. *SP*, Kuang-hsü 7/11/18.

15. Yeh, 5.4.

16. Yang, *Money and Credit*, pp. 84–87. *Ch'ien-chuang* seem comparable, in both origin and function, to the "money-changers" of medieval Bruges, described by DeRoover, pt. 3.

17. *SP*, Kuang-hsü 4/5/25.

18. A 1909 Japanese report divided the native banks of Hankow into two general classes: the larger, which dealt in all aspects of the commerce of the port, and the smaller, which restricted themselves to money exchange and financial services for small merchants. Both classes were included under the generic term *ch'ien-chuang*. (Tōa dōbunkai, 6: 608–9.)

19. *SP*, Kuang-hsü 4/4/3.

20. Yeh, 1.7; IGC, *Decennial Reports, 1892*, p. 177; Su, *Hsien-tai-hua*, p. 113.

21. *SP*, T'ung-chih 13/1/25 and Kuang-hsü 7/11/18.

22. Nishizato, 1: 10–11.

23. *SP*, Kuang-hsü 4/1/13, recounts how a *ch'ien-chuang* and several mercantile firms, all run by Kiangsi natives, simultaneously failed because of interlocking credit relations.

24. Tōa dōbunkai, 6: 610–12.

25. Caine to Wade, 1 March 1872, FO 228/515.

26. Chang Kuo-hui, p. 94.

27. *SP*, Kuang-hsü 4/8/1. Of course, in Hankow such proximity frequently also implied local-origin ties.

28. *SP*, Kuang-hsü 13/4/11.

29. Report of Li Han-chang, T'ung-chih 8/10/19, HPYJCS.

30. Reports of T'an Yen-hsiang, T'ung-chih 6/5/12, and of Li Han-chang, T'ung-chih 6/8/8, both HPYJCS.

31. Chinese People's Bank, pp. 730–31. See also Jones, "Finance in Ningpo," p. 60 and *passim*.

32. Patrick Hughes, "Report on Trade at Hankow, 1877," FO 17/788.

33. *SP*, T'ung-chih 13/1/25.

34. *SP*, Kuang-hsü 8/10/8.

35. Tsungli yamen records for Hankow commonly report the use of *ch'ien-chuang* banknotes in the foreign trade of the port, as does *SP*, Kuang-hsü 7/11/18. Jones notes that widespread use of these notes (*ch'ien-p'iao*) in the foreign trade began at Shanghai about 1858 ("Finance in Ningpo," p. 71). If this is correct, it would seem that, rather than spawning the proliferation of native credit instruments at Shanghai, after the opening of the port the foreign trade lagged some sixteen years behind in making use of the facilities already widely employed in the domestic trade.

36. *SP*, Kuang-hsü 8/10/8.

37. *SP*, T'ung-chih 13/11/9, Kuang-hsü 4/3/21, Kuang-hsü 7/intercalary/6; Mizuno, p. 291. The *kuo-chang* system as practiced by Ningpo and Shaohsing banks is described in Nishizato, 1: 10–11.

38. *SP*, T'ung-chih 13/1/25 and T'ung-chih 13/11/9.

39. *SP*, Kuang-hsü 8/8/28.

40. *SP*, Kuang-hsü 4/10/20.

41. Examples appear in reports of T'an Yen-hsiang, T'ung-chih 6/5/12, and of Li Han-chang, T'ung-chih 8/10/18 and Kuang-hsü 4/2/20, all HPYJCS; Medhurst to Alcock, 28 March 1868, FO 228/456; Hankow Taotai Ho to U.S. Consul Shepard, 26 November 1877 and 25 December 1877, Post Records, U.S. Consulate, Hankow, USNA.

42. *SP*, Kuang-hsü 9/12/1.

43. *SP*, Kuang-hsü 7/11/21.

44. *SP*, Kuang-hsü 3/10/24 and T'ung-chih 13/11/9.

45. *SP*, T'ung-chih 13/11/9. A similar business slump, which resulted in the linked failure of five Hankow *ch'ien-chuang*, is reported in *IWL*, 27 November 1866.

46. Francis W. White, "Hankow," in IGC, *Reports on Trade*, 1877, p. 14.

47. *SP*, Kuang-hsü 4/1/13, Kuang-hsü 4/3/21, and Kuang-hsü 4/4/3.

48. *SP*, Kuang-hsü 3/6/2.

49. Jones, "Finance in Ningpo," p. 77.

50. Nishizato, 1: 13.

51. Yeh, 1.6; WMCIA, "Tien-tang-yeh."

52. *SP*, T'ung-chih 13/2/14. A recent study that reassesses the myth of imperial indifference to contractual obligations among merchants is R. H. Brockman, "Commercial Contract Law in Late Nineteenth-Century Taiwan," in Jerome A. Cohen, R. Randle Edwards, and Fu-mei Chang Chen, eds., *Essays on China's Legal Tradition* (Princeton, 1980), pp. 76–136.

53. Report of Kuan-wen, T'ung-chih 4/1/20; see also reports of Kuan-wen, T'ung-chih 5/3/10, of T'an Yen-hsiang, T'ung-chih 6/1/29, of Li Han-chang, T'ung-chih 8/11/19, and of Weng T'ung-chüeh, Kuang-hsü 1/11/13; all HPYJCS.

54. *SP*, Kuang-hsü 3/12/6.

55. Tseng Kuo-ch'üan, memorial of T'ung-chih 5/10/26, Tseng, 2.6–7. This

case subsequently cost Magistrate Li his office, but not because his sentencing of Yeh was considered inappropriate to the offense. Rather, Li was censured for not having noted that as a degree holder (by purchase) Yeh was not subject to ordinary criminal punishments until he had been stripped of his status.

56. *SP*, Kuang-hsü 4/3/21, Kuang-hsü 4/5/20, Kuang-hsü 7/11/18, and scattered mentions in other issues.

57. *SP*, Kuang-hsü 3/6/2.

58. Drysdale, Ringer and Company to Caine, 13 November 1868, FO 228/456; *SP*, Kuang-hsü 7/7/5.

59. *SP*, Kuang-hsü 7/11/18.

60. IGC, *Reports on Trade*, 1865, p. 41.

61. *NCDN*, 15 March 1871.

62. Nishin bōeki kenkyūjo, 1: 133.

63. *1920 HC*, 5.28, and diagram of "Han-k'ou ch'ien-yeh kung-so," unpaginated diagram section; Ho, *Hui-kuan*, p. 105. Another source records that the Chekiang, Anhwei, and Kiangsi guilds amalgamated first and that the Hupeh guild was the last to join (Nishin bōeki kenkyūjo, 1: 136–37).

64. Diagram of "Han-k'ou ch'ien-yeh kung-so," unpaginated diagram section, *1920 HC*.

65. The new institution was known as the "P'iao-pang kung-hui" and also included several new, Chinese-owned modern banks of Hankow. (Tōa dōbunkai, 6: 616; Chang Shou-po, p. 30.)

66. Niida, p. 504.

67. Johnson to Low, 20 September 1870, and Johnson to Cadwallader, 21 January 1875, *DUSCH*. See also Morse, *Trade and Administration*, pp. 145–46, 157.

68. Report of Hankow Customs Commissioner Thomas Dick, 13 February 1878, in IGC, *Haikwan Banking System*, p. 71.

69. Report of Li Han-chang, T'ung-chih 11/11/29, HPYJCS.

70. *SP*, Kuang-hsü 3/10/2.

71. Sources for this incident are *SP*, T'ung-chih 13/1/25, T'ung-chih 13/2/3, and T'ung-chih 13/2/14; *NCDN*, 11 March 1874 and 8 April 1874. An instructive comparison may be drawn with the similarly disastrous campaigns of the dukes of Burgundy to prohibit commercial credit in fifteenth-century Bruges; see DeRoover, pp. 339–40 and 351.

72. A similar proclamation was issued by the Shanghai Financial Guild in 1873; see Nishizato, 1: 14, and Jones, "Finance in Ningpo," p. 71.

73. Ts'ai, vol. 6, no. 1–2, p. 78.

74. See, for example, *SP*, Kuang-hsü 4/4/3, and Nishin bōeki kenkyūjo, 1: 137.

75. Diagram of "Han-k'ou ch'ien-yeh kung-so," unpaginated diagram section, *1920 HC*.

76. The Shanghai Financial Guild dated from the mid-eighteenth century and was a monopoly of the Ningpo-Shaohsing bankers; see Tu, *Shang-hai hang-yeh hsing-chih*, and Nishizato, 1: 14. According to McElderry (p. 44), it was reconstituted around 1883, apparently as a more inclusive organization. This step was probably a response to the financial collapse in that city during that year.

77. Su, *Hsien-tai-hua*, pp. 113–14, 332.

78. On the modern character of negotiable paper—a feature conspicuously lacking in the banking systems of medieval Europe—see DeRoover, pp. 3, 550.

Chapter Six: The State and Commerce

1. See, e.g., Sjoberg, pp. 136, 183.

2. The first citation is from the geographer Glenn Trewartha (p. 82); the second is from the influential historian Ch'ü T'ung-tsu (p. 168).

3. See, e.g., Hou, pp. 251–83.

4. Morse, *Gilds*, p. 27; Moulder, p. 66.

5. Imahori, *Kōzō*, esp. pp. 301–3.

6. Dawson, p. 58.

7. Hatano, p. 3 and *passim*; see also Terada, p. 7.

8. Saeki, "Sansei shōnin," p. 1. A disciple of Naitō Konan, Saeki uses Naitō's term *dokusai seiji* (autocracy) in preference to *zettaishugi* (absolutism), favored by Japanese Marxist historians. However, his specific invocation of the reign of Louis XIV of France makes clear that his reference is the same. Briefly, Saeki's argument develops the "Naitō hypothesis" that autocratic rule in China began with the fall of the great T'ang clans and was intensified by each succeeding dynasty through the Ch'ing. Large groups of urban merchants, which sprang up during the Five Dynasties period, contributed to the perpetuation of this autocratic rule. See esp. Saeki's articles "Tō Azia sekkai no tenkai—sōsetsu" (General theory of the development of the East Asian world), and "Chūgoku kinsei ni okeru dokusai kunshū no keizaisatsu" (The economic policies of the autocratic rulers of modern China), *Chūgokushi kenkyū*, 2: 6–8, 61–62.

9. Fujii, esp. pt. 1; Teng, *Chung-kuo li-shih*, esp. "Ts'ung Wan-li tao Ch'ien-lung" (From Wan-li to Ch'ien-lung); P'eng Tse-i, "Shou-kung-yeh te fa-chan"; Wei and Lu, *Shang-pan k'uang-yeh*.

10. Myers, p. 79. See also Metzger, "State and Commerce."

11. See, e.g., Ch'üan and Kraus, *Rice Markets and Trade*; Yang, "Government Control"; Sybille van der Sprenkel, "Urban Social Control," in Skinner, ed., *City in Late Imperial China*, pp. 609–32.

12. See, respectively, *Hsien-chuang-i-kung nien-p'u*, p. 75; Parker, "Salt," FO 228/525; *1818 HC*, 12.10. Ten-boat mutual responsibility groups for harbor-dwelling merchants were also instituted at Hankow around 1837; see Na-erh-ching-o and Chou Chih-ch'i, memorial of Tao-kuang 17/2/3, CPA.

13. Murphey, "City as a Center of Change," pp. 357–58.

14. Mary C. Wright, *The Last Stand of Chinese Conservatism: The T'ung-chih Restoration, 1862–1874* (Stanford, 1957), p. 149.

15. Kuan-wen, memorial of T'ung-chih 3/7, cited in Beal, pp. 143–48. See also Yeh-chien Wang, *Land Taxation in Imperial China, 1750–1911* (Cambridge, Mass., 1973), pp. 72, 80.

16. *HPTC*, 50.3–4.

17. *Hsien-chuang-i-kung nien-p'u*, p. 74; Lin, *Cheng-shu*, various reports during his tenure as Hukwang governor-general.

18. In 1873 the town was shaken by a rumor that the central government was about to demand that all domestic customs receipts be forwarded directly to Peking, but this report proved unfounded. (*NCDN*, 4 August 1873.)

19. Kuan-wen, memorial of Hsien-feng 11/9, *CPIWSM*, T'ung-chih reign, 2.4–8; Kuan-wen, memorial of T'ung-chih 1, "Ts'ai-cheng," MCA; *HPTC*, 50.12–13.

20. On the establishment of likin in Hupeh, see Hu Lin-i, *I-chi* (1866 and 1875), *passim*; Wang Chia-pi, "Pien-nien wen-kao"; *HPTC*, ch. 50; *SP*, Kuang-

hsü 6/11/4. The best secondary source on the likin's early history remains Beal, *Likin*. See also Kwang-Ching Liu, "The Ch'ing Restoration," in Fairbank, pp. 409–90.

21. Tseng Kuo-ch'üan, memorial of T'ung-chih 5/8, *HPTC*, 50.27; Ch'en Ming-chin, memorial of Kuang-hsü 14/1, *IWL*, 3 March 1888.

22. Pien, 5.43–44.

23. *HPTC*, 50.28–29.

24. Hsiao Yao-nan, ch. 2.

25. *HPTC*, 50.68.

26. Parker, *China*, p. 235.

27. *1867 HC*, 20.2.39–40; *1884 HS*, 3.21.

28. Pien, 5.23, 5.43–44.

29. Hill, *Twenty-five Years*, p. 10.

30. A good example appears in *SP*, Kuang-hsü 13/4/12.

31. *1884 HS*, 3.21.

32. *SP*, Kuang-hsü 6/11/4 and Kuang-hsü 6/11/6.

33. Pien, 6.3–5.

34. WMCIA, "Yao-ts'ai."

35. Pien, 6.3.

36. I know of no standard work in any language on late imperial Chinese brokers. My remarks here draw upon Ch'ü Chih-sheng, "Ya-hang"; Feng, "Ya-shui"; Kosaku, p. 240ff; Negishi, *Baiban*, pp. 112–15; Shiba, "Chūgoku toshi," pp. 189, 192; Shiba, *Commerce and Society*, p. 165ff; Yang, "Government Control," pp. 193–94; Yokoyama, pp. 149–70, 175–85; and Susan Mann Jones, "The Organization of Trade at the County Level: Brokerage and Tax Farming," *Select Papers from the Center for Far Eastern Studies*, 3 (1978–79), pp. 70–99. I have also profited from several conversations with Professor Jones on this subject.

37. On the twentieth-century transformation of brokerage functions, see esp. Feng, p. 1069ff, and Jones, "Organization of Trade," pp. 85–87.

38. On brokerage policies of early Ch'ing emperors, see Uchida, "Gakō seido," pp. 52–54, and Feng, p. 1067.

39. Yen Ssu-sheng, memorial of Ch'ien-lung 10, Yen, 5.35; Tōa dōbunkai, 7: 247–54; Uchida, "Gakō seido," p. 62.

40. Yen, 5.33–36.

41. Hu Lin-i's collected writings contain many documents relating to his brokerage reforms. Most important are his memorials of Hsien-feng 5/10/6 and Hsien-feng 6/3/24, *I-chi* (1875), 4.10–12 and 8.14–17. See also Hu's memorial of Hsien-feng 9/5/21, CPA; Wang Chia-pi, *ts'e* 3; *HPTC*, ch. 50; Uchida, "Gakō seido." The Tōyō Bunko, Tokyo, holds a collection of 176 brokerage licenses issued in various provinces under the system of reforms pioneered by Hu Lin-i. Seventy-seven of these are from Hupeh, including 48 from the Hsien-feng reign, 15 from the T'ung-chih, and 14 from the Kuang-hsü. One additional Hupeh brokerage license, from Hankow in the Hsüan-t'ung reign, is held at the Wuhan Municipal Archives. Of the 77 Tōyō Bunko licenses from Hupeh, 18 are for grain brokers, 11 are for cotton cloth and 6 for raw cotton, 8 are for wood and wood products, 7 are for meat and fish, 6 are for paper products, and the remainder are divided between several other commodities. In all respects other than date of issue, name of broker, commodity, and location, the licenses are identical, all bearing the complete text of the Board of Revenue's revised regulations, originally drafted by Wang Chia-pi and Hu Lin-i.

42. On the growth of provincial fiscal autonomy, beginning with the inno-

vations of Hu Lin-i and his contemporaries, see P'eng Yü-hsin, "Ts'ai-cheng kuan-hsi."

43. Hu Lin-i, *I-chi* (1875), 4.12. On all surviving brokerage licenses in the Tōyō Bunko and the Wuhan Municipal Archives, the Board of Revenue authorizes their sale to "lower gentry and brevet official rank holders" (*sheng-chien chih-hsien*), as well as commoners.

44. Hu Lin-i, *I-chi* (1875), 8.17; Uchida, "Gakō seido," p. 60.

45. *1920 HC*, 12.12.

46. WMCIA, "Yao-ts'ai."

47. Hu Lin-i, *I-chi* (1875), 8.17.

48. A full transcription of the 1678 Hankow Rice Brokers' Guild regulations appears in Negishi, *Shina no girudo*, pp. 244–45. On the subsequent history of the trade, see Abe, "Beikoku jukyū."

49. *SP*, Kuang-hsü 6/8/13.

50. Yen, 5.33; Yü-t'ai, memorial of Tao-kuang 21/11/28, CPA.

51. Yen, 5.33–36.

52. See regulations no. 13–16 of brokerage licenses in Tōyō Bunko and Wuhan Municipal Archives collections.

53. Hughes to Wade, 4 May 1874, FO 228/537; Gardner to Walsham, 25 August 1886, FO 228/831. Peter Golas reports a similar case from eighteenth-century Peking; see Golas, "Early Ch'ing Guilds," in Skinner, ed., *City in Late Imperial China*, p. 570.

54. *HPTC*, ch. 50. For a comparable phenomenon in Europe, see DeRoover, pp. 229–30.

55. Report of Hankow Customs Commissioner Thomas Dick, 13 February 1878, in IGC, *Haikwan Banking System*, pp. 70–71.

56. Several "public pawnshops" (*kung-tien*) of Hankow are described in *SP*, Kuang-hsü 7/intercalary/25. It appears that these institutions were guaranteed and at least partially capitalized by the county administration.

57. On the magnitude of the Ch'ing administration's investment in commerce, see Fujii, no. 3, p. 73; Hatano, *passim*; Terada, p. 7; Yang, *Money and Credit*, p. 99. On the Shan-hou-sheng and Cheng-yuan banks, see, respectively, *SP*, Kuang-hsü 8/10/8; Tseng Kuo-ch'üan, memorial of T'ung-chih 5/10/26, Tseng, 2.6–7. For an analogous phenomenon in Europe, see DeRoover, p. 280.

58. *1884 HS*, "Kung-k'uan pu," pp. 3–4. Upon his arrival, Chang Chih-tung took this practice a step further by depositing his entire viceregal treasuries with the Wuhan pawnbrokers to generate interest; see WMCIA, "Tien-tang-yeh."

59. Saeki, *Chūgokushi kenkyū*, 2: 315. On this practice generally, see Lien-sheng Yang, "Economic Aspects of Public Works in Imperial China," in his *Excursions in Sinology* (Cambridge, Mass., 1969), pp. 244–45.

60. *1884 HS*, "Kung-k'uan pu," p. 1.

61. Memorials of Hupeh Governors Yang Chien, Chia-ch'ing 21, Ch'ang Ming, Chia-ch'ing 13, Yang Mao-t'ien, Tao-kuang 3/4/21, and Chao Ping-yen, Tao-kuang 25, all in "Ts'ai-cheng," MCA. See also Na-erh-ching-o and Chou Chih-ch'i, memorial of Tao-kuang 17/2/3, CPA. The standard work on the sale of degrees and ranks is Hsü Ta-ling, *Chüan-na chih-tu*.

62. Memorials of Hu Lin-i, Hsien-feng 8/5/14, and Li Han-chang and Kuo Pai-yin, T'ung-chih 11/7/14, both in "Ts'ai-cheng," MCA.

63. Wang Feng-sheng, 1.1. Saeki Tomi discusses several other pre-Taiping contributions made by Hankow salt merchants in *Chūgokushi kenkyū*, 2: 290.

64. Pien Pao-ti, memorial of Kuang-hsü 10, Pien, 6.3.

65. Yeh, 5.3.

66. Hu Lin-i, memorial of Hsien-feng 5/3/11, *I-chi* (1875), 8.11.

67. On the "one-percent port contribution," see WMCIA, "Yao-ts'ai." Evidence of later trade-specific solicitations is found in a proclamation of the Hankow taotai dated Hsüan-t'ung 2/5/30, which denounces irregularities in the collection of an established "merchant contribution" (*shang-chüan*) of 350 taels per year levied on the rice merchants of the T'u-tang neighborhood of Hankow (Wuhan Municipal Archives).

68. Letters of 21 November 1866 and 28 January 1867, Hankow to Shanghai Private Letter Book (C55/1), JMA; Pien Pao-ti, memorial of Kuang-hsü 9/11, Pien, 5.56–59. A suggestion of this sort of activity in pre-Taiping Hankow appears in Yeh, 5.1, and a general discussion of government borrowing from merchants in pre-Taiping China is Saeki, "Sansei shōnin," p. 5. For a European parallel, see DeRoover, pp. 85–88.

69. Li Han-chang, memorial of Kuang-hsü 5/3/28, Li Han-chang, ch. 9.

70. Pien Pao-ti and P'eng Tsu-hsien, memorial of Kuang-hsü 10/9, Pien, 6.51–53.

71. Lin reported his Hankow investigation in a memorial of Tao-kuang 18, which is summarized in Hsin-pao Chang, *Commissioner Lin and the Opium War* (Cambridge, Mass., 1964), pp. 36–37. For the procommercial attitudes of other early-nineteenth-century Hupeh officials, see, e.g., Chou T'ien-chüeh, memorial of Tao-kuang 19/5/25, and Yü-t'ai, memorial of Tao-kuang 21/10/20, both CPA.

72. Morita, *Suirishi*, esp. p. 92. For an example of a Hupeh official's endorsement of these projects, see Yü-t'ai, memorial of Tao-kuang 21/10/20, CPA.

73. Kuan-wen, memorial of Hsien-feng 11/4, *CPIWSM*, Hsien-feng reign, 78.3–4; Hu Lin-i, letter to Tan Shao-tsun, *I-chi* (1875), 65.10.

74. Yeh, 5.3.

75. *SP*, Kuang-hsü 6/7/26.

76. Wolseley, p. 387.

77. Allen to Walsham, 2 September 1889, FO 228/878.

78. *SP*, Kuang-hsü 8/3/2.

79. Hu Lin-i, letter to Ch'en Ch'iu-men, Hsien-feng 8, *I-chi* (1866), 4.78; memorial of Hsien-feng 6/12/3, *I-chi* (1875), 14.2; memorial of Hsien-feng 6/3/24, *I-chi* (1875), 8.15.

80. By 1859 Hu could boast of his success in generating funds for his troops by these means (memorial of Hsien-feng 9/5/21, CPA). His immediate successors as governor, Yen Shu-sen and Tseng Kuo-ch'üan, also reported ever-increasing revenues from these sources; see, e.g., Tseng, memorial of T'ung-chih 6/3/27, Tseng, 3.28–29.

81. Hu Lin-i, memorial of Hsien-feng 9/5/21, CPA; Tseng Kuo-ch'üan, directive to Hupeh Bureau, Tseng, "Kung-tu," 1.2–3.

82. Proclamation of the Hupeh Bureau, 29 June 1861, FO 228/313; *SP*, Kuang-hsü 8/3/28.

83. Li Han-chang, memorial of Kuang-hsü 5/2/21, Li Han-chang, ch. 9. The Hupeh Bureau did not oversee the expenditure of commercial revenues, which was the task of a separate organ known originally as the General Commissariat (*tsung-liang-t'ai*), then after 1866 as the General Military Supply Bureau (*chün-hsu tsung-chü*), and finally after 1880 as the General Reconstruction Bureau (*shan-*

hou tsung-chü). However, officers of these organs all overlapped or were intimate with those of the Hupeh Bureau. See Tseng, 1.16–18; *HPTC*, 50.27.

84. Tseng Kuo-ch'üan, directive to the Hupeh Bureau, T'ung-chih 5, Tseng, "Kung-tu" section, 1.3; Pien Pao-ti, memorial of Kuang-hsü 9, Pien, 15.43–44; *SP*, Kuang-hsü 8/3/28.

85. See, e.g., Hu Lin-i, *I-chi* (1866), 6.23–26, 10.27–28; Kuan-wen, memorial of T'ung-chih 1, "Ts'ai-cheng," MCA; Tseng, 3.28–29.

86. "Sui-shou teng-chi," Kuang-hsü 2, entries for Kuang-hsü 2/3/6, Kuang-hsü 2/4/16, Kuang-hsü 2/10/30, and scattered mentions elsewhere throughout the year, MCA.

87. Pien Pao-ti, memorial of Kuang-hsü 10, Pien, 7.26–27.

88. Li Han-chang, memorial of Kuang-hsü 4/4/10, Li Han-chang, ch. 8.

89. Pien Pao-ti, memorials of Kuang-hsü 10, Pien, 6.3–5, 5.45–48.

90. T'an Chün-p'ei, memorial of Kuang-hsü 12/5, T'an, 5.18–20.

91. Pien, 6.5; T'an, 5.19.

92. IGC, *Tea, 1888*.

93. *IWL*, 25 September 1886 and 3 December 1892; Chang Chih-tung, 12.18–20.

94. Fan, 5.1–7.

95. WMCIA, "Tien-tang-yeh."

96. *SP*, Kuang-hsü 5/1/17.

97. Medhurst to Alcock, 18 February 1868, FO 228/505; Medhurst to Alcock, 28 March 1868, FO 228/456; Drysdale, Ringer and Co. to Caine, 13 November 1868, FO 228/456; Caine to Alcock, 25 January 1869 and 13 August 1869, FO 228/476; Caine to Wade, 18 November 1870, FO 228/494; Caine to Wade, 1 March 1872, FO 228/515.

98. WMCIA, "Yeh-k'ai-t'ai."

99. WMCIA, "Chu-mu shih-ch'ang."

100. Pien Pao-ti, memorial of Kuang-hsü 8/12, Pien, 4.1–3.

101. Lin Tse-hsü, *Jih-chi*, entries for Tao-kuang 17/3/4 (p. 234), Tao-kuang 18/10/11 (p. 308); *idem*, *Kung-tu*, p. 18.

102. Hsü Ta-ling, ch. 5 and 7.

103. WMCIA, "Yao-ts'ai."

104. Hu Lin-i, memorial of Hsien-feng 8/5/14, "Nei-cheng," MCA. See also Fan, 4.30; Yeh, 5.3. On the sale of substantive offices generally, see Hsü Ta-ling, ch. 6.

105. *1867 HC*, 14.54–60.

106. Fan, 5.6; Ts'ai, vol. 5, no. 9, p. 34.

107. This sort of award is regularly reported in memorials from Hupeh officials in "Nei-cheng" and "Ts'ai-cheng" files, MCA. On Liu Jen-shan, see WMCIA, "Yao-ts'ai."

Chapter Seven: Local Origin in an Immigrant City

1. See esp. Ho, "Geographic Distribution."

2. Crissman, p. 185.

3. *Ibid.*, p. 201.

4. H. E. Hobson, in IGC, *Reports on Trade*, 1869, p. 28. For a Chinese view of this phenomenon, see *1920 HC*, 12.11–12.

5. Ho, *Ladder of Success*, p. 233.

6. On Chungking, see Tou, ch. 1; Hu Chao-hsi, pt. 3. Peking also developed "immigrant city" features, though for different reasons.

7. Yeh, 1.2.

8. *1818 HC*, 12.18. See also Rowe, "Urban Control," pp. 97–98.

9. "Feng-su chih," in Hsü Huan-t'ou, ed., p. 2.

10. "Hu-k'ou chih," in Hsü Huan-t'ou, ed., p. 1. Figures for Peking and for American cities are from Sidney Gamble, *Peking: A Social Survey* (New York, 1921), pp. 105, 412.

11. Oliphant, p. 566. See also Cornaby, p. 39.

12. A useful study of interregional migration, with emphasis on the Sung but reference to later periods as well, is Hozumi Fumio, "Ryūminko" (An investigation of vagabonds), *Keizai ronsō*, 75, nos. 1 and 6 (1965), pp. 1–20, 1–15.

13. Translated in Ho, "Geographic Distribution," p. 122. See also Ho, *Hui-kuan*, esp. p. 67.

14. The thirteen are *Chang-shih san-hsiu chia-p'u*, *Chang-shih tsung-p'u*, *Feng-shih tsung-p'u*, *Han-k'ou Lao-shih ts'u-p'u*, *Han-shih tsung-p'u*, *Han-yang Yao-shih ts'u-p'u*, *Hung-shan-miao Lo-shih tsung-p'u*, *Kuan-ch'iao Ling-shih tsung-p'u*, *Kuei-shih tsung-p'u*, *Liu-shih tsung-p'u* (1924), *Liu-shih tsung-p'u* (1932), *Yao-shih tsung-p'u*, *Yeh-shih tsung-p'u*.

15. On Chang Hsien-chung in Ma-ch'eng, see Hu Chao-hsi, pp. 87–89. Part 3 of Hu's book details the westward migrations of both the Yüan-Ming and Ming-Ch'ing transitions.

16. *SP*, Kuang-hsü 3/12/6. Another of the many Lower Yangtze migrants to Hankow in this period was an Anhwei man who fled the rebels in 1862, reported in John, p. 205; see also Foster, p. 150.

17. Gingell to Bruce, 10 March 1863, *BPP 1864*, 63, no. 3302, p. 40.

18. The county origins of many lower-class Hankow residents are recorded in litigation reports in Chinese and foreign government archives and in newspapers. Examples are reports of Weng T'ung-chüeh, Kuang-hsü 3/3/26 and Kuang-hsü 3/5/20, HPCSOJ; Chinese-language report dated T'ung-chih 1/8/30, FO 682/1797; *SP*, Kuang-hsü 4/4/29, Kuang-hsü 9/4/6, and Kuang-hsü 9/5/3.

19. *SP*, Kuang-hsü 4/4/29, e.g., reports on a Huang-p'i native who relocated to Hankow, first worked as a barber for incoming sailors, and subsequently became an itinerant fruit peddler.

20. Hsiao Chih-chih, "Ma-t'ou kung-jen." On Hunanese within this workforce, see esp. WMCIA, "Chu-mu shih-ch'ang."

21. *1884 HS*, 2.22.

22. The rise of these elements is well chronicled in *SP* and *IWL*. I have made a preliminary attempt to analyze its consequences for local history in my articles "Urban Control" and "Rebellion and Its Enemies." An anticipated sequel to the present volume will address the subject in greater detail.

23. *1867 HC*, 8.35.

24. Oliphant, p. 566.

25. *SP*, Kuang-hsü 5/7/26, describes the family of a porter in Hankow; *SP*, T'ung-chih 11/8/21, tells of the family life of a small-time gambler; Yeh, 2.5 and 4.7, recounts the lives of several poor households (*hsiao-chia*) in the city.

26. Wilson to London office, 5 March 1862, LMS; A. G. Reid, "Dr. A. G. Reid's Report of the Health of Hankow for the Half Year Ended 31st March 1872," *Customs Gazette*, January-March 1872, p. 44.

27. A. G. Reid, "Dr. A. G. Reid's Report on the Health of Hankow for the Half Year Ended 30th September 1871," *Customs Gazette*, April-September 1871, p. 55.

28. See esp. George Rudé, *Paris and London in the Eighteenth Century* (New York, 1973), pp. 3–5 and *passim*.

29. *BPP 1865*, 52, no. 3489, p. 122.

30. Weber, *Religion of China*, p. 90.

31. Examples appear in Fan, 3.8; *1920 HC*, 15.26–29; *Yeh-shih tsung-p'u*, 5.1; Niida, p. 508.

32. Skinner, "Introduction: Urban and Rural in Chinese Society," in Skinner, ed., *City in Late Imperial China*, p. 266. Skinner develops these ideas at greater length in "Mobility Strategies."

33. John, p. 90.

34. R. de Luca, "Report on Hupeh," in IGC, *Salt*, p. 80.

35. *TYSY*, 3.13; *1818 HC*, 12.17; Yeh, 5.20; *SP*, Kuang-hsü 9/12/1.

36. *1818 HC*, 12.10.

37. John, letter of 5 November 1861, LMS.

38. Fan, 3.8, 5.19–20, and *passim*; Yeh, 1.6.

39. Fan, ch. 3, 4, and 5. A representative sojourner of several decades, Wu Pang-chih, and permanent moves by the sojourners Hsiang Lin-mao and Yao Pi-ta are mentioned in Fan, 3.7–8.

40. *Yeh-shih tsung-p'u*, ch. 1–6. See also WMCIA, "Yeh-k'ai-t'ai."

41. *BPP 1865*, 52, no. 3489, p. 123.

42. Cha, 1.9.

43. *1818 HC*, 6.33; John, letter of 5 November 1861, LMS.

44. This and the following paragraphs draw upon numerous fragmentary sources, including *1867 HC*, 27.136; *1920 HC*, 5.22–29; reports of Kuan-wen, T'ung-chih 5/3/10, of T'an Yen-hsiang, T'ung-chih 6/5/12, and of Pien Pao-ti, Kuang-hsü 9/10/21, all HPYJCS; reports of Kuo Po-yin, T'ung-chih 7/12/15, of Weng T'ung-chüeh, Kuang-hsü 1/9/7 and Kuang-hsü 3/3/26, and of Li Han-chang, Kuang-hsü 4/12/4, all HPCSOJ; report of Kuo Po-yin, T'ung-chih 8/3/20, TLYM, "Hu-pei Che-chiang Feng-t'ien"; litigation dated T'ung-chih 1/8/30, FO 682/1797; and *SP*, Kuang-hsü 9/4/3, Kuang-hsü 9/4/6, Kuang-hsü 9/5/3, Kuang-hsü 9/7/21, and Kuang-hsü 9/17/27.

45. *1920 HC*, 5.22–29. In this, Hankow parallels major early European centers of interregional trade, in which retail commerce remained a closely guarded monopoly of local natives; see DeRoover, p. 16.

46. Isolated examples of Hankow natives who became major merchants were Li Hsiang-hsing, a major salt merchant of the Chia-ch'ing era, and Feng Chieh-an, active at Shanghai in the 1880's (HPTCCY, *ts'e* 6; *SP*, Kuang-hsü 9/12/26). Hankow natives, moreover, maintained *hui-kuan* of their own at other Yangtze ports, such as Chungking and I-ch'ang. Yet in general Hupeh natives played a negligible role in trade outside their own local, and in some cases regional, systems. See Su, *Hsien-tai-hua*, pp. 52–54. Rare examples of indigenous Hankow literati were the families that produced Hsiung Po-lung in the seventeenth century and Hu Chao-ch'un in the nineteenth; see *1867 HC*, ch. 27, and *1920 HC*, 20.2.39–40.

47. The activities of these lineages are suggested in their genealogies, cited in n. 14, above.

48. See esp. the movements of the Han clan, described in *Han-shih tsung-p'u*.

49. Fujii, no. 1, pp. 15 and 26; Chang Shou-po, frontispiece.

50. On the history of Huang-p'i natives in Hankow, see *1920 HC*, 5.22–29; *CCJP*, 23 August 1962, 21 July 1964, 9 October 1979. On underemployment in Hankow among natives of these surrounding counties, see *SP*, Kuang-hsü 9/4/6 and Kuang-hsü 9/5/3; Rowe, "Rebellion and Its Enemies," pp. 86–87, 100–101.

51. Detailed data on one family of Mien-yang merchants may be found in *Liu-shih tsung-p'u* (1924). Information on the Huang-pang and Han-pang is provided by Ts'ai, vol. 6, no. 1–2. See also Chapter 2, above.

52. For examples see Chang Ying-han, memorial of Chia-ch'ing 25/6/12, "Hsing-k'o t'i-pen," MCA; report of Kuang-hsü 13/5, HPYJCS; *1920 HC*, 12.12.

53. Nakamura, "Kokō bei no ryūtsū"; Kitamura, p. 2; Fujii, no. 1, p. 26.

54. Chu, p. 239; Shigeta, "Kishu shōnin," pp. 612–13. See also Chapter 4, above.

55. Fujii, esp. pt. 2; Shigeta, "Kishu shōnin." Brief discussions in English of the activities of the Hui-chou merchants in Ch'ing China may be found in Ho, *Ladder of Success*, pp. 233–34, and Skinner, "Mobility Strategies," pp. 344–45.

56. *TYSY*, 7.7.

57. *Ibid.*, 8.22.

58. Ssu Yen-shao of Wu-yüan county, for example, was a leading timber merchant at Hankow in the eighteenth century (Shigeta, "Kishu shōnin," p. 598).

59. *Ibid.*, pp. 603, 605, 610–14. Three such Hui-chou dealers were Chin Lieh-kuang, Chin Luan, and Wang Kuang-she.

60. Biographies of Hui-chou merchants at Hankow drawn upon for these and subsequent remarks appear in Fan, 3.7–8, 3.13, 4.19, 4.24, 5.1–8, 5.10, 5.13, and 5.19; *1867 HC*, 19.10–11, 20.2.22–23, and 22.8–9; *1920 HC*, 13.22–23.

61. *TYSY*, 7.7.

62. Chang Shou-po, pp. 21–25; Chang P'eng-fei, ed., pp. 70–71.

63. Among Saeki's several studies on this subject are "Sansei shōnin"; "Shinchō no kyōki to Sansei shōnin" (The Shansi merchants and the rise of the Ch'ing), in *Chūgokushi kenkyū*, 2: 263–321. See also Terada, *Sansei shōnin*. For an English-language summary of the activities of the Shansi and Shensi merchants, see Skinner, "Mobility Strategies," pp. 345–47.

64. Fujii, no. 2, p. 33.

65. *SSHK*, 1.21–28.

66. There were at least seventeen different product- or service-specific guilds of Shansi and Shensi merchants in Hankow, and at one point the provincial club identified 24 distinct commodities traded there by its members (*SSHK*, 1.15, 1.20). On Fen-chou wine distribution at Hankow, see *1920 HC*, 5.28.

67. *SSHK*, 1.20.

68. TLYM, "Hu-pei Han-k'ou O-shang pei-p'ien."

69. Fan, 3.16. On Shansi merchants' involvement in the Liang-Huai system, see esp. Terada, chap. 2.

70. *NCDN*, 18 April 1877.

71. *BPP 1863*, 73, no. 3104, p. 133; *BPP 1865*, 53, no. 3489, p. 123. See also Tōa dōbunkai, 7: 248–49.

72. These dealerships were the targets of a cleanup campaign launched in the 1830's by Lin Tse-hsü (Lin, *Cheng-shu*, pp. 588–89). IGC, *Reports on Trade*, 1869, p. 28.

73. Mayers, p. 451.

74. The six were Russell and Co.'s Apun, Jardine's Yowloong (Yu Lung), Heard and Co.'s Coe Lun and Seating (Liu Shao-tsung), and Dent's Sheng Heng-shan and Yang Hui-shan. (Hao, pp. 227–34; see also pp. 51–53.)

75. R. E. Bredon, "Hankow Despatch no. 459," 28 November 1887, in IGC, *Tea, 1888*, pp. 16–17; Shigeta, "Kishu shōnin," p. 613; Chu, p. 237; Hao, p. 170; Chang Shou-po, p. 23. Because of this privileged access to foreign goods, Cantonese merchants at Hankow in the late nineteenth century pioneered the type of "department store" (*pai-huo kung-szu*) common in modern Chinese cities; see WMCIA, "Pai-huo-yeh."

76. One British consul reported that "Chinese, usually Cantonese, are invariably placed in charge of foreign goods protected by transit passes" (*BPP 1866*, 71, no. 3587, p. 121). Cantonese warehouse workers were employed by Cantonese merchants as well.

77. "Nearly all Europeans who are building enter into contracts only with Canton men, who are much more expensive, but much more to be relied upon as builders." (R. Wilson, letter of 22 December 1862, LMS. See also *NCDN*, 16 June 1876.)

78. Roxby, p. 277.

79. On the role of these merchants in Ch'ing commerce, see Nishizato, "Nimbō shōnin"; Jones, "Ningpo *Pang*." On the home areas, see Shiba, "Ningpo and Its Hinterland"; Jones, "Finance in Ningpo"; James Cole, "Shaohsing: Studies in Ch'ing Social History," Ph.D. diss., Stanford Univ., 1975.

80. Chang Shou-po, p. 22; *1920 HC*, 5.25.

81. In addition to Ning-Shao handling of gold and silver as specie, Ning-Shao artisans at Hankow were known for their fine handicraft work in these metals (*1920 HC*, 12.11).

82. Nishizato, no. 1, p. 8; IGC, *Reports on Trade*, 1869, p. 28; Hao, p. 53. Shih Fu-jun, noted in Chapter 2, was one such Ningpoese river merchant; see Alabaster to Fraser, 19 April 1880, and Alabaster to Wade, 7 July 1880, both FO 228/651.

83. *1920 HC*, 13.13.

84. Report of Li Han-chang, T'ung-chih 10/1/24, HPYJCS.

85. Augustine Heard and Co. archives, Baker Library, Harvard University, cited by Hao, p. 175.

86. Chang Shou-po, frontispiece.

87. Information on men from these areas appears in biographies in Fan, 2.22, 2.32, 5.1–7, 5.35, and 5.38; Yeh, 1.7; *1867 HC*, 19.13–14 and 20.8–9; *1884 HS*, 3.13; *1920 HC*, 5.22–29. See also report of Kuan-wen, T'ung-chih 5/3/10, and of Hankow taotai, Kuang-hsü 13/5, HPYJCS; report of Weng T'ung-chüeh, Kuang-hsü 1/9/7, and of Li Han-chang, Kuang-hsü 4/12/1, HPCSOJ; and report of Kuo Po-yin, T'ung-chih 8/3/20, TLYM, "Hu-pei Che-chiang Feng-t'ien"; Ts'ai, vol. 5, no. 10, p. 41.

88. Yeh, 1.10.

89. The Hui-chou Guild of the city, for instance, took cultivating of this remembrance as first among its stated goals (*TYSY*, "Chüan-shou," p. 1).

90. *Yeh-shih tsung-p'u*, 3.6, 3.14, 4.1.

91. *1867 HC*, 19.13–14.

92. Jones, "Ningpo *Pang*," p. 77. A similar argument is advanced by Skinner, "Urban Social Structure," in Skinner, ed., *City in Late Imperial China*, p. 540.

93. Chinese People's Bank, pp. 730–31.

94. Jing Su and Lo Lun, *Landlord and Labor in Late Imperial China: Case Studies from Shandong*, ed. and trans. Endymion Wilkinson (Cambridge, Mass., 1978), pp. 135–36.

95. An early-twentieth-century survey of boatmen in Shanghai, conducted by the South Manchurian Railroad, revealed that slightly more than half still devoted at least a portion of their time to agricultural labor. Yokoyama Suguru, in reporting this finding, argues that it applies to earlier periods and to other urban localities as well (Yokoyama, pp. 158–59).

96. Several examples are discussed in letter of Hankow agent, 21 March 1867, Hankow to Shanghai Private Letter Book (C55/1), JMA; John, letter of 5 November 1861, LMS; *1867 HC*, 19.13–14.

97. *1920 HC*, 13.13.

98. *1867 HC*, 20.2.16–17.

99. *Yeh-shih tsung-p'u*, 15.23, 15.37, 16.1.

100. WMCIA, "Wang-yü-hsia."

101. *Yeh-shih tsung-p'u*, 1.81–82.

102. *Han-k'ou Lao-shih ts'u-p'u*.

103. See, e.g., Hsü Huan-t'ou, ed., "Ming-sheng chih," p. 2.

104. *TYSY*, 8.62–63; Niida, pp. 503, 505.

105. *Ta-Ch'ing lü-li*, ch. 8, "Jen-hu i-chi wei ting," pp. 1–9.

106. *Ibid.*, "Pieh-chi i-ts'ai," p. 1.

107. *SP*, Kuang-hsü 1/10/16.

108. Yeh, 1.2.

109. *SP*, Kuang-hsü 1/10/16.

110. Skinner, "Urban Social Structure," in Skinner, ed., *City in Late Imperial China*, p. 539.

111. Fan, ch. 3–5. Because of Fan's inconsistent format in reporting such items as local origin, registration, and occupation, precise quantification is impracticable.

112. Fan, 3.14, 3.17, 5.10; *Yeh-shih tsung-p'u*, 15.23.

113. *TYSY*, 8.36, 8.39, 8.43–44, 8.47, 8.49.

114. Fan, 3.7–8 (Hsiang Ta-fu, Hsiang Ta-te), 3.13–17 (Sun Shih-lou, Wu Shih-ch'ao, Fang Hui-ko); *1920 HC*, 13.22–23 (Wu Chang-keng); *1884 HS*, 3a.7 (Hung Ju-k'uei); Wang Pao-hsin, 2.19 (Ting P'ing-yüan, Yüan Sun-kai, Wu Shao-po, Hung Ch'in-yu). Wang Pao-hsin specifically comments on the prevalence of this phenomenon.

115. Wang Lan is noted in *1867 HC*, 14.20–21; his descendants Wang Ch'uan-i and Wang Chiung-an appear in *1867 HC*, 19.13–14, and Wang Pao-hsin, 2.19.

116. *SP*, Kuang-hsü 1/10/16.

117. Fujii, no. 4, p. 119ff. Fujii argues (no. 4, pp. 128–29) that a record of a merchant's having "established registration" (*chan-chi*) in the host county often signifies merely that he had filed for a supplementary "commercial registration" there, rather than that he had formally emigrated from his former county of registration. In Hankow, the term used for change of registration into the county was not *chan-chi* but *ju-chi*. Although *chan-chi* was used in a few cases, I find no evidence that it was not intended to be synonymous with *ju-chi*, that is, to signify a permanent and complete change of registration. As such, it was inherited by the reregistrant's descendants.

118. Ho, *Ladder of Success*, p. 234.
119. *1818 HC*, 15.40.
120. Fujii, no. 4, pp. 123–25.
121. *SP*, Kuang-hsü 1/10/16.
122. *1884 HS*, 3a.13; *1867 HC*, 19.10–11.
123. *Hu-pei hsüeh-cheng ch'üan-shu* (Records of the Hupeh provincial director of studies), Ch'ien-lung 59, cited in *SP*, Kuang-hsü 1/10/16.
124. *SP*, Kuang-hsü 1/10/16.
125. *Ibid.*
126. *SP*, Kuang-hsü 1/10/18.
127. *Ibid.*
128. *Ibid.*
129. WMCIA, "Chu-mu shih-ch'ang."
130. See *TYSY*, *chüan shou*, p. 1; *SSHK*, 1.14.
131. An example of inns catering to a single provincial group, in this case Szechwanese, is found in *SP*, Kuang-hsü 5/8/29.
132. *SP*, Kuang-hsü 4/9/1; Rowe, "Urban Control," p. 90.
133. *SP*, Kuang-hsü 3/10/2.
134. Report of Li Han-chang, T'ung-chih 8/7/5, HPYJCS.
135. *SP*, Kuang-hsü 4/5/25.
136. *SP*, Kuang-hsü 5/1/17.
137. See, e.g.: on boatmen, Yeh, 6.7, and *SP*, Kuang-hsü 2/8/16; on porters, report of Hsü Tsung-ying, Kuang-hsü 9/3/5, HPYJCS; on factory hands, report of Weng T'ung-chüeh, Kuang-hsü 3/3/26, HPCSOJ. Yokoyama, pp. 189–96, discusses this phenomenon in late imperial China.
138. WMCIA, "Wang-yü-hsia."
139. Tōa dōbunkai, 7: 248–49.
140. Report of Weng T'ung-chüeh, Kuang-hsü 3/3/26, HPCSOJ.
141. Report of Li Han-chang, Kuang-hsü 4/12/4, HPCSOJ.
142. Report of Pien Pao-ti, Kuang-hsü 9/10/21, HPYJCS.
143. Report of Kuan-wen, T'ung-chih 5/3/10, HPYJCS; see also Fujii, no. 3, pp. 66–70.
144. See, e.g., *SP*, Kuang-hsü 4/1/13 and Kuang-hsü 4/5/20.
145. Report of Li Han-chang, T'ung-chih 6/8/8, HPYJCS.
146. Imahori, *Kōzō*, esp. preface and pp. 1, 274, 295ff. A brief synopsis of the *kyōdōtai* argument and its application to Chinese cities appears in Shiba, "Toshi," p. 191. For an English-language introduction to the theory, see Kamachi Noriko, John K. Fairbank, and Ichiko Chūzō, *Japanese Studies of Modern China since 1953* (Cambridge, Mass., 1977), pp. xxiii–xxv. For a Japanese critique of *kyōdōtai* arguments, see Hatada Takashi, *Chūgoku sonraku to kyōdōtai riron* (Chinese villages and the theory of *kyōdōtai*) (Tokyo, 1973).
147. See, e.g., Fujii, no. 2, pp. 32–33, no. 3, pp. 76–78, and no. 4, p. 133; Hatano, pp. 60–61; Terada, p. 7; Levy and Shih, *Modern Chinese Business Class*.
148. Report of Kuan-wen, T'ung-chih 4/1/20, HPYJCS; report of Kuo Po-yin, T'ung-chih 8/3/20, TLYM, "Hu-pei Che-chiang Feng-t'ien."
149. Ch'ing-pao, memorial of Chia-ch'ing 25/2/23, "Hsing-k'o t'i-pen," MCA.
150. Oliphant, p. 566.
151. Yeh, 5.3.
152. Tou Chi-liang notes that the staffs of Shansi banks in nineteenth-century Chungking were all Shansi natives, who were housed within the bank precincts and were not allowed out in the evening to mingle with people from other provinces (Tou, p. 161).
153. Cited in Thompson, p. 175.

154. "The Hankow dialect is very poor, consisting of only 316 syllables, against the Pekingese 420. . . . [It] is in many regards in a transitional state, and not so fixed as the Pekingese." (Parker, "Hankow Dialect," p. 308.)

155. Many such disputes are reported in *SP*. I hope to discuss them more fully in another context.

156. *NCH*, 29 June 1872. The Wuhan local historian P'an Hsin-tsao has told me he believes that Cantonese were the least-assimilated sojourner group in late-nineteenth-century Hankow, whereas Lower Yangtze groups (people from Hui-chou, Kiangsi, and Ningpo) were among the most assimilated. P'an placed Shansi men at some point between these two extremes.

157. Representative cases are those of Cheng Tzu-yün (Fan, 4.18), Hu Hsiao-lan (Fan, 5.35), Chu Hung-shu (*1867 HC*, 20.2.16–17), Hu Yüan (*1920 HC*, 15.4), and Li Pi-ch'ün (*1920 HC*, 15.26).

158. E.g., the father of Wu Chang-keng (*1867 HC*, 19.10–11).

159. E.g., Wang Pi-hsiang (*1818 HC*, 25.46) and Wu Chang-keng (*1867 HC*, 19.10–11).

160. *SP*, Kuang-hsü 9/4/3; Rowe, "Rebellion and Its Enemies," pp. 88–89, 99–100.

161. Ho, *Hui-kuan*, p. 107 (translation mine).

162. Tou, pp. 18, 80, and *passim*.

163. All three men were from Hui-chou. Fan, 3.13; *TYSY*, 8.44.

164. On assimilation by marriage, see Tou, pp. 82–83; Fujii, no. 2, p. 46ff and no. 4, p. 140; and Peter Golas, "Early Ch'ing Guilds," in Skinner, ed., *City in Late Imperial China*, pp. 564–65.

165. Rozman, p. 88.

166. Skinner, "Urban Social Structure," in Skinner, ed., *City in Late Imperial China*, p. 539.

167. Melson and Wolpe, p. 1126. As the Japanese sociologist Chie Nakane has observed, Chinese seem to have developed a tolerance for such multiple identities. In contrast to the Japanese, for whom "one group [identity] is always preferred while the others are secondary," the Chinese "find it impossible to decide which group is the most important of several. So long as the groups differ in nature [as, clearly, did ascriptive native identity and deliberately chosen locational identity in Hankow] the Chinese see no contradiction and think it perfectly natural to belong to several groups at once." (Chie Nakane, *Japanese Society* [Harmondsworth, England, 1973], p. 22.)

168. Curtin, "Geographical Centrality." In this recent state-of-the-field analysis, Curtin presents his notion of "locational solidarity" in these terms: "People who live in a particular place—city or village—share advantages, disadvantages, and interests with other people who live in the same place. A spatial location can therefore be a source of human solidarity alongside a common social class, a common religion, or a common way of life." (Cited by permission of the author.)

169. Geertz, p. 12.

170. Thrupp, p. 228.

Chapter Eight: Guild Structure

1. Clement F. R. Allen, describing the city's new Shansi-Shensi guildhall. FO, *Diplomatic and Consular Reports*, 1888, p. 14.

2. *1920 HC*, 5.22–34. The reasons for this underestimation will be discussed below.

3. For example, in the work of H. B. Morse, Niida Noboru, and Imahori Seiji. For a summary discussion, see Shiba, "Toshi," p. 191.

4. See, for example, the confusion acknowledged by a local Japanese reporter in Nishin bōeki kenkyūjo, 1: 965; also *SP*, Kuang-hsü 5/11/20.

5. Katō, "Hang"; Shiba, *Commerce and Society* (source of citation, p. 1). See also Ma, p. 60; Shiba, "Toshi," p. 189.

6. Chesneaux, p. 117.

7. See Jones, "Ningpo *Pang*," p. 78.

8. *1920 HC*, 1.19.

9. See *SP*, Kuang-hsü 5/11/20; Mizuno, p. 294.

10. Morse, *Gilds*, pp. 7–9; MacGowan, p. 134.

11. *TYSY*, 8.15.

12. Etzioni, p. 3.

13. Failure to take these two steps was, however, no sure indication of a group's limited size or resources. The salt merchants' trade association, for example, though one of the most powerful and prestigious such groups in the city, did not publish official regulations or move into its own permanent guildhall until 1889. (*1920 HC*, 5.29.)

14. Dawson, p. 84. See also *Present Day Impressions*, pp. 218–19.

15. Sources consulted on this matter include *Ta-Ch'ing lü-li*, *Ta-Ch'ing lü-li hui-chi pien-lan*, *Ta-Ch'ing hui-tien*, *Ta-Ch'ing hui-tien shih-li*, and *Hu-pu tse-li*.

16. *TYSY*, 3.2–3.

17. *Ta-Ch'ing lü-li hui-chi pien-lan*, 15.2–3.

18. *SP*, Kuang-hsü 5/11/20.

19. "Han-k'ou ch'a-yeh kung-so kuei-t'iao" (Regulations of the tea trade of Hankow [1889]), reproduced in Tōa dōbunkai, 2: 672–74, and in Ch'üan, *Hang-hui*, pp. 182–85.

20. The Tea Guild's confrontation with other creditors of the bankrupt British firm Mackeller and Co. provides a good example. See Chapter 4, above, and FO 228/436.

21. Examples are provided in *TYSY*, 8.22, 8.57, 8.60, 8.74–76; *SSHK*, 1.10, 2.25.

22. *TYSY*, 3.13; *1920 HC*, 5.22.

23. Ho, "Geographic Distribution," pp. 20–21; Tou, pp. 21–23. Ho identifies the first *hui-kuan* in China as that of Wu-hu (Anhwei) natives at Peking during the Ming Yung-le reign (1403–24).

24. Ho, *Hui-kuan*, p. 74; Rozman, p. 132.

25. IGC, *Decennial Report, 1892*, p. 191.

26. Ho, "Geographic Distribution," pp. 121–22, and *Hui-kuan*, pp. 67, 74.

27. Yeh, 6.2; Liu Wen-tao, 1.1.5.

28. *1920 HC*, 5.24; "Han-k'ou Chiang-hsi hui-kuan kung-i" (Regulations of the Kiangsi Hui-kuan at Hankow [n.d.]), reproduced in Tōa dōbunkai, 2: 562, and in Ch'üan, *Hang-hui*, p. 106.

29. The list appearing in *1920 HC*, 5.22–34, was compiled in the early Republican period by the leaders of the All-Hankow Guild Alliance. It lists 179 guilds of various types, usually supplying data on guildhall locations, founding dates, constituency, goals, and building history. Its chief limitations for the study of local guild history are that (1) it includes only organizations that owned their

own meeting halls and so excludes the apparently far greater number of *pang* that rented or borrowed facilities, and (2) it lists only groups still in existence when it was compiled, thus eliminating, e.g., those that might not have survived the Taiping devastations and thereby skewing the sample in favor of later types of organization. Nevertheless, it remains uniquely useful and even permits some guarded quantification. In the remainder of this chapter, references to specific Hankow guilds not otherwise annotated have been drawn from this source. The document has previously been studied by Ho Ping-ti, although not as intensively, and in some instances my observations coincide with those of Professor Ho. In many respects, Ho's work represents the point of departure for my analysis of late imperial guilds.

30. Membership criteria are recorded for 123 of the 179 guilds. Of these 123, 81 were reported founded before 1889, and we can safely estimate that an additional 10 were also founded before this date. The remaining 32 guilds were either reported (23) or estimated (9) to have been founded after 1890. I have eliminated two of the 91 founded before 1889 from further consideration, since they merely represent separate physical premises belonging to organizations included elsewhere in the list. Of the remaining 89, a total of 45 (i.e., 51 percent) contained local-origin restrictions among their requirements for membership and 44 (49 percent) did not.

31. Hamilton, "Merchant Associations," p. 57.

32. *SSHK*, ch. 1; *SP*, Kuang-hsü 4/8/21.

33. *SSHK*, ch. 1; Niida, p. 510.

34. Report of Pien Pao-ti, Kuang-hsü 9/10/21, HPYJCS; Tōa dōbunkai, 6: 610–12.

35. *SSHK*, 1.15. References to individual guild members by *hao* (name of firm) predominate in the Shansi-Shensi Guild's lists of various project donors (e.g., *SSHK*, 1.11, 1.21–28, 2.13).

36. Niida, p. 509.

37. See, e.g., the characteristic reference to members of various Hankow *hui-kuan* as "guests of the association" (*hui-k'o*) (*SP*, Kuang-hsü 5/4/10).

38. These six include those of the Hui-chou *hui-kuan* (reproduced in *TYSY*, 8.74–76), the Shansi-Shensi *hui-kuan* (in *SSHK*, 2.9–11), and the Kiangsi *hui-kuan* (in Tōa dōbunkai, 2: 562, and Ch'üan, *Hang-hui*, p. 106), as well as the trade associations governing rice brokers (in Negishi, *Shina no girudo*, pp. 244–45), tea dealers (in Tōa dōbunkai, 2: 672–74, and Ch'üan, *Hang-hui*, pp. 182–85), and scalemakers (in Tōa dōbunkai, 2: 641–42, and Ch'üan, *Hang-hui*, pp. 133–34). The fact that business firms might belong to more than one guild has been established for nineteenth-century Lukang, Taiwan; see DeGlopper, p. 646.

39. For the process by which these 45 were selected, see note 30, above.

40. *SSHK*, prefaces, p. 1; Niida, p. 504.

41. Skinner, "Introduction: Urban Social Structure in Ch'ing China," in Skinner, ed., *City in Late Imperial China*, p. 543.

42. *Ibid.*

43. Chang Shou-po, p. 23.

44. Ch'üan, *Hang-hui*, p. 101. I borrow the terms "simplex" and "multiplex" from Philip Kuhn's work on nineteenth-century militia organization. Tou, p. 57, arrives at a similar distinction, which he terms "simple" (*chien-i*) and "complex" (*fan-fu*).

45. *1920 HC*, 12.11.

46. *SSHK*, 1.20.

47. *1920 HC*, 5.22; Negishi, *Chūgoku no girudo*, p. 143.

48. *SSHK*, 2.38.

49. Hsü, ed., "Ming-sheng chih," p. 2.

50. *TYSY*, 8.62–63.

51. *SP*, Kuang-hsü 4/3/8.

52. Skinner, "Introduction: Urban and Rural in Chinese Society," in Skinner, ed., *City in Late Imperial China*, p. 271. No source is cited for this information.

53. Ch'üan, *Hang-hui*, pp. 94–95.

54. P'eng Tse-i, "Hang-hui," p. 74.

55. Hamilton, "Merchant Associations," p. 62. Studying Swatow local-origin clubs, Hamilton was struck by the fact that the catchment area designated as "home" varied considerably for Swatow clubs at, e.g., Shanghai and Nanking. He concludes that "individuals who in one location would invidiously distinguish between themselves, would in another location join the same association. . . . Hence, such clubs did not necessarily reveal an intense loyalty to a particular social system." Although some groups (Hui-chou men, for example) were less flexible about their home area's boundaries than were Swatow men, Hamilton's observations are compatible with my earlier conclusions about the role of extraction and distribution networks in determining patterns of local-origin club formation.

56. See esp. Imahori's discussion of the "guild-merchant" in his *Kōzō*, p. 295ff, and Shiba's summary interpretation of Imahori's views in "Toshi," p. 191. The work of other Japanese scholars on Chinese guilds often reflects a similar point of view; see, e.g., Nishizato, 1: 10–11.

57. Ho, "Geographic Distribution," p. 122.

58. See Melson and Wolpe, p. 1119; also Gary Hamilton, "Regional Associations."

59. *1920 HC*, 5.34.

60. Tōa dōbunkai, 2: 641–42; Ch'üan, *Hang-hui*, pp. 133–34.

61. Negishi, *Shina no girudo*, pp. 244–45.

62. Teng, p. 183.

63. That is, 44 of the 89 pre-1889 guilds for which membership criteria are known. Of the remaining 45, 20 were both local origin and trade restrictive, and 25 were local origin restrictive only. See note 30, above.

64. *SP*, Kuang-hsü 8/5/29.

65. *SP*, Kuang-hsü 5/3/7.

66. This account of the timber trade is based primarily upon WMCIA, "Chumu shih-ch'ang," with additional information supplied by *SP*, Kuang-hsü 2/4/22 and Kuang-hsü 9/7/24, and *Ying-wu-chou hsiao-chih*.

67. This account is drawn primarily from WMCIA, "Yao-ts'ai," with additional material provided by *1920 HC*, 5.22; "Yao-pang ta-chieh" (Medicine guild street), *CCJP*, date unknown; and Ch'üan, *Hang-hui*.

68. Stinchcombe, p. 154.

69. Ho, *Hui-kuan*, p. 102 (translation mine). See also Tou, p. 18 and *passim*.

70. See esp. Shigeta, "Kishu shōnin," p. 597.

71. *1920 HC*, 5.22.

72. On the Financial Guild, see Chapter 5, above; on the Tea Guild, see Chapter 4. In the later nineteenth century the Shansi-Shensi *hui-kuan* was still popu-

larly known as the "Ten Guilds," even though it had more than twenty component *pang*.

73. *1920 HC*, 5.27.

74. *1920 HC*, 5.34.

75. *SSHK*, 1.11 and *passim*.

76. *1920 HC*, 12.11; Chang Shou-po, pp. 22–23.

77. Chang Shou-po, p. 25.

78. Tou, p. 34ff.

79. Tu, "Shang-hai hang-hui hsing-chih."

80. Negishi, *Chūgoku no girudo*, pp. 36–43. Negishi provides a schematization of the multiplex Cantonese provincial guild at Shanghai, within which fifteen component *pang* were arranged in a clear, nested hierarchy.

81. *Ibid.*, p. 39.

82. A useful article synthesizing such research is Melson and Wolpe, "Modernization and the Politics of Communalism." I follow them in employing the concept of "social mobilization" suggested in Deutsch, "Social Mobilization and Political Development."

83. Rudolph and Rudolph, esp. pp. 33, 63–68.

84. *Ibid.*, p. 99.

85. Melson and Wolpe, pp. 1123, 1125.

86. *1920 HC*, 5.30.

87. *NCH*, 9 November 1867.

88. *SSHK*, 2.9.

89. *Ibid.*, 2.35.

Chapter Nine: Guild Functions

1. Thrupp, p. 19ff.

2. Ho, *Hui-kuan*, p. 67.

3. Ch'üan, *Hang-hui*, pp. 94–95.

4. *SP*, Kuang-hsü 6/9/5.

5. "Han-k'ou kuan-mei ch'uan-hu kung-so kung-i" (Regulations of the official Coal Boatmen's Guild of Hankow), cited in Ch'üan, *Hang-hui*, p. 110.

6. *SSHK*, 3.9–11; *TYSY*, ch. 4.

7. On trade diasporas generally, see Philip D. Curtin, *Economic Change in Precolonial Africa: Senegambia in the Era of the Slave Trade* (Madison, Wis., 1975), pp. 59–66; on the role of religion, see esp. p. 66.

8. *SSHK*, 1.7.

9. *SP*, Kuang-hsü 2/4/22.

10. *SP*, Kuang-hsü 4/8/21.

11. Allen to Walsham, 2 September 1889, FO 228/878.

12. *SP*, Kuang-hsü 7/10/25.

13. *TYSY*, ch. 2.

14. *Ibid.*, 8.78.

15. *SP*, Kuang-hsü 7/intercalary/25; *1867 HC*, 6.16.

16. *TYSY*, ch. 5.

17. *Ibid.*, 8.7.

18. Ts'ai, vol. 6, no. 3, p. 43; Hsü, ed., "Ming-sheng chih," p. 2.

19. *TYSY*, 7.7.

20. Saeki, "Sansei shōnin," pp. 7–8. Of course, there was probably a connection between agricultural limitations and the decision of a particular local-origin community to devote itself to trade. For a comparable European case, see Pirenne, pp. 82–83, on the rise of Venice.

21. As noted in Fujii, pt. 4.

22. See, e.g., reports of Li Han-chang, Kuang-hsü 6/8/28 and T'ung-chih 11/11/29, HPYJCS.

23. Nishin bōeki kenkyūjo, p. 965.

24. *SP*, Kuang-hsü 9/7/24.

25. *SP*, Kuang-hsü 5/4/10.

26. *1920 HC*, 5.31.

27. "Han-k'ou mi-shih kung-so chih ting pang-kuei" (Regulations of the Hankow Rice Brokers' Guild), reproduced in Negishi, *Shina no girudo*, pp. 244–45.

28. *1920 HC*, unpaginated diagram section.

29. Mizuno, p. 293.

30. See, e.g., *SP*, Kuang-hsü 2/2/8; Mizuno, p. 293; Tōa dōbunkai, 2: 641–42.

31. See report of Li Han-chang, T'ung-chih 11/11/29, HPYJCS.

32. See report of Li Han-chang, Kuang-hsü 6/8/28, *ibid.*

33. *SP*, Kuang-hsü 5/4/25, cited in P'eng Tse-i, "Hang-hui," p. 84.

34. See the case of the tung-oil dealers of Hankow, discussed in Chapter 6, above.

35. "Han-k'ou Chiang-hsi hui-kuan kung-i" (Regulations of the Kiangsi Guild of Hankow), cited, e.g., in Tōa dōbunkai, 2: 562. Western observers frequently commented upon the "openness" of Chinese guilds to all merchants who met the general guidelines for admission; see, e.g., *Present Day Impressions*, p. 218.

36. This point is made strongly in Ch'üan, *Hang-hui*, p. 106ff, and in P'eng Tse-i, "Hang-hui," p. 77.

37. *SP*, Kuang-hsü 5/4/25, cited in P'eng Tse-i, "Hang-hui," p. 84; Tōa dōbunkai, 2: 641–42.

38. *SP*, Kuang-hsü 5/11/20.

39. See Hu Lin-i's reasoning on the desirability of hereditary brokerage licensing, discussed in Chapter 6, above.

40. Mayers, p. 445.

41. Ch'üan, *Hang-hui*, pp. 115, 182ff.

42. P'eng Tse-i, "Hang-hui," pp. 71–73, 102. In a more recent article, P'eng has identified an earlier period of rapid growth in the number of "exclusionary" guilds, approximately from 1790 to 1840. He argues that this signified a general rigidification of the economy in these years and concludes that, paradoxically, "the independent development of [urban] commercial capital proceeded at the expense of the development of the overall economy," which was then in a period of stagnation. (P'eng Tse-i, "Shou-kung-yeh te fa-chan," pp. 50, 52.)

43. See Esherick, p. 69 and *passim*.

44. Imahori, *Kōzō*, pp. 298–301; Nishizato, 2: 209ff.

45. The great Japanese student of Chinese customary law, Niida Noboru, argued on the basis of research on the Hankow Shansi-Shensi Guild that "this type of organization, the *hui-kuan*, at least by the late Ch'ing displayed as a body autonomous powers and liabilities separate from those of its individual members." Yet he doubted whether it could be said to have fully progressed, in the language of German legal philosophy, from the *Genossenschaft* ("company," "guild," "association," or "partnership") to the *Körporschaft* ("corporate group" or "corporation"). (Niida, p. 516.) In my more broadly based study of Hankow guilds, I find that throughout the nineteenth century such organizations often assumed a distinct legal personality, but, as far as I can determine, no

corresponding concept of limited liability pertained to make the guilds "corporations" in a Western legal sense. Our interest here, however, is primarily in the mobilization of capital and manpower, areas in which guilds did act as corporate groups.

46. Cited in Ch'üan, *Hang-hui*, p. 110.

47. See, e.g., *TYSY*, 8.7 and 8.60; *SSHK*, 2.35.

48. *TYSY*, 6.47–49.

49. *Ibid.*, 1.8.

50. *Ibid.*, 8.15.

51. *SSHK*, map legend, p. 4.

52. Allen to Walsham, 2 September 1889, FO 228/878; *1920 HC*, 5.29–30.

53. "Han-k'ou mi-shih kung-so chih ting pang-kuei," in Negishi, *Shina no girudo*, pp. 244–45.

54. "Han-k'ou Chiang-hsi hui-kuan kung-i," in Tōa dōbunkai, 2: 562.

55. "Wu-Han t'ien-p'ing t'ung-yeh hang-kuei" (Regulations of the Scale-makers' Guild of Wuchang and Hankow), in Tōa dōbunkai, 2: 641–42.

56. See Shimizu, pp. 116–26.

57. "Han-k'ou ch'a-yeh kung-so kuei-t'iao," in Tōa dōbunkai, 2: 672–74.

58. Cited in Ch'üan, *Hang-hui*, p. 110.

59. *1920 HC*, 5.29–30. The Kwangtung Guild likewise levied a percentage on all members' commercial transactions to finance guildhall reconstruction between 1878 and 1891; Ch'üan, *Hang-hui*, p. 95.

60. See, e.g., *SSHK*, 2.36.

61. Yeh, 5.9.

62. IGC, *Salt*, p. 102.

63. *SP*, Kuang-hsü 7/intercalary/25; Caine to Wade, 1 March 1872, FO 228/515.

64. Su, "Chin-tai-hua," first year's report, p. 122.

65. IGC, *Decennial Report, 1892*, p. 191.

66. *TYSY*, 3.2–3, 3.13, 7.7–9, 8.15, and 8.39.

67. *Ibid.*, 8.47–48. See also *ibid.*, 3.6–12, 7.52, 7.56–57, 8.7, 8.25, 8.54, and 8.60.

68. *Ibid.*, 7.52–53.

69. Discussions of the 1796–1805 reconstruction project appear in *ibid.*, 7.52–54, 8.23–30, 8.57–59, and 8.62–63.

70. *Ibid.*, 8.60.

71. *Ibid.*, ch. 6. I hope to present and analyze some of these documents in another context.

72. The term *wu-chi* apparently signified that the property holder (in this case the Hui-chou Guild) held title to the structure but not to the lot upon which it was built. See Shiba, "Ningpo and Its Hinterland," p. 418.

73. *TYSY*, 8.76.

74. *Ibid.*, 6.33.

75. *Ibid.*, 6.46–49.

76. *Ibid.*, 8.29.

77. *Ibid.*, 6.49.

78. Fan, *passim*.

79. *SP*, Kuang-hsü 5/7/12.

80. *SP*, Kuang-hsü 6/10/9 and Kuang-hsü 7/7/28.

81. Little information has survived about the guildhall's original construction or this first major repair. For what sources we have, see: *SSHK*, prefaces, p. 1, and 1.7; *1920 HC*, 5.24; Niida, p. 504.

82. *1920 HC*, 5.24. See also *SSHK*, 1.10 and 2.44.

83. *SSHK*, 1.11–12, 1.17.

84. *Ibid.*, diagram section and 1.11–12; *SP*, Kuang-hsü 4/3/8, Kuang-hsü 7/9/25; FO, *Diplomatic and Consular Reports*, 1888, p. 14.
85. *SSHK*, diagram section, p. 1, and 3.44; *1920 HC*, 5.24.
86. *SSHK*, 1.12 and 1.17; *SP*, Kuang-hsü 4/3/8 and Kuang-hsü 7/9/25.
87. *SSHK*, 1.14.
88. *Ibid.*, 1.14–15.
89. *Ibid.*, 1.21, 1.28, and ch. 1, *passim*.
90. *Ibid.*, 2.35.
91. *Ibid.*, 2.36.
92. *Ibid.*, 2.45.
93. *Ibid.*, 2.35–40; Niida, p. 515.
94. *SSHK*, 2.9–11.
95. *Ibid.*, 2.35.
96. *Ibid.*, 2.45–47.
97. Frank H. H. King, *Money and Monetary Policy in China 1845–1895* (Cambridge, Mass., 1965), pp. 51–68.
98. Frederic Wakeman, Jr., "The Canton Trade and the Opium War," in Fairbank, ed., p. 178.
99. Shimizu, pp. 125–26.
100. IGC, *Decennial Report, 1892*, p. 179. See also Allen to Walsham, 2 September 1889, FO 228/878; P'eng Tse-i, "Hang-hui," p. 79.
101. Cited in Ch'üan, *Hang-hui*, p. 110.
102. *1920 HC*, 5.24; Niida, pp. 503, 505.
103. *SP*, Kuang-hsü 2/4/22.
104. I hope elsewhere to study in detail the history of benevolent-hall organization in Hankow. For guild-sponsored benevolent halls in other major commercial centers, see Rhoads, p. 104; Tu, "Shang-hai hang-hui hsing-chih."
105. *TYSY*, 3.12, 7.56–57, 8.28–30.
106. *1920 HC*, 5.23.
107. *SSHK*, 2.44.
108. *Ibid.*; *TYSY*, 8.26–27.
109. *SSHK*, 1.10.
110. *TYSY*, 8.26–27; *1867 HC*, 6.16; *SSHK*, 2.11 and 2.41.
111. *TYSY*, 7.52.
112. *Ibid.*, 7.15. On guild-sponsored schools generally, see Ho, *Ladder of Success*, p. 196ff.
113. *TYSY*, 8.23–25.
114. Ch'en Hui-yen, 4: 587.
115. See *1920 HC*, 5.18.
116. Imahori, *Kōzō*, pp. 286–92.
117. Yeh, 5.1.
118. *SP*, Kuang-hsü 4/10/4, also Kuang-hsü 4/3/8 and Kuang-hsü 4/10/1.
119. Tou, p. 18 and *passim*.
120. *Ibid.*, pp. 33, 80.
121. Skinner, "Introduction: Urban Social Structure in Ch'ing China," in Skinner, ed., *City in Late Imperial China*, p. 549.

Chapter Ten: Guilds and Local Power

1. *1920 HC*, 5.24.
2. *SP*, Kuang-hsü 9/4/3; report of Li Han-chang, Kuang-hsü 6/8/28, HPYJCS.
3. *SP*, Kuang-hsü 13/4/30; Allen to Walsham, 2 September 1889, FO 228/878; "Rules for the Weighing of Teas at Hankow," 1 May 1886, FO 228/831.
4. IGC, *Salt*, p. 102.
5. Shimizu, pp. 116–26.
6. Tōa dōbunkai, 2: 565–66.

7. On Kiangsi, see "Han-k'ou Chiang-hsi hui-kuan kung-i," in Tōa dōbunkai, 2: 562, and *SP*, Kuang-hsü 6/10/9; on Ningpo and Hui-chou, see *TYSY*, 6.33.

8. *TYSY*, 8.74–76, 7.7–9.

9. *SSHK*, 1.15. The Hunanese timber merchants' Liang-hu hui-kuan had a similar leadership structure, with headmen of each of the component *pang* serving in rotation as managers of the overall multiplex guild (WMCIA, "Chu-mu shih-ch'ang").

10. *SSHK*, 2.9.

11. *SP*, Kuang-hsü 4/3/8.

12. Etzioni, p. 3.

13. Manipulation by commercial capitalist "bosses" is suggested most emphatically by Imahori and other Japanese scholars adhering to the *kyōdōtai* theory of Chinese economic organization.

14. See, e.g., *TYSY*, 7.7, and the description of the Hankow Tea Guild election in Hsü Jun, p. 14.

15. "Guilds," in *Present Day Impressions*, p. 218. On liveried members in preindustrial English guilds, see Thrupp, p. 12.

16. *SSHK*, diagram section, p. 1.

17. A particularly forceful argument for broker domination appears in Uchida, "Gakō seido," p. 70.

18. Tu, "Shang-hai hang-hui hsing-chih." Tu's conclusions are based on his study of the organizational history of Soochow-Sungkiang cotton-cloth dealers at Shanghai.

19. Katō, p. 67.

20. Imahori, *Kōzō*, p. 274.

21. Yeh, 5.1–2.

22. *SSHK*, 2.11.

23. Tou, pp. 24–25.

24. *Ibid.*, pp. 28–29.

25. *1920 HC*, 15.28.

26. Jones, "Ningpo *Pang*," p. 84ff. A similar attenuation of the importance of family in determining organizational leadership within a changing urban environment was found among London aldermen by Thrupp, p. 83.

27. *1920 HC*, 15.28.

28. *TYSY*, 8.25.

29. *SP*, Kuang-hsü 13/4/30 and Kuang-hsü 4/3/8; *SSHK*, 2.41.

30. See, e.g., Negishi, *Shina no girudo*, pp. 244–45; Tōa dōbunkai, 2: 641–42; *SSHK*, 1.10, 1.14, and 2.9; *TYSY*, 7.54 and 8.7.

31. For sanctions against guild members, see regulation five, "Han-k'ou mi-shih kung-so chih ting pang-kuei," in Negishi, *Shina no girudo*, pp. 244–45.

32. Gardner to Walsham, 25 August 1886, FO 228/831, and discussion of this incident in Chapter 4, above.

33. Morse, *Gilds*, p. 5. See also *Present Day Impressions*, p. 219.

34. Dahl, esp. pp. 89–91, 164.

35. Katō, p. 66.

36. Tou, esp. pp. 32–38.

37. Negishi, *Shina no girudo*, pp. 316–19; Imahori, *Kōzō*, pp. 295–301.

38. On Sha-shih, see Hu Lin-i, endorsement on petition of Ching-I-Shih taotai, Hsien-feng 7/7, in Hu Lin-i, *I-chi* (1866), 8.31–34; IGC, *Decennial Reports, 1892–1901* (Shanghai, 1902), pp. 248–49; also Su, *Hsien-tai-hua*, pp. 51–52. Shanghai's Swatow Opium Guild, reported in Hamilton, "Merchant Associa-

tions," illustrates a roughly similar broad-based guild cooperation in pursuit of concrete economic interests.

39. Edward Rhoads, *China's Republican Revolution: The Case of Kwangtung, 1895–1913* (Cambridge, Mass., 1975), pp. 24–25, 36–37.

40. Elvin, "Gentry Democracy," pp. 42–43. For the influence of Tou Chi-liang on Elvin's work, see Elvin, *Pattern*, p. 293.

41. Skinner, "Introduction: Urban Social Structure in Ch'ing China," in Skinner, ed., *City in Late Imperial China*, pp. 522, 552.

42. *SP*, Kuang-hsü 6/9/5.

43. "Hu-pei Han-k'ou-chen chieh-tao t'u"; "Wu-Han ch'eng-chen ho-t'u"; *1920 HC*, 5.22–34.

44. Yeh, 1.1–2; Liu Wen-tao 1.1.6. The term "trade confederation" seems preferable to "guild confederation" for these pre-Taiping associations, since often the individual trades represented did not yet have inclusive trade guilds.

45. *SP*, Kuang-hsü 9/4/3; Ts'ai, vol. 6, no. 1–2, p. 77.

46. WMCIA, "Yao-ts'ai."

47. *1920 HC*, 5.19; Hankow Benevolent Hall Alliance, *Yen-ko chi ch'ing-k'uang*. On the "winter defense," see, e.g., *SP*, Kuang-hsü 4/4/3. I hope to present a fuller study of the winter defense in another context. A similar citywide merger of benevolent halls occurred in Canton around 1900; see Rhoads, "Merchant Associations," p. 104.

48. See *1867 HC*, 6.15–17; *1920 HC*, 5.15–16.

49. See Rowe, "Rebellion and Its Enemies."

50. *1920 HC*, 5.18.

51. Chang Chih-tung, 12.18–20; WMCIA, "Chu-mu shih-ch'ang."

52. *1920 HC*, 5.22 and 5.29. The All-Hankow Guild Alliance relinquished governmental functions upon the founding of the Chinese Republic, but it continued to represent Hankow guilds and guildsmen at least through the 1920's.

53. WMCIA, "Chu-mu shih-ch'ang."

54. *TYSY*, 2.2–3.

55. *Ibid.*, 7.9.

56. Lin, *Jih-chi*, p. 275 (entry for Tao-kuang 18/1/8).

57. *Ibid.*, p. 282 (entry for Tao-kuang 18/3/23).

58. *SSHK*, 1.7.

59. *TYSY*, 3.3.

60. *Ibid.*, 8.22, 8.47–48, 8.57, 8.60, 8.62–63, 8.74–76.

61. *SSHK*, 1.10, 2.35.

62. *1920 HC*, 5.24.

63. Report of Li Han-chang, T'ung-chih 8/7/5, HPYJCS.

64. See Rowe, "Rebellion and Its Enemies."

65. WMCIA, "Yao-ts'ai."

66. *Ibid.* This tax was irregular and probably extralegal, being imposed by the local administration for its own use; the date it was initiated has not been recorded. Chang Chih-tung abolished it in the early 1890's.

67. *IWL*, 9 December 1891.

68. T. T. Ch'ü, p. 168.

69. Weber, *City*, p. 83.

70. *Ibid.*

71. Elvin, *Pattern*, p. 293.

72. Imahori, *Kōzō*, p. 303.

73. Wolf, p. 2. Anthropologists have often characterized informal nexes on the local level as "networks" of personal relations rather than bounded "groups" or "organizations." See, e.g., J. A. Barnes, "Networks and the Polit-

ical Process," in Marc J. Swartz, ed., *Local Level Politics: Social and Cultural Perspectives* (Chicago, 1968), pp. 107–30; J. Clyde Mitchell, "Theoretical Orientations in African Urban Studies," in Michael Banton, ed., *The Social Anthropology of Complex Societies* (New York, 1966), pp. 37–68; J. Clyde Mitchell, *Social Networks in Urban Situations: Analyses of Personal Relationships in Central African Towns* (Manchester, 1969). According to Lapidus, p. 187, it was just such personal networks that constituted the real basis of power and urban autonomy in medieval Muslim cities. Although personal networks also played a role in China, there the main repositories of power were bounded, formal organizations—the guilds.

Conclusion

1. I have made preliminary attempts to treat these complex issues in "Urban Control" and "Rebellion and Its Enemies."

2. Hilary Beattie, *Land and Lineage in China: A Study of T'ung-ch'eng County, Anhwei, in the Ming and Ch'ing Dynasties* (Cambridge, 1979), esp. pp. 93–94 and 114–15.

3. Lapidus, p. 4.

4. Dahl, p. 86. It should be clear that I use "pluralism"—both in a social sense to refer to the multiplicity of subethnic and occupational groups in Hankow and in a political sense to refer to the structure of decision-making power that involved representatives of these groups—in order to describe an existing condition rather than to prescribe an ideal. For a thoughtful study of the pluralist idea and the hazards involved in its use, see John Higham, "Ethnic Pluralism in Modern American Thought," in Higham, *Send These to Me: Jews and Other Immigrants in Urban America* (New York, 1975), pp. 196–230.

5. See Georg Simmel, "Large Cities and Mental Life," in Pitirim A. Sorokin, Carl C. Zimmerman, and Charles J. Galpin, eds., *A Systematic Sourcebook in Rural Sociology* (Minneapolis, 1932), esp. 1: 247; Louis Wirth, "Urbanism as a Way of Life," *American Journal of Sociology*, 44 (1938), esp. p. 15; Robert Redfield, "The Cultural Role of Cities," in *The Papers of Robert Redfield* (Chicago, 1962), esp. 1: 333.

6. Richard Wilson, letter of 3 July 1886, Hankow Letter Book, Vol. 6, LMS.

7. See, e.g., discussions of the careers of Ts'ai Fu-ch'ing and Hsü Jung-t'ing, in P'i, pp. 66–67. Ts'ai began as the Hankow agent for a Ningpo marine-products firm, and Hsü as a dealer in hides and medicinal herbs. On the activities of urban merchants in 1911, see P'i, "Shang-hui ho shang-t'uan"; Esherick, *Reform and Revolution*; Rhoads, "Merchant Associations"; and esp. Marie-Claire Bergère, "The Role of the Bourgeoisie," in Mary C. Wright, ed., *China in Revolution: The First Phase, 1900–1913* (New Haven, 1968), pp. 229–96.

Selected Bibliography

Characters for the names of authors of Chinese and Japanese works cited here can be found in the Character List.

Abe Takeo, "Beikoku jukyū no kenkyū—Yōsei shi no isshō to shita mita" (Supply and demand of grain in the Yung-cheng period), in Abe, *Shindaishi no kenkyū* (Studies in Ch'ing history), Tokyo, 1971, pp. 411–522.

Annales de la propagation de la foi, 10–25 (1837–53).

Balazs, Etienne, *Chinese Civilization and Bureaucracy*, New Haven, 1964.

———, "Les Villes chinoises," *Recueil de la Société Jean Bodin*, 6 (1954), pp. 239–61.

Beal, Edwin G., Jr., *The Origins of Likin, 1853–1864*, Cambridge, Mass., 1958.

Bishop, Mrs. J. F., *The Yangtze Valley and Beyond*, London, 1899.

Blakiston, Thomas W., *Five Months on the Yangtze*, London, 1862.

Bowers, Alexander, "The Yang-tze-kiang and the New Treaty Ports," *The Chinese and Japanese Repository*, 1 (1864), pp. 269–70.

Bryson, Mrs., *John Kenneth Mackenzie, Medical Missionary to China*, London, 1891; repr. San Francisco, 1977.

Cha Shen-hsing, *Ching-yeh-t'ang shih-chi* (Collected poems from the Ching-yeh studio), n.d.

Chang Chih-tung, *Nan-p'i Chang kung-pao cheng-shu* (Political writings of Chang Chih-tung), 1901.

Chang Kuo-hui, "Shih-chiu shih-chi hou-pan-ch'i Chung-kuo ch'ien-chuang te mai-pan-hua" (The compradorization of Chinese native banks in the second half of the nineteenth century), *Li-shih yen-chiu*, 6 (1963), pp. 85–98.

Chang P'eng-fei, ed., *Han-k'ou mao-i chih* (Commercial gazetteer of Hankow), 1918.

Chang-shih san-hsiu chia-p'u (Genealogy of the Chang family, third revision), 1876.

Chang-shih tsung-p'u (Genealogy of the Chang clan), 1948.

Chang Shou-po, *Tsui-chin Han-k'ou kung-shang-yeh i-pien* (Handbook of current industry and commerce in Hankow), 1911.

Ch'ang-chiang jih-pao (Yangtze River daily), occasional articles on Wuhan local history, 1960–80.

Chao-Li-Ch'iao Tea Factory with Central China Normal University, Department of History, *Tung-ch'a chin-hsi* (Yang-lou-tung tea, past and present), Wuhan, 1980.

Ch'en Hui-yen, "Wu-ch'ang chi-shih" (A record of events at Wuchang), in *T'ai-p'ing t'ien-kuo tzu-liao ts'ung-k'an* (Collected sources on the Taiping Heavenly Kingdom), Shanghai, 1953, pp. 577–606.

Ch'en Hung-mou, *P'ei-yuan-t'ang ou-ts'un kao* (Draft writings from the P'ei-yuan studio), 1866.

Chesneaux, Jean, *The Chinese Labor Movement, 1919–1927*, Stanford, 1968.

China Directory, 1874, Hong Kong, 1874; repr. Taipei, 1971.

"Chinese Partnerships: Liability of the Individual Members," *Journal of the Royal Asiatic Society, China Branch*, n.s. 22, no. 1 (1887), pp. 39–52.

Chinese People's Bank, Shanghai Branch, comp., *Shang-hai ch'ien-chuang shih-liao* (Historical materials on Shanghai native banks), Shanghai, 1960.

Chin Ta-k'ai, "Wu-han ch'eng-chen te yen-pien" (The evolution of the Wuhan cities), *Hu-pei wen-hsien*, 5 (October 1967), pp. 62–67.

Ch'ing Palace Archives, National Palace Museum, Taipei.

Chou-pan i-wu shih-mo (Complete record of barbarian management), 1929–31; repr. Taipei, 1970–71.

Chu, T. H., *Tea Trade in Central China*, Shanghai, 1936.

Ch'ü Chih-sheng, "Chung-kuo te ya-hang" (Chinese brokers), *She-hui k'o-hsueh tsa-chih*, 4 (December 1933), pp. 480–90.

Ch'ü, T'ung-tsu, *Local Government in China under the Ch'ing*, Cambridge, Mass., 1962.

Ch'üan Han-sheng, "Ch'ing-ch'ao chung-yeh Su-chou te mi-liao mao-i" (The rice trade of Soochow in the mid-Ch'ing), *Bulletin of the Institute of History and Philology, Academia Sinica*, 34 (1969), pp. 71–86.

———, *Chung-kuo hang-hui chih-tu shih* (History of the guild system in China), Shanghai, 1933.

——— and Richard Kraus, *Mid-Ch'ing Rice Markets and Trade: An Essay in Price History*, Cambridge, Mass., 1975.

Cooper, T. T., *Travels of a Pioneer of Commerce (in Pigtails and Petticoats)*, London, 1871.

Cornaby, W. Arthur, *Rambles in Central China*, London, 1896.

Crissman, Lawrence W., "The Segmentary Structure of Urban Overseas Chinese Communities," *Man*, 2, no. 2 (1967), pp. 185–204.

Curtin, Philip, "Geographical Centrality and Colonial Dependence," paper prepared for the Eighth International Economic History Congress, Budapest, August 1982.

Customs Gazette, 1871–74.

Dahl, Robert A., *Who Governs? Democracy and Power in an American City*, New Haven, 1961.

Dawson, F. L., Jr., "Law and the Merchant in Traditional China: The Ch'ing Code, *Ta-Ch'ing lü-li*, and Its Implications for the Merchant Class," *Papers on China*, 2 (1948), pp. 55–92.

Dean, Britten, *China and Great Britain: The Diplomacy of Commercial Relations 1860–1864*, Cambridge, Mass., 1974.

———, "Sino-British Diplomacy in the 1860s: The Establishment of the British Concession at Hankow," *Harvard Journal of Asiatic Studies*, 32 (1972), pp. 71–97.

DeGlopper, Donald, "Social Structure in a Nineteenth-Century Taiwanese Port City," in G. William Skinner, ed., *The City in Late Imperial China*, Stanford, 1977, pp. 633–50.

DeRoover, Raymond, *Money, Banking, and Credit in Medieval Bruges*, Cambridge, Mass., 1948.

Deutsch, Karl W., "Social Mobilization and Political Development," in Jason L. Finckle and Richard W. Gable, eds., *Political Development and Social Change*, New York, 1966, pp. 205–26.

Du Halde, J. B., *A Description of the Empire of China and Chinese Tartary*, London, 1738.

Eberhard, Wolfram, *Collected Papers*, Volume I: *Settlement and Social Change in Asia*, Hong Kong, 1967.

———, "Data on the Structure of the Chinese City in the Pre-Industrial Period," *Economic Development and Cultural Change*, 4 (1956), pp. 253–68.

———, *Social Mobility in Traditional China*, Leiden, 1962.

Elgin, Lord, *Letters and Journals of James, Eighth Earl of Elgin*, ed. Theodore Walrond, London, 1872.

Elvin, Mark, "The Gentry Democracy in Chinese Shanghai, 1905–14," in Jack Gray, ed., *Modern China's Search for a Political Form*, London, 1969, pp. 41–65.

———, "Market Towns and Waterways: The County of Shanghai from 1480 to 1910," in G. William Skinner, ed., *The City in Late Imperial China*, Stanford, 1977, pp. 441–74.

———, *The Pattern of the Chinese Past*, Stanford, 1973.

——— and G. William Skinner, eds., *The Chinese City Between Two Worlds*, Stanford, 1974.

Esherick, Joseph W., *Reform and Revolution in China: The 1911 Revolution in Hunan and Hubei*, Berkeley, 1976.

Etzioni, Amitai, *Complex Organizations*, Englewood Cliffs, N.J., 1964.

Fairbank, John K., ed., *The Cambridge History of China*, Volume X: *Late Ch'ing*, Part One, Cambridge, 1978.

Fan K'ai, *Han-k'ou ts'ung-t'an* (Hankow compendium), 1822; repr. Taipei, 1974.

Fei Hsiao-tung, *China's Gentry: Essays on Rural-Urban Relations*, Chicago, 1953.

Feng Hua-te, "Ho-pei sheng ya-shui hsing-chih chih yen-pien" (The changing nature of brokerage taxes in Hopeh), in Fang Hsien-t'ing, ed., *Chung-kuo ching-chi yen-chiu* (Studies on the Chinese economy), Changsha, 1938, vol. 2, pp. 1067–80.

Feng-shih tsung-p'u (Genealogy of the Feng clan), 1946.

Feuerwerker, Albert, *China's Early Industrialization: Sheng Hsuan-huai and Mandarin Enterprise*, Cambridge, Mass., 1958.

Foster, Mrs. Arnold, *In the Valley of the Yangtze*, London, 1899.

Fu I-ling, *Ming-Ch'ing shih-tai shang-jen chi shang-yeh tzu-pen* (Merchants and commercial capital during the Ming and Ch'ing dynasties), Peking, 1956.

Fujii Hiroshi, "Shin'an shōnin no kenkyū" (A study of the Hsin-an merchants), *Tōyō gakuhō*, 36 (1953–54), no. 1, pp. 1–44; no. 2, pp. 32–60; no. 3, pp. 65–118; no. 4, pp. 115–45.

Geertz, Clifford, *Peddlers and Princes: Social Development and Economic Change in Two Indonesian Towns*, Chicago, 1963.

Gill, William, *The River of Golden Sand*, London, 1883.

Great Britain, Foreign Office, Archives. Public Record Office, London.

———, *Commercial Reports by Her Majesty's Consuls in China*, Nos. 1–6 (1880–85).

———, *Diplomatic and Consular Reports on Trade and Finance: China. Report for the Year 1887 on the Trade of Hankow*, Annual Series, No. 380, 1888.

Great Britain, House of Commons, *British Parliamentary Papers*, 1861–66.
Green, Henrietta, *Henrietta Green, a Memoir*, Ashford, England, 1891.
Hamilton, Gary G., "Nineteenth Century Chinese Merchant Associations: Conspiracy or Combination?," *Ch'ing-shih wen-t'i*, 3, no. 8 (December 1977), pp. 50–71.
———, "Regional Associations in the Chinese City: A Comparative Perspective," *Comparative Studies in Society and History*, 21 (July 1979), pp. 346–61.
Han-k'ou Lao-shih ts'u-p'u (Genealogy of the Lao lineage of Hankow), 1755.
Han-k'ou Shan-Shen-hsi hui-kuan chih (Gazetteer of the Shansi-Shensi Hui-kuan of Hankow), ed. Hou P'ei-chün, 1896.
Han-k'ou Tzu-yang shu-yüan chih-lüeh (Brief gazetteer of the Tzu-yang Academy of Hankow), ed. Tung Kuei-fu, 1806.
Hankow Benevolent Hall Alliance, *Ko shan-t'ang ch'uang-li yen-ko chi shih-yeh ch'ing-k'uang* (History and activities of the various benevolent halls), Hankow, 1945.
Han-shang hsiao-wen chi (Collected poems of the Leisure Moments Society of Hankow), ed. Huan Ying-ch'ing, 1911.
Han-shih tsung-p'u (Genealogy of the Han clan), 1946.
Han-yang fu-chih (Gazetteer of Hanyang prefecture), 1747.
"Han-yang fu yü-t'u" (Map of Hanyang prefecture), 1901.
Han-yang hsien-chih (Gazetteer of Hanyang county), 1818.
Han-yang hsien-chih (Gazetteer of Hanyang county), 1867.
Han-yang hsien-shih (Unofficial gazetteer of Hanyang county), 1884.
"Han-yang hsien yü-t'u" (Map of Hanyang county), 1901.
Han-yang Yao-shih ts'u-p'u (Genealogy of the Yao lineage of Hankow), 1923.
Hao, Yen-p'ing, *The Comprador in Nineteenth-century China: Bridge Between East and West*, Cambridge, Mass., 1970.
Hatano Yoshihiro, *Chūgoku kindai kōgyōshi no kenkyū* (Studies in the history of modern industry in China), Kyoto, 1961.
Hill, David, *Hoopeh, China: Its Claims and Call*, York, 1881.
———, *Twenty-five Years in Central China, 1865–1890*, London, 1891.
Ho Ping-ti, *Chung-kuo hui-kuan shih lun* (On the history of *Landsmannschaften* in China), Taipei, 1966.
———, "The Geographic Distribution of *Hui-kuan* (*Landsmannschaften*) in Central and Upper Yangtze Provinces," *Tsinghua Journal of Chinese Studies*, n.s. 5, no. 2 (December 1966), pp. 120–52.
———, *The Ladder of Success in Imperial China: Aspects of Social Mobility, 1368–1911*, New York, 1962.
———, "The Salt Merchants of Yang-chou: A Study of Commercial Capitalism in Eighteenth-Century China," *Harvard Journal of Asiatic Studies*, 17 (1954), pp. 130–68.
Hou Wai-lu, *Chung-kuo feng-chien she-hui shih lun* (On the history of Chinese feudal society), Peking, 1973.
Hsia-k'ou hsien-chih (Gazetteer of Hsia-k'ou county), 1920.
Hsiao Chih-chih, "Han-k'ou tsu-chieh" (The Hankow concession area), *Wuhan ta-hsueh hsueh-pao*, 4 (1978), pp. 77–80.
———, "Wu-han ma-t'ou kung-jen ko-ming tou-cheng shih" (The revolutionary struggles of Wuhan dockworkers), unpublished discussion paper, 1972.
Hsiao, Kung-chuan, *Rural China: Imperial Control in the Nineteenth Century*, Seattle, 1960.

Hsiao Yao-nan, *Hu-pei ti-fang chi-yao* (Outline of river control works in Hupeh), 1924.
Hsien-chuang-i-kung nien-p'u (Chronological biography of Yü-t'ai), ca. 1865.
Hsü Huan-t'ou, ed., *Han-k'ou hsiao-chih* (Brief gazetteer of Hankow), 1914.
Hsü Jun, *Hsu Yü-chai tzu-hsu nien-p'u* (Autobiography of Hsü Jun), Shanghai, 1910.
Hsü Ta-ling, *Ch'ing-tai chüan-na chih-tu* (The system of sales of official ranks and degrees in the Ch'ing period), *Yen-ching hsueh-pao*, Special Issue 22 (1950).
Hu Chao-ch'un, *Hu-shih i-shu* (Surviving works of Hu Chao-ch'un), ca. 1915.
Hu Chao-hsi, *Chang Hsien-chung t'u-Shu k'ao-pien* (An investigation of Chang Hsien-chung's butchery of Szechwan), Chengtu, 1980.
Hu Lin-i, *Hu wen-chung-kung i-chi* (Complete works of Hu Lin-i), 1866; repr. Taipei, 1972.
———, *Hu wen-chung-kung i-chi* (Complete works of Hu Lin-i), 1875.
"Hu-pei Han-k'ou-chen chieh-tao t'u" (Street map of Hankow), 1877.
Hu-pei t'ung-chih (Consolidated gazetteer of Hupeh), 1920.
"Hu-pei t'ung-chih chih-yü" (Collected materials for a prospective Hupeh provincial gazetteer), comp. Hung Liang-p'in, manuscript, ca. 1885.
Hu-pu tse-li (Statutes and precedents of the Board of Revenue), 1865; repr. Taipei, 1972.
Huc, M., *A Journey Through the Chinese Empire*, New York, 1859.
Hung Liang-chi, *Ch'ien-lung fu-t'ing-chou-hsien t'u-chih* (Atlas of administrative units under the Ch'ien-lung reign), 1803.
Hung-shan-miao Lo-shih tsung-p'u (Genealogy of the Lo clan of Hung-shan-miao), 1918.
Imahori Seiji, *Chūgoku no shakai kōzō* (Chinese social structure), Tokyo, 1953.
———, "Shindai ni okeru goka no kindaika no hasu" (The modernization of business partnerships in the Ch'ing period), *Tōyōshi kenkyū*, 17, no. 1 (1956), pp. 1–49.
Inspectorate General of Customs, *Chinese Life-boats, Etc.*, Special Series No. 18, Shanghai, 1893.
———, *Customs Rules and Regulations for the Shipment and Discharge of Cargo, and Harbour and Pilotage Regulations in Force at the Treaty Ports*, Customs Papers No. 5, Shanghai, 1876.
———, *Decennial Reports, 1882–1892*, Shanghai, 1893.
———, *Reports of the Commissioners of Customs on the Practices at Each Port in the Matter of Privileges Conceded and the Facilitation of Business Generally*, Office Series No. 8, Shanghai, 1869.
———, *Reports on the Haikwan Banking System and Local Currency at the Treaty Ports*, Office Series No. 13, Shanghai, 1878.
———, *Reports on Trade at the Ports in China Open by Treaty to the Foreign Trade*, Shanghai, 1865–89.
———, *Salt, Production and Taxation*, Office Series No. 81, Shanghai, 1906.
———, *Tea, 1888*, Special Series No. 11, Shanghai, 1889.
I-wen-lu, Shanghai, 1879–99.
Jardine, Matheson and Co., Archives, University Library, Cambridge University.
John, Griffith, *A Voice from China*, London, 1907.
Jones, Susan Mann, "Finance in Ningpo: The 'Ch'ien Chuang,' 1750–1880," in

W. E. Willmott, ed., *Economic Organization in Chinese Society*, Stanford, 1972, pp. 47–77.

———, "The Ningpo *Pang* and Financial Power at Shanghai," in Mark Elvin and G. William Skinner, eds., *The Chinese City Between Two Worlds*, Stanford, 1974, pp. 73–96.

Kankō kokurisha, comp., *Kankō annei* (Guide to Hankow), 1916.

Katō Shigeshi, "On the Hang, or the Associations of Merchants in China," *Memoirs of the Research Department of the Tōyō Bunko*, 8 (1936), pp. 65–80.

Kennedy, Thomas L., "Chang Chih-tung and the Struggle for Strategic Industrialization: The Establishment of the Hanyang Arsenal, 1884–1895," *Harvard Journal of Asiatic Studies*, 33 (1973), pp. 154–82.

Kitamura Hironao, "Shindai no shōnin shichō ni tsuite" (On commercial markets in the Ch'ing period), *Keizaigaku zasshi*, 28, no. 3 (1952), pp. 1–19.

Kokuryūkai, comp., *Tōa senkaku shishi kiden* (Records and biographies of pioneer East Asian patriots), Tokyo, 1933; repr. Tokyo, 1966.

Kosaku Torizō, *Chūgoku bōeki kikō no kenkyū* (A study of the commercial structure of China), Tokyo, 1949.

Kuan-ch'iao Ling-shih tsung-p'u (Genealogy of the Ling clan of Kuan-ch'iao), 1883.

Kuang-hsü Hu-pei yü-ti chi (Atlas of Hupeh in the Kuang-hsü reign), 1894.

Kuei-shih tsung-p'u (Genealogy of the Kuei clan), 1935.

Lapidus, Ira Marvin, *Muslim Cities in the Later Middle Ages*, Cambridge, Mass., 1967.

Latourette, Kenneth Scott, *The History of Christian Missions in China*, New York, 1929.

Lettres édifiantes et curieuses, écrites des missions étrangères, Vols. 9–13: *Mémoires de la Chine*, Lyon, 1819.

Levy, Marion J., Jr., and Shih Kuo-heng, *The Rise of the Modern Chinese Business Class*, New York, 1949.

Lewis, Charlton M., *Prologue to the Chinese Revolution: The Transformation of Ideas and Institutions in Hunan Province, 1891–1907*, Cambridge, Mass., 1976.

Li Han-chang, *Ho-fei Li chin-k'o-kung cheng-shu* (Political writings of Li Hanchang), 1900.

Li Shao-ling, *Wu-han chin-hsi t'an* (Wuhan past and present), Wuhan, 1957.

Li-tai chih-kuan piao (Schedule of official posts under the successive dynasties), 1780; repr. Taipei, 1965.

Liang-Huai yen-fa chih (Gazetteer of the salt administration of Liang-Huai), 1905.

Lin Tse-hsü, *Lin Tse-hsü chi: jih-chi* (Collected works of Lin Tse-hsu: diary), Peking, 1962.

———, *Lin Tse-hsü chi: kung-tu* (Collected works of Lin Tse-hsu: official proclamations), Peking, 1963.

——, *Lin wen-chung-kung cheng-shu* (Political writings of Lin Tse-hsu), Taipei, 1965.

Little, Archibald John, *The Far East*, London, 1905.

———, *Through the Yangtze Gorges*, London, 1898.

Liu, Kwang-Ching, *Anglo-American Steamship Rivalry in China, 1862–1874*, Cambridge, Mass., 1962.

Liu-shih tsung-p'u (Genealogy of the Liu clan), 1924.

Liu-shih tsung-p'u (Genealogy of the Liu clan), 1932.

Liu, Ts'ui-jung, *Trade on the Han River and Its Impact on Economic Development, c. 1800–1911*, Taipei, 1980.

Liu Wen-tao, *Han-k'ou-shih chien-she kai-k'uang* (Outline history of the municipality of Hankow), Hankow, 1930.

London Missionary Society, Archives, School of Oriental and African Studies, London.

———, *First Report of the Hankow Hospital, in Connection with the London Missionary Society*, Hankow, 1868.

———, *Report of the London Mission Hospital at Hankow*, Hankow, reports for 1877–78, 1882–83, 1883–85, and 1887–88.

Lu Chien-ying, *Lu wen-chieh-kung tsou-i* (Memorials of Lu Chien-ying), Taipei, n.d.

Ma, Lawrence J. C., *Commercial Development and Urban Change in Sung China (966–1279)*, Ann Arbor, 1971.

McElderry, Andrea Lee, *Shanghai Old-Style Banks (Ch'ien-chuang) 1800–1935*, Ann Arbor, 1976.

MacGillivray, D., *A Century of Protestant Missions in China*, Shanghai, 1907.

MacGowan, D. J., "Chinese Guilds," *Journal of the North China Branch of the Royal Asiatic Society*, 21, no. 3 (1886), pp. 133–92.

Margary, Augustus Raymond, *Notes of a Journey from Hankow to Ta-Li-Fu*, Shanghai, 1875.

Mayers, W. F., N. B. Dennys, and C. King, *The Treaty Ports of China and Japan: A Complete Guide*, London, 1867.

Melson, Robert, and Howard Wolpe, "Modernization and the Politics of Communalism: A Theoretical Perspective," *American Political Science Review*, 64 (December 1970), pp. 1112–30.

Metzger, Thomas, "The State and Commerce in Imperial China," *Asian and African Studies*, 6 (1970), pp. 23–46.

———, "T'ao Chu's Reform of the Huaipei Salt Monopoly," *Papers on China*, 16 (1962), pp. 1–39.

Ming-Ch'ing Archives (Number One Historical Archives), Peking.

"Chu-p'i tsou-che, nei-cheng" (Palace memorials, internal bureaucratic matters).

"Chu-p'i tsou-che, nung-min yün-tung" (Palace memorials, peasant movements).

"Chu-p'i tsou-che, ts'ai-cheng" (Palace memorials, fiscal administration).

"Hsing-k'o t'i-pen" (Routine memorials, Board of Punishments).

"Kung-k'o t'i-pen" (Routine memorials, Board of Works).

"Sui-shou teng-chi" (Records of imperial correspondence).

Mizuno Kōkichi, *Kankō* (Hankow), Tokyo, 1907.

Morita Akira, *Shindai suirishi kenkyū* (Studies on the history of water conservancy in the Ch'ing period), Tokyo, 1974.

———, " 'Shōku henran' ni tsuite" (On Chinese merchant guides), *Fukuoku daigaku kenkyūjohō*, 16 (1972), pp. 1–28.

Morse, Hosea Ballou, *The Gilds of China*, London, 1909.

———, *The Trade and Administration of China*, New York, 1908.

Mote, F. W., "The Transformation of Nanking, 1350–1400," in G. William Skinner, ed., *The City in Late Imperial China*, Stanford, 1977, pp. 101–54.

Moulder, Frances, *Japan, China, and the Modern World Economy*, Cambridge, 1977.

Murphey, Rhoads, "The City as a Center of Change: Western Europe and China," *Annals of the Association of American Geographers*, 44 (1954), pp. 349–62.

———, *The Outsiders: The Western Experience in India and China*, Ann Arbor, 1977.

———, *Shanghai: Key to Modern China*, Cambridge, Mass., 1953.

———, *The Treaty Ports and China's Modernization: What Went Wrong?*, Ann Arbor, 1970.

Myers, Ramon, "Merchants and Economic Organization During the Ming and Ch'ing Period: A Review Article," *Ch'ing-shih wen-t'i*, 3, no. 2 (December 1974), pp. 77–93.

Nakamura Jihei, "Shindai Kokō bei no ryūtsū no ichimen" (One aspect of the circulation of Hukwang rice during the Ch'ing), *Shakai keizai shigaku*, 18, no. 3 (1952), pp. 53–65.

Negishi Tadashi, *Baiban seido no kenkyū* (A study of the compradore system), Tokyo, 1948.

———, *Chūgoku no girudo* (Chinese guilds), Tokyo, 1953.

———, *Shina no girudo no kenkyū* (A study of Chinese guilds), Tokyo, 1938.

Niida Noboru, "Shindai no Kankō San-Sensei kaikan to San-Sensei hō" (Shansi and Shensi *hui-kuan* and guilds at Hankow during the Ch'ing dynasty), *Shakai keizai shigaku*, 13, no. 6 (September 1943), pp. 497–518.

Nishin bōeki kenkyūjo, *Shinkoku tsūshō soran* (Guide to Chinese commerce), Shanghai, 1892.

Nishizato Yoshiyuki, "Shinmatsu no Nimbo shōnin ni tsuite—Sekkō zaibatsu no naritachi ni kansuru" (On the Ningpo merchants in the late Ch'ing: an investigation into the origins of the Chekiang financial clique), *Tōyōshi kenkyū*, 26, nos. 1 and 2 (1967), pp. 1–29, 71–89.

North-China Daily News, Shanghai, 1869–79.

North-China Herald, Shanghai, 1858–90.

Oliphant, Laurence, *Narrative of the Earl of Elgin's Mission to China and Japan in the Years 1857, '58, '59*, New York, 1860.

Oxenham, E. L., "History of Han Yang and Hankow," *China Review*, 1, no. 6 (1873), pp. 283–84.

———, *On the Inundations of the Yangtze-Kiang*, London, 1875.

P'an Hsin-tsao, *Wu-han-shih chien-chih yen-ko* (The founding and history of Wuhan), Wuhan, 1956.

P'an Lei, *Sui-ch'u-t'ang chi* (Collected writings from the Sui-ch'u studio), n.d.

Pao Shih-ch'en, *An-Wu ssu-chung* (Four strategies for the pacification of Kiangsu), 1846.

Parker, E. H., *China: Her History, Diplomacy, and Commerce*, London, 1901.

———, "The Hankow Dialect," *China Review*, 3, no. 5 (1875), p. 308.

P'eng Tse-i, "Ch'ing-tai ch'ien-ch'i shou-kung-yeh te fa-chan" (The development of handicrafts in the early Ch'ing), *Chung-kuo shih yen-chiu*, 1981, no. 1, pp. 43–60.

———, *Chung-kuo chin-tai shou-kung-yeh shih tzu-liao, 1840–1949* (Materials on the history of modern Chinese handicrafts, 1840–1949), Peking, 1957.

———, "Shih-chiu shih-chi hou-ch'i Chung-kuo ch'eng-shih shou-kung-yeh shang-yeh hang-hui te ch'ung-chien ho tso-yung" (The reestablishment and functions of Chinese urban handicraft and commercial guilds in the second half of the nineteenth century), *Li-shih yen-chiu*, 1965, no. 1, pp. 71–102.

P'eng Yü-hsin, "Ch'ing-mo chung-yang yü ko sheng ts'ai-cheng kuan-hsi"

(Fiscal relations between the central and provincial governments in the late Ch'ing), *She-hui k'o-hsueh tsa-chih*, 1946; repr. in *Chung-kuo chin-tai-shih lun-ts'ung* (Essays on modern Chinese history), vol. 2, no. 5, Taipei, 1962, pp. 3–45.

———, "K'ang-Jih chan-cheng ch'ien Han-k'ou yang-hang ho mai-pan" (Foreign firms and compradores at Hankow before the War of Resistance to Japan), *Li-lun chan-hsien*, February 1959, pp. 22–29.

Percival, William Spencer, *The Land of the Dragon: My Boating and Shooting Excursions to the Gorges of the Upper Yangtze*, London, 1889.

P'i Ming-hsiu, "Wu-ch'ang shou-i chung te Wu-Han shang-hui ho shang-t'uan" (The merchant associations and merchant militia of Wuchang and Hankow during the Wuchang Uprising), *Li-shih yen-chiu* 1982, no. 1, pp. 57–71.

Pien Pao-ti, *Pien chih-chün tsou-i* (Memorials of Pien Pao-ti), 1894.

Pirenne, Henri, *Medieval Cities: Their Origins and the Revival of Trade*, Princeton, 1969.

Present Day Impressions of the Far East and Prominent and Progressive Chinese at Home and Abroad, London, 1917.

Rawski, Evelyn Sakakida, *Agricultural Change and the Peasant Economy of South China*, Cambridge, Mass., 1972.

Rhoads, Edward, "Merchant Associations in Canton, 1895–1911," in Mark Elvin and G. William Skinner, eds., *The Chinese City Between Two Worlds*, Stanford, 1974, pp. 97–118.

Richtofen, Ferdinand von, *Letters, 1870–1872*, Shanghai, n.d.

Robson, William, *Griffith John, Founder of the Hankow Mission*, New York, n.d.

Rörig, Fritz, *The Medieval Town*, Berkeley, 1967.

Rowe, William T., "Rebellion and Its Enemies in a Late Ch'ing City: The Hankow Plot of 1883," in Tang Tsou, ed., *Political Leadership and Social Change in China: Select Papers from the Center for Far Eastern Studies*, 4, Chicago, 1979–80, pp. 71–111.

———, "Urban Control in Late Imperial China: The *Pao-chia* System in Hankow," in Joshua A. Fogel and William T. Rowe, eds., *Perspectives on a Changing China: Essays in Honor of Professor C. Martin Wilbur*, Boulder, Colo., 1979, pp. 89–112.

Roxby, Percy M., "Wu-Han: The Heart of China," *Scottish Geographical Magazine*, 32 (1916), pp. 266–79.

Rozman, Gilbert, *Urban Networks in Ch'ing China and Tokugawa Japan*, Princeton, 1973.

Rudolph, Lloyd I., and Suzanne Hoeber Rudolph, *The Modernity of Tradition: Political Development in India*, Chicago, 1967.

Saeki Tomi, *Chūgokushi kenkyū* (Studies in Chinese history), vol. 2, Kyoto, 1971.

———, *Shindai ensei no kenkyū* (A study of the Ch'ing salt administration), Kyoto, 1956.

———, "Shindai ni okeru Sansei shōnin" (The Shansi merchants in the Ch'ing dynasty), *Shirin*, 60, no. 1 (January 1977), pp. 1–14.

Shen-pao, Shanghai, 1872–88; repr. Taipei, 1964.

Shiba Yoshinobu, "Chūgoku toshi o meguru kenkyū gaikyō—hōseishi o chūshin ni" (A survey of studies on Chinese cities, with emphasis on legal history), *Hōsei shi kenkyū*, 23 (1974), pp. 185–206.

———, *Commerce and Society in Sung China*, ed. Mark Elvin, Ann Arbor, 1970.

———, "Ningpo and Its Hinterland," in G. William Skinner, ed., *The City in Late Imperial China*, Stanford, 1977, pp. 391–440.

———, "Urbanization and the Development of Markets in the Lower Yangtze Valley," in John Winthrop Haeger, ed., *Crisis and Prosperity in Sung China*, Tucson, 1975, pp. 13–48.

———, "Shindai Kishu shōnin no ichimen" (One perspective on the Hui-chou merchants in the Ch'ing period), *Jimbun kenkyū*, 19, no. 8 (1968), pp. 587–626.

Shigeta Atsushi, "Shinsho ni okeru Konan beishichō no ikkōsatsu" (An investigation of Hunan rice markets in the early Ch'ing), *Tōyō bunka kenkyūjo kiyo*, 10 (November 1956), pp. 427–98.

Shimizu Taiji, *Shina no kazoku to sonraku* (Kinship and village in China), Tokyo, 1928.

Simon, G-Eugène, *La Cité chinoise*, Paris, 1885.

Sjoberg, Gideon, *The Preindustrial City*, New York, 1960.

Skinner, G. William, ed., *The City in Late Imperial China*, Stanford, 1977.

———, "Marketing and Social Structure in Rural China," Parts 1 and 2, *Journal of Asian Studies*, 24 (1964–65), pp. 3–44, 195–228.

———, "Mobility Strategies in Late Imperial China: A Regional Systems Analysis," in Carol A. Smith, ed., *Regional Analysis*, New York, 1976, vol. 1, pp. 327–64.

Smith, F. Porter, *The Rivers of China*, Hankow, 1869.

Stinchcombe, Arthur L., "Social Structure and Organizations," in James G. March, ed., *Handbook of Organizations*, New York, 1965, pp. 142–93.

Su Yün-feng, "Chung-kuo chin-tai-hua chih ch'u-yü yen-chiu: Hu-pei sheng" (A regional study of China's modernization: Hupeh province). First year's report (1974), second year's report (1975), third year's report (1976). Manuscripts prepared for the Regional Modernization Project, Institute of Modern History, Academia Sinica, Taipei.

———, *Chung-kuo hsien-tai-hua ch'u-yü yen-chiu: Hu-pei sheng 1860–1916* (Modernization in China, 1860–1916: A regional study of social, political, and economic change in Hupeh Province), Taipei, 1981.

Ta Ch'ing hui-tien (Institutes of the Ch'ing dynasty), 1899.

Ta Ch'ing hui-tien shih-li (Institutes and precedents of the Ch'ing dynasty), 1899.

Ta Ch'ing lü-li (Statutes and precedents of the Ch'ing dynasty), 1870.

Ta Ch'ing lü-li hui-chi pien-lan (Guide to the statutes and precedents of the Ch'ing dynasty), 1888.

T'an Chün-p'ei, *T'an chung-cheng tsou-kao* (Draft memorials of T'an Chün-p'ei), 1902.

Teng T'o, *Lun Chung-kuo li-shih chi-ko wen-t'i* (On several problems in Chinese history), 2d ed., Peking, 1979.

Terada Takanobu, *Sansei shōnin no kenkyū* (A study of the Shansi merchants), Kyoto, 1972.

Thompson, R. W., *Griffith John, the Story of Fifty Years in China*, New York, 1908.

Thrupp, Sylvia, *The Merchant Class of Medieval London*, Ann Arbor, 1962.

The Times, London. 1855–89.

Tōa dōbunkai, *Shina keizai zensho* (Complete handbook of the Chinese economy), Osaka, 1908–9.

Tōa dōbunkai chōsa hensambu, *Shina kaikōjo shi* (Guide to the open ports in China), Shanghai, 1924.

Tou Chi-liang, *T'ung-hsiang tsu-chih chih yen-chiu* (A study of local origin organizations), Chungking, 1946.

Trewartha, Glenn T., "Chinese Cities: Origins and Functions," *Annals of the Association of American Geographers*, 42 (1952), pp. 69–93.

Ts'ai I-ch'ing (Ts'ai Fu-ch'ing), "Hsien-hua Han-k'ou" (Leisurely chats about Hankow), series of twelve articles, *Hsin-sheng yueh-k'an*, vol. 5, no. 5, through vol. 6, no. 6 (dates unknown).

Tseng Kuo-ch'üan, *Tseng chung-hsiang-kung tsou-i* (Memorials of Tseng Kuo-ch'üan), 1903.

Tsungli yamen, Archives, Institute of Modern History, Academia Sinica, Taipei.

"Hu-pei Che-chiang Feng-t'ien Fa-Ying-Mei-O chiao-pu" (Negotiations with the French, British, Americans, and Russians in Hupeh, Chekiang, and Fengtien), A-7-3.

"Hu-pei chiao-she O-jen i-wei-chieh ko-an" (Resolved and unresolved cases of negotiations with Russians in Hupeh), A-7-5.

"Hu-pei Han-k'ou O-shang pei-p'ien" (The defrauding of a Russian merchant at Hankow, Hupeh), A-7-5.

"Hu-pei Han-k'ou Ying-kuo tsu-ti an" (Cases regarding property leased by Britain in Hankow, Hupeh), A-9-1.

"Hu-pei Ying-jen chiao-she" (Negotiations with British subjects in Hupeh), A-7-2.

Tu Li, "Ya-p'ien chan-cheng ch'ien Shang-hai hang-hui hsing-chih chih shan-pien" (Changes in the character of Shanghai guilds before the Opium War), paper presented to the Conference on the Sprouts of Chinese Capitalism, Nanking, May 1981.

Uchida Naosaku, "Baiban seido no kenkyū" (A study of the compradore system), *Shinakenkyū*, 48 (1938), pp. 1–22.

———, "Chūgoku ni okeru shōgyō chitsujo no kiso—gakō seido no saikentō" (The foundation of China's commercial structure: a reexamination of the brokerage system), *Hitotsubashi ronsō*, 22, no. 2 (August 1949), pp. 49–73.

———, "Yōkō seido no kenkyū" (A study of the foreign-firm system), *Shinakenkyū*, 50 (1939), pp. 187–212.

United States Consulate at Hankow, *Despatches from United States Consuls in Hankow, 1861–1906*. File Microcopies of Records in the National Archives, No. 107, Washington, 1947.

———, Post Records, U.S. National Archives, Washington.

Waley, Daniel, *The Italian City-Republics*, New York, 1969.

Wang Chia-pi, "Pien-nien wen-kao" (Chronological draft correspondence notebooks), manuscript. 1844–82.

Wang Feng-sheng, *Ch'u-pei Chiang-Han hsuan-fang pei-lan* (Survey of Yangtze and Han River conservancy works in Hupeh), 1832.

Wang Pao-hsin, *Chi Han-k'ou ts'ung-t'an* (Continuation of the Hankow compendium), 1916; repr. Wuchang, 1932.

Wang Yün-wu, ed., *Tao-Hsien-T'ung-Kuang ssu-ch'ao tsou-i* (Memorials from the Tao-kuang, Hsien-feng, T'ung-chih, and Kuang-hsu reigns), Taipei, n.d.

Weber, Max, *The City*, New York, 1958. Original German edition 1921.

———, *From Max Weber: Essays in Sociology*, ed. H. H. Gerth and C. Wright Mills, New York, 1958.

———, *The Religion of China*, New York, 1951.

———, *The Theory of Social and Economic Organization*, New York, 1964.

Wei Ch'ing-yuan and Lu Su, *Ch'ing-tai ch'ien-ch'i te shang-pan k'uang-yeh ho tzu-pen-chu-i meng-ya* (Early Ch'ing commercial mining and the sprouts of capitalism), Peking, 1981.

Wesleyan Missionary Society, *The Five Annual Reports of the Hankow Medical Mission Hospital*, Shanghai, 1870.

———, *Seventh Report of the Hankow Medical Mission Hospital*, Shanghai, 1872.

Williams, Samuel Wells, *The Middle Kingdom*, New York, 1883.

———, "The Topography of Hupeh," *Chinese Repository*, 19 (1850), pp. 101–2.

Wolf, Eric R., "Kinship, Friendship, and Patron-Client Relations in Complex Societies," in Michael Banton, ed., *The Social Anthropology of Complex Societies*, New York, 1966, pp. 1–22.

Wolseley, Garnet J., *Narrative of the War with China in 1860*, London, 1862; repr. Wilmington, Del., 1972.

"Wu-Han ch'eng-chen ho-t'u" (Combined map of the Wu-Han cities), 1890; repr. Wuhan, 1980.

Wuhan Municipal Archives, Wuhan. Miscellaneous documents.

Wuhan Municipal Commercial and Industrial Alliance, "Han-yang Ying-wu chou chu-mu shih-ch'ang shih-lüeh" (Brief history of the bamboo and timber market at Hanyang's Parrot Island), manuscript, 1964.

———, "Wu-han pai-huo-yeh te su-yüan" (Origins of Wuhan's department store business), manuscript, n.d.

———, "Wu-han p'iao-hao chih-t'an" (A discussion of the Shansi banks of Wuhan), manuscript, 1961.

———, "Wu-han-shih Wang-yü-hsia shih-p'in ch'ang yen-ko" (History of the Wang-yü-hsia food processing plant of Wuhan), manuscript, 1959.

———, "Wu-han tien-tang-yeh lüeh-t'an" (A discussion of the pawnbroking business of Wuhan), manuscript, 1962.

———, "Wu-han yao-ts'ai hang-yeh li-shih yen-ko" (History of the medicinal herbs trade of Wuhan), manuscript, n.d.

———, "Wu-han Yeh-k'ai-t'ai yao-tien chien-shih" (Short history of the Yeh-k'ai-t'ai medicine store of Wuhan), manuscript, n.d.

Wuhan Progressive Education Institute, *Wu-han ti-fang li-shih chiao-ts'ai* (Teaching materials on Wuhan local history), Wuhan, 1968.

"Ya-t'ieh" (Brokerage licenses), collection located at Tōyō Bunko, Tokyo.

Yang, Lien-sheng, "Government Control of Urban Merchants in Traditional China," *Tsinghua Journal of Chinese Studies*, 4, no. 1 (1972), pp. 186–206.

———, *Money and Credit in China*, Cambridge, Mass., 1952.

Yao Hsien-hao, ed., *Chung-kuo chin-tai tui-wai mao-i shih tzu-liao* (Materials on the history of China's modern foreign trade), Peking, 1962.

Yao-shih tsung-p'u (Genealogy of the Yao clan), 1930.

Yazaki, Takeo, *Social Change and the City in Japan: From the Earliest Times Through the Industrial Revolution*, Tokyo, 1968.

Yeh-shih tsung-p'u (Genealogy of the Yeh clan), 1873.

Yeh Tiao-yüan, *Han-k'ou chu-chih tz'u* (Songs of the bamboo branches of Hankow), 1850.

Yen Ssu-sheng, *Ch'u meng-shan fang ch'üan-chi* (Complete works from the mountain retreat of Ch'u), n.d.

Ying-wu-chou hsiao-chih (Brief gazetteer of Parrot Island), ed. Hu Feng-tan, 1873.

Yokoyama Suguru, *Chūgoku kindaika no keizai kōzō* (The economic structure of China's modernization), Tokyo, 1972.

Character List

Well-known names and terms, such as Shanghai and Peking, and personal names cited for purposes of illustration only are omitted. Authors of Chinese and Japanese works cited in the Bibliography are included in the listing here.

Abe Takeo 安部健夫
an 岸
An-hua 安化
An-I hui-kuan 安益會館
an-shang 岸商
Arao Kiyoshi 荒尾精
bushi 武士
Cha Shen-hsing 查慎行
ch'a-chan 茶棧
ch'a-chuang 茶庄
ch'a-hao 茶號
ch'a-hu 茶戶
ch'a-k'o (duty) 茶課
ch'a-k'o (merchant) 茶客
ch'a-li 茶釐
ch'a-shang 茶商
ch'a-shui 茶稅
Ch'a-yeh kung-so 茶業公所
chan 棧
chan-chi 佔籍
chan-hang 棧行
chan-huo 棧夥
chang 丈
Chang-chia-k'ou 張家口
Chang Chih-tung 張之洞
Chang Hsien-chung 張獻忠
Chang Kuo-hui 張國輝
Chang Liang-chi 張亮基
Chang Lien-teng 張連登
Chang Ou-fang 張藕芳
Chang P'eng-fei 張鵬飛
Chang Shou-po 張壽波
Chang T'ien-chüeh 張添爵
Chang Yin-pin 張寅賓
ch'ang-kuan 常關
Ch'ang Ta-ch'un 常大淳
Ch'ang-te 常德
chao-chi ku-fen 招集股分
Chao-li-ch'iao 趙李橋
Chao-shang chü 招商局
chao-shang pien-t'ung shih-pan 招商變通試辦
Chao Shu-chih 趙淑智
Chao Yü 趙玉
Che-Ning kung-so 浙寧公所
chen 鎮
Chen-chiang 鎮江
Chen-hai 鎮海
Ch'en-chou 辰州
Ch'en-hsien 郴縣
Ch'en Hui-yen 陳徽言
Ch'en Hung-mou 陳宏謀

Ch'en-Kuei hui-kuan 郴桂會館
Ch'en Ming-chin 陳明謹
Cheng chieh 正街
Cheng Lan 鄭蘭
cheng-lun 整輪
ch'eng 城
ch'eng-fa 成法
ch'eng-huang 城皇
Ch'eng I-lo 程儀洛
ch'eng-tan 成單
chi 籍
Chi-an 吉安
chi-chiu 祭酒
Chi-shan 佶山
chi-shen 祭神
ch'i-chü 契據
ch'i-hang 齊行
ch'i-p'iao 期票
Ch'i-yang 祁陽
Ch'i-yang hui-kuan 祁陽會館
ch'i-yeh 企業
ch'i-yüeh 契約
chia 家
Chia chieh 夾街
Chia-yü 嘉魚
Chiang-Han 江漢
Chiang-Han kuan 江漢關
Chiang-hsia 江夏
chiang-t'ang 講堂
Chiang-tu 江都
ch'iao-yü 僑寓
chieh 街
chieh-chü 借據
chien-i 簡易
Chien-jung kung-so 建絨公所
ch'ien 錢
ch'ien-cho 錢桌
ch'ien-chuang 錢庄
ch'ien-p'iao 錢票
ch'ien-p'u 錢舖
Ch'ien-t'ang 錢塘
ch'ien-tien 錢店
ch'ien-yin 鈐印
chih-chao 執照
chih-hsien 職銜
chih-shang 職商
Chih-yeh kung-so 紙業公所
chih-yüan 職員
Chin-chüan chü 晉捐局
chin-shih 進士
Chin Ta-k'ai 金達凱
Chin-t'ing hui-kuan 金庭會館
ching-chi 經紀
Ching-chou 荊州
Ching-huo kung-so 京貨公所
ching-kuan 經管
Ching-shan 京山
ching-shih 經世
ching-shou 經手
ching-shou-jen 經手人
Ching-te-chen 景德鎮
ching-ying 經營
Ch'ing-chang chü 清丈局
ch'ing-mien 情面
ch'ing-tan 清單
chiu-chiu shang-pu chüan 九九商埠捐
chiu-chung 就中
Ch'iu Hsing-shu 裘行恕
chou 州

Chou Tsuan-wen 周纘文
ch'ou 籌
chu 駐
chu-ch'üan yeh 主權業
chu-shih 主事
Ch'u-an 楚岸
ch'u-fen 處分
ch'uan-chü 船局
ch'uan-hang 船行
ch'uan-hu 船户
Ch'uan-k'ou [illegible]口
ch'uan-p'iao 船票
ch'uan-szu 船司
chuang 庄, 莊
Ch'un-ch'iu lou 春秋樓
Chung chieh 中街
Chung-chou hui-kuan 中州會館
chung-pao 中飽
chung-pu 中埠
ch'ung 衝
Ch'ung-yang 崇陽
chü 局
chü-chien 居間
Chü-jen 居仁
chü-jen 舉人
chü-min 居民
chü-min hsing-jen 居民行人
Ch'ü Chih-sheng 曲直生
chüan 捐
chüan-na 捐納
chüan-shu 捐輸
Ch'üan Han-sheng 全漢昇
Ch'üan Teh 全德
chün-ch'eng 君丞
Chün-chou 均州
chün-hsiang 軍餉
chün-hsü chü 軍需局
chün-hsü tsung-chü 軍需總局
chün-kung 軍功
chün-ying 軍營
dokusai seiji 独裁政治
fa-shang sheng-hsi 發商生息
fan (peddler) 販
fan (troublesome) 煩
fan-fu 繁複
Fan K'ai 范鍇
Fan Kuo-t'ai 樊國太
fan-yin-tien 飯飲店
fang 坊
Fang Hsien-t'ing 方顯廷
fang-sheng 放生
Fen (river) 汾
Fen-chou 汾州
fen-hsün tao 分巡道
fen-hua 分化
fen-i ts'ai-ch'an 分異財產
fen-kung 分工
Feng-ch'eng t'ang 鳳城堂
feng-chien 封建
feng-chien hang-hui 封建行會
Feng Hua-te 馮華德
feng-lun chih li 封輪之例
Fo-shan 佛山
fu-chi 附籍
fu-chi ying-shih 附籍應試
Fu I-ling 傅衣淩
fu-tung-shih 副董事
Fujii Hiroshi 藤井宏
hai-kuan 海關
Han (river) 漢
Han-ch'uan 漢川
Han-chung 漢中
Han-Huang-Te 漢黃德

Han-k'ou ch'a-yeh kung-so 漢口茶業公所
Han-k'ou ch'ien-yeh kung-so 漢口錢業公所
Han-k'ou hsiao-chih 漢口小志
Han-k'ou jen 漢口人
Han-k'ou ko-t'uan lien-ho-hui 漢口各團聯合會
Han-k'ou shang-wu chü 漢口商務局
Han-k'ou ts'ung-t'an 漢口叢談
Han-k'ou tz'u-shan-hui 漢口慈善會
Han-nan 漢南
Han-pang 漢幫
Han-pao 漢報
Han-yang 漢陽
hang 行
hang-kuei 行規
hang-li 行釐
hang-t'ou 行頭
hang-yung-ch'ien 行用錢
hao 號
Hatano Yoshihiro 波多野善大
Heng-chou 衡州
Ho Ping-ti 何炳棣
ho-po so 河泊所
Ho Wei-chien 何維鍵
Hou chieh 後街
hou-ch'üeh 候缺
Hou-hu 後湖
hou-pu 候補
Hou Wai-lu 侯外廬
Hsi-hu 西湖
hsia-fei 匣費
Hsia-k'ou 夏口
hsia-lu 下路
hsia-pa-hang 下八行
hsia-shang 匣商
Hsiang (river in Hunan) 湘
Hsiang (river in Hupeh) 襄
hsiang 巷
hsiang-ch'ing 鄉情
hsiang-hui 香會
Hsiang-li 湘釐
hsiang-li 鄉釐
hsiang-pao 相保
hsiang-shih 襄事
Hsiang-t'an 湘潭
hsiang-t'u 鄉土
Hsiang-yang 襄陽
hsiang-yung 鄉勇
hsiao-chia 小家
Hsiao Chih-chih 肖致治
hsiao-hang 小行
Hsiao-ho 小河
Hsiao-kan 孝感
hsiao-kuan 小官
hsiao-mao 小貿
hsiao t'uan-t'i 小團體
Hsiao Yao-nan 蕭耀南
Hsieh-hsing kung 協興公
Hsieh Yüan 謝元
hsien-ch'eng 縣丞
hsien-chih 限制
hsien-hsüeh 縣學
Hsien-ning 咸寧
Hsien-t'ao 仙桃
Hsin-an 新安
Hsin-an fang 新安坊
Hsin-an ma-t'ou 新安碼頭
hsin-cheng 新政
hsin-hsia 新匣
Hsin-hui 新會
Hsin ma-t'ou 新碼頭
hsin-p'iao 新票

Hsin-t'an 新灘

hsin-t'ieh 新帖

Hsing-an 興安

Hsiu-ning 休寧

Hsiung Po-lung 熊伯龍

Hsü Jun 徐潤

Hsü Lin-han 徐臨漢

Hsü Ta-ling 徐大齡

Hsü Wen-kao 徐文高

hsün-chien 巡檢

Hsün-li 循禮

hsün-szu wei-yüan 巡司委員

hu 户

Hu Chan-men 胡戰門

Hu Chao-ch'un 胡兆春

Hu Chao-hsi 胡昭曦

Hu I-tieh 胡一爹

Hu Lin-i 胡林翼

hu-pao 互保

Hu-pei sheng chih-pu chü 湖北省織布局

Hu-pei t'ung-sheng yen-ch'a-ya-li tsung-chü 湖北通省鹽茶牙釐總局

hua-p'iao 花票

Hua-pu chieh 花布街

Huai-ch'ing 懷慶

Huai-ch'ing hui-kuan 懷慶會館

Huai-nan 淮南

Huai-pei 淮北

Huai-yen kung-so 淮鹽公所

Huang-chou 黃州

Huang-hua 黃花

Huang-kang 黃岡

Huang-pang 黃幫

Huang-p'i 黃陂

Hui-chou 徽州

hui-i 會議

hui-k'o 會客

hui-kuan 會館

hui-shou 會首

hui-shou lao-yeh 會首老爺

hung-ch'a pang 紅茶幫

Hung Liang-chi 洪亮吉

Hung T'an 洪覃

Hung Tzu-chien 洪滋鑑

huo 夥

Huo-ch'iu 霍丘

huo-li 貨釐

huo-lu 火路

huo-tao 火道

I-ch'ang 宜昌

i-chung 義塚

i-chü 義舉

i-hsüeh 義學

i-lu 義路

I-lü kung-so 瘞旅公所

I-ning 義寧

i-pu 義埠

i-shang-i-kuan 亦商亦官

i-shih 議事

i-tu 義渡

I-yang 益陽

Imahori Seiji 今堀誠二

Jen-I 仁義

ju-chi 入籍

k'a 卡

k'ai-chung-fa 開中法

kang 綱

kang-fa 綱法

k'ang-ch'ü 康衢

Kankō kokurisha 漢口鶴唳社

Kao Heng 高恒

Kitamura Hironao 北村敬直

ko-hao 各號

Ko hui-kuan kung-so lien-ho-hui 各會館公所聯合會
Kokuryūkai 黑龍會
Kosaku Torizo 上坂酉三
k'o 課
k'o-chan 客棧
K'o Feng-shih 柯逢時
k'o-hang 客行
k'o-pang 客幫
k'o-shang 客商
k'ou-an 口岸
ku-huo 雇夥
Ku-kang t'ang 古岡堂
ku-shang 賈商
K'uai Te-piao 蒯德標
kuan 關
kuan-hang 官行
kuan-pan 官辦
kuan tao 關道
Kuan-ti 關帝
Kuan-tu chü 官渡局
kuan-tu shang-pan 官督商辦
Kuan-wen 官文
kuan-yen 官鹽
Kuan Yü 關羽
Kuei-yang 桂陽
kung 公
kung-ch'ai 公差
kung-cheng jen 公正人
kung-cheng shih-shen 公正士紳
kung-i 公議
kung-ku chü 公估局
kung-kung 公共
kung-pang 工幫
kung-so 公所
kung-te ch'ien 功德錢
kung-tien 公店
kung-t'ui 公推
k'ung-p'iao 空票
kuo-chang 過賬
kuo-k'o 國課
kuo-lung cheng-kao 過籠蒸糕
Kuo Wen-i 郭文毅
kyōdōtai 共同体
lao-ch'eng 老成
lao-chia 老家
Lao-ho-k'ou 老河口
lao-hsi 老西
lao-hsia 老匣
lao-tsung 老總
Le-shan t'ang 樂善堂
Lei (river) 耒
Lei I-hsien 雷以諴
lei-shang 累商
Lei-tsu tien 雷祖殿
li (linear measurement) 里
li (monetary measurement) 釐
li (tax district) 里
li-an 立案
Li-Chih 禮智
Li-chin chü 釐金局
Li Han-chang 李瀚章
li-hsü 吏胥
Li-ling 醴陵
li-p'iao 釐票
Li Shao-ling 黎少岑
Li-tai chih-kuan piao 歷代職官表
Liang-hang kung-so 糧行公所
Liang-hu hui-kuan 兩湖會館

Liang-Huai 兩淮
lien-ming pao-cheng 連名保證
Lin-chiang hui-kuan 臨江會館
Lin-hsiang 臨湘
Lin Tse-hsü 林則徐
Ling-hsiao shu-yüan 淩霄書院
Ling-nan hui-kuan 嶺南會館
Liu Hsin-sheng (Liu Jen-hsiang) 劉歆生（劉人祥）
Liu Jen-shan 劉仁山
Liu K'un-i 劉坤一
liu-min 流民
liu-pang 六幫
Liu-tu 六渡
Liu Tzu-t'ao 劉子濤
Liu Wen-tao 劉文島
Liu-yang 瀏陽
Liu Yao-ch'ing 劉堯卿
lo-chi 落籍
Lo K'ai-hsüan 羅開軒
Lu Chien-ying 陸建瀛
lu-k'o 陸課
Lu-shen 盧坤
Lu Su 魯肅
lung-chü 龍局
Lung-wang miao 龍王廟
Ma-ch'eng 麻城
Ma-wang miao 馬王廟
Mai-chu 邁柱
mai-pan 買辦
mai-tien 賣店
men-k'o 門客
men-tou 門斗
meng-i 蒙議
Mi-shih kung-so 米市公所
miao 廟
Mien-hua chieh 棉花街
Mien-pang kung-so 麵幫公所
Mien-yang 沔陽
min 民
min-ch'uan 民船
min-pan 民辦
Mizuno Kōkichi 水野幸吉
Morita Akira 森田明
mu 畝
mu-fu 幕府
mu-pin 幕賓
mu-ts'ai 木材
Mu-tso kung-so 木作工所
Nakamura Jihei 中村治兵衛
nan 難
Nan-feng 南豐
Nan-hai 南海
Nan-pang 南幫
Nan-shih 南市
Negishi Tadashi 根岸佶
nei-szu 內私
Niida Noboru 仁井田陞
Nishin bōeki kenkyūju 日清貿易研究所
Nishizato Yoshiyuki 西里善行
O-an 鄂岸
O-chou 鄂州
O-li 鄂釐
pa-k'ai tsung-hang 霸開總行
Pa-sheng 八省

pa-ta-hang 八大行
pa-ta-pang 八大幫
pai-huo kung-szu 百貨公司
Pai Wen-min 白文敏
pan-kung-fei 辦公費
Pan-pien-tien 半邊店
P'an Hsin-tsao 潘新藻
P'an Lei 潘耒
P'an-yü 番禺
pang 幫
pang-hui 幫會
pao 包
pao-ch'a li-chin 包茶釐金
pao-cheng yin 保證銀
pao-chia 保甲
Pao-chia chü 保甲局
pao-chieh 保結
Pao-ch'ing 寶慶
pao-jen 保人
Pao-kung chü 堡工局
Pao Shih-ch'en 包世臣
pao-tan 保單
pao-t'ou 包頭
Pei-pang 北幫
pen-chi 本籍
pen-i 本邑
pen-pang 本幫
P'eng Tse-i 彭澤益
P'eng Yü-hsin 彭雨新
P'eng Yü-lin 彭玉麟
p'i 疲
P'i-huo kung-so 皮貨公所
p'i-lien 毗連
P'i Ming-hsiu 皮明庥
p'iao 票
p'iao-chuang 票庄
p'iao-fa 票法
p'iao-hao 票號
P'iao-pang kung-hui 票幫公會
p'iao-shang 票商
P'iao-shui 漂水
Pien Pao-ti 卞寶第
P'ing-hsiang 萍鄉
p'ing-p'iao 憑票
P'ing-yao 平遙
pu-chi 簿籍
pu-k'uai 捕快
pu-t'ieh 部帖
Pu-yeh kung-so 布業公所
p'u 舖
P'u-ch'eng 蒲城
P'u-ch'i 蒲圻
p'u-fan 舖販
P'u-t'an 蒲潭
ryūtsū keizai 流通經濟
Saeki Tomi 佐伯富
San-i tien 三義殿
Sha-shih 沙市
Sha-yeh kung-so 紗業公所
shan-chü 善舉
shan-hou 善後
shan-hou tsung-chü 善後總局
Shan-Shen hui-kuan shih-pang shou-shih 山陝會館十幫首士
Shan-Shen-li 山陝里
shan-t'ang 善堂
shan-t'ou 山頭
shang-chai p'u-i 商宅僕役
shang-chi 商籍
shang-chüan 商捐
shang-hsüeh 商學
shang-huo 商夥

shang-lu 上路
shang-pa-hang 上八行
shang-pan 商辦
shang-pang 商幫
shang-pen 商本
shang-p'in ching-chi 商品經濟
shang-pu 上埠
shang-shui 商稅
shang-szu 商司
shang-t'uan 商團
shang-t'ung 商銅
shang-wu chü 商務局
Shang-yüan hui-kuan 上元會館
she-ch'ü 社區
She-hsien 歙縣
Shen-chia miao 沈家廟
Shen-pao 申報
shen-shang 紳商
shen-tung 紳董
shen-yüan 紳員
sheng-chien chih-hsien 生監職銜
Sheng Heng-shan 盛恒山
Sheng Shih-feng 盛世豐
Sheng-yü-t'ai 盛裕泰
sheng-yüan 生員
Shiba Yoshinobu 斯波義信
Shigeta Atsushi 重田德
shih 市
shih-chi 市集
shih-chia 時價
shih-chih 實職
Shih Fu-jun 史富潤
shih-hsi 食餼
Shih-kao kung-so 石膏公所
shih-kuan 實官
shih-li 事例
shih-min 市民
shih-shang 士商
Shih Ta-k'ai 石達開
shiminteki na jichi 市民的な自治
Shimizu Taiji 清水泰次
shou-chüan 收捐
shou-jen 首人
shou-shih (chief of affairs) 首事
shou-shih (head gentryman) 首士
shu-hang 舒行
shu-pan 書班
shu-yüan 書院
shui 稅
shui-fan 水販
shui-hui 水會
shui-lung 水龍
shui-tang 水擋
Shun-te 順德
So-ho 索河
Ssu-kuan miao 四官廟
Su-Hu kung-so 蘇湖公所
Su Yün-feng 蘇雲峯
sui-tao sui-mai 隨到隨賣
Sun Ch'u-ch'ih 孫楚池
Sung-chiang 松江
szu-hsia 司匣
szu-shih 司事
szu-tsai Hsi-kiang 死在西江
Ta-chih 大智
Ta Ch'ing i-t'ung-chih 大清一統志
Ta Ch'ing lü-li 大清律例
ta-hang 大行
Ta-ho 大河
Ta-sheng-k'uei 大盛魁

Ta-wang miao 大王廟
Ta-yeh 大冶
ta-yüan 大員
tai 代
T'ai-p'ing 太平
T'ai-yüan 太原
tan 担
Tan-Huai hui-kuan 單懷會館
T'an Chün-p'ei 譚鈞培
t'ang 堂
T'ang Hsün-pang 唐訓邦
T'ang I-yen 唐裔演
tao-t'ai 道臺
tao-t'ung 道通
T'ao Chu 陶澍
Te-an 德安
t'e-pieh shih 特別市
teng-hui 燈會
Teng T'o 鄧拓
Terada Takanobu 寺田隆信
ti-sou 抵鎖
Ti-wai 堤外
t'i-ch'uang shih-yeh 提創實業
t'i-hsi 體惜
tien (shop) 店
tien (temple) 殿
tien-huo 店夥
Tien-pao chü 電報局
tien-p'u 店舖
tien-tung 店東
T'ien-chu chiao 天主教
T'ien-hou 天后
T'ien-hou kung 天后宮
T'ien-men 天門
T'ien-Mien 天沔
T'ien-tu yen 天都奄
T'ien Wei-han 田維翰
ting-tan 定單
t'ing 廳
t'ing-kuan 庭館
t'o-ch'ien 拖欠
Tōa dōbunkai 東亞同文會
Tōa dōbunkai chōsa hensambu 東亞同文會調查編纂部
tonya 問屋
Tou Chi-liang 竇季良
tsa-huo 雜貨
tsai-an 在案
Ts'ai I-ch'ing (Ts'ai Fu-ch'ing) 蔡乙青（蔡輔卿）
Ts'ai-tien 蔡店
ts'ai-tung 財東
tsao-li 皂吏
ts'ao-yün tao 漕運道
tse-kuo 澤國
Tseng Kuo-ch'üan 曾國荃
Tseng Kuo-fan 曾國藩
tso-fang 作房，作坊
tso-pao 作保
tso-shang 坐商
tso-tsa 佐雜
Tso Tsung-t'ang 左宗棠
tsung-chü 總局
tsung-k'a 總卡
tsung-li 總理
tsung-li shou-shih 總理首事
tsung-liang-t'ai 總糧臺
tsung-shang 總商
tsung-tung 總董
ts'ung-chung 從中

tu-hsiao chü 督消局
tu-hsiao tsung-chü 督消總局
Tu Li 杜黎
tu-t'ung 督同
Tu Wen-lan 杜文瀾
t'u-chu 土住
T'u-tang 土壋
T'u Tzu-sung 涂子松
t'uan-lien 團練
tung (capitalist) 東
tung-fang 冬防
Tung-hu 東湖
tung-shih 董事
Tung-t'ing 洞庭
T'ung-ch'eng 桐城
t'ung-chih 同知
t'ung-hsiang 同鄉
t'ung-hsiang-hui 同鄉會
t'ung-hsiang-jen 同鄉人
t'ung-p'an 通判
T'ung-shan 通山
t'ung-shih 統事
t'ung-yeh 同業
T'ung-yeh kung-so 銅業公所
Tzu (river) 資
tzu-chih tzu-li chih kung-t'uan 自治自立之公團
tzu-chin 子金
tzu-jan hang-yeh 自然行業
tzu-k'ou-shui 子口稅
Tzu-yang shu-yüan 紫陽書院
Tz'u-hsi 慈谿
tz'u-shan shih-yeh 慈善事業
Uchida Naosaku 内田直作
wai-szu 外私
Wan-shou kung 萬壽宮
Wang Chia-pi 王家璧
Wang Feng-sheng 王鳳生
Wang Heng-shih 汪衡士
Wang Hui-han 汪會漢
Wang Kuo-chu 汪國柱
Wang Li-ta 王立大
Wang Pao-hsin 王葆心
Wang Ping-en 王秉恩
Wang Shih-liang 汪士良
Wang Wen-i 汪文儀
Wang Yün-wu 王雲五
wei-ch'ih kung-i 維持公益
wei-ch'ih pang-kuei 維持幫規
wei-ch'ih pen-chi 維持本籍
wei-ch'ih shang-yeh 維持商業
Wei Ch'ing-yüan 魏慶遠
wei-shen 委紳
Wei Yüan 魏源
wei-yüan 委員
wen 文
Wen-ch'ang tien 文昌殿
Wen-hsi 聞喜
wen-pang 文幫
weng 翁
Weng T'ung-chüeh 翁同爵
wu-chi 無基
Wu Chi-lung 吳積隆
Wu Ch'uan-hao 吳傳灝
Wu-hsien 吳縣
Wu Hsin-chiu 吳心九
Wu-hu 蕪湖
wu-k'ao ch'iung-min 無靠窮民

Wu-liang tien 無量殿
wu-pang 武幫
Wu Yu-ch'ing 武有慶
Wu-yüan 婺源
ya-ch'ien 牙錢
ya-hang 牙行
ya-i 衙役
ya-shui 牙稅
ya-t'ieh 牙帖
yang-chieh wei-yüan 洋街委員
yang-hang 洋行
Yang-hu 陽湖
yang-lien 養廉
Yang-lou-tung 羊樓洞
Yang-ming shu-yüan 陽明書院
yang-p'iao 洋票
Yang Tse-tseng 楊澤曾
Yao Hsieh-hsing 姚協興
Yao Hsien-hao 姚賢鎬
Yao K'uan-ch'ing 姚冠卿
Yao-wang miao 葯王廟
Yao Yü-k'uei 姚玉魁
Yeh Ch'eng-chüan 葉成佺
Yeh Hung-liang 葉宏良
Yeh-k'ai-t'ai 葉開泰
yeh-li 業釐
Yeh Ming-ch'en 葉名琛
Yeh Tiao-yüan 葉調元
yen 奄
yen-chia 鹽家
yen-chiu shang-yeh 研究商業
yen-fan-tzu 鹽販子
yen-hang 鹽行
yen-k'o 鹽課
yen-li 鹽釐
yen-miao 奄廟
Yen Ssu-sheng 晏斯盛
yen tao 鹽道
yen-tu 鹽督
yen-yün-shih 鹽運使
yin 引
yin-fa 引法
yin-hang 銀行
yin-hao 銀號
yin-kung t'i-yung 因公提用
yin-p'iao 銀票
Ying-wu chou 鸚鵡洲
ying-yeh 營業
Yokoyama Suguru 横山英
Yu-i 由義
Yu-yeh kung-so 油業公所
yü 寓
Yü-chou 禹州
yü-kuan 寓館
yü-mai 預買
Yü Neng-p'ei 余能培
Yü-shan t'ang 禹山堂
Yü Sheng-chu 余繩鑄
Yü Shih-chiung 余士炯
Yü-tai ho 玉帶河
Yü-t'ai 裕泰
Yüan (river) 沅
yüan-chi 原籍
Yüan-ling 沅陵
Yüan-ning hui-kuan 元甯會館
Yüan Pao-heng 袁保恒
Yüeh-k'uei t'ang 粵魁堂
yüeh-shang 月商

yüeh-tai 閱代
Yüeh-yang 岳陽
yün 運
yün-hsüeh 運學
yün-shang 運商
Yün-shang kung-so 運商公所
yün-szu 運司
yün-ts'ang 運艙
Yün Tsu-i 惲祖翼
Yün Yen-ch'i 惲彥琦
zettaishugi 絶對主義

Index

Within the following list, Chinese words have been alphabetized syllable by syllable according to their Wade-Giles romanization, unless this would lead to too great a displacement (as with "Soochow" and "Kwangtung," for example); English words have been alphabetized letter by letter.